FOR THE SAKE OF OUR SALVATION
The Truth and Humility of God's Word

Articles

Tradition & Traditions

Letter & Spirit 6 (2010): 3–9

CONTRIBUTORS

~: Scott W. Hahn :~

Scott W. Hahn, founder of the St. Paul Center for Biblical Theology, holds the Pope Benedict XVI Chair of Biblical Theology and Liturgical Proclamation at St. Vincent Seminary in Latrobe, Pennsylvania, and is professor of Scripture and Theology at Franciscan University of Steubenville, Ohio. He has held the Pio Cardinal Laghi Chair for Visiting Professors in Scripture and Theology at the Pontifical College Josephinum in Columbus, Ohio, and has served as adjunct faculty at the Pontifical University of the Holy Cross and the Pontifical University, Regina Apostolorum, both in Rome. Hahn is the general editor of the *Ignatius Study Bible* and the *Catholic Bible Dictionary*, and is author or editor of more than twenty books, including *Kinship By Covenant: A Canonical Approach to the Fulfillment of God's Saving Promises* (The Anchor Yale Bible Reference Library, 2009), *Covenant and Communion: The Biblical Theology of Pope Benedict XVI* (2009), *Letter and Spirit: From Written Text to Living Word in the Liturgy* (2005), *Understanding the Scriptures* (2005), and *The Lamb's Supper: The Mass as Heaven on Earth* (1999).

~: Brant Pitre :~

Brant Pitre is Professor of Sacred Scripture at Notre Dame Seminary in New Orleans, Louisiana. He received his Ph.D. in Theology from the University of Notre Dame, where he specialized in the study of the New Testament and ancient Judaism and graduated with highest honors. He is the author of *Jesus, the Tribulation, and the End of the Exile* (2005), and the forthcoming *Jesus and the Jewish Roots of the Eucharist* (2011). He is also working on another book, tentatively titled: *Jesus and the Last Supper: Judaism and the Origin of the Eucharist*.

~: Pablo T. Gadenz :~

Pablo T. Gadenz, a priest of the Diocese of Trenton, is Assistant Professor of Biblical Studies at Immaculate Conception Seminary School of Theology at Seton Hall University, South Orange, New Jersey. He received his licentiate in Scripture (S.S.L.) from the Pontifical Biblical Institute (2005) and his doctorate in biblical theology (S.T.D.) from the Pontifical Gregorian University (2008). His published dissertation is titled *Called from the Jews and from the Gentiles: Pauline Ecclesiology in Romans 9–11* (Wissenschaftliche Untersuchungen zum Neuen Testament, 2009). He has published book reviews in *Biblica* and is the translator (from Italian) of the monograph: Filippo Belli, *Argumentation and Use of Scripture in Romans 9–11* (Analecta Biblica 183, 2010). He is a member of the Catholic Biblical Association of America and the Society of Biblical Literature.

~: Michael Maria Waldstein :~

Michael Maria Waldstein is the Max Seckler Professor of Theology at Ave Maria University. He previously taught at the University of Notre Dame before serving as the founding President of the International Theological Institute in Gaming, Austria, where he also held the position of St. Francis of Assisi Professor of New Testament. He served as a member of the Pontifical Council for the Family (2003–2009) and is a member of the the the Board of Trustees of the University of Eichstaett, Germany. He holds a B.A. from Thomas Aquinas College, a Ph.D. from the University of Dallas, an S.S.L. from the Pontifical Biblical Institute in Rome, and a Th.D. from Harvard University in New Testament and Christian Origins. His published works include a critical edition of the four Coptic manuscripts (with English translation) of the *The Apocryphon of John* (1995), a Gnostic text discovered in the Nag Hammadi codices, and a new translation of John Paul II's *Man and Woman He Created Them: A Theology of the Body* (2006), as well as numerous articles on the Gospel of John, gnosticism, St. Thomas Aquinas, John Paul II and Hans Urs von Balthasar in such journals as *Nova et Vetera, Communio, Anthropotes,* and *Journal of Early Christian Studies.*

~: John R. Betz :~

John Betz is Associate Professor of Systematic Theology at the University of Notre Dame. Betz's scholarly interest is in the area of German philosophy and theology from the eighteenth century to the present. Within this period he has been concerned primarily with two thinkers: the enigmatic Lutheran author Johann Georg Hamann (1730–1788), arguably the greatest critic of the Enlightenment, and the twentieth-century Jesuit Erich Przywara (1889–1972), who was a prominent philosophical theologian between the two world wars and is most well known for his 1932 work, *Analogia Entis.* In addition to articles in journals such as *Modern Theology, Pro Ecclesia,* and the *Journal of the History of Ideas,* his publications include the book, *After Enlightenment: The Post-Secular Vision of J. G. Hamann* (2009), and a forthcoming translation, in collaboration with David B. Hart, of the 1962 edition of Przywara's *Analogia Entis.*

~: Germain Grisez :~

Germain Grisez was the Most Rev. Harry J. Flynn Professor of Christian Ethics at Mount St. Mary's University, Emmitsburg, Maryland, from 1979–2009. He is now Professor Emeritus. Previously he taught philosophy at Georgetown University (1957–1972) and Campion College, Regina, Saskatchewan (1972–1979). His most important work is *The Way of the Lord Jesus,* vol. 1: Christian Moral Principles; vol. 2: Living a Christian Life; and vol. 3: Difficult Moral Questions, now published by St. Paul's/Alba House, Staten Island, New York. For more about Grisez, his publications, and his collaboration with various other Catholic scholars, see www.twotlj.org.

~: Joseph C. Atkinson :~

Joseph C. Atkinson is the Associate Professor of Sacred Scripture at the John Paul II Institute in Washington, DC. He specializes in the biblical and theological foundations of the family's role in salvation history (the domestic church) and has lectured widely in America, Ireland, Australia, and India and on the biblical structure of the family, hermeneutics, the Jewish background of the family, and covenantal theology. His published articles include: "Family As Domestic Church: Developmental Trajectory, Legitimacy, And Problems Of Appropriation," and "Nuptiality as a Paradigmatic Structure of Biblical Revelation." EWTN Global Catholic Network has produced a 13-part series with Atkinson on the biblical vision of marriage and family.

~: Brian W. Harrison, O. S. :~

Brian W. Harrison is a priest of the Society of the Oblates of Wisdom. He is scholar-in-residence at the Oblates of Wisdom house of studies in St. Louis, Missouri, and an emeritus Professor of Theology of the Pontifical Catholic University of Puerto Rico. He earned his licentiate (S.T.L.) in theology at the Pontifical University of St. Thomas Aquinas (Angelicum) and his doctorate in systematic theology (S.T.D.) from the Pontifical Athenæum of the Holy Cross in Rome. His doctoral dissertation was *The Teaching of Pope Paul VI on Sacred Scripture, with Special Reference to the Historicity of the Gospels* (1997).

~: Robert L. Fastiggi :~

Robert L. Fastiggi is Professor of Systematic Theology at Sacred Heart Major Seminary in Detroit, where he has taught since 1999. From 1985–1999, he was on the faculty of St. Edward's University in Austin, Texas. He holds an A.B. in Religion from Dartmouth College, and a M.A. and a Ph.D. in Theology from Fordham University. Among the books he has written and edited are *The Natural Theology of Yves de Paris* (1991); *The Mystical Theology of the Catholic Reformation: An Overview of Baroque Spirituality* (with José Pereira, 2006). *De Maria Numquam Satis: The Significance of the Catholic Doctrines on the Blessed Virgin Mary for All People* (edited with Judith Marie Gentle, 2009) Fastiggi serves as the executive editor of the annual New Catholic Encyclopedia Supplements that have been published since 2009, and he is the co-editor of the English translation of the

40th edition of Denzinger-Hünermann's *Enchirdion Symbolorum Definitionum et Declarationum de Rebus Fidei et Morum*, to be published by Ignatius Press.

~: Jeffrey L. Morrow :~

Jeffrey L. Morrow is assistant professor at Immaculate Conception Seminary School of Theology at Seton Hall University in South Orange, New Jersey, where he currently teaches courses in systematic theology and Sacred Scripture. He has forthcoming articles concerning the history of biblical interpretation in *Scottish Journal of Theology*, *New Blackfriars*, and *Pro Ecclesia*.

~: Matthew Levering :~

Matthew Levering is Professor of Theology at the University of Dayton in Dayton, Ohio. Previously he taught theology at Ave Maria University for nine years and in 2006-2007 was the Myser Fellow at the Center for Ethics and Culture at the University of Notre Dame. Since 2007 he has served as Chair of the Board of the Academy of Catholic Theology. He is also co-director of the Center for Catholic-Evangelical Dialogue. Levering is the co-editor of the theological quarterly, *Nova et Vetera*, and co-edits book series for the University of Notre Dame Press, Catholic University of America Press, Sapientia Press, and Brazos Press. He earned his Ph.D. in Systematic Theology from Boston College and is the author or editor of more than twenty books and dozens of articles. His books include: *Christ and the Catholic Priesthood* (2010); *Jewish-Christian Dialogue and the Life of Wisdom* (2010); *Participatory Biblical Exegesis: A Theology of Biblical Interpretation* (2008); *Biblical Natural Law: A Theocentric and Teleological Approach* (2008), *Ezra and Nehemiah: A Theological Commentary* (2007), *Sacrifice and Community: Jewish Offering and Christian Eucharist* (2005), *Scripture and Metaphysics: Aquinas and the Renewal of Trinitarian Theology* (2004), and *Christ's Fulfillment of Torah and Temple: Salvation According to St. Thomas Aquinas* (2002).

~: Thomas J. McGovern :~

Thomas J. McGovern is a priest of the Opus Dei prelature who works in Dublin, Ireland. He earned his doctorate in theology from the University of Navarre, in Pamplona, Spain, writing his dissertation on: "The Inspiration and the Interpretation of Sacred Scripture in Chapter 3 of the Vatican II Dogmatic Constitution on Divine Revelation, *Dei Verbum*." He is a memer of the editorial committee for the English translation of the *Navarre Bible*. His articles have been published in *Position Papers* (Dublin); *Forum Katolishce Theologie* (Augsburg); *Irish Theological Quarterly*; *Josephinum Journal of Theology*; *Scripta Theologica* (Pamplona); and *Annales Theologici* (Rome). His books include: *Priestly Celibacy Today* (1998);

Priestly Identity: A Study in the Theology of Priesthood (2002); and *Generations of Priests* (2010). His article in this volume was first published in *Homiletic and Pastoral Review* 92 (November 1992): 10–19.

~: Joseph H. Crehan, S. J. :~

Joseph H. Crehan (1906–1981), a Jesuit priest, earned his doctorate at the Pontifical Gregorian University in Rome and taught theology at Heythrop College, and St. John's College in England. He served on the editorial board and as principal author of many of the entries in the three-volume *A Catholic Dictionary of Theology* (1962–1971). He was also the author of *The Theology of St. John* (1965); *Early Christian Baptism and Creed: A Study in Ante-Nicene Theology* (1950), and was the translator and annotator of Athenagoras's "Embassy for the Christians" and "The Resurrection of the Dead," published in the Ancient Christian Writers series. His article in this volume was originally published in *The Journal of Theological Studies*, New Series 6 (1955): 87–90.

~: Thomas F. Stransky, C. S. P. :~

Thomas F. Stransky, a Paulist priest, is rector emeritus of Tantur Ecumenical Institute for Theological Studies in Jerusalem, where he served from 1987–1998. He was one of the original staff members of the Vatican's Secretariat for the Promotion of Christian Unity, serving with Cardinals Augustin Bea and Johannes Willebrands, the first two secretariat presidents. Among his books are *Roman Catholic Theologies and Agendas: Since Vatican Council II (1962–65) into the 1990s* (1991). His article in this volume was originally published in *American Ecclesiastical Review* 143 (1960): 376–383.

~: Peter Paul Zerafa, O. P. :~

Peter Paul Zerafa (b. 1929) is a member of the Dominican Order. He had a long career as a professor of sacred Scripture. He taught for nearly 30 years at the Angelicum in Rome (1960–1989), as well at the Pontifical Institute Regina Mundi, Rome (1964–1983) and many other institutions. Zerafa was a consultor to the Pontifical Commission for the New Vulgate, and a member of the commission in charge of producing the second edition of the Maltese Bible. His books include: *Wisdom in Proverbs* 1:20–33; 8:1–31 (1967), and *The Wisdom of God in the Book of Job* (1978). His article in this volume was originally published in the *Angelicum* 39 (1962): 92–119.

~: Augstin Cardinal Bea, S.J. :~

Augustin Cardinal Bea (1881–1968), was a Jesuit priest with a long distinguished career as a biblical scholar, serving at the Pontifical Biblical Institute and the Pontifical Gregorian University among other places. Cardinal Bea served on the Pontifical Biblical Commission under Pope Pius XII and influenced the formation of the pope's encyclical, *Divino Afflante Spiritu* (1943). He also collaborated from 1941–1948 in the project to prepare a new Latin translation of the Psalter. A close adviser to Pope John XXIII, he had a shaping influence on the Second Vatican Council's documents on non-Christian religions, religious freedom, and divine revelation. His books include: *The Unity of Christians* (1963) and *The Word of God and Mankind* (1962), from which the selection in this volume is drawn. It was originally published with permission of the Continuum International Publishing Group in *Letter & Spirit*, vol. 1 (2005).

~: Paul Cardinal Taguchi :~

Paul Cardinal Taguchi (1902–1978) was Archbishop of Osaka, Japan, serving from 1941–1978. He was elevated to the College of Cardinals by Pope Paul VI in 1973. Cardinal Taguchi studied at the Pontifical Urbaniana University and Pontifical Athenaeum St. Apollinare in Rome. The essay in this volume was originally published in *L'Osservatore Romano* (May 15, 1975), and was reprinted in John Steinmueller, *The Sword and the Spirit* (Waco, TX: Stella Maris, 1978), 87–108.

~: Romano Guardini :~

Romano Guardini was a priest and theologian and one of the most important figures in Catholic intellectual life in twentieth-century Germany. His books include: *The Spirit of the Liturgy* (1918); *The Church and the Catholic* (1922); *Letters from Lake Como* (1927); *Sacred Signs* (1929); *Pascal for our Time* (1935); *The Conversion of St. Augustine* (1935); *The Lord* (1937); *The World and the Person* (1939); *The Last Things* (1940); *The Death of Socrates* (1943); *Prayers from Theology* (1948); *The End of the Modern World* (1950); *Power and Responsibility* (1951); *In Praise of the Book* (1951); *Rilke's Duino Elegies* (1961); *The Humanity of Christ* (1958); *The Wisdom of the Psalms* (1963); *The Church of the Lord* (1965). The essay in the current volume of *Letter & Spirit*, was originally published as "Heilige Schrift und Glaubenswissenschaft," in the German review, *Die Schildgenossen* (1928). This marks the first time Guardini's text has been translated into English.

~: Scott G. Hefelfinger :~

Scott G. Hefelinger is Adjunct Professor of Philosophy at the International Theological Institute in Trumau, Austria. After completing a degree in music composition and writing a number of musical works, he earned a Master of Sacred Theology (S.T.M.) degree from the Institute, where he is currently pursuing his licentiate of Sacred Theology (S.T.L.). His recent work is forthcoming in *Logos: A Journal of Catholic Thought and Culture* and *Antiphon: A Journal for Liturgical Renewal*.

Letter & Spirit 6 (2010): 11-19

Introduction

In this volume of *Letter & Spirit*, we examine one of the most fundamental mysteries of the Christian faith, the mystery of the truth and inspiration of the sacred Scriptures as the Word of God. Christianity has never been a religion of the book, although from the beginning Scripture has played a vital role in the lives of believers and the mission of the Church.

The New Testament testifies that the first Christians understood both the Jewish Scriptures and the apostolic writings to be of divine origin, authority, and power. We know from the oldest surviving extra-biblical records that every celebration of the Eucharist on the Lord's Day began with readings from "the memoirs of the apostles and the writings of the prophets."[1]

Early on, Christians began the custom of venerating the Scriptures. They kissed the book of the Gospels before opening and reading it. They began their liturgies with a solemn procession in which they bore the Gospel book to the altar and "enthroned" it in a place of honor. "The entrance of the Gospel makes visible [Greek: *emphainei*] the coming of the Son of God and his entrance into this world," St. Germanus I, the seventh-century Patriarch of Constantinople, wrote in his famous explanation of the divine liturgy.[2]

There was more than symbolism at work in these rituals of respect. During the imperial persecutions, bishops, priests, and lay people endured torture and death rather than hand over or reveal the hiding places of "the Lord's Scriptures."[3] Church Fathers such as Origen taught that the book of the Gospels was to be revered as the Eucharist was—as "the Body of the Lord."[4]

Indeed, a profound unity was felt between the Word and the Eucharist. As St. Jerome put it: "When we approach the [eucharistic] mystery, if a crumb falls to the ground we are troubled. Yet when we are listening to the Word of God, and God's Word and Christ's flesh and blood are being poured into our ears yet we pay no heed, what peril should we not feel?"[5] The first Christians believed that

---

1   St. Justin Martyr, *First Apology*, Chaps. 65–67, in *Ante-Nicene Fathers*, 10 vols., eds. Alexander Roberts and James Donaldson (Peabody, MA: Hendrickson, 2004 [reprint]), 1:185.

2   St. Germanus of Constantinople, *Ecclesiastical History and Mystical Contemplation*, 24, in *On the Divine Liturgy*, trans. and introd. Paul Meyendorff (Crestwood, NY: St. Vladimir's Seminary, 1984), 73.

3   See Gregory Dix, *The Shape of the Liturgy*, new ed. introd. Simon Jones (New York: Continuum, 2005 [1945]), 24–27; compare Rev. 6:9.

4   Origen, *Homilies on Exodus*, Hom. 13, 3, in *Patrologiae Cursus Completus: Series Graeca*, ed. J. P. Migne, 161 vols. (Paris: Garnier and J. P. Migne, 1857–1866), 12:391. Hereafter abbreviated: *PG*. Eng. trans. in Origen, *Homilies on Genesis and Exodus*, The Fathers of the Church 71 (Washington, DC: Catholic University of America, 1982).

5   St. Jerome, *Commentary on the Psalms*, Ps. 147, in *Corpus Christianorum: Series Latina* (Turnhout: Brepols, 1953–), 78:337–378.

God's Word was living and active, at work in those who believe.[6] Pronounced in the Church's sacred liturgy, this Word was performative and efficacious, accomplishing what it proposed—bringing the believer into contact with the living God. Each of the Church's sacraments, St. Augustine taught, was "a kind of visible word [Latin: *verbum visibile*]."[7]

The first Christians cherished the Scriptures as the very Word of God written in human words, inspired by the Spirit of God.[8] But their faith was not a faith in written texts. It was faith in the living Word, in the event preserved and in some way mysteriously prolonged in these texts—the encounter with the divine person, Jesus Christ. The Scriptures themselves testified that Jesus is the Word of God, long spoken by the Father through the mouths of his prophets but in these last days come in human flesh in the person of his only Son.[9]

Verbum caro factum est. These words from the prologue of the Gospel of John, rendered in the Latin of the Vulgate, the first common translation of the Bible, encapsulate the mystery: "And the Word was made flesh." Christianity is not a religion of the book. It is the religion of the incarnate Word of God. The Christian believes that this Word is the eternal Word, the *Logos*, the divine Wisdom and creative Reason through whom God created the heavens and the earth in the beginning.[10] The Christian believes that this divine Word, in the fullness of time, humbled and emptied himself, accommodating himself to our weakness, condescending to share in our humanity by dwelling among us in the form of a man, a servant to others.[11]

At the heart of the mystery and mission of the Word incarnate lies the mystery of the sacred Scriptures. The Scriptures are central to the divine pedagogy and economy of salvation that they attest to. The history that unfolds in the pages of the Old Testament documents a dialogue, a kind of courtship, in which God, through his patriarchs and prophets, addresses to Israel and the nations an invitation to share in the blessings of his divine life, to live as children of God in his covenant family and kingdom. The history of salvation is depicted as beginning in pure gift, with a series of divine speech acts: *Dixitque Deus fiat.* "And God said: 'Let there be ...'" God is depicted speaking the world into being, writing what the Church Fathers and saints would later call the *liber naturae*, the book of nature. The human person is the culmination of God's creation, made a *creatura Verbi*, a

---

6   See Heb. 4:12; 1 Thess. 2:13.

7   St. Augustine, *Tractates on the Gospel of John*, Tract. 80, 3, in *A Select Library of Nicene and Post-Nicene Fathers of the Christian Church*, 1st series, 14 vols., ed. Philip Schaff (Peabody, MA: Hendrickson, 1994 [reprint]), 7:344; compare 1 Pet. 1:23; Eph. 5: 26.

8   1 Thess. 2:13; 2 Thess. 3:16; 2 Pet. 1:21.

9   Heb. 1:1.

10   2 Pet. 3:5; John 1:3; Col. 1:15–16; Heb. 11:3; compare Ps. 33:6, 9.

11   Gal. 4:4; Phil. 2:5–11.

creature of the Word, as later Church writers would term it. Born of the creative Word of God, the human person is shown throughout the pages of the Scriptures as having been created for a relationship with the Creator, summoned to live in filial dialogue with the Father.

The history that unfolds in the New Testament records how God's Word was made flesh in order to fulfill all that God had promised beforehand in the Scriptures.[12] Jesus' resurrection from the dead is depicted as the vindication of his interpretation of the Scriptures. On the night of his resurrection, he is shown teaching his disciples the meaning of his new covenant in light of the Scriptures and how the written text is to become living Word in the celebration of the divine liturgy. "And beginning with Moses and all the prophets, he interpreted to them in all the Scriptures the things concerning himself ... and how he was known to them in the breaking of the bread."[13]

The theology and apologetics of the early Church, not to mention her pastoral practice, consisted almost entirely of interpretation and commentary on the Scriptures in light of the words and deeds of Christ.[14] The apostles considered themselves to be servants of the Word of God. St. Paul described himself as "a minister according to the divine office which was given to me ... to make the Word of God fully known."[15] The apostolic Church charted her growth in terms of the growth of God's Word.[16] And the New Testament writings, which preserve the apostolic preaching and witness to Christ, profess the same motive and purpose as that preaching—to bring men and women into saving contact with the "words of eternal life," through which they would meet the living Word of God.[17]

> That ... which we have heard, which we have seen with our eyes, which we have looked upon and touched with our hands, concerning the Word of life ... we are writing.[18]

> These were written that you may believe that Jesus is the Christ, the Son of God, and that believing you may have life in his name.[19]

---

12 Compare Matt. 26:56; Mark 14:49; Luke 24:27, 32, 45; John 5:39.

13 See Luke 24:27, 35.

14 See for example, Rom. 1:2; John 2:22; Acts. 15:6; 17:2, 11; 18:28; Rom. 1:2; 15:4; 1 Cor. 15:3, 4; compare John 14:25–26.

15 1 Cor. 14:36; 2 Cor. 2:17; Act. 6:4; Col. 1:25.

16 Compare Acts 6:7; 12:24; 19:20.

17 John 6:63, 68.

18 1 John 1:1–4.

19 John 20:31.

The Christian faith, then, is rooted in this mystery of a God who communicates, a God who has chosen to enter into a dialogue of love with his creatures through the gift of his Word—incarnate in Christ and inspired in the pages of the Scripture. The mystery of the written Word, the *Verbum Dei Scriptum*, participates in this greater mystery—the mission of the incarnate Word, the *Verbum Dei Incarnatum*.

~:~

These mysteries give shape to the theme and subject matter of this volume of *Letter & Spirit.* Theologians traditionally have considered these mysteries under the heading of *the inspiration and truth* of sacred Scripture or, to use a slightly older nomenclature, *the inspiration and inerrancy* of Scripture. In the modern period, the orthodox Catholic understanding of these categories was set forth in the great Scripture encyclicals of the popes—Leo XII's *Providentissimus Deus* (1893), Benedict XV's *Spiritus Paraclitus* (1920), and Pius XII's *Divino Afflante Spiritu* (1943)—and codified in Second Vatican Council's dogmatic constitution on divine revelation, *Dei Verbum* (1965).[20]

In essence, the Church has always taught that Scripture partakes of the mystery it imparts—that there is a profound interrelation between the Word incarnate and the Word inspired. Pius XII expressed it this way:

> For as the substantial Word of God became like human beings in all things 'except sin,' so the words of God, expressed in human language, are made like to human speech in every respect except error. In this consists that "condescension" of the God of providence, which St. John Chrysostom extolled with the highest praise and repeatedly declared to be found in the sacred books.[21]

It is important to remember that this analogy of the Word inspired and the Word incarnate—and the Church's teaching on the truth and inerrancy of Scripture—grows out of the lived experience of the early Church. Following the christological hymn in St. Paul's Letter to the Philippians,[22] the Church Fathers took note of the

---

20 See Pope Leo XIII, *Providentissimus Deus* [The God of All Providence], Encyclical Letter on the Study of Scripture (November 18, 1893); Pope Benedict XV, *Spiritus Paraclitus* [The Holy Spirit, the Comforter], Encyclical Letter Commemorating the Fifteenth Centenary of the Death of St. Jerome (September 15, 1920); Pope Pius XII, *Divino Afflante Spiritu* [Inspired by the Divine Spirit], Encyclical Letter Promoting Biblical Studies (September 30, 1943); Second Vatican Council, *Dei Verbum* [The Word of God], Dogmatic Constitution on Divine Revelation, (November 18, 1965). Texts in *The Scripture Documents: An Anthology of Official Catholic Teachings*, ed. Dean P. Béchard (Collegeville, MN: Liturgical Press, 2002).

21 Pius XI, *Divino Afflante Spiritu* 20, quoting Heb. 4:15.

22 See Phil. 2:5–11.

deep humility of the divine expressed in the incarnation—the humility of the Son of God's *kenosis*, his self-emptying to be born of a woman in the form of an infant. Many saw an analogy between the humility and condescension of the incarnation and the humility and condescension of the Word of God expressed in the poverty of human language.

In the Scriptures, God adapts his Word to our weakness in order to communicate with us, Origen said:

> He condescends and accommodates himself to our weakness,
> like a schoolmaster talking a "little language" to his children, like
> a father caring for his own children and adopting their ways.[23]

The Word inspired follows the same pattern of lowliness and humble service as the Word incarnate. As the Word was made incarnate for our salvation, so also the Scriptures are inspired for the sake of our salvation. This image is a commonplace in the writings of the Fathers and Churchmen of the Middle Ages; so is the notion that the Scriptures contain no error, as God cannot lie.[24] St. Thomas Aquinas held that "Sacred Scripture was divinely appointed to manifest the truth necessary for salvation."[25] The enduring sense of the Church was well expressed in the Middle Ages by St. Anselm of Canterbury:

> There is nothing that we preach profitably for spiritual salvation
> that sacred Scripture, made fruitful by the miracle of the Holy
> Spirit, has not expressed or does not contain within itself.[26]

~:~

One of the ironies of history is that it was the Reformation's insistence upon *sola Scriptura* that first forced the issue of the truth and inspiration of Scripture.

---

23 Origen, *Fragments on Deuteronomy*, 1, 21 (PG 17:24), quoted in Stephen D. Benin, *The Footprints of God: Divine Accommodation in Jewish and Christian Thought* (Albany: State University of New York, 1993), 12.

24 Tit. 1:2.

25 Latin: "Sacra Scriptura ad hoc divinitus est ordinata ut per eam nobis veritas manifestetur necessaria ad salutem." St. Thomas Aquinas, *Quaestiones Quodlibetales* [Miscellaneous Questions], quod. 1, q. 6, art. 1; compare Aquinas, *Summa Theologiae* [Summary of Theology], pt. 1a-2ae, q. 106, art. 4, reply obj. 2; pt. 1a-2ae, q. 108, art. 2, contra.

26 Latin: "Nihil utiliter ad salutem praedicamus, quod sacra Scriptura, Spiritus Sancti miraculo fecundata, non protulerit aut intra se non contineat." St. Anselm, *De Concordia Praescientiae Dei cum Libero Arbirtrio* [The Compatibility of God's Foreknowledge, Predestination, and Grace with Human Freedom], q. 3, chap. 6, in *Patrologiae Cursus Completus: Series Latina*, ed. J. P. Migne, 221 vols (Paris: Garnier and J. P. Migne, 1844–1864), 158:528B. Eng. trans. in *Anselm of Canterbury: The Major Works*, eds. Brian Davies and G. R. Evans (New York: Oxford, 2008), 435–474.

In seeking to undermine the Church's interpretive authority by insisting that "Scripture alone" was sufficient for salvation, the reformers unwittingly set in motion a series of intellectual processes by which the Bible eventually came to be secularized during the Enlightenment and the subsequent rise of liberal theology and historical-critical exegesis in the nineteenth and twentieth centuries.

Nowadays, this secular approach to Scripture is the preferred and incontestable methodology in the academy and in many seminaries and ecclesial centers of higher learning. And as the modern period has progressed into what is now regarded as "post-modernity," it has become plain to see: removed from their origin and context in the Church's living traditions of faith and worship, the Scriptures possess no inherent authority and there is no necessary reason to presume that they are true, accurate, or reliable. In the academy today, the Bible is often treated as simply another ancient text, the veracity of which is subject to the skeptical evaluations and criteria of an elite of secular authorities.

Much of biblical interpretation today begins with the assumptions, not of faith, but of a positivistic rationality that denies the truth or historicity of any claims or events that cannot be demonstrated by means of the natural sciences; in other words, it begins by denying the possibility of what the Scriptures assert on every page—that God can act and speak in human history, that the material and natural world is open to a world that is spiritual and supernatural.

Practically speaking, that means today's dominant methodology for reading Scriptures starts by presuming that many of the events recorded in the Scriptures—including one of the central truth claims of the Christian faith, Christ's bodily resurrection from the dead—did not actually take place. The consequences of this interpretive method have been disturbing, some would say devastating, not only for theology and exegesis, but for all aspects of the Church's faith, worship, mission, and spiritual life. These consequences have not been confined to Catholicism; indeed, they have spread to every Christian confession.[27]

The widespread erosion in the assumption that Scripture is the true Word of God forms the broader context for the articles and studies in this volume of *Letter & Spirit*. As we see it, the work we present in these pages is no ivory tower exercise. It is no exaggeration to say that at stake in this discussion is the future of the identity of the Church and the mission of the Word incarnate. If the Scriptures cannot be trusted to communicate the truth about God and his saving message, if they do not bring us to the encounter with the living God who speaks his Word, then it must be asked: what is the meaning and purpose of the Church?

In previous eras, the Church proclaimed the Word with confidence that it was the good news, the *Verbum Vitae* ("Word of life") that spoke to the deepest yearnings and desires of the human condition. Believers could entrust themselves to this Word, order their lives by it; they could seek in it the highest beauties and

---

27   See the important investigation by G. K. Beale, *The Erosion of Inerrancy in Evangelicalism: Responding to the Challenges to Biblical Authority* (Wheaton, IL: Crossway, 2008).

truths and the meaning of history. The Word marked out the new horizons of their identity and the new direction of their lives in Christ. In a world they understood to be passing, amidst a generation they understood to be crooked and perverse, the Christian would live by the light of this Word—"holding fast the Word of life" in anticipation of the day of Christ, the day when he will come again.[28]

This certainty has been shaken, and the repercussions can be felt everywhere in the Church and in the broader secular civilization of the West. At least since the time of St. Jerome, the Church has recognized an essential and reciprocal relationship between the Scriptures and Christ—that faith in Christ is indissolubly bound up with how we approach the testimony about Christ that we find in the Scriptures.[29] Jerome argued that ignorance of the Scriptures means ignorance of Christ. In our day we can see very clearly what he was talking about. The widespread skepticism concerning the truth of Scripture has accompanied a widespread crisis of faith in Christ and in God.

So it becomes crucial that we take up afresh the theological question of Scripture's inspiration and truth. We believe that means recovering the ancient analogy by which the Word inspired is understood in light of the Word incarnate. For us, this analogy is the key to avoiding the two false snares of modern biblical interpretation—on the one hand, a fideism or fundamentalism that denies the human character of the Word, and on the other, a critical skepticism that denies the divine character of the Word.

The analogy of the Word incarnate and the Word inspired suggests a fruitful approach to the mysterious realities by which the divine was made human in order to make the human divine. This is the reality no less of sacred Scripture than it is of Jesus Christ. And this analogy suggests a hermeneutic that unites faith and reason, and roots the reading of the sacred page in the continuities of the Church's liturgical tradition and rule of faith.

We agree with the consistent teaching of the Catholic magisterium that the study of literary genres and historical context is indispensable for understanding the literal meaning of the sacred texts. But we also believe with the Church that any interpretation of Scripture is incomplete and ultimately inadequate if it stops at the "letter" of the text and does not reckon with the spiritual message—the saving truths that God desires to communicate to his Church through the sacred text.

To extend the metaphor between inspiration and the incarnation, we might suggest that much of today's scholarship is guilty of a kind of "scriptural Ebionism." The Ebionites were Jewish Christians who believed that Christ, while a great prophet, was nonetheless only a man and not the divine and eternal Word of God. Much scholarship today is based on a similar conviction about the Scriptures—that

---

28 Phil. 2:15–16.

29 See St. Jerome, *Commentary on Isaiah*, Prol., in *Patrologiae Cursus Completus: Series Latina*, ed. J. P. Migne, 221 vols (Paris: Garnier and J. P. Migne, 1844–1864), 24:17.

while perhaps strangely beautiful specimens of ancient literature, they are only that. We must recover a sense of the "theandric" mystery of the sacred Scriptures. As Christ is fully God and fully human and hence cannot be understood apart from this "theandric" or divine-human reality, neither can the Scriptures be understood apart from their dual authorship—by "men moved by the Holy Spirit spoke from God."[30]

If historical and literary study is indispensable to the interpretation of Scripture, the reckoning of the text in light of the mystery of its inspiration and divine authorship is even more so. With the saints and Fathers of the Church, the exegete must be open in humility to the influence of the Holy Spirit, guided by confidence in the methods of reason and by a lively sense that he is in prayerful dialogue—what the ancients called *lectio divina*—with the Word of God.

⁜

The articles and studies in the pages that follow were composed in the wake of the month-long Synod of Bishops convened at the Vatican, October 5–26, 2008, by Pope Benedict XVI to examine the subject of "The Word of God in the Life and Mission of the Church." They were thus written well in advance of *Verbum Domini*, Benedict's official response to the Synod, which he issued in the weeks before this volume was to be published. It is perhaps providential, however, that this volume of *Letter & Spirit* anticipates and addresses many of the profound themes and concerns in the new papal document.

Verbum Domini represents the most authoritative papal statement on sacred Scripture in more than sixty years—and it is perhaps the most comprehensive official Catholic treatment of the subject ever.[31] Benedict proposes a deeper, more richly Marian, ecclesial and eucharistic reflection on the analogy of the Word incarnate and the Word inspired. He writes: "As the Word of God became flesh by the power of the Holy Spirit in the womb of the Virgin Mary, so sacred Scripture is born from the womb of the Church by the power of the same Spirit."[32]

Benedict forcefully restates the Church's traditional teaching that the Word of God is true. He quotes at length from the decisive passage in the Second Vatican Council's *Dei Verbum*:

> As the Council's teaching states ... the inspired books teach the
> truth: "since, therefore, all that the inspired authors, or sacred
> writers, affirm should be regarded as affirmed by the Holy Spirit,

---

30   1 Pet. 1:21.

31   Pope Benedict XVI, *Verbum Domini* ["The Word of the Lord"], Post-Synodal Apostolic Exhortation on the Word of God in the Life and Mission of the Church (September 30, 2010) (Boston: Pauline, 2010).

32   Benedict XVI, *Verbum Domini*, 19.

we must acknowledge that the books of Scripture firmly, faithfully and without error, teach that truth which God, for the sake of our salvation, wished to see confided to the sacred Scriptures. Thus, 'all Scripture is inspired by God and is useful for teaching, for reproof, for correction and for training in righteousness, so that the man of God may be proficient, equipped for every good work' (2 Tim. 3:16–17, Greek)."[33]

If the Scriptures are to be read and interpreted properly as the Word of God, we must have the correct understanding of their inspiration and truth, according to Benedict: "Whenever our awareness of its inspiration grows weak, we risk reading Scripture as an object of historical curiosity and not as the work of the Holy Spirit in which we can hear the Lord himself speak and recognize his presence in history."[34]

Benedict suggests the need for deeper study of the relationship between the process of inspiration and the truth of the sacred texts. "Here I would express my fervent hope that research in this field will progress and bear fruit both for biblical science and for the spiritual life of the faithful," he writes.[35]

Hence, we offer the research and reflections in these pages as a humble response to the Pope's hopes, which we share. It is our fervent hope that this volume of *Letter & Spirit* will contribute to the progress of biblical science, the spiritual life of the faithful, and the mission of the incarnate Word—that the Word of the Lord might grow and prevail mightily.[36]

---

33 Benedict XVI, *Verbum Domini*, 19, quoting *Dei Verbum*, 11.

34 Benedict XVI, *Verbum Domini*, 19.

35 Benedict XVI, *Verbum Domini*, 19.

36 See Acts 19:20.

Letter & Spirit 6 (2010): 21-45

FOR THE SAKE OF OUR SALVATION:
The Truth and Humility of God's Word

∻ Scott W. Hahn ∻

St. Paul Center for Biblical Theology

Christian tradition has always seen a close relationship between the pages of Scripture and the person of Jesus Christ. Both are designated the Word of God because both participate in the mystery of God revealing himself and his will in human form. Scripture is the Word inspired; Christ is the Word incarnate. In the former, the divine Word is expressed in human language; in the latter, the divine Word is enfleshed in human nature. The two mysteries are interpenetrating and mutually illuminating.

The implications of this analogy may be drawn out in different ways. Most obviously, the doctrine of inspiration is akin to the doctrine of the incarnation because it entails a historical manifestation of the Word in a divine-and-human form.[1] Further contemplation reveals that the inerrancy of Scripture is a parallel reflection of the sinlessness of Christ, for both are immune to the privations of truth and love which we call error.[2] So too, on a hermeneutical level, the inspired Word must be read in a way that takes full account of its interconnectedness with the incarnate Word.[3] This is to say that biblical exegesis must investigate the historical meaning of Scripture as well as its theological meaning, the two being properties of its human and divine dimensions respectively.

Building on the foundation of this tradition, I propose that more can be said to elucidate the relationship between Christ and the Bible. My aim in what follows is to advance a twofold thesis. First, I argue that the Church's perspective on Scripture derives from Christ's perspective on Scripture. It is Jesus who sets

---

1   This point is made in the Second Vatican Council's document on divine revelation: "For the words of God, expressed in human language, have become like unto human speech, just as the Word of the eternal Father, when he took on himself the flesh of human weakness, became like unto human beings." *Dei Verbum* [The Word of God], Dogmatic Constitution on Divine Revelation, (November 18, 1965). Translations and section numbers for conciliar, papal, and curial documents cited in this article follow those given in *The Scripture Documents: An Anthology of Official Catholic Teachings*, ed. and trans. by Dean P. Béchard (Collegeville, MN: Liturgical Press, 2002) unless otherwise indicated.

2   This point is made by Pope Pius XII in his 1943 encyclical on biblical studies: "For as the substantial Word of God became like to men in all things 'except sin' (Heb. 4:15), so the words of God, expressed in human language, are made like to human speech in every respect except error." *Divino Afflante Spiritu* [Inspired by the Divine Spirit], Encyclical Letter Promoting Biblical Studies (September 30, 1943), 20.

3   See, for example, Pope John Paul II, Address on the Interpretation of the Bible in the Church (April 23, 1993), 6–11.

the parameters for what the Church believes and teaches about the Bible, and so it follows that our theology of biblical inspiration must proceed from certain fixed points regarding its origin, authority and truthfulness that are established by the teaching of Christ. Second, I am convinced that Scripture's humble human expression is a mirror image of the humility of Jesus. By this I mean that inspired Scripture, like the incarnate Son, embodies the merciful condescension of God in a way that confronts our intellectual pride and calls us to a humility of heart and mind "for the sake of our salvation."[4]

The Authority and Truth of the Word

Though rarely stated in these terms, the Christian vision of the Bible must be determined by Christ's vision of the Bible.[5] Just as we look to Jesus as the perfection of the human vocation, so also we look to him as "the pioneer and perfecter of our faith."[6] Christian belief in the authority and mystery of Scripture is no exception to this principle. By his teaching and example, the Word made flesh transmits to his followers a right understanding of the Word made Scripture.

The gospels have much to say about Jesus' perspective on the Bible.[7] The shape of his thinking on this subject is revealed through the many appeals to the sacred text that occur in his preaching, in his private temptations, and in his polemical engagement with opponents. Virtually everywhere, dispersed throughout all the putative strata and hypothetical sources that are said to underlie the canonical gospels, Jesus appears as one committed to thinking and acting in accord with biblical revelation. Statistical analysis indicates that Jesus referenced the texts of

---

4   The celebrated phrase from *Dei Verbum*, 11.

5   For a development of this thesis by a Protestant scholar, see John W. Wenham, *Christ and the Bible* (Guildford, Surrey: Eagle, 1993). Note also the work of R. D. Wilson, "Jesus and the Old Testament," *The Princeton Theological Review* 24 (1926): 632–661.

6   Heb. 12:2.

7   I recognize that the gospels preserve the *ipsissima vox Christi* ("the genuine voice of Christ") and not always the *ipsissima verba Christi* ("the very words of Christ"). Even so, the Pontifical Biblical Commission insists in its 1964 instruction that the evangelists used "different words to express what he [Jesus] said, not keeping to the very letter, but nevertheless preserving the sense." *Sancta Mater Ecclesia* [Holy Mother Church], Instruction on the Historical Truth of the Gospels (April 21, 1964), 9. My approach to the gospels takes full account of this and is fundamentally aligned with the perspective of the *Catechism of the Catholic Church* as elucidated by Joseph Cardinal Ratzinger (now Pope Benedict XVI) in *Gospel, Catechesis, Catechism: Sidelights on the Catechism of the Catholic Church* (San Francisco: Ignatius, 1997), 64: "The *Catechism* trusts the biblical word. It holds the Christ of the gospels to be the real Jesus. It is also convinced that all the gospels tell us about this same Jesus and that all of them together help us, each in its own way, to know the true Jesus of history, who is no other than the Christ of faith." For scholarly defenses of the historical veracity of the Gospel accounts, see Craig S. Keener, *The Historical Jesus of the Gospels* (Grand Rapids, MI: Eerdmans, 2009); Craig L. Blomberg, *The Historical Reliability of the Gospels*, 2nd. ed. (Downers Grove, IL: IVP Academic, 2007); and Paul Rhodes Eddy and Gregory A. Boyd, *The Jesus Legend: A Case for the Historical Reliability of the Synoptic Jesus Tradition* (Grand Rapids, MI: Baker Academic, 2007).

the Old Testament thirty-nine times throughout the four gospels.[8] However, this figure fails to do justice to the data, since countless other times he alludes to the biblical writings in more subtle and sophisticated ways—adopting their wording, utilizing their images, expounding their themes. It is no exaggeration to say that the mind of Jesus was saturated with the teachings and concerns of the Scriptures.

The question of primary importance is how Jesus viewed the nature of the Bible. What kind of "theology of Scripture" is presupposed by his teaching? How did he account for its sanctity and religious authority? There can be no doubt that Jesus maintained a remarkably high view of the biblical Word. His most basic conviction is the notion that Scripture has its origin in God. For Christ, the words of the Bible are the words of his Father, and so its written assertions are nothing less than divine assertions preserved in readable form. Evidence for this outlook appears, for instance, in Matthew 19:4–5, where Jesus regards "what Scripture says" and "what God says" as one and the same thing.[9] In discussing the divine plan for married life, he tells the Pharisees that "he who made" (*ho ktisas*) man and woman in the beginning is also the One who said (*eipen*): "For this reason a man shall leave his father and mother and be joined to his wife, and the two shall become one."[10] According to Jesus, the voice of the world's Creator is the same voice that speaks through the human words of the Book of Genesis.

A similar perspective may be adduced from Mark 12:36, where Jesus refers to David being "in the Holy Spirit" (*en tō pneumati tō hagiō*) when he composed the words of Psalm 110. He envisions David, the human psalmist, participating in a supernatural movement of the Spirit when he uttered words that ultimately point to his messianic identity. What is remarkable about this statement is the way that Jesus conceptualizes sacred Scripture as a product of divine and human activity unfolding simultaneously in the process of composition. Because the Spirit superintended the writing of the Scriptures, there is a divine causality that must be recognized and accounted for; at the same time, the concept of a human author scrawling his thoughts on papyrus is just as naturally a part of the picture. So Jesus not only ascribes the biblical writings to the agency of God or his Spirit, but he also affirms the conscious involvement of human authors. In addition to David's role in the composition of Psalm 110, he speaks of other portions of the Bible being written by figures such as Moses,[11] Isaiah,[12] and Daniel.[13]

---

8   For the thirty-nine explicit quotations attributed to Jesus, see Richard N. Longenecker, *Biblical Exegesis in the Apostolic Period*, 2nd. ed. (Grand Rapids, MI: Eerdmans, 1999), 42–43.

9   For this and similar phenomena in the writings of the New Testament, see B. B. Warfield, "'It Says:' 'Scripture Says:' 'God Says,'" in *The Works of Benjamin B. Warfield*, vol. 1 (Grand Rapids, MI: Baker, 1981), 283–332.

10   Gen. 2:24.

11   John 5:46–47.

12   Mark 7:6.

13   Matt. 24:15.

An immediate consequence of Scripture's divine origin is its supreme authority. If the Bible enshrines the discourse of God, it must thereby express the will of God. Jesus reveals this perspective as his own in several places in the gospels, most memorably during his showdown with the devil in the wilderness. In the Matthean account of the temptations of Jesus, the Messiah repels his assailant with three quotations from the Old Testament Scriptures. In all three, he introduces the citation with the preface, "it is written" (*gegraptai*), a formula used in emergent Judaism and throughout the New Testament to summarize the belief that Scripture, precisely in its canonical expression, is the incontrovertible foundation for religious faith and life.[14] Jesus confirms this by his first quotation against the devil in Matthew 4:4: "Man shall not live by bread alone, but by every word that proceeds from the mouth of God."[15] Insofar as Scripture communicates words that come from God, it lays down inviolable standards that must never be ignored or transgressed.

This perspective is again manifest when Jesus states in John 10:35 that "Scripture cannot be broken" (*ou dunatai luthēnai hē graphē*). In this context, he is rebutting a charge that his claim to be the Son of God amounts to blasphemy. In order to prove otherwise, he appeals to Psalm 82:6, where the judges of Israel are described as "gods" insofar as God's authority was entrusted to them to administer divine justice according to divine law. Jesus reasons that if a divine appellation can be given to men who enact and enforce the Law of God, then no objection can be made for one who performs the works of God.[16] The argument has force, he insists, because the binding authority of Scripture can never be annulled or invalidated. Its testimony is altogether unbreakable. Moreover, the solemn weight of divine authority extends to every part of Scripture, even to its individual words. This is clear from the fact that Jesus' whole argument turns on the use of the term "gods" in Psalm 82.

Finally, if Jesus holds that Scripture comes from God, and that its teachings are invested with divine authority, does it follow for him that Scripture is divinely truthful?[17] The answer that emerges from the gospels is an emphatic yes. Although there is no one passage where Jesus makes this deduction in so many words, the Gospel tradition gives us ample warrant for drawing the conclusion. Consider, for

---

14   Matt. 4:4, 7, 10.

15   Deut. 8:3.

16   See John 10:37–38.

17   It should be pointed out that the biblical notion of "truth" conveys the idea of reliability as well as factuality. Thus, it not only entails an accurate presentation of the way things are or were, but it provides sufficient ground for one's trust and confidence as well. For an important survey of the topic, see Roger Nicole, "The Biblical Concept of Truth" in *Scripture and Truth*, eds. D. A. Carson and John D. Woodbridge (Grand Rapids, MI: Baker, 1992), 287–298. For an analysis of truth as grounded in God's faithfulness to the covenant, see Oswald Loretz, *The Truth of the Bible*, trans. David J. Bourke (New York: Herder and Herder, 1968).

instance, Christ's high priestly prayer in John 17:1–26. Petitioning the Father on behalf of his disciples, he states: "your word is truth."[18] Now, granted, Jesus is not speaking specifically about the Bible in this passage. Nevertheless, the assertion is deprived of meaning if in fact the written Word of God is tainted with misinformation and false representations of reality. The statement affirms something that is true in general; it is not an assertion that characterizes one particular form of God's Word over against another. Instead, it seems that Jesus is explicating the positive content of Israel's belief that "God is not man, that he should lie."[19] Besides, we never see Christ correcting the Scriptures from his transcendent vantage point as the Son of God, as one who knows the Father in a uniquely divine way.[20] Neither does he make merely tentative proposals on the basis of biblical testimony. His every reference to Scripture is made with an unshakeable trust in its reliability.

Similar confidence in the truthfulness of Scripture is displayed when Jesus invokes its prophetic oracles. Christ firmly believed that the Old Testament "must" (*dei*) be brought to fulfillment in him, especially in the events of the Triduum, for the Scriptures had determined in advance that he should be handed over to enemies,[21] reckoned with transgressors,[22] lifted up on the cross,[23] and brought through suffering into glory.[24] It is hard to imagine such a weight of divine necessity on the mind of Jesus unless he was convinced of the absolute truth of the sacred texts. Yet Jesus maintained that the entire Old Testament bore witness to his messianic mission. The testimony of Scripture stretching from the Law and the prophets to the psalms is such that God's plan of salvation is climactically realized in him.[25] For Jesus, then, the Old Testament is anything but a haphazard collection of writings bundling together diverse and contradictory viewpoints. There is a unified plan and perspective throughout, an authentic christological focus that is intended by God. But a unity of purpose at this level presupposes an underlying consistency which would seem to rule out any serious deviation from the truth. It takes only a few dissonant notes to spoil the harmony of a grand symphonic performance.

All of this takes on greater significance when we consider that Jesus' whole mission was "to bear witness to the truth"[26] and to enable his disciples to "know

---

18   John 17:17.

19   Num. 23:19.

20   Matt. 11:27.

21   Matt. 26:54.

22   Luke 22:37.

23   John 3:14.

24   Luke 24:25–26.

25   See Luke 24:44.

26   John 18:37.

the truth" by adherence to his word.[27] He claims for himself a personal veracity that, for any other man, would be audacious at best and intolerable at worst. Not even the prophets of Israel, who spoke by the Spirit of God, could make such all-encompassing claims for their teaching. Yet the Gospel tradition lacks any statement or comment that might suggest Jesus was prone, or even potentially liable, to err in his speech. All that he teaches is delivered with absolute authority and without the attachment of disclaimers or qualifications. His words are put forward as a stable foundation of rock upon which to build one's life in preparation for the final judgment.[28] For these reasons, the authority and reliability of God's Word in Scripture can be said to stand or fall with the authority and reliability of God's Word incarnate. The two are inseparably united at the deepest level.

The Perspective of the Ancient Church

The perspective of Jesus on Scripture was immediately taken over as the perspective of the ancient Church. The teaching of the New Testament as well as the earliest Christian writers is merely an echo of the voice of Christ on this subject. In all essentials, from the Bible's divine origin to its divine authority and truthfulness, there is a consistency and continuity of doctrinal outlook. Even where developments beyond the express teaching of Jesus are evidenced, it is usually an effort to make explicit what is already implicit in his words.

Regarding the divine origin of the Bible, one can find no clearer statement than Paul's affirmation in 2 Timothy 3:16–17: "All Scripture is inspired by God and profitable for teaching, for reproof, for correction, and for training in righteousness, that the man of God may be complete, equipped for every good work." The crucial expression of the passage is "inspired by God," which in Greek is the compound adjective *theopneustos*, meaning "breathed by God." Owing to the influence of the Latin Vulgate, which rendered the expression *divinitus inspirata*, the Church has traditionally spoken of the divine inspiration of Scripture. This is perfectly legitimate as theological terminology, but it should be pointed out that *inspirare* typically means "to breath into," as its usage in the Vulgate Old Testament makes evident.[29] *Theopneustos*, however, designates a "breathing out" or "breathing forth" of the Scriptures from God as their Source.

The description is obviously anthropomorphic, recalling how human words are merely a breath, a type of exhaling accompanied by a momentary sound. However, this does not mean that Paul thought of the breath of God as something so fleeting and insubstantial. On the contrary, the conceptual background of the expression lies in the Old Testament, where the Lord's *n š mâ* or "breath" is

---

27   John 8:31–32.

28   Matt. 7:24–27.

29   For example, Gen. 2:7; Wisd. 15:11; Sir. 4:11.

the instrument of his infinite power. It brought all of creation into being[30] and performed such mighty feats of deliverance as blasting a path of escape through the Red Sea.[31] To say that Scripture is "God-breathed" is to speak of its divine origin as well as its divine potency as a word that never fails to accomplish God's purpose.[32]

It is precisely the supernatural source and power behind the Scriptures that makes them "profitable" for Christian teaching. Since God himself brought forth the divine books, they are supremely authoritative for various forms of religious instruction,[33] especially moral formation, as indicated here by their ability to equip the believer "for every good work." It likewise accounts for the characterization of the biblical texts as *hiera grammata*, "sacred writings," for they partake of the holiness of God who produced them.[34]

Despite the importance of Paul's instruction in 2 Timothy, it is only a partial statement on the nature of the Bible. Not only is the scope of the biblical canon left unspecified,[35] but the participation of human authors goes unmentioned as well. In other words, the historical process by which God breathed the Scriptures into being receives no attention. For this dimension of the mystery, which was clearly affirmed by Jesus,[36] we have to look at other passages which describe the Bible as a book that is simultaneously human and divine.

The most important is Peter's affirmation in 2 Peter 1:20–21: "First of all," he declares, "you must understand this, that no prophecy of Scripture is a matter of one's own interpretation, because no prophecy ever came by the impulse of man, but men moved by the Holy Spirit spoke from God." This saying extends our vision beyond that of the Pauline text by considering the involvement of human participants in Scripture's composition. On the one hand, Peter is anxious to deny that biblical prophecy is a strictly natural phenomenon, as though the prophets of Israel communicated only what they imagined the future would bring. In the apostle's judgment, it is reductionistic and simply wrong to equate prophecy with human speculation about the will of God for his people or about his plan for the

---

30   Ps. 33:6.

31   2 Sam. 22:16.

32   Isa. 55:11.

33   Paul also voices this conviction in Rom. 15:4 and 1 Cor. 10:11.

34   2 Tim. 3:15.

35   Contextually it is clear that Paul has the Old Testament in mind, for Timothy could not have known the books of the New Testament "from childhood" (2 Tim. 3:15). Nevertheless, it should be pointed out that the expression "all Scripture" (*pasa graphē*) is distributive in meaning, extending to every document that is legitimately classified as scriptural. Technically, then, the assertion is not limited to the writings familiar to Timothy. Paul is establishing a formal principle that is directly applied to the Old Testament and yet equally applicable to the scriptural texts of the New Testament. See Maximilian Zerwick, *Biblical Greek Illustrated by Examples* (Rome: Pontifical Biblical Institute, 1963), 189.

36   For example Mark 12:36; John 5:46–47.

days ahead. On the other hand, Peter counters such mistaken notions with the conviction that every prophecy of Scripture comes about by a supernatural opera-tion of the Spirit. Prophetic illumination is nothing less than a gift from God that the prophet is called to mediate to the people of God. Though a certain emphasis is placed on the prophet's role of speaking a divine message in oral form (vs. 21), the statement also has in view the permanent expression of prophetic speech in the written texts of the Bible (vs. 20).

Peter describes the divine influence upon the prophets in terms of men being "moved" by the Spirit. The use of *pherein* ("to carry along") in the passive voice underscores the primacy of God's activity in directing and impelling the prophet according to his purpose. The Spirit, whose influence is decisively more than mere assistance, determines what the prophet utters, much as a strong wind determines the course and nautical speed of a ship driven out to sea.[37] By the same token, the saying does not imply that the prophets were merely passive instruments manipu-lated by an irresistible force. Peter has in mind the writing prophets of the Bible, and these must not be confused with ecstatic prophets whose faculties were seized by the Spirit and put to use in an altered state of consciousness.[38] Rather, the prophets whose writings became part of the Bible were free and active participants in a concurrent movement of divine and human activity.

Furthermore, because the prophecies of Scripture were given "by" (*hypo*) the divine Spirit, and because the prophets articulated words that originated "from" (*apo*) God as their divine source, Peter concludes that readers have every reason to place full confidence in their message. This, in part, is why he insists that the prophetic word is so "sure."[39] Guaranteed by God, prophetic oracles can always be trusted to reach their fulfillment, even if they appear to be delayed and are forced to suffer the ridicule of scoffers who advance heretical counterclaims (topics of discussion in 2 Peter 2–3).

The supreme authority of Scripture, implied in different ways in the Pauline and Petrine texts just examined, is no less apparent elsewhere in the New Testament. One thinks of the ubiquitous occurrence of the formula, "it is written" (*gegraptai*), to introduce biblical citations.[40] Mirroring the conventional practice of Judaism in general and of Jesus in particular, the earliest Christians held the scriptural Word in such high regard that its authority required no assertion. If it stands written in the Bible, its binding force and prophetic certainty are beyond question.

---

37   As in Acts 27:15, 17.

38   One thinks of the example of King Saul, who was "turned into another man" when the Spirit of the LORD came mightily upon him and caused him to prophecy (1 Sam. 10:6).

39   2 Pet. 1:19.

40   Acts 1:20; 13:33; 15:15; Rom. 1:17; 2:24; 3:4; 1 Cor. 1:19; 2:9, among others.

Part of the reason for this is the belief that God speaks directly to his people through the biblical texts. Regardless of when the books of Scripture may have been written, the speech of God traverses the ages to address the present situation of the faithful. An example of this appears in Hebrews 3:7, where the Holy Spirit is said to speak the words of Psalm 95:7–8 to believers in the first century. The passage is put forward as immediately relevant to the original recipients of the Book of Hebrews, not because the ancient psalmist had this community in mind when he wrote, but because the Spirit "says" (*legei*, present tense) what the Psalm says in the here and now. The voice of the human author had long since fallen silent, and yet the voice of God, proceeding from eternity, is contemporary with every generation that encounters his Word. Once again, the divine authority of Scripture follows from its divine origin, and this prevents its relevance from being locked up in an irretrievable past.

Finally, if the ancient Church embraced the teaching of Jesus on the divine character and authority of Scripture, was it also convinced of the Bible's divine truthfulness? Here too the evidence supports a decisive yes. But as with Jesus, there is no one passage we can pinpoint that articulates the conviction in so many words. Instead, the total witness of the New Testament displays such an undiluted confidence in the testimony of Scripture that no other conclusion seems possible. Beyond this, there are a few particulars from which a doctrine of the Bible's trustworthiness may be inferred. For example, recall that Jesus equated the words of Scripture with the words of God,[41] and then spoke of the Father's word as "truth."[42] Working from these premises, one can deduce that the Bible, being the written Word of God, must be as truthful as God himself in all that it affirms.[43] This same logic appears to undergird the faith of the apostolic Church. For the early Christian community also believed that the words of Scripture are *ta logia tou theou*, "the oracles of God."[44] And not only so, but the same Church taught that God can never be the author of falsehood or deception; rather, his divine majesty is *ho apseudēs theos*, "the God who never lies."[45]

But whatever explicitness is lacking in the New Testament regarding the reliability and truth the Bible, this belief is stated clearly and unambiguously in the writings of the earliest ecclesiastical authors. Consider, for example, the first-century testimony of St. Clement of Rome, who states in his letter to the Corinthians that the Holy Scriptures are "true" and that "nothing unrighteous or

---

41   Matt. 19:4–5.

42   John 17:17.

43   For the importance of establishing the inerrancy of Scripture as a logical deduction from revealed premises, see Roger Nicole, "Induction and Deduction with Reference to Inspiration," in *Standing Forth: Collected Writings of Roger Nicole* (Fearn, Ross-shire: Mentor, 2002), 151–158.

44   Rom. 3:2; see also Acts 1:16; 4:24–25; 28:25; Heb. 1:5–13.

45   Titus 1:2.

counterfeit is written in them."[46] Similarly, in the middle of the second century, St. Justin Martyr counters accusations against the internal consistency of the Bible with the emphatic declaration: "I am positive that no passage [of Scripture] contradicts another."[47] Likewise, before the close of the second century, St. Irenaeus of Lyons contends that "the Scriptures are indeed perfect, since they were spoken by the Word of God and his Spirit."[48] Without statements to the contrary, either in the New Testament or in the earliest mainstream traditions, we are left to conclude that the historical picture is one of unbroken continuity regarding a Christian perspective on the Bible. From Jesus to the apostolic Church to the pastors and theologians of the second century there is full unanimity of conviction on Scripture's divine origin, divine authority, and divine truthfulness.

The Perspective of the Contemporary Magisterium

Although it lies beyond the scope of the present essay, the continuance of this perspective can be traced through the patristic and medieval periods up to the very threshold of modernity.[49] It was not until the rise of rationalist biblical criticism in the eighteenth and nineteenth centuries that the longstanding Christian consensus on the nature of Scripture seemed in danger of collapse, or at least destined for a thoroughgoing modification. At stake was the mystery of Scripture as such, the belief that the biblical Word comes from God, that it carries the authority of God, and that it reflects the character of God as One who is faithful and true.

The Church's response to this new climate of criticism and its frequent rejection of traditional positions on the Bible began in earnest at the First Vatican Council (1869–1870) and continued for nearly a century, culminating at the Second Vatican Council (1962–1965). The decades between these conciliar events witnessed numerous ecclesiastical interventions, especially papal encyclicals devoted to scriptural studies (1893, 1920, 1943) and periodic statements issued by the Pontifical Biblical Commission (founded in 1902). Careful study of these pronouncements reveals, not only an openness to legitimate developments in the field

---

46   St. Clement of Rome, *Letter to the Corinthians*, 45, 2–3, in *The Apostolic Fathers: Greek Texts and English Translations*, 3rd. ed., ed. and trans. Michael W. Holmes (Grand Rapids, MI: Baker Academic, 2007), 105.

47   St. Justin Martyr, *Dialogue with Trypho*, Chap. 65, in *Writings of Saint Justin Martyr*, The Fathers of the Church: A New Translation (New York: Christian Heritage, 1948), 251.

48   St. Irenaeus, *Against the Heresies*, Bk. 2, Chap. 28, 2; adapted from *The Ante-Nicene Fathers*, 10 vols., eds. Alexander Roberts and James Donaldson (Peabody, MA: Hendrickson, 2004 [reprint]), 1:399.

49   For an extensive historical and theological treatment of inspiration, see the remarkable work of Christianus Pesch, *De Inspiratione Sacrae Scripturae* [The Inspiration of Sacred Scripture] (Friburgi Brisgoviae: Herder, 1906). Similar works of note include Augustin Bea, *De Inspiratione Scripturae Sacrae* [The Inspiration of Sacred Scripture] (Rome: Pontifical Biblical Institute, 1930) and Sebastianus Tromp, *De Sacrae Scripturae Inspiratione* [The Inspiration of Sacred Scripture], 5th. ed. (Rome: Pontifical Gregorian University, 1953).

of biblical science, but also a heightened concern to preserve intact the doctrinal patrimony of the Church regarding the supernatural character of the Bible.

The First Vatican Council affirmed the divine origin of Scripture by asserting its divine authorship. Although the language of God as "author" is not part of the referential language of the Bible itself, this became the preferred terminology in Christian theology, going back at least to Pope Gregory the Great in the sixth century,[50] to capture the essential meaning of inspiration. In the words of the Council:

> These [books of Scripture] the Church holds to be sacred and canonical, not because, having been composed by simple human industry, they were later approved by her own authority, nor merely because they contain revelation without error, but because, having been written by the inspiration of the Holy Spirit, they have God for their author and were delivered as such to the Church.[51]

Inspiration is thus defined as a mystery of divine authorship in the literary sense of the term.[52] The definition is further clarified by setting it against misconceptions that had gained currency in nineteenth-century theological discourse.[53] Every major statement of the Church on the subject has since reaffirmed the designation of God as the divine author of the Scriptures.[54] This would become an enduring benchmark of orthodoxy in the debate over "the Biblical Question" in the twentieth century.

---

50 Pope St. Gregory the Great, *Morals on the Book of Job*, Pref. 1, 2 (Oxford: John Henry Parker, 1844).

51 First Vatican Council, *Dei Filius* [The Son of God], Dogmatic Constitution on the Catholic Faith, (April 24, 1870), Chap. 2.

52 Even scholars who are otherwise disinclined to see a literary meaning in the Latin *auctor* in earlier Church pronouncements acknowledge that Vatican I describes God as the literary author of the books of Scripture. For example, see Bruce Vawter, *Biblical Inspiration* (Philadelphia: Westminster, 1972), 22–24. On the use of this language in connection with inspiration, see Augustin Bea, "Deus Auctor Sacrae Scripturae: Herkunft und Bedeutung der Formel" [Divine Author of Sacred Scripture: Origin and Meaning of the Formula], *Angelicum* 20 (1943), 16–31.

53 The mistaken positions are those of Daniel Haneburg and Johann Jahn. The first popularized a view of inspiration in which the books of Scripture were written in a strictly human way but were later approved and endorsed by the Church. The second advanced a thesis that inspiration was equivalent to a charism of negative assistance whereby the biblical authors were prevented from asserting untruths but were otherwise left to write as they pleased. Neither position is acceptable because neither accounts for the historic Christian belief that Scripture is the Word of God and not merely the words of men.

54 See Pope Leo XIII, *Providentissimus Deus* [The God of All Providence], Encyclical Letter on the Study of Scripture (November 18, 1893), 41; Pope Benedict XV, *Spiritus Paraclitus* [The Holy Spirit, the Comforter], Encyclical Letter Commemorating the Fifteenth Centenary of the Death of St. Jerome (September 15, 1920), 3; Pius XII, *Divino Afflante Spiritu*, 1; and *Dei Verbum*, 11.

Of course, the human contribution to Scripture also demanded attention and clarification. In patristic theology, the concurrent authorship of the Bible was often compared to a musician playing an instrument, an analogy that served to underscore the primacy of God's role vis-à-vis the hagiographer's subordinate role in the composition of the biblical writings.[55] In medieval scholasticism, especially in the theology of Thomas Aquinas, the notions of God as the *auctor principalis* and the sacred writer as the *auctor instrumentalis* came into vogue as a way of describing the twofold efficient causality that produced the Bible.[56]

However helpful one regards these traditional notions, they lacked the fuller development that modern times demanded.[57] Thus, Pope Leo XIII advanced the discussion somewhat by describing the charism of inspiration as touching both the intellect and will of the sacred writer: "For, by supernatural power, God so moved and impelled them to write—he was so present to them—that the things which he ordered, and those only, they, first, rightly understood, then willed faithfully to write down, and finally expressed in apt words and with infallible truth."[58] Even fuller is the statement proffered by Vatican II: "In composing the sacred Books, God chose and employed certain men, who, while engaged in this task, made full use of their faculties and powers, so that, with God acting in them and through them, they as true authors committed to writing everything and only those things that he wanted written."[59] Hence, not only is the human dimension of Scripture affirmed along with the divine, echoing the teaching of Jesus and the early Church, but a new appreciation for the depth of the mystery is evidenced as well. That is, we are led to see that instrumental causality is nothing less than a participatory causality: God operated "in" and "through" the human authors without suppressing their faculties, overriding their freedom, or preventing their personalities from making a distinct imprint on the biblical texts. In a way that exceeds our comprehension, the sacred authors were true authors caught up into the action of God transmitting his Word in written form.

---

55   For early attestations of the analogy, see Athenagoras, *A Plea for the Christians*, 9 (in *Ante-Nicene Fathers*, 2:133); and Pseudo-Justin, *Exhortation to the Greeks*, 8 (*in Cohortatio ad Graecos; De Monarchia; Oratio ad Graecos*, ed. Miroslav Marcovich Patristische Texte und Studien 32 [New York: De Gruyter, 1990]).

56   See, for example, St. Thomas Aquinas, *Quaestiones Quodlibetales* [Miscellaneous Questions], Quod. 7, q. 6, art. 1, reply obj. 1. Note that the traditional concept of instrumental authorship is not a relegation of the human writer to a secondary status, making him less than a true author. To the contrary, it signals an elevation of the writer's natural faculties through participation in the supernatural activity of God, the principal author.

57   It should be noted that Pius XII insisted on the usefulness of patristic and Thomistic concepts of instrumentality in assisting modern theologians to describe the nature and effects of biblical inspiration with greater precision. *Divino Afflante Spiritu*, 19.

58   Leo XIII, *Providentissimus Deus*, 41.

59   *Dei Verbum*, 11.

Naturally, the belief that Scripture has a divine *auctor* who inspired its human writers entails the corresponding belief that Scripture carries the weight of divine *auctoritas*. This had never been in doubt in the course of the Church's history any more than it was in the mind of Jesus or his earliest followers. Nevertheless, the challenges of the modern age called for a firm restatement of the fact. On this front, one can do no better than reference the Second Vatican Council, where the authority of the Bible is invoked in connection with theological studies and the various ministries which flow from it. According to the Council, just as the soul animates and enlivens the body, so the study of Scripture must be "the soul" that brings vitality and life to sacred theology.[60] More fundamentally, the Church's teaching office views itself under the authority of the Word: "this magisterium is not superior to the Word of God but is its servant. It teaches only what has been handed on to it. At the divine command and with the help of the Holy Spirit, it listens to this devoutly, guards it with dedication and expounds it faithfully."[61] Suffice it to say, then, that no amount of criticism or skepticism, emanating either from within or without the contemporary Church, has been able to dislodge the conviction that the written Word of God is supremely authoritative for determining the faith and life of the pilgrim Church on earth.

Lastly, the Church remains fully convinced that the inspired Scriptures are trustworthy and true. In this respect too she walks in step with her Lord and her ancient forebears in the faith. But this is also where the Church has encountered the stiffest resistance from the ranks of the modern academy. No one conversant in twentieth-century theology doubts that biblical inerrancy is one of the watershed issues of our time. Here the pressures have been greatest to leave behind, or at least significantly modify, the traditional understanding of Scripture's total immunity from error in favor of a new paradigm that allows factual inaccuracies to stand alongside the truths enshrined in its sacred pages.

It is important to point out, however, that those who dispute the absolute truthfulness of Scripture do not attempt to make their case on historical grounds. They could hardly do so, given the sweeping consensus of the tradition. Rather, the push to limit the inerrancy of the Bible is based on a revised theological methodology. Traditionally, the Bible's freedom from error was maintained as a logical consequence of its divine inspiration. If God is the principal author of Scripture, and God, who is infinite Truth, can only assert what is true, then it follows deductively that the Word of God in Scripture can only contain truth.[62] This is precisely the logical structure of Leo XIII's teaching on inerrancy:

---

60   *Dei Verbum*, 24.

61   *Dei Verbum*, 10.

62   One finds this same line of reasoning in the *Catechism*: "God is Truth itself, whose words cannot deceive. This is why one can abandon oneself in full trust to the truth and faithfulness of his word in all things." *Catechism of the Catholic Church*, 2d. ed. (Vatican City: Libreria Editrice Vaticana, 1997), no. 215.

> For all the books that the Church receives as sacred and canonical are written wholly and entirely, with all their parts, at the dictation of the Holy Spirit. And so far is it from being possible that any error can coexist with inspiration, that inspiration not only is essentially incompatible with error but excludes and rejects it as absolutely and necessarily as it is impossible that God himself, the supreme Truth, can utter that which is not true. This is the ancient and unchanging faith of the Church.[63]

Today, however, the deductive method has been sidelined by an inductive method that attempts to define the extent of inerrancy on the basis of exegesis.[64] This approach involves sifting the texts of the Bible to determine, on a case by case basis, where their assertions are reliable and where they are "deficient in truth"[65] that is, reflective of the limitations and imperfections of their human authors. Needless to say, with so many difficulties present in the sacred text, contemporary scholars typically view inerrancy as something restricted to its religious teaching on faith, morals, and sacred history, with matters touching on profane history, geography, and science being subject to the more or less faulty apprehension of the sacred writers. Some would impute error to Scripture's religious teaching as well.[66]

But the Church herself has never endorsed this new methodology or its consequences. Holding firm the doctrinal stance of Leo XIII, subsequent popes have taught that "we can never conclude that there is any error in Sacred Scripture" and that even its historical texts must be said to "rest on the absolute truth of the facts."[67] More than once the Church has been forced to correct the mistaken view that biblical inerrancy extends only to matters of "faith and morals."[68] The Pontifical Biblical Commission likewise affirmed in its 1964 instruction that the

---

63   Leo XIII, *Providentissimus Deus*, 40–41.

64   The distinction in methodology is sometimes described as an *a priori* approach, which deduces inerrancy from revealed premises, and an *a posteriori* approach, which works from the written text of Scripture and makes an inductive conclusion based on observations made by the interpreter.

65   This is the memorable expression of Cardinal Franz König made during deliberations over Vatican II's treatment of divine revelation. See Alois Grillmeier, "Dogmatic Constitution on Divine Revelation, Chapter III," in *Commentary on the Documents of Vatican II*, ed. Herbert Vorgrimler (New York: Herder and Herder, 1969), 3:205.

66   For example, Raymond E. Brown, *The Critical Meaning of the Bible* (New York: Paulist, 1981), 16.

67   Benedict XV, *Spiritus Paraclitus*, 5–6.

68   Pius XII, *Divino Afflante Spiritu*, 1; see also Pius XII's *Humani Generis* [The Human Race], Encyclical Letter on Certain False Opinions Threatening to Undermine the Foundations of Catholic Doctrine (August 12, 1950), 22.

four Gospels are faithful witnesses to Jesus and that their inspiration by the Holy Spirit renders them "immune from all error."[69]

The question is whether the unrestricted inerrancy of Scripture remains the teaching of the Church today. It is beyond dispute that this was its official position leading up to Vatican II. But many find in the Council's 1965 document *Dei Verbum* signs of a new and fundamentally different perspective.[70] Can we finally say, after a century of heated debate and strident restatements of the Bible's unlimited truthfulness, that the Church has reversed directions and come to accept that the Scriptures are only imperfectly accurate? The whole question turns on a single statement in *Dei Verbum*:

> Therefore, since everything asserted by the inspired authors or sacred writers should be regarded as asserted by the Holy Spirit, it follows that we must acknowledge the Books of Scripture as teaching firmly, faithfully, and without error the truth that God wished to be recorded in the sacred writings for the sake of our salvation.

Here the Council contends that every human assertion in the Bible is at the same time a divine assertion made by the Holy Spirit, and that as a consequence of this, the scriptural texts teach truth *sine errore*, "without error." This sounds like little more than a faithful restatement of the Church's established teaching on Scripture's unrestricted inerrancy. However, the document also remarks that the truth which resides in the written Word is recorded "for the sake of our salvation." This last expression is the peg on which countless scholars hang the weight of an alleged development in the Church's perspective. The argument is that Scripture's freedom from error is now linked with truth insofar as it pertains to the saving purposes of God. Truths not directly linked with our salvation, it is said, do not enjoy the same privilege of being preserved from error.

This reading of the document is firmly entrenched in modern Catholic scholarship. Nevertheless, I would contend that the wording of the Constitution does not support such an interpretation. To begin with, the grammar of the text does not in fact delimit the kind of truth under discussion. The prepositional phrase *nostrae salutis causa*, "for the sake of our salvation," functions as an adverbial phrase modifying the verbal expression, *consignari voluit*, "wished to be recorded." As such, it elucidates the purpose behind God's desire to put his truth in the Bible without differentiating between different classes of truths it may be said to

---

69 Pontifical Biblical Commission, *Sancta Mater Ecclesia*, 11.

70 Brown, *Critical Meaning*, 19, says: "Many of us think that at Vatican II the Catholic Church 'turned the corner' in the inerrancy question by moving from the *a priori* [approach] toward the *a posteriori* in the statement of *Dei Verbum* 11."

express.[71] Secondly, the lengthy footnote attached to this sentence cites multiple sources from the tradition which speak of Scripture's comprehensive conformity to the truth. Thus, in agreement with the document's use of footnotes in general, the references in the present footnote underscore the continuity of the Council's teaching with theological and magisterial positions of the past. Thirdly, analysis of the debates and earlier schemas that led to the final draft of *Dei Verbum* reveal a concern among the majority of the Council fathers, prompting even the intervention of Pope Paul VI, to avoid a wording of the text that would limit Scripture's inerrancy to "saving truth," an expression which could easily be misinterpreted to mean the truths of faith and morals and nothing beyond.[72] Fourthly, since the preceding clause insists that everything (*omne id*) asserted by the human authors is likewise asserted by the Holy Spirit, a restricted inerrancy reading leaves no way to avoid imputing misstatements of fact to the divine author.[73] Yet earlier papal statements declare such a proposition flatly "impossible."[74] Fifthly, it borders on inconceivable that the Council fathers were introducing a development of doctrine with virtually no indication that they were doing so and no explanation as to why the time was ripe for taking such a momentous step. If this were the case, the Council could only be charged with dodging a grave responsibility to the people of God. Taken together, the cumulative force of these observations supports the contention that *Dei Verbum*'s teaching on biblical truth stands in doctrinal continuity with previous ecclesiastical teaching on the inerrancy of Scripture. One can legitimately speak of a new emphasis on the Bible's salvific purpose, but not of a fundamental departure from the Church's historic position on its unlimited truthfulness.

In summary, I am convinced that Jesus and the Church of both ancient and modern times share a common outlook on the nature of Scripture. Adherence to the divine origin, authority, and truth of the written Word is upheld consistently and without compromise down through the centuries. It could not be otherwise, I would contend, for these aspects of the biblical mystery are part of the Christian

---

71 In essence, the prepositional phrase answers the question "why" God put his truth in the Bible, not "what kind" of truth is recorded there without error. See Augustin Cardinal Bea, S.J., *The Word of God and Mankind*, trans. Dorothy White (Chicago: Franciscan Herald, 1967), 187–191.

72 The penultimate schema spoke of the Scriptures teaching *veritatem salutarem*, but the text was amended to read *veritatem* without adjectival qualification. See Bea, *Word of God*, 190; Grillmeier, "Dogmatic Constitution," 3:210–215; also Mark Joseph Zia, "The Inerrancy of Scripture and the Second Vatican Council," *Faith & Reason* 31 (2006): 175–192.

73 Consider the succinct words of Luis Alonso-Schökel, "Inspiration," in *Sacramentum Mundi: An Encyclopedia of Theology* (New York: Herder and Herder, 1969), 3:150: "Since Scripture is inspired by God, it follows that it cannot assert any falsehood: otherwise God himself would be commending falsehood to us on his own authority."

74 For example, Leo XIII, *Providentissimus Deus*, 40.

deposit of faith which was "once for all delivered to the saints."[75] From Pentecost to the present day, the Church has maintained Christ's perspective on the Bible as her own.

The Humility of the Word

It is no surprise that people find it difficult to embrace this "high view" of Scripture advocated by Jesus and the Church. The claims of faith inherent in this perspective are not only unverifiable from a scientific standpoint, but they seem utterly improbable from a rational and aesthetic standpoint. To put it bluntly, the written Word of God strikes many as too human to be divine. Unnumbered intellectuals throughout history have thus faced the scandal of the Bible and chosen to reject it. In this way too the inspired Word treads the path of the incarnate Word and mirrors its mystery.

In point of fact, Scripture will always be a reflection of the Word made flesh. According to the traditional christological analogy,[76] the union of divinity and humanity in Jesus can assist our understanding of the divine and human authorship of the Bible, just as the perfect sinlessness of Jesus is comparable to the perfect truthfulness of the Bible. But what of the cruciformity of Jesus? What of the fact that he was despised as an uneducated and ordinary man claiming to wield divine authority? Even in this respect the Scriptures bear the image of the crucified Messiah. For the texts of the Bible, by presenting their mighty claims in such modest wrappings, are offensive to human pride and elicit the contempt of the sophists of every age.

Too often the humble form of the Scriptures is passed over and left underdeveloped in Christian theology.[77] In one sense, this is perplexing, given the common acknowledgement that the Bible is not just authentically human but sometimes scandalously human. I suspect that many exegetes and theologians find it too awkward and uncomfortable to make this a focus of concentrated study. Or if they seize upon Scripture's "imperfections" it is with the aim of knocking down traditional conceptions of its sublime flawlessness. Neither of these is a helpful reaction to the humility of the written Word. Instead, I propose that study of this problem offers rich theological insight as well as personal and pastoral applications.

I should first summarize what constitutes "the humble style of biblical language."[78] By this I mean those less-than-appealing features of the Word that

---

75 Jude 3.

76 See nn 1–2 above.

77 A significant exception is the work of the eighteenth-century Lutheran intellectual, Johann Georg Hamann, who placed considerable stress on the humility of Scripture. See especially John R. Betz, "Hamann's London Writings: The Hermeneutics of Trinitarian Condescension" *Pro Ecclesia* 14 (2005), 191–234, as well as Betz's article in the present volume.

78 The expression comes from St. Augustine, *Confessions* Bk. 12, Chap. 27, 37, in *A Select Library*

represent stumbling blocks to a belief in the Bible's divine perfection.[79] For instance, one thinks of Scripture's frequent use of anthropomorphisms and anthropopathisms to speak of God, who is otherwise said to be "spirit."[80] Many have scorned these as the crude conceptions of an uncultivated people. One could also point to Scripture's unpolished diction and grammatical solecisms, features that make the Word off-putting to educated minds with more refined literary tastes.[81] So too, its penchant for hyperbole and poetic license and approximation fails to captivate those who think that the Bible should have nothing to do with colloquial parlance and speak only with scientific exactitude. Still more scandal is afforded by the numerous alleged discrepancies that make the Bible appear inconsistent with itself, with the documents of ancient history, and with the findings of modern archeology. The collective impression of these "blemishes" causes proud minds to recoil and refuse consent. It is a reminder that unbelief will always remain an option and even the default position of many who find no way to account for Scripture's apparent lack of sophistication.

The question is whether these humble aspects of the Word should stand as barriers to our acceptance of its supernatural authority and reliability. I think not. In fact, I find the mode of biblical communication to be perfectly harmonious with the mystery of Christ himself. The same rationale that underlies the incarnation of the eternal Word also informs the inspiration of the scriptural Word. Neither is intelligible except as an instance of divine condescension—what Chrysostom called the *synkatabasis* of God.[82] This is the theological proposition that God bends down to make contact with human persons in ways that are fitted to their capacity to receive him.[83] It means that God lowers himself in view of our weakness with the aim of lifting us up by his strength. Thus, divine accommodation is not primarily a matter of how the human dimension of revelation limits the divine but of how the divine is made known and rendered comprehensible through the

---

of *Nicene and Post-Nicene Fathers of the Christian Church*, 1st series, 14 vols., ed. Philip Schaff (Peabody, MA: Hendrickson, 1994 [reprint]), 1:186.

79   Of course, the presence of these features in Scripture does not rule out the superb literary talents of an Isaiah or an Amos, the style-consciousness of a Luke, the elegant simplicity of a James, or the rhetorical sophistication shown by the author of the Book of Hebrews.

80   Isa. 31:3; John 4:24.

81   Jerome, for example, delighted in classical eloquence but initially rebelled at "the uncouth style" of the Bible (*Epistulae* 22.30). Commenting on this reaction, Benedict XV remarks that Jerome at first "failed to discern the lowly Christ in his lowly Scriptures" (*Spiritus Paraclitus*, 10). Augustine, who likewise struggled to accept the unimpressive style of the Bible (*Confessions* Bk. 3, Chap. 5, 9), held that educated persons drawn to the Church must be taught Christian humility lest they be repelled by the "carnal coverings" of scriptural language (*On the Catechizing of the Uninstructed*, Chap. 9, 13).

82   See his *Homilies on Genesis*, 17, 1.

83   For a superb analysis of this theme in historical theology, see Stephen D. Benin, *The Footprints of God: Divine Accommodation in Jewish and Christian Thought* (Albany: State University of New York, 1993).

human. The Word incarnate accomplished this by the assumption of a human nature; the Word inspired achieves this by making use of simple human language. The challenge is to keep the full reality of condescension in view as we interpret the Bible. Even when God packages his perfection and power in lowly tangible forms, we must not allow their sensible exterior to blindfold us to their supernatural interior.

Here it is worthwhile to revisit the christological analogy. After all, the supreme instance of condescension is the kenosis of the Son, who "emptied himself" to become a man.[84] Certainly this entails the eternal Word accepting various limitations and weaknesses of the human condition. The New Testament testifies that Jesus experienced such things as fatigue,[85] hunger,[86] astonishment,[87] grief,[88] and extreme distress.[89] Ultimately, he "humbled himself" to the point of accepting death, "even death on a cross."[90] Yet virtually none of these empirical observations, which verify the full humanity of Jesus, force us to conclude that Christ divested himself of his divinity or surrendered his inherent impeccability. The weaknesses apparent on the surface of Jesus' historical life do not cancel or diminish his unseen perfection. At no point did he cease to be "the truth,"[91] the sinless and guileless Word of the Father.[92]

The same is true of the written Word of God. Despite its concrete expression in human language—even plain and sometimes imperfect language—it does not cease to be the divine discourse of God. The Word incarnate was intensely human, yet he never sinned. So too, the Word inspired is intensely human, yet it never errs. Once again it is Jesus who is the key to understanding the mystery of Scripture as simultaneously human and divine, as imperfect in appearance but perfect in reality. In this respect, the Church's belief in inspiration and inerrancy is simply an extension of her faith in the incarnation.

A similar logic echoes in other halls of theology as well. The notion that God accommodates himself to human weakness by conveying his Word in humble form finds confirmation in Mary's maternal gift of the Word, in the apostles' preaching of the Word, and in the liturgy's actualization of the Word. These events too may be said to illuminate the mystery of divinity and humility coming together in the Scriptures.

---

84 Phil. 2:7.

85 John 4:6.

86 Matt. 4:2.

87 Mark 6:6.

88 John 11:35.

89 Luke 22:44.

90 Phil. 2:7–8.

91 John 14:6.

92 Heb. 4:15; 1 Pet. 2:22.

Consider first a *mariological* analogy, in which biblical inspiration parallels the Mother of God cooperating with the Spirit of God to bring forth the divine Word. As in the concurrent authorship of the Scriptures, here we have the synchronized actions of two persons, one human and one divine. And just as the sacred writers acted fully and freely under the influence of the Spirit in giving written form to the inspired Word, so Mary acted in perfect unison with the Spirit in giving flesh to the eternal Word. Moreover, because her involvement in the action of God was grounded in a free consent and receptivity to his grace, we can speak of a non-competitive, participatory causality in bringing forth the Word. Mary's fiat, in other words, was no mere passive resignation to the divine plan but rather an active and dynamic embrace of her mission. In her words of acceptance, *genoito moi kata to rēma sou*, "let it be to me according to your word,"[93] the optative mood indicates an ardent wish or desire on her part.[94]

Notice again how the divine Word is communicated by means of the humblest human instrument. Mary was an unknown peasant girl from an obscure village under the heel of Roman domination. Human pride would think it absurd to look with favor upon the low estate of a self-professed *doulē*, a "slave girl,"[95] and yet this is precisely in keeping with the pattern of divine condescension. That the Lord's lowliest creations should be made instruments of his saving power is one of the hallmarks of salvation history.

A second parallel may be called a *kerygmatic* analogy. By this I mean the correlation between biblical inspiration and the preaching of the apostolic Church. Like the sacred writers of Scripture, the apostles brought the life-transforming Word to the world by the power of the Spirit. As a result, their proclamation of the gospel was not reducible to mere human words but was suffused with the plenary authority of God. Paul states as much when he tells the Thessalonians: "when you received the word of God which you heard from us, you accepted it not as the word of men but as what it really is, the word of God."[96] Similar to biblical inspiration, by which the words of God are given permanent expression in the written words of men, the apostolic witness to Jesus was the articulation of a divine Word that effected the permanent founding of the Church in history.

Here too the humility of the Word and those who bear it is pronounced. On the one hand, the gospel kerygma itself, which Paul calls *ho logos ho tou staurou*, "the word of the cross," is a word of foolishness to the sages and sophists of the age.[97] Many indeed take offense at the message of a rejected and humiliated Messiah, for

---

93   Luke 1:38.

94   Ignace de la Potterie, *Mary in the Mystery of the Covenant*, trans. Bertrand Buby (New York: Alba House, 1992), 34–35.

95   Luke 1:38, 48.

96   1 Thess. 2:13.

97   1 Cor. 1:18.

it confounds the expectations of reason and throws it into confusion. On the other hand, the humility of the kerygma is something in which the apostles participate in a very personal way. Being subjected to the same dishonor as the Word they declare, they are treated "like men sentenced to death" and even as "the refuse of the world."[98] One need only peruse the list of Paul's afflictions in 2 Corinthians 11:23–33 to get a sense of how profoundly the mission of the apostles integrates them into the scandal of the cross and the foolishness of divine condescension embodied in God's Word.

A third parallel is a *liturgical* analogy. If biblical inspiration consists of the Spirit conveying the Word of God through fallible human instruments, the liturgical celebration is where the Spirit continues to bear the Word into the world through a canonized series of human gestures and utterances. This is accomplished through proclamation as well as sacramental administration. In the eucharistic assembly, the biblical Word is enunciated so that just as its divine message came fresh to the first recipients of the biblical books, so in the context of worship it speaks anew to God's people and invites them to respond with the same "obedience of faith."[99] Likewise, by the simultaneous action of the Spirit (epiclesis) and human speech (words of consecration), the Word is made present (confection) and made food (communion). This makes every occasion of sacramental worship a new intervention of God in history, a new event of salvation.[100]

Here the power of God working through human weakness is unmistakable. The functions of the priestly ministry indicate that God continues to use the frailest of natural means to accomplish his supernatural purposes. Empowered by grace, the priest is made to act in the person of Christ, speaking his words, repeating his movements, and setting before us the paschal sacrifice that redeemed the world. And the humble elements of bread and wine that stand helpless before the transubstantiating Word—these are the lowly signs that will be made the Lord's greatest gift. It is difficult to imagine a more self-abnegating form by which the divine Word should signal his presence among us.

Clearly the humility of the Word, primarily in Christ and secondarily in Scripture, points to a recurrent pattern in God's efforts to reach the human family with his love. In effect, there is a typology of divine condescension which must be recognized and contemplated in our theology. This is true not only objectively, as impressed in the events and instruments of salvation, but also, as I hope to show, in our subjective response.

---

98 1 Cor. 4:9, 13.

99 Rom. 1:5; 16:26.

100 See, for example, Jeremy Driscoll, "The Word of God in the Liturgy of the New Covenant" *Letter & Spirit* 1 (2005), 87–100. For more extensive analysis, consult Scott Hahn, *Letter and Spirit: From Written Text to Living Word in the Liturgy* (New York: Doubleday, 2005).

Recognition of Scripture's humility invariably raises the question of its purpose. Why should God express himself and his will[101] in the humble letter of the Bible? My own conviction is that it invites reason to embrace the knowledge of faith, and that it confronts pride with a summons to intellectual humility.

The humility of the Word first of all represents a challenge to the supremacy of reason in the apprehension of reality. Reason, we are prone to forget, has inherent limitations with which one must come to terms. Not only is the intellectual faculty incapable of demonstrating the mysteries of faith disclosed through revelation, but it is also incapable of discovering the plans and purposes of God in history. This is a serious handicap when it comes to interpreting the Bible. It is not that we should retreat into fideism in our study of Scripture, but that we should avoid the irrationality of pure rationalism. One can say that reason functions properly when it accepts its limitations and acknowledges that there are questions it cannot answer. However, when reason comes to see that the act of faith is itself a reasonable act, it can then proceed to an investigation of truth beyond the philosophical and empirical. This is what Joseph Cardinal Ratzinger (now Benedict XVI) terms "a hermeneutic of faith" and urges must become a part of modern biblical studies.[102] Only through supernatural faith is one given access to a transcendent order of knowledge in which the Bible is perceived, not merely as a cultural document or historical artifact in need of decipherment, but as the living Word of God demanding a response from us. In such a context, one discovers that the all-too-human language of Scripture is a manifestation of the foolishness of God that exceeds human wisdom.[103]

Beyond this, I believe that the humble expression of the Word invites us to be healed of intellectual arrogance. This is obviously related to the foregoing comments about reason and its limits. But the fact is that even when faith and reason are working in tandem, the latter is tempted to impose unreasonable restrictions on the former. In the realm of biblical studies, this takes the form of methodological skepticism, otherwise known as "a hermeneutic of suspicion."[104] Not only does

---

101 Recall that Vatican II describes the revelatory form of God's Word as both personal and propositional: "By divine Revelation God wished to manifest and communicate the both *himself* and the eternal decrees of *his will* concerning the salvation of mankind" (*Dei Verbum*, no. 6, Flannery edition; emphasis added). This personal aspect of revelation is linked with the "sacramentality" of Scripture, on which see F.X. Durrwell, *In the Redeeming Christ: Toward a Theology of Spirituality*, trans. Rosemary Sheed (New York: Sheed and Ward, 1963), 37–53; and Mary Healy, "Inspiration and Incarnation: The Christological Analogy and the Hermeneutics of Faith," *Letter & Spirit* 2 (2006), 27–41.

102 This was one of the primary theses of his famous Erasmus Lecture delivered in New York in 1988. For the text, see Joseph Ratzinger, "Biblical Interpretation in Conflict: The Question of the Basic Principles and Path of Exegesis Today" in *God's Word: Scripture–Tradition–Office*, eds. Peter Hünermann and Thomas Söding, trans. Henry Taylor (San Francisco: Ignatius Press, 2008), 91–126.

103 See 1 Cor. 1:25.

104 For Pope Benedict XVI's critique of this and other philosophical missteps in the critical study

this approach mean that the Bible's sincerity and truthfulness must be proven before it can be accepted, but that the interpreter stands in a position of judgment over the Word, measuring its claims according to his or her own standards.

This is to turn things upside down. The folly of divine condescension urges that we lay aside our hypercriticism and our educated conceit in approaching the biblical Word. It calls for an intellectual kenosis in which the mind adjusts itself to the mode of God's revelation by, in a sense, lowering itself to the same level. An intellect that is humble and receptive to the Word in modest dress is one that tunes itself to the higher wisdom of God and receives the insight that is withheld from "the wise and understanding."[105] It recognizes the truth that God's power is made perfect in weakness.[106]

We have only to turn to the gospels to see what this means in practice. For Jesus embodies the response of personal humility that the form of the written Word requires. Hearing the Scriptures as the voice of the Father, he allowed himself to be formed by its message in all aspects of his human development. His commitments as a devout Jew meant that the rhythms of life followed the dictates of the Hebrew Scriptures as proclaimed in the weekly synagogue liturgies and the yearly temple festivals. Jesus' detailed familiarity with the entire corpus of biblical writings bears witness to his full participation in the religious observances of his people. Even at the point of agony and death the memorized words of the Psalter fall from his parched lips.[107] Everywhere his posture toward the Bible is one of docility and total adherence to its authority and truth.

This is remarkable considering that Christ is the Word of God begotten from eternity.[108] He is the full disclosure of God in the world, the living sacrament of the kingdom of God which he proclaims.[109] This being so, Jesus' submission to the Bible can only be called an act of extreme humility. It is a profound gesture of

---

of Scripture, see Scott W. Hahn, *Covenant and Communion: The Biblical Theology of Pope Benedict XVI* (Grand Rapids: Brazos, 2009), especially 25–40.

105 Matt. 11:25.

106 See 2 Cor. 12:9. The Church has long recognized the value of this principle in connection with the difficulties of the Bible. Augustine, for example, in correspondence with Jerome, holds together a doctrinal commitment to the inerrancy of Scripture with a hermeneutic of humility in interpreting problematic texts. He firmly believes "that not one of their [biblical] authors has erred in writing anything at all," and yet when he stumbles across a passage which "seems contrary to truth," he concludes either that the text was miscopied, mistranslated, or that he simply "failed to understand it" (*Letter* 82). Translation from *Saint Augustine: Letters*, vol. 1, The Fathers of the Church: A New Translation (New York: Fathers of the Church, Inc., 1951), 392. Leo XIII cited this very statement in recommending such an approach to all interpreters of the Bible (see *Providentissimus Deus*, 41). The passage is also referenced in the final footnote of *Dei Verbum*, 11.

107 Mark 15:34 = Ps. 22:1; Luke 23:46 = Ps. 31:5.

108 John 1:1.

109 For the christology implied in Jesus' proclamation of the kingdom, see Pope Benedict XVI, *Jesus of Nazareth* (New York: Doubleday, 2007), 46–63.

self-abasement for the Word made flesh to surrender himself in reverent obedience to the Word made Scripture. Hence, for the interpreter, responding to the humility of the biblical Word means imitating its humble appropriation by the incarnate Word. His example suggests it, and his very words demand it: "Take my yoke upon you, and learn from me; for I am gentle and lowly in heart."[110]

Concluding Reflections

Reflection on the foregoing suggests several ideas that, as I see the matter, must inform our perspective on the nature and purpose of sacred Scripture. These include implications as well as recapitulations touching on the truth and humility of God's Word.

First, the incarnation of the Word, far from being an isolated truth, is Christianity's most illuminating truth. It reveals a pattern of divine wisdom that is replicated in myriad forms in the drama of salvation history. The theological use of analogy brings to light many of these imprints of the Word becoming flesh. Inspiration, for instance, is elucidated by the christological mystery, and yet similar lines may be drawn that reveal mariological, kerygmatic, and liturgical analogies as well. More than mere illustrative helps, these are rooted in the typology of God's actions in history and as such testify to the unity of the divine plan of salvation.

Second, the Church's perspective on the nature of Scripture is entirely derivative. In all essential respects it is the perspective of Jesus Christ himself which she received as a sacred trust to be faithfully transmitted. Hence the testimony of the Lord regarding the divine excellence of the Bible was embraced from the very beginning as normative for the Christian community. This obliges the Church, not only to promote the fullness of the doctrine and to provide clarification whenever necessary, but to appropriate the inspired Word as Jesus himself did in his historical life. Scripture must shape her thinking and empower her preaching as well as become her prayer and define her way of life. Anything less than this falls short of a total conformity to Christ.

Third, the biblical Word participates in the very mystery it communicates. This is to say that Scripture comes to us in the same manner as the Son comes to us—as divinity clothed in humanity, as majesty cloaked in humility. Like the suffering Messiah, the Bible has all the outward appearance of poverty and weakness; it too is subject to misunderstanding, rejection, and denigration. But this in no way diminishes the full reality that the Church perceives in the Word. The incarnational analogy urges assent to the divine and human dimensions of Scripture without confusion or separation; there can be no legitimate emphasis on one at the expense of the other. Just as the mystery of the God-man is received by the Church in faith, despite reason's inability to demonstrate it or to exhaust its intelligible content, so too the truth of inspiration is proposed for belief, despite

---

110 Matt. 11:29.

apparent evidence to the contrary. Being a mirror reflection of the Word incarnate, the Word inspired is a treasure in earthen vessels, a communication of the highest divine truths in the humblest of human forms.

Finally, the humility of the Word is a test of our faith and a protest against pride. Reason is liable to take offense at the lowliness of scriptural expression, finding it improbable that God should speak through such a drab and uneven collection of human writings. Still less convincing to reason is the proposition that Scripture is completely and comprehensively true. This makes a posture of faith and humility indispensable to biblical interpretation at every level. For the wisdom of God in Christ is characteristically cruciform, and so it will only appear as foolishness in the eyes of an unbelieving world. Yet the Cross and the canon are the saving power of God for all who receive the Word with the faith that sustains the Church.

Apropos to this closing note, I offer for consideration the incisive words of Benedict XVI, who recently addressed the International Theological Commission on the importance of becoming little in order to perceive the wonders of Christian truth. In contrast to academic currents that make reason the measure of things divine, he remarks: "Then there is the other way of using reason, of being wise—that of the man who recognizes who he is; he recognizes the proper measure and greatness of God, opening himself in humility to the newness of God's action. It is in this way, precisely by accepting his own smallness, making himself little as he really is, that he arrives at the truth."[111]

---

111 Homily, Mass with the International Theological Commission (Dec. 1, 2009), in *L'Osservatore Romano*, Weekly Edition in English (Dec. 9, 2009), 6.

Letter & Spirit 6 (2010): 47-66

THE MYSTERY OF GOD'S WORD:
Inspiration, Inerrancy, and the Interpretation of Scripture

❧ Brant Pitre ☙

Notre Dame Seminary

What is the Bible? Is it divinely inspired? If so, does it teach the truth? To what extent is it free from error? How should we interpret Scripture? What rules should be followed and what methods employed in order to properly understand the sacred text?[1]

These are questions that Christians of every stripe have asked over the centuries. The purpose of this essay is to explore how the Catholic Church in particular answers these questions and what the Church teaches and believes about the Bible. We will consider three fundamental issues—the inspiration, inerrancy, and interpretation of Scripture—concentrating on the official teachings of the Catholic magisterium, the Church's bishops in union with the Pope.[2]

Catholic doctrine on Sacred Scripture can be found in several key sources: the teachings of the ecumenical councils of Trent (1546), Vatican I (1870), and Vatican II (1965); the three papal encyclical letters on the Bible, written by Leo XIII (1893), Benedict XV (1920), and Pius XII (1943); and the summary statement of Catholic doctrine on Scripture given in the official *Catechism of the Catholic Church*, promulgated by John Paul II (1992). Taken together, these documents provide everything we need for an overview of magisterial teachings on sacred Scripture. Unfortunately many of these sources, especially the papal encyclicals on Scripture, are often not studied closely by students in biblical studies; hence we will attempt to familiarize readers with them by quoting them directly. Moreover, since the Second Vatican Council's 1965 Dogmatic Constitution on Divine Revelation *Dei*

---

1   This is a revised and expanded version of an essay that first appeared in Michael Bird and Michael Pahl, eds., *The Sacred Text: Excavating the Texts, Exploring the Interpretations, and Engaging the Theologies of the Christian Scriptures*, Gorgias Précis Portfolios 7 (Piscataway, NJ: Gorgias, 2010), 177-197.

2   For a collection of magisterial documents on sacred Scripture, see *The Scripture Documents: An Anthology of Official Catholic Teachings*, ed. Dean P. Béchard (Collegeville, MN: Liturgical Press, 2002). Hereafter abbreviated *SD*. For the original Latin texts, see Heinrich Denzinger, ed., *Enchiridion Symbolorum Definitonum et Declarationum de Rebus Fidei et Morum* [Handbook of Creeds, Definitions and Declarations concerning Matters of Faith and Morals] (Freiberg: Herder, 1911); Eng.: *The Sources of Catholic Dogma* (Fitzwilliam, NH: Loreto, 2002). See also *Enchiridion Biblicum: Documenti della Chiesa sulla Sacra Scrittura* [Documents of the Church Concerning Sacred Scripture], eds. Alfio Filippi and Erminio Lora, 2nd. ed. (Bologna: Dehoniane, 1993). Hereafter abbreviated *EB*. For original Latin texts of Church council documents, see Norman P. Tanner, *Decrees of the Ecumenical Councils*, 2 vols. (Washington, DC: Georgetown University, 1990).

Verbum (Lat: the "Word of God") constitutes the most recent and most thorough conciliar teaching on the Bible, we will pay primary attention to its presentation of Catholic doctrine.

By reading *Dei Verbum* in continuity with the papal encyclicals, as well as the earlier Church councils, we will attempt to offer an overview of a distinctively Catholic approach to the Bible. As we will see, contrary to what is sometimes assumed about the Catholic Church and the Bible, when studied carefully the teachings of the magisterium—especially as formulated at the Second Vatican Council—present us with a beautiful, challenging, and inspiring vision of the splendor of God's Word as found in the pages of the sacred text.

The Inspiration of Sacred Scripture

The first teaching that demands our attention is the one that lays the foundation for all of the others: Catholic doctrine on scriptural inspiration. At Vatican II, the Pope and the bishops summarized the Church's teaching on the inspiration of Scripture with the following words:

> The divinely revealed realities, which are contained and pre-sented in the text of Sacred Scripture, *have been written down under the inspiration of the Holy Spirit.* For Holy Mother Church, relying on the faith of the apostolic age, accepts as sacred and canonical the books of the Old and New Testaments, *whole and entire, with all their parts,* on the grounds that, written under the inspiration of the Holy Spirit, *they have God as their author,* and have been handed on as such to the Church herself.[3]

Several aspects of this teaching merit our attention. First, Vatican II directly ties the doctrine of inspiration to the reality of divine revelation. This is an important starting point, especially since the first two chapters of *Dei Verbum* are devoted to expounding the nature of divine revelation and its transmission.[4] For our purposes here, we need only note that in Catholic teaching, there are two orders of knowl-edge: (1) the order of "natural reason" and (2) the order of "supernatural divine revelation."[5] Scripture belongs in a special way to the latter, insofar as it both

---

3   Second Vatican Council, *Dei Verbum* [The Word of God], Dogmatic Constitution on Divine Revelation, (November 18, 1965) (*SD*, 19–31). All translations of *Dei Verbum* contained herein are from Austin Flannery, *Vatican Council II: Vol. 1: The Conciliar and Post Conciliar Documents,* rev. ed. (Northport: Costello, 1996), 750–765. Unless otherwise noted, emphasis in quotations from Vatican II is added.

4   Unfortunately, an examination of these two chapters is beyond the scope of this essay. For a famous study, see Joseph Ratzinger, "Revelation Itself," and "The Transmission of Divine Revelation," in *Commentary on the Documents of Vatican II,* 5 vols., ed. Herbert Vorgrimler (New York: Herder and Herder, 1967–1969), 3:170–198.

5   "By natural reason man can know God with certainty, on the basis of his works. But there

contains and presents "divinely revealed realities" (Lat.: *divinitus revelata*). In other words, the Council begins this section by affirming that Scripture is no ordinary book, but contains the supernatural revelation of God.

Second, notice that Vatican II clearly teaches that inspiration is not limited to certain parts of Scripture. Rather, all of the books of Old and New Testaments, "whole and entire, with all their parts" (*cum omnibus eorum partibus*) are divinely inspired. With these words, the Council is reaffirming the traditional doctrine of *plenary*, rather than partial, inspiration. Where does the Council get this formula? In the footnote to *Dei Verbum* 11, Vatican II cites two key sources. The first is the dogmatic teaching of the First Vatican Ecumenical Council, which defined that the books of the Bible, "whole with all their parts" (*integri cum omnibus suis partibus*) are "written by the inspiration of the Holy Spirit."[6] The second is a 1915 decree of the Pontifical Biblical Commission, which spoke of "the Catholic dogma regarding the inspiration of Sacred Scripture," whereby "everything (*omne*) the sacred writer asserts, expresses, and suggests must be held to be asserted, expressed, and suggested by the Holy Spirit."[7]

As we will see throughout this essay, this is but the first of many instances in which Vatican II will invite us to interpret its teaching on Scripture with a *hermeneutic of continuity* rather than a *hermeneutic of rupture*.[8] As Pope Benedict XVI has stated, the former approach to interpreting the documents of Vatican II emphasizes "renewal in the continuity" of the one Church of Christ, whereas the latter approach "risks ending in a split between the preconciliar Church and the postconciliar Church."[9] For its part, *Dei Verbum* itself encourages a hermeneutic of continuity and renewal rather than discontinuity and rupture by repeatedly citing modern magisterial teachings, as well as patristic and medieval sources, in the official footnotes to the text.

Third, and perhaps most important of all, in *Dei Verbum*, the Catholic doctrine of inspiration is ultimately an affirmation of the *divine authorship* of Scripture: the books of Scripture are inspired because they "have God as their author" (*Deus*

---

is another order of knowledge, which man cannot possibly arrive at by his own powers: the order of divine revelation." *Catechism of the Catholic Church*, 2d. ed. (Vatican City: Libreria Editrice Vaticana, 1997), no. 50. See also René Latourelle, *Theology of Revelation* (New York: Alba House, 1966).

6   First Vatican Council, *Dei Filius* [The Son of God], Dogmatic Constitution on the Catholic Faith (April 24, 1870), 2 (*SD*, 14–18, at 16–17).

7   Pontifical Biblical Commission, *On the Parousia or the Second Coming of Our Lord in the Letters of St. Paul the Apostle* (June 18, 1915) (*SD*, 207–208).

8   See Pope Benedict XVI, Address to the Roman Curia (December 22, 2005), in *L'Osservatore Romano*, Weekly Edition in English (January 4, 2006), 4–6. This address is also available in a recent volume dedicated to interpreting the documents of Vatican II with a hermeneutic of continuity and renewal. See Matthew L. Lamb and Matthew Levering, *Vatican II: Renewal within Tradition* (New York: Oxford University, 2008), ix–xv.

9   Benedict XVI, Address (December 22, 2005), quoted in Lamb and Levering, *Vatican II*, x.

habent auctorem). In the final analysis, when the Church affirms the doctrine of inspiration, it answers the perennial question of who authored the Scriptures by declaring in no uncertain terms: "God is the author of sacred Scripture."[10] Once again, in taking this position, Vatican II explicitly cites and employs the language of Vatican I, which taught that inspiration is not the result of the books of the Bible being "later approved" of the Church; nor is it because they contain "revelation without error"; rather the books are inspired because they "have God for their author."[11]

The Mystery of Dual Authorship

Such a bold doctrine of inspiration raises several questions: If God is the author of Scripture, what role did the human authors have to play? Does the Church's affirmation of divine authorship negate or neglect the human dimension of Scripture? By no means. In the same breath in which Vatican II teaches the divine authorship of Scripture, it also proclaims with equal force the truly human authorship of the sacred texts. Compare the very next lines:

> To compose the sacred books, *God chose certain men who*, all the while he employed them in this task, *made full use of their powers and faculties* so that, though he acted in them and by them, it was *as true authors* that they consigned to writing whatever he wanted written, and no more.[12]

This emphasis on the full use of the human faculties and powers by the individual authors of the books of Scripture is something on which it is critical to insist. As anyone who has read the Bible knows, any doctrine of inspiration that fails to take into account the diversity of human voices within Scripture ultimately fails to reckon with the reality of the biblical texts. And once again, in affirming the full human authorship of Scripture, Vatican II cites earlier magisterial teachings, in this case Pope Pius XII's 1943 encyclical letter promoting the historical study of Scripture, *Divino Afflante Spiritu*. Pius taught that "the inspired writer, in composing the sacred Book, is the living and reasonable instrument of the Holy Spirit," such that by using "his faculties and powers" any reader of the Bible can infer "the special character of each" human author "and, as it were, his personal traits."[13]

Catholic doctrine does not stop at merely affirming the fully divine and fully human authorship of Sacred Scripture. It also goes on to propose a striking analogy for illuminating the relationship between them:

---

10   *Catechism*, no. 105.

11   *Dei Filius*, 2 (*SD*, 16–17).

12   *Dei Verbum*, 11 (*SD*, 24).

13   Pope Pius XII, *Divino Afflante Spiritu* [Inspired by the Divine Spirit], Encyclical Letter Promoting Biblical Studies (September 30, 1943), 33 (*SD*, 115–139, at 128).

> Indeed, *the words of God*, expressed in the words of men, *are in every way like human language, just as the Word* of the eternal Father, when he took on himself the flesh of human weakness, *became like men.*[14]

With these words, Vatican II is claiming that the mystery of dual authorship—divine and human—can best be understood by the equally ineffable (but equally true) mystery of the incarnation. In the incarnation, the eternal "Word" of God "became flesh and dwelt amongst us," fully human, yet fully divine.[15] Once again, the Council's immediate source for this analogy is Pius XII's landmark encyclical, *Divino Afflante Spiritu.* There the Pope taught:

> As the substantial Word of God became like to men in all things "except sin" (Heb. 4:15), so the words of God, expressed in human language, are made like to human speech in every respect except error. In this consists that "condescension" of the God of providence, which St. John Chrysostom extolled with the highest praise and repeatedly declared to be found in the Sacred Books.[16]

In short, the Catholic Church proposes an *incarnational analogy* for understanding the mystery of Scripture's inspiration. By means of this analogy it affirms in the strongest possible terms both the divine authorship of Scripture as well as the free, full, and reasonable human authorship of the sacred texts. Like the mystery of the incarnation itself, the mystery of dual authorship is a testament to both the truth and humility of the Word incarnate and the Word inspired.[17]

The Inerrancy of Sacred Scripture

The next teaching that demands our attention is what the 1915 decree of the Pontifical Biblical Commission—as cited by Vatican II in the footnote to *Dei Verbum* 11—refers to as "the Catholic dogma of the inerrancy (*inerrantia*) of Scripture."[18]

---

14   *Dei Verbum*, 13 (*SD*, 25).

15   John 1:14. On the Catholic doctrine of the incarnation, see *Catechism*, nos. 456–483.

16   Pius XII, *Divino Afflante Spiritu*, 37 (*SD*, 129).

17   See Mary Healy, "Inspiration and Incarnation: The Christological Analogy and the Hermeneutics of Faith," *Letter & Spirit* 2 (2006): 27–41; J. H. Crehan, "The Analogy between *Dei Verbum Incarnatum* and *Dei Verbum Scriptum* in the Fathers," *Journal of Theological Studies* 6 (1955): 87–90.

18   Pontifical Biblical Commission, *On the Parousia or the Second Coming of Our Lord in the Letters of St. Paul the Apostle* (June 18, 1915), cited in *Dei Verbum*, 11 (*SD*, 24; compare *SD*, 207–208). See also Pius XII, *Divino Afflante Spiritu*, 46, who speaks of "the traditional teaching regarding the inerrancy of sacred Scripture." (*SD*, 132).

The doctrine of inerrancy flows directly from the doctrine of inspiration. The two cannot be understood apart from one another; nor can they be separated from one another without detriment to both. That is why Vatican II's teaching on the inerrancy of Scripture follows immediately on the heels of its doctrine of inspiration. After affirming that the human authors wrote only what God wanted written, and no more, the Council states:

> Since therefore, *all that the inspired authors or sacred writers assert, must be held as asserted by the Holy Spirit*, we must acknowledge that *the books of Scripture teach truth*—which God, for the sake of our salvation, wished to see confided to the sacred writings—firmly, faithfully, and *without error.* [19]

Three aspects of this important text demand our attention. First, although it is frequently overlooked, Vatican II situates its teaching on inerrancy in the context of plenary inspiration: "all (*omne*) that the inspired authors or sacred writers assert" must be regarded as "asserted by the Holy Spirit" (*assertum a Spiritu sancto*). This is a staggering claim, but one entirely consistent with the teaching on divine authorship we analyzed above. Second, on the basis of plenary inspiration, the Council goes on to affirm ("therefore") that the Bible teaches "truth" (*veritatem*)—firmly, faithfully, and "without error" (*sine errore*). With these words we find reference to the Bible's freedom from error, commonly referred to by Catholic theologians as the doctrine of inerrancy.[20] Third and finally, the specific reason for the inerrancy of Scripture is given: it is "for the sake of our salvation" (*nostrae salutis causa*) that God inspired the sacred authors to teach truth without error. These points sum up Vatican II's teaching on the truth of Scripture and its freedom from error.

Now, it is important to note here that since the Second Vatican Council a debate has arisen among scholars about how to interpret the teaching of *Dei Verbum* 11. Specifically, the debate revolves around whether or not the second half of the sentence in *Dei Verbum* 11 limits the extent of the inerrancy of Scripture. Indeed, some scholars claim that the text teaches a form of *limited inerrancy.*[21] They

---

19 *Dei Verbum*, 11 (SD, 24). Since there is debate about how to interpret this text, I have adapted Flannery's translation to follow the Latin as closely as possible. The original reads: "Cum ergo omne id, quod auctores inspirati seu hagiographi asserunt, retineri debeat assertum a Spiritu Sancto, inde Scripturae libri veritatem, quam Deus nostrae salutis causa, litteris sacris consignari voluit, firmiter, fideliter et sine errore docere profitendi sunt."

20 For example, Augustine Bea, *De Inspiratione et Inerrantia Sacrae Scripturae: Notae Historicae et Dogmaticae* [The Inspiration and Inerrancy of Sacred Scripture: An Historical and Doctrinal Study] (Rome: Pontifical Biblical Institute, 1954).

21 For example, Ronald D. Witherup, *Scripture: Dei Verbum*, Rediscovering Vatican II; (New York Paulist, 2006), 93: "The lack of error pertains not to every jot and tittle of Scripture but to that essential truth necessary for our salvation. This seems to qualify the type of inspiration found in the Bible. Inspiration, then, does not concern historical or scientific content but religious content, specifically, moral and doctrinal truths essential to salvation."

argue that the phrase "for the sake of our salvation" limits inerrancy to the saving truth found in Scripture; assertions in Scripture that are not directly "salvific" are not protected from error in the same way.[22] To support this interpretation, they note that the Council used the phrase "without error" (*sine errore*) rather than the noun "inerrancy" (*inerrantia*), suggesting that it was departing from the teaching on inerrancy found in earlier magisterial documents.[23]

Other scholars, however, argue that the limited inerrancy position is a based on a misinterpretation of *Dei Verbum* 11.[24] In support of this interpretation, they note that in the original Latin, the expression "for the sake of our salvation" is an adverbial phrase modifying the word "consign," not an adjectival phrase modifying the word "truth."[25] In other words, this clause tells us God's *purpose* in protecting Scripture from error; it does not limit *what kind* of truth in Scripture is protected from error.[26] From this perspective, Vatican II is simply "reaffirming inerrancy in a way both new and yet also in agreement with traditional teaching."[27] In support of this, I would add that *Dei Verbum* itself suggests as much by choosing to cite two modern magisterial affirmations of "the *absolute inerrancy* of Scripture" in the first footnote to the teaching on inspiration.[28]

Although we cannot go into the details of this debate in such a short essay, it is important for the reader to grasp its basic contours, not least because similar debates over inspiration and inerrancy are taking place in the ecumenical sphere, in Christian communities outside the Catholic Church.[29] However, because the interpretation of Vatican II's teaching is disputed among Catholic scholars, I would like to make several basic arguments in favor of the latter position, while recogniz-

---

22 So Aidan Nichols, *The Shape of Catholic Theology: An Introduction to its Sources, Principles and History* (Collegeville, MN: Liturgical Press, 1991), 131–140.

23 So Alois Grillmeier, "Chapter III: The Divine Inspiration and Interpretation of Sacred Scripture," in *Commentary on the Documents of Vatican II*, 5 vols., ed. Herbert Vorgrimler (New York: Herder and Herder, 1967–1969), 3:199–246, at 204–205, 234–235.

24 For example, Denis Farkasfalvy, *Inspiration and Interpretation: A Theological Introduction to Sacred Scripture* (Washington, DC; Catholic University of America, 2010), 221–235. An earlier version of this section appeared as Farkasfalvy, "Inspiration and Interpretation," in Lamb and Levering, *Vatican II*, 77–100.

25 Farkasfalvy, *Inspiration and Interpretation*, 226–227, n. 26.

26 Augustine Cardinal Bea, *The Word of God and Mankind* (Chicago: Franciscan Herald, 1967), 184–192, at 191. See also "Inspiration," in *Catholic Bible Dictionary*, ed. Scott W. Hahn (New York: Doubleday, 2009), 381–391.

27 Farkasfalvy, *Inspiration and Interpretation*, 229.

28 The first footnote to *Dei Verbum*, 11 cites the Pontifical Biblical Commission, *On the Parousia*, and the Sacred Congregation of the Holy Office, Letter (December 22, 1923), both of which explicitly speak of "the Catholic dogma of the inspiration and inerrancy of sacred Scripture" (*dogmate catholico de inspiratione et inerrantia sacrarum Scripturarum*). (DS 3629; EB 415, 499).

29 For an exploration of the issue by a leading Protestant exegete, see G. K. Beale, *The Erosion of Inerrancy in Evangelicalism: Responding to New Challenges to Biblical Authority* (Wheaton: Crossway, 2008).

ing that the final interpreter of the Council is of course the living magisterium of the Catholic Church.[30]

A Hermeneutic of Continuity

First, if we interpret Vatican II's teaching on Scripture with a hermeneutic of continuity, then the weight of probability is tipped heavily in favor of absolute (or complete) inerrancy. The reason: previous magisterial teachings on Scripture are unequivocal on this point.

For example, in 1870, Vatican I dogmatically proclaimed that the canonical books of Scripture contain "revelation without error" (*sine errore*)—the exact Latin phrase used by Vatican II.[31] Likewise, in his 1893 encyclical, Pope Leo XIII taught that Scripture is "entirely immune from all error" (*ab omni omnino errore immunes*).[32] Significantly, he also declared that the complete inerrancy of Scripture is not merely a theological opinion but rather "the ancient and unchanging faith of the Church."[33]

In 1920, Pope Benedict XV repeated Leo's teaching and proclaimed "the absolute immunity of Scripture from error" (*de absoluta Scripturarum a quibusvis erroribus immunitate*) as "the ancient and traditional belief of the Church."[34] Finally, and perhaps most significantly, in 1943, Pius XII began his historic encyclical by declaring Scripture's "freedom from any error whatsoever" a "solemn definition of Catholic doctrine."[35] Note: none of these papal teachings are passing remarks; the manner in which the doctrine of absolute inerrancy of Scripture is formulated and the frequency with which it is proposed clearly identify it as a truth of faith.[36]

---

30   In 2008, Pope Benedict XVI called a Synod of Bishops to discuss "The Word of God in the Life and Mission of the Church." After the Synod, the following proposition (no. 12) was given to Pope Benedict: "The Synod proposes that the Congregation for the Doctrine of the Faith clarify the concepts of 'inspiration' and 'truth' in the Bible, along with their reciprocal relationship, in order to better understand the teaching in *Dei Verbum* 11. In particular, it is necessary to emphasize the specific character of Catholic Biblical hermeneutics in this area." (Quoted in Farkasfalvy, *Inspiration and Interpretation*, 237). Currently, we are still awaiting such a magisterial clarification.

31   *Dei Filius*, 2 (*SD*, 16–17).

32   (Author's translation.) Pope Leo XIII, *Providentissimus Deus* [The God of All Providence], Encyclical Letter on the Study of Scripture (November 18, 1893), 20 (*SD*, 37–61, at 54–55).

33   Leo XIII, *Providentissimus Deus*, 20 (*SD*, 55).

34   Pope Benedict XV, *Spiritus Paraclitus* [The Holy Spirit, the Comforter], Encyclical Letter Commemorating the Fifteenth Centenary of the Death of St. Jerome (September 15, 1920), 16 (*SD*, 81–111, at 87). In the same section, the Pope also speaks of "the absolute truth" (*absolutamque veritatem*) and "immunity from error" (*erroris immunitatem*), stating that "no error can occur in the inspired text," and that "divine inspiration extends to every part of the Bible without the slightest exception and that no error can occur in the inspired text."

35   Pius XII, *Divino Afflante Spiritu*, 1 (SD, 116).

36   See Second Vatican Council, *Lumen Gentium* [Light to the Nations], Dogmatic Constitution on the Church (November 21, 1964), 25, in Flannery, *Vatican Council II*.

Second, as we saw above, Vatican II also teaches the plenary inspiration of Scripture. The logical result of plenary inspiration is complete inerrancy. Look closely again at the two parts of how the Council formulates its teaching:

1. *Since*, all that the inspired authors or sacred writers assert, must be held as asserted by the Holy Spirit,

2. we *therefore* must acknowledge that the books of Scripture teach truth— which God, for the sake of our salvation, wished to see confided to the sacred writings—firmly, faithfully, and without error.[37]

It is only when the doctrine of complete inspiration (the first half of the sentence) is separated from the doctrine of inerrancy of Scripture (the second half of the sentence) that the *Dei Verbum* 11 can be interpreted as somehow limiting inerrancy. It makes no sense to affirm that inspiration is unlimited, but that inerrancy, the direct result of inspiration, is somehow limited. If everything asserted by the sacred writers is asserted by the Holy Spirit then, both logically and theologically, everything asserted by the sacred authors must be free from error.

Third, in the footnote to the teaching on the truth of Scripture, Vatican II explicitly cites two previous papal condemnations of limited inerrancy.[38] Although these magisterial condemnations are frequently overlooked, they are critical to correctly interpreting the Council's teaching, since Vatican II wished to bring them to our attention:

> But it is absolutely wrong and forbidden, either to narrow inspiration to certain parts only of Holy Scripture, or to admit that the sacred writer has erred. For the system of those who, in order to rid themselves of these difficulties, do not hesitate to concede that divine inspiration regards the things of faith and morals and nothing beyond, because (as they wrongly think) in a question of the truth of falsehood or a passage, we should consider not so much what God has said as the reason or purpose that he had in mind in saying it—this system cannot be tolerated.[39]

> "It is absolutely wrong and forbidden, either to narrow inspiration to certain passages of Holy Scripture, or to admit that the sacred writer has erred," since divine inspiration "not only is essentially incompatible with error but excludes it and rejects it as absolutely and necessarily as it is impossible that God himself, the supreme Truth,

---

37 *Dei Verbum*, 11 (*SD*, 24). See also Farkasfalvy, *Inspiration and Interpretation*, 226–227.

38 *Dei Verbum*, 11, n. 5 (*SD*, 24, n. 22).

39 Leo XIII, *Providentissimus Deus*, 20 (*SD*, 55).

can utter that which is not true. This is the ancient and constant faith of the Church." This teaching, which our predecessor Leo XIII set forth with such solemnity, we also proclaim with our authority, and we urge all to adhere to it religiously.[40]

It is not apparent how these citations can be reconciled with the view that *Dei Verbum* is limiting the inerrancy of Scripture. As we have demonstrated, Vatican II's overall teaching on the Bible stands in direct continuity with previous papal and conciliar teachings and indicates this fact by repeatedly citing them in the footnotes. Hence, if this passage were actually restricting the scope of inerrancy, then this would be the only footnote in *Dei Verbum* that indicates a rupture with previous magisterial teaching rather than continuity. I find this intrinsically implausible and exegetically untenable. Instead, the most probable interpretation is that Vatican II, like the passages from the papal encyclicals that it chooses to cite, is reaffirming—in a positive and concise way—the ancient and traditional Catholic doctrine of the complete inerrancy of Scripture.

A final support for this reading is offered by the most recent magisterial interpretation of *Dei Verbum* 11, given in 1998 by the Congregation for the Doctrine of the Faith and signed by the congregation's Prefect Cardinal Joseph Ratzinger (now Pope Benedict XVI). The Congregation asserts that "the absence of error (*absentia erroris*) in the inspired sacred texts," is an example of *a divinely revealed article of faith* of the highest order, of like status with the solemnly defined christological dogmas or the doctrine of the real presence of Christ in the Eucharist.[41] The Congregation supports its interpretation by citing *Dei Verbum* 11, as well as Pope Leo's condemnation of limited inerrancy.

A Hermeneutic of Trust

With that said, it is important to clarify what the absolute inerrancy of Scripture does and does not mean. In particular, we want to briefly distinguish the Catholic doctrine from other concepts of inerrancy that may be found outside the Catholic Church, such as in Protestant fundamentalism.[42] For within different Christian communities the idea of biblical inerrancy takes various forms, some of which are very different from, and even incompatible with, magisterial teaching on the matter.

---

40 Pius XII, *Divino Afflante Spiritu*, 3 (*SD*, 116–117).

41 See Congregation for the Doctrine of the Faith, "Commentary on the Concluding Formula of the *Professio Fidei*," (June 29, 1998), 5, in *L'Osservatore Romano*, Weekly Edition in English (July 15, 1998), 3–4, at 3. Text also in *Acta Apostolicae Sedis* 90 (1998): 549.

42 For a discussion of the problems with fundamentalist interpretation and how it differs from Catholic doctrine, see Pope John Paul II, Address to the Pontifical Biblical Commission (April 23, 1993), 6 (*SD*, 170–180, at 174–175): Pontifical Biblical Commission, *On the Interpretation of the Bible in the Church*, Sec. I, Par. F. (*SD*, 244–317, at 273–275).

First, the Catholic doctrine of inerrancy does *not* mean that subsequent manuscripts of sacred Scripture are somehow preserved from any textual errors, omissions, or alterations. To the contrary, it is precisely the task of textual criticism—which Catholics have been doing at least since the time of Origen in the early third century—to establish the most probable form of the original text. As Pius XII affirms, the sacred writer "is not to be taxed with error" simply because "copyists have made mistakes."[43]

Second—and this is very important—the Catholic concept of absolute inerrancy presupposes *a correct interpretation of the biblical text*. This means that a passage of Scripture must be interpreted in accord with the literary genre of the text as well as the actual intentions of the human author. It should go without saying that any interpretation of Scripture that disregards the genre and historical context of the writings is bound to end up accusing the text of error—and not without justification. This is particularly true of those portions of Scripture that in both ancient and modern times have been interpreted as making "scientific" claims that are questionable and or verifiably false.

The classic example of this is the debate over texts of Scripture that depict the shape of the sky as being "like a skin" or a "dome."[44] As St. Augustine points out, those who interpret these expressions literally and use this to cast doubt on "the trustworthiness of the Scriptures" ultimately "do not understand the style of the divine utterances."[45] Augustine argues that these descriptions can and should be understood "figuratively"; or, as we might say, these descriptions are *phenomenological* descriptions of the appearance of the sky.[46] It is in this context that Augustine concludes: the biblical authors "knew about the shape of the sky, whatever might be the truth of the matter. But the Spirit of God who was speaking through them did not wish to teach people about such things which would contribute nothing to their salvation."[47] Significantly, this statement from Augustine about figurative language and "scientific" statements in the Bible is quoted by both Leo XIII and

---

43   Pius XII, *Divino Afflante Spiritu*, 3 (*SD*, 116–117).

44   See Ps. 104:2; Isa. 40:22 (Lat.). See St. Augustine, *On the Literal Meaning of Genesis*, Bk. 2, Chap. 9, 20, in *On Genesis*, trans. Edmund Hill, (Hyde Park, NY: New City, 2002), 201–203.

45   Augustine, *Genesis*, Bk. 2, Chap. 9, 20.

46   Augustine, *Genesis*, Bk. 2, Chap. 9, 20. We still use such phenomenological language today. For example, when the Psalmist speaks about the "rising" of the sun being "from the end of the heavens" (Ps. 19:6), the text is no more making an objective "scientific" claim about the relationship between the sun and earth than is the modern weathercaster who speaks about "sunrise" being at 6:00 a.m. Just as no one who understood the idiom would accuse the weathercaster of affirming an astronomical error, neither should we accuse the sacred text of having erred on this point. In neither case is a properly "scientific" claim even being made. Instead, both are speaking in a phenomenological way about what the sun appears to do as it "rises" in the sky, according to ordinary speech. As such, both statements are true.

47   Augustine, *Genesis*, Bk. 2, Chap. 9, 20.

Pius XII in their encyclicals on Scripture,[48] as well as by *Dei Verbum* in its footnote on the inerrancy of Scripture.[49] As Pius XII says, following both Augustine and St. Thomas Aquinas:

> The first and greatest care of Leo XIII was to set forth the teaching on the truth of the sacred Books and to defend it from attack. Hence with grave words did he proclaim that *there is no error whatsoever if the sacred writer, speaking of things of the physical order, "went by what sensibly appeared," as the Angelic Doctor says, speaking either in figurative language or in terms that were commonly used at the time and many instances are in daily use at this day, even among the most eminent men of science.* For "the sacred writers or to speak more accurately"—the words are St. Augustine's—"the Holy Spirit, who spoke by them, did not intend to teach men these things"—that is to say, the essential nature of the things of the universe—"things in no way profitable to salvation."[50]

In other words, in the case of an apparent 'scientific' error, one has to ascertain exactly what the biblical author is asserting. As Leo had pointed out long ago, the authors of Scripture "did not seek to penetrate the secrets of nature."[51] Rather, they used "ordinary language" to describe the world around them "in a way men could understand and were accustomed to."[52] Once again, the incarnational anal-

---

48   Leo XIII, *Providentissimus Deus*, 18 (SD, 54); Pius XII, *Divino Afflante Spiritu*, 3 (SD, 116–117).

49   *Dei Verbum* 11, n. 5.

50   Pius XII, *Divino Afflante Spiritu*, 3 (SD, 116–117).

51   Leo XIII, *Providentissimus Deus*, 18 (SD, 54).

52   It is worth noting here that *Dei Verbum* 11, n. 5, also quotes St. Thomas Aquinas, *Disputed Questions On Truth*, q. 12, art. 2, contra., resp. In this text, Aquinas draws directly on Augustine, *Genesis*, Bk. 2, Chap. 9, 20, when taking up the disputed question: "Does Prophecy Deal with Conclusions which Can Be Known Scientifically?" In his answer, Aquinas says that "All those things the knowledge of which can be useful for salvation are the matter of prophecy, whether they are past, or future, or even eternal, or necessary, or contingent. But those things which cannot pertain to salvation are outside the matter of prophecy." However, he immediately goes on to add that by "necessary for salvation," he means "necessary for the instruction in the faith or the formation of morals." Strikingly, he asserts that "many things which are proved in the sciences can be useful for this [that is, salvation]." Even more striking, he also asserts that "we find that mention of these is made in Holy Scripture." For this reason, Aquinas ultimately answers the question in the affirmative: "Conclusions which are demonstrated in the sciences can belong to prophecy." He even gives a pastoral reason for inspired prophecy containing things which can be known scientifically: "Although conclusions of the sciences can be known in another way than through prophecy, it is not superfluous for them to be shown by prophetic light, for through faith we cling more firmly to what the prophets say than we do to the demonstrations of the sciences. And in this, too, the grace of God is praised and his perfect knowledge is shown forth." *The Disputed Questions on Truth*, 3 vols. (Chicago: Regnery, 1952–1954), 2:112–113. Hence, for Aquinas, while Scripture does contain truths which can be proved through the sciences, it only contains those which are necessary for salvation.

ogy helps shed light on the mysterious humility of God's inspired Word, which really has been "made like to human speech *in every respect* except error."[53]

Third, according to Pope Pius XII, inerrancy *does* mean that Scripture's "freedom from any error whatsoever" also applies to *"matters of history,"* which should not be seen as "in no way connected with faith."[54] What does this mean? For one thing, it must be immediately noted that Church's view of the historical truth of Scripture also presupposes correct interpretation: that is, there must be an actual historical intent on the part of the biblical author. This is of course not always the case for every book of the Bible—for example, the Psalms and the Wisdom literature—nor even for every passage in a particular book—for example the parables in the Gospels, or allegories and apocalyptic imagery found throughout the Bible. Moreover, Pius XII also recognizes the presence of *"approximations"* in the language of Scripture that must be taken into account, so that what appears to be "historical error" often ends up being rather "the customary modes of expression" used by ancient historiographers.[55] One might think here of the differences in detail between the various gospel accounts of Jesus' words at the Last Supper.[56] However, with these qualifications in mind, the Church does indeed affirm the overall "historical truth of sacred Scripture."[57] As Pope Benedict XV wrote:

> *Those too who hold that the historical portions of Scripture do not rest on the absolute truth of the facts but merely upon what they are pleased to term their relative truth, namely, what people then commonly thought are ... out of harmony with the Church's teaching ...* For whereas physics is concerned with "sensible appearances" and must consequently square with phenomena, history, on the contrary, must square with the facts, since history is the written account of events as they actually occurred.[58]

This teaching may come as something of a surprise, given the climate of historical skepticism that has characterized a great deal of modern biblical scholarship. However, it is the logical outcome of the doctrine of plenary inspiration, in which "everything asserted by the sacred authors"—including their historical assertions— is held to be "asserted by the Holy Spirit."[59] Given the reality of inspiration, the Catholic Church teaches that whenever a biblical author actually makes an histori-

---

53 Pius XII, *Divino Afflante Spiritu*, 37 (SD, 129).
54 Pius XII, *Divino Afflante Spiritu*, 1 (SD, 116).
55 Pius XII, *Divino Afflante Spiritu*, 38 (SD, 129–130).
56 Compare Matt. 26:26–29; Mark 14:22–25; Luke 22:14–23.
57 Pius XII, *Divino Afflante Spiritu*, 3 (SD, 117).
58 Benedict XV, *Spiritus Paraclitus*, 22 (SD, 89).
59 *Dei Verbum*, 11 (SD, 24).

cal assertion, these assertions are also true, in accordance with the intentions of the author.[60]

Fourth and finally—and this cannot be stressed too much—from a Catholic perspective, the doctrine of inerrancy does *not* mean that there are no *apparent* errors, *apparent* contradictions, or other serious difficulties littered throughout the Scriptures. To the contrary, the Popes have repeatedly encouraged Catholic commentators to both recognize such difficulties and arduously seek solutions to them.[61] Once again, *Dei Verbum* gives us clear guidance in this matter by citing in the footnote Augustine's guideline for how Catholic exegetes should deal with an apparent error in Scripture.[62] In a brilliant letter to St. Jerome, Augustine affirms that the authors of Scripture were "completely free from error," and lays down this general rule:

> And if in these writings I am perplexed by anything which appears to me opposed to truth, I do not hesitate to suppose that [1] either the manuscript is faulty, or [2] the translator has not caught the meaning of what was said, or [3] I myself have failed to understand.[63]

In other words, the Catholic doctrine of inspiration and inerrancy ultimately calls the biblical interpreter to adopt what might be called *a hermeneutic of trust*—as opposed to the hermeneutic of skepticism that has been so widespread in the modern period. From an interpretive posture of trust, the truth of the biblical text is presumed and the Scripture is always given the benefit of the doubt. Such a hermeneutic is not uncritical naiveté, but rather an eminently reasonable response to the divine authorship of Scripture. Indeed, from a Catholic perspective, the truth of Scripture is not something that an individual interpreter derives as a result of inductive analysis, but a truth that is received as divinely revealed. All of this, of course, calls for the exercise of the virtues of patience and humility on the part of the biblical scholar. It is much easier to accuse the sacred text of error than to admit with Augustine the possibility that "I myself have failed to understand." But if all of Scripture is indeed the inspired Word of God, then it seems reasonable to suggest that a hermeneutic of trust is exactly the posture that a person of "faith" (*pistis*)—which in Greek also means "trust"—should take.[64]

---

60 See Bea, *Word of God*, 189–190.

61 For example, see Pius XII, *Divino Afflante Spiritu*, 44 (*SD*, 131).

62 St. Augustine, *Letter 82*, Chap. 1, 3, is cited in *Dei Verbum*, 11, n. 5. Significantly, Augustine's letter is also cited in two of the encyclicals on Scripture. See Benedict XV, *Spiritus Paraclitus*, 14 (*SD*, 87); Leo XIII, *Providentissimus Deus*, 21 (*SD*, 56).

63 Augustine, *Letter 82*, Chap. 1, 3, in *A Select Library of Nicene and Post-Nicene Fathers of the Christian Church*, 1st series, 14 vols., ed. Philip Schaff (Peabody, MA: Hendrickson, 1994 [reprint]), 1:350.

64 As an example of this posture, see the comments of Pope Benedict XVI, *Jesus of Nazareth*

The Interpretation of Scripture

The third and final issue is slightly less controversial but no less central: Catholic teaching regarding the interpretation of Sacred Scripture. Once again, it is no coincidence that *Dei Verbum's* discussion of biblical interpretation comes *after* its teachings on inspiration and inerrancy, for it presupposes them:

> Seeing that, in sacred Scripture, God speaks through men in a human fashion, it follows that *the interpreter of sacred Scripture, if he is to ascertain what God has wished to communicate to us, should carefully search out the meaning which the sacred writers really had in mind*, that meaning which God had thought well to manifest through the medium of their words.[65]

Notice that this teaching on interpretation emphasizes both the *human authorship* of Scripture ("the meaning which the sacred authors really had in mind") as well as the *divine authorship* ("the meaning which God thought well to manifest through their words"). Both must be taken into account and neither isolated from the other if the exegete is to properly interpret the inspired text. It is worth pointing out that this emphasis distinguishes Vatican II's methodology of interpretation from much modern exegesis, in which attention is given solely to what the human author intended to affirm.[66]

How then do we discover what the human author intended? In one of the lengthiest and most detailed sections of *Dei Verbum*, Vatican II has this to say:

> In determining the intention of the sacred writers, attention should be paid, (among other things), to literary genres. This is because truth is presented and expressed differently in historical, prophetic, or poetic texts, or in other styles of speech. *The interpreter has to look for that meaning which a biblical writer intended and expressed in his particular circumstances, and in his historical and cultural context, by means of such literary genres as were in use at his time.* To understand correctly what a biblical writer intended to assert, due attention is needed both to the customary and characteristic ways of feeling, speaking, and narrating which were current in his time, and to the social conventions of the period.[67]

(New York: Doubleday, 2007), xxi–xxii, who sums up his "methodology" with the pithy, and surprisingly controversial phrase: "I trust the Gospels."

65   *Dei Verbum*, 12 (*SD*, 24–25).

66   On this point, see Robert Barron, "Biblical Interpretation and Theology: Irenaeus, Modernity, and Vatican II," *Letter & Spirit* 5 (2009): 173–191.

67   *Dei Verbum* 12 (cf. *SD* 24-25). The translation provided here is from Tanner, *Decrees of the*

From this important passage, we are able to distill several tools for Catholic exegetes to use in determining the intentions of the human author. First, exegesis must pay attention to *literary genres*. This means asking questions like: What kind of book is this? What is the literary form of the work? Is it poetry, prophecy, history? How one answers this question will have a direct effect on the interpretation of the text. Second, the exegete must also closely examine the *language* of the sacred text and its "characteristic ways of speaking." This means asking questions such as: What is the precise meaning of the words used? What is their denotation as well as their connotation? Is the human author using a particular idiom, such as hyperbole or double entendre? Finally, both literary and linguistic analysis must be accompanied by a close study of *history* and *culture*: What is the "historical and cultural context" in which the text was composed? What were the "social conventions of the period" that can shed light on the text? In sum, these four tools—literature, language, history, and culture—are Vatican II's primary means of discovering the intention of the human authors.

Once again, in making these statements, we can see the Council building in a very explicit way on the earlier teachings of the papal encyclicals on the Bible. In this case, *Dei Verbum* 12 footnotes Pius XII's lengthy discussion of historical exegesis in *Divino Afflante Spiritu*, in which the pontiff vigorously promoted the study of "grammar, philology ... history, archaeology, ethnology, and other sciences" as well as close scrutiny of the literary "modes of expression" used in the biblical text.[68] Pius, in turn, had been building on Benedict XV's teaching that "all interpretation rests on the literal sense"—that is, on "a careful study of the actual words so that we may be perfectly certain what the writer really does say."[69] Indeed, well before Benedict XV, Leo XIII had insisted that exegetes study the original languages of Scripture and "the practice of scientific criticism," and carry out "historical investigation" of the biblical texts.[70] Once again we see that a close reading of *Dei Verbum* reveals a hermeneutic of renewal in continuity. Far from proposing a rupture with earlier Church teaching, *Vatican II is explicitly incorporating modern developments from the papal encyclicals on Scripture*, developments that support authentic scientific, literary, and historical criticism of the Bible.

However, this is not the end of the interpreter's task. Given the reality of inspiration, simply determining what the human authors intended does not exhaust the task of exegesis.[71] Indeed, to stop with the human authors leaves exegesis

---

Ecumenical Councils, 976 (slightly adapted), since the rendition of this important passage in Flannery, *Vatican II*, is deficient in several aspects.

68   See Pius XII, *Divino Afflante Spiritu*, 33–43 (SD, 128–131).

69   Benedict XV, *Spiritus Paraclitus*, 50–54 (SD, 100–102).

70   Leo XIII, *Providentissimus Deus*, 17 (SD, 52–53).

71   On this point, see Joseph Cardinal Ratzinger, "Biblical Interpretation in Conflict," in *God's Word: Scripture—Tradition—Office* (San Francisco: Ignatius, 2008), originally published in Joseph Ratzinger, "Biblical Interpretation in Crisis: On the Question of the Foundations and

incomplete, for there is another author involved: God. Hence, the exegete must also discover what the divine author intended. Surely this is the more difficult task. How does one accomplish it? According to *Dei Verbum*, the answer is as follows:

> But since sacred Scripture must be read and interpreted with its divine authorship in mind, no less attention must be devoted to *the content and unity of the whole Scripture*, taking into account *the living Tradition of the entire Church* and *the analogy of faith*, if we are to derive their true meaning from the sacred texts.[72]

As the *Catechism of the Catholic Church* rightly points out, in the above passage, the Second Vatican Council was proposing "three criteria" (*criteria tria*) for discovering what the divine author of Scripture intended.[73]

The Council's first criterion for discovering the divine author's intention is to interpret any given text in the canonical context of the Bible as a whole, that is, according to "the content and unity of the whole Scripture" (*contentum et unitatem totius scripturae*).[74] This means that the meaning of a given portion of Holy Scripture, say, in the Old Testament, can legitimately be interpreted in light of another portion, say, the New Testament. Even though such texts may have different human authors, both texts have the same divine author. This gives them a unity that is supernatural but nonetheless real. Indeed, given the divine authorship of Scripture, it is not only fitting that Scripture interpret Scripture; correct interpretation actually requires that the biblical canon as a whole be taken into account.

The second criterion for discovering what the divine author intended is more controversial, since historically it has constituted a dividing line between Catholic and Protestant exegesis. According to Vatican II, the biblical text must not only be interpreted in the light of Sacred Scripture as a whole, but in the light of "the living Tradition of the entire Church" (*vivae totius ecclesiae traditionis*).[75] In Catholic doctrine, sacred Tradition is also the Word of God, which has its origin in "the preaching of the apostles," is continued in the Church," in her doctrine, life, and worship," and is witnessed in a special way in "the sayings of the holy Fathers," that is the Church Fathers of the first centuries.[76] All of these are guided by the help of the Holy Spirit. And because the Holy Spirit is likewise the author of Scripture,

---

Approaches of Exegesis Today," in *Biblical Interpretation in Crisis: The Ratzinger Conference on the Bible and the Church*, ed. Richard John Neuhaus (Grand Rapids, MI: Eerdmans, 1989).

72 *Dei Verbum*, 12 (*SD*, 24–25).

73 *Catechism*, no. 111.

74 *Dei Verbum*, 12 (*SD*, 24–25); cf. *Catechism*, no. 112.

75 *Dei Verbum*, 12 (*SD*, 24–25); cf. *Catechism*, no. 113.

76 *Dei Verbum*, 8 (*SD*, 22–23). On the relationship between sacred Scripture and sacred Tradition, see *Dei Verbum*, 7–10 (*SD*, 21–23); *Catechism*, nos. 74–83. For an exhaustive modern study, see Yves Congar, *Tradition and Traditions: An Historical and a Theological Essay* (London: Burns and Oates, 1966).

in order to discover the intention of the divine author, Scripture must not be inter-preted apart from Tradition—as if the two were opposed to one another—but in the light of that Tradition, led by the same Spirit of God. As St. Paul says: "Stand firm and hold to the traditions [Gk.: *paradosis*] which you were taught by us, either by word of mouth or by letter."[77]

The third and final criterion: the interpreter must take into account what Vatican II calls "the analogy of faith" (Lat.: *analogiae fidei*).[78] This somewhat more obscure term is a reference to "the coherence of the truths of faith among them-selves and within the plan of revelation."[79] In other words, the interpreter must also take into account the doctrine of the Church, as expressed in the ordinary and universal teachings of the living magisterium. Yet again, Vatican II is drawing this language from Leo XIII's encyclical on the Bible, in which he states that "the analogy of faith should be followed"—that is, "Catholic doctrine, as authoritatively proposed by the Church."[80] While this may seem like putting the doctrinal cart before the exegetical horse, note the reason for the Pope's teaching: "Seeing that *the same God is the author both of the sacred books and of the doctrine committed to the Church* ... it follows that all interpretation is foolish and false which either makes the sacred writers disagree with one another, or is opposed to the doctrine of the Church."[81]

No doubt this might strike non-Catholics as problematic, but consider two points. First, whether or not one agrees with the premises, the logic of the teaching is consistent. If the same Holy Spirit who authored the Scripture also guides the magisterium in the formulation and teaching of Church doctrine, then "sound doctrine"[82] is an aid, not an obstacle, to discovering what the divine author of Scripture intended because both Scripture and sound doctrine are true. Second, a good case can be made that any Christian who accepts a *closed canon* implicitly ac-knowledges the importance of Church doctrine in interpreting Scripture. Indeed, the very fact that Christians accept that there is a single definitive canonical list of books implies an acceptance of this third criterion, because the canonical list of books is nothing other than an *extrabiblical Church doctrine*.[83] There is no inspired table of contents for Scripture; the canon is a Church doctrine, not found in the

---

77 2 Thess. 2:15.

78 *Dei Verbum*, 12 (*SD*, 24–25); cf. *Catechism*, no. 114.

79 *Catechism*, no. 114.

80 Leo XIII, *Providentissimus Deus*, 14 (*SD*, 48). The "analogy of faith" is also mentioned in Pius XII, *Divino Afflante Spiritu*, 24 (*SD*, 125).

81 Leo XIII, *Providentissimus Deus*, 14 (*SD*, 48).

82 Titus 1:9.

83 See *Catechism*, no. 120, for the Catholic doctrine of the canon, citing the definitive canonical lists of the councils of Rome (A. D. 382), Florence (1442), and Trent (1546). I owe this point to my good friend, Michael Barber.

Bible itself, one believed by both Catholics and non-Catholics alike.[84] If the doctrine of the canon is an aid to interpretation, then it is consistent to suggest that other Church doctrines are as well.

In short, in addition to the incarnational analogy of inspiration discussed above, the official Catholic doctrine of biblical interpretation proposes what might be called an *incarnational* and *ecclesial hermeneutic*—one that gives equal emphasis to the human and divine authorship of Scripture, as interpreted in the context of Christ's Church. Discovering what the human author intended necessitates focusing on the literal sense of the text in its historical context. Hence the importance of literary and historical criticism. Discovering what the divine author intended means interpreting the biblical text in three broader contexts: Scripture, Tradition, and the doctrines of the Church. Hence the importance—indeed the necessity—of theological exegesis done in an ecclesial context.

All that the Prophets Have Spoken

By way of conclusion, we can now briefly summarize what we have learned about inspiration, inerrancy, and interpretation, and briefly tie each of these to the teaching of Scripture itself.

According to Catholic doctrine, the Bible is nothing less than the inspired Word of God, written under the very breath of the Holy Spirit. In making such an audacious claim, the Church is drawing directly on the teaching of Paul, who affirms that "all Scripture is inspired by God [Gk.: *theopneustos*, literally, "God-breathed"], and profitable for teaching, for reproof, for correction, and for training in righteousness, that the man of God may be complete, equipped for every good work."[85]

Given the reality of divine inspiration, the Church also affirms that the Scriptures are to be believed. They teach the truth—firmly, faithfully, and without error. Again, proposing this doctrine, the Church is simply following the model of Jesus in the Gospels, who declares that "Scripture cannot be nullified,"[86] and upbraids the disciples on the road to Emmaus by saying: "O foolish men, and slow of heart to believe all [Gk.: *pasin*] that the prophets have spoken!"[87] Notice that Jesus does not limit the trust his disciples are to place in the inspired Word: *all* that the prophets have spoken is to be believed. Jesus sets no limits on the truth of Scripture; neither does the Catholic Church. Indeed, from a historical perspective, it is worth noting that Jesus himself no doubt shared the ancient Jewish belief in

---

84 Unfortunately, we do not have the space here to enter into the debate over the Old Testament canon. Suffice it so say that my point stands merely on the basis of the New Testament canonical list of books, which is likewise an extrabiblical Church doctrine. *Dei Verbum* 8 points out that, "By means of this same Tradition the full canon of the sacred books is known to the Church."

85 2 Tim. 3:16.

86 John 10:35.

87 Luke 24:25.

the inspiration and inerrancy of Jewish Scripture. According to Josephus, first-century Jews believed both that the Scriptures were "inspired" and that "there is no discrepancy in what is written."[88]

Finally, the Catholic doctrine of interpretation adopts an incarnational and ecclesial approach to the exegesis. This approach recognizes Scripture's fully human elements and difficulties as well as its divine origin and ecclesial destination. In this, the Church once again follows the New Testament itself, which declares that in the Scriptures—especially the letters of Paul—"there are some things hard to understand, which the ignorant and unstable twist to their own destruction."[89] It is precisely for this reason that, "no prophecy of Scripture is a matter of one's own interpretation [*idias epilusis*]."[90] Rather, the written Word of God must be interpreted in the living light of sacred Scripture as a whole, sacred Tradition, and the doctrines of the faith, so that it not be "a dead letter" but rather become for "the children of the Church ... strength for [the] faith, food for the soul, and a pure and lasting font of the spiritual life."[91]

---

88 Josephus, *Against Apion*, Bk. 1, 7, 37, in *The Works of Josephus*, trans. William Whiston (Peabody, MA: Hendrickson, 1994 [reprint]), 776.

89 2 Pet. 3:16.

90 2 Pet. 1:20.

91 *Dei Verbum*, 24 (*SD*, 29–30); cf. *Catechism*, no. 111.

Letter & Spirit 6 (2010): 67-91

Magisterial Teaching on the Inspiration and Truth of Scripture
Precedents and Prospects

~: Pablo T. Gadenz :~
Seton Hall University

Following the 2008 Synod of Bishops on "The Word of God in the Life and Mission of the Church," the Pontifical Biblical Commission took up a new subject for study, namely, the inspiration and truth of the Bible. The reason for this choice was at least twofold. First, the commission was ready to tackle a new subject following the publication, earlier in 2008, of its document, *The Bible and Morality*.[1] Second, the Synod itself, in one of the fifty-five "final propositions" it submitted to Pope Benedict XVI, had recommended that the concepts of the inspiration and truth of the Bible be clarified by the Vatican's Congregation for the Doctrine of the Faith.[2] Since the biblical commission is a consultative body to the doctrinal congregation on biblical matters, it was only natural that it should take up this proposal.

Thus far, the biblical commission has dedicated its 2009 and 2010 plenary meetings to the study of the Bible's inspiration and truth.[3] It is unclear how many more annual meetings will be dedicated to this subject.[4] It is also unclear when, or in what form, the outcome of the commission's study will be published, if at all.[5] In light of these developments, it is timely to review the existing magisterial

---

1 Pontifical Biblical Commission, *The Bible and Morality: Biblical Roots of Christian Conduct* (Vatican City: Libreria Editrice Vaticana, 2008).

2 "The Synod proposes that the Congregation for the Doctrine of the Faith clarify the concepts of the inspiration and truth of the Bible, as well as their reciprocal relationship, in order to make the teaching of *Dei Verbum*, 11, better understood. In particular, it is necessary to highlight the originality of Catholic biblical hermeneutics in this area." Synod of Bishops, 12th Ordinary General Assembly, List of Propositions, 12. Available (in Italian) online at: http://www.vatican.va/roman_curia/synod/documents/rc_synod_doc_20081025_elenco-prop-finali_it.html.

3 Regarding the April 20–24, 2009 plenary meeting, the Vatican Information Service explained that "attention will be given to a new study entitled 'Inspiration and Truth of the Bible.'" (April 16, 2009) (http://visnews-en.blogspot.com/2009/04/plenary-assembly-of-pontifical-biblical.html). For the April 12–16, 2010 meeting, the Vatican reported that "the members of the commission will turn their attention to the subject of 'Inspiration and Truth of the Bible.' As the first stage of its study, the commission has chosen to concentrate its efforts on verifying how the themes of inspiration and truth appear in the various texts of the Bible." (April 10, 2010) (http://visnews-en.blogspot.com/2010/04/plenary-assembly-of-pontifical-biblical.html).

4 On several occasions, the Pontifical Biblical Commission has spent four or more years studying individual subjects. See the description at: http://www.vatican.va/roman_curia/congregations/cfaith/pcb_documents/rc_con_cfaith_pro_14071997_pcbible_en.html .

5 In recent years, the commission has indeed published some well-known documents as a result of

teaching on the inspiration and truth of the Bible, since any new document would necessarily rest on the foundation of existing precedents.

The chief documents that set forth the Church's teaching in this area are those of various ecumenical councils: the Second Vatican Council's Dogmatic Constitution on Divine Revelation, *Dei Verbum*, as well as documents from the Councils of Florence, Trent, and Vatican I. Also of importance are the three papal encyclicals on biblical matters—*Providentissimus Deus* of Pope Leo XIII (1893), *Spiritus Paraclitus* of Pope Benedict XV (1920), and *Divino Afflante Spiritu* of Pope Pius XII (1943). In addition, there are several other papal and Vatican curial publications, including the "Instruction on the Historical Truth of the Gospels" (1964) of the Pontifical Biblical Commission, as well as its "Responses" from the early part of the last century.[6]

The first goal of this essay, then, is to provide a review of the magisterial teaching set forth in these documents. Specifically, the following headings having a certain logical order will be considered: inspiration as divine authorship; the inspired human authors; truth or inerrancy as a consequence of inspiration; inerrancy and the salvific purposes of Scripture; biblical truth and biblical interpretation; and the analogy between incarnation and inspiration.[7] The second goal of this essay is to consider the future prospects by suggesting some ideas that may likely be taken into account or treated in more detail in any new document to be issued on the Bible's inspiration and truth. Such ideas can be adduced by considering the events of the 2008 Synod, recent theological work, and perhaps most especially the teaching of Pope Benedict XVI, including his earlier work as a theologian and as prefect of the Congregation for the Doctrine of the Faith.[8] For example, at the

---

its studies, but this is not always the case. See Pontifical Biblical Commission, *The Interpretation of the Bible in the Church* (Vatican City: Libreria Editrice Vaticana, 1993), and Pontifical Biblical Commission, *The Jewish People and Their Sacred Scriptures in the Christian Bible* (Vatican City: Libreria Editrice Vaticana, 2002). The norms governing the biblical commission, ever since its reorganization by Pope Paul VI in 1971 such that it was no longer an organ of the magisterium but became a consultative body, indicate that its conclusions are "submitted to the Supreme Pontiff before being turned over for the use of the Sacred Congregation of the Doctrine of the Faith." The current commission study of the Bible's inspiration and truth might result, therefore, in a document from the doctrinal congregation or even a papal document sometime in the future. See Pope Paul VI, *Sedula Cura* [The Solicitous Care], Apostolic Letter Issued *Motu Proprio* on New Laws Regulating the Pontifical Biblical Commission (June 27, 1971), 10, in *The Scripture Documents: An Anthology of Official Catholic Teachings*, ed. Dean P. Béchard (Collegeville, MN: Liturgical Press, 2002), 149. Hereafter abbreviated *SD*. Latin text in *Enchiridion Biblicum: Documenti della Chiesa sulla Sacra Scrittura: Edizione bilingue* [Documents of the Church on Sacred Scripture: Bilingual Edition] 2nd ed., eds. Alfio Filippi and Erminio Lora (Bologna: Dehoniane, 1993), 734. Hereafter abbreviated *EB* and cited by paragraph number.

6   See Béchard's discussion of these early "Responses" in *SD*, 318–329.

7   These headings basically correspond to the topics and order of treatment in the document of the Second Vatican Council, *Dei Verbum* [The Word of God], Dogmatic Constitution on Divine Revelation, (November 18, 1965), 11–13 (*SD*, 24–25; *EB* 686–691).

8   Regarding Pope Benedict's personal interest in the topic, see his Address to the Plenary

level of general principle, one thinks of the pope's emphasis on interpreting the Second Vatican Council, not with a "hermeneutic of discontinuity and rupture" but "in the continuity of the one subject-church that the Lord has given to us."[9] One can imagine that this principle will help to guide the work of those involved in preparing any new document on biblical inspiration and truth.

Inspiration as Divine Authorship

It is helpful to begin by situating the teaching on inspiration within the overall context of the Catholic understanding of revelation, that is, of the revealed Word of God. Ultimately, this revelation is the Word of God incarnate, Jesus Christ.[10] As the young theologian Joseph Ratzinger explained in an essay written during the Second Vatican Council, "We have to reach beyond the positive sources of Scripture and Tradition to their inner source: the revelation, the living Word of God, from which Scripture and Tradition both spring."[11] Scripture is a privileged witness to this revelation which is Christ.[12] Indeed, as Vatican II's *Dei Verbum* indicates, Scripture is inspired and hence "expresses in a special way" the revelation of Christ preached by the apostles.[13] Even if the words of Scripture cannot fully express the infinite Word of God who is Christ, nonetheless the "sacred Scriptures contain the Word of God [Lat.: *verbum Dei continent*], and, because they are inspired [*quia inspiratae*], they truly are the Word of God [*vere verbum Dei sunt*]."[14]

Assembly of the Pontifical Biblical Commission (April 23, 2009), in *L'Osservatore Romano*, Weekly Edition in English (April 29, 2009), 3, 5, at 3: "You have gathered…to study a very important topic: *Inspiration and Truth of the Bible.* This subject not only concerns theology, but the Church herself. …The topic you have addressed furthermore responds to a concern that I have very much at heart, because the interpretation of Sacred Scripture is of capital importance for the Christian faith and for the life of the Church." Also, back in 1999 when Ratzinger was prefect of the Congregation for the Doctrine of the Faith, the congregation sponsored a symposium in order "to be informed more comprehensively about the current situation" regarding "open questions and urgent problems" that remain "regarding *the inspiration and truth of the Bible*, the canon, the relationship between the Old and New Testaments, and the general criteria of Christian biblical interpretation" [emphasis added]. Joseph Ratzinger and Tarcisio Bertone, "Presentation," in *L'Interpretazione della Bibbia nella Chiesa: Atti del Simposio* [The Interpretation of the Bible in the Church: Acts of the Symposium], Atti e Documenti 11 (Vatican City: Libreria Editrice Vaticana, 2001), 7–8, at 7.

9   Pope Benedict XVI, Address to the Roman Curia (December 22, 2005), in *L'Osservatore Romano*, Weekly Edition in English (January 4, 2006), 4–6, at 5.

10   John 1:1, 14.

11   Joseph Ratzinger, *God's Word: Scripture, Tradition, Office*, eds. Peter Hünermann and Thomas Söding, trans. Henry Taylor (San Francisco: Ignatius, 2008), 41–89, at 50. The quotation is from an essay titled "The Question of the Concept of Tradition: A Provisional Response," originally published in 1965 in a volume co-authored with Karl Rahner.

12   Christ "is revelation in the proper sense." Ratzinger, *God's Word*, 56; also, "Scripture bears witness" to "the abiding reality of Christ"; at 57.

13   *Dei Verbum*, 8 (*SD*, 22; *EB* 679).

14   *Dei Verbum*, 24 (*SD*, 29; *EB* 704). In *Dei Verbum*, 9, we similarly read that "Sacred Scripture is the utterance of God [Latin: *locutio Dei*] inasmuch as it is consigned to writing under the

Of course, as the Council recognized, this Word of God is "spoken through human agents and in human fashion."[15] We will discuss the human authors of Scripture in the following section, but for now let us consider how the fact of inspiration is associated with the divine authorship of Scripture.[16] The New Testament itself asserts that "all Scripture is inspired" [Gk.: *theopneustos*], that is, literally, "God-breathed."[17] In the sacred writings, "human beings, moved by the Holy Spirit, spoke from God."[18] Based on these and other biblical texts,[19] as well as the statements of patristic and medieval writers,[20] the Church's magisterium has often over the centuries referred to the fact of biblical inspiration in terms of divine authorship. The Council of Florence (1442) affirms that "one and the same God is the author of the Old and the New Testament—that is, the Law and the prophets and the Gospel—since the saints of both testaments spoke under the inspiration of the same Spirit."[21]

A century later, the Council of Trent (1546), takes up the same formulation regarding the divine authorship of the biblical books; however, in response to the challenges of the Reformation, the Council emphasizes also the unwritten traditions. The first decree of the Council's fourth session states that the Council "accepts and venerates with an equal measure of piety and reverence all the books

---

inspiration of the divine Spirit [*divino afflante Spiritu*]." (*SD*, 23; *EB* 682). Regarding this passage, which also says that sacred Tradition "hands on fully and completely" the Word of God, Ratzinger comments that "only Scripture is defined in terms of what it *is*: it is stated that Scripture *is* the Word of God consigned to writing. Tradition, however is described only functionally, in terms of what it *does*: it hands on the Word of God, but *is* not the Word of God." Joseph Ratzinger, "Dogmatic Constitution on Divine Revelation, Chapter II: The Transmission of Divine Revelation," in *Commentary on the Documents of Vatican II*, ed. Herbert Vorgrimler, trans. William Glen-Doepel, 5 vols. (New York: Herder, 1969), 3:181–198, at 194.

15   *Dei Verbum*, 12 (*SD*, 24; *EB* 688).

16   "*God is the author of sacred Scripture.*" *Catechism of the Catholic Church*, 2nd ed. (Vatican City: Libreria Editrice Vaticana, 1997), no. 105; emphasis in the original.

17   2 Tim. 3:16.

18   2 Pet. 1:20.

19   For a discussion of 2 Tim. 3:14–17; 2 Pet. 1:16–21; and other biblical texts related to biblical inspiration (such as Isa. 34:16; Neh. 9:3, 20; Mark 12:36; Acts 1:16; 4:25; and Heb. 3:7) and inerrancy (such as John 10:35; Luke 24:44; and Acts 1:16), see Valerio Mannucci, *Bibbia come Parola di Dio: Introduzione Generale alla Sacra Scrittura* [The Bible as Word of God: General Introduction to Sacred Scripture], 17th ed. (Brescia: Queriniana, 2002), 132–134, 246.

20   Still recognized for its thorough treatment of inspiration in the writings of patristic and medieval writers, as well as in the ancient councils, is the classic work, Christiano Pesch, *De Inspiratione Sacrae Scripturae* (Freiburg: Herder, 1906 [1925 reprint]), 38–201.

21   Council of Florence, *Cantate Domino* [Sing Praises to the Lord], Bull of Union with the Copts (February 4, 1442), in *Decrees of the Ecumenical Councils*, 2 vols., ed. Norman P. Tanner (Washington: Georgetown University, 1990), 1:572; (*EB* 47). Even earlier, at the Second Council of Lyons (1274), in the Profession of Faith of Michael Palaeologus, there is a formula stating that God is the one author of the New and Old Testaments (*EB* 40). The Greek text here uses the word *archēgos* for "author" (Latin: *auctor*), indicating more clearly that the expression "God is the author of the Scriptures" also means broadly that God is their originator or founder.

of the Old and New Testaments, since the one God is the author of both, together with the traditions concerning both faith and morals."[22]

Against a climate of rationalism, the First Vatican Council (1870) confirmed this teaching of the earlier councils and further developed it by rejecting two false or incomplete theories of inspiration. The Council held that the biblical books are "sacred and canonical, not because, having been composed by simple human industry, they were later approved by her own authority, nor merely because they contain revelation without error, but because, having been written by the inspiration of the Holy Spirit [Lat.: *Spiritu sancto inspirante conscripti*], they have God for their author and were delivered as such to the Church."[23]

The Council thus explains that inspiration is to be understood in terms of divine authorship. Inspiration, which renders the biblical books sacred and canonical, does not mean that the Church subsequently approved books that were written only by human industry.[24] Moreover, it is insufficient, although not incorrect, to say that inspiration is a negative assistance against error (as if it were merely a form of infallibility), since inspiration understood as divine authorship also involves a positive influence on the human author.

Vatican I's teaching on inspiration is doctrinally defined in one of the canons at the end of the document, with an anathema pronounced on "anyone [who] does not receive as sacred and canonical the complete books of the sacred Scripture with all their parts, as the holy synod of Trent enumerated them, or denies that they were divinely inspired."[25] Also notable is the canon's insistence that inspiration is plenary ("complete books...with all their parts").

Finally, the Second Vatican Council, in *Dei Verbum* (1965), incorporates the teaching of the earlier councils in its own discussion of inspiration as divine authorship:

> The divinely revealed truths that are contained and presented in the text of sacred Scripture have been written down under the inspiration of the Holy Spirit. Relying on the faith of the apostolic age, Holy Mother Church holds as sacred and canonical the complete books of the Old and New Testaments, with all their parts, on the grounds that, written under the inspiration

---

22 Council of Trent, *Decretum Primum: Recipiuntur Libri Sacri et Traditiones Apostolorum* [First Decree: Acceptance of the Sacred Books and Apostolic Traditions], (April 8, 1546) (*SD*, 3–4, at 3; *EB* 57).

23 First Vatican Council, *Dei Filius* [The Son of God], Dogmatic Constitution on the Catholic Faith, (April 24, 1870), Chap. 2 (*SD*, 14–17, at 16; *EB* 77).

24 For some background on the Catholic authors who held the theories rejected by Vatican I, see Raymond F. Collins, "Inspiration," in *The New Jerome Biblical Commentary*, eds. Raymond E. Brown, Joseph A. Fitzmyer, and Roland E. Murphy (Englewood Cliffs, NJ: Prentice Hall, 1990), 1023–1033, at 1029.

25 *Dei Filius*, Canon 4 (*SD*, 17; *EB* 79).

of the Holy Spirit (compare John 20:31; 2 Tim. 3:16; 2 Pet.
1:19–21; 3:15–16), they have God as their author, and they have
been handed on as such to the Church herself.[26]

Besides listing several supporting biblical citations, *Dei Verbum* 11 concludes by
explicitly quoting 2 Timothy 3:16–17. Summarizing, we could say that "what the
New Testament expressed by referring to God-breathed Scripture is achieved by
saying: 'God is the author of Scripture.'"[27]

Turning to papal and curial teaching on inspiration and divine authorship,
we highlight three select documents. First, Leo XIII, in *Providentissimus Deus*, repeated the teaching of Vatican I that inspiration is plenary as he rejected attempts
to restrict it in any way: "It is absolutely wrong and forbidden either to narrow
inspiration to certain parts only of holy Scripture or to admit that the sacred writer
has erred"; in particular, "the system of those who…do not hesitate to concede that
divine inspiration regards the things of faith and morals and nothing beyond…
cannot be tolerated."[28] Second, the Congregation for the Doctrine of the Faith, in
its declaration *Dominus Iesus* (2000), pointed out the uniqueness of the Old and
New Testaments as inspired texts:

> The Church's tradition…reserves the designation of *inspired
> texts* to the canonical books of the Old and New Testaments,
> since these are inspired by the Holy Spirit.[29]

Third, in a 2009 address to the Pontifical Biblical Commission, Pope Benedict
re-emphasized the divine authorship of the Scriptures. Referring to Vatican II,
he noted that "the Council recalls first of all that God is the author of sacred

---

26   *Dei Verbum*, 11 (*SD*, 24; *EB* 686). This sentence has a footnote referring, among other things, to
the teaching of the First Vatican Council quoted above (*EB* 77).

27   Richard F. Smith, "Inspiration and Inerrancy," in *The Jerome Biblical Commentary*, eds. Raymond
E. Brown, Joseph A. Fitzmyer, and Roland E. Murphy (Englewood Cliffs, NJ: Prentice Hall,
1968), 499–514, at 503.

28   Pope Leo XIII, *Providentissimus Deus* [The God of All Providence], Encyclical Letter on
the Study of Scripture (November 18, 1893), 40 (*SD*, 55; *EB* 124). Leo was writing against
the opinions of Catholic authors who had suggested, especially after the definition of papal
infallibility at Vatican I, that inspiration and inerrancy should similarly be restricted to faith
and morals. See the discussion in Collins, "Inspiration," 1030; and Antonio M. Artola and José
M. Sánchez Caro, *Biblia y Palabra de Dios* [Bible and Word of God], Introducción al Estudio
de la Biblia 2 (Estella: Verbo Divino, 1990), 224–225. Later documents, such as the 1907
Decree of the Holy Office *Lamentabili* (*EB* 200, 202), the encyclical of Benedict XV *Spiritus
Paraclitus* (*EB* 448, 455), and the encyclical of Pius XII *Divino Afflante Spiritu* (*EB* 538) all refer
back to the teaching of Vatican I and Pope Leo on the plenary character of inspiration and on
inspiration as divine authorship.

29   Congregation for the Doctrine of the Faith, *Dominus Iesus* [The Lord Jesus], Declaration on
the Unicity and Salvific Universality of Jesus Christ and the Church (Vatican City: Libreria
Editrice Vaticana, 2000), 8.

Scripture"; he went on to reiterate that the Holy Spirit is "the invisible and transcendent Author."[30]

It is helpful to note that this teaching on the inspiration of Scripture, including the understanding of inspiration as divine authorship, is a teaching of the highest level of authority, on account of the doctrinal definition of Vatican I. As the Congregation for the Doctrine of the Faith has explained, such teachings are doctrines "of divine and catholic faith which the Church proposes as divinely and formally revealed and, as such, as irreformable."[31] Thus, any future document will undoubtedly reiterate this teaching. At the same time, a future document will likely explain further what is meant by saying that God is the "author" of Scripture. For example, to speak of the divine author and the human authors of Scripture is to speak using *analogy*; in this analogy, however, God's authorship has priority (as the "primary analogate"). As St. Thomas Aquinas explained, this is because God as author can "signify his meaning, not by words only (as man also can do), but also by things themselves."[32] God's authorship thus also includes the very events of salvation history.

The Nature of Inspiration: Scripture's Human Authors

In *Dei Verbum*, after the statement on divine authorship quoted above, there is a statement about the inspired human authors:

> In composing the sacred books, God chose and employed certain men who, while engaged in this task, made full use of their faculties and powers so that, with God himself acting in them and through them, they as true authors [*veri auctores*] committed to writing everything and only those things that he wanted written.[33]

30　Pope Benedict XVI, Address (April 23, 2009), 3.

31　Congregation for the Doctrine of the Faith, "Commentary on the Concluding Formula of the *Professio Fidei*," (June 29, 1998), 5, in *L'Osservatore Romano*, Weekly Edition in English (July 15, 1998), 3–4, at 3. Text also in *Acta Apostolicae Sedis* 90 (1998): 549. Hereafter abbreviated *AAS*; available online: http://www.vatican.va/archive/aas/index_sp.htm. For a discussion of exactly what falls under the dogmatic definition of Vatican I, see Artola and Sánchez Caro, *Biblia*, 144–145.

32　St. Thomas Aquinas, *Summa Theologiae*, pt. 1a, q. 1, art. 10. Text in *Summa Theologica*, 3 vols. (New York: Benziger Brothers, 1947), 1:7. See also the *Catechism*, no. 117: "Thanks to the unity of God's plan, not only the text of Scripture but also the realities and events about which it speaks can be signs."

33　*Dei Verbum*, 11 (*SD*, 24; *EB* 686).

This statement clarifies that the human authors of Scripture are not merely secretaries but true authors who write using all of their abilities but who nevertheless write only those things God wanted written.[34]

The emphasis in *Dei Verbum* on the human authors as *veri auctores* caps a development seen in the documents leading up to Vatican II. Earlier papal statements, using the scholastic terminology of instrumental causality, speak of God as the principal cause of the Scriptures, with the sacred author as his instrument. For example, Leo writes, in a passage that also discusses inerrancy:

> Hence, because the Holy Spirit employed men as his instruments, we cannot therefore say that it was these inspired instruments, who, perchance, have fallen into error, and not the primary author. For, by supernatural power, God so moved and impelled them to write—he was so present to them—that the things which he ordered, and those only, they, first, rightly understood, then willed faithfully to write down, and finally expressed in apt words and with infallible truth. Otherwise, it could not be said that God was the author of the entire Scripture.[35]

Benedict XV, in describing St. Jerome's teaching on inspiration, also uses the language of instrumentality; nonetheless he also affirms that, according to Jerome, "the individual authors of these books worked in full freedom under the divine afflatus, each of them in accordance with his individual nature and character. ...Each of them uses his own gifts and powers," so that one can speak of a "partnership of God and man [*Dei cum homine communitatem*]."[36] Pius XII emphasizes that the sacred author, as an instrument of the Holy Spirit, is a "living and reasonable" instrument, in keeping with human nature. He indicates therefore that the interpreter should "endeavor to determine the peculiar character and circumstances of the sacred writer, the age in which he lived, the sources written or oral to which he had recourse, and the forms of expression he employed."[37]

---

34 Thus, a "verbal dictation" theory of inspiration is rejected. In this regard, the Catholic understanding of inspiration differs, for example, from a Muslim understanding; see Ralph Del Colle, "Inspiration and Inerrancy in Scripture," *Chicago Studies* 47 (2008): 25–38, at 35–36. Several older magisterial texts have in fact used the Latin verb *dictare* to refer to biblical inspiration (and to oral traditions as well), but the Latin verb has a broader range of meaning than the English "dictate"; see the discussion in Mannucci, *Bibbia*, 156.

35 Pope Leo XIII, *Providentissimus Deus*, 41 (*SD*, 55–56; *EB* 125).

36 Pope Benedict XV, *Spiritus Paraclitus* [The Holy Spirit, the Comforter], Encyclical Letter Commemorating the Fifteenth Centenary of the Death of St. Jerome (September 15, 1920), 3 (*SD*, 84; *EB* 448).

37 Pope Pius XII, *Divino Afflante Spiritu* [Inspired by the Divine Spirit], Encyclical Letter Promoting Biblical Studies (September 30, 1943), 19 (*SD*, 128; *EB* 556–557).

Thus the stage was set for the further step in *Dei Verbum*, with its mention of the human authors as "true authors." The language of instrumentality is avoided,[38] at least in part to leave open the possibilities for further theological reflection in the future.[39] The Council's terminology has been repeated various times in subsequent years.[40] For instance, Pope Benedict has referred to the divine and human authors of Scripture by speaking of a "divine-human synergy...God really speaks to men and women in a human way."[41]

Regarding the nature of inspiration and Scripture's divine and human authorship, one possible area for development in a future document regards the role of the Church.[42] Already prior to the Council, Karl Rahner theorized about inspiration in connection with the apostolic Church;[43] however, he did so in such a way that the Scriptures seemed to be unduly subordinated.[44] In his book, *Jesus of Nazareth*, Pope Benedict offers a more promising reflection, pointing out the mutual relationship between Scripture and Church:

> At this point we get a glimmer, even on the historical level, of what inspiration means: The author does not speak as a private, self-contained subject. He speaks in a living community. ...One

---

38 See the synoptic presentation of the various schemas of *Dei Verbum*, with the proposed emendations for this section, in Francisco Gil Hellín, ed., *Concilii Vaticani II Synopsis: Constitutio Dogmatica de Divina Revelatione Dei Verbum* [Vatican II Synopsis: The Dogmatic Constitution on Divine Revelation, *Dei Verbum*] (Vatican City: Libreria Editrice Vaticana, 1993), 88–89.

39 For interesting background, see Jared Wicks, "Six Texts by Prof. Joseph Ratzinger as *Peritus* Before and During Vatican Council II," *Gregorianum* 89 (2008): 233–311, at 277–280 (302–305 for the original German). The young Ratzinger, in a lecture given in Rome to German-speaking bishops on October 10, 1962, the eve of the opening of the Council, critiqued the preparatory schema on revelation on this point, recommending that the Council "refrain from describing in detail the process of inspiration" (at 278) and avoid "dogmatically defining" any theory, thus leaving "the way open for further thinking" (at 279). For the text of the preparatory schema on inspiration (which incorporated passages from the encyclicals of Popes Leo XIII and Pius XII), see Gil Hellín, *Synopsis*, 183.

40 For example, see Pope John Paul II, Address Commemorating the Twenty-Fifth Anniversary of *Dei Verbum* (December 14, 1990), 4 (*SD*, 164–165). See also the *Catechism*, no. 106.

41 Benedict XVI, Address (April 23, 2009).

42 For a discussion of various approaches to inspiration, see Walter Vogels, "Three Possible Models of Inspiration," in *Scrittura ispirata: Atti del Simposio Internazionale sull'Ispirazione* [Inspired Scripture: Acts of the International Symposium on Inspiration], ed. Antonio Izquierdo, Atti e Documenti 16 (Vatican City: Libreria Editrice Vaticana, 2002), 61–79.

43 Karl Rahner, *Inspiration in the Bible*, 2nd ed., trans. Charles H. Henkey and Martin Palmer, Quaestiones Disputatae 1 (New York: Herder, 1964), 53: "The inspiration of holy Scripture is nothing else than God's founding of the Church, inasmuch as this applies to precisely that constitutive element of the apostolic Church which is the Bible."

44 See the discussion in James T. Burtchaell, *Catholic Theories of Biblical Inspiration since 1810: A Review and Critique* (Cambridge: Cambridge University, 1969), 254–255.

could say that the books of Scripture involve three interacting subjects.[45]

Thus, in addition to the human authors and God, Benedict refers to the "collective subject, the 'People of God.'...The People of God—the Church—is the living subject of Scripture; it is in the Church that the words of the Bible are always in the present."[46] What we see here is a reflection on inspiration that takes into account the broader "dialogical" understanding of revelation that was advanced at the time of Vatican II. We will return to consider this ecclesial understanding of inspiration further below, in our discussion of biblical interpretation.

Can Error Coexist with Inspiration?

Closely connected to the Church's teaching on biblical inspiration is its teaching on the truth and inerrancy of Scripture. In general, this means that the intended affirmations of Scripture are without error. Scripture's truth and inerrancy are often explained deductively—as a consequence or effect of its inspiration. This deductive argument appears rather simple: if the Scriptures are inspired such that God is their author then it follows that they "teach the truth."[47] For example, consider how *Dei Verbum* presents the deduction; after stating that the human authors are "true authors" who "committed to writing everything and only those things that [God] wanted written," the text continues:

> Therefore, since [*Cum ergo*] everything asserted by the inspired authors or sacred writers should be regarded as asserted by the Holy Spirit, it follows that [*inde*] we must acknowledge the books of Scripture as teaching firmly, faithfully, and without error the truth that God wished to be recorded in the sacred writings for the sake of our salvation.[48]

If we compare this statement with *Providentissimus Deus*, we certainly note some significant differences (to which we will return shortly), but the basic deductive argument that reasons from inspiration to truth and inerrancy is the same.

> And so far is it from being possible that any error can coexist with inspiration, that inspiration not only is essentially incompatible with error, but excludes and rejects it as absolutely and necessarily as it is impossible that God himself, the Supreme

---

45 Pope Benedict XVI, *Jesus of Nazareth: From the Baptism in the Jordan to the Transfiguration*, trans. Adrian J. Walker (New York: Doubleday, 2007), xx.

46 Benedict XVI, *Jesus of Nazareth*, xxi.

47 *Catechism*, no. 107: "The inspired books teach the truth."

48 *Dei Verbum*, 11 (SD, 24; EB 687).

Truth, can utter that which is not true. This is the ancient and unchanging faith of the Church, solemnly defined in the Councils of Florence and of Trent, and finally confirmed and more expressly formulated by the Council of the Vatican.[49]

It is interesting to note that Pope Leo understands inerrancy to be first, a consequence of inspiration (inspiration "excludes and rejects" error), and second, a truth of faith ("the ancient and unchanging faith of the Church").[50] These two ideas were confirmed in the Congregation for the Doctrine of the Faith's 1998 commentary on the new formula for the *Professio Fidei*, the public profession of faith required of those who hold certain offices of Church governance or who teach subjects dealing with faith and morals in universities and seminaries.

The congregation's commentary first discusses the order of the truths specified by the three propositions found at the conclusion of the Profession of Faith—first, truths contained in the Word of God which the Church sets forth to be believed as divinely revealed; second, truths on faith and morals set forth by the Church as to be held definitively; and third, sure teachings which have not been defined or proposed as definitive, but which nonetheless require the religious submission of will and intellect. The congregation then lists examples of these truths, including one regarding the inerrancy of Scripture—"the absence of error in the inspired sacred texts [*absentia erroris in scriptis sacris inspiratis*]." The congregation asserts this to be among the truths of the first order—that is, a truth that is to be believed as divinely revealed.[51]

---

49 Leo XIII, *Providentissimus Deus*, 40–41 (*SD*, 55; *EB* 124–125). The first sentence of this quotation (*EB* 124) is one of the texts given in the footnote to the statement in *Dei Verbum* 11, just quoted. The deductive logic is also evident in a phrase that follows shortly thereafter: "Those who maintain that an error is possible in any genuine passage of the sacred writings either pervert the Catholic notion of inspiration or make God the author of such error" (*Providentissimus Deus*, 41; *SD*, 56; *EB* 126; which is also cited in the same footnote in *Dei Verbum* 11).

50 Later documents make the same two points. For example, Benedict XV notes first that "Jerome further shows that the immunity of Scripture from error or deception is necessarily bound up with its divine inspiration and supreme authority. He says...that it was taught him as the doctrine of the Fathers and generally received" (Benedict XV, *Spiritus Paraclitus*, 5 [*SD*, 86; *EB* 450]). Second, he says that "St. Jerome's teaching on this point serves to confirm and illustrate what our predecessor of happy memory, Leo XIII, declared to be the ancient and traditional belief of the Church touching the absolute immunity of Scripture from error" (*Spiritus Paraclitus*, 5 [*SD*, 87; *EB* 452]). Similarly, Pius XII quotes the just-cited passage of *Providentissimus Deus*, and then comments: "This teaching, which our predecessor Leo XIII set forth with such solemnity, we also proclaim with our authority" (Pius XII, *Divino Afflante Spiritu*, 4 [*SD*, 117; *EB* 540]).

51 Congregation for the Doctrine of the Faith, "Commentary," 11; *AAS* 90 (1998): 549. To better appreciate this statement, it is instructive to review the whole list of examples given in the commentary for truths of the first order: "the articles of faith of the Creed; the various christological dogmas and Marian dogmas; the doctrine of the institution of the sacraments by Christ and their efficacy with regard to grace; the doctrine of the real and substantial presence of

Thus the commentary affirms that the inerrancy of Scripture is a truth of faith. Moreover, the commentary's footnote refers precisely to the two texts we have just considered—from *Providentissimus Deus* and *Dei Verbum*—thus implicitly confirming that the inerrancy of Scripture is a consequence of inspiration. The juxtaposition of these two texts also suggests that they should be read in continuity with one another. Hence, even before considering to what exactly the teaching on biblical inerrancy and truth extends and how to apply it, we must understand it as a truth of faith that follows as a consequence of the dogma of inspiration.

The theological manuals written prior to Vatican II make similar points,[52] as do various biblical scholars writing during and after the Council,[53] thus confirming the consistent argument in magisterial documents that the truth or inerrancy of Scripture follows necessarily from its inspiration.

Inerrancy and the Salvific Purposes of Scripture

Given this seemingly settled tradition of understanding, it is somewhat surprising that the *Instrumentum Laboris* or working document of the 2008 Synod of Bishops expressed a different relationship between inspiration and inerrancy. Indeed, the working document appeared to understand inerrancy as somehow restricted. Instead of saying, "therefore, since" Scripture is inspired, "it follows that" it teaches the truth, the translated Latin text says that "although [*quamvis*] all parts of Sacred

---

Christ in the Eucharist and the sacrificial nature of the eucharistic celebration; the foundation of the Church by the will of Christ; the doctrine on the primacy and infallibility of the Roman Pontiff; the doctrine on the existence of original sin; the doctrine on the immortality of the spiritual soul and on the immediate recompense after death; the absence of error in the inspired sacred texts; the doctrine on the grave immorality of direct and voluntary killing of an innocent human being."

52 See, for example, Sebastianus Tromp, *De Sacrae Scripturae Inspiratione* [The Inspiration of Sacred Scripture], 6th ed. (Rome: Gregorian University, 1962), 113, 120–124.

53 For example, during the Council and in reference specifically to the Gospels, Joseph Fitzmyer wrote that the "evangelists were inspired by the Holy Spirit to compile and write down the accounts as they did. This inspiration guarantees their Gospel truth, which is free from error. …The consequence of inspiration is inerrancy, that is, immunity from formal error in what is affirmed." Joseph A. Fitzmyer, "The Biblical Commission's Instruction on the Historical Truth of the Gospels," *Theological Studies* 25 (1964): 386–408, at 401. Fitzmyer then explains, like Pius XII before him, that the truth of Scripture has to be understood in light of the literary genres found in the Bible: "There is poetical truth as well as historical truth, rhetorical truth as well as legal truth, mythical truth as well as the Gospel truth." See also Luis Alonso Schökel, *The Inspired Word: Scripture in the Light of Language and Literature*, trans. Francis Martin (New York: Herder, 1965), 324–325: "The principle of inerrancy is easy to understand: God cannot be deceived, nor can he deceive us. If God proposes something in the Scriptures, it is true and cannot be false. …The deduction is simple. God has spoken, and God cannot utter falsehood. It does no good to take refuge in the distinction between the divine and the human in the Scriptures; the truth is divine, the error human—such a distinction has no basis in the nature of the inspired text." While Alonso Schökel wrote this book before the promulgation of *Dei Verbum*, its later 1986 edition (in Spanish) nonetheless leaves this part essentially unchanged: see *La Palabra Inspirada: La Biblia a la Luz de la Ciencia del Language*, 3rd ed., Academia Christiana 27 (Madrid: Ediciones Cristiandad, 1986), 313–314.

Scripture are inspired, yet [*tamen*] its inerrancy refers only [*tantummodo*] to 'the truth, which God, for the sake of our salvation, wished to be recorded in the sacred writings.'"[54]

It was on account of this statement that a discussion over inerrancy arose at the Synod,[55] and as a result, that the final proposition quoted at the beginning of this essay was formulated. It is interesting to note, however, that in his address to the Pontifical Biblical Commission, delivered six months after the Synod, Pope Benedict follows *Dei Verbum* very closely, rather than the formulation in the *Instrumentum Laboris*:

> Therefore, since all that the inspired authors or hagiographers state is to be considered as said by the Holy Spirit, the invisible and transcendent Author, it must consequently be acknowledged that "the books of Scripture, firmly, faithfully and without error, teach that truth which God, for the sake of our salvation, wished to see confided to the sacred Scriptures."[56]

From another perspective, the statement advancing a "restricted inerrancy" view is not surprising given the theological discussion that has taken place since Vatican II regarding how to interpret paragraph 11 of *Dei Verbum*, and especially the meaning of the phrase "for the sake of our salvation."

For example, some have asserted the need for the Church to move beyond the supposedly "aprioristic and unhistorical thinking that has dominated teaching on inerrancy since the age of the Fathers."[57] Indeed, some have gone so far as to

---

54 Synod of Bishops, "The Word of God in the Life and Mission of the Church," *Instrumentum Laboris* (May 11, 2008), 15(c) (Lat.: "Quamvis omnes Sacrae Scripturae partes divinitus inspiratae sint, tamen eius inerrantia pertinet tantummodo ad 'veritatem, quam Deus nostrae salutis causa Litteris Sacris consignari voluit'" [*Dei Verbum*, 11]), in *L'Osservatore Romano*, Weekly Edition in English (June 25, 2008), I–XV, at V, although the translation there is faulty. (The translation above is my own.) Compare Brian W. Harrison, "Does Vatican Council II Allow for Errors in Sacred Scripture?" *Divinitas* 52 (2009): 279–304.

55 "There's an interesting discussion about the inerrancy of the Bible. There's long been debate in Catholicism between 'restricted inerrancy,' which holds that only some portions of the Bible are free from error (usually understood as that which concerns salvation), and 'unrestricted inerrancy,' meaning that everything in the Bible is true, although in the sense of truth which the Bible itself intends." John Allen, "Synod on the Bible: Shaping the Imaginations of 1.2 Billion Catholics" [Online Edition] (October 10, 2008) (http://ncronline.org/blogs/all-things-catholic/synod-bible-shaping-imaginations-12-billion-catholics). Compare Allen, "The Synod on the Bible Looks for Middle Ground," [Online Edition] (October 17, 2008): "Cardinal Francis George of Chicago, widely seen as one of the leading thinkers at the senior levels of the Church, said in an interview this week that the second option [the 'unrestricted inerrancy' option] better represents 'where we're at today,' but acknowledged that the issue hasn't been resolved." (http://ncronline.org/blogs/all-things-catholic/synod-bible-looks-middle-ground-poignant-press-conference).

56 Benedict XVI, Address (April 23, 2009).

57 Alois Grillmeier, "Dogmatic Constitution on Divine Revelation, Chapter III: The Divine

suggest that "at Vatican II the Catholic Church 'turned the corner' in the inerrancy question by moving from the *a priori* toward the *a posteriori* in the statement of *Dei Verbum* 11."[58] In other words, rather than argue in an *a priori* and deductive way from Scripture's inspiration to its truth and inerrancy, one should take stock of the difficulties in the Bible and then come up with a properly limited understanding of the Bible's inerrancy and truth.

In this regard, the interventions of various Council fathers, most famously Cardinal Franz König of Vienna, are recalled, in which examples of "errors" in Scripture were set forth.[59] As a result, Raymond Brown and others have argued that Vatican II taught a limited view of inerrancy—not a quantitative limit, "but a qualitative one whereby all Scripture is inerrant to the extent that it serves the purpose for which God intended it. Recognition of this type of limitation is implicit in the statement made at Vatican II."[60] Brown concedes, however, that this view still faces "the problem of finding a criterion: How exactly does one know what God wanted put into the Scriptures for the sake of our salvation?"[61] It should be noticed that, given such a criterion, one is back to the *a priori* and deductive argument, the only difference being that the lines have been re-drawn. In other words, if one holds to any form of inerrancy, at some point the *a priori* and deductive argument will be invoked.

As for the proper interpretation of the phrase "for the sake of our salvation," it is helpful to recall that the penultimate schema or draft of *Dei Verbum* 11 instead spoke of "saving truth" (*veritatem salutarem*), in order to make reference also to the events of salvation history. Many Council fathers expressed concerns about this terminology, as it appeared to restrict inerrancy to matters of faith and morals, an

---

Inspiration and the Interpretation of Sacred Scripture," in Vorgrimler, *Commentary*, 3:199–246, at 206.

58　Raymond E. Brown, *The Critical Meaning of the Bible* (New York: Paulist, 1981), 18. Brown goes on to say that, "The statement is not without an ambiguity that stems from the compromise nature of *Dei Verbum*. …The result is often a juxtaposition of conservative older formulations with more open recent formulations." On this point, Pope Benedict's comments regarding the proper hermeneutic of continuity for interpreting the Council can be helpful for moving the discussion forward: "The hermeneutic of discontinuity risks ending in a split between the pre-conciliar Church and the post-conciliar Church. It asserts that the texts of the Council as such do not yet express the true spirit of the Council. It claims that they are the result of compromises in which, to reach unanimity, it was found necessary to keep and reconfirm many old things that are now pointless. However, the true spirit of the Council is not to be found in these compromises but instead in the impulses toward the new that are contained in the texts." Benedict XVI, Address (December 22, 2005).

59　On König's intervention, see the discussion in Grillmeier, "Chapter III," 3:205–210.

60　Raymond E. Brown, *An Introduction to the New Testament*, Anchor Bible Reference Library (New York: Doubleday, 1997), 31. For a recent critique of this position, see Denis Farkasfalvy, *Inspiration and Interpretation: A Theological Introduction to Sacred Scripture* (Washington: Catholic University of America, 2010), 187, 230, 232–233, 238.

61　Brown, *Introduction*, 31.

idea that, as we have seen, was condemned by Leo XIII. The doctrinal commission overseeing the drafting process was of the opinion that this terminology did not introduce any "material limitation" to the truth of Scripture, but rather indicated its "formal specification."[62] The matter was brought to the attention of Pope Paul VI, who, sharing the concern of the Council fathers, asked the doctrinal commission to consider omitting the expression, in part because it could be open to wrong interpretation.[63] After Cardinal Augustin Bea, a trusted adviser of the Pope, explained the matter to the commission, it voted to drop the adjective "saving" and replace it with the clause "for the sake of our salvation." This clause went on to become part of the definitive text.[64]

The end result, it appears, can be summed up in the following words from a contemporary textbook: "A limitation on biblical truth is something which Catholic tradition has wished to avoid by every means."[65] Of course, along with

---

62 See Giovanni Caprile, "Tre Emendamenti allo Schema sulla Rivelazione: Appunti per la Storia del Testo" [Three Amendments to the Schema on Revelation: Notes for the History of the Text], *La Civiltá Cattolica* 117 (1966): 214–231, at 224; see also Gil Hellín, *Synopsis*, 90–91. An English translation of the commission's Latin explanation is found in Harrison, "Vatican Council II," 288: "This expression does *not* imply any *material limitation* to the truth of Scripture, rather, it indicates Scripture's *formal specification*, the nature of which must be kept in mind in deciding in what sense everything *affirmed* in the Bible is true—not only matters of faith and morals and facts bound up with the history of salvation" (emphasis in Latin original).

63 Caprile, "Tre Emendamenti," 226. See also Farkasfalvy, *Inspiration*, 186, 229.

64 Cardinal Bea explains the meaning of the phrase in his commentary on *Dei Verbum*. "Now we must consider whether the 'truth' (that is, the truth "which God wanted put into the sacred writings for the sake of our salvation") implies some limit set to the inerrancy of Scripture, meaning that it taught 'without error' not everything that it asserts but only all that concerns our salvation (or those things also which closely and directly affect our salvation). ...Our question, therefore, about the possible existence of a limit set to inerrancy refers, not to the events in which God truly reveals himself, but to those events which form their historical setting, and which Scripture frequently describes in great detail. Does the inerrancy asserted in this document cover also the account of these historical events? In other words, is the historical background also described 'without error'?...For my own part I think that this question must be answered affirmatively, that is, that these 'background' events also are described without error. In fact, we declare in general that there is no limit set to this inerrancy, and that it applies to all that the inspired writer, and therefore all that the Holy Spirit by his means, affirms. ...If therefore the Council had wished to introduce here a new conception, different from that presented in these recent documents of the supreme teaching authority, which reflects the beliefs of the early fathers, it would have had to state this clearly and explicitly. Let us now ask whether there may be any indications to suggest such a restricted interpretation of inerrancy. The answer is decidedly negative. There is not the slightest sign of any such indication. On the contrary everything points against a restrictive interpretation. ...In fact, the phrasing we now have does not admit of any such interpretation, because the idea of salvation is no longer directly linked with the noun 'truth', but with the verbal expression 'wanted put into the sacred writings'; in other words, the phrase in which the text speaks of salvation explains God's purpose in causing the Scriptures to be written, and not the nature of the truth enshrined therein." Augustin Cardinal Bea, *The Word of God and Mankind*, trans. Dorothy White (Chicago: Franciscan Herald Press, 1967), 189–191. Brown, *Critical Meaning*, 19, n.22, finds Bea's explanation to be a "much more conservative interpretation" than his own.

65 Artola and Sánchez Caro, *Biblia*, 231 (my translation).

statements avoiding a limitation on biblical truth, there have been various magisterial statements which provide principles for how it should be interpreted. Before turning to these statements in the next section, one final point can be considered here, namely, the emphasis in *Dei Verbum* 11, on the "truth" of Scripture rather than on its "inerrancy."

The emphasis on the inerrancy of Scripture in the pre-conciliar period was the result, in part, of the necessity of defending the Bible against rationalist and modernist criticism.[66] It was also due to the "noetic" emphasis of the neo-scholastic theology that characterized the manuals of that period. Revelation was understood as the communication of a set of truths; these truths could be formulated as propositions which then demanded the assent of faith.[67] Within this framework, it is not surprising that there was an emphasis on the inerrant character of the propositions revealed in Scripture. As we have seen, at Vatican II there was a development in the understanding of revelation: God reveals not merely propositions demanding assent, but reveals himself. Christ is the revelation of the Father; thus, revelation is not only propositional but also personal, not only informational but relational. Given this bigger picture regarding the understanding of revelation, there similarly is a bigger picture in which to situate the understanding of inerrancy.[68] Indeed, the Council sought to indicate this larger context by speaking, beginning in the

---

66 See Alonso Schökel, *Inspired Word*, 311: "Toward the end of the last century [19th century], the arms of the enemy were directed against the supposed errors of the Bible in an effort to force a breach and enter the sanctuary of inspiration in order to destroy it. The Bible had to be defended; and this is the time when our manuals on inspiration were conceived and constructed. It is not strange, then, that they were surrounded by such great walls of arguments and replies in those sections which dealt with inerrancy. It would be disrespectful and unfitting to dismantle these walls, which still have a function, but we must stop to consider whether or not the wall is the essence of the city, or whether peaceful habitation of the city is not something more important."

67 Aidan Nichols, in his study of the foremost neo-scholastic theologian of the first half of the twentieth-century, Reginald Garrigou-Lagrange, presents Garrigou-Lagrange's definition of revelation as the "[f]ree and essentially supernatural divine agency, by which God…manifested religious truths…in such a way that subsequently they can be infallibly proposed by the Church." Aidan Nichols, *Reason with Piety: Garrigou-Lagrange in the Service of Catholic Thought* (Naples, FL: Sapientia, 2008), 34–35, quoting Garrigou-Lagrange, *De Revelatione per Ecclesiam Catholicam Proposita* [Revelation Declared through the Catholic Church]. Contrast this view with what Tracey Rowland writes about Joseph Ratzinger's understanding of revelation: "For Ratzinger, revelation is not a collection of statements—revelation is Christ himself." Tracey Rowland, *Ratzinger's Faith: The Theology of Pope Benedict XVI* (Oxford: Oxford University, 2008), 49.

68 Rowland, *Ratzinger's Faith*, 51, further explains Ratzinger's understanding of revelation: "The purpose of this dialogue between God and the human person is not so much the transmission of information but rather the transformation of the person in the life of the Trinity. For Ratzinger this is not a matter of removing the intellectual component of faith but understanding it as a component in a wider whole."

third of the five schemas (including the preparatory schema),[69] of the "truth" of Scripture, rather than its inerrancy.[70]

Biblical Truth and the Interpretation of the Bible

Stating the principle of the Bible's inerrancy and truth is relatively easy, but applying it is more difficult, as we have already suggested.[71] Thus, ever since the time of Pope Leo XIII, there have been magisterial statements that explain how biblical truth and inerrancy are to be understood. These statements are the necessary complement to the statements considered above that resist the restriction of biblical truth. They not only are of assistance in explaining various difficulties encountered in the Bible, but they also refer to various principles of biblical interpretation, which, from the perspective of a Catholic hermeneutic, are important to grasp so as not to fall into a fundamentalist understanding of inerrancy.[72]

First, Leo explained how the Bible should be understood with regard to the truths of natural science. Quoting St. Augustine, Leo writes:

> "The Holy Spirit…did not intend to teach men these things (that is to say, the essential nature of the things of the visible universe), things in no way profitable to salvation." Hence they did not seek to penetrate the secrets of nature, but rather described and dealt with things in more or less figurative language, or in terms which were commonly used at the time and that in many instances are in daily use at this day.[73]

---

69 For a synopsis and explanation of the five schemas of this part of the document, see, for example, Mannucci, *Bibbia*, 252–258. On the positive formulation using the word "truth," Mannucci writes that "the Bible is the book of God, not because it is without error, but because it teaches without error the Truth of God" (at 255; my translation). For a Latin synopsis for this part, see Gil Hellín, *Synopsis*, 90–93.

70 Alonso Schökel, *Inspired Word*, 324: "No part of the Bible contains error. …This is the significance of the negative formula, 'inerrancy.' And though it is universally applicable to the Bible, it presupposes a very restricted view of biblical truth. It has the advantage of all such specific formulas of being precise, but the danger begins when it is allowed to dominate the whole consideration of truth in the Bible, thus reducing the Scriptures to a catalogue of formal propositions. …In order to avoid this, we must put the question of inerrancy in the larger context of the truth of the Bible. Then the negative universality and precision of the term 'inerrancy' will work to best advantage."

71 Alonso Schökel, *Inspired Word*, 325: "The general principle which follows quite simply from the veracity of God, can get quite complicated when we start to apply it."

72 See the critique of fundamentalist interpretation in Pontifical Biblical Commission, *On the Interpretation of the Bible in the Church*, Sec. I, Par. F. (*SD*, 244–317, at 273–275; *EB* 1381–1390).

73 Leo XIII, *Providentissimus Deus*, 39 (*SD*, 54; *EB* 121), citing Augustine, *On the Literal Interpretation of Genesis* (Bk. 2, Chap. 9). This quotation of Augustine, which makes reference to salvation, is cited in *Dei Verbum* 11, in the footnote accompanying the phrase "for the sake of our salvation."

Hence, one should not consider as errors expressions used to describe things as they appear to the senses (for example, the sun rising).[74] Pope Leo also explained that the principle set forth with regard to natural sciences would also "apply to cognate sciences and especially to history."[75]

This last statement led some scholars, including Marie-Joseph Lagrange, to raise questions regarding the kinds of history recorded in the Bible. In 1905, a decree of the Pontifical Biblical Commission responded to this historical question, addressing whether it may be admitted "that those books of sacred Scripture regarded as historical...sometimes narrate what is not history properly so-called and objectively true, but only have the appearance of history." The commission gave a nuanced reply: "Negative, except in the case...when it can be proved...that the sacred writer intended not to give a true and strict history but to set forth, under the guise and form of history, a parable or an allegory or some meaning distinct from the strictly literal or historical sense of the words."[76]

This response, with its focus on the intention of the sacred author and the kind of literature involved, anticipates what Pius XII says in *Divino Afflante Spiritu* regarding the importance of discovering the literal sense and of determining the literary genre. On the literal sense, he writes "that the supreme rule of interpretation is to discover and define what the writer intended to express"[77]; regarding literary genres, "the Catholic commentator...should also make a prudent use of this means, determining, that is, to what extent the manner of expression or the literary mode adopted by the sacred writer may lead to a correct and genuine interpretation."[78] Thus, for Pius, critical study of the Bible and the defense and explanation of the Bible's inerrancy go together:

> Not infrequently...when some persons reproachfully charge the sacred writers with some historical error or inaccuracy in the recording of facts, on close examination it turns out to be nothing else than those customary modes of expression and narration peculiar to the ancients.[79]

---

74 Apparently, Brown does not see much of a distinction between interpreting inerrancy and limiting inerrancy. Hence, he asserts that "Pope Leo XIII...excluded natural or scientific matters from biblical inerrancy, even if he did this through the expedient of insisting that statements made about nature according to ordinary appearances were not errors." Brown, *Critical Meaning*, 15.

75 Leo XIII, *Providentissimus Deus*, 40 (SD, 54; EB 123).

76 Pontifical Biblical Commission, *Response Concerning the Narratives in the Historical Books of Sacred Scripture Which Have Only the Appearance of Being Historical* (June 23, 1905) (SD, 188; EB 161). See also Benedict XV, *Spiritus Paraclitus*, 6 (SD, 89–90; EB 456–460), who responds to this question rather strongly, reflecting the controversies of the anti-Modernist period.

77 Pius XII, *Divino Afflante Spiritu*, 19 (SD, 128; EB 557).

78 Pius XII, *Divino Afflante Spiritu*, 21 (SD, 129; EB 560).

79 Pius XII, *Divino Afflante Spiritu*, 21 (SD, 130; EB 560).

The Pontifical Biblical Commission further addressed the question of history with regard to biblical truth and inerrancy in its "Instruction on the Historical Truth of the Gospels" (1964). This was another landmark document advocating appropriate use of historical-critical methods by Catholic biblical scholars. With regard to the gospels, the instruction states that "the truth of the narrative is not affected in the slightest by the fact that the evangelists report the sayings or the doings of our Lord in a different order, and that they use different words to express what he said, not keeping to the very letter, but nevertheless preserving the sense."[80] The instruction also reaffirms the Church's teaching on inspiration and inerrancy by advising the exegete to "bear in mind...that the gospels were written under the inspiration of the Holy Spirit, and that it was he who preserved their authors immune from every error."[81] As did *Divino Afflante Spiritu*, the instruction sees the proper use of the historical-critical method and a legitimate freedom for the Catholic biblical scholar as compatible with the Church's traditional doctrine on inerrancy.

Returning to *Dei Verbum* 11, we can situate the principle that the Scriptures were written "for the sake of our salvation" in the same context as the principles we have just reviewed. Rather than introduce a limitation, the phrase "for the sake of our salvation" provides help both for understanding inerrancy correctly and for interpreting the text correctly, as it reminds us of the purpose for which God had the Scriptures written.

In its next paragraph, however, *Dei Verbum* has still more to say regarding the relationship between biblical truth and biblical interpretation:

> To determine the intention of the sacred writers, one must attend to such things as 'literary forms' *[genera litteraria]*. For truth is differently presented and expressed in various types of historical writings, in prophetic or poetic texts, or in other modes of speech.[82]

By advising the interpreter to pay attention to literary genres and to the circumstances of the historical time-period in which the biblical texts were written, this paragraph, like previous documents, refers to various scholarly methods of biblical interpretation. The interpretive task does not end, however, with the application of such methods. Indeed, the document continues by proposing a further interpretive principle: "Sacred Scripture must also be read and interpreted in the light of the

---

80 Pontifical Biblical Commission, *Sancta Mater Ecclesia* [Holy Mother Church], Instruction on the Historical Truth of the Gospels (April 21, 1964), IX (*SD*, 227–235, at 231; *EB* 651). On this point, see also *Dei Verbum*, 19 (*SD*, 28; *EB* 698): the Evangelists "related to us an honest and true account of Jesus" so that "we might know 'the truth' concerning the things about which we have been instructed" (citing Luke 1:2–4).

81 Pontifical Biblical Commission, *Sancta Mater Ecclesia*, XI (*SD*, 232; *EB* 653).

82 *Dei Verbum*, 12 (*SD*, 25; *EB* 689).

same Spirit by whom it was written."[83] Three criteria which the interpreter should take into account are then indicated for implementing this principle: "the content and unity of the whole of Scripture,...the entire living tradition of the Church and the analogy of faith."[84] In particular, the first of these criteria corresponds to "canonical exegesis,"[85] and so the question can be asked, again linking biblical truth and biblical interpretation as was done with other principles, whether a canonical perspective can shed some light on biblical truth.[86] It would not be surprising if the Pontifical Biblical Commission's current study of inspiration and truth explores this subject further.

Pope Benedict XVI himself takes up another one of the criteria, that of paying attention to how a passage is read within the living Tradition of the whole Church. Drawing on the common patristic and medieval teaching that distinguishes the literal and the spiritual senses, the Pope in *Jesus of Nazareth* explains that while the interpreter must seek "to discover the precise sense the words were intended to convey at their time and place of origin,"[87] it is also necessary

> to keep in mind that any human utterance of a certain weight contains more than the author may have been immediately aware of at the time. When a word transcends the moment in which it is spoken, it carries within itself a "deeper value." This "deeper value" pertains most of all to words that have matured in the course of faith-history. For in this case the author is not simply speaking for himself on his own authority. He is speaking from the perspective of a common history that sustains him and that already implicitly contains the possibilities of its future, of the further stages of its journey. The process of continually rereading and drawing out new meanings from words would not have been possible unless the words themselves were already open to it from within. At this point we get a glimmer, even on

---

83   *Dei Verbum*, 12 (*SD*, 25; *EB* 690).

84   *Dei Verbum*, 12 (*SD*, 25; *EB* 690). These three criteria are repeated in the *Catechism*, nos. 112–114, and Benedict XVI frequently makes reference to them.

85   Pope Benedict XVI, Address to the Synod of Bishops (October 14, 2008), in *L'Osservatore Romano*, Weekly Edition in English (October 22, 2008), 13: "One must interpret the text taking into consideration the unity of all of Scripture. Today this is called canonical exegesis; at the time of the Council this term did not yet exist, but the Council expressed the same thing: it is necessary to take into account the unity of the entirety of Scripture." See also Benedict XVI, *Jesus of Nazareth*, xviii–xix.

86   Two attempts to understand the truth of Scripture in light of the canon are found in: Mannucci, *Bibbia*, 246, 264–271; and Giancarlo Biguzzi, "Il Problema della Verità Biblica nel Nuovo Testamento" [The Problem of Biblical Truth in the New Testament], in Izquierdo, *Scrittura Ispirata*, 233–248.

87   Benedict XVI, *Jesus of Nazareth*, xix.

the historical level, of what *inspiration* means. The author does not speak as a private, self-contained subject. He speaks in a living community, that is to say, in a living historical movement not created by him, nor even by the collective, but which is led forward by a greater power that is at work. There are dimensions of the word that the old doctrine of the fourfold sense of Scripture pinpointed with remarkable accuracy. The four senses of Scripture are not individual meanings arrayed side by side, but dimensions of the one word that reaches beyond the moment.[88]

From this point, the Pope goes on to explain that in addition to speaking about the divine author and the human authors of Scripture, we should also speak of the collective subject "People of God" as author in some sense, as "the deeper 'author' of the Scriptures."[89] "The People of God—the Church—is the living subject of Scripture; it is in the Church that the words of the Bible are always in the present."[90] This living subject of the Church is always guided by the "Spirit of truth...into all the truth."[91] First, during the period of the oral preaching of the Gospel message up to the time of the writing of the gospels, the Holy Spirit guides the "remembering" of the apostles and the early Church,[92] so that the four written gospels, "whose historicity the Church affirms without hesitation, faithfully hand on what Jesus...actually did and taught for their eternal salvation."[93] Second,

---

88 Benedict XVI, *Jesus of Nazareth*, xix–xx (emphasis added). On the four senses of Scripture, see the *Catechism*, nos. 115–118.

89 Benedict XVI, *Jesus of Nazareth*, xxi.

90 Benedict XVI, *Jesus of Nazareth*, xxi.

91 John 16:13.

92 See John 2:22; 12:16; 14:26.

93 *Dei Verbum*, 19 (*SD*, 27; *EB* 698). Along these lines, and specifically with regard to the Gospel of Luke, see Benedict XVI: "If we have good reason to be convinced that the Holy Scriptures are '*inspired*,' that they matured in a special sense under the guidance of the Holy Spirit, then we also have good reason to be convinced that precisely these specific aspects of the Lukan tradition preserve essential features of the original figure of Jesus for us." *Jesus of Nazareth*, 182; emphasis added. And again, with regard to the Gospel of John, Benedict writes: "This means that the Gospel of John...does not simply transmit a stenographic transcript of Jesus' words and ways; it escorts us, in virtue of understanding-through-remembering, beyond the external into the depth of words and events that come from God and lead back to him. As such, the Gospel is 'remembering,' which means that it remains faithful to what really happened and is not...a violation of historical events. Rather, it *truly* shows us who Jesus was. ...It shows us the real Jesus." *Jesus of Nazareth*, 234–235; emphasis added. Parallels can be drawn between the Pope's comments on remembering and recent work on the historicity of the Gospels: "In the immediate testimony of the witness, that which lives on in deep memory, the witness 'sees' what is disclosed in what happens, the empirical event requiring to be seen as the revelation of God, fact and meaning coinhering. But memory is also remembered and understanding grows. In what is no doubt the most reflective Gospel testimony we have, that of John, the immediacy of memory is by no means lost. Rather, the ongoing process of remembering interpretation

even after the writing of the New Testament, the effects of inspiration are not exhausted, as the living subject of the Church interprets the Scriptures in the same Spirit in whom they were written, grows in understanding of the Scriptures, and thus, "constantly advances toward the fullness of divine truth."[94]

The Word Incarnate and the Word Inspired

Finally, it is helpful to recall the analogy that magisterial documents have made between the incarnation and biblical inspiration. The encyclical, *Divino Afflante Spiritu*, was the first magisterial document to make this comparison. In a section discussing how biblical inspiration is compatible with the various ways that ancient authors expressed their thought (for example, using idioms, hyperbole, paradox, and the like), Pius XII remarks that none of these ways

> is excluded from the sacred books, provided the way of speaking adopted in no wise contradicts the holiness and truth of God. ... For as the substantial Word of God became like to men in all things "except sin" (Heb 4:15), so the words of God, expressed in human language, are made like to human speech in every respect except error. In this consists that "condescension"...of the God of providence, which St. John Chrysostom extolled.[95]

Hence, the analogy is used, on the one hand, to affirm inerrancy, and on the other, to provide guidance (regarding literary genres) as to how inerrancy should be understood. *Dei Verbum* takes up the analogy between incarnation and inspiration in paragraph 13, immediately following the discussion of biblical interpretation in 12. The wording is in many ways similar to that of *Divino*.

> Hence, in sacred Scripture, with the truth and holiness of God remaining always inviolate, the marvelous "condescension" of eternal wisdom is clearly shown. ...For the words of God,

---

ponders and works to yield its fullest meaning." Richard Bauckham, *Jesus and the Eyewitnesses: The Gospels as Eyewitness Testimony* (Grand Rapids, MI: Eerdmans, 2006), 507–508.

94   *Dei Verbum*, 8 (SD, 22; EB 680). See also Benedict XVI: "The Church's remembering is not merely a private affair. ...It is a being-led by the Holy Spirit, who shows us the connectedness of Scripture, the connection between word and reality, and, in doing that, leads us 'into all the truth.' This also has some fundamental implications for the concept of *inspiration*. ...But because the author thinks and writes with the memory of the Church, the 'we' to which he belongs opens beyond the personal and is guided in its depths by the Spirit of God, who is the Spirit of truth. In this sense, the Gospel itself opens up a path of understanding, which always remains bound to the scriptural word, and yet from generation to generation can lead, and is meant to lead, ever anew into the depth of all the truth." *Jesus of Nazareth*, 234; emphasis added.

95   Pius XII, *Divino Afflante Spiritu*, 20 (SD, 129; EB 559).

expressed in human language, have become like unto human speech, just as the Word of the eternal Father, when he took on himself the flesh of human weakness, became like unto human beings.[96]

While it does not include the parallel found in *Divino* between the phrases "except sin" and "except error," it nonetheless does make reference, like the encyclical, to the "truth and holiness" of God remaining intact.[97] As a result, "truth" is considered in all three paragraphs of Chapter 3 of *Dei Verbum* dealing with the inspiration and interpretation of Scripture (paragraphs 11–13); it is considered in the context of or in relation to inspiration (para. 11), interpretation (para. 12), and the incarnation (para. 13).

Later in the document, there is a further reference to the analogy, within the context of the liturgy: "The Church has always venerated the divine Scriptures just as she venerates the Body of the Lord, never ceasing to offer to the faithful, especially in the sacred liturgy, the bread of life, received from the one table of God's Word and Christ's Body."[98]

Pope John Paul II also referred to this analogy in his 1993 address to the Pontifical Biblical Commission, noting the "strict relationship uniting the inspired biblical texts with the mystery of the incarnation,"[99] and referring to the two passages just quoted from *Divino* and *Dei Verbum*. Drawing from the analogy, the Pope first cautions against the tendency of some Christians who reject "the mysteries of scriptural inspiration and the incarnation…by clinging to a false notion of the Absolute" and who thus ignore "the human circumstances of the Word of

---

96 *Dei Verbum*, 13 (*SD*, 25; *EB* 691). For further discussion, including a synopsis of the two magisterial texts, see Antonio Izquierdo, "La Escritura Inspirada y la Encarnación del Verbo" [Inspired Scripture and the Incarnation of the Word], in Izquierdo, *Scrittura ispirata*, 249–282.

97 In the redaction of the conciliar text, there were proposed emendations involving all of these phrases; see the various proposals and the responses of the Council's theological commission in Gil Hellín, *Synopsis*, 105–107. See also the discussion in Miguel Angel Tábet, "Ispirazione, Condiscendenza Divina ed Incarnazione nella Teologia di Questo Secolo" [Inspiration, Divine Condescension and Incarnation in the Theology of this Century], *Annales Theologici* 8 (1994): 235–283, at 265–266.

98 *Dei Verbum*, 21. The *Catechism*, nos. 101 and 103, refers respectively to *Dei Verbum*, 13 and 21, and thus places the analogy at the very beginning of its treatment of Scripture. See the discussion in Tábet, "Ispirazione," 266.

99 Pope John Paul II, Address to the Pontifical Biblical Commission (April 23, 1993), 6 (*SD*, 170–180, at 173).

God."[100] On the other hand, the Pope also indicates that "Catholic exegesis must be careful not to limit itself to the human aspects of the biblical texts."[101]

In a possible future document, the analogy could be deepened by considering the Church in relation to the incarnate Word, on the one hand, and in relation to the inspired Word, on the other. In fact, *Dei Verbum* already points in this direction, saying that "the spouse of the incarnate Word, the Church, taught by the Holy Spirit, strives to attain day by day a more profound understanding of the sacred Scriptures."[102] As we have seen, the writings of the current Pope stress the role of the Church as the living subject which receives God's revelation with faith and then progresses to the full understanding of that revelation. In this regard, if the relationship of the Church as the spouse of the incarnate Word is such that "the two shall become one"[103]—that is, the Church becomes the Body of Christ—then with the analogy one can perhaps similarly relate the mystery of inspiration to the Church. As he has said, there is "an interwoven relationship between Church and Bible, between the People of God and the Word of God."[104]

The Mystery of the Lord who is the Word

Consideration of the analogy between the incarnation and the inspiration of the Bible also reminds us that through the inspired words of Scripture we enter into the mystery of the Word made flesh.[105] Through the truth of Scripture, we enter into the mystery of the One who is truth itself.[106] Ultimately, this is what the Church's teaching on the inspiration and truth of Scripture enables us to do: it helps us recognize Scripture as a sure and authoritative witness of the Word.

In his reflection at the opening of the 2008 Synod, Benedict began by meditating on the text of Psalm 119:89: "Your Word, Lord, stands forever; it is firm as the heavens."[107] In his address, he alluded to many of the points we have considered: the inspiration and truth of Scripture, its divine and human authors,

---

100 John Paul II, Address (April 23, 1993), 8 (*SD*, 175). In this regard, some scholars refer to biblical fundamentalism as a kind of monophysitism; see Izquierdo, "Escritura Inspirada," 257.

101 John Paul II, (April 23, 1993), 9 (*SD*, 175). The "absolutization" of the historical-critical method is seen as a kind of nestorianism; see Izquierdo, "Escritura Inspirada," 257.

102 *Dei Verbum*, 23 (*SD*, 29; *EB* 703).

103 Eph. 5:31–32; see Gen 2:24.

104 Joseph Ratzinger, "What in Fact is Theology?" in Joseph Ratzinger, *Pilgrim Fellowship of Faith: The Church as Communion*, eds. Stephan Otto Horn and Vinzenz Pfnür, trans. Henry Taylor (San Francisco: Ignatius, 2005), 29–37, at 33.

105 John 1:14.

106 See John 14:6.

107 New American Bible translation.

the Word and the Church. We close by quoting excerpts from his reflection, which help us appreciate the grandeur of the written Word of God.

> This refers to the solidity of the Word. It is solid, it is the true re-ality on which one must base one's life. …Only the Word of God is the foundation of all reality, it is as stable as the heavens and more than the heavens, it is reality. Therefore, we must change our concept of realism. The realist is the one who recognizes the Word of God, in this apparently weak reality, as the founda-tion of all things. Realist is the one who builds his life on this foundation, which is permanent. …We are always searching for the Word of God. …Just reading it does not mean necessarily that we have truly understood the Word of God. The danger is that we only see the human words and do not find the true actor within, the Holy Spirit. …We must always look for the Word within the words. Therefore, exegesis, the true reading of Holy Scripture, is not only a literary phenomenon, not only reading a text. It is the movement of my existence. It is moving towards the Word of God in the human words. Only by conforming ourselves to the mystery of God, to the Lord who is the Word, can we enter within the Word, can we truly find the Word of God in human words. …Only God is infinite. And therefore his Word too is universal and knows no boundaries. Therefore by entering into the Word of God we really enter into the divine universe. We escape the limits of our experience and we enter into the reality that is truly universal. Entering into communion with the Word of God, we enter a communion of the Church that lives the Word of God. … We go towards the depths, in the true grandeur of the only truth, the great truth of God.[108]

---

108 Pope Benedict XVI, Address at the Opening of the Synod of Bishops (October 6, 2008), in *L'Osservatore Romano*, Weekly Edition in English (October 8, 2008), 5.

Letter & Spirit 6 (2010): 93-140

Analogia Verbi
The Truth of Scripture in Rudolf Bultmann and Raymond Brown

∽: Michael Maria Waldstein :∽

Ave Maria University

At its core, the debate about modern exegesis is not a dispute among historians: it is rather a philosophical debate. Only in this way can it be carried on correctly; otherwise we continue with a battle in the mist. In this respect, the exegetical problem is identical with our time's struggle about the foundations as such. …The exegete should approach the exegesis of the text not with a ready-made philosophy, not with the dictate of a so-called modern or scientific worldview, which determines in advance what is permitted to be and what is not permitted to be. He may not exclude a priori that God is able to speak as himself in human words in the world. — Joseph Cardinal Ratzinger[1]

God, who spoke in the past, speaks without any break with the bride of his beloved Son, … All that the inspired authors or sacred writers affirm is to be held as affirmed by the Holy Spirit. — Second Vatican Council[2]

"There is a big difference between still believing something and believing it again: still believing that the moon acts on plants shows stupidity and superstition; believing it again is a sign of philosophy and reflection."[3] Georg Christoph Lichtenberg's irony in this aphorism expresses his firm faith in the irresistibly victorious power with which the natural science shaped by Francis Bacon and René Descartes was sweeping all superstition from the table. Everything in the universe follows

---

1   Cardinal Joseph Ratzinger, "Biblical Interpretation in Crisis," The Erasmus Lecture (January 27, 1988), in *The Essential Pope Benedict XVI: His Central Writings and Speeches*, eds. John F. Thorton and Susan B. Varenne (San Francisco: HarperSanFrancisco, 2007), 243–258, at 253, 255.

2   Second Vatican Council, *Dei Verbum* [The Word of God], Dogmatic Constitution on Divine Revelation, (November 18, 1965), 8, 11, in *The Scripture Documents: An Anthology of Official Catholic Teachings*, ed. Dean P. Béchard, S.J. (Collegeville, MN: Liturgical Press, 2002), 19–31.

3   Georg Christoph Lichtenberg (1742–1799), *Sudelbücher* [Sketchbooks], Bk. E, 52, written in the early 1770's. For an English translation, see *The Waste Books*, trans. and introd. R. J. Hollingdale (New York: New York Review Books, 2000).

mathematical laws, without exception. There are no spiritual mystical forces that descend from the moon. The old herb woman who still goes into the woods at half moon to pick her medicinal herbs is behind the times. She "still believes." "Believing again" is legitimate as long as it is based on science,[4] but not on the grounds of mere "philosophy and reflection."

Lichtenberg also writes, "If you only understand chemistry, you don't understand it rightly."[5] Is mathematical physics the only thing one needs to understand outside of chemistry? Or must one go even outside that master discipline to ask whether the choices made by Bacon and Descartes at the origin of modern science, which includes the choice of mechanics as the one true mode of understanding replacing all others, are good choices? This is the philosophical question at the root of the debate about the truth of Scripture.

During the debates about the truth of Scripture at the Second Vatican Council, Cardinal Franz König of Vienna argued, "Peer reviewed science in Near Eastern studies shows in addition that in the sacred books historical accounts and accounts bearing on matters of natural science at times fall short of the truth."[6] The final text of the Council's *Dei Verbum* should be read as agreeing with Cardinal König, Cardinal Aloys Grillmeier argues, even though this agreement "cannot be grasped immediately in the actual words *[Wortlaut]* of the text," but must be inferred from the history of the text's redaction and the surrounding discussion.[7]

An intense debate took place during the Council about the phrase, "the truth, which God, for the sake of our salvation, willed to be recorded in the sacred letters."[8] As Grillmeier points out, Pope Paul VI personally asked the Council's Theological Commission to change the original "saving truth" into "the truth, which God, for the sake of our salvation" to avoid the impression that the truth taught "without error" is limited to matters of faith and morals.[9]

Nevertheless Grillmeier concludes in a more subtle manner that the assurance of the truth of Scripture is in fact limited to statements that directly bear on salvation.

---

4   Recent evidence shows that there is "a semilunar periodicity of neurotransmitter-like substances from heart-stimulating plants." Wolfgang Schad, "Lunar Influence on Plants," *Earth, Moon, and Planets* 85 (1999): 405–409, at 408.

5   Lichtenberg, *Sudelbücher*, Bk. J, 860.

6   Franz Cardinal König, Address to the Plenum of the Council (October 2, 1964); quoted according to Aloys Grillmeier, "Kommentar zu Kapitel III der Konstitution über die Göttliche Offenbarung *Dei Verbum*" [Commentary on Chapter III of the Constitution on Divine Revelation *Dei Verbum*] in *Lexikon für Theologie und Kirche* [Lexicon of Theology and the Church], 11 vols. (Freiberg: Herder, 1993–2001) 2:528–558, at 532.

7   Grillmeier, "Kommentar," 2:528.

8   *Dei Verbum*, 11.

9   See Grillmeier, "Kommentar," 2:536–537.

There are immediate saving statements and narratives, in which this formal aspect *salutis causā* [for the sake of salvation] is fully verified. There are also parts of Scripture, however, that only perform an auxiliary function in relation to these immediate saving truths. Here there can be—from the point of view of the secular sciences—a falling short of the truth. Here we must recognize the facts without prejudice or fear. The question of inerrancy must not become a matter of bad conscience or cramped attitudes. ...

Everything in Scripture has a share in "the truth, which God, for the sake of our salvation, willed to be recorded," either *immediately* and *by its contents* or *mediately* and *in virtue of its service* to the saving statement. ...Items in Scripture that are, from the point of view of the secular sciences, not right or not exact, must not be seen in isolation, nor should one call them simply "errors." All of this must be left in the whole of Scripture and should be judged in its service to the saving Word.[10]

A different reading of *Dei Verbum 11* is proposed by Cardinal Augustin Bea.

Does the text we have before us now imply a restrictive interpretation of inerrancy? Here also the answer is firmly negative. The first proof of this is seen in the fact that all those (and in the first place the Pope himself) who had been anxious to prevent the possible misunderstanding that might have arisen from the expression "the saving truth" have instead accepted the present form, which means that they consider that this does not present the same danger of misunderstanding. ...

Let us then conclude: all that the inspired writers assert is asserted through them by the Holy Spirit. Consequently, in all their assertions the sacred books teach "firmly, faithfully and without error, what God wanted put into them for the sake of our salvation."[11]

I had accepted Grillmeier's reading of *Dei Verbum* early in my studies and continued to maintain it without much philosophy and reflection until a thesis written in 2002 by one of my students in Austria, David Bolin (now Fr. Thomas, O.S.B.), convinced me that I was wrong. I now believe again in the truth of Scripture

---

10   Grillmeier, "Kommentar," 2:549–550.

11   Augustin Cardinal Bea, *The Word of God and Mankind* (Chicago: Franciscan Herald, 1967), 190–191; emphasis added.

without the nuance of "falling short of the truth." Philosophy and reflection, which belongs to those who believe again, cannot be credited to my account, however, because they were (at least to begin with) not my own.

During one of the open discussion sessions of the 2008 Synod of Bishops on "The Word of God in the Life and Mission of the Church," Peter Cardinal Turkson dramatically raised the question of the truth of Scripture.[12] The *Instrumentum Laboris* ("Working Document")[13] distributed before the Synod, he argued, turns the text of *Dei Verbum* 11 on its head by adding the word "only," so as to limit the inerrancy of Scripture. Heated discussions followed in the coffee breaks after this intervention. I heard even normally measured and balanced people complain angrily about the attempt by "fundamentalists" to turn the clock back to the time before Vatican II. Here is a comparison between the *Instrumentum* and *Dei Verbum*, translated in parallel from the Latin (emphasis added).

Although all parts of sacred Scripture are divinely inspired,	*Since* therefore *all* that the inspired authors or sacred writers affirm is to be held as affirmed by the Holy Spirit,
nevertheless, its inerrancy applies *only* to	*therefore* one must profess that the books of Scripture teach
"the truth *that* God, for the sake of our salvation, wanted to be recorded in the sacred letters"	the truth, *which* God, for the sake of our salvation, wanted to be recorded in the sacred letters, firmly, faithfully and without error
—*Instrumentum Laboris*, Pt. 1, Chap. 2, A	— *Dei Verbum*, 11

In the Council text, the word "all" plays a role that is parallel but opposite to the *Instrumentum*: "truth" applies to "all that the sacred authors affirm" since "all … is to be held as affirmed by the Holy Spirit," while the *Instrumentum* admits some errors as long as they are not directly related to salvation. When one combines *Dei Verbum's* reason for the truth of Scripture, "All is to be held as affirmed by the Holy Spirit," with the statement, "Some errors are affirmed in Scripture," the conclusion inevitably follows, "These errors are to be held as affirmed by the Holy Spirit."

---

12   In the open discussion session of October 7, 2008.

13   Synod of Bishops, "The Word of God in the Life and Mission of the Church," *Instrumentum Laboris* (May 11, 2008). Available online at: http://www.vatican.va/roman_curia/synod/index.htm.

Like the *Instrumentum*, Grillmeier's commentary omits the reason, "affirmed by the Holy Spirit," which is astonishing, considering Grillmeier's famous care and precision as a scholar. From his commentary alone, one could not infer that this sentence is present in *Dei Verbum* 11. There is not even the slightest allusion to it in Grillmeier's text. What could have moved him to avoid this text?

On a very general level, it is not difficult to answer this question. All who reflect about their Christian faith in the modern age experience the pressure of the scientific picture of the world or, more exactly, of the choices and philosophical premises implicit in that scientific picture. These premises, which lie in the voluntaristic nominalism of William of Ockham and the choice of mathematical mechanics as the master science of nature by Bacon and Descartes, destroy the metaphysics of analogy and participation required for understanding the *analogia verbi* ["analogy of the Word"] in *Dei Verbum* 11.

The purpose of this essay is to illustrate the power of this pressure in two cases. Rudolf Bultmann completely submits to it, but attempts to neutralize its consequences in a Lutheran dialectic. Raymond Brown resists it, but not without a highly dramatic struggle. Following the recent stimulating study of the truth of Scripture by Denis Farkasfalvy,[14] the essay pursues the close connection between Scripture and the Eucharist in Christ's spousal gift of self, "I am yours and you are mine." For this reason, the backbone of the essay's argument is Raymond Brown's interpretation of the eucharistic passage John 6:54–57. The argument's method is to apply the "hermeneutics of the gift"[15] to the question of the truth of Scripture, as suggested by St. Bernard.

> "He spoke and they were made" (Psalm 148:5). Yet, he who made me by merely speaking, by speaking once, certainly remade me *by speaking* much *and by doing* wonders ["Do this in memory of me"]. …In the first work he gave me myself; in the second *himself,* and where *he gave himself,* he gave me back to myself. As one given and given back, I owe myself for myself, and owe myself twice. What shall I render to God for himself? Even if I could give myself back to him a thousand times, what am I [compared] to God?[16]

---

14 Denis Farkasfalvy, *Inspiration & Interpretation: A Theological Introduction to Sacred Scripture* (Washington, DC: Catholic University of America, 2010). See especially Chapter Four: "The Eucharistic Provenance of the Christian Bible."

15 The "hermeneutics of the gift" is the theological method adopted by Pope John Paul II. See *Man and Woman He Created Them: A Theology of the Body*, trans. Michael Waldstein (Boston: Pauline, 2006), 179.

16 St. Bernard of Clairvaux, *De Diligendo Deo* [On Loving God], Chap. 5, 15, in *Bernard of Clairvaux: Selected Works*, The Classics of Western Spirituality (New York: Paulist, 1987), 173–206; emphasis added.

Bultmann on the Truth of Scripture

One can grasp Bultmann's overall vision under five headings: truth, sin, God, Scripture, and Jesus.[17]

Truth. At the very foundations of Bultmann's thought, which was complete in its essential outlines before his encounter with Martin Heidegger, there lies the philosophical thesis that being human in the authentic sense does not mean being an object in the cosmos with a certain nature or essence; it means "existing"; and existing means being a historical possibility which continually realizes itself through decision. "The free deed is the expression of our existence; in fact, only in the free deed, and nowhere else, do we exist in the authentic sense, since the free deed is nothing but our existence itself ... "[18]

One can recognize in this thesis a post-Kantian form of the nominalism of William of Ockham (1288–1348), who radicalized the voluntaristic theses of his teacher Duns Scotus (1265–1308). There was a storm of protest in the Islamic world about Pope Benedict XVI's 2006 Lecture at the University of Regensburg and its claim that Mohammed's practice of imposing Islam by violence implies a voluntaristic denial of human rationality. This storm has deflected attention from a similar accusation of voluntarism made shortly afterwards much closer to home.

> The decisive statement in [the Byzantine emperor's] argument against violent conversion [as practiced by Mohammed] is this: not to act in accordance with reason is contrary to God's nature. The editor, Theodore Khoury, observes: For the emperor, as a Byzantine shaped by Greek philosophy, this statement is self-evident. But for Muslim teaching, God is absolutely transcendent. His will is not bound up with any of our categories, even that of rationality. Here Khoury quotes a work of the noted French Islamist R. Arnaldez, who points out that Ibn Hazm went so far as to state that God is not bound even by his own Word, and that nothing would oblige him to reveal the truth to us. Were it God's will, we would even have to practice idolatry. ...
>
> In all honesty, one must observe that in the late Middle Ages we find trends in theology which would sunder this synthesis between the Greek spirit and the Christian spirit. In contrast

---

17   For a more detailed analysis of Bultmann, see my three interrelated articles: "The Foundations of Bultmann's Work," *Communio* 14 (1987): 115–145; "Hans Jonas's Construct 'Gnosticism': Analysis and Critique," *Journal of Early Christian Studies* 8 (2000): 341–372; "The Evolution of Bultmann's Interpretation of John and Gnosticism," *Lateranum* 70 (2004): 313–352.

18   Rudolf Bultmann, "Welchen Sinn hat es, von Gott zu Reden?" [What is the Point of Talking about God?], in *Glauben und Verstehen: Gesammelte Aufsätze*, vol. 1 (Tübingen: Mohr-Siebeck, 1933), 26-37, here 35. Eng.: *Faith and Understanding I*, ed. Robert W. Funk (London: S.C.M., 1969).

with the so-called intellectualism of Augustine and Thomas, there arose with Duns Scotus a voluntarism which, in its later developments, led to the claim that we can only know God's *voluntas ordinata* ["ordained will"]. Beyond this is the realm of God's freedom, in virtue of which he could have done the opposite of everything he has actually done. This gives rise. …to the image of a capricious God, who is not even bound to truth and goodness. God's transcendence and otherness are so exalted that our reason, our sense of the true and good, are no longer an authentic mirror of God, whose deepest possibilities remain eternally unattainable and hidden behind his actual decisions.

As opposed to this, the faith of the Church has always insisted that between God and us, between his eternal Creator Spirit and our created reason there exists a real analogy, in which—as the Fourth Lateran Council in 1215 stated—unlikeness remains infinitely greater than likeness, yet not to the point of abolishing analogy and its language. God does not become more divine when we push him away from us in a sheer, impenetrable voluntarism; rather, the truly divine God is the God who has revealed himself as *Logos* ["Word, Reason"]. …[19]

Duns Scotus's student, William of Ockham, radicalizes his teacher's emphasis on divine free will to the point of nominalism, that is, "name-ism." He argues that God could command us to hate him, in which case hatred rather than love would be good. "Good" is thereby reduced to a mere *name imposed at will.*

Ockham's nominalism cuts the bonds of analogy and participation that unite God and creatures and thus obscures the interior goodness of creatures. It sees their order as an order God happens to have imposed on them from the outside, one among many orders he could have imposed. It regards natural beings as artifacts, not as natural beings, not as having an interior principle of order toward the good. They reflect the free divine power, not the divine being, goodness and wisdom. They have no inner participation in the being and goodness of God.

Charles Taylor points out the close connection between nominalism and Bacon's proposal of mechanics as the master science of nature.

---

19 Benedict XVI, "Faith, Reason and the University : Memories and Reflections," (December 12, 2006), in *The Regensburg Lecture*, ed. James V. Schall (South Bend, IN: St. Augustine, 2007). Also available online at: http://www.vatican.va/holy_father/benedict_xvi/index.htm.

> This [voluntaristic and nominalist] line of thought even contributed in the end to the rise of mechanism: the ideal universe from this point of view is a mechanical one.[20]

> In nominalism, the super-agent who is God relates to things as freely to be disposed of according to his autonomous purposes. ...The purposes of things are extrinsic to them. The stance is fundamentally one of instrumental reason. ...The shift will not be long in coming to a new understanding of being, according to which, all intrinsic purpose having been expelled, final causation drops out, and efficient causation alone remains. There comes about what had been called "the mechanization of the world picture." And this in turn opens the way for a view of science in which a good test of the truth of a hypothesis is what it enables you to effect. This is the Baconian view ... [21]

Luther was strongly influenced by Ockham, mainly by way of the Ockhamist Gabriel Biel (1420–1495). Bacon inherited the same philosophical premises in his Calvinist theological training.[22] Bultmann inherited them in his Lutheran formation, though in a post-Kantian form.

Bultmann's entire ontology is based on the voluntaristic principle, "The free deed is nothing but our existence itself." One can observe the crucial role of this principle with particular clarity in his doctrine of knowledge, and his correlative doctrine of truth.

> If *human existence* is *temporal-historical*, and thus concerned in every concrete Now with itself, not merely by choosing in every concrete Now one among many possibilities that offer themselves, but, in doing so, by grasping ever again a possibility of itself, if, I say, the Being of human existence is thus *Being-able-to-be*, because each Now is essentially new and receives its meaning precisely now, now through its decision, and therefore not from a timeless meaning of the world, then the question of truth has meaning only as the question of *the one truth of the moment, my moment.*[23]

---

20 Charles Taylor, *Sources of the Self: The Making of the Modern Identity* (Cambridge, MA: Harvard University, 1989), 82.

21 Charles Taylor, *A Secular Age* (Cambridge, MA: Belknap, 2007), 97–98.

22 See Steven Matthews, *Theology and Science in the Thought of Francis Bacon* (Aldershot: Ashgate, 2008).

23 Rudolf Bultmann, *Theologische Enzyklopädie*, ed. Eberdhard Jüngel and Klaus W. Müller (Tübingen, Mohr-Siebeck, 1984), 50; Eng: *What is Theology*, trans. Roy A. Harrisville (Philadelphia: Fortress, 1997).

"The truth of the moment" refers to something correlative to decision, namely, to a certain challenge in the light of which I understand myself in a concrete moment. "The *whole* truth, *my* truth, is in question. I want to understand *myself*."[24]

Sin. Yet, I am not able to live exclusively in the truth. I also live in "the sphere of the objective" which is cut off from the challenge of the moment. This sphere arises inexorably from the inner dynamism of knowledge. It is here that Bultmann first deploys the Kantian account of "objective beings" as mere phenomena.[25] Negatively, the corruption of authentic truth consists in a detachment from the challenge of the moment; positively, it consists in objectification, in the formation of a sphere of objective being and truth that can be universal and timeless. Modern natural science, according to Bultmann, is the prime example of this corruption of truth in our age, just as Roman Catholicism was at the time of Luther.

One of the main philosophical forces at the very origin of natural science is the ambition for power over nature as articulated by Bacon and Descartes. According to Bacon, "Human knowledge and power coincide in the same. ...For nature is not conquered except by obeying."[26] On this point, Bacon's secretary, Thomas Hobbes, agrees with his employer. "Knowledge is for the sake of power."[27] The extent of the power sought by Bacon is vast: "the power and empire of the human race itself over the universe of things."[28] Bacon's choice of mechanics as the master-science of nature follows from his choice of power as the end. "Aristotle [said it] best. Physics and mathematics give rise to practical science and mechanics."[29]

Descartes studied Bacon before he began his first major work in natural philosophy.[30] In his Discourse on Method (1637), he lays down the goal of his philosophy in agreement with Bacon.

> It is possible to reach knowledge that will be very useful to life, and instead of the speculative philosophy which is now taught in the schools [that is, Aristotelian-Scholastic philosophy] we can find a practical one, by which, knowing the force and the actions of fire, water, air, stars, the heavens, and all the other bodies that

---

24　Bultmann, *Theologische Enzyklopädie*, 49.

25　See Bultmann, *Theologische Enzyklopädie*, 195.

26　Francis Bacon, *The New Organon, or New Directions Concerning the Interpretation of Nature*, Bk. 1, 3; James Spedding, ed., *The Works of Francis Bacon*, 14 vols. (London: Longman, 1857–1874), 1:157.

27　Thomas Hobbes, *Elementa Philosophiae* [Elements of Philosophy], Pt. 1, 1; *De Philosophia* [On Philosophy] par. 6, in *Opera Philosophica* [Philosophical Works], 3 vols., ed. William Molesworth (London: John Bohn, 1839), 1:6.

28　Bacon, *New Organon*, Bk. 1, 129; *Works*, 1:222.

29　Bacon, *The Advancement of Knowledge*, Bk. 3, Chap. 6; *Works*, 1:576.

30　The documentary evidence for Descartes' relation to Bacon is gathered in René Descartes, *Oeuvres de Descartes* [Works of Descartes], 12 vols., ed. by Charles Adam and Paul Tannery (Paris: Librairie Philosophique J. Vrin, 1983), 12:479, n. a.

surround us as distinctly as we know the various skills of our artisans we can employ them in the same way for all the uses for which they are fit, and so make ourselves masters and possessors of nature.[31]

Bultmann accepts the Baconian-Cartesian notion of science, including the self-limitation of reason to the task of discovering mechanical laws in nature. Following Immanuel Kant, he denies the existence of an objective natural world. Far from discovering such a world, human "knowledge" constitutes it in an act of power. When the mind forces the truth of the moment to hold still, when it thus lifts that truth into objectivity, it gives rise to the "objective" natural world according to patterns and causal laws that lie in the structure of the mind rather than in things.[32]

As a member of the modern age I cannot escape agreeing with current natural science. The only responsible way for me to practice historical critical scholarship is in complete agreement with that science. The universe follows mathematical laws, without exception. I must accordingly deny that miracles are possible, which immediately turns the historicity switch of the Gospels to the "off" position. God is entirely absent from the cosmos.

Although it is inevitable for me, objectification poses a grave threat to human existence. By living "according to" the objective world and its stable relations, I can evade the challenge of the moment to find security in objective truth. In this observation, Bultmann applies the Lutheran doctrine of justification by faith alone without works of the law to the order of knowledge and being.[33]

On this background one can grasp Bultmann's concept of sin. Sin is the refusal of the challenge of the moment, rooted in the desire for security and expressed in the flight away from the moment into the sphere of the objective.[34] Sin is boasting in human power. The enemy is not, as it was for Luther, Catholic boasting in the salvific power of good works and indulgences available for purchase, but scientific boasting in human power and life-improving consumer goods, the modern equivalent of indulgences, also available for purchase.

> The existential meaning of hell is not that of an image of a physical place below the world full of torments. Instead, it is the recognition of the power of evil, indeed, the evil of the poisoned and poisoning atmosphere which humankind has created for itself when we began to assume that we could create *security through scientific knowledge* and the ability to dominate the earth. With this attitude, the world does become hell. Such confusion leads

---

31 Descartes, *Discourse on Method*, Pt. 6; *Oeuvres*, 6:61–62.

32 See Bultmann, *Theologische Enzyklopädie*, 107.

33 See Bultmann, *Theologische Enzyklopädie*, 39–40.

34 See Bultmann, *Theologische Enzyklopädie*, 85, 91, 93, 131–132.

to the battle of all against all. Here are the *roots of our doubts*, our questioning the meaning of life.[35]

Bultmann's analysis of scientific-technological power over nature as the main issue of our times resembles in some respects what Benedict XVI says about Bacon, though Benedict is far from condemning science as sin. He recognizes much truth in it.[36]

> We must take a look at the foundations of the modern age. These appear with particular clarity in the thought of Francis Bacon. ...But what is the basis of this new era? It is the new correlation of experiment and method that enables man to arrive at an interpretation of nature in conformity with its laws and thus finally to achieve "the triumph of art over nature" (Bacon, *New Organon*, Bk. 1, 117). ...
>
> Anyone who reads and reflects on these statements attentively will recognize that a disturbing step has been taken: up to that time, the recovery of what man had lost through the expulsion from paradise was expected from faith in Jesus Christ: herein lay "redemption." Now, this "redemption," the restoration of the lost "paradise," is no longer expected from faith, but from the newly discovered link between science and praxis. It is not that faith is simply denied; rather it is displaced onto another level—that of purely private and other-worldly affairs—and at the same time it becomes somehow irrelevant for the world.
>
> This programmatic vision has determined the trajectory of modern times and it also shapes the present-day crisis of faith which is essentially a crisis of Christian hope. Thus hope too, in Bacon, acquires a new form. Now it is called: *faith in progress*.[37]

God. The first two points of this sketch (truth and sin) constitute the dialectic which lies at the roots of Bultmann's thought. This dialectic has two sharply distinct sides: one side is the non-objectified challenge of the moment; the other is

---

35 Antje Bultmann Lemke, "Bultmann's Papers," in Edward Hobbs, ed., *Bultmann, Retrospect and Prospect: The Centenary Symposium at Wellesley* (Philadelphia: Fortress, 1985), 11–12; emphasis added.

36 See esp. the conclusion of Benedict's "Faith, Reason and the University," quoted at the end of this essay.

37 Pope Benedict XVI, *Spe Salvi* [In Hope We Are Saved], Encyclical Letter on Christian Hope (November 30, 2007), 16–17 (Washington, DC: United States Conference of Catholic Bishops, 2007).

the sphere of objectified truth, the world of escape from the challenge, the world of science and sin.

Given these two sides, it is clear that Bultmann must locate God exclusively on the side of existential challenge.

> What is the question of God if not the question, "What is truth?" When the question of truth is posed accurately as the question of the moment, can it be anything but the question of God? For God, if he is thought at all, is thought as the power which rules the Now, as the challenge spoken into the Now.[38]

This definition of God must be taken in its full philosophical rigor. One must resist the temptation of distorting it by conforming it to the metaphysics of analogy and participation that informs the mainstream of the Christian tradition in conformity with its roots in Greek philosophy. For Bultmann, God does not have "being." God is the challenge of the moment and nothing besides. No being stands behind this challenge. For that being would be "objective," it would be something one can "talk about," something pulled down into the human sphere, something which is not necessarily felt as a challenge, something, therefore, which is contrary to the deepest nature of God as absolute Lord.

> The knowledge of God is the *knowledge of the challenge of the moment*. His call becomes heard as the demand which the moment places on us. God is invisible for the objectifying vision of scientific research.[39]

Scripture. The definition of God as the challenge of the moment does not imply that the voice of the moment is automatically God. If this were so, God would be available to philosophical analysis, because the moment is a universal human phenomenon. In fact, however, God is only available to faith in his historical revelation; he is a concrete historical Word spoken from beyond the moment into the moment.[40]

Can this revelation be identified? Yes, God is scriptural; God is a linguistic event which occurs when the Word of Scripture is proclaimed and preached.

> All proclamation points to Scripture, not as to its accidentally first stage, but as to that of which it speaks, namely, revelation. This first revelation, and nothing else, *is* revelation. ...Thus Scripture is the authority, the only authority for theology.[41]

---

38   Bultmann, *Theologische Enzyklopädie*, 50.
39   Bultmann, *Theologische Enzyklopädie*, 57.
40   See Bultmann, *Theologische Enzyklopädie*, 63.
41   Bultmann, *Theologische Enzyklopädie*, 169.

Bultmann thus affirms the principle *sola Scriptura* ("Scripture alone") in the most radical form possible. God himself is *sola Scriptura*.

Jesus. The definition of God as the linguistic event which occurs when the historical word of Scripture is proclaimed into my moment can be further specified. Jesus Christ is this Word of God.

> *God's revelation as a historical event is thus Jesus Christ as the Word of God.* This Word was instituted in the contingent historical event Jesus of Nazareth and it is alive in the tradition of the Church. The fact of Jesus Christ does not take on importance as a fact which is visible outside of the proclamation, but only as a fact which we encounter in the proclamation, as a fact made present by the proclamation. Jesus Christ is the Word.[42]

Bultmann makes two fundamental assertions in this text. On the one hand he asserts that Jesus is the unique Word of God. On the other hand he excludes any objective or metaphysical implications from this assertion. Jesus is significant for faith, not as a person with certain objective characteristics, divine or otherwise, but as the preached Jesus. The traditional dogma of his divinity is contrary to the inner meaning of revelation, because it falsely objectifies God. In the world of objective history, Jesus is simply a mere man, one among other human beings, with no supernatural attributes. However, he *does become significant when he is preached as God's definitive Word. As preached, his significance is indeed paramount and exclusive.*

Bultmann: Critical Reflections from a Catholic Perspective

On the positive side, one must acknowledge that Bultmann understood and lived central aspects of our modern situation with remarkable clarity and intensity. He did not blink at the clash between the modern scientific worldview and the Christian faith, but faced it head on. His critique of power is particularly incisive and anticipates many facets of the post-modern critique.

But there are problems in the manner in which he interprets the struggle and attempts to bring its forces together into a new synthesis. In attempting to resolve the clash between the scientific worldview and the Christian faith, he takes a violent shortcut: He uncritically accepts the mechanist worldview and then stages an all out witch-hunt on it. By pressing it into such a Lutheran dialectic he grants it too much and too little. Too much because he does not criticize it in detail; and too little because he condemns it entirely as an expression of sin and negates the elements of truth in it.

Perhaps the most central objection against Bultmann from a Catholic perspective is that he abandons the assent to the fundamental goodness of the world as God's creature. His neo-Kantian Lutheran ontology does not allow any other

---

42   Bultmann, *Theologische Enzyklopädie*, 95.

position. The objective world is the result of an inauthentic mode of human knowledge, namely, science. Far from being caused by God it arises as a self-enclosed objectification from human sin. In this respect Bultmann's ontology is close to gnosticism. Gift, in particular the gift of being, plays no role in it. A "hermeneutics of the gift" cannot get even the slightest foothold in this ontology.

Almost equally important from a Catholic perspective is the objection that Bultmann does not sufficiently respect the historical, literal meaning of the biblical texts as normative. To preach the Word of God as located in the non-objective sphere of existential challenge requires great conceptual clarity, a clarity which became possible only after the development of Bultmann's dialectical doctrine of knowledge. The ancient Christians did not have this clarity. If ancient Christian texts are mired in objectification, then Bultmann gives them too much credit when he interprets them as really proclaiming the non-objective Word of God. He reads them against their meaning. In his 1988 Erasmus Lecture, then-Cardinal Joseph Ratzinger points particularly to the interplay between historical critical scholarship and natural science in Bultmann's antagonistic reading.

> Modern exegesis, as we have seen [Bultmann was the example given], completely relegated God to the ungraspable, the non-worldly, and thus the ever inexpressible, but only in order to then be able to treat the biblical text itself as an entirely worldly thing, according to the methods of the natural sciences. In relation to the text it practices *physiologein* [reasoning in the manner of natural science]. As a "critical" science it claims an exactness and certitude similar to natural science. This claim is false, because it is based upon a misunderstanding of the dynamism and depth of the word.[43]

---

43   Cardinal Joseph Ratzinger, "Biblical Interpretation in Crisis," The Erasmus Lecture (January 27, 1988); published as "Biblical Interpretation in Crisis: On the Question of the Foundations and Approaches of Exegesis Today," in Richard J. Neuhaus, ed., *Biblical Interpretation in Crisis: The Ratzinger Conference on Bible and Church* (Grand Rapids MI: Eerdmans, 1989), 17–18; translation revised. For the German text, which includes some sections not present in this official English translation delivered by Ratzinger, see "Schriftauslegung im Widerstreit: Zur Frage nach Grundlagen und Weg der Exegese heute," in Joseph Ratzinger, *Wort Gottes: Schrift—Tradition—Amt* (Freiburg: Herder, 2005), 83–116, at 106. Two independent English translations of the longer German text are available: "Biblical Interpretation in Conflict: The Question of the Basic Principles and Path of Exegesis Today," in Joseph Ratzinger, *God's Word: Scripture—Tradition—Office*, trans. Henry Taylor (San Francisco: Ignatius, 2008); "Biblical Interpretation in Conflict: On the Foundations and the Itinerary of Exegesis Today," trans. Aidan Walker, in José Granados, Carlos Granados, and Luis Sánchez-Navarro, eds., *Opening up the Scriptures: Joseph Ratzinger and the Foundations of Biblical Interpretation* (Grand Rapids, MI: Eerdmans, 2008), 1–29.

Bultmann protests emphatically, "Scripture is the authority, the only authority for theology."[44] But in fact, a neo-Kantian doctrine of knowledge determines what can, and what cannot, be Word of God. What is required to let the biblical text unfold its own dynamism is an "open philosophy." Two fundamental ideas characterize such an open philosophy, according to Ratzinger's Erasmus Lecture: human beings are open to transcending the world toward God; and God is able to open them from within by the gift of communion with himself.

Ratzinger singles out St. Thomas Aquinas as providing the true starting point by his metaphysics and theology of analogy and participation.

> Thomas Aquinas grasped these two ideas metaphysically in the principles of analogy and participation and thus made possible an open philosophy that is capable of accepting the biblical phenomenon in all its radicalism. Instead of the dogmatism of a supposedly scientific world picture, the challenge for today is to think further in the direction of such an open philosophy, in order to find once again the presuppositions for understanding the Bible.[45]

The development of such an open philosophy based on Aquinas, centered on analogy and participation, can prevent pressing the biblical text into a closed philosophy.

> At its core, the debate about modern exegesis is not a dispute among historians: it is rather a philosophical debate. Only in this way can it be carried on correctly; otherwise we continue with a battle in the mist. In this respect, the exegetical problem is identical with our time's struggle about the foundations as such. …
>
> The exegete should approach the exegesis of the text not with a ready-made philosophy, not with the dictate of a so-called modern or scientific worldview, which determines in advance what is permitted to be and what is not permitted to be. He may not exclude a priori that *God is able to speak as himself in human words in the world*.[46]

---

44 Bultmann, *Theologische Enzyklopädie*, 169.

45 Ratzinger, "Schriftauslegung im Widerstreit," 109. This passage is missing from "Biblical Interpretation," as delivered. For an English translation, see Granados, *Opening up the Scriptures*, 23.

46 Ratzinger, "Biblical Interpretation," 16, 19; "Schriftauslegung im Widerstreit," 104, 107; emphasis added; translation revised.

Raymond Brown on the Truth of Scripture

One of my advisors for my doctoral thesis on John at Harvard, a scholar close to Bultmann, warned me against Brown's commentary on John. "It is vitiated by a strong Catholic metaphysical bias and by an animus against the scientific discoveries made by Bultmann and his school, particularly John's close relation to gnosticism. Bultmann and Nag Hammadi are dirty words for Brown."

As happens at times with wayward students, this warning warmed my interest and I invested much time in studying Brown's commentary. Particularly in comparison with Bultmann, I found it to be a work of refreshing sanity and common sense in its use of the tools of historical criticism. I also found deep theological insight in it. I was therefore not surprised when, during the seminar that followed his 1988 Erasmus Lecture, Cardinal Ratzinger praised Brown, who was present among the participants at the seminar. The Cardinal expressed his wish that Germany had more exegetes who were as deeply rooted in the Catholic tradition and as faithful to the magisterium as Brown was.

Given this context, it is with reluctance that I focus on Brown's reading of the truth of Scripture in his 1980 essay "The Human Word of the Almighty God."[47] The essay proposes a violently simple and impatient solution of the complex problem of the truth of Scripture, a solution that comes in the end quite close to Bultmann. It cuts the Gordian knot of biblical truth with one stroke of the Enlightenment sword by claiming, "God does not speak." According to Brown, *Dei Verbum 11* ("All that the inspired authors and sacred writers affirm is to be held as affirmed by the Holy Spirit") is simply false. God is unable to speak as himself in human words in the world.

The best way to approach Brown's essay, I am convinced, is with a rigorous application of canonical criticism in light of Brown's work as a whole, especially his 1955 dissertation on the *sensus plenior* and his commentary on John. Such a canonical reading relativizes the thesis of the essay as a thesis at odds with Brown's real intentions.

First, however, let us focus on the essay in itself, outside the canon, as Brown himself would advise us in determining the *sensus literalis*. The clarity and simplicity of the thesis, "God does not speak," even if it is in the end too clear and simple, is extremely helpful for what Lichtenberg calls "philosophy and reflection."

> Many of us think that at Vatican II the Catholic Church "turned the corner" in the inerrancy question. ...Those who wish to read *Dei Verbum* in a minimalist way [that is, as involving minimal change in the Church's position] can point out that the sentence immediately preceding the one I just quoted says that every-

---

47 Raymond E. Brown, "The Human Word of the Almighty God," in *The Critical Meaning of the Bible* (New York: Paulist, 1981), 1–22. The essay was first delivered as a lecture in 1980 at Georgetown University.

thing in Scripture is asserted by the Holy Spirit and can argue that therefore "what God wanted put into the Scripture for the sake of our salvation" (which is without error) means every view the human author expressed in Scripture. However, there is noncritical exegesis of Church documents as well as noncritical exegesis of Scripture. Consequently, to determine the real meaning of *Dei Verbum* one must study the discussions in the Council that produced it, and one must comb a body of evidence that can be read in different ways. [Footnote:] The evidence is given and interpreted in the Grillmeier article.[48]

Brown explains what he means by a critical exegesis of Church documents. When the Catholic Church changes her mind, he argues, it is her practice "gracefully to retain what was salvageable from the past and to move in a new direction with as little friction as possible."[49] The original draft of *Dei Verbum*, which Brown classifies as "far-right" and "ultraconservative," suffered a stinging defeat in 1962, "and so it became a matter of face-saving that in the revisions and in the final form of the constitution the ultraconservatives should have their say."[50] The supposed face-saving left many traces, but its principal trace is the sentence, "All that the inspired authors and sacred writers affirm is to be held as affirmed by the Holy Spirit."

It is not easy to work out Brown's hypothesis in detail. Is he saying that the centrist majority allowed the ultraconservative minority to add a statement which they, the centrists, considered false? Is he saying that the centrists voted for that false statement to be included in an authoritative formulation of Catholic doctrine simply to perform a face-saving maneuver on behalf of their ultraconservative fellow-bishops? Would not the use of falsehood as official doctrine, just to avoid clerical friction, be rather shamelessly vapid horse trading? Is this a likely historical critical reconstruction of what actually happened at Vatican II, even leaving aside the Catholic belief that the Council's deliberation was guided by the Holy Spirit?

At the beginning of his essay Brown assures the reader. "First, I fully accept the Roman Catholic doctrine of the Bible as the Word of God and the whole discussion assumes that fact."[51] He adds that there is a need for discussion because a "real struggle" is going on about how the Roman Catholic doctrine is to be understood.

> The real struggle, which is between the Catholic center and the Catholic far right, does not imperil the Catholic doctrine

---

48   Brown, *Critical Meaning of the Bible*, 18–19.

49   Brown, *Critical Meaning of the Bible*, 18, n. 41.

50   Brown, *Critical Meaning of the Bible*, 18.

51   Brown, *Critical Meaning of the Bible*, 3.

of the Bible as the Word of God, which both accept. In this
instance, as in most others, the struggle concerns the *meaning* of
the doctrine. It gets nasty only when the far right claims that its
understanding of the doctrine constitutes doctrine.[52]

Brown sees an apparent contradiction in the phrase "Word of God" that needs to
be resolved.

> *"The word of God" … is a human word, for God does not speak.*
> But it is *of* God, and not simply a human composition about
> God. The Bible makes us confront the seeming contradiction of
> a divine self-revelation in human terms.
>
> This is no minor issue, because if God did not actually speak
> words (external or internal) one must admit clearly and firmly
> that every word in the history of the human race, including the
> biblical period, is a time-conditioned word, affected by limita-
> tions of human insight and problems. The attribution of a Word
> to God, to Jesus, or to the Church would not enable that word
> to escape limitation.[53]

In a footnote at the end of this text Brown writes:

> This statement is sometimes translated hostilely as a denial of
> absolute truth. There is a God and God is truth; and so there
> is absolute truth. The affirmation made above would mean only
> that every human perception of that truth is *partial*. The op-
> posite affirmation would be that a human statement about God
> can be exhaustive.[54]

Brown's argument in this footnote is very condensed and not fully clear. One possible way of understanding it is as an argument by *reductio ad absurdum* ("reduction
to the absurd"). The conclusion to be established is, "God does not speak." As in
any *reductio*, one assumes the opposite of the conclusion to see what follows. Let
us assume, then, that God does speak human words, not in the sense of producing
them by his own vocal chords or as actually distinct inner words, but in the sense
of affirming the truth expressed by these words.

What follows from this assumption, according to Brown? The absolute truth,
with which God is identical, is fully exhaustive. In the one Logos, God expresses
himself and all things. Therefore, if God affirms the truth in a statement made by

52   Brown, *Critical Meaning of the Bible*, 3.

53   Brown, *Critical Meaning of the Bible*, 1, 4.

54   Brown, *Critical Meaning of the Bible*, 4, n. 8.

human words, that statement must be fully exhaustive, which is absurd. No human statement can be exhaustive, because all our perception of the truth expressed in words is partial. Therefore it is absurd to claim that God himself speaks in human words.

This argument makes a rather obvious mistake. From the statement, "God affirms the truth in a statement made by human words," it jumps to the statement, "God affirms the comprehensive truth in that statement." Why should God be incapable of affirming a partial truth, precisely what is affirmed in a particular statement, as long as it is "absolutely" true in the sense of being really true?

The main bulk of Brown's article, in fact, follows another path to the same conclusion, a path Brown considers proper to the historical critical study of Scripture. "My contribution will be entirely from the vantage point of biblical criticism."[55] Among other possible paths, Brown foregoes that of systematic theology.

> I do not plan to consider the Word of God … in the context … of systematic theology (for example, whether there is a magisterial position or a unanimous theological position on what 'the Word of God' means). [Footnote:] In any case, it would be almost impossible to show that past writers or magisterial statements were dealing with the problem to be discussed here, for *its particular nuance stems from modern biblical insights*.[56]

What are the modern biblical insights that supersede the point of view of systematic theology to such a degree that, even if there were a position of the magisterium or a consensus of Catholic theology as a whole on the meaning of "Word of God," it would be "almost impossible to show" its relevance, because the problem to be discussed is so new? These insights must indeed be weighty, if they can nuance the very problem so substantially that all past writers and magisterial statements become irrelevant.

Brown lays out the modern biblical insights in two sections, one of them devoted to revelation, that is, to intra-biblical claims to direct speech by God ("Thus says the Lord"), the other to inspiration, that is, to the claim that the Bible as a whole is the Word of God, even when no such direct intra-biblical divine speech is involved.

Under the heading of "revelation" Brown first considers claims by the prophets that they pass on words received from God. The redaction history of prophetic oracles is the main insight that leads Brown to conclude that these oracles are not, in fact, words directly received from God, but words formulated by the prophets. The prophets encountered a divine "message," but the mode of that "message"

---

55 Brown, *Critical Meaning of the Bible*, 5.
56 Brown, *Critical Meaning of the Bible*, 5, n. 11; emphasis added.

was not verbal. Brown does not explain how a "message" from God can be made intelligible to a human being without any concepts or words. "The message is the message of God, but the words are words of Jeremiah."[57]

Brown makes the same point about the Decalogue. "The question of whether a revealing God ever communicates in words comes to a head in an Old Testament perspective in the encounter between Moses and God on Sinai. In Jewish thought this was the supreme experience of God."[58] Brown once again uses redaction history (the two extant versions of the Decalogue) to argue that the Ten Commandments are not words spoken by God, but "human formulations of a less specified revelation of divine moral demand."[59] How a divine moral demand could be communicated to a human being without specific statements in inner or outer words is, once again, a point Brown does not explain.

For the words of Jesus, Brown changes the basis of his argument. His principal point (emphasized in the text below) resembles the *reductio ad absurdum* argument analyzed above.

> In the words of Jesus it is dubious that one encounters *an unconditional, timeless Word spoken by God*. The Son of God who speaks in the first three Gospels is a Jew of the first third of the first century, who thinks in much of the world view of this time. The Jesus of the Fourth Gospel, who is pre-existent, does claim to have heard words in the presence of his Father and to have brought them to earth ... but when one examines the words of the Johannine Jesus critically, they are often a variant form of the tradition known in the synoptics.[60]

Redaction criticism plays an important role, but the whole question is decided ahead of time in the very first sentence by the phrase "an unconditional, timeless word spoken by God." As in the *reductio* analyzed above, there is a mistaken jump in Brown's argument. Conditioned, time-bound words can be true. Why should God's use of them to affirm a truth involve their being suddenly stripped of their conditioned, time-bound nature?

Words of the risen Jesus present a special problem in Brown's mind, because through his resurrection Jesus attained an unconditional, timeless existence. His words, therefore, could qualify as attaining an unconditional, timeless character. Yet, the redaction history of these words once again suggests that they are conditioned and time-bound. They are later human formulations of encounters with Jesus that involved entirely non-verbal encounters and revelations.

---

57   Brown, *Critical Meaning of the Bible*, 9.

58   Brown, *Critical Meaning of the Bible*, 9–10.

59   Brown, *Critical Meaning of the Bible*, 10.

60   Brown, *Critical Meaning of the Bible*, 12; emphasis added.

What we seem to have is a communication by the risen Jesus that was only later vocalized in words as the various communities and writers came post factum to understand the import of the revelation. The category of "speaking" may be an inadequate way to describe the unique, eschatological encounter with the risen Jesus—an approximation of this revelation to ordinary experience. If so, the study of the "words" of the risen Jesus (who has passed *beyond* the limitations of human circumstances) may reflect the thesis that only human beings speak words and that revelation by the Word of God really means divine revelation to which human beings have given expression in words.[61]

This text concludes Brown's treatment of "Word of God" under the heading of "revelation," that is, of words about which the Bible itself claims that they are directly spoken by God. If in all these instances it can be shown that God does not speak, then the conclusion follows *a fortiori* for the "Word of God" under the heading of "inspiration," which covers the whole Bible, including words about which the Bible itself does not claim that they are directly spoken by God.

Brown's argument under the heading "inspiration" is much simpler. Historical critical exegesis has shown that Scripture contains errors, both in secular matters and in matters of faith and morals bearing on eternal salvation. An example of the latter, Brown argues, is the denial of immortality in Job 14:13–22 and Sirach 14:16–17; 17:22–23; 38:21. If Scripture were the word of God in the sense that God himself affirms what the text affirms, such errors should be impossible.

In what sense, then, is Scripture the word of God. It is not of God in the sense of being a word affirmed or asserted by God, in which case one could rely on God's truthfulness. It is of God in the sense of being only of man, but of man as an attempt to express a non-verbal "message" or "revelation" that is of God. This human attempt often falls into error. Nevertheless, the Bible as a whole is a reliable divine communication, because errors in one book are relativized when that book is placed in the canon of Scripture as a whole.

If one discovers religious errors, one does not seek to explain them away; one recognizes that God is willing to work with human beings in all their limitations, and that each author's contribution is only part of a larger presentation of biblical truth. …We have spent too much time protecting the God who inspired the Scriptures from limitations that he seems not to have been concerned about. The impassioned debate about inerrancy tells us less about divine omnipotence (which presumably allows

---

61   Brown, *Critical Meaning of the Bible*, 14.

God to be relaxed) than about our own insecurity in looking for absolute answers.[62]

Omnipotence is not the point, one must object against this evasive text. The point is truth or falsity. It is easy for God to feel relaxed (and for Brown to feel secure) about the truth of Scripture if he does not say anything.

Brown's "Human Word of the Almighty God" in Context

Brown's argument for the conclusion that God does not speak is an argument, he claims, that is drawn from insights gained by modern historical critical studies of the Bible. On the surface, the insights are mainly those of tradition and redaction criticism (in Part One of the essay) and the errors of Scripture both in secular matters and in matters of faith and morals (in Part Two of the essay).

Let us focus on Part One, which is more important and revealing. When one compares the arguments from tradition and redaction criticism with the conclusion they are supposed to establish, one notices a disproportion in universality. The arguments about the redaction history of prophetic oracles suggest that in some cases what the prophets call "words of God" in the most direct sense ("Thus says the Lord") are, in fact, mere human words, subsequently placed on the lips of God. At least in these particular cases, the arguments suggest, God did not speak. It is logically impossible to get the full universality of the conclusion, "God does not speak (God never speaks)," from these arguments. Might not one or the other prophetic oracle really be a verbatim rendition of actual words of God?

Another sort of argument is clearly involved in Brown's mind to supply the missing universality of his conclusion. One might suppose that it is the argument he sketches at various points as a *reductio ad absurdum*. If God spoke in human words, these words would have to be comprehensive, unconditional and timeless. No human words can have these qualities. Therefore, it is absurd to hold that God speaks in human words.

I do not think that this argument represents the true heart of Brown's concerns or that he invested the full power of his most considered thought in it. It sounds like a memory of his early neo-Scholastic training, a bad memory. In order to identify the argument (or, rather, the force) that pushes Brown, it is helpful to draw out an important corollary from the thesis that God does not speak.

If God does not speak, if only human beings speak, then the literal sense of Scripture is exclusively a human sense. There is no divine intention and affirmation in the letter of Scripture that needs to be taken into account in determining the literal sense, although a non-verbal divine message has passed to the inspired writer. The theologically neutral discipline of historical critical exegesis, which is practiced as a secular discipline in the academy, is the competent discipline to

---

62   Brown, *Critical Meaning of the Bible*, 17–18.

determine the sense of the letter. It is the only competent discipline and it is sufficiently competent. It does not need explicitly theological principles, such as those
affirmed in the final paragraph of *Dei Verbum* 12, which speaks about reading
Scripture in the same Spirit in which it was written: according to the unity of
Scripture; its reading in the Tradition; and the analogy of faith. These theological principles would have a bearing on the literal sense of Scripture only if God
himself affirmed what the text says. Just as mathematical physics does not need any
theological principles, because it deals with matters that are intelligible in terms
of this world alone, so also the historical critical exegesis of Scripture, because the
literal sense of Scripture is exclusively human. Brown repeats this corollary like a
mantra throughout the essay: historical critical exegesis is in charge of the literal
sense. That is the consensus in the scientific academy.

In his 1955 dissertation, by contrast, Brown defines the literal sense as follows.

> The literal sense is that which both the Holy Spirit and the
> human author directly and proximately intended, and which
> the words directly convey, either properly or metaphorically.
> The literal sense must be intended by both God and the human
> author.[63]

This definition is closely related to *Dei Verbum* 11. "All that the inspired authors
or sacred writers affirm is to be held as affirmed by the Holy Spirit." According
to Brown's 1955 definition of the literal sense, God *does* speak in it. He speaks by
intending the sense of the words of Scripture. God himself, not only the human
author, affirms the truth conveyed by these words. One can hold God himself
accountable, not only the human author. Are you telling me the truth? If the
meaning is intended by God, the answer is clear. The truthfulness of truth itself
guarantees the truth of the words, understood rightly.

If God himself speaks in the literal sense, a method appropriate to merely
human speech will not be sufficient. Theological principles for determining the
literal sense will have to be used, above all the principles mentioned by *Dei Verbum*
12: Scripture must be read "in the same Spirit by whom (or in whom) it was written *[eodem Spiritu quo scripta est]*."

What Brown asserts in his 1955 definition of the literal sense is precisely
what he denies twenty-five years later in the thesis that "God does not speak." The
main difference is the disappearance of the *analogia verbi*, that is, of analogy and
participation in the use of the terms "speak, intend, affirm, word" for both God
and human beings.

---

63 Raymond E. Brown, *The Sensus Plenior of Sacred Scripture* (Baltimore: St. Mary's University,
1955), 4–5; emphasis in original.

Let us focus on the concept of analogy. In the Psalmist's line: "I will sing of your steadfast love ... for you have been a fortress for me,"[64] "love" is an analogical term, "fortress" is a metaphor. God loves, properly speaking, but is a fortress only in an improper, transferred sense. A fortress is more truly a fortress than God is, but God is more truly love than human love is, even though we know and name human love first. Nevertheless, although "love" is used in a proper sense, it is not used univocally, because "between the Creator and the creature no likeness can be expressed without the need of expressing a greater unlikeness."[65]

In human speech one must distinguish the outer act of pronouncing words and the interior mental act of conceiving a statement. The outer act of speech, understood as producing sounds, can be said of God only metaphorically, because God has no body. Just as God does not walk, properly speaking, so he does not make sounds. The second, the inner speech in concepts, can be said analogously, just as "God knows" is analogous. In fact, the only speech that is truly and fully speech in that interior sense is God's own eternal speech, in which he expresses the truth about himself and all things by his interior Word.[66] "God spoke only once, once only because he keeps on speaking for ever. For He is one single, uninter-rupted, and eternal speech act."[67] Finite human interior speech is an analogical participation in this true and full speech. Although God cannot make sounds by vocal cords, he can use sounds or letters to express his knowledge.

It is on this basis that the theological tradition understands Scripture as the Word of God. If God speaks the truth comprehensively in his eternal Word, he can *a fortiori* take up human words to speak in an analogous sense. He can affirm a partial truth in finite human words, since these words are analogous participations in his eternal Word. This *analogia verbi* was Brown's conviction in his dissertation. Brown's argument in the 1980 essay is thus rooted in the rejection of the *analogia verbi*. God never speaks.

The Analogia Verbi in Brown's Commentary on John

The *analogia verbi* is much more resoundingly present in Brown's 1966 commentary on John than in his 1955 dissertation. My Bultmannian thesis advisor was quite right to see a pervasive Catholic metaphysics in that commentary. Given Luther's roots in nominalist philosophy, he labored hard to eliminate the metaphysics and

---

64 Ps. 59:16.

65 Fourth Council of the Lateran, "Constitution on the Error of the Abbot Joachim" (1215), in Henirich Denzinger, ed., *Enchiridion Symbolorum Definitonum et Declarationum de Rebus Fidei et Morum* [Handbook of Creeds, Definitions and Declarations concerning Matters of Faith and Morals], 32nd. ed. (Freiberg: Herder, 1963), 806; Eng.: *The Sources of Catholic Dogma* (Fitzwilliam, NH: Loreto, 2002).

66 John 1:1.

67 St. Bernard, *Sermons on Various Subjects*, 5, 2; as translated in Farkasfalvy, *Scripture & Interpretation*, 205, n. 2.

theology of analogy and participation, which had become unintelligible to him. With his nominalist glasses he inevitably saw analogy and participation as human boasting in competition against God. I have my own goodness (says the papist), which I can raise up as a claim before God. God must reward me for it, because it is truly my own. In the project of de-Hellenization Bultmann follows out Luther through Kant to the bitter end, as one can see in his commentary on John.[68]

The following passage from Brown's commentary on John 6:54–57 provides a sharp contrast to Bultmannian de-Hellenization. It exemplifies how analogy and participation are built into the very foundations of Brown's reading of John.

> A comparison of verses 6:54 ["The one who feeds on my flesh and drinks my blood has eternal life]" and 56 ["The one who feeds on my flesh and drinks my blood remains in me and I in him"] shows that to have eternal life is to be in close communion with Jesus; it is a question of the Christian's remaining (*menein*) in Jesus and Jesus' remaining in the Christian. In verse 27 Jesus spoke of the food that lasts (*menein*) for eternal life, that is, an imperishable food that is the source of eternal life. In verse 56 the *menein* is applied not to the food but to the life it produces and nourishes. Communion with Jesus is really a participation in the intimate communion that exists between Father and Son. Verse 57 ["Just as the living Father sent me, and I live because of the Father, so the one who feeds on me will live because of me"] simply mentions the communion between Father and Son with an assumption that the reader will understand. ... Verse 57 is a most forceful expression of the tremendous claim that Jesus gives *man a share in God's own life*, an expression far more real than the abstract formulation of 2 Peter 1:4 ["sharers in the divine nature"]. And so it is that, while the synoptic Gospels record the institution of the Eucharist, it is John who explains what the Eucharist does for the Christian. Just as the Eucharist itself echoes the theme of the covenant ("blood of the covenant"—Mark 14:24), so also the mutual indwelling of God (and Jesus) and the Christian may be a reflection of the covenant theme. Jeremiah 24:7 and 31:33 take the covenant promise, "You will be my people and I shall be your God," and give it the intimacy of working in man's heart.[69]

---

68 See my "Evolution of Bultmann's Interpretation of John and Gnosticism."

69 Raymond E. Brown, *The Gospel According to John*, 2 vols., Anchor Bible 29 (New York: Doubleday, 1966), 1:292–293.

From a Bultmannian perspective, it is precisely the analogy of the term "life" and the "real" participation in divine life that spoil Brown's reading of John 6. He is simply re-chewing Greek rational metaphysics, which John has shed by affirming the paradox of incarnation, the supreme offense against Greek reason. "The event of the revelation is a question, is an offense. *This and nothing else is meant by, The Word became flesh.*"[70] Brown misses the point most fundamentally when he writes about "the intimate communion that exists between Father and Son." Nothing exists between Father and Son. Father and Son are just the standard Greek fantasy about a supra-mundane divine world, a slight variation on Middle-Platonic and Gnostic motifs. As moderns, whose thinking is scientifically sophisticated, we cannot "still believe" that this Platonizing fantasy is true. We cannot go back behind Kant.

This is the first feature to be highlighted in Brown's text, namely, the solidity of the metaphysics and theology of analogy and participation in his reading of John. For Brown, Father and Son are not Greek fantasies. They are the real source of being, life and communion. "Life" and "communion" are said analogously of them and us; we receive a real participation in this life and communion above all in the Eucharist. What Bultmann dismisses as background overcome by John, Brown affirms as true. It is difficult to exaggerate this contrast. Brown and Bultmann are polar opposites in their reading of John.

The second feature of Brown's commentary on John 6:54–57 is the sense of the Word's presence. The text of John, which resumes the covenant promise, mediates a present "intimacy of working in man's heart." It is in the present that the God of the covenant says, "You are mine and I am yours," just as the Son says to the Father, "All that is mine is yours and what is yours is mine."[71] One can hardly overlook Brown's own faith in this reading of John. It is a reading, not only by a historical scholar, who ascertains a past act of speech as an uninvolved observer, but by a living man who is addressed by a living act of speech and apprehends it as a true testimony in personal faith: "I believe you." Brown does not write, "It was John who explained back then in Hellenistic categories what the Eucharist was back then thought to do for Hellenistic Christians; we today, of course, think quite differently, because we know that the universe follows exceptionless mathematical laws." He writes, "It is John who explains what the Eucharist does for the Christian."

Particularly the second feature shows that Brown's understanding of the literal sense in this passage is not sufficiently expressed in his definition of the literal sense in the *New Jerome Biblical Commentary*.

---

70   Rudolf Bultmann, *Das Evangelium des Johannes*, 21st ed. (Göttingen: Vandenhoeck & Ruprecht, 1986), 39; emphasis added. Eng.: *The Gospel of John: A Commentary*, trans. G. R. Beasley-Murray (Oxford: Blackwell, 1971).

71   John 17:10.

> Most exegetes, if we may judge from their commentaries on Scripture, would be working with a definition of the literal sense closely resembling the following. *The sense which the human author directly intended and which the written words conveyed.*[72]

This definition is not a sufficient account of what Brown himself actually does as an exegete of John 6:54–57. It does not account for the present divine act of speech, the present divine testimony apprehended by personal faith. Brown's definition in his dissertation does more justice to his actual exegesis.

> The literal sense is that which both the Holy Spirit and the human author directly and proximately intended, and which the words directly convey, either properly or metaphorically. The literal sense must be intended by both God and the human author.[73]

In his opening meditation for the 2008 Synod, Benedict XVI reflected on a passage from Psalm 118 (verses 89–94) precisely along these lines of the Word's presence. The final words of the passage contain the urgent appeal, which is that of every believer in the present: "I am yours; save me." In hearing the Word of God, Benedict XVI comments, we do not only hear someone's past speech, as would be the case in mere human speech, but we also hear a present act of speech.

> It is a great danger … in our reading of Scripture that we stop at the human words, words from the past, past history, and we do not discover the present in the past, the Holy Spirit who speaks to us today in the words of the past. In this way we do not enter the interior movement of the Word, which in human words conceals and reveals divine words. Therefore, there is always a need for seeking. We must always look for the Word within the words. …
>
> With his incarnation he said: I am yours. And in baptism he said to me: I am yours. In the Holy Eucharist, he says ever anew: I am yours, so that we may respond: Lord, I am yours. In the way of the Word, entering the mystery of his incarnation, of his being among us, we want to appropriate his being, we want to expropriate our existence, giving ourselves to him who gave himself to us.

---

72 Raymond E. Brown, Joseph Fitzmyer, and Roland Murphy, eds., *New Jerome Biblical Commentary* (Englewood Cliffs, NJ: Prentice-Hall, 1990), 1148.

73 Brown, *Sensus Plenior*, 4–5; emphasis in original.

"I am yours." Let us pray the Lord that we may learn to say this
Word with our whole being. Thus we will be in the heart of the
Word. Thus we will be saved.[74]

What Benedict focuses on, particularly in the latter part of this text, which concludes his meditation, is the covenantal theme of self-gift and communion, which
Brown focuses on in his comments on John 6:54–57. It is here that one finds the
heart of the sense of presence of the Word. This sense of presence is possible only
if someone really intends the meaning of the words in the present. It cannot be the
human intention of John alone, because he spoke (and wrote) and then fell silent. If
the literal sense were an exclusively human sense, if God did not speak as himself
in it, the sense of presence would be lost. Against his own theoretical hermeneutical writings, Brown's commentary agrees with the *analogia verbi*.

Dei Verbum 8 helps to drive home this sense of the Word's presence. "God,
who spoke in the past, speaks without any break with the bride of his beloved Son."
In the spousal dialogue it is very important exactly who speaks to whom and when
exactly. One may well be able to exchange marriage vows by proxy, letting someone
else speak for oneself, even by authorized letters, but the consummation of the
vows, the full gift of self, "I am yours," and its renewal in the total bodily gift of self
throughout married life must be a present living word spoken in person. Unless
God himself speaks to the bride as himself, he does not give the spousal gift of self,
"I am yours." In that case, all we have is the memory of past words of a bridegroom
who has long been dead, if he ever existed. This is the sharp existential point of
the sword of God's word in the *analogia verbi*. This is what is really at stake in *Dei
Verbum* 11, "All that the inspired authors or sacred writers affirm is to be held as
affirmed by the Holy Spirit."

Brown's Denial of the Analogia Verbi

Brown's 1980 essay on the "Word of God" throws this *analogia verbi* overboard in a
spasm of de-Hellenization. No analogy, no participation connects the word of the
Bible with the eternal Word. God does not speak. The *analogia verbi* disappears
in a flash. By the same token, the analogy and participation of life must disappear
as well. Is Brown ready to pay this price? Clearly not! He would have to renounce
everything he says about John and the Eucharist. His commentary on John has
more weight than his theoretical 1980 essay. In the seminar following the Erasmus
Lecture, he emphasized again and again in discussion with Cardinal Ratzinger
that he does not see himself as a theoretician of the historical critical method, but
primarily as a practitioner (more on this below).

---

74 Pope Benedict XVI, Address at the Opening of the 12th Ordinary General Assembly of the
Synod of Bishops (October 6, 2008). Available oneline at: http://www.vatican.va/roman_curia/
synod/index.htm.

Nevertheless, it remains a fact that he says in his 1980 essay, "God does not speak." What force is responsible for this sudden denial of the *analogia verbi*, which is so deeply at odds with the fundamental intentions of Brown's work as a whole? Let us formulate the question slightly differently. What force in contemporary academic culture is most directly opposed to the metaphysics and theology of analogy and participation? Once the question is formulated in this way, the answer suggests itself of its own accord: modern natural science and its nominalist philosophical premises. The academy has great power to socialize its members into a "full obedience of intellect and will" with respect to these philosophical premises, which historically came to constitute this particular mode of natural science in its present form. Peer review is one of the modes in which this power is exercised, but there are many other capillary and atmospheric modes. Structures of plausibility and intellectual customs are slowly built up by this pressure and Enlightenment prejudices thereby achieve the status of the self-evident. The universe follows mathematical laws, without exception.

Brown is clearly aware of the power of Enlightenment prejudices and he openly resists it to some degree. He responds to those who attack the historical critical method by conceding that it carries some such prejudices. At the same time, he adds qualifiers that all but eliminate his concession. The method carries them only in some instances and only as external accretions.

> Rhetorically I would wish to ask … what is there in the nature of the historical critical method that should have ever prevented its practitioners from being members of the believing community, and is … [one] not blaming a method for the prejudices of some who employ it. It is true that, as a child of the post-Enlightenment, biblical criticism has tended to be almost doctrinaire in its skepticism about the transcendent, for example, in ruling out of court any evidence that Jesus worked miracles … But it is time that we identify such prejudices as regrettable accretions rather than as intrinsic principles of the method.[75]

Brown's claim that Enlightenment prejudices are quite external to the historical critical method may *de iure* ["in principle"] be true, simply considering redaction criticism, for example, as a technique in the abstract. *De facto* ["in fact"] however, this claim is simply false. The phrase "regrettable accretions rather than intrinsic principles" underestimates the capillary and atmospheric action of Enlightenment prejudices in the historical-critical method as it has actually been practiced in the academy. Brown correctly locates the thesis, "There are no miracles," near the top of the list of Enlightenment philosophical prejudices. Yet, his own thesis, "God

---

75   Raymond E. Brown, "What the Biblical Word Meant and What it Means," in *Critical Meaning of the Bible*, 23–44.

does not speak," is simply another one of these prejudices, not far from the top either. That this obvious fact escaped his own notice is a sign of the great power of Enlightenment prejudices in academic practice.

In his "Addendum," written after the seminar on the Erasmus Lecture, Brown sees himself as untouched by philosophical prejudices. Already in the seminar discussion, he had deflected Cardinal Ratzinger's philosophical critique of Bultmann by claiming he himself, like many in the Anglo-Saxon world, were practitioners of the historical-critical method, interested in facts, not bound by abstract philosophical theories.

> Much of Cardinal Ratzinger's paper is directed against the philosophy that he detects in historical-critical exegesis. ...The Cardinal argues, "The debate about modern exegesis is not a dispute among historians; it is rather a philosophical debate." ...
>
> To explain my divergence here I must speak of my training. *I obtained a master's degree in philosophy, writing on the philosophical background of Einstein,* before I did any graduate biblical studies. ...Yet, like many Americans and Anglo-Saxons who did not do their graduate biblical studies in Germany, *I never had laid out for me a master philosophy* according to which I should practice exegesis. My biblical training was highly historical critical. ...
>
> I recognize that what the Cardinal has described has been the philosophy of many practitioners of the method, but *the fact that I could learn the method entirely differently calls into question whether the flaws are in the method itself.* I do recognize philosophical questions about the historical critical method, but in my judgment *they are not questions about the possibility of the supernatural.* ... I hope that such a practical rather than a philosophical approach is not simply an American versus a German way of thinking.[76]

The question: "Can God speak as himself with human words in the world?" is, in fact, very well described as one of the "questions about the possibility of the supernatural." With noticeable pride Brown mentions his Master's thesis about the philosophical background of Einstein. "Einstein, on whom I wrote my thesis, is unimpeachable! Germans may revel in philosophy. We Americans are more practical. We are interested in facts. We are scientists, like Einstein at Princeton. We only do philosophy as far as we need it for science!" Einstein, of course, was a

---

76 Raymond E. Brown, "Addenda," in Neuhaus, *Biblical Interpretation in Crisis,* 37–49, at 44–47; emphasis added.

German, and Einstein's most direct intellectual ancestor Descartes, who supplied the master philosophy for Einstein, was not American either. America, Alexis de Tocqueville observes in his chapter on "Philosophical Method of the Americans," is the country "where the precepts of Descartes are least studied and are best applied. ...The Americans do not read the works of Descartes ... but they follow his maxims."[77] Brown did not learn the historical-critical method quite as differently as he thinks. Like Bultmann, he identifies with the scientific academy, apparently unaware of the violent self-limitation of reason to the master paradigm of mathematical mechanics in the wake of Bacon and Descartes. Bultmann realized the philosophical implications of this self-limitation more clearly.

Brown radicalizes his Enlightenment prejudices in the essay, "What the Biblical Word Meant and What it Means." He makes a sharp distinction between what the Bible meant in the past (when it was written, the literal meaning of the Bible) and what the Bible means at present (in the life of the Church, which is not its literal, but its ecclesiastical meaning, a kind of typological application). The Church's authority as an interpreter of the Bible extends only to the latter meaning. The Church has no authority to speak about the literal sense. Neutral historical critical scholarship is fully in charge of what the Bible meant, of the literal sense; the non-neutral Church is free to play only with the ecclesiastical sense. The two meanings can diverge to the point of sharp tension.

> What a passage *means* to Christians is the issue for the Church— not the semi-historical issue of what it *meant* to the person who wrote it. ...To the best of my knowledge the Roman Catholic Church has never defined the literal sense of a single passage of the Bible. ...[The Church was not wrong] at Trent in insisting that its doctrine of seven sacraments, eucharistic sacrifice, and priestly ordination were a valid interpretation of Scripture—an interpretation of what by symbiosis Scripture had come to mean in Church life, but not necessarily an interpretation of what it meant in the mind of those who wrote the pertinent passages.[78]

One reason why what the Bible meant cannot be determined by the Church (for example by the application of the theological principles of the literal sense in *Dei Verbum* 12: the unity of Scripture, its reading in the tradition, and the analogy of faith) is the theological neutrality of the historical-critical method. "What 'Matthew and Luke meant' is the literal sense of their Gospels; and critical scholars, whether Catholic or Protestant, have to use the same methods in determining

---

77 Alexis de Tocqueville, *Democracy in America*, Vol. 2, Pt. 1, Chap. 1. (New York: Library of America, 2004), 483–488.

78 Brown, *Critical Meaning of the Bible*, 40–41.

the sense."[79] Catholics, Protestants and atheists have to use the same method in mathematical physics. For the Church to intervene in determining the literal sense of Scripture would be the equivalent of her intervening in mathematical physics, as she did with disastrous consequences in the case of Galileo.

It is fascinating to observe that in proceeding more and more radically along this familiar line of the Enlightenment liberation of historical-critical exegesis from the bonds of ecclesiastical dogma, Brown comes to a point in his argument at which he suddenly takes a stand. A deeper Brown, the Brown of the book on the *sensus plenior* and of the commentary on John, suddenly emerges.

> Yet *personally* I would not accept ... [the view that] allows the literal meaning and the church interpretation to be contradictory in the strict sense. If one takes an example from the few doctrines that I have mentioned above as including or presupposing specific historical facts, some would not be disturbed by a situation in which historical criticism would make it virtually certain that Jesus was conceived normally, even though church doctrine speaks of a virginal conception. Yet that is modernism in the classic sense whereby doctrines are pure symbols that do not need to be correlated at all with the facts of which they speak.[80]

It is certainly a curious rhetorical situation for Brown to find himself in. He brings the accusation of modernism against those among his fellow Catholics who would deny the fact of Mary's virginity on the historical-critical level of the literal sense (what the Bible meant) while generously allowing their Church to affirm it as a dogma and as the ecclesiastical sense of Scripture (what the Bible means, the legitimate playpen for Church authority).

Particularly interesting is the word "personally," which I emphasized in quoting the text above. We hear the personal, deeper Brown, who takes a stand. In order to unfold this deeper Brown, one can hardly do better than to turn to Joseph Fitzmyer who has a kinship with Brown on many levels.

> If the meaning of a biblical text could take on a meaning different from its originally expressed—and I would add, originally intended—meaning, then how could one say that the Bible is still the source par excellence of divine revelation, the means that God has chosen to convey to generation after generation of his people what his plans, his instructions, and his will in their regard actually are. This characteristic of the written Word of

---

79   Brown, *Critical Meaning of the Bible,* 36.

80   Brown, *Critical Meaning of the Bible,* 41; emphasis added.

God demands that there be a basic homogeneity between what it meant and what it means, between what the inspired human author sought to express and what he did express, and what is being said by the words so read in the Church of today. *This, then, is the major problem that the literal sense of Scripture raises today, and one with which theologians and exegetes have to deal.* ...The literal sense is the goal of a properly oriented historical-critical interpretation of Scripture. By "properly oriented" I mean the use of that method with the presupposition of Christian faith that one is interpreting the written Word of God couched in ancient human language, with a message not only for the people of old, but also for Christians today.[81]

What Fitzmyer calls "the major problem that the literal sense of Scripture raises today" is precisely the problem raised by Brown's essay on the Word of God. Fitzmyer's language partly converges with Brown's, particularly in the use of "message," which, for the Brown of the essay, is an entirely non-verbal form of divine communication, secondarily and often erroneously translated by human beings into words. Yet, Fitzmyer also brings out what Brown must unavoidably mean by "message." He calls the words of the Bible "the means that God has chosen to convey to generation after generation of his people what his plans, his instructions, and his will in their regard actually are." The formulation "chosen to convey," particularly the verb "convey," is close to what Brown says about the literal sense in his dissertation. "The literal sense is that which both the Holy Spirit and the human author directly and proximately intended." A divine intention is present in the words of Scripture. In these words, God speaks as himself. Fitzmyer's formulation is close to *Dei Verbum 11*, "All that the inspired authors and sacred writers affirm is to be held as affirmed by the Holy Spirit."

Consistent with this emphasis, Fitzmyer points out that the historical critical interpretation of Scripture needs to be oriented by the presupposition of faith that God is indeed speaking in this text. A theologically neutral orientation of the method will ultimately be a false orientation that will fail to do justice to the literal sense of the text. Brown himself makes the following argument for the necessity of faith as an orientation for exegesis. "Good sense in interpreting is the first and most indispensable fruit of faith."[82] The text quoted from his commentary on John proves his point, whatever his theoretical essay on the Word of God may say to contradict it.

The position formulated by Fitzmyer seems to be Brown's real intention in the 1980 essay on the Word of God when one considers his work as a whole. It

---

81 Joseph Fitzmyer, *The Interpretation of Scripture: In Defense of the Historical-Critical Method* (Mahwah, NJ: Paulist, 2008), 89, 91; emphasis added.

82 Brown, *Sensus Plenior*, 8.

would be interesting to work out in detail how one should label the meaning of Brown's text in this rereading of his 1980 essay in light of Fitzmyer. Should it be called *sensus canonicus* or *sensus plenior* or *sensus caritativus?* At any rate, it is the *sensus literalis* of Brown's text in his commentary on John 6:54–57.

From Brown's Literal Sense to Aquinas's Spiritual Sense

The *Catechism of the Catholic Church* describes the "spiritual sense" of Scripture:

> According to an ancient tradition, one can distinguish between two *senses* of Scripture: the literal and the spiritual, the latter being subdivided into the allegorical, moral and anagogical senses. The profound concordance of the four senses guarantees all its richness to the living reading of Scripture in the Church.
>
> The *literal sense* is the meaning conveyed by the words of Scripture and discovered by exegesis, following the rules of sound interpretation: "All other senses of sacred Scripture are based on the literal."
>
> The *spiritual sense.* Thanks to the unity of God's plan, not only the text of Scripture but also the realities and events about which it speaks can be signs.
>
> 1. The *allegorical sense.* We can acquire a more profound understanding of events by recognizing their significance in Christ; thus the crossing of the Red Sea is a sign or type of Christ's victory and also of Christian baptism.
>
> 2. The *moral sense.* The events reported in Scripture ought to lead us to act justly. As St. Paul says, they were written "for our instruction."
>
> 3. The *anagogical sense* [Greek: *anagoge*, "leading up"]. We can view realities and events in terms of their eternal significance, leading us toward our true homeland: thus the Church on earth is a sign of the heavenly Jerusalem.[83]

Many Scripture scholars consign this text to the antiquity to which it belongs as "an ancient tradition." "The individual doctrines that the *Catechism affirms have no*

---

83   *Catechism of the Catholic Church,* 2d. ed. (Vatican City: Libreria Editrice Vaticana, 1997), nos. 115–117.

other authority than that which they already possess."[84] This one possesses none. It is just that, an ancient tradition. It was not even mentioned in *Dei Verbum*.

Brown's dissertation stands unimpressed by this argument against the spiritual sense.

> The typical sense is generally defined in the textbooks as: "that meaning by which the things, which are signified by the words of Scripture, signify according to the intention of the Holy Spirit yet other things." In other words, some "thing" about which the text of Scripture speaks literally is used by God to foreshadow something else. ("Thing" is here used in a wide sense, referring to persons, actions, events, laws, et cetera.). ...*The existence of types in the Bible is a dogma of faith.*[85]

If the existence of the spiritual sense is "a dogma of the faith," then its presence in the *Catechism is simply the reaffirmation of the formidable authority which it already possesses.*

Brown's position in his dissertation can be sustained on the basis of the two main features drawn above from his commentary on John 6:54–57: analogy/participation and the presence of the divine act of speech. Analogy and participation as affirmed in Brown's commentary on John 6:54–57 necessarily give rise to a great semiotic system, a system of signs and sacraments, that includes all creatures. A sign is that which, when known, makes known something else. If all creatures share in God's being, then all are signs (*semeia*) of God in some way. What we understand about them and express by words makes God known, in some instances only in the manner of metaphor (for example, in the words "rock, fortress, lion"), in others by way of analogy (for example, in the words "being, life, knowledge, love").

At the beginning of his account of the sacraments, Thomas Aquinas argues that all signs of the sacred can be called "sacraments." His first argument against his own position is the following.

> All sensible creatures are signs of sacred things, according to Romans 1:20, "the invisible things of God are clearly seen, being understood by the things that are made." But not all sensible things can be called sacraments. Therefore, not every sign of a sacred thing is a sacrament.[86]

---

84 Joseph Cardinal Ratzinger, "The *Catechism of the Catholic Church* and the Optimism of the Redeemed," *Communio* 20 (1993): 469–484, at 479. Emphasis added.

85 Brown, *Sensus Plenior*, 10–11, emphasis added.

86 Thomas Aquinas, *Summa Theologiae* [Summary of Theology], pt. 3a, q. 60, art. 2, obj. 1, in *Summa Theologica*, 3 vols. (New York: Benzinger Brothers, 1947).

The body of the article lays down the anthropological principle of the sacramental semiotic system: human beings are by their very nature semiotic animals. "Signs are given to human beings, because it belongs to them to make their way through the known to the unknown." In the fullest and most specific sense of "sacrament," a sign is a sacrament when it not only signifies what is sacred, but when God's holiness reaches out through it to make a person holy. This effective gift of the sacred takes place above all in the Eucharist, as Brown understands it in the text of John. Yet, in a broader sense, "sacrament" includes all signs of the sacred.

The response to the first argument turns on this distinction. Granted, not all creatures are sacraments in the full and specific way the Eucharist is. Still, in the wider sense all of them are, because they are necessarily signs of the sacred.

Two important points need to be added. First, the sacramental function of creatures as signs does not attach to them from the outside, if God is truly "more interior than my innermost."[87] As the innermost source of being, God shapes the sign-function of creatures not from the outside, but most deeply from within. God alone can give such a sign-function to creatures. No creature can use another to signify in this manner. It is a divine mode of signification through things. Together with analogy and participation, of course, this interior signification of creatures will become unintelligible in the degree to which one takes nominalist premises for granted.

Second, the semiotic system is not only metaphysical (manifesting God through the very being of all creatures), but historical, due to God's plan as it is worked out in history. It is above all here, in this historical dimension, that the spiritual sense of Scripture is at home. If history is directed toward a goal, its earlier phases will point ahead to the goal, just as the first part of a planned trip points ahead to the remainder. The early phases of the plan are signs of the plan's overall intention. One clearly sees this signification only when one is able to see the whole plan, at least in outline. Once again, this signification is not just accidentally attached to events, though a certain divine freedom in an accidental and still significant disposition of events should not be excluded.

If the divine act of speech reflected in Brown's commentary on John 6:54–57 is a real event, what happens in this semiotic system? What happens when God (to use Ratzinger's formulation in the Erasmus Lecture) "speaks as himself in human words in the world"? The necessary consequence of this unheard-of event is the fusion of the two kinds of signification. God's speech through words takes up and absorbs into itself his signification through the things signified by the words.

One needs to focus on two points about speech and things to grasp the impact of this fusion. First, it is only in full speech that one finds a personal testimony

---

87   St. Augustine, *Confessions*, Bk. 3, Chap. 6, 11, in *A Select Library of Nicene and Post-Nicene Fathers of the Christian Church*, 1st series, 14 vols., ed. Philip Schaff (Peabody, MA: Hendrickson, 1994 [reprint]), 1:63. Translation altered.

that can be grasped by personal faith (I believe you) while things are, in comparison, mute. Second, it is only in things that one finds full reality in all its depth while spoken or written words are, in comparison, mere signs. In the eternal Logos, both sides (sign and reality) simply coincide. The fusion of the two significations in human speech has, therefore, a profound impact on both sides: God's Word gives speech to things: things become a testimony in which God himself affirms a truth that can be grasped by personal faith. And the reality of things gives weight and depth to the words beyond their usual power. It is somewhat like a man giving flowers to a woman while saying, "I love you. I am yours and you are mine." The words give eloquence to the flowers and the flowers give reality and depth to the words. It is only somewhat like the spiritual sense because, just as God alone can signify through things, so he alone can speak through words that integrate the signification of things into themselves. The man who gives flowers cannot truly absorb the significance of the flowers into his words, because their sign-value does not flow, at root, from his intention. The significations remain separate, even if they are complementary.

The spiritual sense, understood as a fusion between the meaning of words and the signification of things is truly a sense of Scripture. What is at stake in it is not the significance of things alone, which remains relatively mute, but the meaning of the words of Scripture, enriched by its fusion with the signification of things. It is a strict and inescapable extension of the literal sense, due to the power of the divine speech act in the literal sense, which cannot be limited to the words, because God is the innermost source of being that gives to all beings their specific semiotic note and value.

The Account of the Spiritual Sense in Thomas Aquinas

Thomas Aquinas sees the spiritual or mystical sense of Scripture as necessarily arising in this manner from the literal sense, that is, as arising precisely because that literal sense is intended by God and therefore absorbs the signification of things. Once again, "Thing is here used in a wide sense, referring to persons, actions, events, laws, et cetera."[88] In his late *Lectura Romana on Peter Lombard* he sees this expansion of meaning as a necessary property of Scripture that is found in no other text.

> The mystical meaning is that which arises, not from the signification of the words, but from that of the things signified by the words. In other sciences, only words are passed on as signs to signify things, because their author is man, who can only signify things through words alone. In this Scripture even the things signified by the words signify something else. This is because

---

88 Brown, *Sensus Plenior*, 10.

the Holy Spirit ordained that those things signified by the words would signify something further.[89]

In the *Summa Theologiae*, not long after the *Lectura Romana*, his argument is similar.

> The author of Scripture is God, in whose power it is not only to fit vocal sounds to the act of signifying (which man can do as well), but even things themselves. And therefore, while in all sciences vocal sounds signify, this science [namely, God's teaching in Scripture] alone has the property that the very things signified by vocal sounds signify something in turn. That first signification, by which vocal sounds signify things, belongs to the first sense, which is the historical or literal sense. The signification by which in turn the things signified by the vocal sounds signify other things is called the spiritual sense, which is grounded on the literal and presupposes it.[90]

The division of the spiritual sense into three senses—allegorical, moral and anagogical—is clear and transparent. It turns first on the distinction between practical truth (moral sense) and theoretical truth, and then within theoretical truth on the distinction between the preliminary truth of history (allegorical sense) and the definitive truth of the end (anagogical sense).[91] In the traditional order followed by Thomas, the two theoretical senses frame the practical sense.

Allegorical Sense: Littera gesta docet ("The letter shows things done"). Of the senses that express theoretical truth, the allegorical bears on the unity of the divine plan as it works itself out on a still imperfect level within the *gesta*, the deeds and events of history ("things" in the wide sense). It includes two main relations between distinct historical periods in this plan: the Old Testament in relation to its fulfillment by Christ; and the earthly life of Christ in relation to its fulfillment in the life of the Church on earth.

For example, when Scripture presents Christ himself as the Eucharist in the literal sense, "This is my body ... this is my blood of the covenant,"[92] it speaks through the reality of the Eucharist itself about the innermost unity of the Church. This allegorical reading is supported by the literal sense of Paul's statement,

---

89   St. Thomas, *Lectura Romana in Primum Librum Sententiarum Petri Lombardi* [Roman Lectures on the First Book of the Sentences of Peter Lombard], prol. 4.1, reply obj. 3 (Toronto: Pontifical Institute of Mediaeval Studies, 2006).

90   Aquinas, *Summa Theologiae*, pt. 1a, q. 1, art. 10, contra.

91   See St. Thomas Aquinas, *Quaestiones Quodlibetales* [Miscellaneous Questions], quod. 7, q. 6, art. 2, contra.

92   Mark 14:22–24.

"Because there is one bread, we who are many are one body, for we all participate in the one bread."[93]

Moral Sense: The moral sense answers the question of practical truth, "What am I to do?" In the same literal statement about Christ in the Eucharist,[94] God directs an appeal to the eucharistic assembly for each individual person and the Church as a whole to conform its actions to the reality of the eucharistic Christ.[95]

Anagogical Sense: The whole of God's plan is most of all intelligible in terms of its end. The anagogical sense depends on the signification by which the whole plan, including the present life of the Church militant, points ahead to that end. When the letter speaks about the Eucharist, it speaks through the very reality of the Eucharist about the definitive city, the bride and wife of the Lamb,[96] in which the reciprocal vow between bride and bridegroom, "I am yours and you are mine," is consummated.

The traditional order of senses is intelligible. The inner logic of history (allegorical sense) is the basis for understanding the moral sense. For example, the objective fact of the Church's Eucharistic unity as a historical fact encountered in experience (which is the object of the allegorical sense of literal statements about Christ) is the proximate basis for understanding the moral sense in the concrete. Both the allegorical and the moral sense are ultimately completed by the orientation of everything to the end (anagogical sense). Both the Church's eucharistic unity and the eucharistic morality built on it are intelligible only as anticipations of the definitive city built by the slaying of the Paschal Lamb and by the consummation of the marriage between the Lamb and the city: I am yours and you are mine. The anagogical sense is the most sapiential.

In his *Quaestiones Quodlibetales*, Thomas argues in detail that not all four senses are found in all passages of Scripture.[97] The following presentation follows this text closely, but uses the Eucharist as the example to preserve the thematic focus of the whole essay.

Only One Sense: Some passages, for example the description of the definitive Jerusalem in Revelation 20–21, bride of the slaughtered Lamb, have no spiritual sense at all, only a literal sense. Unless one has a clear grasp of "literal sense," this statement may appear strange. The literal sense is whatever the words really mean. Revelation 20–21 with its rich symbolic vocabulary is one of the most Spirit-filled passages in the whole of Scripture. All of this belongs to the literal sense. Such complex symbolism is not an example of the allegorical sense. It is part of the literal sense in describing the reality of the city. Since the city is the definitive reality, it

---

93   1 Cor. 10:17.

94   Mark 14:22–24.

95   See Donald J. Keefe, "Toward a Eucharistic Morality," *Communio* 2 (1975): 99–125.

96   Rev. 20–21.

97   See Aquinas, *Quaestiones Quodlibetales*, quod. 7, q. 6, art. 2, reply obj. 5.

signifies nothing beyond itself. It is for this reason that this text cannot have a spiritual sense. "What belongs according in the literal sense to the state of glory is traditionally interpreted in no other way [than the literal], because it is not the figure of something else, but figured by everything else."[98]

Two Senses: "What is said morally according to the literal sense is traditionally interpreted only allegorically."[99] For example, "I give you a new commandment, that you love one another as I have loved you,"[100] the literal sense of which is the moral norm taught by Christ, speaks through that norm allegorically about the eucharistic gift of self as constitutive of the Church's life. It is not clear why Thomas does not consider the anagogical sense as a possibility in literally moral texts. The whole second part of the *Summa* treats moral matters as a great anagogical movement toward God. Why could the moral norm of love not point anagogically to the fulfilled eucharistic love that will be the principle of life of the glorified Church?

Three Senses: When the literal sense of Scripture speaks about the Church it cannot be interpreted allegorically. Paul's statement about the Church, "Because there is one bread, we who are many are one body,"[101] has a literal, moral and anagogical sense, but not an allegorical sense, because it already refers in the sense of the letter to the final object of the allegorical sense, namely, the life of the Church. The only exception to this rule for Thomas are literal statements about the early Church, which can be interpreted allegorically with reference to the present Church.

Four Senses: All four senses are found in passages of the Old Testament about saving events and deeds, which point ahead to Christ and in passages of the New Testament about Christ, which point ahead to the Church. The example of the Eucharist given above illustrates the latter. "This is my body … this is my blood of the covenant"[102] speaks literally about Christ in the Eucharist, allegorically about the unity of the Church, morally about a eucharistic norm of action, and anagogically about the very end, the wedding of the Lamb.

Literal Statements about Christ as the Center of the Spiritual Sense

It is unfortunate that in his dissertation Brown has a decided preference for the term "typical sense" rather than "spiritual" or "mystical sense." In this preference, he follows the rather abstract neo-Scholastic discussion, which centered on the allegorical sense of Old Testament types, leaving the moral and anagogical sense as well as literal statements about Christ in relative obscurity. The search for allegorical types of Christ resulted in many forced and artificial constructions that

---

98   Aquinas, *Quaestiones Quodlibetales*, quod. 7, q. 6, art. 2, reply obj. 5.

99   Aquinas, *Quaestiones Quodlibetales*, quod. 7, q. 6, art. 2, reply obj. 5.

100 John 13:34.

101 1 Cor. 10:17.

102 Mark 14:22–24.

make no distinction between the literary technique of allegory and the allegorical sense. What might work in an inventive literary allegory is then assumed to be the spiritual sense of the words. It is not surprising that the typical sense does not enjoy Brown's favor. It embodies for him one of the main flaws in traditional exegesis that needs to be overcome by historical criticism faithful to the literal sense.

In actual Christian life, the main texts of Scripture in which God speaks to the Church in the spiritual sense are the Gospels and apostolic letters when they speak in the literal sense about Christ, as in the example of the Eucharist given above. Let us return to the concluding passage of Benedict XVI's meditation for the opening of the 2008 Synod on the Word of God.

> With his incarnation he said: I am yours. And in baptism he said to me: I am yours. In the Holy Eucharist, he says ever anew: I am yours, so that we may respond: Lord, I am yours. In the way of the Word, entering the mystery of his incarnation, of his being among us, we want to appropriate his being, we want to expropriate our existence, giving ourselves to him who gave himself to us.
>
> "I am yours." Let us pray the Lord that we may learn to say this word with our whole being. Thus we will be in the heart of the Word. Thus we will be saved.

The sentence, "In the Holy Eucharist, he says ever anew: I am yours, so that we may respond: Lord, I am yours," can be taken as an entrance door into reading the spiritual sense of the words, "This is my body ... this is my blood of the covenant."[103] These words speak in their literal sense about Christ in the Eucharist, but, precisely because it is God who is speaking, he is speaking to us through the very reality of the eucharistic Christ, because that very reality is turned by his providence toward us now, toward our present moment: "I am yours."

In the present moment, in which the eucharistic assembly hears the Word of God about the Eucharist, it hears a present testimony of the covenantal God expressed not only through the words, but through the full richness and depth of the eucharistic Christ himself and it can embrace this testimony with the bride's words to her bridegroom, "My beloved is mine and I am his."[104]

Where in the letter of Scripture does God primarily speak to us through the very reality signified by the literal sense? The answer is clear. "God, who spoke in many partial and various ways of old to the fathers through the prophets, has spoken to us in the last of these days through [his] Son."[105] When he explains how

---

103 Mark 14:22–24.

104 Song 2:16.

105 Heb. 1:1–2.

the spiritual sense of biblical words about Christ arises out of their literal sense, Thomas Aquinas shows indirectly why this particular instance of the spiritual sense is indeed so central. In the *Quaestiones Quodlibetales* he goes first through the threefold basis of the spiritual senses in literal statements about Jesus, and then through the three senses themselves.

> What belongs to the head is prior to what belongs to the
>   members, for the body is truly Christ's,
> (1) and what is done in him is a figure of Christ's mystical body
>   and what is done in it,
> (2) so that it is in him, Christ, that we must find the exemplar
>   for living.
> (3) It is also in Christ that the future glory is shown to us
>   already now.
> For this reason, that which is said according to the *letter* about
>   Christ himself, the head,
> (1) can be set forth *allegorically*, referring to his mystical body,
> (2) and *morally*, referring to our acts that must be formed anew
>   following him himself,
> (3) and *anagogically*, inasmuch as in Christ the way of glory is
>   shown to us.[106]

The fundamental reason for the spiritual sense of literal statements about Christ is that "the body is truly Christ's": I am yours and you are mine. It is created by Christ's complete eucharistic gift of self. This interior and constitutive mutual relation between Christ and his body gives rise to the spiritual sense. It is primarily when God speaks to the eucharistic assembly in the literal sense about Christ that he speaks through "things," namely, through the very reality of his Son in his act of giving himself. He speaks in all three dimensions, about the journey of history experienced by the Church in the present, about what we should do as members of that Church, and about the final goal toward which we tend.

This speech through his Son has, therefore, an interior ordination to his sacramental real presence in the Eucharist, which is irreducible to the words of Scripture, including its spiritual sense. God's speech in Scripture, including the spiritual sense, is completed by Christ's saving deed in his real presence. "Unless you eat the flesh of the Son of Man and drink his blood, you do not have life within yourselves."[107]

> There is a close connection between Scripture and the Eucharist.
> "The Church has always venerated the divine Scriptures just as

---

106 Aquinas, *Quaestiones Quodlibetales*, quod. 7, q. 6, art. 2, reply obj. 5. Emphasis added.
107 John 6:53.

she venerates the Body of the Lord, since, especially in the sacred liturgy, she unceasingly receives and offers to the faithful the bread of life from the table both of God's Word and of Christ's Body" (*Dei Verbum*, 21). In the Bible, God himself speaks the words of his love in human words in the course of the long history of his covenant with his people. "All that the inspired authors and sacred writers affirm is to be held as affirmed by the Holy Spirit" (*Dei Verbum*, 11). The Eucharist concentrates these many words of God in the Lord's bodily gift of self to his own, whom he "loves to the end" (John 13:1). For this reason, the Eucharist is a hermeneutical principle of Scripture, just as Scripture is an unfolding and explanation of the Eucharist.

The written word does not, however, contain the totality of the eternal Logos made man. The incarnate Word, which is at the same time God's definitive deed, transcends the written word. The power of the written word, therefore, lives from the remaining presence of this greater Deed-Word. Our transformation by hearing and receiving the word happens by the power that is at work in the eucharistic real presence of the Deed-Word. The Word of God that consists of Scripture is a mode of the presence of the Lord that points toward the Eucharist. The presence of the Lord in the Word calls for his presence in the Eucharist.

In both modes of presence, God is also deeply hidden, accessible only through the love of the Holy Spirit poured out in the heart, visible only for the eyes of faith that have gained sight through this love. Without an interior relation of love to the Lord, the letter of Scripture remains dead. Revitalizing the Word of God in the life of the Church stands and falls thus with the renewal of faith in Christ today.[108]

Conclusion

The choice of Brown's commentary on John 6:54–57 as the central thematic focus made the argument of this essay rather easy. A more difficult text would have been Brown's commentary on the end of 2 Maccabees, if he had written one. "So I myself will here bring my story to a halt. If it is well written and elegantly dispositioned, that is what I myself desired; if it is poorly done and mediocre, that was all

---

108 Proposal of the German bishops at the 2008 Synod of Bishops on the Word of God. This proposal was accepted in a much abbreviated form in the Synod's Final List of Propositions, Prop. 3. Available online at: http://www.vatican.va/roman_curia/synod/index.htm.

I could manage."[109] There is little to be seen in this text, at least on the immediate level, of spousal dialogue and eucharistic self-gift. If the *analogia verbi* is true and God affirms what the human author affirms, then God affirms the mediocrity of 2 Maccabees—and speaks the truth. Yet God does not say about himself, "That is all I could manage."

Farkasfalvy suggests a fruitful line of argument in the analogy between incarnation and inspiration. As he points out, in the incarnation there is one person in two natures; in Scripture there is one written word with two affirmations, human and divine, proceeding from two distinct agents.[110] The human author's "I" cannot simply be identified with the divine "I." Many difficult questions of the *analogia verbi* remain to be addressed. One of the most interesting proposals is Origen's extended account of the analogous use of "gospel" in the first book of his commentary on John.[111] The difficulties mentioned by Cardinals König and Grillmeier as well as Bultmann and Brown do not disappear, but are intensified if one accepts *Dei Verbum* 11. The present essay simply proposes the *lectio difficilior* ("the more difficult reading") as the *lectio potior* ("the stronger reading").

It is easy to slice through the Gordian knot of this *lectio difficilior* with one stroke of the Enlightenment sword, as Bultmann does. He simply submits to the pressure of Baconian and Cartesian Nominalist premises transported by natural science in its present, academically established form. The universe follows mathematical laws, without exception. "Sire, I did not need this hypothesis," Pierre-Simon Laplace famously responded when Napoleon asked him why his five-volume Mécanique Céleste ("Celestial Mechanics") did not mention God. Laplace's response, some argue, is not a "philosophical commitment."

> It is, rather, the best research strategy that has evolved from our long-standing experience with nature. …Over centuries of research we have learned that the idea "God did it" has never advanced our understanding of nature an iota, and that is why we abandoned it.[112]

The final claim, "and that is why we abandoned it," is false. We abandoned it because in the founders of modern science, above all in Bacon and in Descartes, we chose power over nature as the end of understanding and therefore chose mathematical mechanics as the supreme way of understanding. "God did it" cannot, as a matter of principle, be a factor within a mathematical mechanical account, just as goodness or beauty cannot play any role in it. The claim that this is the one true way of

---

109 2 Macc. 15:37–38.

110 See Farkasfalvy, *Inspiration & Interpretation*, 219–220.

111 See Farkasfalvy, *Inspiration & Interpretation*, 233, n. 33.

112 See Jerry A. Coyne, "Seeing and Believing: The Never-Ending Attempt to Reconcile Science and Religion, and Why it is Doomed to Fail," *The New Republic* (February 4, 2009).

understanding nature, replacing all others, is an imposition of the will to power; it is not an insight gained in the simple experience of attempting to understand nature. Nevertheless, the academic mainstream affirms this claim.

> What is the nature of reality? Where did all this come from? … Traditionally these are questions for philosophy, but philosophy is dead. Philosophy has not kept up with modern developments in science, particularly physics. Scientists have become the bearers of the torch of discovery in our quest for knowledge.[113]

Posing as the latest and most sophisticated contribution to the debate between science and religion, this proclamation of the death of philosophy unwittingly proclaims its life. It is simply a restatement of Kant's thesis of the impossibility of metaphysics and the self-limitation of reason to the Baconian-Cartesian project.[114] Quantum mechanics may differ from Newtonian mechanics, but it is still mathematical mechanics. It is a curious irony of history that the school of Aristotle produced the *Questions of Mechanics* (which show both a clear awareness of the power of mechanics and a lack of interest in increasing such power) and that Bacon appeals to this Aristotelian text in his proposal for scientific knowledge.[115]

> Aristotle [said it] best. Physics and mathematics give rise to practical science and mechanics.[116] Inquiries into nature have the best result when the physical is brought to its term in the mathematical.[117] We give this precept: everything in nature relating both to bodies and powers must be set forth (as far as may be) numbered, weighed, measured, determined. *For it is works we are in pursuit of, not speculations.* Physics and mathematics, in due combination, give rise to practical science.[118]

Bultmann does not raise the fundamental question whether this Baconian limitation of reason by the interests of power is legitimate. He simply takes the absence of God from the mechanical cosmos as inevitable and attempts to neutralize it in

---

113 Stephen Hawking and Leonard Mlodinow, *The Grand Design* (New York: Bantam, 2010), 5.

114 See, for example, Immanuel Kant, *Prolegomena to Any Future Metaphysics*, 4:275 (Cambridge: Cambridge University, 2004).

115 For the importance of the Pseudo-Aristotelian *Questions of Mechanics* for the development of modern science, particularly for Galileo, who wrote a commentary on the text, see Paul Rose and Stillman Drake, "The Pseudo-Aristotelian *Questions of Mechanics* in Renaissance Culture," *Studies in the Renaissance* 18 (1971): 65–104.

116 Bacon, *Advancement of Knowledge*, Bk. 3, Chap. 6; *Works* 1:576.

117 Bacon, *New Organon*, Bk. 2, 8; *Works*, 1:235.

118 Bacon, *Parasceve ad Historiam Naturalem et Experimentalem* [Preparative for Natural and Experimental History], Apho. 7; *Works* 1:400; emphasis added.

a neo-Kantian Lutheran dialectic between sin and justification. Science is sin; it is boasting in human power; it is resistance against God as Lord. Yet, I cannot escape science and pretend that I am not a modern. I inescapably accept mathematical mechanical laws as the true way of understanding nature. I thereby create hell on earth. While I remain a sinner, the word of God smashes the self-security of my scientific reason and thereby liberates me to exist authentically in the challenge of the moment. *Simul justus et peccator* ("at the same time righteous and a sinner"). I am simultaneously an enlightened modern (enlightened with the light of science, which is the darkness of sin, producing hell) and a believer (enlightened by the truth of a divine Word that cannot enlighten my darkness). Scripture speaks to me now as the sovereign voice of God, but what it says will for ever remain unknown to me, because to know it would be to objectify it sinfully into sin.

> The Word of the Spirit never takes on form, never becomes concrete; it never becomes outward and objective, but is merely "picked up" at times in a sort of existential faith, a faith, however, which by no means truly exists because it vanishes as soon as it appears. Here everything remains uncertain, including the certitude of our uncertainty in the presence of the self-revealing God.[119]

Brown recognizes the catastrophe of this Bultmannian path. He resists the pressure of nominalist premises, because he is deeply rooted in the Catholic tradition. His roots are fragile, however, and his resistance is a highly dramatic struggle with partly disastrous outcome, as documented by his 1980 essay and its main thesis, "God does not speak." Still, in his practice as an exegete, as exemplified by his comments on John 6:54–57, he holds on to two key truths threatened by nominalist premises, namely, analogy/participation and the sense of the presence of a divine act of speech.

Brown's affirmation of these two truths opens up from within itself into the fuller understanding of the truth of Scripture, including the divinely intended literal sense and the spiritual sense as understood by Thomas Aquinas. What we can learn from Brown as readers of Scripture is to hold on to the same two truths.

Analogy/Participation: A renewal of the study of nature on the philosophical basis of analogy and participation is the most urgent need of exegesis, as Benedict XVI argues in his Regensburg lecture.

> Modern scientific reason has to assume simply as a given that there are rational structures of matter and that there is a cor-

---

119   Heinrich Schlier, "A Brief Apologia," in *We are Now Catholics: Rudolf Goethe, Martin Giebner, Georg Klunder, Heinrich Schlier,* ed. Karl Hardt (Westminster, MD: Newman, 1959), 187–215, at 205.

respondence between our spirit and the prevailing rational structures of nature, on which the path of its method is based. Yet the question why this [given] is a fact is a real question, and one which has to be remanded by the natural sciences to other modes and planes of thought—to philosophy and theology.

For philosophy and, albeit in a different way, for theology, listening to the great experiences and insights of the religious traditions of humanity, and those of the Christian faith in particular, is a source of knowledge, and to ignore it would be an unacceptable narrowing of our listening and responding. Here I am reminded of something Socrates said to Phaedo. In their earlier conversations, many false philosophical opinions had been raised, and so Socrates says: "It would be easily understandable if someone became so annoyed at all these false notions that for the rest of his life he despised and mocked all talk about being—but in this way he would be deprived of the truth of being and would suffer a great loss."

The West has long been endangered by this aversion to the fundamental questions of its reason, and can only suffer great harm thereby. The courage to engage the whole breadth of reason, and not the denial of its grandeur—this is the program with which a theology grounded in biblical faith enters into the debates of our time. "Not to act reasonably, not to act with *logos*, is contrary to the nature of God," said Manuel II, according to his Christian understanding of God, in response to his Persian interlocutor. It is to this great *logos*, to this breadth of reason, that we invite our partners in the dialogue of cultures. To rediscover it constantly is the great task of the university.[120]

The renewal of the study of nature, overcoming the limits imposed on reason by nominalism as well as the Baconian-Cartesian will to power, is a huge task that will occupy generations of scientists, philosophers and theologians. At the very roots of that renewal, the metaphysics of analogy and participation needs to be thought through afresh, especially what follows from it for the semiotic system, the sacramental organism of signs.

The Divine Intention in the Literal Sense: In Scripture, God speaks as himself by human words in the world. If it is indeed God who is speaking, then we may "believe again" in the full truth of Scripture's literal sense and its full richness unfolded in the spiritual sense. Believing again is a sign of genuine philosophy and

---

120 Benedict XVI, "Faith, Reason and the University," translation revised.

reflection, of an open philosophy that is able to affirm the *analogia verbi* reaffirmed by Vatican II. "God, who spoke in the past, speaks without any break with the bride of his beloved Son. ...All that the inspired authors or sacred writers affirm is to be held as affirmed by the Holy Spirit."[121]

In conclusion, we can return to the text by St. Bernard quoted at the introduction of this article. It expresses the two truths in powerfully synthetic and deeply suggestive form.

> "He spoke and they were made" (Ps. 148:5). Yet, he who made me by merely speaking, by speaking once, certainly remade me *by speaking* much *and by doing* wonders ["Do this in memory of me"]. ...In the first work he gave me myself; in the second *himself,* and where *he gave himself,* he gave me back to myself. As one given and given back, I owe myself for myself, and owe myself twice. What shall I render to God for himself? Even if I could give myself back to him a thousand times, what am I [compared] to God?[122]

---

121 *Dei Verbum*, 8, 11.

122 St. Bernard, *De Diligendo Deo*, Chap. 5, 15; emphasis added.

Letter & Spirit 6 (2010): 141-179

Glory(ing) in the Humility of the Word
The Kenotic Form of Revelation in J. G. Hamann

~: **John R. Betz** :~

University of Notre Dame

Nature vanishes before your Word. Here is the holy of holies; the whole of creation is but a forecourt compared to what we see in your Word.

J. G. Hamann[1]

These old rags have saved me from the pit, and I pride myself in them like Joseph in his colored coat.

J. G. Hamann[2]

In the first volume of *The Glory of the Lord*, Hans Urs von Balthasar writes: "At the threshold of modernity stands a uniquely tragic figure … because in this figure all lines seem to converge—the concerns of strict Lutheranism, of classical education and culture, and of a theological aesthetics that would embrace them both in a genuine encounter—and yet, he remained a figure out of joint with his times and his thought never came to fruition."[3] This figure, whose relevance von Balthasar wished to recover and who stands obscurely in the background of von Balthasar's own theological project, was Johann Georg Hamann (1730–1788), otherwise known as "the Magus of the North."[4] While von Balthasar's reading of Hamann

---

1 Johann Georg Hamann, *Londoner Schriften* [London Writings], ed. Oswald Bayer and Bernd Weissenborn (München: Verlag C. H. Beck, 1993), 109 (*SW* 1:49). Page numbers in parentheses refer to the otherwise standard edition of Hamann's works, *Sämtliche Werke* [Complete Works], ed. Josef Nadler, 6 vols. (Vienna: Herder Verlag, 1949–1957). See also *Londoner Schriften*, 59 (*SW* 1:4): "The Word of this Spirit is just as great a work as creation, and just as great a mystery as the redemption of human beings; indeed, this Word is the key to the works of the former and the mysteries of the latter." At the outset I would like to dedicate this article to Oswald Bayer, who almost singlehandedly has brought Hamann back to the attention of modern theology, and who in so many ways has made this minor contribution possible. I would also like to express my sincere gratitude to Scott Hahn for graciously soliciting, inspiring, and in every way encouraging the development of this article – and for reminding me of what the communion of saints looks like.

2 Johann Georg Hamann, *Briefwechsel* [Correspondence], ed. Walther Ziesemer and Arthur Henkel, 7 vols. (Wiesbaden: Insel Verlag, 1955–1975), 1:341. (Hereafter cited as *Briefwechsel* by volume).

3 Hans Urs von Balthasar, *The Glory of the Lord: A Theological Aesthetics*, vol. 1: Seeing the Form (San Francisco: Ignatius, 1982), 80. (Revised translation).

4 See the chapter on Hamann, the only Protestant, in *The Glory of the Lord: A Theological Aesthetics*, vol. 3: Studies in Theological Style: Lay Styles (San Francisco: Ignatius, 1985),

is concerned with Hamann's aesthetics, broadly conceived, in the following I will be concerned more specifically with Hamann's understanding of Scripture, which holds much promise, I would argue, for biblical hermeneutics today. This promise, I submit, consists chiefly in Hamann's profound sensitivity to the *kenotic form* of divine revelation. While this form is commonly seen in the life and mission of the Son—the locus classicus for which is the so-called christological hymn of Philippians 2:5–11—what is distinctive to Hamann is that in the midst of his conversion in 1758 he also discovered this form in Scripture, seeing therein an analogous kenosis, and an analogously hidden glory, of the Holy Spirit. As von Balthasar observes, "The same wonder that fills Hamann at the depletion of God in the servant figure of Christ fills him when he contemplates it in the Holy Scriptures, for there 'old rags' are twisted into ropes to pull man out when he lies trapped like Jeremiah in the miry pit, and one must, with Paul, venture to speak of the foolishness and infirmity of God."[5]

To be sure, Hamann is not the origin of discussions of kenosis in the modern period, which can be traced back earlier to Lutheran controversies of the seventeenth century between the faculties of Giessen and Tübingen over the extent and implications of divine kenosis in Christ.[6] But it is with Hamann, arguably, that the full scope and Trinitarian implications of this doctrine are first seen; and it is primarily in this that his largely unrecognized significance to von Balthasar's theology consists. In the following, therefore, building on von Balthasar's study of Hamann in the third volume of *The Glory of the Lord*, my aim will be to determine what we could still learn from Hamann today: first, regarding a Christian aesthetics that is attentive to the kenotic form of divine revelation in general; second, regarding the kenotic form of Scripture in particular, which bears greatly, I would argue, upon the Church's understanding of the Bible and divine inspiration; and, finally, regarding the corresponding humility that is required not only to understand the works of the Trinity *ad extra* ("toward the outside"), but to see their glory—to see glory, as Hamann did, not only in the humble presence of God in creation, and not only in the servant-form (*Knechtsgestalt*) of Christ, but also in the "rags" of Scripture. Given Hamann's relative obscurity in the English-speaking world, however, and in order to establish his significance, I necessarily begin with a brief introduction to his role in the history of ideas.

239–278. Though Hamann was an ardent Lutheran and, being from Prussia, had little if any contact with the Catholic Church of his time, it is notable that his final years were spent among the Catholic "Münster Circle," in which context he was received as something of a saint and buried by the Catholic priest Franz Friedrich von Fürstenberg (1728-1810). See John R. Betz, *After Enlightenment: The Post-Secular Vision of J. G. Hamann* (Oxford: Wiley-Blackwell, 2009), 293–311.

5   Von Balthasar, *Glory of the Lord*, 3:251.

6   For a brief history of the doctrine of kenosis in modernity, see Graham Ward, "Kenosis: Death, Discourse and Resurrection," in *Balthasar at the End of Modernity*, eds. Lucy Gardner, David Moss, Ben Quash, Graham Ward (Edinburgh: T & T Clark, 1999), 15–68.

Hamann in the History of Ideas

In the history of ideas Hamann is typically remembered, if he is remembered at all, as an important but enigmatic critic of the Enlightenment—whose *Socratic Memorabilia* (1759),[7] which is addressed to Immanuel Kant, reminded his friend of the principle of Socratic ignorance, emphasized the importance of faith to reason, and presented Socrates as a type and herald of Christian wisdom; whose *Aesthetica in Nuce* ("Aesthetics in a Nutshell") (1762) upbraided J. D. Michaelis, arguably the father of modern biblical criticism, for failing to appreciate the allegorical and typological depths of Scripture, and modern philosophy for its corresponding insensibility to the text of creation; whose *Philological Ideas and Doubts* (1772) took his disciple J. G. Herder to task for naturalizing the "sacrament" of language; whose *Metakritik* (1784) of Kant's critical philosophy drew attention to the cultural, linguistic, and historical mediation of all ostensibly pure, rational thought; and whose *Golgatha und Scheblimini* (1784), which was directed against Moses Mendelssohn's *Jerusalem*, thoroughly deconstructed the secular foundations of Mendelssohn's political philosophy and his corresponding, politically expedient representation of Judaism as a religion of reason.[8]

Admittedly, these and other writings are little known and studied today, due largely to the difficulties of Hamann's highly allusive, cryptic, and (in Mendelssohn's phrase) "dark and puzzling" style.[9] And we can be sure that it is partly on account of the notorious darkness of his style that he came to be known as the "Magus of the North."[10] But von Balthasar's claim that Hamann's thought never came to fruition is debatable, since Hamann was a mentor to the influential Herder and Friedrich Heinrich Jacobi, and was admired, if not fully understood, by a host of prominent intellectuals and cultural icons: from Johann Wolfgang

---

7   See James C. O'Flaherty, *Hamann's Socratic Memorabilia: A Translation and Commentary* (Baltimore: Johns Hopkins, 1967).

8   For more on these works and subjects, see generally Betz, *After Enlightenment*. For English translations of some of his key works, see Johann George Hamann, *Writings on Philosophy and Language*, ed. Kenneth Haynes (Cambridge: Cambridge University, 2007).

9   See Moses Mendelssohn, "Rezensionsartikel," in *Briefe, Die Neueste Literatur Betreffend (1759–1765)* [Letters Concerning the Latest Literature], ed. Eva J. Engel, in *Gesammelte Schriften* [Collected Works] (Stuttgart-Bad Cannstatt: Friedrich Frommann Verlag, 1991), 5/1:200–206.

10 As Matthias Claudius put it regarding the peculiarity of Hamann's style: "He has wrapped himself in a midnight robe, but the golden little stars shining from it here and there betray him, and allure, so that one does not regret the effort [required to understand him]." See Claudius, *Sämtliche Werke* [Complete Works] (Gotha: Perthes Verlag, 1902), 23. Compare Friedrich Schlegel's assessment: "With his divinatory profundity [Hamann] stood alone in the literature of his time, for which his peculiar religious orientation was already alienating and all the more inaccessible given that his sibylline leaves and hieroglyphic intimations are even more veiled in the dark raiment of symbolic allusions." Friedrich Schlegel, "Geschichte der Alten und Neuen Literatur" [History of Ancient and Modern Literature], in *Kritische Neuausgabe* [Critical New Edition], ed. Hans Eichner (Munich: Verlag Ferdinand Schöningh, 1961), 6: 378.

von Goethe, who regarded him as the "brightest mind of his day,"[11] to F. W. J. Schelling and G. W. F. Hegel, who regarded him, respectively, as a "prophet" and a "genius," to Søren Kierkegaard, who hailed him not only as "the greatest humorist in Christendom," but as one of the "most brilliant minds of all time."[12] As Hegel observed in his lengthy two-part review of Hamann's works, "Herder and especially Jacobi (leaving aside Goethe's … thorough appraisal) spoke of him … and appealed to him as one who was destined to come, who was in complete possession of the mysteries, of which their own revelations were simply a reflected glory."[13] And, in fact, it would be difficult to find in this period of German intellectual life a figure whose influence was so obscurely but powerfully present, operating like a dark center of gravity among the more familiar stars—particularly when one considers that Herder, Jacobi, Goethe, Hegel, Schelling, and Kierkegaard all made claims to being Hamann's heir or interpreter, as though their own literary, philosophical, or spiritual credentials somehow depended upon it.

While he is better appreciated in Germany, Hamann's importance was not lost on the eminent historian of ideas, Isaiah Berlin, whose provocative monograph on Hamann presents him not only as the *bête noir* ("black beast") of the Enlightenment but as "the pioneer of anti-rationalism in every sphere."[14] Of

---

11   See Kanzler Friedrich von Müller, *Unterhaltungen mit Goethe* [Conversations with Goethe], ed. Renate Grumach (Munich: C. H. Beck, 1982), 109. See in this regard the collection entitled, *Johann Georg Hamann: "Der Hellste Kopf Seiner Zeit"* [The Brightest Mind of his Day], ed. Oswald Bayer (Tübingen: Attempto Verlag, 1998). Moreover, in his journal from Italy, looking back on his own tradition, Goethe goes so far as to call Hamann the "literary father" of the German people. As he put it upon discovering the writings of Vico, "It is truly a beautiful thing if a people can claim such a literary father; one day Hamann will become a similar codex for the Germans." See *Italienische Reise* [Italian Journey] (Weimar: Böhlau 1890), 1:31.

12   See Sören Kierkegaard, *The Concept of Anxiety*, ed. Reidar Thomte (Princeton: Princeton University, 1980), 178, 198. For more on the history of Hamann's reception, see John R. Betz, "Reading Sibylline Leaves: Hamann in the History of Ideas," *Journal of the History of Ideas* 70 (January 2009): 93–118.

13   G. W. F. Hegel, "Hamann's Schriften" [Hamann's Writings], in *Werke* [Works], ed. Eva Moldenhauer and Karl Markus Michel (Frankfurt: Suhrkamp Verlag, 1986), 11:277.

14   Isaiah Berlin, *Three Critics of the Enlightenment: Vico, Hamann, Herder* (Princeton: Princeton University, 2000), 257; Berlin's treatment of Hamann originally appeared under the title, *The Magus of the North: J. G. Hamann and the Origins of Modern Irrationalism*, ed. Henry Hardy (New York: Farrar, Straus, and Giroux, 1993). Berlin's attendant thesis of Hamann's "irrationalism" is highly debatable. Suffice it to say that everything depends upon what one means by "rational" and "irrational." "If by rational one means a type of secular fanaticism that proudly refuses to consider the weakness of reason or the merits of faith and thinks reason alone is capable of providing a sufficient foundation for philosophy and culture, then Hamann was, by comparison, irrational. For his part, however, Hamann thought that the entire project of the Enlightenment was irrational, being founded upon a hypocritical misuse of reason that would end in philosophical confusion and spiritual darkness—since the light of reason (the human logos) is precisely not autonomous, as the Enlighteners claimed, but a dim reflection of the light of the *Logos* upon which every human logos depends. Accordingly, for Hamann, true reason is not reason operating by its own light (which is but a reflected moonlight), but reason invigorated by faith and enlightened by the Holy Spirit." See Betz, *After Enlightenment*, 6, 16, 312–313.

course, given Berlin's own secular prejudices, there is something tendentious in his claims. There is also something misleading in his characterization of Hamann as the ringleader of the German "counter-Enlightenment" (not least of all given Hamann's own desire to clarify the limits of reason and thereby pave the way for genuine, spiritual enlightenment).[15] Additionally, one must take stock of the fact that Berlin's work takes little account of the conclusions of German scholarship, which tends to see Hamann as a "radical Enlightener" among his contemporaries of the Enlightenment.[16] That being said, however, Berlin has a point: for there is no denying the force of Hamann's "metacritique" or the success of his (and his disciple Herder's) "metacritical invasion," particularly his reduction of "pure reason" to language, history, and tradition—the very thing from which the Enlighteners sought to escape. Indeed, the postmodern crisis of reason, as a consequence of the demise of the Enlightenment's overblown doctrine of reason, is something that Hamann had long foreseen and to some extent brought about: not in order to dissolve reason into history (and historical relativism) and not in order to dissolve reason into language (and the interminable "play" of *différance*), but in order to help fallen reason, wounded by pride, discover in history and in language the divine revelation that alone can heal it. For, to sum up his "metacritique," reason must be humbled and shown its dependence, if it is to discover the truth, since truth is found not beyond history or apart from tradition in the vacuum of reason alone, but rather *in* history where God has revealed himself: partially in the dream-like mythology of pre-Christian paganism, but especially in the inspired stories, histories, and sacred poetry of the Hebrews, all of which, for Hamann, constitute a prophetic testament to the person of Christ.

Hamann's Theological Aesthetics

But if Hamann's ideas were not without effect, von Balthasar is nevertheless right that his vision was never transmitted whole, but only in part (as might be expected from an authorship that consisted largely of fragmentary prophetic tracts). Thus, in standard philosophical and literary accounts, Hamann is typically remembered for his *Metakritik* or for his influence upon the proto-Romantic literary movement known as the *Sturm und Drang* ("Storm and Stress"). What is generally lost from view in such accounts, however, is the theological inspiration behind his authorship, which stems from his dramatic conversion in 1758 and

---

15   See Betz, *After Enlightenment*, 1–8, 76–82, 317. See also, Betz, "Reading Sibylline Leaves," 93–102. Regarding Berlin's problematic classification of the Counter-Enlightenment, see also Robert Norton, "The Myth of the Counter-Enlightenment," in *Journal of the History of Ideas* 68 (2007): 635–658.

16   See, for example, Oswald Bayer, *Zeitgenosse im Widerspruch: Johann Georg Hamann als Radikaler Aufklärer* [J. G. Hamann as Radical Enlightener] (München: Pieper Verlag, 1988). See also James C. O'Flaherty's debate with Berlin in "Letters to the Editor," *The New York Review of Books* (November 18, 1993); compare Berlin, "Magus of the North," *The New York Review of Books* (October 21, 1993).

centers upon the *kenotic form* of divine revelation. Indeed, it is here—specifically in Hamann's understanding of divine kenosis—that we find the organizing theme of his thought, which explains everything from his opposition to the Enlightenment and its "abstractions," to his doctrines of creation, history, and Scripture, to the peculiar form of his own mimetic authorship. For in Hamann's view the kenotic or utterly humble form of divine revelation not only showed up the pride of his rationalist contemporaries, who could find no eternal truth in history or tradition, much less in the history and scriptures of a particular people (given the supposed superiority of reason to history and the divide that was thought to lie between the contingent facts of the one and the eternal, necessary truths of the other); it also called for a new aesthetics that would disclose the Word of God in the otherwise "sealed" books of nature and Scripture—books that will remain sealed, according to Hamann, as long as our perception, our aesthetic sense, is unredeemed.

Accordingly, the first point of Hamann's aesthetics, which marks his definitive rejection of every gnosticism (ancient or modern), is that nature and history are significant *and that divine kenosis makes them so.* As such, their evidence need not be doubted (as with René Descartes), much less should they be spurned (as is the tendency of Platonism); nor is there any need to withdraw from them by way of Kant's Platonizing transcendental method into the fortress of pure reason, thinking that their evidence is somehow tainted and unable to provide any certainty for the sciences (this being the chronic fear of all philosophy that seeks certainty apart from faith). On the contrary, divine kenosis precisely *redeems* nature and history from philosophical skepticism and restores our confidence in them *as* revelation. As Hamann memorably puts it in the *Aesthetica*, "Speak, that I may see you!—This wish was fulfilled by creation, which is a speech [*Rede*] to the creature through the creature; for day to day pours forth speech, and night to night declares knowledge."[17] In other words, with creation God has already responded to our desire to see him and know something about him. For the *Logos* is not simply the hidden ground or ratio of creation; he is also the one who continuously communicates through it as the *Logos*, the Word. But, again, in order to perceive the *Logos* in the kenotic form of his self-revelation, for Hamann (on account of our fallen condition) our senses must be opened, redeemed. As the incarnate *Logos* himself

---

17 Hamann, *SW* 2:198. Compare Ps. 19:1–4. The phrase, "Speak, that I may see you!" refers to a story about Socrates, which has come down to us from Erasmus and, earlier, from Apuleius. See Erasmus, *Apophthegmata* [Aphorisms], Bk. 3, 70, in *Apophthegmata, Libri I–IV*, ed. Tineke Ter Meer (Leiden: Brill Academic, 2010). As the story goes, Socrates once addressed the son of a wealthy man in just these words, *loquere igitur, adolescens, ut te videam* ("Well then, lad, speak so that I can see you."), in order to "see" his talent. What Hamann means in the present context is that creation similarly fulfills the creature's desire to see God's "invisible nature" (see Rom. 1:20). See Hans-Martin Lumpp, *Philologia Crucis: Zu Johann Georg Hamanns Fassung von der Dichtkunst* [Philology of the Cross: Hamann's Conception of Poetry] (Tübingen: Max Niemeyer, 1970), 55. Compare, Hamann, *Briefwechsel*, 1:393: "Creation is a speech, whose thread stretches from one end of heaven to the other."

frequently puts it, establishing the principle that whatever is known is known only in the mode of the knower, we must have "ears to hear." And here we see why, for Hamann, a humble descent into self-knowledge precedes the resurrection of vision, indeed why his *Socratic Memorabilia*, which is dedicated to clearing away rational pretensions of knowledge—so that true knowledge born of poverty of spirit can take root in the soul—precedes his *Aesthetica*.[18]

For Hamann, in any event, philosophy need not and indeed should not seek its *Logos* in abstraction from the senses—this being, for Hamann, the *proton pseudos* ("original error") of philosophy divorced from faith, since philosophy thereby *misses* the accommodating movement of revelation, falls *de facto* into a hamartiological condition, and mistakenly proceeds in its investigations as if creation itself were not a revelation and no other revelation had been given. Rather, for Hamann, the transcendent *Logos*, which is the ultimate desideratum of reason, being the source of reason, is found precisely in the ordinary humble forms where he has revealed himself: in the "words" of creation, in the words of the prophets, and, above all, in the person and words of the Word made flesh, whom "we have seen with our eyes" and "looked upon and touched with our hands."[19] This is why logic—which is sourced in something higher than the necessary truths of reason—cannot and should never be divorced from aesthetics; on the contrary, on account of the accommodating movement of divine kenosis, aesthetics is precisely the route to the *Logos*.

But if divine kenosis establishes that nature and history are significant, that both have something to *say*, this does not alter the fact that they require interpretation. For if human texts can be rich and demanding of interpretation, the books of nature and history are infinitely more so. As Hamann puts it, "*All* the appearances of nature are dreams, faces, riddles, which have their meaning, their secret sense. The book[s] of nature and history are nothing but *ciphers*, hidden signs, which require the same key that interprets holy Scripture and is the point of its inspiration."[20] Further compounding the hermeneutical difficulty, as a consequence of our postlapsarian condition the "verse" or divine poetry of creation is precisely "jumbled," so that we cannot understand it. As Hamann puts it in the *Aesthetica*, "Wherever the guilt may lie (whether outside us or in us): nature leaves for our use nothing but jumbled verse and the *disiecti membra poetae*. It is the task

---

18   See Hamann, *SW* 2:164: "nothing but the *descensus ad inferos* [*Höllenfahrt*: "descent into hell"] of self-knowledge paves the way for our deification." Conversely, for Hamann, nothing is a greater impediment to seeing clearly than pride, since it bars the humble path to self-knowledge and prevents one from seeing the humility of God in creation. In this respect, Hamann's method resembles the patristic model we see in Evagrius, for whom the discipline of the Christian life (*praktiki*), which is all about self-knowledge and the understood need to attain *apatheia* or purity of heart—certainly by the grace of God—precedes the contemplation of God in nature (*theoria physiki*).

19   See John 1:14; 1 John 1:1.

20   Hamann, *Londoner Schriften*, 417 (*SW* 1:308–309).

of the scholar to collect them; of the philosopher, to interpret them; for the poet, to imitate them—or more boldly still!—bring about their destiny."[21]

As a result, in our fallen condition, we no longer experience creation as a divine speaking "to the creature through the creature"—as little as Jesus's unbelieving audience was able to understand his parables,[22] which are the preeminent example of the speech of the *Logos* "to the creature through the creature." Instead, all that we perceive are the fragments of an original poem, which we no longer know how to order or read, and no amount of labor on the part of the scholar or scientist will avail to do anything more than, so to speak, assemble the letters. As Hamann similarly put it to Kant (in the context of Kant's proposal that the two of them collaborate on a physics book for children):

> Nature is a book, a letter, a fable (in the philosophical sense) or however you want to call it. Assuming that we knew all its letters to the greatest possible degree; that we could make out the syllables and pronounce all the words; that we even knew the language in which it was written—Is all of that by itself enough to understand a book, to make judgments about it, to extract its character? In other words, the interpretation of nature involves more than physics. Physics is nothing but the Abc. Nature is an equation of an unknown quantity, a Hebraic word written with nothing but consonants to which the understanding must supply the [vowel] points.[23]

For Hamann, therefore, whatever significance nature and history have will be opaque, especially to rationalists who obtusely interpret them by the light of reason alone and attempt to make them fit the mold of our limited reasoning capacities— a point that Hamann in various ways tried to make to Kant after Kant tried and failed to win him back to the Enlightenment. As he suggestively put it to Kant in the *Socratic Memorabilia*, "But perhaps all of history is ... a riddle that will not be solved unless we plow with another calf than our reason."[24] In other words, by itself reason will never be able to do anything more than scratch the surface of the books of nature and history; it will never be able to fathom their profounder prophetic content. And if this is true of nature and history, for Hamann, it goes without

---

21 Hamann, *SW* 2:198–199. By the phrase *disiecti membra poetae* ("the scattered limbs of the poet"), which comes from Horace (*Satires*, Bk. 1, Sat. 4, 62), Hamann is alluding to the fate of Orpheus who was torn to pieces by the Maenads, and who therefore metonymically stands in the present context for the jumbled and fragmentary verse of creation.

22 Matt. 13:13–15.

23 Hamann, *Briefwechsel*,1:450.

24 See Hamann, *SW* 2:64. As it happens, Hamann's efforts to convert Kant proved as useless as Kant's own efforts to convert him, and yet they remained friends.

saying that it is true of Scripture, which in his view is an even richer, profounder, and more mysterious communication "to the creature through the creature."

So what then, for Hamann, is the hermeneutical key to understanding nature, history, and Scripture, the key that decodes their scrambled and sometimes baffling message? Beginning with the passage from the *Aesthetica* quoted above, Hamann suggests that the poet (in fulfillment of the vocation of Adam in Genesis 2:19) is somehow able to translate the meaning of nature and bring the words of creation to their destiny, that is, to render visible the hidden glory of the Word in the words of creation. And perhaps here we have a clue to his otherwise cryptic statement in the same text:

> Speaking is translation—from an angelic into a human tongue, i.e., thoughts into words,—things into names,—pictures into signs, whether they be poetic, kyriological, historical, symbolic, or hieroglyphic—and philosophical or characteristic."[25]

That is, the task of the poet is to translate the speech of creation, which is already in itself a translation of divine thoughts and ideas. But, for Hamann, the poet or would-be translator of creation is, strictly speaking, a Christian—someone who believes in Christ, is inspired with the Spirit of Christ, and is thereby made into a translator of divine things.[26] Accordingly—picking up on Hamann's suggestion that creation is a kind of "speaking in tongues"—just as the spiritual gift of interpretation is required in order to understand the gift of speaking in tongues,[27] so too the gift of the Spirit is required in order to understand the "angelic tongue" of creation. The same holds true, for Hamann, of the strange stories of the Torah and the "strange tongues" of the prophets.[28] Thus, as with the Old Testament, the hermeneutical key, which begins to unlock the riches of the prophetic books

---

25   See Hamann, *SW* 2:199. For the various kinds of signification Hamann has in mind, see the first section of Johann Georg Wachter's *Naturae et Scripturae Concordia* [The Harmony of Nature and Scripture] (1752). See Betz, *After Enlightenment*, 127–128. For the most detailed investigation of this passage, however, see Xavier Tilliette, "Hamann und die Engelsprache: Über eine Stelle der Aesthetica in Nuce" [Hamann and the Speech of Angels: Concerning a Passage in *Aesthetics in a Nutshell*], in *Acta des Internationalen Hamann-Colloquiums*, ed. Bernhard Gajek (Frankfurt: Vittorio Klostermann, 1979), 66–77.

26   As he strikingly put it to Lindner (*Briefwechsel*, 1:367): "*Christian* or *poet*. Do not be surprised that these are synonyms."

27   See 1 Cor. 14:5–12.

28   Compare Isa. 28:11. To this extent, as we shall see, Hamann follows in the patristic tradition of allegorical exegesis, which similarly finds in Christ the hermeneutical key to the Old Testament. As the traditional maxim has it, "the Old [Testament] is revealed in the New, and the New is hidden in the Old" [Lat.: *vetus in novo patet, novum in vetere latet*].

of nature and history, is faith in Christ, the giver of the Spirit,[29] who "searches everything, even the depths of God."[30]

But, following Hamann, we need to be more precise: we need to specify that the key is Christ *in his servant-form*, in his *Knechtsgestalt*. For it is in view of the kenotic form of the *Logos* in Christ that we are given to understand not only the ultimate prophetic *content* of creation and history but also the analogously *kenotic form* of God's self-revelation throughout creation and history. With regard to content, for example, we are given to understand that creation is an intimation, declared with increasing clarity by the prophets, of the Word's kenotic indwelling of his creation—to the point that Paul can say that "Christ in you" is the mystery hidden since the foundation of the world but now revealed to the saints.[31] At the same time, with regard to form, to the degree that we see the glory of God in the face of Christ, the servant-king, we come to understand that majesty is found *in humility*, and that it is precisely the *humility* of the *Logos* that renders him, the archetype of all reason, invisible and unintelligible to the "proud little mare" of reason alone.[32] Thus, as a fundamental rule for our interpretation of nature, history, and Scripture, Hamann would have us meditate in particular upon the *kenotic form* under which the Word—the *Logos*—appears.

Admittedly, after Paul, there is nothing particularly original in seeing the kenotic form of the incarnate Word, "who, though he was in the form of God, did not count equality with God something to be grasped, but emptied himself [*ekenōsen*] taking the form of a servant."[33] On the contrary, seeing this form is what defines the vision and sensibility of every Christian who has grasped with Peter the radical nature of the incarnation,[34] and with Paul the shocking bathos and outright paradox—the glory in the disgrace—of the cross.[35] What is distinctive to Hamann, however, is that he expands upon Paul's teaching in Philippians, seeing the same kenotic form that is evident in the incarnate Son, his *Knechtsgestalt*, as *the form of the glory of creation and Scripture*. In other words, Hamann sees the kenosis of the Son to be paradigmatic of the way that the *Logos* reveals himself—humbly and kenotically—throughout creation and history, and, among his historical revelations, above all in Scripture.

But what, concretely, does this mean? As far as our understanding of creation is concerned, it means that, creation, while glorious—it is the speech of the *Most High*—can also appear plain, stripped of any greater significance, in a word, mun-

---

29   John 4:10.

30   1 Cor. 2:10.

31   Col. 1:27.

32   See Hamann, *Londoner Schriften*, 346 (SW 2:43).

33   Phil. 2:6.

34   Matt. 16:16.

35   1 Cor. 1:18–29.

dane. To be sure, in part this is due to our fallen condition. As Hamann observes, "Nature is glorious, who can overlook it, [but] who understands its language; for the natural man it is mute and lifeless."[36] To the eyes of faith, however, which have come to see the glory of God in Christ and thus have grown accustomed to seeing majesty in humility, the fact that creation can appear this way—as plain, as ordinary, as mere "nature"—is equally seen to be a function of divine kenosis, of a glory that is so humbly communicated that it can go unnoticed, just as the glory of the incarnate *Logos*, being clothed in utter humility, could go largely unnoticed. Accordingly, like the crucified-resurrected *Logos* to which it bears witness, creation too appears in a strangely double light of majesty and humility, of fullness and "the most complete self-emptying." As Hamann puts it in a core passage from the *Aesthetica*:

> The book of creation contains examples of universal concepts that GOD wished to reveal to the creature through the creature; the books of the covenant contain examples of secret articles that GOD wished to reveal to the creature through the creature. The unity of the author is reflected in the dialect of his works;—in all *one* note of immeasurable height and depth! A proof of the most glorious majesty and of the most complete self-emptying! A marvel of such infinite calm [*Ruhe*] that makes GOD seem like nothing, so that one is forced either to deny his existence or be a beast (Ps. 73:21–22); but at the same time of such infinite power, which fills all in all, that one does not know how to save oneself from his most penetrating activity![37]

The same is true, as we shall see in greater detail below, of the Old Testament: it too exhibits a strangely double light of glory and humility. The only difference is that, in comparison to creation, the glory of its divine origin is arguably still more hidden, inasmuch as the Old Testament is an even profounder revelation. One could even say, the profounder the revelation—the more fully it approximates God's self-revelation in Christ—the more hidden beneath a kenotic form it will be: the more it will have the form not simply of truth-in-mystery, but of majesty-in-

---

36 Hamann, *Londoner Schriften*, 152 (*SW* 2:91). Of course, reason should be able to grasp that nature is creation, that is, a divine artifact, as Paul says in Rom. 1. For reason is perfectly capable of tracing effects upward to a divine cause. By the same token, reason should be able to infer from the order of creation something about the intelligence and wisdom of the Creator. One could even argue that reason can see that creation, inasmuch as it is a divine expression, is a kind of divine language. But this is not to say that reason, unenlightened by faith, can understand the language (the Logos) in and through which it is spoken or see that it is a kenotic communication "to the creature through the creature." On the contrary, as we have seen, apart from faith, the language of creation will be indecipherable.

37 Hamann, *SW* 2:204.

humility, indeed, wisdom-in-folly. Accordingly, in comparison to creation (which is but a preliminary revelation of the *Logos*), one might speak hyperbolically of the still more "immeasurable height and depth" of the Old Testament, whose glory and wisdom are still more hidden from the wise and learned,[38] inasmuch as they are concealed beneath an even greater self-emptying. This is why in the absence of faith in Christ, who is their ultimate prophetic content, many of the stories of the Old Testament, far from being transparently divine, can appear nonsensical and even offensive. Indeed, one could read the Old Testament and come away with nothing; just as some see nothing in the testimony of creation.[39] Read with the eyes of faith, however, which have been sensitized to the humility of divine revelation—and are thereby equipped to see light in the darkness, as it were, and make sense of what is otherwise obscure to reason—the Old Testament is seen to be an even more mysterious and even more gloriously concealed, but at the same time, paradoxically, even more intimate communication "to the creature through the creature."[40]

For this reason, then, among the historical self-revelations of the *Logos*, the revelation given to Israel and recorded in Scripture is preeminent; for it is here, in a form proportionate to the *Logos*, that the *Logos* (in anticipation of his incarnation) is most fully revealed. But this is not to deny the significance of earlier revelations to the pagan world. On the contrary, following Hamann, who in turn develops the patristic tradition concerning the *logos spermatikos*, a sensibility enlightened by divine kenosis will delight to discover revelations of the *Logos*—in the form of traces, analogies, and typological foreshadowings—throughout human history. For, according to this view, there is no history that is not already *Heilsgeschichte* ("salvation history") and, as such, the history of the *Logos* kenotically communicating himself to human beings for the purposes of our salvation. Nor, for Hamann, should one be deterred by the folly of the form through which such revelations are sometimes given, as is the case with much of pagan mythology. On the contrary, a "philology of the cross," which is attentive to the wisdom-in-folly of divine revelation, will find unexpected meanings in much of the poetry and literature of the pagan world. As Hamann observes, seeing in Greek mythology a presentiment of divine kenosis: "Even the pagans knew to weave a little word of these mysteries into their mythology. Jupiter transformed himself into a miserable, shivering, and half-dead cuckoo dripping with rain in order to enjoy the favor of his lawful wife—And the Jew, the Christian rejects his king because he coos like a hen around his chicks,

---

38 Matt. 11:25.

39 Rom. 1:18–23.

40 See Hamann *Londoner Schriften*, 152 (SW 1:91): "Nature is glorious. … But Scripture, the Word of God, the Bible, is more glorious, is more perfect." Compare *Londoner Schriften*, 251 (SW 1:190): "Next to the wealth of God in nature, which arose out of nothing, there is no greater creation than the transformation [through Scripture] of human concepts and impressions into heavenly and divine mysteries."

contending in a meek and lowly form for the rights of his love."[41] Indeed, reading pagan literature with Hamann, who reclaims the teaching of the early Church, we find that the ultimate, unconscious witness of paganism is to the incarnate and glorified Word. As he puts it, "The mustard seed of *anthropomorphosis* and *apotheosis*, which is hidden in the *hearts* and *mouths* of all religions, is manifest here in the full stature, in the middle of the garden, of a *tree* of *knowledge* and *life*—all *philosophical* contradictions and the entire *historical* puzzle of our existence are resolved by the *original testimony* of the *incarnate Word*."[42]

In view of this rough sketch of Hamann's aesthetics we can now see why von Balthasar accorded such importance to him, indeed, why von Balthasar's theology is profoundly indebted to him. And in this regard, by way of summary, one might speak of three basic insights. Firstly, Hamann saw that truth, the *Logos*, is found not by abstraction from the aesthetic sphere but precisely through the aesthetic sphere, since this is the theater, the dramatic stage, so to speak, of divine kenosis—thereby suggesting the very method of von Balthasar's theologicial project. Secondly, in von Balthasar's view, Hamann saw the *form* of true glory—glory not as the world conceives of it, but "glory as *kenosis*, not only of the incarnate Son, but also of the [Father], who by creating reaches into nothingness, and of the Holy Spirit, who conceals himself, as Hamann strikingly puts it, 'under all kinds of rags and tatters,' 'under the rubbish' of the letter of Scripture."[43] In other words, Hamann perceived that this striking coincidence of opposites—of *glory and kenosis, majesty and abasement*—is mysteriously proper to *all* of the persons of the Trinity: that their shared glory consists precisely in their shared humility, their reciprocal *kenosis*. Accordingly—and this will be a point of great importance in what follows—Hamann saw that divine glory as manifested in creation and the economy of salvation is a glory that is *hidden*, a glory, as it were, *in disguise*, a

---

41   Hamann, *Briefwechsel*, 1:394; compare Matt. 23:37. For Hamann, therefore, there can be no ultimate opposition between Christ and Dionysus, the cross and pagan antiquity (as Friedrich Nietzsche had supposed); on the contrary, it is in the revelation of the Gospel and the folly of the cross that we see what the inspired pagan poets were unconsciously trying to say. See also, *ZH* 1:352: "Do we not find in Hosea: 'I am like a moth to Ephraim, like rot to the people of Judah' (Hos. 5:12). Does he not often change himself into a golden rain in order to win the love of a people and a soul. Is his justice not jealous about the bowels of his mercy and his love for the children of men. And what great projects did he have necessary in order to blind—that I should speak so humanly—the first [his justice]. How many amorous pursuits does he engage in to make us sensitive and to keep us faithful. Must he not abduct us, must he not often use force against his will—Tell me, how could it have occurred to the pagans to convert the glory of Olympus into the image of an ox, which eats grass?" The "golden rain" is an allusion to the story of Danaë and the manner of Zeus's entrance into her chamber; the reference to God's righteousness is an allusion to Zeus's wife, Hera, who represents justice and order and whom Zeus deceived by his transformations; the reference to the ox is to the rape of Europa. See Harry Sievers, *Johann Georg Hamanns Bekehrung* [Hamann's Conversion] (Zürich: Zwingli Verlag, 1969), 126–135.

42   Hamann, *SW* 3:192.

43   Balthasar, *Glory of the Lord*, 1:80–83.

glory, moreover, that is often so obscure, so hidden beneath a contrary, seemingly paradoxical form (*sub contrario*), as to be offensive to those who cannot perceive it and who, lacking the eyes of faith, duly reject it—whether in their rejection of the testimony of creation,[44] or in their rejection of the Crucified,[45] or in their rejection of Scripture. Thirdly, by way of analogy, Hamann found his way to a genuine universality, thereby steering between the extremes of a narrow pietism that would shut out the world and a liberal Christianity that is so open to the world as to be indistinguishable from it, and which invariably dilutes into "religion" the saltiness of the Gospel's claims.[46] In other words, seeing Christ *as the root*,[47] as the Alpha and the Omega,[48] as the beginning and the end, Hamann saw how to reclaim the significance of human history and culture (namely, as the medium of divine self-revelation) without in the least compromising a radical Christocentrism.[49] Thus von Balthasar observes, Hamann was "alone in seeing that the real problem was how to construct a theory of beauty in such a way that in it the total aspiration of worldly and pagan beauty is fulfilled while all glory is at the same time given to God in Jesus Christ."[50]

Finally, Hamann points the way for further theological reflection. For if one follows Hamann in seeing a shared kenotic form in the works of the Trinity *ad extra*, and if one follows him in seeing this form as constitutive of divine rev-

---

44   Rom. 1:19–24.

45   1 Cor. 1:18.

46   See Hamann, *Londoner Schriften*, 106 (SW 1:46): "There is but one truth; but it has countless analogies [*Gleichungen*] and expressions." Thus von Balthasar laments that Hamann's theological vision did not have greater influence than that of Schleiermacher. See *Glory of the Lord*, 3:277: "How little was needed and [Hamann] could have become the theological mentor and 'familiar spirit' of German Idealism (instead of [Friedrich] Schleiermacher), exceeding his actual historical influence, and so determined the theological climate for more than a century."

47   Col. 1:15.

48   Rev. 1:8.

49   See Balthasar, *Glory of the Lord*, 3:246: "Hamann never deviated one iota from this consistent and unbroken Christocentrism." Compare Hamann, *Londoner Schriften*, 431 (SW 2:48): "It would be more possible to live without one's heart and head than to live without him. He is the head of our nature and all our powers, and the source of movement, which can no more stand still in a Christian than the pulse can stand still in a living man."

50   Balthasar, *Glory of the Lord*, 1:81. And, true enough, seen in light of the larger theological context, what was briefly and singularly united in Hamann (both a full-blooded theological aesthetics, which sought to take in the whole of human history, literature, and culture, and an uncompromising Christocentrism) eventually split off into two antithetical directions within Protestantism: on the one hand, a subjective theology of feeling and culture in the Romantic spirit of Schleiermacher; on the other hand, an objective, dogmatic, dialectical theology in the tradition of Kierkegaard and the early Karl Barth. What was thereby lost from view was a genuine synthesis of Protestant Christocentrism (with all its subjective passion) and Catholic universalism (with all its objectivity and sacramental vision of reality). And looking back to Hamann, it was this synthesis that von Balthasar sought to reclaim for his own analogical, Christocentric theology of history and culture.

elation—whether in creation, or in the Old Testament, or in the servant-form of Christ—it is but a step to saying that this form, which is exhibited by the economic Trinity, affords a speculative glimpse of the kenotic form of the life of the Trinity *ad intra* ("unto itself"), as a divine life of mutually self-emptying relations.[51] One could argue that Hamann points the way to a higher and more fitting doctrine of divine unity and simplicity: not by way of a rational affirmation of monotheism (because God *must* be one or because God *must* be free of composition, as the axiom of divine simplicity would have it), but by way of faith in the God who is *one* because, in the form of three persons, each existing fully in the other, he is perfect, complete, self-emptying love.

Thus far, with reference to von Balthasar's work, we have been concerned with Hamann's aesthetics, broadly conceived. It is notable, however, that Hamann's aesthetics arose out of his interpretation of Scripture and that the proper interpretation of Scripture (in a polemic against J. D. Michaelis) was the principal theme of his *Aesthetica in Nuce*. Indeed, Hamann's conversion took place precisely through his reading of Scripture, specifically through his reading of the Old Testament. Moreover, it was his discovery of the kenotic form of the Word, majestically hidden in the pages of the Old Testament, that first opened his eyes to the kenotic form of the Word everywhere else.[52] In the apt phrase of Joachim Ringleben, "The Bible was his *Hen* ["One"] because it disclosed the *Pan* ["All"]."[53] It would be impossible, therefore, to overestimate the importance Hamann attached to Scripture. And yet, remarkably, his understanding of Scripture is probably the most neglected aspect of his thought. In the rest of this essay, therefore, my concern will be to elucidate Hamann's biblical hermeneutics, ultimately in order to determine what promise, if any, it holds for the Church today.

Hamann's Conversion: A Dramatic Transposition

To judge from the manner of Hamann's conversion, he was destined to be a sign of contradiction. The *lumières* of the Enlightenment, most notably Voltaire, had little patience or tolerance for the Old Testament: as a literary work it was com-

---

51   See John R. Betz, "Hamann's *London Writings*: The Hermeneutics of Trinitarian Condescension," *Pro Ecclesia* 14 (Spring 2005): 191–234.

52   See Hamann, *Londoner Schriften*, 132 (*SW* 1:72): "God has revealed everything in his Word." Compare *Londoner Schriften*, 59 (*SW* 1:4): "The Word of this Spirit is just as great a work as creation, and just as great a mystery as the redemption of human beings; indeed, this Word is the key to the works of the former and the mysteries of the latter." See also Joachim Ringleben, "'Rede, Daß ich Dich Sehe': Betrachtungen zu Hamanns Theologischem Sprachdenken" ["Speak, That I Might See You": Reflections on Hamann's Thought Regarding Religious Speech], *Neue Zeitschrift für Systematische Theologie und Religionsphilosophie* 27 (1985): 222: "The Bible was to him precisely the book above all books, the book *of* books: *liber instar omnium* [the book of books]. What was said there opened his eyes to all speech; and the very one whom the Bible revealed he saw again everywhere."

53   Ringleben, "Gott als Schriftsteller: Zur Geschichte eines Topos" [God as Author: The History of a Theme], in Bayer, *Johann Georg Hamann*, 37.

monly considered rubbish, certainly inferior to the classics of pagan antiquity; but, more to the point, many considered it morally offensive, even execrable.[54] And yet, ironically enough, Hamann's conversion took place precisely through the Old Testament, which, together with the New Testament, he subsequently came to regard and value as a work greater than all the works of pagan antiquity and, indeed, greater than the work of creation itself: "Nature is glorious. ... But Scripture, the Word of God, the Bible, is more glorious, is more perfect ... it is the wet nurse that gives us our first food, the milk that makes us strong."[55] So how did Hamann, one of the most literate men of his age, come to this unpopular view?

As for the circumstances of his conversion, they remind us of Augustine; and, in fact, Hamann's confessional *London Writings* (1758) bear striking similarities to Augustine's own *Confessions*—not least of all in that both ardently defended the Old Testament against the scoffing critics of their age. So too, on a more personal level, both had reached a point of desperation, both were led to "pick up and read" the Bible, and both were overwhelmed by how deeply it penetrated their heart, spoke to their own situations, and filled them with unexpected grace. According to Hamann's own account, his conversion began when, after a *second* reading of the entire Old Testament, he was moved to deep reflection on the story of Cain and Abel:

> I thought about Abel, of whom God said: the earth opened its mouth to receive the blood of your brother -- -- and suddenly I felt my heart beat, I heard a voice sighing and wailing in its depths as the voice of blood, as the voice of a murdered brother, who wanted to avenge his blood if I did not at times hear it and should continue to stop up my hears to its voice. -- -- that precisely this made Cain a restless fugitive. I felt at once my heart swelling, it poured itself out in tears, and I could no longer—I

---

54   As Voltaire contemptuously put it in his *Sermon of the Fifty*, "If one can dishonor the divinity with absurd fables, may these fables perish forever. ... My bretheren, you know what horror seized us when we read the writings of the Hebrews together, directing our attention only to those traits that violated purity, charity, good faith, justice, and universal reason, traits we found not merely in every chapter but which, to make things worse, were sanctified in all [...] but [...] it is not here that I wish to examine the ridiculous and the impossible; I concentrate on the execrable." See *Sermon of the Fifty*, ed. J. A. R. Séguin (New York: R. Paxton, 1962), 11. Similar sentiments can be found in some of the earliest critics of the first Christians, such as Celsus, Porphyry, and the Manichees, and in our own day in the writings of popular atheists like Christopher Hitchens and Richard Dawkins, the latter of whom finds the God of the Old Testament to be "arguably the most unpleasant character in all of fiction." See his *The God Delusion* (Boston: Houghton Mifflin, 2006), 31. As we shall see, none of their aspersions would have taken Hamann by surprise.

55   Hamann, *Londoner Schriften*, 152 (*SW* 1:91).

could no longer hide from God that I was the murderer of my brother, that I was the murderer of his only begotten Son.[56]

In other words, feeling himself strangely transposed into the story and its hidden allegorical dimensions, Hamann came to recognize and feel in the murder of Abel his own guilt in the spilling of Christ's blood, and that his previous failure to admit this guilt had made him, like Cain, a restless fugitive. But, he adds in a parallel reflection, no sooner do "we hear the blood of the redeemer crying out in our heart than we feel that its ground has already been sprinkled [... and] that the same avenging blood cries grace to us."[57] That is, to put it simply, Hamann experienced in the middle of his reading of the Old Testament what Lutheran theology means by "law" and "gospel"—the law that convicts us of sin, the gospel of grace that sets us free.[58] Fittingly, therefore, looking back on his conversion, he speaks of being poured "from one vessel into another," seeing in all of this the workings of the Holy Spirit, who over the course of the next several months "continued, in spite of my great weakness, in spite of the long resistance that I had previously mounted against his witness and his stirrings, to reveal to me more and more the mystery of divine love and the benefit of faith in our merciful and only Savior."[59]

By all accounts Hamann's conversion is striking; it is the kind of thing that William James might have recorded in his *Varieties of Religious Experience*[60] had he known about it. What makes it especially interesting, however, given the age in which Hamann lived, is that it occurred through the same Old Testament that many of his contemporaries had come to despise (and at least in this respect the Enlightenment did not deter but precisely lent support to the anti-Semitism of the modern age). What is more, to judge from Hamann's account, the Holy Spirit caused him to *linger* in the Old Testament, which, to his amazement, revealed his own life *through* the history of Israel: "Whoever would compare my life with the travel log of Israel would find that they exactly correspond."[61] In other words, Hamann discovered that the particular history of Israel was also, strangely, a universal story; that Israel's errings were his errings.[62] And in this way, as in a

---

56 Hamann, *Londoner Schriften*, 343 (*SW* 2:41).

57 Hamann, *Londoner Schriften*, 138. (*SW* 1:78).

58 It is not, therefore, that the Old Testament is simply "the Law" and the New Testament is the "Gospel," as an oversimplified account of Lutheran theology would have it, since Hamann had this experience of "law" and "gospel" while reading the Old Testament, and since, as we shall see, the Old Testament is at bottom filled with the grace of Christ.

59 Hamann, *Londoner Schriften*, 343 (*SW* 2:40), *Londoner Schriften*, 345 (*SW* 2:42).

60 William James, *The Varieties of Religious Experience: A Study in Human Nature* (London: Longmans, Green, 1902).

61 Hamann, *Londoner Schriften*, 345 (*SW* 2:42)

62 See Hamann's *Golgatha and Scheblimini* (1784; *SW* 3:311): "According to the analogy of its ceremonial law, the entire history of the Jewish people seems to be a living *primer* to all *historical literature in heaven*, on and *under the earth*, which awakens the mind and heart – – a progressive,

mirror, he came to know himself. Thus, subsequent to his conversion, in reference to Scripture's uncanny power to interpret and probe the hearts of those who read it—even haughty contemporaries, who were wont to ridicule it—Hamann was fond of citing the line from Horace: "What are you laughing at? Change the name and the story is about *you*."[63]

Thus, rather ironically, in the middle of the Enlightenment Hamann had an awakening—one that *ipso facto* placed him in opposition to his age, the "age of reason," which failing to understand Scripture mistakenly placed reason above Scripture. For the going ideology—which Kant enshrined in his popular mani-festo of 1784, entitled "What is Enlightenment?"—self-knowledge was thought to come through reason by way of an internal and unmediated auto-illumination. As Hamann discovered, however, it actually comes by way of the external, historically mediated prophetic Word of Scripture, which is "more sure" than reason[64] and deeper than reason, because it reveals a *Logos* that is higher than reason—indeed, a Logos that, unbeknownst to fallen reason, is the archetype of all true reason. Whereas Kant supposed enlightenment to come through an internal self-critique of reason, reason being for Kant sufficient unto itself, for Hamann it comes ad-ventitiously—as grace—through the critical and transforming power of the Word of God, which is "living and active," even to the dividing of "soul from spirit,"[65] and in this way, through this separation,[66] brings light and the new creation out of the darkness and confusion of our souls. Accordingly, he concludes his brief autobiography:

> with a proof [based on] my own experience, with heartfelt and sincere thanks to God for his saving Word, which I have found tested as the only light not only to come to God, but to know ourselves, as the most valuable gift of divine grace, which sur-passes nature and all its treasures as much as our immortal spirit surpasses the lime of flesh and blood, as the most astonishing

---

diamond-like index pointing to the Jubilees and plans of divine government, spanning the whole of creation from its *beginning* to its *end*."

63   To describe this rhetorical transposition Hamann later used the term "metaschematism," which derives from 1 Cor. 4:6, where Paul says that he has "figuratively applied" (*meteschēmatisa*) his words to Apollos and himself—not for his own benefit, but so that through indirect means the Corinthians will come to the realization that his message (about not boasting in human leaders, see 1 Cor. 3:5–4:5) applies specifically *to them*. See Hamann, *ZH* 4:272: "*Quid rides? de TE fabula narratur*"("Why are you laughing? *You* yourself are the man of the fable.") See also, *Briefwechsel*, 1:396. Compare Horace, *Satires*, Bk. 1, Sat. 1, 69: "*Quid rides? mutato nomine de te fabula narratur*" ("What are you laughing at? Change the name and the story is about you.") For Hamann, the paradigmatic instance of such transposition in the Old Testament is Nathan's parable in 2 Sam. 12.

64   2 Pet. 1:19.

65   Heb. 4:12.

66   See Gen. 1:3.

and praiseworthy revelation of the most profound, most sublime, most marvelous mysteries … of God's nature, attributes, and exceedingly good will chiefly toward us miserable human beings … as the only bread and manna of our souls, which a Christian can no more do without than the earthly man can do without his daily necessities and sustenance—indeed, I confess that this Word of God accomplishes just as great wonders in the soul of a devout Christian, whether he be simple or learned, as those described in it; that the understanding of this book and faith in its contents can be attained by no other means than through the same Spirit, who inspired its authors; that his inexpressible sighs, which he creates in our hearts, are of the same nature as the inexpressible images, which are scattered throughout the Holy Scriptures with a greater prodigality than all the seeds of nature and its kingdoms.[67]

Glory(ing) in the "Old Rags" of Scripture

What is arguably most striking about Hamann's conversion, however, is that he does not dispute the initial impression Scripture affords. On the contrary, following in the tradition of Church fathers like Jerome and Augustine, he readily admits that Scripture's form is not immediately impressive or transparently divine: that, on the face of it, it is a miscellaneous, fragmentary collection of ancient stories and poetry written by people who were by no means the "*literati* [intellectuals] of their *saeculi* [age]."[68] And yet, to Hamann's own amazement, it was precisely through such humble means that he was saved. As he puts it in his brief statement on biblical hermeneutics: "We all find ourselves in a swampy dungeon like the one in which Jeremiah found himself. Old rags served as ropes to pull him out; to them he owed his gratitude for saving him. Not their appearance, but the services they provided him and the use he made of them, redeemed his life from danger (Jer. 38:11–13)."[69]

---

67 See Hamann, *Briefwechsel*, 1:345–346 (*SW* 2:43).

68 Hamann, *SW* 2:169. St. Jerome, for example, initially found the style of Scripture repugnant to his classical sensibility (*Letter* 22, chap. 30, 2); similarly, St. Augustine initially thought the style of Scripture inferior to the works of Cicero (*Confessions*, Bk. 3, Chap. 5, 9). But what Augustine and Jerome discovered, following Origen, was that the divine character of Scripture and the "splendor of its teachings" is "concealed under a poor and humble style." See Origen, *On First Principles*, trans. G. W. Butterworth (Gloucester, MA: Peter Smith, 1973), 267. For more on this topic, see Henri De Lubac, *The Christian Faith* (San Francisco: Ignatius, 1986), 261–289. I wish to express my thanks here to John C. Cavadini for a helpful discussion of this topic, especially as it relates to Origen.

69 Hamann, *SW* 2:169. Compare *Briefwechsel*, 1:341. Von Balthasar comments on this passage in *Glory of the Lord*, 3:251. See n. 6 above.

To be sure, as Hamann recognized, such a humble or "low" style will not suit the tastes or prejudices of proud philosophers or literary critics—no more than it satisfied the literary sensibilities of Christianity's ancient critics, like Celsus or Porphyry. "The talk," he writes, "is not of a revelation that a Voltaire, a [Henry St. John] Bolingbroke, a [Earl of] Shaftesbury would find acceptable [to which one might add more recent critics of Christianity, like Christopher Hitchens and Richard Dawkins]; that would most satisfy their prejudices, their wit, their moral and political fancies."[70] And why? The principal problem, as Hamann sees it, is that his contemporaries, duped by pride into trusting their own reason more than revelation, could not imagine that enlightenment, that salvation, could come through such humble means—as little as first-century Jews under Roman occupation could imagine that the Messiah would come in the form of a suffering servant and carpenter's son.[71]

As Hamann recognized, however, it is not to the proud that Scripture is given (their own pride denies them the gift), but to the lovers of God, whose humility allows them to be enlightened by the Holy Spirit and to recognize in such disguise "the beams of heavenly glory." As he puts it in his *Cloverleaf of Hellenistic Letters* (1762):

> If the divine style elects the foolish—the trite—the ignoble—in
> order to put to shame the strength and ingenuity of all profane
> authors: then it almost goes without saying that eyes that are
> illumined, inspired, and armed with the jealousy of a friend, an
> intimate, a lover are required in order to see in such disguise the
> beams of heavenly glory.[72]

Accordingly, for Hamann, there is an unavoidable subjective element to interpretation of the Bible. One's disposition or attitude is largely what determines what one will see. And in this regard, given the objective humility of Scripture, a corresponding subjective humility would seem to be indispensable. As Hamann puts it, "Humility of heart is therefore the one required disposition and most indispensable

---

70   Haman, *Londoner Schriften*, 68 (SW 1:10). Compare *Londoner Schriften*, 59 (SW 1:4): "As little as an animal is capable of reading the fables of Aesop, Phaedrus, and *la Fontaine*—or, even if it were able to read them—it would not be able to make such bestial judgments regarding the sense of the stories and their justification as human beings have made in criticizing and philosophizing about the book of God."

71   Matt. 13:55. And yet, as Hamann was surprised to find, it was through this particular "style" that God was pleased to reveal himself—just as, throughout Scripture, God elects not the powerful, not those of noble birth, but precisely the weak to shame the strong, and even the foolish to shame the supposedly wise, and in general "what is low and despised in the world, even things that are not" (or are reckoned not) in order "to bring to nothing things that are." (1 Cor. 1:26–31.)

72   Hamann, SW 2:171.

preparation for reading the Bible."[73] Indeed, it would seem to be a precondition for entering the "hermeneutical circle" and experiencing the illumination that Hamann describes. For, in order to discover the glory of the Holy Spirit hidden in the humility of the letter, one must read Scripture in like mind—in the same Spirit of humility that originally inspired it: "The lowliest images contain a meaning that is unlocked when we read the Word of God with simplicity and humility—with precisely the simplicity and humility that the Spirit of God assumed when by this means he revealed himself to man."[74]

In the same work, with regard to the objective humility of Scripture, Hamann then continues with a reference to Paul's dictum in 2 Corinthians 4:7 that we have this "glory in earthen vessels," but now applies this to the earthen quality of the divine style: "We have this treasure of divine documents, as Paul says, *'en ostrakinois skeuesin ina ē hyperbolē tēs dynameōs ē tou theou kai mē ex ēmōn'* [in earthen vessels, to show that the transcendent power is from God and not from us]."[75] To which he adds, "we can be sure that the *stylus curiae* [style of the curia] of the Kingdom of Heaven remains the meekest and humblest, especially when compared to that of the Asian courts."[76] Indeed, he says, "the external appearance of the letter bears a greater resemblance to the untamed foal of an ass, that beast of burden, than to the proud stallions that spelled Phaeton's demise."[77] In other words, Hamann daringly suggests, far from being externally glorious, the form of Scripture, as a vehicle of the Word of God, is more like the ass on which Christ rode into Jerusalem.[78] But, as his allusion equally makes clear, this does not prevent Scripture from conveying

---

73 Hamann, *Londoner Schriften*, 158 (SW 1:97).

74 Hamann, *Londoner Schriften*, 163 (SW 1:102). Compare Origen, *On First Principles*, 306: "These treasures require for their discovery the help of God, who alone is able to 'break in pieces the gates of brass' [Is. 45:2] that conceal them and to burst the iron bars that are upon the gates."

75 Hamann may have taken this from Origen, who says the same thing in *On First Principles*, Bk. 4, 7, where he also observes that "if it had been the hackneyed methods of demonstration used among men and preserved in books that had convinced mankind, our faith might reasonably have been supposed to rest in the wisdom of men and not in the power of God." See *On First Principles*, 267.

76 Hamann, SW 2:171. Compare SW 2:171–172: "According to all the textbooks of rhetoric, journalistic and epistolary styles belong to the *humili generi dicendi* [humble class of speech], of which class there remain few analogies in ancient Greek. And yet it is with just this kind of taste that one must judge the books of the New Testament, and in this respect they are to a certain extent original." For a discussion of the Christian notion of a so-called "low style" or *sermo humilis* as it develops out of Augustine, is received in the western tradition, and relates to and radically transforms classical understandings of the *sermo sublimis* or "elevated style," see Erich Auerbach's famous study, *Mimesis*, trans. Willard R. Trask (Princeton: Princeton University, 1953), 72–73, 151–152.

77 Hamann, SW 2:171–172. The reference is to the brazen Phaeton, son of Helios, who could not manage his father's horses and, as a result, nearly scorched the earth before being struck down by Zeus.

78 Compare Matt. 21:1–5.

a divine content and, as it were, leading one to the true Jerusalem that is above.[79] On the contrary, for Hamann, it is as if divine revelation does not come in any other way—and that one must be wary of any purported revelation that does not come in a similarly humble form.[80]

For Hamann, therefore, as a first rule of exegesis, one must see the style of Scripture as an extraordinary testament to the humility of the Holy Spirit, who condescended to inspire the sounds and letters of human language and charge them with divine purpose. But, following Hamann, we have not yet appreciated the depth of the Holy Spirit's kenosis in the inspiration of Scripture until we appreciate the extent to which in inspiring human authors He also accommodated "human inclinations and concepts, indeed even prejudices and weaknesses."[81] And here we have, as it were, a second rule of biblical exegesis—one that goes a long way toward addressing (and obviating) criticisms of the Old Testament on the basis of the violence it contains or the primitive science it represents.[82] Accordingly, Hamann's understanding of kenosis bears a certain similarity to doctrines of accommodation that have been current in theology at least since the nineteenth century, which found in the concept a convenient way of excusing Scripture, in particular the Old Testament, for its otherwise humble and, in the words of a notable English divine, "most unspiritual appearance."[83]

But, while Hamann's understanding of kenosis bears a certain similarity to going doctrines of accommodation, one must immediately add and emphasize that

---

79 Gal. 4:26.

80 See 2 Cor. 11:14.

81 See Hamann, *Londoner Schriften*, 68 (*SW* 1:10). Compare *Londoner Schriften*, 251 (*SW* 1:190): "Next to the wealth of God in nature, which arose out of nothing, there is no greater creation than the transformation [through Scripture] of human concepts and impressions into heavenly and divine mysteries; this omnipotence [which transforms] human language into the thoughts of the Cherubim and Seraphim."

82 For, to take the obvious example of Genesis, a doctrine of accommodation helps one to appreciate the creation narratives as accommodating the natural philosophy of the time, and not confuse biblical inerrancy with what we mean today by scientific explanation. So too, as far as the violence of the Old Testament is concerned, a doctrine of accommodation helps one to see it as a reflection of the violent culture of the time and—this being the case—a testament to the humility of the Holy Spirit who lowered himself to communicate divine mysteries in its everyday language. Of course, following Origen in Bk. 4 of *On First Principles*, one could go further and deny that certain passages of Scripture have any literal meaning at all; and that the initial offense they cause is simply a provocation to read more deeply and spiritually in order to discover the hidden treasure they contain.

83 See Charles Gore, "The Holy Spirit and Inspiration," in *Lux Mundi* [Light of the World]: *A Series of Studies in the Religion of the Incarnation* (London: John Murray, 1904), 240. As Gore goes on to say of the Old Testament, "Its material sacrifices, its low standard of morals, its worldliness, were constantly being objected to by the gnostic and Manichaean sects, who could not tolerate the Old Testament canon. 'But you are ignoring,' the Church replied, 'the gradualness of the Spirit's method.' He lifts man [little by little] he condescends to man's infirmity: he puts up with him as he is, if only he can at the last bring him back to God."

it is not exhausted by a doctrine of accommodation and differs significantly from it. For the humility of Scripture (and, for that matter, of creation) is not merely the function of a necessary accommodation to our senses and spiritual weakness. A doctrine of kenosis, taken in this sense, would still be too Platonic—the humility of the form (of creation, of Scripture) being here merely the terminus of a downward and, in the colloquial sense of the term, "condescending" emanation. Moreover, kenosis, taken in this sense, would be a merely negative concept, a matter of God stooping down, so to speak, as a matter of necessity for our salvation, whereas for Hamann the concept of kenosis is an utterly positive one, representing a free act of love, which loves to give itself to the beloved—even to the point of leaving everything behind. And it was above all by seeing this—seeing the humility of Scripture as the emblem of God's love—that he came to love the humility of the Word.

This difference, between a positive and negative doctrine of kenosis, is especially manifest in how one reads the Old Testament. When proponents of accommodation (or a merely negative doctrine of kenosis) read the Old Testament, they see it as necessarily "limited" and "imperfect," as spiritual "milk" suited to the spiritual infancy of Israel.[84] When Hamann reads the Old Testament, on the other hand, he reads it in light of a positive kenosis of the Holy Spirit, who does not hold anything back but presents himself fully in *Knechtsgestalt*—just as the Son of God is fully present in Christ, but in *Knechtsgestalt*. Consequently, there is no lack of wisdom in the Old Testament (as little as it is lacking in Christ); its wisdom (as with the wisdom of the incarnate *Logos*) is simply hidden beneath a seemingly incongruous form. To be sure, this form is in part an accommodation to our senses and spiritual weakness (as the flesh of Christ is in some sense an accommodation to our senses and the weakness of our spiritual vision). But it is also a positive function of the humility of the Holy Spirit, who does not overtly draw attention to his own Wisdom, the *Logos*, but in the form of an *indirect communication* leaves it for the humble and discerning to find. And, for his part, it seems that Hamann was someone who found it—who discovered the infinite riches of the Logos *in* the Old Testament, the Word kenotically hidden at the bottom of its words. And having found it, he gloried in it.

How different this is from a merely negative doctrine of accommodation, which can see in the Old Testament only its limitations! Whereas Hamann glories in the Old Testament, proponents of accommodation (in the sense described above) are secretly embarrassed by it—and, as a result, are far too accommodating to Christianity's cultured despisers whom they otherwise hope to assuage. This is not to deny that the Old Testament can give an unsettling impression, an impression that might tempt one to embrace Marcion. But, as Hamann found, there is a mystery to its form, which is mysteriously adequate to the depth of the mystery it

---

84 Gore, "Holy Spirit and Inspiration," 256.

conveys. For truth—at least any truth that isn't trivial, like the necessary truths of logic or mathematics—is always "hidden in a mystery."[85] Instead, therefore, of seeing the limitations of the Old Testament, Hamann would have us look deeper and see the infinite wealth hidden in its poverty, the glory hidden in its humility, the light hidden in its darkness, the divine power hidden in its weakness, the wisdom hidden in its "folly." And for this reason, if we are properly to appreciate the form of Scripture, we need to see it in light of the cross.

Wisdom in Folly: The Cruciform Style of Scripture

Needless to say, devout readers will bristle at the notion of the "foolishness" and "infirmity" of God; and understandably so, for God is certainly not foolish, nor is he weak. But once again, for Hamann, following Paul, we have not fully appreciated divine revelation until we have truly grasped how foolish and weak it can appear, what foolish, weak, and insignificant instruments God can use, and, what is more, how all of this accords with God's pleasure. To be sure, after Paul, we are more accustomed to speaking of the wisdom-in-the-folly *of the cross*. But, for Hamann, if our exegesis of Scripture is not to be naïve or disingenuous, we must also appreciate the corresponding wisdom-in-the-folly of *the Old Testament*. In other words, we must own up to the fact, which is obvious to any unbelieving critic, that its stories frequently defy rational comprehension—sometimes because they strike us as fanciful or magical (as with the parting of the Red Sea or the miraculously floating axe head), sometimes because they strike us as morally repugnant (as with the command to sacrifice Isaac or the murder of Sisera, not to mention the actions of Phinehas and the occasional sanction of genocide), and sometimes because they strike us as tasteless, ludicrous, or downright absurd. Understandably, out of piety, we might not want to admit the offence that such stories can cause; but this does not keep them from posing serious hermeneutical challenges for modern interpreters—whether for unbelievers who will readily write them off, following Voltaire, as the crude and foolish imaginations of human authors who "impiously ascribed their work to the supreme being,"[86] or for believers who, embarrassed by them, would rather ignore them, and therefore never raise the question of how they could be divinely inspired.

So, in view of the hermeneutical difficulty, how does Hamann proceed? In what way does he help modern Christians past the apparent impasse? We have already seen that, far from being embarrassed by the form of Scripture, he glories in it. Now we simply have to add that he glories in it just as Paul glories in the cross, seeing a correspondence between the folly of the one and the folly of the other.[87] For, like Paul, but now with regard to the form of the Old Testament, Hamann

---

85   1 Cor. 2:7.

86   See Voltaire, *Sermon of the Fifty*, 11.

87   1 Cor. 1:18–25.

wants us to see the offence; he wants us to recognize the scandal (as if to suggest that faith is not faith in the profoundest sense of the word until it is tested, until one recognizes the offence but still believes).[88] And in this regard he draws our attention to one story in particular, the story of David's bizarre behavior before the court of Gath in 1 Samuel: "So he changed his behavior before them; he pretended to be mad when in their presence. He scratched marks on the doors of the gate, and let his spittle run down his beard."[89]

The reason why this particular story piques Hamann's interest is that it genuinely puts reason to the test. Indeed, here we have precisely the kind of passage that elicited Voltaire's impassioned objection. And yet, where others scoff and turn away,[90] and where even many a believer is perplexed, Hamann would have us see right in the midst of the difficulty a striking revelation. As he puts it in his commentary:

> The Holy Spirit has become an historian of human, foolish, indeed, even sinful deeds in order to dupe Achish like David. David disguised himself; the Spirit of purity and wisdom- -he makes signs on the doors of the gates- - - - - -The Holy Spirit is not satisfied to speak and write like a man- -but as less than a man- -as a foolish, raving madman- -but he poses this way only in the eyes of God's enemies- -he paints the *doors* of the *gates* with signs that no Achish could make any sense of, signs people took for the handwriting of an idiot- -what is more, he lets his spittle run down onto his beard. He seems to contradict and pollute himself by what he inspired as the Word of God.[91]

In other words, for Hamann, the mystery, which is so great that he underscores it with an excess of dashes, is that the Holy Spirit, the Spirit of *Wisdom*, poses this way, "plays the fool," as it were, disguising himself and concealing his glory not only here but throughout the Old Testament.[92] What is more, Hamann observes,

---

88 It is in Hamann, therefore, that we see the modern prototype of Kierkegaard's thought and authorship—the difference being that, whereas Kierkegaard is concerned more exclusively with the offence and scandal of the paradox of the God-man, Hamann is equally focused on the offence and scandal of the form of Scripture. See in this regard especially Kierkegaard's *Philosophical Fragments, Concluding Unscientific Postscript* (1846), and *Practice in Christianity* (1850). For more on the relation between Hamann and Kierkegaard, see John R. Betz, "Hamann before Kierkegaard: A Systematic Theological Oversight," *Pro Ecclesia* 16 (Summer 2007): 299–333.

89 1 Sam. 21:13–14.

90 John 6:66.

91 Hamann, *Londoner Schriften*, 160 (*SW* 1:99).

92 Of course, the Holy Spirit only *plays* the fool, for in this way he *wisely* conceals his wisdom from the "wise and learned" (Matt. 11:25). In this regard, one should note, Scripture is a species—or rather the prototype—of esoteric literature in that it suitably guards from the profane and their

the Holy Spirit condescends even to apparent contradiction—not only clothing his eternal glory in humble stories that have "no form or majesty" that we should regard them,[93] but condescending even further to become an historian of the sins of the people of Israel, thereby "polluting" himself—the *Holy* Spirit—with the "lies of Abraham" and the crimes of David.[94] And what is the result of this shocking, proto-Christological kenosis? In return for thus humbling and abasing himself for the purpose of our salvation, the writing of the Holy Spirit, as Hamann observed, is more often than not despised and rejected by the *literati* of the age.

In the same context, therefore, Hamann takes special interest in the response that David's behavior elicits from Achish—"Achish said to his servants, 'Look, you see the man is mad; why then have you brought him to me? Do I lack madmen, that you have brought this fellow to play the madman in my presence? Shall this fellow come into my house?'"[95] Hamann's commentary on this passage is similarly striking: "Who can read without trembling reverence the story of David, who distorted his gestures, played like a fool, painted the doors of the gate, [and] slobbered on his beard, without hearing in the judgment of Achish an echo of the thinking of an unbelieving joker and sophist of our time."[96] Thus, once again, we see a mysterious correspondence between the form of Scripture and the form of the cross. For, by clothing himself in such stories, the Holy Spirit not only freely condescends to adopt a humble and at times even scandalous form, but, as a result, similarly suffers the rejection and ridicule of human beings. As Hamann observes in the dramatic opening of his brief statement on biblical exegesis: "God an author!—The Creator of the world and Father of human beings is denied and reproved, the God-man was crucified, and the inspirer of God's Word is ridiculed and blasphemed. The

---

acquisitive grasp (see Gen. 3:6) the mysteries it contains. See Ps. 138:6: "For ... he regards the lowly; but the haughty he knows from afar"; compare Matt. 7:6: "Do not give dogs what is holy; and do not throw your pearls before swine"; and Matt. 13:13–17. Written subsequent to his conversion, Hamann's own mimetic writings are of a similar nature: they too, like the Old Testament, have an outward form of folly; their content, however, which is concealed behind a welter of mystifying allusions, is none other than Christ, "the wisdom of God" (1 Cor. 1:24). See *SW* 2:197, where Hamann begins his *Aesthetica in Nuce* with the following epigraph from Horace: *Odi profanum vulgus et arceo. Favete linguis! Carmina non prius audita, Musarum sacerdos, Virginibus puerisque canto.* ("I loathe the profane crowd and repel it. Silence your tongues! I, a priest of the muses, sing to virgins and youths of songs never heard before.") The corollary here is that the knowledge of God is reserved for those possessed of a pure of heart and a childlike disposition—"Let the little children come to me" (Matt. 19:14)—who allow themselves to be instructed by Wisdom and are therefore able to recognize her in such disguise.

93 Compare Isa. 53:2.

94 Hamann, *Londoner Schriften*, 160 (*SW* 1:99). Presumably Hamann is thinking of Abraham's lie to Abimelech that Sarah was his sister (Gen. 20:2).

95 1 Sam. 21:14–15.

96 Hamann, *Londoner Schriften*, 61 (*SW* 1:5).

inspiration of this book is just as great an act of abasement and condescension as the creation of the Father and the incarnation of the Son."[97]

Following Hamann, then, we should not be surprised to see the Old Testament ridiculed and rejected; for if Hamann is right, it is a peculiarity of the kenotic form of divine revelation to be a sign of contradiction.[98] Indeed, to this extent, the *form* of revelation is itself already a sign of eschatological judgment; for it is here already, in view of this kenotic form, that the spirits divide—just as they divide over the kenotic form of the Son. But if this is so, as Hamann would ultimately have us see, this is a judgment that critics bring upon themselves, inasmuch as they are unwilling to see in the kenotic form of revelation the deeper mystery of divine love:

> This marvelous characteristic of his love for human beings, of which Holy Scripture is full, is ridiculed by weak minds, who prefer a human wisdom or a satisfaction of their curiosity ... an agreement with the taste of the time ... to the divine Word. No wonder ... if the Spirit of Scripture is dismissed with just the same indifference, indeed, if the Spirit seems just as mute and useless as the Savior did to Herod, who, notwithstanding his great curiosity and expectation to see him, readily sent him ... back to Pilate (Luke 23:7–11).[99]

In other words, Herod could not *see* Christ, even though he was standing right in front of him; and, for Hamann, it is the same with Scripture. Its critics, whether ancient or modern, whether Celsus or Voltaire—or, most recently, "new atheists" such as Richard Dawkins and Christopher Hitchens—also fail to *see* the Holy Spirit, who is clothed in a similarly humble form. By the same token, as a result of their own judgment, they are unable to perceive the glory of the *Logos* shining from the depths of Scripture's pages. In both cases the outward, humble, scandalous form—and not the inner glory—is all that they see.

But, given this difficulty, the question now becomes all the more pressing how one comes to see differently—how one comes to love the "old rags" of the Old Testament and pride oneself in them as instruments of salvation, which are capable of lifting our souls, like Jeremiah, out of the pit? Needless to say, this is a difficult question, which touches upon the mystery of faith (cf. Mt. 16:7). Following Hamann, however, one condition would seem to be necessary if one is

---

97 Hamann, *Londoner Schriften*, 59 (SW 1:4). Compare *Londoner Schriften*, 68 (SW 1:10).

98 As Christ himself says to the disciples, through whom the divine revelation of the Gospel is to be furthered and who, to the extent that they abide in the truth, are likewise destined to be signs of contradiction, "Blessed are you when people revile you and persecute you and utter all kinds of evil against you falsely on my account ... for in the same way they persecuted the prophets who were before you" (Matt. 5:11–12).

99 Hamann, *Londoner Schriften*, 68 (SW 1:10).

ever to break the seals on the Old Testament: one must perceive the fundamental correspondence between the servant-form of the incarnate Logos and the "old rags" of the Holy Spirit. More precisely, one must read the Old Testament in light of Christ Crucified. For it is through the cross that we are trained to see strength in weakness, glory in disgrace, wisdom in folly, majesty in humility, and it is in precisely such terms, Hamann suggests, that one must also understand and read the Old Testament. As he puts it in a key passage from his *Aesthetica in Nuce*:

> The spirit of prophecy is the testimony of JESUS; this first sign, whereby he revealed the majesty of his *Knechtsgestalt*, transfig-ures the holy books of the covenant into good, old wine, which tricks the stewards' [sic] judgment and strengthens the weak stomach of the art critics. *Lege libros propheticos non intellecto CHRISTO*, says the Punic Church father, *quid tam insipidum & fatuum invenies? Intellege ibi CHRISTUM, non solum sapit, quod legis, sed etiam inebriat.*[100]

Accordingly, as a last and most fundamental rule of biblical hermeneutics, Hamann would have us read Scripture backwards, as it were, through the lens of the cross, which reveals not only the ultimate christological *content* of the Old Testament, whose stories and allegories are at the end of the day a mysterious prophetic witness to Christ,[101] but also the corresponding christological *form* of the Old Testament.

With regard to content, for example, we come to see in the otherwise troubling story of Genesis 22—a story that one can read only with "fear and trembling"—a cryptic allegory of the Father who gave his only Son; so too, in a further revelation, we see in the life of Joseph, the beloved Son of Jacob—in his being stripped of glory, in his being rejected and betrayed by his brothers, in his being handed over to Gentiles, in his descent into a pit, in his being taken for dead, in his rising from the pit, in his being accepted by Gentiles, in his being seated at the right hand of Pharaoh with dominion over all the earth, and in his saving of the world from hunger—a striking allegory and prophetic foreshadow-ing of the incarnation, life, death, resurrection, and mission of the Son of God, who saves from death and spiritual malnourishment all who come to him. As Hamann notes, "When we look at the history of Joseph our experience is like that of certain portraits: from whatever angle we look at it we catch glimpses of the Redeemer looking back."[102] By the same token, we come to see that the form

---

100 Hamann, *SW* 2:212. The quotation is from St. Augustine's *Tractates on the Gospel of John*, Tract. 9, 3: "If you read the prophetic books without understanding CHRIST, what exceedingly insipid and fatuous things you will find! But if you perceive Christ in them, what you read will not only be to your taste, but will also intoxicate you." Compare John 2:9.

101 Luke 24:44.

102 *Londoner Schriften*, 101 (*SW* 1:44).

of the Old Testament—its majestic humility, its wisdom in folly—is a mysterious analogue of the majestic humility of the incarnate Son and the wisdom-in-folly of his cross. In other words, in light of the cross, which takes our burden, even our exegetical burden, we come to see the apparent folly of the Old Testament as an analogous incarnation of Wisdom—of Wisdom *in disguise*, of Wisdom in an unexpected and potentially alienating form. According to the terms of Hamann's aesthetics, therefore, to see as a Christian is an entirely new kind of seeing: it is to see beauty—to see glory—"in a nutshell," i.e., concealed beneath the rough exterior of a *stylus atrox*. And in this regard, I would argue, Hamann lightens the burden of the Church's defense of Scripture—a burden that it has had ever since the fathers of the Church, most notably Augustine, struggled to defend the inspiration of the Old Testament against scoffing critics inside the Church (such as Marcion) and outside the Church (such as the Manichees).

A Postscript on Hamann's Relevance to the Question of Biblical Inerrancy

But if Hamann is to be relevant to biblical hermeneutics today, there is one final question we need to address, and that is: how his understanding of Scripture—specifically, his understanding of the kenotic form of Scripture—bears on the Church's doctrine and contemporary debate concerning biblical inerrancy.[103] Unfortunately, there is no simple answer to this question, since Hamann had nothing directly to say about the topic. In fact, the term "biblical inerrancy" is quite foreign to his vocabulary, representing what is arguably an entirely different mode of response—a very reactionary response—to the particular challenges that came with the Enlightenment. To introduce him into our contemporary debate and guess at his response to it therefore cannot help but seem an anachronism. Moreover, the entire question of biblical inerrancy is itself so vexed that one has little desire to address it in the first place. After all, what do we mean by "biblical inerrancy"?[104] One is tempted to say that the concept is a category mistake, unsuited to any literary work, much less the Bible, which for Hamann (following

---

103 For the Catholic Church's teaching on biblical inerrancy, see the encyclicals *Providentissimus Deus* [The God of All Providence] (1893), *Spiritus Paraclitus* [The Holy Spirit, the Comforter] (1920), and *Divino Afflante Spiritu* [Inspired by the Divine Spirit] (1943), and the Second Vatican Council's *Dei Verbum* [The Word of God] (1965). These and other encyclicals can be found in *The Scripture Documents: An Anthology of Official Catholic Teachings*, ed. Dean P. Béchard (Collegeville, MN: Liturgical Press, 2002).

104 Does it mean, for example, that Scripture is a divine dictation, which could be said to override the sensibilities of Scripture's human authors, rendering them incapable of the slightest historical error? Or does it mean that the intentions of the Holy Spirit with regard to faith, morals and all that is necessary for our salvation are infallibly executed in and through the freedom of the authors he inspired, which honors not only human freedom but also the genius of the Holy Spirit, who is able to accomplish his will in and through the freedom of those he inspires? Does it mean inerrant at the level of the letter, so that we must suppose God to have commanded Abraham to sacrifice Isaac and to have killed the firstborn of Egypt, et cetera, or does it mean inerrant sometimes with regard to the letter, as in the report that Jesus was born in

Robert Lowth) is the *most poetic* of all texts.[105] In any case, the question of biblical inerrancy and its relation to the doctrine of kenosis is not a simple one; nor can it be answered adequately here.

But an attempted answer is perhaps better than none at all given what is at stake with the doctrine of biblical inerrancy and given that, at least indirectly, by way of anticipation, Hamann did have something to say about it. For, in emphasizing the kenotic form of divine revelation as a starting point of Christian reflection, what Hamann helps us to see, if I may dare to say so, is that both sides in this debate are missing the same thing—believers when they trumpet Scripture's infallibility as though this were an obvious virtue or even its greatest virtue; unbelievers when, failing to see any such virtue, they obtusely deride Scripture for its lack of a satisfying form. That is, to put it simply, what both sides fail to register and reflectively consider is the kenotic form of *glory-in-humility* that for Hamann is paradigmatic of divine revelation. For, seen thus, the glory of Scripture consists not in any evident clarity (it is often obscure) or in any evident integrity (it is a miscellaneous collection) or in any evident harmony (its various authors sometimes seem to contradict one another), but in the radical humility of the Holy Spirit, who lies hidden, as a result of his own divine kenosis, under all kinds of "rags and tatters."[106] Indeed, the authority of Scripture will precisely *not* be apparent to unbelievers (as little as the authority of the *Logos* was evident in the servant-form of Christ), and so it is folly on the part of believers to expect them to see it. And, as for believers who are able to see it, who are able to recognize in such disguise "the beams of

---

Bethlehem of Judea in the days of Herod (Matt. 2:1), and at other times inerrant at the level of its figurative meaning or content, of which the external letter is a mere vehicle?

105 See Lowth, *Lectures on the Sacred Poetry of the Hebrews*, trans. G. Gregory, F.A.S. (Boston: Joseph T. Buckingham, 1815), 25–26. In other words, if Scripture is more like divine poetry than a work of logic, and if it is a work of art greater than creation itself, as Hamann maintains, that is, an even more unfathomably rich testament of divine things expressed through human words, images, and concepts, then how could the word inerrant be a sufficient description of it? What, for instance, would we think of someone who came away from a great poem, and *a fortiori* from Scripture, with no other word on his lips to describe it? Would we not think that he had precisely not understood it, that he had not even begun to fathom the wealth of its imagery and the depth of its mystery? Is the Holy Spirit not the *Creator* Spirit? Is he not, in Hamann's phrase, the "Poet in the beginning of days"? Is his work not *more* wonderful than less inspired works of poetry? Is it not more deeply laden with meanings that arrest the understanding and stretch the imagination and leave us awestruck?

106 Hamann, *Londoner Schriften*, 59 (*SW* 1:5); quoted in Balthasar, *Glory of the Lord*, 1:80–81. According to Aquinas, the three formal criteria of beauty are integrity, clarity, and consonance. See *Summa Theologiae*, pt. 1a., q. 39, art. 8. For a masterful treatment of the topic, see Umberto Eco, *The Aesthetics of Thomas Aquinas* (Cambridge, MA: Harvard University, 1988). The question, therefore, which is implicitly taken up by von Balthasar, is how this classical understanding of beauty is to be reconciled with what Hamann discovered about divine revelation. Provisionally, we might say that Aquinas' aesthetics holds true of Christ and of Scripture, but that their beauty is hidden in a kenotic form.

heavenly glory," the word "inerrant" is likely to be the last and least meaningful word on their lips, far behind many exclamations of wonder and praise.

Following Hamann, therefore, this much seems clear: the doctrine of biblical inerrancy must not be taken in isolation from the doctrine of divine kenosis—and for reasons having ultimately to do with the christological mystery of Scripture. But if this is the conclusion to which Hamann leads us, it need not—indeed must not—be understood to diminish the significance of the doctrine of inerrancy, for it too is in some sense indispensable. On the contrary, I submit, the two doctrines require and mutually support one another—the doctrine of kenosis guarding against an all too rational, abstract, and ultimately sterile understanding of the biblical text (as something alien to our humanity); and the doctrine of inerrancy guarding against relativistic uses of the doctrine of kenosis that would present the biblical text as so human and so fully accommodated to the cultural sensibilities of the time as to evacuate its claims of any eternal significance.[107] In other words, hermeneutical problems and distortions of the true character of Scripture arise only when one doctrine is emphasized to the exclusion or neglect of the other— just as Christological problems arise when one emphasizes either the divinity of Christ to the neglect of his humanity, or his humanity to the neglect of his divinity. Accordingly, in a way that is analogous to the conclusions of the Council of Chalcedon, the hermeneutical challenge is to hold the two doctrines together in productive tension, whereby the doctrine of kenosis qualifies what is meant by inerrancy, and the doctrine of inerrancy qualifies what is meant by kenosis.

Sic et Non: *The Problematic Doctrine of Inerrancy*

In practice, however, one doctrine tends to be emphasized more than the other, and often this can be explained by the particular challenge that the Church is facing at a given time. Such seems to be the case with the doctrine of inerrancy. Therefore, before attempting to "balance out" the doctrines, or better, before attempting to hold them in productive tension, it is incumbent upon us first to appreciate the exigency of the doctrine of inerrancy in our modern context, which is precisely to uphold the authority of Scripture as the Word of God in the face of the enormous challenges that came with the Enlightenment and the advent of modern historical criticism. As Oswald Bayer summarizes the challenge, specifically with regard to Kant's critical revolution:

> In Kant the authority hitherto accorded to Scripture is assumed
> by the authority of reason. This can easily be shown point by
> point: *auctoritas, infallibilitas, perfectio, sufficientia, perspicuitas*

---

107 For example, it is conceivable that one could misuse the doctrine of kenosis—and the doctrine of accommodation that it implies—in the service of Bultmann's demythologization program, such that all references to supernatural agencies, for example, demons, are said to be "accommodations" to the world view of ancient Israel.

and *efficacia*, above all the power of self-interpretation, of criticism, of autonomous judgment, and the power to establish norms—all of these effective modes and attributes of Holy Scripture, which can only be effective modes and attributes of the Triune God, are ascribed by Kant to reason.[108]

No longer, therefore, could the authority of Scripture be taken for granted. On the contrary, with the tables now turned, Scripture (hitherto understood to be a corrective to fallen reason) would now have to prove itself before the court of (fallen) reason. As Kant put it in the programmatic preface of the *Critique of Pure Reason*, "Our age is the true age of criticism, to which everything must submit. Both religion and law-making seek to escape it, the one through its holiness, the other through its majesty. But then they arouse against themselves justified suspicion and cannot claim unfeigned respect, which reason grants only to that which can endure its unfettered and public examination."[109]

To be sure, seen in the context in which it arose, the doctrine of inerrancy is a reactionary doctrine, one that goes beyond Scripture's own claim that the "law of the Lord is perfect"[110] or Paul's claim that "all of Scripture is inspired by God and is useful for teaching, for reproof, for correction, and for training in righteousness."[111] For that matter, it is a concept, one could argue, alien to Scripture and the entire ancient world, appealing more to our modern scientific, propositional sensibility. And yet, while it may not be the best way to respond to modern critics and skeptics, given the enormity of the challenge of the Enlightenment, it is entirely understandable—perhaps even necessary—as is the fact that in many Protestant churches today the doctrine of inerrancy has become (arguably more so even than the doctrine of justification) the *articulus stantis vel cadentis ecclesiae*, the doctrine by which the Church stands or falls. Indeed, to the extent that many even in the Church have

---

108 See Oswald Bayer, *Autorität und Kritik: Zur Hermeneutik und Wissenschaftstheorie* [Authority and Criticism: On Hermeneutics and the Theory of the Sciences](Tübingen: Mohr-Siebeck, 1991), 44.

109 Immanuel Kant, *Critique of Pure Reason*, A XII (Cambridge: Cambridge University, 1998), 100–101. Accordingly, after the Enlightenment, neither the authority of Scripture nor the authority of the Church could be taken for granted: they themselves, now stripped of their authority, were held in suspicion and subject to interrogation (a fate not unlike that of the Lord to whom they bear witness). Such is the challenge faced by the Church in the modern world; and it is in this context that the modern doctrine of biblical inerrancy (as an attempt to reaffirm the authority of Scripture) and also the doctrine of papal infallibility (as an attempt to reaffirm the authority of the Church in matters of faith and morals) must be understood. See in the present volume of *Letter & Spirit*, the article by Pablo T. Gadenz, "The emphasis on the inerrancy of Scripture in the pre-conciliar period was the result, in part, of the necessity of defending the Bible against rationalist and modernist criticism." ("Magisterial Teaching on the Inspiration and Truth of Scripture: Precedents and Prospects.")

110 Ps. 19:7.

111 2 Tim. 3:16.

consciously or unconsciously adopted the ideology of the Enlightenment, putting their own opinions before Scripture or the mind of the Church, one could argue that it is nothing less than a matter of ecclesial integrity, safeguarding the much contested authority of Scripture in matters of faith and morals.

Additionally, for the individual believer as well one must appreciate the role the doctrine of inerrancy plays in securing our confidence in Scripture and—rightly understood—preserving the mystery of Scripture.[112] For without due deference to the biblical text, inspired by confidence in the unerring intentions of the Holy Spirit, we ourselves, as individuals, are adrift in a sea of doubts about Scripture, whose authority as the Word of God is *ipso facto* denied. Moreover, its ability to speak to us, to probe our hearts, to interpret *us*, and instruct us in the ways of God is hampered and curtailed. We are resistant to it; we maintain a critical distance; we presume to be *its* judge; and, consequently, having denied Scripture its power to judge our hearts, it fails to have the critical and transforming effect for which it was intended.[113] Simply put, the effective Word finds in us no avenue by which to reach its destination. It is the same point that the Logos makes in the Parable of the Sower: his seed, which is his Word, needs the "good soil" of humility in order to grow.[114] And here, it would seem, an overly critical attitude is just as problematic as the "cares of the world." Thus Hamann says, and is well worth repeating, "Humility of heart is … the one required disposition and most indispensable preparation for reading the Bible."[115]

By the same token, the doctrine of biblical inerrancy keeps us from disregarding passages in Scripture that might otherwise seem trivial, irrelevant, or, on the face of it, even objectionable—alerting us to the fact that, for the Church, Scripture is an organic whole, that no part of it is without purpose, and that, as with creation itself, great depths of significance are often hidden in the most surprising places. Indeed, it is precisely confidence in the unerring intentions of the Holy Spirit that forces us to look for meaning in passages we might, for whatever reason, neglect. And in this, too, the doctrine of inerrancy preserves the mystery of Scripture: it effectively keeps us from a selective approach to Scripture that would be guided not by humility but by our own sensibilities (a danger of which every reader of Scripture must be aware, since it is all too easy to *use* Scripture for one's own purposes and bend it or even twist it into conformity with an agenda or ideology alien to Scripture itself).

---

112 Of course, a literalist conception of inerrancy, which reduces the inerrancy of Scripture to its letter, can have precisely the opposite effect of stripping Scripture of its mystery, flattening its many dimensions, and reducing it to a series of propositional statements and historical claims. This, in any event, would not be a Catholic understanding of inerrancy.

113 See Heb. 4:12.

114 Matt. 13:8.

115 Hamann, *Londoner Schriften*, 158 (*SW* 1:97); quoted in *Glory of the Lord* 1:80–81.

There are good reasons, then, to hold fast to the doctrine of biblical inerrancy—reasons that we might now summarize as follows. Firstly, it serves as a principle of ecclesial integrity, inasmuch as it establishes a common reverence for the Word of God as wholly inspired.[116] Secondly, it keeps us humble, reaffirming that the prophetic word of Scripture is *more sure* (2 Pet. 1:19) than our own fallen reasoning and therefore to be trusted, since it derives from a higher Logos.[117] Thirdly, it keeps us open to the meanings for which the Holy Spirit intended it—so long, that is, that inerrancy is not restricted to the literal sense. Finally, it accords with the Augustinian principle that faith (in authority) *precedes* understanding—as anyone who has learned arithmetic on the authority of a grade school teacher and has gone on to college-level calculus can grasp. And if this is true of dianoetic knowledge, to use a Platonic term, it is all the more true of noetic, i.e., spiritual knowledge, in which no one advances apart from humble deference to those farther along the way. With regard to Scripture, therefore, this means that one must trust its authority and be open to its instruction if one is to make any progress in understanding its content.

But, however justified, the doctrine of biblical inerrancy is not without its problems—at least when it is taken in isolation from the doctrine of divine kenosis and thereby made absolute. Among its problems is that it inevitably makes the debate about Scripture a debate about authority, thereby engaging the Church in an exhausting and ultimately fruitless dialectic with the Enlightenment—with the Church affirming the authority of the light of Scripture[118] and secular modernity affirming the authority of the light of reason (however dim and fallen). More problematically, when it is made the sole and absolute criterion of interpretation, it tends to obscure the humanity, the human face, of Scripture, which includes everything from the personalities and idiosyncrasies of its various authors to the real human history to which its redaction was subject. To be sure, it succeeds in conveying the fact that Scripture is a divine communication *to* "the creature"; it fails, however, to do justice to how thoroughly Scripture is also a communication *through* "the creature." As a result, taken in isolation from the doctrine of kenosis, it skews the nature of revelation as a communication, in Hamann's phrase, "to the creature through the creature." Perhaps most problematic of all, inasmuch as the doctrine of inerrancy presents Scripture as a text of overpowering divinity, it fails to register the extraordinary humility of the Holy Spirit, who lowered himself to speak through our humanity. Granted, it is a doctrine that helps us to appreciate the biblical text as something sacred; it helps us to appreciate its wisdom and make

---

116 2 Tim. 3:16.

117 See, for example, *Londoner Schriften*, 112 (*SW* 1:52–53). Accordingly, one could argue that true reason (or reason redeemed) is reason naturally wedded to the Word (its origin and archetype) and that "secular reason" – the reasoning of the Enlightenment – is reason unnaturally divorced from the Word. For more on this claim, see *After Enlightenment*.

118 See Ps. 119:105.

us receptive of it. By itself, however, it is incomplete. For the more one emphasizes the inerrancy of Scripture, even out of a well-intentioned attempt to defend it, the more one inevitably tends to overlook and perhaps even deny its humility and certainly its "folly." It is, therefore, but one pole in our understanding of Scripture, and by itself cannot lead us to a deeper appreciation of the christological mystery of Scripture—which demands our appreciating its divine and human aspect, its glory-in-humility, its wisdom-in-folly. It is in this sense a preliminary guide, a Virgil, not a Beatrice.

What is needed, therefore, I submit, in addition to a dogmatic affirmation of the inerrancy of Scripture, is a theological sensitivity to the kenotic form, the *christological* form, in which the Word appears—both for the sake of the Church's own reading of Scripture and for its engagement with the modern world. The virtue of thus shifting the ground of debate, I would argue, is that debate is then no longer centered upon the question of authority, which admits of no rational resolution, but instead upon the wonder of divine humility as manifest in Christ, but also in Scripture. Then, with the focus shifted to the humility of revelation, the question becomes one of whether we can see it, or whether our own pride prevents us even from noticing it (given that the humility of revelation often falls *below* our rational expectations). Additionally, it is from this ground that we see what *true* authority really looks like: it is an authority clothed not in dread power, which naturally elicits our defiance, but an authority clothed *in humility and love*, which is arguably the only kind of authority that deserves our obedience, and is the only kind of authority that the Church, if it is to be faithful to its Lord, should ever represent to the world. It is, moreover, then, when the Church is clothed in the humility proper to the Spirit of its Lord, that the grounds of the Enlightenment disappear, when the critics of the Church can see its humility and are thereby prepared to hear its message concerning the Word of God. To such critics one might reply: "Admittedly, Scripture may appear substandard compared to other literary works. Admittedly, it has 'no form or majesty' that would command our attention or approbation.[119] To be sure, it appears to be 'nothing much,' just as the figure of Jesus of Nazareth could seem like 'nothing much'—'Is not this the carpenter's son? Is not his mother called Mary?'[120] But looks can be deceiving, especially when we are unaccustomed to the ways of God. For it is in Jesus that the saints see the glory of the Son of God; in his cross that they discover the power of God; and it is in the fragments of Scripture, and in the rag-tag body of the Church, that they see—similarly hidden—the glory of the Holy Spirit."

---

119 See Isa. 53:2.
120 Matt. 13:55.

Innerancy in Kenosis: The Christological Mystery of Scripture

Seen in light of divine kenosis, the doctrine of biblical inerrancy thus stands in need of certain qualifications. This is true, most obviously, as soon as one considers what one might call the "accommodative" aspect of divine kenosis, i.e., the fact that God humbles himself to accommodate the cultural sensibility of his audience—in the way, for example, that the creation accounts are written in a narrative form not altogether dissimilar to other ancient creation accounts, and in the way that Jesus uses agricultural metaphors that his audience would readily understand.[121] Thus, as a *first* necessary qualification, inerrant need not mean that Scripture is scientifically accurate in a modern sense of the term, as though its veracity or even its perfection could be undermined by the findings of modern natural science.[122]

The doctrine of inerrancy stands in need of qualification, furthermore, if this doctrine is taken to mean that the Bible must be to all appearances flawless and free of inconsistencies. For if Hamann's hermeneutics succeeds in conveying anything it is that the kenotic form of Scripture, far from being necessarily agreeable to (fallen) reason, sometimes strikes us as the opposite of reason—indeed, as scandalous to reason. The same is true of its ultimate christological content. Accordingly, as a *second* qualification of the term, inerrant need not mean that Scripture must or will satisfy rational expectations—either in its form or in its content. On the contrary, to the extent that it is written in a kenotic style, we should expect it to elicit quite the opposite reaction. We should expect many a scholar, for instance, to be put off by its fragmentary appearance, the messiness of its redaction history, its apparent incongruities, and even its apparent contradictions (just as we should expect morally sensible persons to be offended by the violence it contains, and just as we should expect philosophers to balk at the notion of an incarnate and crucified God). Indeed, we should expect them to wonder how so human and seemingly fallible a text could be so perfect and so divinely inspired a text.

To admit this, however, is not to deny the inerrancy of Scripture. It is simply to say that its inerrancy, far from being something obvious, is something that is hidden—in keeping with its christological form. At the same time, it is to recognize that the divine "style" is sublimely indifferent to human standards; indeed, that the perfection of Scripture is somehow bound up with its apparent imperfection—just as the perfect revelation of God in Christ is bound up with the seeming imperfection of his "no form or majesty."[123] As Hamann puts it, "According to

---

121 This not to say that everything in Scripture can be culturally relativized; this would be to assume mistakenly that its ultimate author, the Holy Spirit, did not possess complete knowledge of the future audience that would eventually read it.

122 As Hamann himself points out, Genesis should be understood as a narrative [*Erzählung*] rather than an explanation [*Erklärung*], noting that many of his contemporaries obtusely rejected Scripture on the basis of an erroneous notion that Genesis was something on the order of a scientific explanation. See *Londoner Schriften*, 69 (SW 1:11).

123 Isa. 53:2.

the saying of a well-known exegete *DEI Dialectus, Soloecismus*. The same applies here: *Vox populi, vox DEI*. The emperor says schismam, and the gods of the earth rarely bother to be masters of language. What is sublime in Caesar's style is its carelessness."[124] What makes this passage potentially liberating for the exegesis of the Church, is that (as Hamann gives us to understand), far from being bound to rational standards of orthography, the genius of Scripture, the Holy Spirit who blows where he wills,[125] is precisely beyond them. Indeed, seen in this way, it matters not a whit whether Scripture appears to contain errors or even contradictions; for even these (as judged, say, by modern historical critics) are part of its kenotic form, which is to say, part of its disguise.

And this leads to a *third* qualification, which is also implied by the passage quoted above: "*Vox populi vox DEI*." In other words, in keeping with the nature of prophecy, the voice of *God* is mysteriously and miraculously heard in and through the voice of human beings.[126] Accordingly, inasmuch as Scripture is the "prophetic Word,"[127] inerrant need not mean—and in fact does not mean—that Scripture is written without or to the exclusion of the free will and creativity of the human authors of Scripture.[128] On the contrary, it is characteristic of the kenosis of the Holy Spirit that he humbly lets others speak on his behalf as surrogates of his own authority: that he speaks, in Hamann's phrase, "to the creature *through* the creature."[129] And precisely for this reason we should not be taken aback by but delight in the different personalities and even idiosyncracies that shine through the different biblical authors. As Hamann strikingly puts it: "If the hairs of our head, down to the variation of their color, belong to the *Datis* of divine providence, why should the *straight* and *crooked* lines and strokes of our symbolic and typological (but not hieroglyphic) handwriting not be the counter images and mirror of a

---

124 Hamann, *Londoner Schriften*, 2:171. The allusion is to emperor Sigismund, who is supposed to have said at the Council of Constance (1411–1437): "We don't want any schismam," that is schism, in the Church. When the correct spelling was pointed out to him, namely, "schisma," he replied: "Well, I am an emperor and have greater authority than the grammarians. I can even make another grammar." Quoted in Martin Seils, *Johann Georg Hamann: Eine Auswahl aus Seinen Schriften* [Selected Writings] (Wuppertal: Brockhaus Verlag, 1987), 268.

125 John 3:8.

126 Compare *Londoner Schriften*, 188 (*SW* 1:127): "God ... makes the voice of clay, earth and ash as pleasant, as melodious, as the jubilation of the Cherubim and Seraphim." See also *Londoner Schriften*, 188. Compare 251 (*SW* 1:190): "Next to the wealth of God in nature, which arose out of nothing, there is no greater creation than the transformation [through Scripture] of human concepts and impressions into heavenly and divine mysteries."

127 2 Pet. 1:19.

128 Thus *Dei Verbum* speaks of the "true authors" (*veri auctores*) of Scripture. See Second Vatican Council, *Dei Verbum* [The Word of God], Dogmatic Constitution on Divine Revelation, (November 18, 1965), 11, in *Scripture Documents*, 24–25.

129 Hamann, *Londoner Schriften*, 188 (*SW* 1:127).

theopneustie (2 Tim. 3:16), of an unrecognized central force in which we *live and move and have our being* (Acts 17:28)."[130]

But if the doctrine of inerrancy at certain points breaks down and therefore stands in need of qualification, it does so importantly *not* due to negative external pressures (say, the fact that Scripture does not measure up to the standards of modern science), but for positive reasons owing to the kenotic form of Scripture itself. For this reason the Church need not be defensive about the humility of its Scriptures or their seeming inadequacies; rather, it should glory in them, seeing that their poverty, their apparent weakness, their apparent folly is a reflection of the poverty and apparent weakness of its Lord; knowing, moreover, that they contain mysteries which are hidden from the wise of this world, but are revealed to mere children (see Matt. 11:25), i.e., those members of the Church who, by virtue of their own humility, their own poverty of spirit, are able to perceive them and to recognize "in such disguise the beams of heavenly glory."[131]

So, in conclusion, how can Hamann's biblical hermeneutics help us to think about the question of biblical inerrancy today? On the one hand, Hamann certainly affirms the authority of Scripture as wholly inspired and worthy of our veneration—to know this one need only recall his inspiring coda in praise of Scripture at the conclusion of his autobiography. And to this extent, one could argue, he implicitly affirms the intention behind the doctrine of inerrancy, which is to uphold the authority of Scripture in the face of modern biblical criticism. On the other hand, it is equally clear that Hamann's hermeneutics is driven not so much by a recognition of Scripture's authority, still less by notions of its infallibility, as by wonder at its shocking humility and even its apparent fallibility. Again, this is not to deny the doctrine of inerrancy; for Scripture can appear fallible and yet be infallible, just as the cross can *appear* to be folly and yet *be* the wisdom of God. It does, however, force us to consider more deeply the kenotic form of Scripture as an effect of the Holy Spirit's own authorial kenosis. Otherwise, taken in isolation, the doctrine of inerrancy tends to obscure precisely what Hamann, in the name of a properly *Christian* aesthetics, wanted us to see, namely, the humility and apparent folly of divine revelation.

If, therefore, Hamann's hermeneutics has anything to teach us about biblical inerrancy today, it is that its truth is *relative* to the principle of divine kenosis. For

---

130 Hamann, *SW* 3:240. Admittedly, how the Holy Spirit accomplishes his perfect will in and through the freedom of the human authors of Scripture is a mystery—one that corresponds to the overarching mystery of divine providence (Rom. 8:28). But to judge from the economy of salvation, it would seem that God does not want to save us without us. He does not work through us without our *fiat*, without our consent. For salvation is effected in and through the flesh of Christ, which is the flesh of Mary; and this flesh is, as it were, our human contribution. The same is true here: the *external* Word of Scripture, which is given to our hearing and reading for the purpose of our salvation, in order to prepare us for the indwelling of the *incarnate* Word, is effected in and through the humanity of the "true authors" of Scripture.

131 Hamann, *SW* 2:171.

it is not enough to make declarations about the authority of Scripture; one must go farther and deeper: one must come to the point of seeing the *authority-in-the-humility* of Scripture. It is not enough to make declarations about the truth of Scripture: one must come to the point of recognizing the *truth-in-the-mystery* of Scripture. It is not enough to make declarations about the wisdom of Scripture: one must come to the point of recognizing the *wisdom-in-the-folly* of Scripture. In short, one must come to the point where the doctrine of biblical inerrancy fails, where its logic breaks down and proves to be inadequate to the mystery of divine revelation—especially to the extent that it cannot be squared with contradictions. For inasmuch as the doctrine of inerrancy cannot tolerate contradictions of any kind, it fails to register not only the contradictory form of Scripture—its majesty-in-humility and wisdom-in-folly—but also its deepest content, which is itself a single, *holy contradiction*: the God-man, who is at once the Lion and the Lamb.[132] Thus, once again, following Hamann, an adequate doctrine of Scripture would have to be a *Christological* doctrine of Scripture. For it is then that we are seeing (and reading) not simply as theists, who believe in a God who has authoritatively revealed himself, but as Christians, who can see in the very form of Scripture, in its humility, in its "rags and tatters," a reflection of the incarnate Word it proclaims.

---

132 Compare Hamman *SW* 3:221: "As if we lacked original documents that are sealed (Isa. 29:11–12), because one can no longer read (since Divi Renati Cartesii *Methodus* and B. Joannis Clerici *Ars Critica* have become the primers, the *Wolffianism* and *Machiavellianism* in sheep's clothing, the deceptive *patois* of our Gallic *Pedagogue*), and which one *cannot read on account of the seven* seals on the inside and the back or the *seventy times seven* contradictions of the conquering lion and slaughtered lamb—including a beast that was and is not, but nevertheless is." Compare Rev. 17:8.

Letter & Spirit 6 (2010): 181-190

The Inspiration and Inerrancy of Scripture

❧ Germain Grisez ☙

Mount St. Mary's University

In its document on Catholic faith, *Dei Filius*, the First Vatican Council solemnly defined a proposition concerning the Bible: "If anyone does not accept as sacred and canonical the complete books of sacred Scripture with all their parts, as the Council of Trent listed them, or denies them to be divinely inspired, let that person be anathema."[1] The Church holds the biblical books to be sacred and canonical, Vatican I explained, precisely because they were divinely inspired: "written under the inspiration of the Holy Spirit, those books have God as their author, and as such have been delivered to the Church."[2]

Many scholars have tried to explain *how* the Holy Spirit inspired the Scriptures, but no such account has been generally accepted and endorsed by the Church.[3] The situation is similar to the conflicting theories about grace and free choice that gave rise to the famous controversy *De auxiliis*, which the Church has never settled. In both cases there is a tendency to try to determine precisely what God causes and explain how he can cause it without preempting the human agent's role. However, neither God's creative causality nor the causality of human persons' freely chosen actions need be limited to leave room for the other; and while the Second Vatican Council provides no explanation of *how* the Holy Spirit inspired the Scriptures, the Council says everything essential about divine inspiration in the first paragraph of *Dei Verbum* 11:

> The things divinely revealed which are contained and presented in sacred Scripture in written form have been attested under the influence of the Holy Spirit. For in their entirety the books of both the Old and the New Testaments, with all their parts, are held by holy mother Church from apostolic faith as sacred and canonical, because, written under the inspiration of the Holy

---

1   First Vatican Council, *Dei Filius* [The Son of God], Dogmatic Constitution on the Catholic Faith, (April 24, 1870), Canon 2, in Henirich Denzinger, ed., *Enchiridion Symbolorum Definitonum et Declarationum de Rebus Fidei et Morum* [Handbook of Creeds, Definitions and Declarations concerning Matters of Faith and Morals], 32nd. ed. (Freiberg: Herder, 1963), 3029 (1809 in original Denzinger); Eng.: *The Sources of Catholic Dogma* (Fitzwilliam, NH: Loreto, 2002). Hereafter abbreviated *DS*. All translations in this article of passages quoted from Vatican I and Vatican II are my own.

2   *Dei Filius*, Chap. 2, 7 (*DS* 3006/1787).

3   See Richard F. Smith, "Inspiration and Inerrancy," in *The Jerome Biblical Commentary*, vol. 2, *The New Testament and Topical Articles*, eds. Raymond E. Brown, Joseph A. Fitzmyer, and Roland E. Murphy (Englewood Cliffs, NJ: Prentice-Hall, 1968), 505–512.

Spirit (see John 20:31; 2 Tim. 3:16; 2 Pet. 1:19–21, 3:15–16), those books have God as their author, and as such have been delivered to the Church. In composing the sacred books, God indeed chose human beings whom he employed, while they used their own powers and faculties, so that with him acting in and through them, they, as true authors, would convey in writing all those things and only those things that he wanted [notes omitted].

Wishing to communicate with us, God created the human beings and their actions that caused the Bible to be written and accepted by the Church, with the result that these books convey precisely what God wished to communicate. Everything about the actions contributing to the result was inspired, but that takes nothing at all away from the complex set of factors ordinarily involved in human authorship. As for *how* divine creative causality works, since it is unlike any created causality, speculating about *how* the Holy Spirit did what he did is not just useless but sure to be confusing.

Being inspired, Scripture expresses and bears witness to divine revelation; it is, as Vatican II teaches, "the word of God inasmuch as it is consigned to writing under the influence of the divine Spirit."[4] Vatican II also draws a conclusion crucial for all work in theology: "Now, the sacred Scriptures contain the word of God and, since they are inspired, truly are the word of God; and so the study of the sacred page is as it were the soul of sacred theology."[5]

The New Testament and, within it, the four Gospels are especially important for Catholic theology. Vatican II reaffirms that they originate from the apostles, who preached as Jesus commissioned them to do, and then, along with some of their associates, were influenced by the Holy Spirit in putting the same preaching into writing.[6] The Council also reaffirms that the four Gospels are historical: "they faithfully hand on what Jesus, God's Son, while living among us, really did and taught, up to the day on which he was assumed into heaven."[7] The Council goes on to explain that the Gospel narratives benefited from the apostles' growing insight, while pastoral needs shaped the selection and arrangement of material; but the Gospels "always communicate to us true and genuine accounts of Jesus."[8]

If the Holy Spirit inspired the books of the Bible and they contain what God wanted to communicate to us, it makes obvious good sense to listen attentively to

---

4   Second Vatican Council, *Dei Verbum* [The Word of God], Dogmatic Constitution on Divine Revelation, (November 18, 1965), 9, in *The Scripture Documents: An Anthology of Official Catholic Teachings*, ed. Dean P. Béchard (Collegeville, MN: Liturgical Press, 2002), 19–33.

5   *Dei Verbum* 24.

6   *Dei Verbum*, 18.

7   *Dei Verbum*, 19.

8   *Dei Verbum*, 19.

them in the liturgy, read them privately, and seriously study them, always with one overarching purpose: to hear, understand, and take to heart what God wishes to communicate here and now, either for our benefit or the benefit of those he calls us to serve. But sometimes, even often, we may be puzzled and even perplexed by what we hear and read—and study, perhaps seemingly in vain. "Why didn't the Holy Spirit see to it that things would be clearer to me?" we wonder.

Some cryptic remarks of Jesus explaining the parable of the sower are relevant here:

> And he said to them, "Is a lamp brought in to be put under a bushel, or under a bed, and not on a stand? *For there is nothing hid, except to be made manifest; nor is anything secret, except to come to light.* If any man has ears to hear, let him hear." And he said to them, "Take heed what you hear; the measure you give will be the measure you get, and still more will be given you. For to him who has more will be given; and from him who has not, even what he has will be taken away."[9]

The italicized sentence appears to be the key.[10] It points back to Mark 4:11–12 where Jesus, paraphrasing Isaiah 6:9–10, seems to say he is not explaining his parables to the public at large lest people repent and be forgiven. Obviously, though, he does not want that; so what does he really mean?

Whatever God is revealing is not meant to be permanently puzzling and perplexing. Even the obscurities are there to help communicate the message. But to receive it, we must be careful about what we hear—about whom we choose to listen to. Hearing, reading, and studying Scripture will be beneficial in proportion to what goes into them. If people approach Scripture with sincere faith, their faith will be nourished; but if they approach it without openness to God's communication, their alienation from him will only be deepened.

People can form intimate relationships by sharing secrets, yet even within such relationships people also can have good reasons for keeping secrets from one another, as parents, for instance, hide Christmas presents from their children to heighten the fun. Similarly, our risen Lord Jesus did not at once identify himself to the disappointed disciples on the road to Emmaus; and their ignorance created the context for them to learn gradually by listening to him and to grow in their relationship with him, until they finally recognized him: "Did not our hearts burn within us while he talked to us on the road, while he opened to us the scriptures?"[11]

Revelation as a whole includes more than information and facts. It is God's self-manifestation for the purpose of forming a covenantal relationship with

---

9   Mark 4:21–25, italics added; see alo Luke 8:16–18.

10   See Joel Marcus, *Mark 1–8*, Anchor Bible, 27 (New York: Doubleday, 2000), 318–322.

11   Luke 24:32.

us—the relationship with which he wishes to bless us. Since the success of this divine project depends on our cooperation—openness to understand and effort to appropriate what is being offered—he provides just what we need to engage us, to allow us to be active in suitable ways.

Perplexing messages sometimes are the most effective. Pondering subtle, allusive poetry engages us far more deeply than do the one-dimensional, unambiguous messages usually communicated by the media; puzzling out mysterious remarks of loved ones can lead to ineffable insights into their unique personalities. Similarly, by making things easier for us, the Holy Spirit would deprive us of opportunities to make an effort and so to grow; instead, the Spirit gives us what we need, so that we become who we are to be with God and for him by understanding and appropriating what he offers. Moreover, he speaks to us not only as individuals, but also, and especially, together, and together we must listen to and appropriate his message and be formed into the communities of faith we are called to be. Only the hearing of the whole Church is fully sound. Hearing God's word in the Church, we must move forward together "toward the fullness of divine truth until the words of God are consummated in her."[12]

The Second Vatican Council on Scripture's Inerrancy

Despite the Church's teaching about the divine inspiration of sacred Scripture, many today who work at and study theology seem to assume that the writers might well have made mistakes or even told lies. In recent years, some able and respected Catholic scholars have encouraged that view. For example, Raymond E. Brown, holds that, due to the limitations of its human authors, the Bible contains errors, even on matters religious. It is a mistake, he thinks, to exclude error from the Bible *a priori*; one must look at the evidence and weed out the errors.

Brown is aware that his view is at odds with the Church's teaching prior to Vatican II. But he explains:

> Many of us think that at Vatican II the Catholic Church "turned the corner" in the inerrancy question by moving from the *a priori* toward the *a posteriori* in the statement of *Dei Verbum* 11: "The Books of Scripture must be acknowledged as teaching firmly, faithfully, and without error that truth which God wanted put into the sacred writings for the sake of our salvation." Within its context, the statement is not without an ambiguity that stems from the compromise nature of *Dei Verbum*. The Council in 1962 rejected the ultraconservative schema "On the Sources of Revelation" that originally had been submitted, and so it became a matter of face-saving that in the revisions and in the final form

---

12   *Dei Verbum*, 8.

of the Constitution the ultraconservatives should have their say. The result is often a juxtaposition of conservative older formulations with more open recent formulations. Those who wish to read *Dei Verbum* in a minimalist way can point out that the sentence immediately preceding the one I just quoted says that everything in Scripture is asserted by the Holy Spirit and can argue that therefore "what God wanted put into the Scripture for the sake of our salvation" (which is without error) means every view the human author expressed in Scripture. However, there is noncritical exegesis of Church documents as well as noncritical exegesis of Scripture [note omitted]. Consequently, to determine the real meaning of *Dei Verbum* one must study the discussions in the Council that produced it, and one must comb a body of evidence that can be read in different ways [note omitted].[13]

Brown goes on to mention a few facts about the conciliar debate and one theological interpretation of the evidence. Then he states his view: "Everything in Scripture is inerrant to the extent to which it conforms to the salvific purpose of God."[14]

Though Brown does not speak of the spirit of Vatican II, what he says is a paradigm of the method of those who use that expression to suggest that the Council's real teachings are different from the propositions asserted in its documents. Like many who appeal to the spirit of Vatican II, Brown is a careless exegete of the conciliar text. For he focuses on a single sentence: "The books of Scripture must be acknowledged as teaching firmly, faithfully, and without error that truth which God wanted put into the sacred writings for the sake of our salvation," and

---

13   Raymond E. Brown, S.S., *The Critical Meaning of the Bible* (New York: Paulist, 1981), 18–19.

14   Brown, *Critical Meaning of the Bible*, 19. The theological interpretation Brown cites is the commentary of Alois Grillmeier, "The Divine Inspiration and the Interpretation of Sacred Scripture," in *Commentary on the Documents of Vatican II*, vol. 3, ed. Herbert Vorgrimler (New York: Herder and Herder, 1969), 199–246. However, Grillmeier's examination (at 210–215) of the underlying conciliar documents shows that even before Pope Paul VI's intervention, the Council's Theological Commission was explaining "the truth of salvation" (replaced by the phrase "which God wanted put into the sacred writings for the sake of our salvation") as implying no material limitation of the truth of Scripture but only indicating its formal specification. In his footnote, which I have omitted, Brown mentions another commentary but brushes it aside as "much more conservative": Augustin Cardinal Bea, *The Word of God and Mankind* (Chicago: Franciscan Herald, 1967), 184–193. Though Bea's commentary undermines Brown's position, Bea was not what is usually called conservative: he was an accomplished biblical scholar, creator and leader of the Secretariat for Promoting Christian Unity (1960–1968), a close collaborator of Pope John XXIII, and perhaps the most important person, other than the Pope himself, who was both heavily involved in preparing Vatican II and not a conservative; see also Giuseppe Alberigo, "Conclusion: Preparing for What Kind of Council," in *History of Vatican II*, vol. 1: Announcing and Preparing Vatican Council II, ed. Giuseppe Alberigo, Eng. version ed. Joseph A. Komonchak (Maryknoll, N.Y.: Orbis, 1995), xi–xii.

says those who want to read that "in a minimalist [that is, according to Brown, "ultraconservative"] way can point out that the sentence immediately preceding … says that everything in Scripture is asserted by the Holy Spirit." But what Brown speaks of as two sentences actually are parts of one complex sentence. He quotes one and inaccurately paraphrases the other. Moreover, the complex sentence begins with "Since, therefore," which logically connects it with the preceding sentences, which I quoted above, on the inspiration of *the whole of* Scripture. It also includes "it follows that," which logically connects its two parts. Thus, *Dei Verbum* 11, in fact says:

> Since, therefore, all that the inspired writers or sacred authors assert must be taken as asserted by the Holy Spirit, it follows that the books of Scripture are to be acknowledged as teaching firmly, faithfully, and without error the truth which God wanted to be attested by the sacred text for the sake of our salvation [note omitted]. Therefore, "all Scripture is inspired by God and useful for teaching, for reproving, for correcting, for instruction in justice; that the man of God may be perfect, equipped for every good work" (2 Tm 3:16–17, Greek text).

Brown is mistaken in claiming someone can cite Vatican II as saying "everything in Scripture is asserted by the Holy Spirit." What the Council actually says is that "all that the inspired writers or sacred authors assert must be taken as asserted by the Holy Spirit." This is a significant difference. Scripture contains not only many sentences expressing no proposition, but many sentences that express propositions not asserted by their human authors.[15] As evidence of error in Scripture, for instance, Brown cites, among other things, a passage in the book of Job (14:13–22), which Brown says "many recognize" denies an afterlife.[16] But the passage occurs in one of Job's speeches in a series of dialogues with his supposed friends—and it is

---

15   The distinction between making statements and asserting them is part of the theological tradition that was available to the Council in drafting *Dei Verbum* 11. In showing that every lie is sinful, St. Thomas Aquinas takes up the objection that the evangelists did not sin in writing the Gospels, but at least some of them said things that were false, because different authors report differently what Christ or others said; Thomas answers that in such cases the writers did not assert that those very words were uttered, but that words conveying that sense were uttered (*Summa Theologiae* 2a–2ae, q. 110, art. 3, reply obj. 1). (Thomas also points out that it is inadmissible to say that anything false *is asserted* in the canonical Scriptures, since that would undermine the certitude of faith.) The distinction between what is asserted and what is said without being asserted is one that Thomas uses regularly. For example, in dismissing objections based on mistaken statements quoted from the works of theological authorities such as Augustine and Anselm, he points out that the writers did not *assert* the views expressed in those statements, but only reported them or presented them as opinions: see, for example, *Summa Theologiae*, 1a, q. 77, art. 5, reply obj. 3; q. 100, art. 2, reply obj. 2.

16   Brown, *Critical Meaning of the Bible*, 16.

hardly clear that the author of the Book of Job asserts any of the views asserted by participants in that dialogue.[17]

Moreover, as the expressions, "Since, therefore," and "it follows that" indicate, the two paragraphs of Dei Verbum 11 constitute a carefully crafted argument, which Brown apparently overlooked or ignored. With the sentence fragment he inaccurately paraphrases, Vatican II is not, as he alleges, making a concession to ultraconservatives before getting to its real point. Rather, that sentence fragment states both the conclusion drawn from the preceding paragraph and the premise for the fragment Brown quotes.

The Reasoning of Dei Verbum 11

Like most arguments informally stated, the two paragraphs of *Dei Verbum* 11 leave implicit some elements of the Council's argument. It can be reconstructed in logical form:

(1) In their entirety the books of Scripture, with all their parts, were written under the inspiration of the Holy Spirit.

(2) Books written under the inspiration of the Holy Spirit have God as their author.

(3) In their entirety the books of Scripture, with all their parts, have God as their author.

(4) Books that have God as their author contain and present things divinely revealed and attested to by the inspiration of the Holy Spirit.

(5) In their entirety the books of Scripture, with all their parts, contain and present things divinely revealed and attested to by the inspiration of the Holy Spirit.

(6) Books that contain and present things divinely revealed and attested to by the inspiration of the Holy Spirit were the work of human authors whom God employed, they using their own powers and faculties, to convey in writing all those things and only those things that he wanted.

17　Toward the end of the book, after God speaks to him out of a whirlwind, Job says: "I have uttered what I did not understand, things too wonderful for me, which I did not know" (Job 42:3). And though God says Job has spoken "what is right" *of him* (42:7), he does not endorse everything Job has said. Marvin Pope offers a reading of Job 14:13–15 that differs from Brown's. Pope says: "Job here gropes toward the idea of an afterlife." *Job*, Anchor Bible, 15 (Garden City, NY: Doubleday, 1980), 108.

(7) In their entirety the books of Scripture, with all their parts, were the work of human authors whom God employed, they using their own powers and faculties, to convey in writing all those things and only those things he wanted.

(8) Books that were the work of human authors whom God employed, they using their own powers and faculties, to convey in writing all those things and only those things he wanted, include no proposition asserted by a human author that the Holy Spirit does not also assert.

(9) In their entirety the books of Scripture, with all their parts, include no proposition asserted by a human author that the Holy Spirit does not also assert.

(10) In their entirety the books of Scripture, with all their parts, have three attributes: they contain and present things divinely revealed and attested to by the inspiration of the Holy Spirit (from 5, above), they convey in writing all those things and only those things God wanted (from 7, above), and they include no proposition asserted by a human author that the Holy Spirit does not also assert (from 9, above).

(11) Books having those three attributes are books that teach firmly, faithfully, and without error the truth which God wanted to be attested by the sacred text for the sake of our salvation.

12) In their entirety the books of Scripture, with all their parts, teach firmly, faithfully, and without error the truth which God wanted to be attested by the sacred text for the sake of our salvation.

Restated like this, the premises of the Council's argument obviously not only establish its conclusion, but explain why it is true. In this way they also specify the meaning of the expressions used to state the conclusion. Thus, the meaning of the expression *the truth* in the conclusion must at least include the truth of all the propositions asserted by the human authors.[18] In detaching the sentence on which Brown focuses (12 in my restatement) from the premise he regards as a sop to

---

18   Because the premises do not totally explain the conclusion, expressions in the conclusion can mean more than the premises specify, but not less. Thus, the truth without error that God wanted to convey through the books of Scripture logically must include the truth of all the propositions asserted by the inspired writers, but it can include more—that is, the truth conveyed by the *sensus plenior*, which emerges from considering all the biblical books together and in the context of the entire tradition of the Church's faith.

conservatives (9 in my restatement), Brown rejects Vatican II's conclusion, for he fails to accept (12) *keeping the same meaning and the same judgment.*

Dei Verbum 11 having made it clear that only propositions asserted in the Bible convey truths to be believed, *Dei Verbum* 12 goes on to set out norms for interpreting the biblical books and identifying the propositions asserted. One must take into account not only the human author's literary options (for example, the use of dialogue by the author of Job) and sociocultural context, but other expressions of faith articulated in cooperation with the Holy Spirit—other biblical books, the living Tradition of the Church—and the coherence of all the truths of faith.

Brown says nothing about identifying the human authors' assertions.[19] Still, he does accept something of what the Council prescribes, for he holds that the Bible is an effective instrument of God's saving purpose when it is considered as a whole and proclaimed within the Church's living tradition as a whole. But *only* thus considered, he thinks, can the Bible, despite its errors, lead us to all the truth we need to help us on the way to salvation. In his view, for instance, later Old Testament passages and, especially, the New Testament make clear the truth about the afterlife, thus relativizing the error he thinks he finds in Job.[20] For Brown, any part of the Bible conveys God's Word only when considered as a part of the whole Bible and the Church's Tradition, and interpreted as such. But that is at odds with the teaching of Vatican I and Vatican II, that each of the Bible's books is part of the Bible and is recognized by the Church as divinely inspired.

Brown's implicit rejection of divine inspiration *as Vatican I and Vatican II understood it* is not surprising. Logically, anyone who denies Vatican II's conclusion (that all the propositions asserted by the inspired authors are without error) must deny at least one of the premises from which it follows. Brown implicitly denies not only that the sacred writers cooperated with the Holy Spirit in asserting what they asserted but that they were divinely inspired in the sense taught by both Vatican II and Vatican I—the latter with a solemn definition.[21]

The teaching in *Dei Verbum* 12 about biblical interpretation implies that Catholics are in a better position than Jews or Protestants to interpret the Bible, but Brown's view implies far more: that the Bible cannot mediate God's revelation either to believing Jews and others who do not accept the New Testament or to

---

19 Like most other Scripture scholars, Brown in his exegetical works provides little help for readers who wish to pick out the propositions that the human author of a biblical book is asserting. Indeed, Catholic exegetes seem to have ignored *Dei Verbum* 12; for a commentary on that state of affairs, see Ignace de la Potterie, S.J., "Interpretation of Holy Scripture in the Spirit in Which It Was Written (*Dei Verbum* 12c)," in *Vatican II Assessment and Perspectives: Twenty-five Years After (1962–1987),* vol. 1 (New York: Paulist, 1988), 220–266.

20 See Brown, *Critical Meaning of the Bible,* 19–21.

21 Brown does not intend to deny divine inspiration: "I fully accept the Roman Catholic doctrine of the Bible as the word of God, and the whole discussion assumes that fact." *Critical Meaning of the Bible,* 3. He only implicitly denies inspiration by misinterpreting *truth* in the sentence on which he focuses.

non-Catholic Christians, who do not receive the Bible within the living tradition of the Church as a whole. If one were to take seriously what he says, it even would seem that most Catholics, who cannot possibly study each bit of Scripture in the context of the whole Bible and tradition, would do better not to read the Bible at all—a conclusion Brown surely would not have welcomed.

It does not follow from what I have said that we should look in the Bible for truths—scientific, historical, or other—unrelated to our salvation. It is reasonable to assume that God's saving purpose in communicating with us will have limited the propositions the inspired writers assert to truths we need to know to form our relationship with him and live our lives in response to his love. But this does not amount to agreeing with those who take Vatican II's phrase, "for the sake of our salvation," to be a restriction upon the inerrancy of Scripture. They assume other propositions are asserted in Scripture and might be false. Vatican II denies this, and, in denying it, holds that the Holy Spirit inspires every part of every book of Scripture and makes no false assertions.

Moreover, in practice there is a great difference between these views. Someone who supposes that the Bible contains some false assertions tends to ask whether what is taken as an assertion is true and then looks to extrinsic criteria for an answer. This will lead to excluding some propositions that are saving truths but happen to be hard to understand and/or accept. God's message will be mutilated, and what remains of it will be distorted. By contrast, someone who supposes, as the Church teaches, that the Bible contains no assertions of false propositions is inclined to ask how some things taken as assertions in the Bible can be true. To answer, it will be necessary to seek the statements' meaning in their larger context and ultimate reference to salvation. In the last resort, too, one might conclude—with the help of other parts of the Bible, the whole of tradition, and current documents of the Church's teaching office—that some apparently asserted propositions are not really such. In any case, by truly doing one's best to discover God's message in even the most perplexing passages, one will enjoy the benefit God intended by giving us those passages.

Perplexities regarding the Bible should not be dissolved by assuming the inspired writers erred or lied; rather, it is necessary to struggle with the perplexities, in the conviction that whatever the writers actually assert is God's truth. Often, though, it is hard to tell whether they really are asserting the propositions they seem to assert, or even to know what proposition, if any, an inspired writer meant to express. Since most people can read the Bible only in translations and lack the historical knowledge required to interpret it, they do well to make judicious use of commentaries by competent exegetes, including Raymond Brown, which can help one avoid gross misunderstandings.

Letter & Spirit 6 (2010): 191-224

THE INTERPENETRATION OF INSPIRATION AND INERRANCY AS A HERMENEUTIC FOR CATHOLIC EXEGESIS

~: Joseph C. Atkinson :~
John Paul II Institute

The purpose of this paper is to examine the concepts of divine inspiration and inerrancy, to explore if they are causally connected and to determine the extent of their importance, if any, for the development of an adequate Catholic hermeneutic. Since the rise of modern rationalistic methodologies, the traditional Catholic teaching that Scripture is both divinely inspired and inerrant has been called into question both explicitly and implicitly.[1] This confusion is part of a broader "crisis in biblical interpretation," as Pope Benedict XVI, then Cardinal Joseph Ratzinger, has described it.[2]

At the heart of this hermeneutical crisis is the rejection or weakening of the traditional "incarnational" understanding of Scripture—namely, that the Word of sacred Scripture, like the hypostatic Christ, is at once fully human and fully

---

1 Alexa Suelzer indicates the range and effects of these attacks: "More than 250 years have elapsed since the inauguration of modern biblical research. For much of that time the Old Testament has been submitted to devastating attacks from every quarter. By their denial of the supernatural order, rationalism and deism made the Bible irrelevant as a communication of the Word of God to men; de-Christianized humanism reduced reading the Bible to an aesthetic experience; evolutionism considered all religions a deterministic development from primitive forms, allowing no place for the free intervention of God in history." "Modern Old Testament Criticism," in *The Jerome Biblical Commentary*, eds. Raymond E. Brown, Joseph A. Fitzmyer and Roland E. Murphy (Englewood Cliffs, NJ: Prentice-Hall, 1968), 604. These attacks against the supranatural dimension of Scripture arose from the anthropocentric turn which was effected during the Enlightenment period. Previously, authority was situated in an objectively received text, given with divine sanction. From the Enlightenment onward, authority would reside increasingly within the human intellect alone. Avery Dulles in his treatment of biblical hermeneutics rightly identifies the issue of authority as critical in the controversies over the nature of Scripture: "For many of our contemporaries, the term authority is a pejorative one, evoking suspicion and hostility. ... [The sacred writers] were witnessing to a divine revelation which they had received as a pure gift in trust for others ... to anyone who accepts this claim and belief, the testimony of the biblical witnesses shares, in some sense, in the authority of God himself." "The Authority of Scripture: A Catholic Perspective," in *Scripture in the Jewish and Christian Traditions: Authority, Interpretation, Relevance*, ed. Frederick E. Greenspahn (Nashville: Abingdon, 1982), 14. Hence a conflict arises between the Scriptures and our own autonomous authority. David R. Law identifies several foundations for the present-day crisis in accepting the biblical witness: "the modern emphasis on autonomy," "suspicion of the past," and the "rise of historical scholarship." *Inspiration* (New York: Continuum, 2001), 3–15.

2 See Joseph Cardinal Ratzinger, *Biblical Interpretation in Crisis: The Ratzinger Conference on Bible and Church*, ed. Richard John Neuhaus (Grand Rapids, MI: Eerdmans, 1989).

divine.[3] The written Word, like the incarnate Lord, holds both dimensions—the human and the divine—in a necessary and dynamic relationship. In the modern context, particularly with its anthropocentric focus, this divine-human interplay increasingly has been downplayed or neglected.[4] Modern critical methodologies focus exclusively on the human dimension of the biblical text while neglecting or rejecting the divine dimension, especially the essential issues such as the divine authorship of all parts of Scripture without limitation and its consequent freedom from error.[5]

Historically and theologically these three concepts—divine authorship, plenary inspiration, and inerrancy—have been critical to a proper Catholic exegesis of Scripture. Ultimately, our understanding of Scripture and its interpretation will have to come back to the incarnation of the Word of God. This paper will argue that, as with the incarnation, it is necessary to keep both the human and divine dimensions of Scripture in a healthy, fruitful tension. Only then can we avoid making interpretive errors and encounter the reality of the sacred text.

The Problems in Moden Exegesis

There is a wide consensus that fundamental problems exist in modern biblical exegesis, especially its reliance on diachronic analysis, which emphasizes almost exclusively the historical character and the cultural conditioning of the biblical text.[6] It is important to note that these problems are being raised by those com-

---

3   The foundations for this affirmation are to be found in the prologue to John's gospel (John 1:1–18). As we will see below, the Catholic magisterium solemnly affirmed this strict parallel between the nature of Scriptures and the nature of Christ.

4   This can be seen by the general lack of interest in the concept of inspiration. As Paul Achtemeier notes: "It is surprising and puzzling that the discussion of the doctrine of inspiration, within the past two or three decades, has been notable more by its absence than its presence. It has been honored by being ignored in many circles." *The Inspiration of Scriptures: Problems and Proposals* (Philadelphia: Westminister, 1980), 4.

5   See Ratzinger, *Biblical Interpretation*, 2: "The [critical] methodology itself seems to require such a radical approach: it cannot stand still when it scents the operation of man in sacred history. It must try to remove all the irrational residue and clarify everything. Faith itself is not a component of this method. Nor is God a factor to be dealt with in historical events." Ratzinger acknowledges that improvements have been made but he still urges a profound critique of the critical methods so that what is of value can be saved. See *Biblical Interpretation*, 5.

6   There are numerous works which provide a critical analysis of the state of higher critical methodologies. See Claus Westermann, *Genesis 1–11: A Commentary*, trans. John J. Scullion (Minneapolis: Augsburg, 1984), 567–606; Gordon Wenham, *Genesis 1-15*, Word Biblical Commentary 1 (Waco, TX: Word, 1987), xxv-xlv; Yehezkel Kaufmann, *The Religion of Israel: From its Beginnings to the Babylonian Exile*, trans. Moshe Greenberg (Chicago: University of Chicago, 1960); Issac M. Kikawadia and Arthur Quinn, *Before Abraham Was* (Nashville: Abingdon, 1986); Umberto Cassuto, *A Commentary on the Book of Genesis*, trans. Israel Abrahams (Jerusalem: Magnes, 1961). See generally, Pontifical Biblical Commission, *The Interpretation of the Bible in the Church* (Boston: Pauline, 1993); Ratzinger, *Biblical Interpretation*.

mitted to the use of these methods in their own exegetical work.[7] As a consequence, other methods based on a synchronic approach to the text and which take account of rhetoric, the reality of symbolic and typological thought, and the like—approaches once rejected by critical methodologies—have developed rapidly over the past few decades. Still there is little consensus as to how we can securely arrive at the truth in Scripture.

The struggle over the nature of the Scriptures and their authentic interpretation has not abated in the twenty years since Ratzinger's now classic Erasmus Lecture. At the heart of his concern was the need to challenge certain philosophical assumptions that underlie modern exegetical methodologies.[8]

> The time seems to have arrived for a new and thorough reflection on exegetical method. ... What we *do* need is a critical look at the exegetical landscape we now have, so that we may return to the [biblical] text and distinguish between those hypotheses which are helpful and those which are not. ... Scientific exegesis must recognize the philosophic element present in a great number of its ground rules, and it must then reconsider the results which are based on these rules.[9]

---

7   For example, see Westermann: "Recent Pentateuchal research on the whole shows that one has to treat the classical criteria for source division with much greater caution and that without exception they have lost their certainty." *Genesis 1–11*, 576. Wenham notes: "Some of the most deeply rooted convictions of the critical consensus have been challenged in recent years. ... The striking thing about the current debate is that it emanates from within the heart of critical orthodoxy. ... There is now widespread recognition of the hypothetical character of the results of modern criticism." *Genesis 1-15*, xxxiv-xxxv.

8   Joseph A. Fitzmyer understands the depth of Ratzinger's critique: "Moreover, Cardinal Ratzinger does not find fault with the method only because of what some of its practitioners do with it, but maintains that 'its erroneous application is due to the defects of the method itself ... it contains such significant mistaken assumptions that a reexamination of it is now incumbent upon all who would affirm the perennial importance of God's written Word for the Church.'" *Scripture, the Soul of Theology* (New York: Paulist, 1994), 35. Ratzinger points to the problem of uncritical acceptance of hypothetical conclusions in the modern academy: "[Martin Dibelius and Rudolf Bultmann] believed they had at their disposal the perfect instrument for gaining a knowledge of history. ... Why, even today in large part, is this system of thought taken without question and applied? Since then, most of it has simply become an academic commonplace, which precedes individual analysis and appears to be legitimized almost automatically by application." *Biblical Interpretaion*, 14.

9   Ratzinger, *Biblical Interpretation*, 21–22. It is important to note that Ratzinger calls for a return to the biblical text. Focus had shifted away from the text which, in some cases was seen as not being authoritative since the "canonized text" was considered only the historically and or culturally conditioned stage within an evolutionary process. Subtexts (previous formulations from competing or vanquished theological voices) were thought to be equally valid. Ratzinger's call remains relevant. Our present need is to recover once again the importance of the text as received canonically and as possessing definitive authority for the community of the Church.

This is a startlingly honest call for self-critique that few in the academic biblical establishment have been willing to make.[10] It acknowledges the value of modern critical methodologies inasmuch as they are necessary to establish the human reality of the text. But at the same time, Ratzinger sees how some approaches have distorted the text precisely because of certain faulty underlying presuppositions.[11] Thus a critical evaluation of these methods is needed to affirm those methods and principles that truly establish the historical and human dimensions of the text and to identify those methodologies and presuppositions that are faulty and lead to distorted readings of the text.[12]

Looking back, we can see Ratzinger's Erasmus Lecture as a bold call to rescue historical critical methods from their own inherent weaknesses. According to Ratzinger, Scripture must be studied as not only a historical and literary text, but as a text that claims to reflect the divine Word. Modern exegesis, however, "completely relegated God to the incomprehensible, the otherworldly and the inexpressible in order to be able to treat the biblical text itself as an entirely worldly reality according to natural-scientific methods."[13] But Scripture is the Word of God and is ultimately a communication from him. Thus, any approach that ignores or rejects this dimension inevitably starts from a place of distortion. Critical to the recovery of a proper hermeneutic, then, is the recovery of the divine horizon of Scripture.

For Ratzinger, properly constructed critical methods are necessary to secure the human dimension of the sacred text, but the human words need to be regarded as imbued with the Spirit of God and, as such, always simultaneously a divine Word. Only if a critical method coheres properly with the dual nature of Scripture will it enable us to encounter and explain the biblical text. If there is a disconnect between method and text, such an approach can only distort. It is the thesis of this paper that one can find in the body of Catholic teaching, the Church's magisterium, sound principles by which authentic exegesis can be carried out.

---

10 In today's academic atmosphere, it would be easy to mislabel such criticism as a form of obfuscation. See Fitzmyer's critique of Ratzinger's lecture in *Scripture, the Soul of Theology*, 38, n. 51.

11 "But today, certain forms of exegesis are appearing which can only be explained as symptoms of the disintegration of interpretation and hermeneutics. Materialist and feminist exegesis, whatever else may be said about them, do not even claim to be an understanding of the text itself in the manner in which it was originally intended." Ratzinger, *Biblical Interpretation*, 5.

12 "In order to arrive at a real solution, we must get beyond disputes over details and press on to the foundations. What we need might be called a criticism of criticism." Ratzinger, *Biblical Interpretation*, 6.

13 Ratzinger, *Biblical Interpretation*, 17.

Scripture's "Self-Consciousness" of its Nature

In his hermeneutics, Hans Gadamer has developed what can be described as a "perspectival" approach.[14] That is, one can look at a reality from various viewpoints that may not initially correspond with each other but each of which provides an essential way of looking at the text. In this vein, I wish to propose three essential perspectives that come from Scripture itself and that are critical in arriving at an understanding of Scripture's "self-conscious" awareness of its own nature.

First, there is the witness to the divine encounter that is captured in the scriptural texts.[15] The frequent appearance of phrases such as, "Thus says the Lord,""the Lord said," or "God said," demonstrate that the original biblical authors believed they were recording direct communications from God.[16] The biblical texts then attest to the authors' belief that an external, objective Word of God was given and received within human history.[17] This Word was not a human creation, but rather an authentic Word originating within God, communicated by God adequately through the instrumentality of human language to his people and received integrally by them. The primary activity and the initiative lay with God. The clear emphasis is on the objective Word received.

Second, the Scriptures witness to the permanent validity of this divine Word. Thus, while the text is necessarily conditioned by the culture in which it originates, at the same time it goes beyond those limiting factors. This is clearly enunciated during the prophetic period. Because of its apostasy, Israel was faced with imminent national destruction. In the face of this existential doom, the prophet Isaiah proclaimed a word of ultimate restoration. This Word, delivered from God, was to sustain Israel during its exile; in the midst of all destruction, this Word perdures and alone can be trusted. As Isaiah proclaimed: "The grass withers, the flower droops, but the Word of our God stands forever."[18]

Because the prophetic word enunciates the will of God and is his Word, it is the enduring norm by which history and individual lives will be judged. This perdurance of God's Word is revealed within the structure of salvation history, in which there is a progressive unfolding of the prophetic witness. The Word given is fulfilled generations later in vastly different cultures and circumstances—yet it is always the same Word. The revealed Word constitutes God's relationship with

---

14   See Brice Wachterhauser, 'Gadamer's Realism: The 'Belongingness' of Word and Reality," in *Hermeneutics and Truth*, ed. B. Wachterhauser (Evanston, IL: Northwestern University, 1994) 148–171.

15   Unless otherwise noted, all Scripture translations are my own and are intended to reproduce the original Hebrew and Greek to the extent possible.

16   The expression "Thus says the Lord" is used 389 times; "the Lord said" (846); and "God said" (440).

17   For example, see 1 Thess. 2:13: "Receiving the Word of God through hearing us, you received not a word of men but, as it truly is, a Word of God."

18   Isa. 40:8.

creation and with history and it structures both history and creation.[19] It is not merely descriptive but creative, a Word of power.[20]

Jesus is reflecting traditional Jewish understanding of the revealed Word when he states that Scripture is "not able to be loosened (Greek: *luthēnai*)" which, in essence, means Scripture cannot be broken. All that is written (*graphē*) determines history and will be fulfilled.[21] While any divine communication is given in terms of a specific cultural moment, it also possesses at the same time a quality that prevents it from being bound to that moment alone. Because of this "eternal" dimension to the Scripture, Jesus can state that "man does not live on bread alone but on every word that goes out of the mouth of God."[22] Thus, even the earliest strata of biblical revelation is considered to be of ever-present value, crossing over millennia of cultural changes.

The Word is always more than a recital of history. To see the Bible as only recorded history is to miss its ultimate purpose and to misconstrue the nature of the Scriptures, which is to enable our union with God. The Second Vatican Council's *Dei Verbum* (1965) begins by stating: "Through this revelation, therefore, the invisible God ... speaks to men as friends ... lives among them, so that he may invite and take them into fellowship with himself."[23]

The Word thus becomes the means by which an encounter with God is effected and by which we come into union with him. Paul realizes the relationship of the sacred word to the spiritual life, calling it "the sword of the Spirit,"[24] an essential element for our spiritual warfare. In the Sermon on the Mount, Christ shows that the Word must form the foundation of every Christian's life or one is lost.[25] The Letter to the Hebrews sees the Word as a living reality, sharper than a two-edged sword, that can pierce into the absolute depths of our being, revealing the truth.[26]

---

19   The relationship of Word to creation is evident in Gen. 1, 2, where God's Word structures creation. The relationship between Word and history is manifest in the New Testament's presentation of Jesus as the fulfillment of the Old Testament prophecies, which were always oriented towards their teleological conclusion in him (see Luke 24:27, 44). Thus history is yet determined by the Word of God: "Thus shall my Word be that goes out from my mouth; it shall not return to me empty because it will do (achieve) that for which I delight and cause what I sent it for to thrive." Isa. 55:11.

20   Compare Heb. 1:3.

21   See John 10:35.

22   Matt. 4:4.

23   Second Vatican Council, *Dei Verbum* [The Word of God], Dogmatic Constitution on Divine Revelation, (November 18, 1965), in *The Scripture Documents: An Anthology of Official Catholic Teachings*, ed. Dean P. Béchard (Collegeville, MN: Liturgical Press, 2002), 19–31. Hereafter abbreviated *SD*.

24   Eph. 6:17.

25   Matt. 7:24–27.

26   Heb. 4:12–13: "For the Word of God is living and active (effective) and sharper beyond all two-

Scripture clearly partakes of culturally constructed norms of language and expression, and of history; these parameters must always be respected and understood properly. However, they do not limit the activity of God but rather are the vehicles chosen by him to proclaim his truth for all time. The truth of the Scriptures is not "bound" by cultural conditions to its own frustration but instead is expressed adequately through them. While the Word is bound in history as to expression, history is caught up in the Word as to meaning.

The third point is that as Scripture reaches its fulfillment in Christ, it is revealed that the inscribed Word is intrinsically related to the person of God. Genesis 1 shows that creation is effected by God speaking his Word; later this same Word is spoken to the prophets, which they faithfully receive and announce to God's people. In the prologue to the Gospel of John, there is a two-fold development. First, this Word spoken by God was always with him, and is, in fact, God, himself. Second, this same Word that had been spoken and which shares in the nature of the Creator has taken flesh and walks amongst us. "The Word became flesh and dwelt [*eskēnōsen*] amongst us."[27] Jesus underscores this Word-Person complex when he states, "I am the way, and the truth and the life."[28] Truth is normally understood as propositional truths that cohere with reality. But here, Jesus is saying that truth is a divine Person. This surely is a mystery that goes beyond our ordinary conceptual categories. In both John's prologue and in this saying of Christ, Scripture is witnessing to an ontological bond between the written Word and the person of God. The Word once uttered in creation, now in the incarnation takes flesh and becomes a Person.

The "God-breathed" Scriptures

With the revelation of Christ, the Word can no longer be understood simply as something external to God. Whatever is the precise relationship, it is not extrinsic. This ontological bond between God and Word appears to be the foundation for 2 Timothy 3:16, which introduces a precise term to help us understand the God-Word relationship:

> All Scripture is inspired by God [Gk.: *theopneustos*—literally, *God-breathed*] and is useful for teaching, for reproof, for correction, for training in righteousness.

---

edged swords, penetrating as far as the division of the soul and the spirit, and also of the joints and marrow, and is able to judge the thoughts and intentions of the heart."

27 John 1:1–3. The verb *eskēnōsen* is particularly evocative here because it literally means "to pitch one's tent," an allusion to the Tabernacle, the tent-like structure (*miškan*) where God abided in the midst of Israel. The Word takes flesh from Mary and pitches his tent in order to dwell amongst us.

28 John 14:6.

Two points need to be investigated to understand the full impact of this verse. First, there appears to be some ambiguity in translating the first three words of this text.[29] Paul Achtemeier rightly notes that it is possible to translate this phrase as either "all (or every) Scripture is God-breathed," or as "every inspired Scripture." The first means that all Scripture comes from God and is inspired, while the second makes a distinction between those Scriptures which are inspired by God and those which are not. Achtemeier concludes that "there is no sure way to determine" which way the translation should go. Others disagree strongly with this conclusion.[30]

For example, Richard Smith lays out evidence that makes fairly clear what the natural reading of the text is. He notes that in the previous verse,[31] Paul had referred to the sacred writings that Timothy had learned as a child, that is to the writings of the Old Testament corpus. In 2 Timothy 3:16, Paul clearly refers again to these same writings.[32] The "Scriptures" that Paul is talking about, then, are those that make up Judaism's sacred corpus. Since there is no definite article in the Greek text, the phrase should be read "every Scripture." And since the term "God-breathed" or "inspired," is an adjectival form and parallels the adjective "useful," and since "useful" is a predicate (the writings are useful), it would seem that "God-breathed" should also be treated as a predicate (the writings are God-breathed). This is virtually the same construction found in 1 Timothy 4:4 ("For everything created by God is good, and nothing is to be rejected if it is received with thanksgiving.") To translate this as "every good created thing is not to be rejected" is unacceptable because it opens the possibility that there were some things that were not created good. The translation here in 2 Timothy 3:16, therefore, should be "every Scripture is God-breathed."[33]

Achtemeier contends that "there is no sure way to determine whether the author of this verse wanted to stress that every Scripture is both inspired and useful for teaching … or whether he wanted to stress that inspired Scripture is useful."[34] But this posits a dual form of Scripture (particularly in reference to the Old Testament)—texts that are inspired by God and those that are not. This, however, does not cohere with the beliefs concerning the Old Testament within either the Judaism at the time or the early Christian community.

The second point to consider is the meaning of *theopneustos*, often translated as "inspired." Rightly understood, this Greek word portrays the dynamic relation-

---

29 For one examination of this problem see Achtemeier, *Inspiration*, 106–108.

30 See Richard Smith, "Inspiration and Inerrancy," in *Jerome Biblical Commentary*, 501–502; Edward Young, *Thy Word is Truth* (Grand Rapids, MI: Eerdmans, 1957), 18–23.

31 2 Tim. 3:15.

32 *Graphē* is the New Testament shorthand for Israel's sacred Scriptures. See Luke 4:21; John 2:22; 7:28, 42; 10:35; Rom. 4:3; Gal. 3:8; 1 Tim. 5:18; James 2:23; 1 Pet. 2:6.

33 This seems to be the position of Pierre Grelot, *The Bible, Word of God: A Theological Introduction to the Study of Scripture* (New York: Desclée, 1968), 35, 49, 57.

34 Achtemeier, *Inspiration*, 107.

ship between God and the Scriptures. The word is composed of *theos*, meaning "God" and *pneō*, meaning "to breathe." Literally, the word means "God-breathed." This is closely linked to the Old Testament concept of prophecy where an objective Word of the Lord is received by a member of the community through the gift of prophecy.[35]

Smith shows that this verbal adjective can be taken as either active ("breathing God," that is, giving thoughts about him) or passive ("breathed by God, himself"). However, when this adjectival form is used with God elsewhere, it is normally passive and the four times it is used in pre-Christian literature, *theopneustos* is passive.[36] Smith concludes: "The passive meaning reflects the Jewish notion of the divine origin of Scripture, and the early native Greek-speaking interpreters of the passage unanimously interpreted the word in a passive sense. Scripture, then, is something that has been breathed by God—in other words, the very breath of God himself ... it bypasses consideration of any human causality."[37]

This text, then, gives us a fairly precise understanding of the God-Word relationship. However, it is an understanding that is often at odds with the Latin term "inspiration." David Law points out that "the basic meaning of inspiration is the breathing in of the divine Spirit into a human being who, under the influence of the Spirit, then communicates God's Word to his fellow human beings. These divinely inspired utterances were eventually consigned to written form."[38]

Philologically, "*in-spiration*" lays the emphasis on the divine breathe that enters into a human person who, then inspired, can write certain religious truths. But this is not, strictly speaking, the meaning of *theopneustos*. In fact, this anthropocentric emphasis tends to distance the written word from God. The stress of 2 Timothy 3:16 is that the writings are "breathed out" by God, thus coming from him, with the implication that they are then received by the person he designates. It is this divine origin that gives the writings their authority. In using the idea of breath (*pneustos*), the text links the sacred writings with the interiority of God.[39] It should be noted that while 2 Timothy 3:16 emphasizes the divine origin of the Word, it does not say, nor does it deny, anything about the human dimension of Scripture. This later insight will be the great contribution that the modern era will articulate, especially in the key paragraph 11 of *Dei Verbum*.

---

35 For example, Jeremiah opens his prophecy by saying: "And the Word of the Lord was to me, saying, 'Before I formed you in the womb, I knew you'" (Jer. 1:4–5). Clearly, the prophet is not claiming these words were merely his own personal thoughts about God but rather the content he had received from God.

36 Smith, *Inspiration*, 501–502.

37 Smith, *Inspiration*, 502.

38 Law, *Inspiration*, 49.

39 See 1 Thess. 2:13.

The Word of God and the Words of God

It is clear that the incarnation is critical for any adequate understanding of the nature of Scripture. This was noted by Pope John Paul II, who described the ontological link between the written Word and the Word incarnate this way: "It is true that putting God's words into writing, through the charism of scriptural inspiration, was the first step toward the incarnation of the Word of God." The Pope here invites us to imagine the forming of the first Hebrew Word of revelation and seeing that as the first step by which Christ assumes human flesh. In each, the Word is embodied in a specific manner; they are only different expressions of the same reality. The Pope underscores this by further referring to "the strict relationship uniting the inspired biblical texts with the mystery of the incarnation."[40]

This understanding is reflected in the *Catechism of the Catholic Church's* teaching on the nature of Scripture: "Through all the words of sacred Scripture, God speaks only one single Word, his one utterance in whom he expresses himself completely." The *Catechism* explains with a reference to St. Augustine:

> "You recall that one and the same Word of God extends throughout Scripture, that it is one and the same Utterance that resounds in the mouths of all the sacred writers, since he who was in the beginning God with God has no need of separate syllables; for he is not subject to time."[41]

In this Augustinian view, the many words uttered within time as Scripture are ontologically bound to the one eternal Word, Jesus Christ, and are an expression of him. From this premise, certain conclusions flow. As John Paul II stated: "Just as the substantial Word of God became like men in every respect except sin, so too the words of God, expressed in human languages, became like human language in every respect except error."[42]

We should note, however, that this incarnational understanding conflicts with many of the methodologies and presuppositions of modern exegetical studies. In contemporary practice, we find an overriding conviction that only the human dimension of Scripture can be properly taken into account in exegetical research. When this presupposition is in force, we are left with a text that can only be seen as historically and culturally conditioned, a product of fallible human creators. While it is legitimate to study the texts this way, if the exegete does not move

---

40   Pope John Paul II, Address to the Pontifical Biblical Commission (April 23, 1993), 6 (*SD*, 170–180, at 173–174).

41   *Catechism of the Catholic Church*, 2d. ed. (Vatican City: Libreria Editrice Vaticana, 1997), no. 102.

42   John Paul II, Address (April 23, 1993), 6 (*SD*, 173–174). John Paul notes that this phrasing is from Pope Pius XII's encyclical *Divino Afflante Spiritu* and that it is quoted virtually verbatim by Vatican II in *Dei Verbum*.

beyond the human dimension to consider the divine, such an approach will result inevitably in distorting the text. Rudolf Bultmann is a classical example. He began with the presupposition that miracles cannot happen; thus, other ways had to be found to explain the miracles attributed to Jesus. By this presupposition, the historicity of the gospel accounts are thus jeopardized and the text becomes increasingly distanced from the reader.

Any method that brackets out the divine dimension of Scripture unwittingly effects a dichotomy between the human text and the divine Word who informs the text. This is, in effect, a kind of reverse monophysitism applied to the Scriptures—the divine nature of Scripture is denied, leaving it to possess only a human dimension which, of necessity, is vulnerable to the effects of our fallen state. This error has led the Church to argue for a proper christological understanding of the Scriptures. It is precisely the dynamic interplay between the interpenetrating divine and human aspects of the text that prevents error and allows the truth of the text to be appropriated in fully human terms.

The Mystery of Divine and Human Authorship

Modern critical approaches to Scripture are reflective of the larger cultural concerns of autonomy and human freedom that have developed steadily from the Enlightenment. This driving concern with human autonomy has led to an anthropocentric preoccupation in approaching the text. For many, it seems, it has become impossible to see how a writer can freely exercise his human capacities as an author if there is a controlling divine influence. To this way of thinking, to assert that God is the true origin (*auctor* or "author" in Latin) of Scripture, renders the human agent a passive instrument who contributed nothing. However, as Karl Rahner shows us, fear that the human element is diminished and human freedom abolished in the dual divine-human authorship is ill-conceived. In his study on inspiration, Rahner suggests that rather than diminishing human capacities, the divine presence enhances them:

> Remembering the well-known analogy between the incarnation in the flesh and in the Word ... we may state that the free spontaneity of Christ's humanity was not lessened by the divine Person to whom this human nature belonged; not even though this humanity was first established in a supreme and unparalleled manner in the person of the *Logos* [Word] ... In a similar fashion the same thing happens in the case of the writers if they are authors ... and not just secretaries. They will then be authors no less, but even more so, than they would be in the natural case of human authorship. Inspiration does not restrain what is man's own, but frees it; it implies no act of unimaginable compromise,

but an application of the basic relationship between God and man.[43]

Rather than pitting the divine against the human, Rahner sees how the two cooperate and how, through the union with the divine, the human becomes even more authentically human. Properly understood, divine inspiration requires a fully alive human agent. In this christological paradigm, one does not have to be afraid of a fully human contribution to Scripture nor deny the effect that the divine presence has either on the human agent or on the text.[44] In touching Scripture we are touching on the incarnation.[45] Hence, Vatican II makes the bold statement: "The Church has always venerated the divine Scriptures just as she venerates the body of the Lord." This can only be true if the Scriptures have an ontological connection with the Lord.[46]

---

43   Karl Rahner, *Inspiration in the Bible*, 2nd. rev. ed., Quaestiones Disputatae 1 (New York: Herder and Herder, 1964), 14, n. 4. Cardinal Augustin Bea had made a similar proposal and is quoted by Rahner: "The instrumentality of the human originator has to be considered and interpreted in such a way that it should not only explain the literary special characteristics of the writings themselves, but also that in every accuracy and literalness these human originators are not only secretaries of God but real human authors. ... Its subordination to the divine ... makes human authorship all the more real and intensive," in "Pio XII e le Scienze Bibliche" [Pius XII and the Biblical Sciences], in *Pio XII Pontificus Maximus Postridie Kalendas Martias, 1876–1956* [Festschrift in Honor of Pope Pius XII on his 80th Birthday] (Rome: Typis Polyglottis Vaticanas, 1956), 71, quoted in Rahner, *Inspiration*, 16.

44   John Paul II comments: "It is in the intimate and inseparable union of these two aspects that Christ's identity is to be found, in accordance with the classic formula of the Council of Chalcedon (451): 'one person in two natures.' ... The two natures, without any confusion whatsoever, but also without any possible separation, are the divine and the human." *Novo Millennio Ineunte* [At the Beginning of the New Millennium], Apostolic Letter at the Close of the Great Jubilee of the Year 2000 (January 6, 2001), 21. In applying the Chalcedon formulae to biblical hermeneutics, we see a need to fully re-integrate the divine dimension so that the two natures are never separated.

45   *Dei Verbum*, 21 (*SD*, 28).

46   By contrast, Raymond Brown sees the incarnation paradigm in a different light. He writes: "There is a *kenōsis* involved in God's committing his message to human words. It was not only in the career of Jesus that the divine has taken on the form of a servant (Phil. 2:7). If one discovers religious errors, one does not seek to explain them away; one recognizes that God is willing to work with human beings in all their limitations. ... Cardinal [Franz] König and others had pointed out the kinds of errors that do exist is Scripture." *The Critical Meaning of the Bible* (New York: Paulist, 1981), 17, 19. The *kenōsis* that Paul speaks of in Phil. 2:7 is the preparation for the incarnation. An essential Catholic belief is that God prepared for this through the immaculate conception of Mary, so that Christ would receive a humanity that had not been tainted by sin. To save the world, the eternal Word does go through a *kenōsis*; but it is not Christ taking on a sinful humanity but rather a sinless one. In applying this to the Scriptures, the magisterium, as John Paul II pointed out, draws the parallel exactly. Just as Christ took flesh without sin, so too the Scriptures are God's Word in human words but without error. If this parallel is true, then the question is: how does permitting an understanding of Scripture that contains error impact our understanding of the incarnation?

Magisterial teaching is a child of its own particular times. That is to say, the Church in her formal pronouncements is usually responding to specific critical issues that threaten the faith. Until the Enlightenment, the Christian world held fairly unanimous beliefs about the divine inspiration of Scripture and inerrancy. Consequently, there was little need to formally state these beliefs because these were commonly held doctrines; they all participated in the same cognitive pre-suppositions.[47] Even during the Reformation the issue was not the nature of the sacred text but how that text was to be interpreted. As James Burtchaell notes: "The Reformers and counter-Reformers were disputing whether all revealed truth was in Scripture alone, and whether it could be dependably interpreted by private or by official scrutiny. Despite a radical disagreement of these issues both groups persevered in receiving the Bible as a compendium of inerrant oracles dictated by the Spirit."[48]

The change in the cognitive landscape was due to the increasing influence of Enlightenment ideas, particularly those growing out of its anthropocentric orientation. The resultant "succession of empirical disciplines newly come of age," including archaeology, geology, paleontology, and the development of literary criticism, all raised substantial challenges to traditional beliefs about the Scriptures.[49] These same principles began to inform critical exegetical models and often, as the Pontifical Biblical Commission noted, "these methods ... have shown themselves to be wedded to positions hostile to the Christian faith."[50] As the divine authorship was being rejected, along with the ideas of inspiration and the truthfulness of the witness of Scripture, the magisterium began to issue official clarifications. These were meant to counter critics outside the Church who questioned traditional doctrines, but also were meant to address problematic theories on inspiration and inerrancy by theologians within the Church.

The Spirit, the Church, and the Truth

But what does it mean for the Church to make decisive interventions when theological problems arise? What is the Church's role in determining truth?

---

47 "The rise of modern critical study broke the chain of continuity which had hitherto existed between the modern reader and his medieval and early Christian predecessors. ... The unity of the Bible was the fundamental premise upon which all were agreed." G. W. H. Lampe, "The Reasonableness of Typology," in *Essays on Typology*, G. W. H. Lampe and K. J. Woollcombe (London: SCM, 1957), 14. Bruce Vawter acknowledges that "it would be pointless to call into question that biblical inerrancy in a rather absolute form was a common persuasion from the beginning of Christian times, and from Jewish times before that. For both the Fathers and the rabbis generally, the ascription of any error to the Bible was unthinkable." *Biblical Inspiration* (Philadelpia: Westminster, 1972), 132.

48 James T. Burtchaell, *Catholic Theories of Biblical Inspiration Since 1810* (Cambridge: Cambridge University, 1969), 1–2.

49 Burtchaell, *Catholic Theories*, 2.

50 Pontifical Biblical Commission, *Interpretation of the Bible*, Introd., Sect. A (*SD*, 246).

Interestingly, the Scriptures themselves witness to the Church's indispensable role in the discerning of truth. 1 Timothy 3:15 states that the Church is 'the pillar (*stylos*) and foundation (*hedraiōma*) of the truth.' What this means is fleshed out in the Council of Jerusalem,[51] which, was called by the apostles to resolve a critical issue of faith—how is one saved. What is critical for us is to note their self-conscious understanding of the nature of their proceedings and their final conclusion.

They did not conceive themselves as an organization of men of faith who, through their good will and rational investigation, would reach a conclusion; if that had been the case, their determinations would, at best, be prudential and certainly refutable at later stages.

Instead, the Scriptures witness to a unique fact—that the Church from its inception[52] understood that it was being led into all truth by the Holy Spirit[52] and that through a charism given to the apostolic leadership, truth could be definitively known. During this first debate within the Church, there was an interplay between the human dimension (Scriptural study, argumentation, prayer) and the divine dimension that would guarantee that the Church would know the mind of the Holy Spirit. The Church understood itself as the organic Body of Christ with the capacity and vocation to discern binding truth because Christ was truly present and leading his Church. The Church does not make or create truth but discerns it. Certainly, the Church can grow in its understanding of any truth and articulate it in more profound ways. What it cannot do is overturn prior determinations of truth.[53] This is the fundamental meaning of Tradition.

Just as in the early Church there were various tensions over the nature of salvation, so too from the early 1800's there were radical challenges to the traditional understanding of Scripture. From the outside, these challenges were coming from rationalistic sciences and critical methodologies. Within the Church, however, there were also some theologians proposing different theories to effect a rapprochement between the new worldview and traditional dogma, often by rejecting some fundamental truth that the Church had already discerned.[54] This was a time of great tension and the Church was forced to respond magisterially to these dangers. The decrees and encyclicals of this period need to be read within this larger context.

We can sympathize with the situation of the popes and Church officials, given the virtual hegemony of rationalistic categories of thought in our own modern world. Many today have rejected the organic nature of the magisterium

---

51 See Acts 15.

52 See John 16:13.

53 Dogmatic truth is different from "prudential decisions" that must be made from time to time for the best interests (*bene esse*) of the Church. The latter do not touch on matters of faith and morals and are by nature reformable according to circumstance.

54 See Burtchaell, *Catholic Theories*, 2.

and instead substitute a mechanical model in its place. This leads to a situation in which one selectively chooses from magisterial teaching those parts that support a particular theological opinion and ignore those parts that challenge it. Alternatively, one pits certain magisterial teachings against others to achieve support for specific theological positions. Such a mechanical understanding cannot account for the divine presence and guarantee which Christ, himself, gives to the Church. With the mechanistic model of the Church, our ability to know the truth with certainty is gravely diminished. The organic understanding of the Church, deeply rooted in the Pauline epistles, coheres more deeply with the nature of truth, and safeguards our ability to know the truth with certainty.

The Development of the Doctrine of Inspiration

It is clear that the last one hundred fifty years has seen a profound evolution in our understanding of the Scriptures. This does *not* mean that what was believed earlier was erroneous or rejected. In principle, growth in Christian doctrine conserves what has already been determined, allows for a continuing deeper grasp of the truth, and enables a more precise articulation of doctrine.[55] To oppose the "truth of the past" to the "truth of the present" comes from a confusion over the nature of truth and institutes a falsifying tyranny of the present moment.

One can perceive a theological trajectory in the Church's understanding of Scripture. With each stage, the understanding of the human involvement in Scripture has become more secure. Initially, as in the christological debates, this security was gained primarily through the identification of theological errors. Later, once the theological ground had been cleared, positive constructions could be made that demonstrated the full interplay between the divine and human, without a diminution of either's role. To properly understand the development of magisterial teaching, it is necessary to closely examine the surrounding context.

The decrees of the Council of Trent were written in response to the challenge of the Reformation. In emphasizing the absolute authority of the Word of God, the Reformers were not arguing over the nature of the sacred texts *per se*. Both sides accepted the Scriptures in terms of the commonly held opinion of that day—that they were inerrant divine oracles. Martin Luther wrote: "We may trust unconditionally only in the Word of God and not in the teachings of the [Church] Fathers; the teachers of the Church can err and have erred. Scripture never erred."[56]

---

55   See John Henry Newman, *An Essay On Development Of Christian Doctrine*, Chap. 5 (Notre Dame, IN: University of Notre Dame, 1989 [1845]), 169–206.

56   Paul Althaus citing Luther in *The Theology of Martin Luther* (Philadelphia: Fortress, 1966), 6 n. 12, cited by John D. Woodbridge, "Some Misconceptions of the Impact of the 'Enlightenment' on the Doctrine of Scripture," in *Hermeneutics, Authority and Canon*, eds. D. A. Carson and John D. Woodbridge (Grand Rapids, MI: Zondervan, 1986), 413, n. 50. There are some who dispute Luther's high view of Scripture. However see John Montgomery, "Lessons from Luther on the Inerrancy of Holy Writ," in *God's Inerrant Word* (Minneapolis: Bethany Fellowship, 1973), 67 where Montgomery also offers Adolf von Harnack's testimony: "It happened that his

Likewise John Calvin called the Scriptures: "the inerring standard," asserting that it was "free from every stain or defect," and "the certain and unerring rule."[57] In his commentary on 2 Timothy 3:16 ("All Scripture is inspired by God and is useful for teaching, for reproof, for correction, for training in righteousness."), Calvin states: "We owe to the Scripture the same reverence which we owe to God; because it has proceeded from him alone, and has nothing belonging to man mixed with it."[58]

If these ideas were novel or an attack on the faith of the Church, the magisterium would have had to respond to refute them. But Trent never mentioned the matter. On the other hand, Trent did establish that all the books found in the Catholic canon, including the so-called deuterocanonical books rejected by the Reformers as "apocrypha," were indeed sacred Scripture. The Council underlined this by stating that God is author of all these books: "[The Synod] venerates ... all the books both of the Old and of the New Testament—seeing that one God is the author of both [testaments]." Trent also gave voice to the then-current understanding of inspiration: the Scriptures were "dictated, either by Christ's own word of mouth, or by the Holy Ghost."[59] While this gives expression to the immediacy of God's participation in Scripture, it does not explicitly take up the issue of human agency. However, this realistic sense of the authorship of God will be used centuries later in formal definitions that establish Scripture as free from all error-precisely because God is author.[60]

The other key point—and perhaps the most important one in that contemporaneous situation—was Trent's insistence that there was an intrinsic relationship between the Word and the Church. The Scriptures not only had a divine origin but were also "preserved in the Catholic Church by a continuous succession."[61] Both the divine and the ecclesial dimensions of Scripture were necessary.

The reality of an authentic human dimension to the Scriptures was only discerned slowly. What proved difficult was to understand the interplay between human agency and divine inspiration. From the late sixteenth century, beginning with Leonhard Leys (also known as Lessius) onwards, theories were put forward

---

[Luther's] church arrived at the most stringent doctrine of inspiration." *God's Inerrant Word*, 69, citing *Outlines of the History of Dogma* (Boston: Beacon Press, 1957 [1898]), 561–562.

57   The sources in Calvin (*Institutes of the Christian Religion*, 1:149; *Commentaries on the Twelve Minor Prophets*, 1:506; and *Commentary on the Psalms*, 5, 2), are cited by John H. Gerstner in "The View of the Bible Held by the Church: Calvin and the Westminster Divines," in *Inerrancy*, ed. Norman L. Geisler (Grand Rapids, MI: Zondervan, 1979), 391.

58   John Calvin, *2 Corinthians and the Epistles to Timothy, Titus, and Philemon*, trans. Thomas Allan Smail, Calvin's New Testament Commentaries 10 (Grand Rapids, MI: Eerdmans, 1996).

59   Council of Trent, *Decreee Concerning Acceptance of the Canonical Scriptures and Apostolic Traditions* (April 8, 1546) (*SD*, 3).

60   Pope Leo XIII, *Providentissimus Deus* [The God of All Providence], Encyclical Letter on the Study of Scripture (November 18, 1893), 20 (*SD*, 37–61, at 54–55).

61   *Decree Concerning the Canonical Scriptures*, (*SD*, 3).

that saw inspiration primarily in the content of the Scripture and not the actual words.[62]

Lessius and others suggested that not every word of Scripture had to be inspired by the Holy Spirit and formed by the Spirit in the writers' mind. Moreover, they suggested that not all scriptural truths and statements came from the Holy Spirit and that texts could be approved as Scripture after they had been written as long as there was no error in them.[63] While it was laudable that these theories sought to understand the human author as making a genuine contribution to the composition of Scripture, some of these early hypotheses ended up limiting the idea of inspiration such that the whole text was not inspired. The question was right but the formula was wrong. In attempting to enhance the human dimension, the divine aspect was diminished.

By the time of Vatican I (1869–1870), there were a number of theories focused on the meaning and extent of inspiration. Two in particular were dealt with by the Council.[64]

Daniel von Haneberg in 1850 rejected plenary verbal inspiration—that is, the belief that God had inspired the actual words of the whole scriptural text, both Old and New Testaments. Instead, he suggested the Bible had three possible types of inspiration: *antecedent* (the passive human author received words directly from God); *concomitant* (God inspired the idea but the sacred author provided the words with God preventing him from making errors); and *consequent* (the sacred author writes the book without divine assistance and later the Church accords it canonical status). Haneberg's approach tended to divide Scripture into human and divinely controlled elements. It should be noted, however, that Haneberg assumes inerrancy as a mark of canonicity.

Another theory taken up by Vatican I is Johann Jans's "assistance theory," by which inspiration is understood as the divine assistance given to protect a written text from error.[65] This is a minimalist understanding of inspiration that limits the activity of God to assuring that the text contains no error. The actual wording of the text is primarily a human achievement, having little or no relation to the influence of God.

Vatican I, in its decree on revelation, intervened to respond to these and similar ideas:

---

62 See Burtchaell, *Catholic Theories*, 88–120, esp. 98–99. In essence, God is responsible for the content which is inspired, whereas man is responsible for its expression, with the proviso that a specific divine assistance was given to make sure the human expression were apt. Hence, these theories were also called "concomitant" or "divine-assistance" theories of inspiration.

63 See the excellent analysis in Burtchaell, *Catholic Theories*, 44–58.

64 Vawter, *Inspiration*, 70-71.

65 See Burtchaell, *Catholic Theories*, 50–51.

> These books the Church holds to be sacred and canonical not because she subsequently approved them by her authority after they had been composed by unaided human skill, nor simply because they contain revelation without error, but because, being written under the inspiration of the Holy Spirit, they have God as their author, and were as such committed to the Church.[66]

The decree also affirms several key principles that provide the framework by which the human-divine agency question can be properly worked out. First, it assumes there are no errors in the text. This was not in dispute and did not need to be defined. It was simply the *sententia communis*—the commonly held position of the Church. Thus, the inerrancy of Scripture is simply mentioned in passing as an accepted reality. Second, the decree carefully delineates the dynamic relationship between the Church and the Scriptures. The Church cannot "make" a text inspired; this comes from God alone. The Church can only discern and acknowledge what is the Word of God. Implicitly, the decree formally acknowledges the substantial reality of both Church and Scripture in such a way that neither collapses before or is absorbed by the other. Vatican I, then, provides the necessary precision that will allow for a proper articulation of the Church-Word relationship at a later date. This decree opened the way to see that the Church and Scripture exist in a positive dialectical relationship, each informing the other. Third, the Scriptures have authority not because of some subsequent confirmation by the Church but precisely because God is author. Consequently, that which is not inspired and that which is not authored by God cannot be his Word, nor can it be part of the canon. The decree does not particularly help in securing the human dimension of Scripture but it does provide essential precisions that will later help in the articulation of the Church's relationship to the Word.[67] Fourth, the decree affirms positively that inspiration resides in the books that were inspired, and not just the human writers.[68]

Discerning the "Limits" of Inerrancy

Following Vatican I, questions emerged about the nature of inspiration. The problem was that a number of the proposed solutions tended in fact to limit inspiration or inerrancy. In 1870 Cardinal Johannes Baptist Franzelin, advanced a theory that tried to separate out divine formal matters of dogma from its human expression.

---

66 First Vatican Council, *Dei Filius* [The Son of God], Dogmatic Constitution on the Catholic Faith (April 24, 1870), 2, 7 (*SD*, 14–18, at 16–17). As Vawter notes, "It is also quite clear that [Vatican I] intended to reject most firmly the opinions of Haneberg and Jan." *Inspiration*, 70–71.

67 *Dei Verbum*, 10 (*SD*, 23), deals with this issue in terms of the magisterium, Tradition and Scripture and shows how the magisterium "is not above the Word of God, but serves it, teaching only what has been handed on." This is the clearest articulation of the Church-Word relationship and is dependent on Vatican I's earlier precision.

68 See Burtchaell, *Catholic Theories*, 74.

The divine author was said to be responsible for dogmatic thought whereas the human author was responsible for the manner of expression.[69] Another approach was to limit inerrancy only to issues of faith and morals. Blessed John Henry Newman used the phrase *"obiter dicta"* to suggest that Scripture was composed of inspired religious, dogmatic teachings, but also of *obiter dicta* (other side issues) that were not authoritative. This formulation did not explicitly state that the *obiter dicta* could be erroneous. However, in his private correspondence, Newman wrote about his belief in partial inspiration that extended only to Scripture's teachings on matters of faith and morals.[70] During this same period, François Lenormant and Salvatore Di Bartolo were examples of those explicitly proposing limited inspiration. However, Pope Leo XIII's encyclical, *Providentissimus Deus*, effectively put an end to these theories.

The immediate cause for *Providentissimus Deus* was the public defense of Alfred Loisy (who would later be excommunicated) by Maurice d'Hulst, the rector of the Institut Catholique de Paris. Leo also wanted to directly address the issues that "rationalists" (such as Loisy) had raised and which had seemingly undermined the reliability of the Scriptures. But the fuller intention of the encyclical was to encourage better scriptural studies in the Church and provide authoritative principles for the development of proper exegesis.[71]

Confronting the anthropocentric turn of the age and the development of rationalistic methodologies in science and in exegesis, Leo focused on the supernatural element of the Scriptures by establishing that God is truly the author of Scripture in a meaningful, concrete way, and not just as a vague force or influence.

> For, by supernatural power, he so moved and impelled them to write ... that the things which he ordered, and those only, they, first, rightly understood, then willed faithfully to write down, and finally expressed in apt words and with infallible truth. Otherwise, it could not be said that he was the author of the entire Scripture. ... "Therefore," says St. Augustine, "since they wrote the things which he showed and uttered to them, it cannot be pretended that he is not the writer; for his members executed what their Head dictated."[72]

---

69 See Vawter, *Inspiration*, 72; Burtchaell, *Catholic Theories*, 120.

70 See Burtchaell, *Catholic Theories*, 78. Newman's original essay ("On the Inspiration of Scripture," *The Nineteenth Century* 15:84 [February 1884] and his subsequent tract ("What is of Obligation for a Catholic to Believe concerning the Inspiration of the Canonical Scriptures" [May 1884]) are available online: http://www.newmanreader.org/works/miscellaneous/scripture.html.

71 See Jean Levie, *The Bible, Word of God in Words of Men* (London: Geoffrey Chapman, 1961), 61.

72 Leo XIII, *Providentissimus Deus*, 20 (*SD*, 56).

We should note that here, perhaps for the first time in the Church's magisterium, there is an opening for the human-divine interplay active in Scripture where man is not merely passive. Clearly, the focus is still on the primary authorship of God who communicates to the writer who writes only what God wills; therefore what is written is from God. Yet it is also clear that there is genuine communication going on in which the writer understands rightly what is communicated, commits himself to faithfully reproducing what he has been given, and then uses appropriate words. The human will and capacities are clearly active in this process, as Leo describes it. The key is that the writers are never acting independently. They are part of an organic whole in which the Head is speaking to them, but in such a way that their personalities or wills are not annihilated.

In addressing the numerous theories circulating at that time, Leo rejected the idea of partial inspiration in the strictest terms:

> But it is absolutely wrong and forbidden, either to narrow inspiration to certain parts only of holy Scripture, or to admit that the sacred writer has erred. ... For all the books which the Church receives as sacred and canonical are written wholly and entirely, with all their parts, at the dictation of the Holy Ghost.[73]

In this sweeping decree, Leo confirms, contrary to Jahn and Haneberg, that inspiration extends to all the parts of the Scripture that are canonical. This response also counters the weakness of Franzelin's proposal of limited inspiration for Leo seems to apply inspiration to the words of the sacred books. Each book "wholly and entirely" comes about at the "dictation of the Holy Spirit." Thus the Scriptures could not be divided into formal ideas and material words, as Franzelin had proposed. It would seem rather that inspiration touches the very words of Scripture—yet how that happens is not yet discerned.[74]

Inspiration and Inerrancy: Their Intrinsic Relationship

To avoid possible contradictions and problems in the biblical texts, some theologians had urged that one could have an inspired text with some parts safeguarded from error (those pertaining to faith and morals) while other parts are not so protected from error. Leo rejects this suggestion as well, stating that only an integral vision of inspiration was acceptable.

---

73   Leo XIII, *Providentissimus Deus*, 20 (*SD*, 56).

74   While the consequence of this teaching would seem to lead to verbal inspiration, at best it can only be said perhaps to be implicit. "In the production of a literary document thought and word are so intimately bound together that it seems artificial to separate the two. ... Consequently, inspiration extended not only to the biblical ideas but also to the words—not that God dictated the words to the writer, but the writers' selection of words was constantly under the directing and driving force of God's inspiration" Smith, "Inspiration and Inerrancy," 511.

> So far is it from being possible that any error can coexist with
> inspiration, that inspiration not only is essentially incompatible
> with error, but excludes and rejects it as absolutely and necessar-
> ily as it is impossible that God himself, the supreme Truth, can
> utter that which is not true.

This statement affirms that if any text is inspired it cannot err. Therefore, it is
useless when faced with difficulties in the text to propose that somehow the text
is fully inspired yet part of it has erred. As Leo presents his case, this is logically
impossible. His reason again goes back to the nature of God. Inspiration means
that God is producing the text, the whole text, such that it is truly his Word. For
the text to be in error is to either deny that God inspired the text or to assert
that God can speak that which is not true. Nor can biblical scholars get out of
difficulties by positing that the human author has erred but not God. Again, this
is illogical because the text ultimately is authored by God. There is a triple helix,
as it were, of divine-human authorship, inspiration, and inerrancy, and this cannot
be broken.

Leo established the inerrancy of Scripture in absolute terms. Bruce Vawter,
who does not agree with the traditional doctrine of inerrancy,[75] candidly notes
that "the Pope's preoccupation throughout [the encyclical] was with the question
of scriptural inerrancy. ... In Leo's mind the sacred books were wholly inerrant (*ab
omni omnino errore immunes*) precisely because of their divine authorship."[76] Leo
put it this way:

> All the Fathers and Doctors agreed that the divine writings,
> as left by the hagiographers, are free from all error ... for they
> were unanimous in laying it down, that those writings, in their
> entirety and in all their parts were equally from the afflatus of
> Almighty God, and that God, speaking by the sacred writers,
> could not set down anything but what was true.[77]

The encyclical establishes the doctrine of plenary inerrancy in several ways. First,
by asserting that God really is the author of all the sacred texts. What is written
by the human writers is also "set down by God" and therefore must be true. No
wedge can be driven between the humanly written words and God's Word. They
are one and the same reality. "We cannot therefore say that it was these inspired
instruments who, perchance, have fallen into error, and not the primary author. ...

---

75   See Vawter, *Inspiration*, 147, 151.

76   Vawter, *Inspiration*, 73.

77   Leo XIII, *Providentissimus Deus*, 21 (*SD*, 56).

Otherwise, it could not be said that he was the author of the entire Scripture. ...
Such has always been the persuasion of the Fathers."[78]

Thus, the text is both man's word and God's, with God being the primary
Author or efficient cause. In essence, the human words coincide with God's Word
and are not something other than of God. Given the interpenetration of human
words with the divine Word, the intrinsic and inseparable relationship of inspiration to inerrancy, and the Church's teaching that all the canonically received
Scriptures are wholly and completely inspired, Leo concludes: "It follows that
those who maintain that an error is possible in any genuine passage of the sacred
writings, either pervert the Catholic notion of inspiration, or make God the author
of such error."[79]

Given the grave crisis of biblical interpretation that was occurring in his day,
Leo supplements his logical argumentation by invoking the ecclesial guarantee for
what he is presenting. He states that his teaching on inspiration and inerrancy is
nothing other than the ancient faith of the Church.

> [The canonical books] are written wholly and entirely, with all
> their parts, at the dictation of the Holy Ghost ... that inspira-
> tion not only is essentially incompatible with error, but excludes
> and rejects it as absolutely and necessarily as it is impossible that
> God himself, the supreme Truth, can utter that which is not
> true. This is the ancient and unchanging faith of the Church,
> solemnly defined in the Councils of Florence and of Trent, and
> finally confirmed and more expressly formulated by the Council
> of the Vatican.[80]

Benedict XV's 1920 encyclical, *Spiritus Paraclitus,* did not add anything new
but reinforced the principles that *Providentissimus Deus* had laid down, confirming
what "our predecessor of happy memory, Leo XIII, declared to be the ancient and
traditional belief of the Church touching the absolute immunity of Scripture from
error."

Benedict's expressed concern was that despite this ancient and traditional
teaching, there were "even children of the Catholic Church" who rejected it.[81]
Accordingly, he used his encyclical to clarify some misappropriations of Leo's

---

78 Leo XIII, *Providentissimus Deus,* 20 (SD, 56).

79 Leo XIII, *Providentissimus Deus,* 21 (SD, 56).

80 Leo XIII, *Providentissimus Deus,* 20 (SD, 56).

81 Pope Benedict XV, *Spiritus Paraclitus* [The Holy Spirit, the Comforter], Encyclical Letter
Commemorating the Fifteenth Centenary of the Death of St. Jerome (September 15, 1920), 18
(SD, 81–111, at 87, 88).

words. Benedict also helped to further advance the Church's understanding of the extent of inspiration—affirming the proposal that inspiration extends "to every phrase—and, indeed, to every single word of Scripture."[82]

Pope Pius XII begins his encyclical *Divino Afflante Spiritu* (1943) by reiterating his allegiance to Leo's teaching and establishing *Providentissimus Deus* as foundational for Catholic exegesis—indeed it is "the supreme guide in biblical studies." While this encyclical has subsequently been interpreted as a liberating break with the Church's traditional teaching, such a reading is not supported by Pius's text. Pius himself states that he is "ratifying and inculcating all that was wisely laid down by our predecessor [Leo]."[83]

Divino Afflante Spiritu must instead by understood as a genuine development in exegetical approaches that is in unquestionable continuity with the teachings of *Providentissimus Deus*. Pius specifically reaffirmed the Church's teaching against continued attempts to restrict inerrancy to only matters of faith and morals. Pius concurs with Leo's rejection of any limits to the Bible's inspiration:

> When subsequently some Catholic writers, in spite of this solemn definition of Catholic doctrine—by which such divine authority is claimed for the "entire books with all their parts" as to secure freedom from any error whatsoever—ventured to restrict the truth of sacred Scripture solely to matters of faith and morals, and to regard other matters, whether in the domain of physical science or history, as *obiter dicta* [incidental or collateral] and—as they contended—in no wise connected with faith … Leo … justly and rightly condemned these errors.[84]

In his desire to demonstrate the truthfulness of Scripture, Pius urged "prudent use" of some newer approaches to scriptural interpretation for the express purpose of "explaining the sacred Scripture and in demonstrating and proving its immunity from all error."[85] Most importantly, Pius gave formal approval to the study of literary forms, thus allowing the human dimension of the text to be fully explored.[86]

---

82 Benedict XV, *Spiritus Paraclitus*, 19 (*SD*, 88).

83 Pope Pius XII, *Divino Afflante Spiritu* [Inspired by the Divine Spirit], Encyclical Letter Promoting Biblical Studies (September 30, 1943), 2 (*SD*, 115–139, at 88).

84 Pius XII, *Divino Afflante Spiritu*, 1 (*SD*, 88).

85 Pius XII, *Divino Afflante Spiritu*, 38 (*SD*, 129).

86 "For the ancient peoples of the East, in order to express their ideas, did not always employ those forms or kinds of speech which we use today; but rather those used by the men of their times and countries." Pius XII, *Divino Afflante Spiritu*, 36 (*SD*, 128–129). As Levie points out, this study was not to be "a subjective process" but "an objective investigation of the intentions of the authors of times past." *Bible, Word of God*, 167. Indeed, Pius intended this study to help

The justification for allowing this confident and rigorous investigation into the human dimension of the divine Word lies in the relationship of Scripture to the incarnation. Pius establishes a strict relationship between the Word inspired and the Word incarnate:

> For as the substantial Word of God became like to men in all things, "except sin," so the words of God, expressed in human language, are made like to human speech in every respect, except error.[87]

Pius' deepening understanding of the human dimension of Scripture, to be gained through prudent study of its literary structures, and his emphasis on the christological structure of Scripture, represent enormous advances. It should be kept in mind that Pius articulated several precisions necessary to keep the divine-human relationship in balance. First, the Word of God is fully human ("like to men in all things"); there is no room for any docetic understanding of the Scripture.[88] Second, the words of Scripture are truly God's words "expressed in human language." The divine origin is clear. Finally, Pius affirmed that the words of Scripture are human in every way except error. In this analogy, to speak of error in Scripture would be comparable to speaking of sin in the incarnate Christ. Pius thus proposes a christological paradigm that makes possible a dynamic understanding of Scripture.[89]

Vatican II and the Truth of Sacred Scripture

The Second Vatican Council's *Dei Verbum* marked a major contribution to the development of the Church's magisterial teaching on the nature of revelation. Yet, as in the case of Pius XII and *Divino Afflante Spiritu*, some have sought to portray *Dei Verbum* as a break from the Church's tradition. For example, Vawter maintains that the Council did its best to withdraw "from the traditional yet unofficial

---

us grasp the genuine dynamics and structures of human language: "When then such modes of expression are met within the sacred text, which, being meant for men, is couched in human language, justice demands that they be no more taxed with error than when they occur in the ordinary intercourse of daily life." *Divino Afflante Spiritu*, 39 (SD, 130).

87 Pius XII, *Divino Afflante Spiritu*, 37 (SD, 128).

88 See Levie, *Bible, Word of God*, 164.

89 Pius XII was not giving blanket approval to historical critical methods. As Levie notes about the encyclical, it is "very circumspect, as precise as it is balanced in its demarcation of the limits of each of the rules it lays down." *Bible, Word of God*, 143. The same Pius was later to issue the encyclical, *Humani Generis* in which he "deplored a certain too free interpretation of the historical books of the Old Testament." Although these books do not conform to contemporary historical methods, he said, 'they "do nevertheless pertain to history in a true sense." *Humani Generis* [The Human Race], Encyclical Letter on Certain False Opinions Threatening to Undermine the Foundations of Catholic Doctrine (August 12, 1950), 38 (SD, 143).

designation of [Scripture] as inerrant."[90] The Council, in his interpretation, limits inerrancy by teaching that the sacred writers were inspired but that "a certain truth only is ascribed to [them], and that only as it is the vehicle of a divine salvific intention."[91]

This is typical of a certain reading of *Dei Verbum's* crucial paragraph 11 that has gained hold in the years since the Council.[92] This reading is opposed by the official reading of the text, which understands *Dei Verbum* to be in continuity with the Church's traditional teaching, only articulating that teaching positively, giving space for both the divine and human dimensions of the text. At the root of these two vying interpretations are very different presuppositions about the nature of Scripture, the dynamic human-divine relationship, and the role of the Church and Tradition in securing the truth.

To understand what the Council fathers intended in *Dei Verbum*, we need to study the stages in the document's evolution,[93] as well as the official determinations given by the Council's theological commission. It is also crucial that we not separate the document from the organic, continuous teaching of the Church, but rather see it as firmly rooted in that Tradition. Paying attention to these criteria prevents misunderstandings from taking root and directs us instead towards a richer appreciation of the authentic nature of the biblical text itself and its central salvific role in the Body of Christ, the Church. In turn, we will find in *Dei Verbum's* christocentric emphasis the principles by which the modern biblical crisis can be addressed properly.

---

90 Vawter, *Inspiration*, 147

91 Vawter, *Inspiration*, 147. Elsewhere Vawter has written: "'Biblical inerrancy' or 'infallibility' in the fundamentalist sense ... is the product of the scientific age in the age of rationalism, a simplistic response to both. It is definitely not one of the authentic heritages of mainline Christianity." "Creationism: Creative Misuse of the Bible," in *Is God a Creationist?: The Religious Case against Creation-Science*, ed. Roland Mushat Frye (New York: Scribner, 1983). 76.

92 Vawter acknowledges what he calls "a certain tension" between the *Dei Verbum* and the "earlier pronouncements emanating from ecclesiastical authority." *Inspiration*, 148. And Raymond E. Brown illustrates how modern exegetes separate what Jesus or Paul affirms from historical reality: "I do not believe that demons inhabit desert places or the upper air, as Jesus and Paul thought. ... Jesus and Paul were wrong on this point. They accepted the beliefs of their times about demons, but those beliefs were superstitious." "The Myth of the Gospels Without Myth," *St. Anthony Messenger* (May 1971): 47–48

93 "In accordance with the legitimate method of the interpretation of conciliar documents in general, here also the whole discussion in the Council and the Theological Commission must be used as sources for a better understanding." Alois Grillmeier, "Chapter III: The Divine Inspiration and Interpretation of Sacred Scripture," in *Commentary on the Documents of Vatican II*, 5 vols., ed. Herbert Vorgrimler (New York: Herder and Herder, 1967–1969), 3:199–246, at 209.

In keeping with the nature of the Council, *Dei Verbum's* aim was not to proclaim any new doctrines but rather to enunciate authentic Catholic teaching in modern terms. Indeed, the Council fathers begin *Dei Verbum* by confirming the document's organic link to the magisterial patrimony, stating that they were "following in the footsteps of the Council of Trent and of the First Vatican Council."[94] This would not seem to suggest the Council intended any radical redefinition of the Church's understanding of Scripture.

In addressing inspiration, *Dei Verbum* begins with the epistemological question of the adequacy of language and its relationship to revelation. Again it affirms its continuity with the Tradition—quoting Vatican I to state that the purpose of revelation is to enable religious truth to be known "with solid certitude and with no trace of error."[95] Human language is thus capable of expressing the truth free from error. This is followed by a declaration that "sacred Scripture is the Word of God," which is further specified as "consigned to writing under the inspiration of the divine Spirit."[96] This teaching, as we have seen, flows directly from Scripture itself, and is a simple reaffirmation of the Church's constant belief.

Given the turbulent climate of biblical studies in the decades prior to the Council, it was not surprising that no other topic was more greatly debated by the Council fathers than that of inspiration and inerrancy. As Ratzinger later commented, with the introduction of the first draft of *Dei Verbum* "the inevitable storm broke."[97] Both those seeking greater ecumenical openness and those seeking to change the Church's teaching on inerrancy fought against the acceptance of the traditional sounding first draft. The atmosphere was so tense that seven days after its introduction, Pope Paul VI removed the text from the Council and set up a commission to reformulate it.[98] The bishops as a whole were clearly divided as to what the Church should teach on this issue and it was evident that for some, the document on revelation was not merely to be "updated." Among the contentious issues involved were the material completeness and sufficiency of Scripture, the role of modern exegetical endeavors, Tradition, the inerrancy of Scripture, and the historicity of the Gospels.[99] The often heated debates led to another direct intervention by Paul VI asking for clarification of the latter three issues, including

---

94 *Dei Verbum*, 1 (*SD*, 19).

95 *Dei Verbum*, 6 (*SD*, 21; Latin: "'firma certitudine et nullo admixto errore'").

96 *Dei Verbum*, 9 (*SD*, 23).

97 Joseph Ratzinger, "Dogmatic Constitution on Divine Revelation: Chapter II, The Transmission of Divine Revelation," in *Commentary on the Documents of Vatican II*, 5 vols., ed. Herbert Vorgrimler (New York: Herder and Herder, 1967–1969), 160.

98 Ratzinger, "Divine Revelation," 161.

99 Ratzinger, "Divine Revelation," 155–166.

inerrancy.[100] Only when the Council's Theological Commission gave a definitive interpretation and the wording of the draft was changed to prevent the notion of inerrancy from being restricted or limited, was the text of *Dei Verbum* finally approved.

The original draft of chapter 3 of *Dei Verbum* (paragraphs 11–13) was entitled "The Interpretation of Inerrancy" and it used traditional propositional language. In the conciliar spirit of *aggiornomento* ("bringing up to date"), the Council sought to articulate its doctrine in a positive fashion. Thus, negative formulations, such as "inerrancy," were transformed into positive constructions, such as "truths of salvation." Some Council fathers wanted to move beyond *aggiornomento* and argued that the document admit that Scripture, rather than being without error, actually spoke in a way that was wanting in truthfulness (*deficere a veritate*).[101] Cardinal Franz König led those favoring this move toward a conciliar declaration of limited inerrancy. Others opposed the effort as a novelty that stood in opposition to all magisterial teaching on the subject.

To advance his argument, Cardinal König rose during the debates and cited three well-known exegetical problems: First, in Mark 2:26, Jesus states that David went into the House of the Lord and ate the bread there at the time when Abiathar was the High Priest. This appears to be in conflict with 1 Samuel 21, which dates the incident to the high priesthood of Ahimilech. Second, Matthew 27:9–10, attributes the prophecy concerning Judas's death to Jeremiah when it appears that the citation is actually from Zechariah 11:12–13. Finally, Cardinal König cited Daniel 1:1 that puts the conquest of Jerusalem in the third year of Jehoiakim, while Jeremiah puts it in the fourth year of his reign.[102]

No Council father stood up to counter these assertions. Of course, these apparent discrepancies have long been recognized and possible solutions could have been proffered, including one from St. Augustine.[103] For instance, in Mark

---

100 Ratzinger, "Divine Revelation," 164.

101 See Grillmeier, "Divine Inspiration," 206.

102 *Acta Synodalia Sacrosancti Concilii Oecumenici Vaticani II* [Synodal Acts of the Ecumenical Council Vatican II], 32 vols. (Rome: Typis Polyglottis Vaticanis, 1970–), vol. 3, pt. 3, 275–276.

103 Augustine was well aware of the problem but, precisely because he believed Scripture to be inspired and God's Word, he believed there can be no error. Consequently he sought to resolve what appeared to be a discrepancy. He first noted that Jeremiah's name "is not contained in all the codices." He personally could not accept this as a solution as too many codices did have the name. (This is a good example of textual criticism.) He then made the acute observation that if Matthew had made an error, it would surely have been pointed out to him by someone reading the text. Therefore the explanation must lie elsewhere. Augustine assumed therefore that God had a reason to have Matthew report this and remarked how "all the holy prophets, speaking in one spirit, continued in perfect unison with each other in their utterances." This resonates somewhat with the idea of being able to refer to all the prophets by mentioning one

2:26 the preposition (*epi*) could mean "in the time of" and would thus only indicate that Abiathar was still alive at the time but was not necessarily the High Priest.[104] The attribution of the quote to Jeremiah in Matthew 27 can be seen as a device by which the name Jeremiah stands for the whole book of the prophets or, given that the quoted text from Matthew contains elements from both Zechariah and Jeremiah in it, only the greater prophet has been mentioned.[105] The apparent dating problem in Daniel might be resolved in a number of ways, including taking into account differences between the Babylonian and Israelite methods of reckoning time.[106]

Archbishop Paul-Pierre Philippe strenuously objected to Cardinal König's proposal, arguing that moving the Council in this direction would contradict the constant magisterial teaching of the Church. The original draft of *Dei Verbum* had stated in unambiguous language that the Scriptures were "absolutely immune from error."[107] Given that the Vatican's Supreme Congregation of the Holy Office

---

major one. *The Harmony of the Gospels*, Bk. 3, Chap. 7, 28–30, in *A Select Library of Nicene and Post-Nicene Fathers of the Christian Church*, 1st series, 14 vols., ed. Philip Schaff (Peabody, MA: Hendrickson, 1994 [reprint]), 1:191–192.

104 See also the solution of William L. Lane, *The Gospel of Mark* (Grand Rapids, MI: Eerdmans, 1974), 115–116 in which he cites Mark 12:26 ("have you not read in the book of Moses, concerning the bush") where the reference is simply the place in the scrolls where reports of this incident can be found. The idea here is that Mark can use *epi* to mean the general place of something. In the passage challenged by Cardinal König, the idea would be that "in the era that Abiathar was still alive and had been High Priest sometime during that era." In other words, while *epi* indicates a place or time, it has the sense of pointing in the more generalized direction of something.

105 See Walter C. Kaiser, Jr., ed., *Hard Sayings of the Bible* (Downers Grove, IL: InterVarsity, 1996), 399–400. This book notes that the prophecies of Zechariah are mentioned four times in the New Testament but the prophet's name is never associated with them. This suggests that the solution may come from the fact that the prophets were collected together and Jeremiah, leading the corpus, became the way to refer to them all.

106 In Babylonian reckoning, the first regnant year counted only after the year of ascension to the throne. See Jack Finegan, *Handbook of Biblical Chronology: Principles of Time Reckoning in the Ancient World and Problems of Chronology in the Bible* (Princeton, NJ: Princeton University, 1964), 314–317. It is interesting to note that D. J. Wiseman suggested several ways of solving this dating problem in Daniel: "If Daniel … is here using the Babylonian system of dating (post-dating, allowing for a separate "accession" year) while Jeremiah (Jer. 25:49; 46:2) follows the usual Palestinian-Jewish antedating (which ignores "accession-years"), there is no discrepancy." "Notes on Some Problems in the Book of Daniel," in *Some Historical Problems in the Book of Daniel*, ed. D. J. Wiseman (London: Tyndale, 1965), 17. These are not necessarily the only solutions but they do show ways in which difficulties can be addressed. This requires the texts be read in their Semitic context, with an understanding of biblical literary techniques, historical and linguist constructs, and cultural norms. Using only a Western lens, the text would naturally seem to contain "errors."

107 The original draft reads: "Ex hac divinae Inspirationis extensione ad omnia, directe e necessario sequitur immunitas absoluta ab errore totius sacra scripturae." *Acta Synodalia Sacrosancti*, vol.

had created this initial draft, it would seem likely that this language was intended to reflect the commonly held doctrine of the Church. But in pursuing the goal of *aggiornamento*, the Council wanted a new draft that would positively address the issues at hand. Thus began a lengthy and contentious amendment process.

In the end, the debate on inerrancy focused on the wording of a single phrase in paragraph 11. The third draft of the document stated that what was asserted by the human authors was also asserted by the Holy Spirit. At this stage, the draft still retained the word "inerrancy" as a title.[108] With the fourth draft, this term was dropped and the reality of inerrancy is positively described in the following phrase: "The whole books of Scripture with all of their parts teach firmly, faithfully, wholly and without error the saving truth [*veritatem salutarem*]."[109] However, it quickly became apparent that the expression *veritatem salutarem* was going to be problematic. If *veritatem* (truth) is modified by *salutarem* (saving), the text would imply that only texts concerned with faith and morals were inerrant. This, of course, was what Cardinal König and others had been advocating. Archbishop Philippe countered:

> If it says the holy books "teach the saving truth [*veritatem salutarem*] without error," it seems inerrancy is restricted to matters of faith and morals. ... Such a circumscription of the object of inerrancy is not possible. I think therefore that this formulation cannot be harmonized with the enduring doctrine of the magisterium of the Church. ... Therefore, it must not be said that the holy Scripture "teach" the saving truth without error because it then introduces a division amongst the assertions of the Scriptures themselves, as if they taught some truths which pertained to salvation without error, and then others not having such content and hence are not under inerrancy.[110]

I, pt. 3, 18. See also Grillmeier, "Divine Inspiration," 199–200: "The text ... presented to the Council fathers in the first session was ... Chapter II, "De Scripturae Inspiratione, Inerrantia et Compositione Litteraria" [The Inspiration of Scripture, Inerrancy, and Literary Composition]. ... Thus the 'absolute inerrancy' of Scripture is stated here in very strong terms."

108 See Vawter's analysis, *Inspiration*, 146.

109 *Acta Synodalia Sacrosancti*, vol. 4, pt. 1, 355.

110 *Acta Synodalia Sacrosancti*, vol. 4, pt. 2, 979–980 (Lat.: "Si dicatur libros sacros 'veritatem salutarem ... sine errore docere,' videtur inerrantia restringi ad res fidei et morum ... talis circumscriptio obiecti inerrantiæ admitti non potest. Censeo enim hæc dicta cum firma doctrina Magisterii Ecclesiæ componi non posse. Igitur, non est dicendum libros sacros veritatem salutarem sine errore 'docere,' quia tunc discrimen insinuatur inter ipsas Scripturæ assertiones, quasi aliæ veritates ad salutem pertinentes sine errore docerent, dum aliæ tale contentum non haberent ac proinde inerrantiæ non subessent.")

The *relators* from the Council's Theological Commission weighed in during the debates and clarified why the term *veritatem salutarem* was used in the fourth draft. They stated that it had been inserted in order to satisfy the requests from the Council fathers so that the effect of inspiration (*effectus inspirationis*), which presumably refers to inerrancy, would be expressed positively (*positive exprimeretur*), and that the object of inerrancy would be clearly circumscribed (*clare circumscriberetur*).[111] Certainly paragraph 11 begins positively by speaking of truth in affirmative terms (what the human writers affirm, God affirms), thus avoiding the earlier negative concept of "language without errors." It thus provided one way in which inerrancy could be applied to a text.[112]

It was evident, however, that *veritas salutaris* could be read as limiting inerrancy and this raised grave concerns. As Alois Grillmeier noted, the September 22, 1965 vote of the Council demonstrated that "the fathers feared this false interpretation" of the phrase.[113] The fathers asked the Theological Commission to provide the meaning of the term *veritas salutaris*. The Commission replied: "The expression *salutaris* should in no way imply that Scripture is not, in its totality, inspired and the Word of God."[114] Despite this precise explanation, a number of Council fathers were not satisfied that the inerrancy of Scripture was safeguarded. "A large number of fathers"[115] suggested that the *salutaris* be deleted so that *truth* would not be restricted. "Their reasoning," Grillmeier records, "was that the expression 'truth of salvation' would, as against the documents of the teaching office, limit inerrancy to matters of faith and morals."[116] Finally, Paul VI sent a letter to the president of the Theological Commission suggesting that the commission consider dropping

---

111 See *Acta Synodalia Sacrosancti*, vol 4, pt. 1, 358; vol. 4, pt. 2, 979. Vatwer understands that the Council fathers wanted to "sharply circumscribe" inerrancy (*Inspiration*, 145), but he reads the Latin *clare* in a somewhat adversarial manner; the term is better translated "clearly circumscribe." This better coheres with *Dei Verbum* 11's beginning statements about biblical affirmations.

112 For instance, when a parable is spoken, the historical reality of the events depicted in the parable is not being asserted. What is being asserted is the contents of the parable (its teaching) and the historical fact that it was spoken.

113 Grillmeier, "Divine Inspiration," 211. "In its reply ... the Theological Commission had to go into the main difficulty: 'the truth of salvation' (*veritas salutaris*) restricts inerrancy to statements on faith and morals (*res fides et morum*) and is thus contrary to the documents of the [Church's] teaching office."

114 Grillmeier, "Divine Inspiration," 213. The problem is that some would separate inspiration from a guarantee of truthworthiness. Leo XIII went to the heart of that question: "So far is it from being possible that any error can co-exist with inspiration, that inspiration not only is essentially incompatible with error, but excludes and rejects it as absolutely and necessarily as it is impossible that God himself, the supreme Truth, can utter that which is not true." *Providentissimus Deus*, 20 (*SD*, 55).

115 Grillmeier, "Divine Inspiration," 211.

116 Grillmeier, "Divine Inspiration," 211.

the phrase *truths of salvation* altogether.[117] All of this textual history suggests that not only the Pope, but a significant number of the world's bishops, were concerned to preserve the organic continuity of the Church's teaching on scriptural inerrancy.

In the end, after much struggle, *veritem salutarem* was indeed dropped and in its place another phrase substituted—"the truth, which God wanted put into sacred writing for our salvation [*veritatem, quam Deus nostrae salutis causa litteris sacris consignari voluit*]." Vawter candidly observes, "There is no doubt that the change was papally instigated and was intended to pacify certain conservative reactions." He also acknowledges that the change was made because "a significant number of the fathers objected to the earlier formulation [*veritatem salutarem*] as a reversion to the old idea that inerrancy could be limited."[118] With the new language, all but five Council fathers voted for the final draft. That suggests that virtually all of those who had been alarmed by the possibility that limited inerrancy might creep into the conciliar text were satisfied that the final language would preclude such a misinterpretation.

The last piece in the interpretive puzzle is the value of footnotes. The footnotes appended to paragraph 11 were used to ensure a proper interpretation of the text as a whole, and in particular, the phrase "that truth which God wanted put into sacred writings for the sake of salvation."[119] Grillmeier notes: "Another way of avoiding a misunderstanding of *veritas salutaris* seemed to be the addition of a note in the official text. This was to give sources for the expression (such as Augustine and the Council of Trent), as well as to protect it against abuse and wrong interpretation by references to the encyclicals *Providentissimus Deus* and *Divino Afflante Spiritu*."

This is precisely what the notes to the final text of paragraph 11 hoped to do as well—as an examination of the references chosen demonstrates. The most important footnote, number 5, is attached to the section that deals with the truth-claims of Scripture. This section contains the critical phrase "truth which God wanted ... for the sake of salvation [*veritatem, quam Deus nostrae salutis causa*]."[120] There is a problem with the standard English translation of this section because the footnote number is placed mid-sentence just before "for the sake of salvation," seemingly implying that the references have nothing to do with that phrase. However, an

---

117 Grillmeier, "Divine Inspiration," 213. See also Vawter, *Inspiration*, 146.

118 Vawter, *Inspiration*, 146.

119 Grillmeier, "Divine Inspiration," 211.

120 The conciliar text refers to the standard collection of magisterial teachings, the *Enchiridion Biblicum: Documenti della Chiesa sulla Sacra Scrittura* [Documents of the Church Concerning Sacred Scripture], eds. Alfio Filippi and Erminio Lora, 2nd. ed. (Bologna: Dehoniane, 1993); hereafter abbreviated *EB*. The references are to *Providentissium Deus*, 18, 20–21 (*EB* 121, 124, 126–127); and *Divino Afflante Spiritu*, 3 (*EB* 539).

examination of the Latin text shows that the footnote is actually placed at the end of the sentence and thus covers all that the sentence affirms.

The fact is, the passages cited by *Dei Verbum* 11 contain the strongest and most authoritative language in the magisterium concerning the plenary inspiration of Scripture and the consequential plenary inerrancy which flows from that and makes a causal connection between the two. The footnotes refer to the following teachings:

> It is absolutely wrong and forbidden, either to narrow inspiration to certain parts only of Holy Scripture, or to admit that the sacred writer has erred.[121]

> So far is it from being possible that any error can coexist with inspiration, that inspiration not only is essentially incompatible with error, but excludes and rejects it as absolutely and necessarily as it is impossible that God Himself, the supreme Truth, can utter that which is not true.[122]

> ... that those writings, in their entirety and in all their parts were equally from the afflatus of Almighty God, and that God, speaking by the sacred writers, could not set down anything but what was true.[123]

> "It is absolutely wrong and forbidden either to narrow inspiration to certain passages of holy Scripture, or to admit that the sacred writer has erred ... as it is impossible that God himself, the supreme Truth, can utter that which is not true. This is the ancient and constant faith of the Church."[124]

The magisterium's strongest articulation of plenary inspiration and inerrancy, *Providentissimus Deus* 20, is referenced twice in this footnote. Thus, it seems reasonable to assume that the footnotes were crafted to reassure the Council fathers that the Church's traditional teaching on inerrancy was being preserved. As a final assurance, paragraph 11 ends with a quote from 2 Timothy 3:16: "All Scripture is divinely inspired." What is unusual here is that the Council mentions specifically the "Greek text" of the Scripture, probably to point readers to the term *theopneustos*

---

121 Leo XIII, *Providentissimus Deus*, 20 (*SD*, 55; *EB* 124).

122 Leo XIII, *Providentissimus Deus*, 20 (*SD*, 55; *EB* 124).

123 Leo XIII, *Providentissimus Deus*, 21 (*SD*, 56; *EB* 126–127).

124 Pius XII, *Divino Afflante Spiritu*, 3; Leo XIII, *Providentissimus Deus*, 20 (*SD*, 117; *EB* 539).

("God-breathed") found uniquely in this text. This term, in all probability, holds the key to the proper interpretation of the nature of Scripture.

Given the Council's desire to "update" the presentation of the Church's doctrine, it is understandable that traditional language yielded to more positive formulations. At the same time, *Dei Verbum* presents a richer and more developed understanding of the nature of the truth-claims in Scripture, one that accounts for the interpenetrating authorial-divine affirmations. Despite the tensions and indeed diametrically opposed opinions in the Council as to the meaning and extent of inspiration and inerrancy, the idea of limited inerrancy or inspiration was not endorsed. To have done so, as a significant number of Council fathers understood, would have entailed rejecting the whole of the Catholic Tradition.[125] Indeed, given the history of the text that we have just reviewed, it is difficult to see how *Dei Verbum* could credibly be interpreted as advocating a position of limited inerrancy.[126]

Christological Perspective

A final element of *Dei Verbum* that can help in resolving the modern crisis in biblical interpretation is its christological structure. Both the Council as a whole and *Dei Verbum* itself had a decidedly christological emphasis that acted as a kind of "hermeneutical control." Beyond the numerous references to Christ as the Word, paragraph 13 of *Dei Verbum* draws the direct parallel made between the incarnation and Scripture: "For the words of God have been made like human discourse, just as the Word of the eternal Father was in every way made like men."

This christological dimension of the Word must always be accounted for in any exegetical encounter with the Word. In fact, it becomes the clue to unravel the modern exegetical crisis. In the first centuries, the Church had to unravel the "exegetical" crisis of the Word enfleshed. What was the true nature of Jesus Christ? Faithful to the written Word and guided by the Holy Spirit, the Church was able to articulate what she had always experienced. Jesus is truly God and truly man,

---

125 Augustin Cardinal Bea, "Vatican II and the Truth of Sacred Scripture," *Letter and Spirit*, 1 (2005): 173–178.

126 On this point, it must be said that there must be credible limits to which one can push the interpretation of a text—whether it be the Scriptures or conciliar documents. To go beyond this limit is no longer to be working with the text or to be bound by it, but rather to be controlled by something outside of the text. There must also be congruence between interpretation and the markers of objective reality—such as history, true literary forms, authoritative traditional understanding, and the coherence of the Scriptures as a whole. Otherwise we are caught in a world of deconstructionism, left with only a disintegrated text, rudderless, and wandering aimlessly. It is only as we seek the objectivity of truth that we are drawn up into reality that frees us from all false images and which allows us to enter into true communion with our fellow man, with our true selves, and finally with God.

yet without sin. If this is a true analogy, the exegetical crisis over the nature of the Word inscribed needs to be resolved in a similar manner.[127] This is eminently valid because the enfleshed Word and the inscribed (written) Word are intrinsically linked, as the prologue to John's gospel asserts.

Because the Word became flesh, it can be now posited that what one says of the Word inscribed should also be said of Christ. The Scriptures therefore, like the *Logos's* incarnated presence, are truly human and truly divine, yet without error. Thus, through the analogy of the Word incarnate and the Word inspired, it becomes possible to understand with greater depth St. Jerome's insight that knowledge of Scripture is knowledge of Christ.[128]

---

127 Fitzmyer, among others, has reservations about applying this incarnational understanding to the Scriptures: "[Hans Urs von] Balthasar also calls Scripture 'the body of the *Logos*' and denies that this patristic idea, according to which both the Eucharist and Scripture mediate to the faithful the one incarnate *Logos*, is 'a merely arbitrary piece of allegorizing.' ... But what else is it? This is a good example of the scholarly *Schwarmerei* ["excessive or unwholesome sentiment"] to which those who advocate a spiritual exegesis of Scripture are led. It is not 'exegesis' at all; it is eisegesis." *Scripture, the Soul of Theology*, 91.

128 Jerome stated the point negatively: "Ignorance of the Scriptures is ignorance of Christ [*Ignoratio enim Scripturarum ignoratio Christi est*]." *Commentary on Isaiah* 1:1, Prol., quoted in *Dei Verbum*, 25 (*SD*, 30).

Letter & Spirit 6 (2010): 225-246

RESTRICTED INERRANCY AND THE "HERMENEUTIC OF DISCONTINUITY"

~: Brian W. Harrison, O. S. :~
Oblates of Wisdom Study Center

The nature and scope of biblical inerrancy, or the truth of Sacred Scripture, has not in recent decades been a popular topic in the writings of Catholic theologians and biblical scholars. According to the standard international bibliography of Christian scholarship, Louvain University's *Elenchus Bibliographicus*, not one publication by a Catholic writer has mentioned either the truth or inerrancy of Scripture in its title since 1995, and only three have done so since 1983.[1] The most recent authoritative and comprehensive general survey of modern Catholic biblical scholarship, the Pontifical Biblical Commission's document *The Interpretation of the Bible in the Church*, includes no clear statement of Catholic doctrine on the guaranteed truth of Scripture; it mentions the subject only once, very briefly, and in passing.[2]

The long-dormant question of inerrancy has been reawakened, however, as a result of the Synod of Bishops held in Rome in October 2008, dedicated to the "The Word of God in the Life and Mission of the Church." This issue was explicitly raised at the Synod and news reports indicated that the ensuing discussion brought to light disagreements and uncertainties among the assembled bishops as to whether the Second Vatican Council (1963–1965) allows for the possibility of error in sacred Scripture. Accordingly, one of the Synod's final propositions requested that the Vatican's Congregation for the Doctrine of the Faith "clarify the concepts of the inspiration and truth of the Bible, as well as their reciprocal relationship, so that the teaching of *Dei Verbum* 11 may be better understood."[3] No doubt as a result of that request, this issue was chosen as the key theme

---

1 See Prosper Grech, "Quid est Veritas? Rivelazione e Ispirazione: Nuove Prospettive" [What is Truth? Revelation and Inspiration: New Perspectives], *Lateranum* 61 (1995): 413–424; G. Blandino, "The Inspiration and Truth of Sacred Scripture," *Teresianum* 39 (1988): 465–477; and Andrés Ibañez Arana, "Inspiración, Inerrancia e Interpretación de la S. Escritura en el Concilio Vaticano II" [Inspiration, Inerrancy and Interpretation of the Sacred Scriptures in the Second Vatican Council], *Scriptorium Victoriense* 33 (1986): 5–96, 225–329; and 34 (1987): 5–44). The 2010 edition of the *Elenchus* will presumably add a fourth publication to this minuscule collection, namely, my article, "Does Vatican Council II Allow for Errors in Sacred Scripture?" *Divinitas* 52:3 (2009): 279–304. Since 1983, just fifteen other Catholic books or articles referenced in the *Elenchus* have the word "inspiration" in their titles.

2 Pontifical Biblical Commission, *The Interpretation of the Bible in the Church* (September 21, 1993), Sec. I, Para. F, in *The Scripture Documents: An Anthology of Official Catholic Teachings*, ed. Dean P. Béchard, S.J. (Collegeville, MN: Liturgical Press, 2002), 244–317, at 273. Hereafter abbreviated *SD*.

3 Synod of Bishops, 12th Ordinary General Assembly, List of Propositions, 12. Available

for discussion at both the April 2009 and April 2010 plenary sessions of the Pontifical Biblical Commission, a consultative body of the doctrine congregation. At this writing, nothing as yet has been published regarding the results of the Commission's deliberations. Nonetheless it seems an opportune time to review the current status of the question regarding Catholic teaching on inerrancy.

In this essay I will first review classical Catholic doctrine on the issue, then I will argue that the crucial text of Vatican II—paragraph 11 of the Council's Dogmatic Constitution on Divine Revelation, *Dei Verbum* (1965)[4]—should be read in harmony with this tradition—that is, with what Pope Benedict XVI has identified as a "hermeneutic of continuity." This will involve a critical analysis, from the standpoint of both faith and reason, of a widespread tendency to read this conciliar text according to a "hermeneutic of discontinuity," or rupture, with our doctrinal heritage.[5]

The Drift of Catholic Academic Thought

To gain a bird's-eye view of the prevailing direction in which Catholic academic thought on this matter has travelled over the last hundred years, we can juxtapose three brief statements separated by intervals of approximately half a century:

First, from 1907, is Pope Pius X's condemnation of the following statement: "Divine inspiration does not extend to the whole of sacred Scripture in such a way as to preserve each and every one of its parts free from all error."[6]

Second, from 1950 is this statement by Pope Pius XII in his encyclical letter, *Humani Generis*: "For some boldly pervert the sense of the [First] Vatican Council's definition regarding God as the author of Holy Scripture, and again put forward the opinion—already repeatedly condemned—that the Bible's immunity from error pertains only to what it hands down in matters concerning God, morals, and religion. They even wrongly speak of a human sense of the sacred books beneath which their divine sense lies hidden, and declare that only the latter is infallible."[7]

(in Italian) online at: http://www.vatican.va/roman_curia/synod/documents/rc_synod_doc_20081025_elenco-prop-finali_it.html.

4   Second Vatican Council, *Dei Verbum* [The Word of God], Dogmatic Constitution on Divine Revelation, (November 18, 1965) (*SD*, 19–31).

5   For his understanding of the hermeneutics of continuity and discontinuity, see Pope Benedict XVI, Address to the Roman Curia (December 22, 2005), in *L'Osservatore Romano*, Weekly Edition in English (January 4, 2006), 4–6, at 5.

6   Pope St. Pius X, *Lamentabili Sane* [With Truly Lamentable Results], Syllabus Condemning the Errors of the Modernists (July 3, 1907), prop. 11, in Henirich Denzinger, ed., *Enchiridion Symbolorum Definitonum et Declarationum de Rebus Fidei et Morum* [Handbook of Creeds, Definitions and Declarations concerning Matters of Faith and Morals], 32nd. ed. (Freiberg: Herder, 1963), 3411; Eng.: *The Sources of Catholic Dogma* (Fitzwilliam, NH: Loreto, 2002). Hereafter abbreviated *DS*. Pius ordered (*mandavit*) that each of the sixty-five propositions in his syllabus were "to be held by all as reprobated and proscribed [*reprobatas ac proscriptas ab omnibus haberi*]" (*DS* 3466).

7   Pius XII, *Humani Generis* [The Human Race], Encyclical Letter on Certain False Opinions

Finally, there is this statement, found in the *Instrumentum Laboris*, or working paper, prepared for the Synod of Bishops in 2008: "Although all parts of Sacred Scripture are divinely inspired, inerrancy pertains only to 'that truth which God wanted put into sacred writings for the sake of salvation' (*Dei Verbum*, 11)."[8]

The contrast between the last statement and the preceding two is clear. Whereas the papal pronouncements strongly emphasize that, as a consequence of the entire Bible's divine authorship, it is completely free from error, the 2008 statement interprets Vatican II's Constitution on Divine Revelation as teaching one version of a thesis that we may conveniently describe as *restricted biblical inerrancy*—the thesis that what the sacred writers say on certain subjects, or express in certain ways, may at times be untrue. According to the version of this thesis attributed here to *Dei Verbum* 11, certain things in the Bible are there "for the sake of our salvation" while others are not; and while the former are guaranteed to be free from error, the latter are not.

It is noteworthy that this 2008 statement is not just an individual theologian's interpretation of Vatican II's teaching. It is embedded in the working paper intended to be the starting point for the Synod's deliberations. This document, developed following a year of consultation with Scripture scholars, theologians, and bishops from around the world, would seem to suggest then, that the "restrictive" reading of *Dei Verbum* has become very widespread, perhaps even the conventional wisdom, in the Catholic academy. Of course, the *Instrumentum Laboris* does not enjoy any magisterial status and the Synod itself eventually refrained from endorsing this position. Nevertheless, it seems deeply significant that this restrictive understanding of inerrancy—in undeniable discontinuity with the Church's Tradition—had within half a century of its most recent condemnation by the magisterium, attained such a high level of scholarly and ecclesial acceptance.

"Unrestricted" Inerrancy in the Biblical Encyclicals

To understand the significance of this drift in Catholic thought, we will now recall several more extensive expositions of key principles found in the three papal encyclicals dedicated exclusively to the study of Scripture.

Threatening to Undermine the Foundations of Catholic Doctrine (August 12, 1950), 22 (*DS* 3887; *SD*, 141)

8   Synod of Bishops, "The Word of God in the Life and Mission of the Church," *Instrumentum Laboris* (May 11, 2008), 15(c) (Latin: "Quamvis omnes Sacrae Scripturae partes divinitus inspiratae sint, tamen eius inerrantia pertinet tantummodo ad 'veritatem, quam Deus nostrae salutis causa Litteris Sacris consignari voluit'" [*Dei Verbum 11*].) In the English-language translation, the first clause of this sentence was poorly translated in such a way as to explicitly call into question the full extent of the Bible's divine inspiration: "With regards [*sic*] to what *might be* inspired *in the many parts* of Sacred Scripture"; emphasis added. The translations into all other vernaculars posted on the Vatican website accurately reflected the Latin text. Available online at: http://www.vatican.va/roman_curia/synod/index.htm.

The most fundamental and explicit magisterial assertions of unrestricted biblical inerrancy come from Pope Leo XIII's *Providentissimus Deus* (1893).[9] Never in eighteen centuries had any pope or Church council issued anything comparable to this encyclical—an authoritative and wide-ranging coverage of the whole field of biblical studies, including both theoretical and practical aspects, in light of new rationalist and "scientific" challenges to the Bible's crediblity. First, the Pope asserts that "it is absolutely wrong and forbidden either to narrow inspiration to certain parts only of holy Scripture *or to admit that the sacred writer himself has erred.*"[10]

We note that Leo is insisting here that everything the Bible's *human* authors write is inerrant; for he sees their words as being simultaneously the Word of God. This is worth dwelling upon. The Pope does not present the doctrine of unrestricted inerrancy as an independent, self-standing point of divine revelation. Rather, he affirms it as a revealed truth directly arising from, and inseparably joined to, a still more basic element of the deposit of faith: the *divine authorship* of the entire Bible, as defined by three previous ecumenical councils:

> Inspiration not only is essentially incompatible with error, but excludes and rejects it as absolutely and necessarily as it is impossible that God himself, the supreme Truth, can utter that which is not true. This is the ancient and unchanging faith of the Church, solemnly defined in the Councils of Florence and Trent, and finally confirmed and expressly formulated by the [First] Council of the Vatican.[11]

The Pope then goes on to cite the last-mentioned First Vatican Council as follows:

> The Church holds [the biblical books] as sacred and canonical not because, having been composed by human industry, they were afterwards approved by her authority; nor just because they contain revelation without error, but because, having been written under the inspiration of the Holy Spirit, they have God for their Author.[12]

Furthermore, the pontiff asserts, the concept of divine authorship may not be reduced to some kind of supernatural enlightenment by which the Holy Spirit guided and protected the human writers' thoughts while not necessarily bearing

---

9   Pope Leo XIII, *Providentissimus Deus* [The God of All Providence], Encyclical Letter on the Study of Scripture (November 18, 1893) (*SD*, 37–61), also in *Enchiridion Biblicum: Documenti della Chiesa sulla Sacra Scrittura* [Documents of the Church Concerning Sacred Scripture], eds. Alfio Filippi and Erminio Lora, 2nd. ed. (Bologna: Dehoniane, 1993). Hereafter abbreviated *EB*.

10   Leo XIII, *Providentissimus Deus*, 20 (*SD*, 55; *EB* 124).

11   Leo XIII, *Providentissimus Deus*, 20 (*DS* 3292–3293; *EB* 124–125; *SD*, 55).

12   Leo XIII, *Providentissimus Deus*, 20 (*SD*, 55–56; *EB* 125 [citing *DS* 3006; *EB* 77].

responsibility for the precise words in which they chose to express those thoughts. Rather, Leo says, divine authorship means that, by supernatural power,

> [God] impelled and moved [the human authors] to write, and assisted them in writing, in such a way that they first rightly understood, then willed faithfully to write down, and finally expressed in apt words and with infallible truth, all the things which he ordered and those things only [Latin: *ea omnia eaque sola, quae ipse iuberet*]. Otherwise he would not be the author of the whole of sacred Scripture.[13]

The conclusion drawn by Leo in *Providentissimus Deus* bases full inerrancy on what he sees as the doctrinal "bed-rock" in this matter. "It follows," he concludes, "that those who maintain that an error is possible in any genuine passage of the sacred books either pervert the Catholic notion of inspiration or make God the author of such error."[14] In short, all Scripture is divinely inspired; divine inspiration means divine authorship; and divine authorship means that everything uttered in writing by the human writers has been uttered by God.

Pope Benedict XV, in his 1920 encyclical *Spiritus Paraclitus*,[15] was concerned to correct certain resurgent errors that were only superficially compatible with Leo's teaching in *Providentissimus Deus*. Here is the first example he gives:

> [Certain contemporary authors] are willing to acknowledge that inspiration itself does indeed extend to every statement—and even to every single word—in the Bible. But then, appealing to a distinction between the primary or religious and the secondary or profane element in Scripture, they narrow down and restrict the effects of inspiration—above all, absolute truth and immunity from error—to that primary or religious element.[16]

There is an evident similarity between this thesis, rejected by the Pope in 1920, and the assertion we quote from the *Instrumentum Laboris* in 2008. In practice, in the work of interpreting a given biblical text, any differences between these two statements would probably approach vanishing point. Let us suppose that, in studying a certain part of Scripture, I begin by asking myself, "What is the *primary or religious element* in this passage?" with the assumption that while this "religious" element is guaranteed by the Holy Spirit to be free from error, other

---

13   Leo XIII, *Providentissimus Deus*, 20 (*SD*, 55–56; *EB* 125).

14   Leo XIII, *Providentissimus Deus*, 21 (*SD*, 56; *EB* 126).

15   Pope Benedict XV, *Spiritus Paraclitus* [The Holy Spirit, the Comforter], Encyclical Letter Commemorating the Fifteenth Centenary of the Death of St. Jerome (September 15, 1920) (*SD*, 81–111).

16   Benedict XV, *Spiritus Paraclitus*, 19 (*SD*, 88; *EB* 454).

elements in the text would remain "error-prone." In asking this question I would be mentally dividing the Scripture passage into two compartments with virtually the same boundaries and specific content as those I would have discerned if my initial question had been, "What does this passage say *for the sake of our salvation?*" In any case, the assumption in both cases is precisely what *Spiritus Paraclitus* is rejecting. There simply can be no error-prone content in any biblical passage, since its integral divine authorship rules out the very possibility of error.[17]

Since *Spiritus Paraclitus*, the hermeneutical method that has been most extensively developed—and, with due precautions, increasingly approved by the Church's magisterium—has been the discernment in Scripture of a greater diversity of *literary genres* than was previously recognized. While certain sections of the Bible may superficially look like "straight" history, they are now widely understood as having been intended by their human and divine authors as instances of parable, allegory, or some other ancient Near Eastern forms of writing in which at least some expressions were not intended to be taken as exact and literal statements of fact.

Benedict XV had rebuked scholars who "take refuge too readily"[18] in this approach, but he tacitly left room for future harmonious doctrinal development here by leaving in place his predecessor Pius X's cautious acknowledgement that some parts of the Bible might be open to a valid reinterpretation along such lines. The Pontifical Biblical Commission, in a papally confirmed response to a question in 1905, expressed disapproval, as a general rule, of the then-novel theory that some "narratives ... are historical in appearance only." It conceded, however, that some passages of Scripture might prove to be of this nature, while warning that in any given case this was "not to be easily or rashly admitted."[19]

---

17 Benedict goes on to censure certain other unsound or even sophistical theories used in the early twentieth century in an effort to reconcile *Providentissimus Deus* with seemingly erroneous statements in Scripture: for instance, the theory of "relative" truth, or history "according to appearances," according to which the Bible's "truth" is sometimes merely what was then commonly *thought* to be true; and the appeal to presumed "tacit quotations," wherein the sacred writer supposedly reports the error-prone statements of non-inspired writers or speakers, but without indicating to the reader that he is doing so (*EB*, 456, 461). There has been little resurgence in recent decades of these particular theories, which have now generally been replaced, among apologists for inerrancy, by a broader appeal to the nature and diversity of biblical literary genres.

18 Benedict XV, *Spiritus Paraclitus*, 26 (*SD*, 90; *DS* 3654; *EB* 461). Benedict admonished those biblical scholars "[who] claim to find certain literary genres in the sacred books that cannot be reconciled with the entire and perfect truth of God's word, or who suggest such origins of the Bible as would weaken—if not destroy—its authority."

19 Pontifical Biblical Commission, *Response Concerning the Narratives in the Historical Books of Sacred Scripture Which Have Only the Appearance of Being Historical* (June 23, 1905) (*SD*, 188; *EB* 161; *DS* 3373).

Pius XII and the Analogy of Word Inspired and Word Incarnate

During the period between the world wars, many Catholic exegetes, mindful of the biblical commission's guidelines and caveats, continued making further use of this appeal to diverse literary genres, and of other critical approaches—for the most part without incurring any Vatican censures. This paved the way for the third encyclical devoted to biblical studies, Pope Pius XII's *Divino Afflante Spiritu* (1943).[20] Many years later, after Pius's death, the idea was floated that this encyclical had "opened new doors" for Catholic Scripture scholars.[21] According to this reading, Pius supposedly authorized principles or approaches in biblical studies that had been forbidden by his predecessors. Even though this posthumous assessment of *Divino Afflante Spiritu* has now become mainstream among those who hold to a "restricted" view of inerrancy,[22] it has no foundation either in the text of the encyclical itself or in the most authoritative scholarly commentaries that accompanied its publication.[23] Indeed, Pius himself, only seven years after his purportedly revolutionary encyclical, insisted on its full doctrinal continuity with the preceding encyclicals and sharply denounced disturbing trends in Scripture scholarship—including, as we have mentioned above, any claim of restricted inerrancy. In *Humani Generis* (1950) he summed up his criticisms as follows:

> Everyone sees how foreign all this is to the principles and norms of interpretation rightly fixed by our predecessors of happy memory, Leo XIII in his encyclical *Providentissimus Deus*, and Benedict XV in the encyclical *Spiritus Paraclitus*, as also by ourselves in the encyclical *Divino Afflante Spiritu*.[24]

What Pius had really done in *Divino Afflante Spiritu* was to express his satisfaction and encouragement to biblical scholars who had been working in ways that had already been recognized as legitimate—at least tacitly, cautiously, or in seminal form—by the Church's magisterium. In particular, Pius spoke of progress made

---

20 Pope Pius XII, *Divino Afflante Spiritu* [Inspired by the Divine Spirit], Encyclical Letter Promoting Biblical Studies (September 30, 1943) (*SD*, 115–139).

21 A provocative article that gave the initial impetus to this thesis was Luis Alonso Schökel, "Dove Va L'Esegesi Cattolica?" [Where is Catholic Exegesis Going?], *La Civiltà Cattolica* (September 3, 1960): 449–460. Alonso's claim was that back in 1943 Pius XII himself "was very conscious of opening a new and wide door through which many novelties would be entering the precincts of Catholic exegesis," at 456.

22 Joseph A. Fitzmyer has called Pius's encyclical a "liberating" and "revolutionary" document that lifted the "dark cloud of reactionism that hung over" Catholic biblical studies. *The Biblical Commission's Document, "The Interpretation of the Bible in the Church": Text and Commentary* (Rome: Pontifical Biblical Institute, 1993), 19–20.

23 See Augustin Bea, "L'Enciclica 'Divino afflante Spiritu,'" [The Encyclical Divino Afflante Spiritu], *La Civiltà Cattolica* (November 10, 1943): 212–224.

24 Pius XII, *Humani Generis*, 24 (*SD*, 141; *EB* 613).

in the study of literary genres and "ancient Near Eastern modes of thought and writing."[25] However, recent commentators who emphasize this "progressive" aspect of the encyclical gloss over or ignore the fact that, for Pius, studies in this area were worthy of further pursuit largely because they were proving to be a new means toward a deeply traditional end—upholding the Catholic dogma that biblical inerrancy is unrestricted in terms of subject-matter. This observation recurs as a *leitmotif* throughout the encyclical.

In his introductory paragraph, Pius praises Leo XIII's zeal to correct "certain Catholic writers [who] had dared to restrict the truth of sacred Scripture solely to matters of faith and morals, and to regard other matters, whether in the domain of physical science or history, as 'obiter dicta' [incidental] and—as they contended—in no wise connected with faith."[26] The Pope then proclaims in the opening line of Part I that "the first and greatest concern of Leo XIII" was to defend the Church's faith that there is "no error whatsoever" in Scripture—not even in regard to "profane" matters. Pius follows this immediately with his own solemn confirmation of Leo's teaching on unlimited inerrancy.[27]

He returns to this theme repeatedly. In a memorable analogy, Pius affirms that just as "the substantial Word of God became like to men in all things 'except sin,' so the words of God, expressed in human language, are made like to human speech in every respect, except error."[28] He goes on to stress that studying biblical literary forms and modes of expression is an important prerequisite for "explaining the sacred Scripture and demonstrating and proving its immunity from all error."[29] The value of such studies for apologetics is recommended again and again in succeeding paragraphs, as the Pope exhorts scholars to continue their research in all the relevant ancillary sciences in order to deal with biblical difficulties that remain unresolved.[30] Scholars must persevere, he says, in the quest for solutions that will be in accord both with the "certain conclusions of the profane disciplines" and with the Church's "traditional teaching that sacred Scripture is free from all error."[31]

The very urgency with which Pius calls on Catholic exegetes to seek a convincing harmony between Scripture and these "profane" or secular areas of knowledge underlines the profound discontinuity between his understanding of inerrancy and that of contemporary writers and teachers who praise his "progres-

---

25 See *EB* 555–565.

26 Pius XII, *Divino Afflante Spiritu*, 1 (SD, 116; EB 538).

27 Pius XII, *Divino Afflante Spiritu*, 3–4 (SD, 116–117; EB 539–540).

28 Pius XII, *Divino Afflante Spiritu*, 37 (SD, 129; EB 559; Latin: "Sicut enim substantiale Dei Verbum hominibus simile factum est quoad omnia 'absque peccato' (Heb. 4:15), ita etiam Dei verba, humanis linguis expressa, quoad omnia humano sermoni assimilia facta sunt, excepto errore.")

29 Pius XII, *Divino Afflante Spiritu*, 38 (SD, 129; EB 560).

30 See Pius XII, *Divino Afflante Spiritu*, 39–46, (EB 560–564).

31 Pius XII, *Divino Afflante Spiritu*, 46 (SD, 132; EB 564).

sive" encyclical while denying the need for any such harmonization. On the soothing assumption that divine inspiration was never intended to guarantee the Bible's truth in these "non-salvific" matters of history and empirical science, they regard the very attempt to uphold its inerrancy in these areas as naïve, futile, and unnecessary. Thus, rather than seek the solutions to biblical difficulties as Pius urged, they "solve" these problems by simply denying that they *are* problematical for believers.

Vatican II and the Limits of Inerrancy

This brings us to Vatican II, the authority of which Catholic advocates of restricted inerrancy invariably invoke. I will advance here a critique of the restricted inerrancy view and of the appeal to *Dei Verbum* 11 to justify this view. I will use as my point of reference the statement in the 2008 *Instrumentum Laboris*, since it expresses clearly and succinctly the thesis I am criticizing. Here it is again:

> Although all parts of sacred Scripture are divinely inspired, inerrancy pertains only to "that truth which God wanted to put into the sacred writings for the sake of our salvation" [*Dei Verbum* 11].

The following objections can be made to this interpretation of the conciliar statement cited here: The word "only" (*tantummodo*), complementing and reinforcing the adversative first clause ("Although ..."), is a gratuitous addition. No Latin word or expression in the conciliar text corresponds to it. Second, translations such as "*that* truth which God wanted *put into* (or *confided to* or *consigned to*) the sacred writings" are not accurate. There is no restrictive adjective "that" (*eam* or *illam*) in the Latin original. The original Latin term, *consignare*, does not mean "consign." This English derivative needs both a direct and an indirect object; we *consign* something *to* someone or something else. The Latin verb means "record," and so takes only a direct object. This in turn means that *litteris sacris* ("the sacred writings") is not in the dative case, but is an instrumental ablative.

So the Council's true meaning in *Dei Verbum* 11 is that the whole Bible—not just certain parts or themes within it—is the *means whereby*, or the *form in which*, God wanted his saving truth to be recorded. The Bible is not being depicted as a sort of receptacle for both salvifically relevant and salvifically irrelevant utterances. A more accurate translation, bringing out the idea that everything the biblical authors affirm is *both* "for the sake of our salvation" *and* free from error, would be as follows:

> Since, therefore, all that the inspired authors or hagiographers affirm must be held as affirmed by the Holy Spirit, we must in consequence acknowledge that, by means of the books of Scripture, the truth that God, for the sake of our salvation,

wanted recorded in the form of the sacred writings is taught firmly, faithfully, and without error.

The gloss of the *Instrumentum Laboris* interpolating "only" into the second clause renders the above sentence incompatible with both faith and reason. With faith, because the first clause alone is sufficient to make it clear that *everything* affirmed by the inspired authors is true. For it says that we must hold everything they affirm to be affirmed also by the Holy Spirit—who cannot err. It is incompatible with reason because adding "only" would turn the whole sentence into a *non sequitur* so egregious that no Church council could possibly have intended to teach it—one in which the conclusion not only does not follow from the premises, but is radically incompatible with them. For it would make the sentence say that *since all* that the inspired authors affirm is affirmed also by the Holy Spirit, *therefore only some of* what they affirm (namely, what is relevant to salvation) is guaranteed to be true.

Further support for my reading of *Dei Verbum* 11 can be found in the final sentence of the paragraph, which follows immediately after the sentence we have been discussing. The Council fathers appeal to 2 Timothy 3:16–17 as biblical support for what they have just said ("Thus [*Itaque*], 'All Scripture is inspired by God and is profitable ...'"). Here the Council makes still clearer that its intention in the previous sentence is to teach that everything in sacred Scripture is *both* inspired by God *and* relevant for our salvation. The Latin *itaque* here makes no sense otherwise.

During the drafting of *Dei Verbum*, the official *relator* told the Council fathers that the purpose of the amendment specifying the "salvific" character or purpose of biblical truth was not to imply that some affirmations of the sacred writers may be false, but rather to help believers to explain and defend the Catholic belief that all of them are true. The *relator* said:

> By the term "salvific" (*salutarem*) it is by no means suggested that sacred Scripture is not in its integrity the inspired Word of God. ... This expression does *not* imply any *material limitation* of the truth of Scripture; rather, it indicates Scripture's *formal specification*, the nature of which must be kept in mind in deciding in what sense all things *affirmed* in the Bible are true—not only matters of faith and morals and facts bound up with the history of salvation. For this reason the [doctrinal commission overseeing the drafting process] has decided that the expression should be retained.[32]

---

32 "Lat. : Voce 'salutaris' nullo modo suggeritur S. Scripturam non esse integraliter inspiratam et verbum Dei. ... Hæc expressio *nullam* inducit *materialem limitationem* veritatis Scripturæ, sed indicat eius *specificationem formalem*, cuius ratio habeatur in diiudicando quo sensu non tantum res fidei et morum atque facta cum historia salutis coniuncta ... sed omnia quæ in Scriptura *asseruntur* sunt vera. Unde statuit Commissio expressionem esse servandam." *Acta Synodalia Sacrosancti Concilii Oecumenici Vaticani II* [Synodal Acts of the Ecumenical Council Vatican II],

The idea of a "material limitation" to biblical truth would be the idea that a certain number of the affirmations made by the sacred authors are immune from error, while the rest are not. This, in effect, is the hermeneutic adopted by the authors of the *Instrumentum Laboris* and others who, interpret *Dei Verbum* 11 restrictively. Since the Council we can observe two basic ways in which scholars advance this idea of a material limitation to Scripture. Some commentators claim openly that there are biblical affirmations which enjoy no divine protection from error because they are not recorded "for the sake of our salvation." Others ostensibly give assent to Vatican II's confirmation that all biblical affirmations are guaranteed to be true; but they effectively deny this teaching by giving it a sophistical "reinterpretation." Like those commentators in the first group, they interpret *Dei Verbum* 11 as implying that some things in the Bible are *not* there "for the sake of our salvation" and thus are not guaranteed to be free from error. But they then go on to maintain that this purportedly "non-salvific" character of some biblical propositions is enough to disqualify them from being true *affirmations* of the biblical text.

Arguably the most influential exposition of this version of restricted inerrancy—one that has reached countless thousands of professors, clergy, seminarians, and other students—is that of the Jesuit scholar, Roderick MacKenzie,[33] writing in the most widely-used English-language edition of the Vatican II documents in the initial post-conciliar period. In a personal footnote to *Dei Verbum* 11, which is not visibly distinguished from the official conciliar footnotes among which it is inserted, MacKenzie writes:

> It is *only* [in matters concerning salvation] that the veracity of God and the inerrancy of the inspired writers are engaged. ... The [text] is authoritative and inerrant in what it affirms about the revelation of God and the history of salvation. *According to the intentions of its authors, divine and human, it makes no other affirmations.* [34]

---

32 vols. (Rome: Typis Polyglottis Vaticanis, 1970–), vol 4, pt. 5, 708; emphasis in original. This explanation was presented when the draft under discussion affirmed that the books of Scripture "teach saving truth [*veritatem salutarem*] without error"; but it clearly applies equally to the final text, in which the adjective *salutarem* was replaced by an adjectival clause similar in meaning: "veritatem, quam Deus nostræ salutis causa Litteris Sacris consignari voluit."

33 MacKenzie, rector of the Pontifical Biblical Institute from 1963 to 1969, is not identified as the author of the comments on *Dei Verbum* in or near the conciliar text itself. However, his signature appears on the introductory essay preceding the text of the Dogmatic Constitution, and an editorial note at the beginning of the book says that the unofficial notes to each conciliar document are the work of the scholar "whose name is at the end of the essay introducing the document." Walter M. Abbott, ed., *The Documents of Vatican II* (London: Geoffrey Chapman, 1967), xiv; see also 110.

34 Abbott, *Vatican II*, 119, n. 31; emphasis added.

In other words, a *biblical* affirmation—in contrast, it would seem, to the affirmations found in all other kinds of literature—is to be identified and distinguished from other types of utterance not by looking at its "structural" linguistic features (choice of words, literary genre, rules of grammar and syntax, etc.), but simply by noting that it treats of a certain predetermined and privileged *theme* or *topic*. That is, by giving priority to its matter, not its form: to *what* the writer is talking about, not *how* he talks about it. This approach would have exegetes ask, "Is this text about a matter concerning salvation? Is it about the revelation of God and the history of salvation?" If the exegete concludes that it is not, then he can safely assume—according to this reading of *Dei Verbum* 11—that the sacred writer is not intending to affirm anything at all.

This reading in effect resorts to a kind of hermeneutical sleight-of-hand that enables the exegete to deny the "affirmed" status of what really are affirmations made by the inspired authors. It amounts to an attempt to reconcile the Catholic dogma of biblical inerrancy with an admission that the Bible does indeed contain errors. But this kind of radical reinterpretation—verbally professing a Catholic dogma while altering the meaning the Church herself has always given to it—was anathematized by Vatican Council I.[35] Moreover, an analysis of the references in the official footnote to this sentence in *Dei Verbum* 11 (footnote 5) reinforces the conclusion that the Council is intent on upholding the traditional doctrine—that *all* the inspired authors' affirmations are free from error, even in matters of history and science.[36]

Inerrancy in Catholic Teaching Since Vatican II

So far we have looked at the basic evidence from the Council itself, arguing from the approved text and footnotes, as explained by the official *relatio*, or explanation of the text. But it is important to note that high Church authorities during the post-conciliar period have also rejected the kind of hermeneutic that seeks to read a doctrine of restricted inerrancy into the "salvation" clause of *Dei Verbum* 11.

No scholar was better qualified than Cardinal Augustin Bea, S. J., to testify authoritatively to the intent of the conciliar text. At Vatican II he presided at the key meeting of the Theological Commission during which the wording of this sentence about inerrancy in *Dei Verbum* 11 was finalized. Shortly after the Council, he published a work[37] that includes several pages on the redactional history and

---

35   Vatican I solemnly defined, "If anyone shall say that sometimes, in accordance with the progress of science, dogmas declared by the Church are to be given a meaning different from that which the Church has understood and understands, let him be anathema" (*DS* 3043).

36   These footnote references are discussed in detail in my "Does Vatican Council II Allow for Errors in Sacred Scripture," 288–295. A slightly amplified version of this article, republished in *Living Tradition* 145–146 (March-May 2010), is available online at www.rtforum.org/lt/lt145. html.

37   Augustin Bea, *La Parola de Dio e l'Umanità: La Dottrina del Concilio Sulla Rivelazione* (Assisi:

correct interpretation of this sentence. Bea's verdict is unambiguous: "Let us ask, therefore, if the *text we have now* implies a restrictive interpretation of inerrancy. Here also the answer is certainly negative."[38]

Even before Bea's commentary was published, the Congregation for the Doctrine of the Faith had sent a letter to the presidents of all the world's bishops' conferences and to all major religious superiors, warning against wrong and dangerous interpretations of the Council that had begun to circulate almost immediately after its conclusion.[39] Heading the congregation's list of ten widespread false interpretations was this:

> Some, purposely disregarding Tradition, have recourse to sacred Scripture, but restrict the scope and force of biblical inspiration and inerrancy, and hold false views on the historical value of the texts.[40]

In 1993, John Paul II gave an allocution to commemorate the fiftieth and hundredth anniversaries of the encyclicals *Divino Afflante Spiritu* and *Providentissimus Deus*, respectively. He confirmed Pius XII's analogy between God's Word in Scripture and the incarnate Word, describing it this way:

> The strict relationship uniting the inspired biblical texts with the mystery of the incarnation was expressed by the encyclical *Divino Afflante Spiritu* in the following terms: "Just as the substantial Word of God became like to men in all things except sin (Heb. 4:15), so the words of God, expressed in human language, are made like to human speech in every respect except error." Repeated almost literally by the conciliar Constitution *Dei*

Citadella Editrice, 1967), 187–190. Eng.: *The Word of God and Mankind* (Chicago: Franciscan Herald, 1967).

38 Bea, *La Parola de Dio*, 190 (Italian: "Domandiamo pertanto, *se l'attuale testo* comporti una interpretazione restrittiva dell'inerranza o no. Anche qui la risposta è senz'altro negativa."); emphasis in original. The emphasis is due to the fact that Bea is here comparing the final, approved text to that of an earlier draft that was arguably more open to a restrictive interpretation.

39 Congregation for the Doctrine of the Faith, *Cum Oecumenicum Concilium* [The Ecumenical Council], Circular Letter to the Venerable Presidents of the Episcopal Conferences and Religious Superiors on certain opinions and errors arising from false interpretations of the Decrees of the Second Vatican Council, (July 24, 1966), in *Acta Apostolicae Sedis* [Official Acts of the Holy See] 58 (1966): 659–661. Hereafter abbreviated *AAS*; available online: http://www.vatican.va/archive/aas/index_sp.htm.

40 Congregation for the Doctrine of the Faith, *Oecumenicum Concilium*, 661 (Lat.: "Imprimis occurrit ipsa Sacra Revelatio: sunt etenim qui ad Sacram Scripturam recurrunt Traditione consulto seposita, sed Biblicae inspirationis et inerrantiae ambitum et vim coartant et de historicorum textuum valore non recte sentient.")

Verbum (13), this statement sheds light on a parallelism rich in meaning.[41]

We have seen above how emphatically Pius XII insisted that the Bible's inerrancy is unrestricted in its scope; John Paul, in confirming his predecessor's statement here, could not have understood it in any other sense. Not only are the words written by the human authors said to be "words of God" himself, but the parallel with the incarnation demands by its very nature that the Bible's exemption from error not be limited to what it says on certain themes. Otherwise the parallel would imply—not just mistakenly but blasphemously—that Christ's exemption from sin is also limited in some way.

A similar observation can be made concerning the 1998 affirmation of biblical inerrancy by the Congregation for the Doctrine of the Faith. Both the wording and the context of the congregation's statement demonstrate that it intends to affirm unrestricted inerrancy. In a doctrinal note accompanying a revision of Church law promulgated by Pope John Paul II, the congregation includes "the absence of error in the inspired sacred writings"[42] among those truths that are "divinely revealed" and hence requiring "the assent of theological faith."[43] This "absence of error" is affirmed absolutely—that is, without any qualifications; by the ordinary rules of language, that is already sufficient to exclude restricted inerrancy. The first reference cited by the congregation is to Leo's assertion in *Providentissimus Deus* that unrestricted inerrancy is "the ancient and constant faith of the Church."[44] As we have seen, this assertion by Leo is arguably the strongest and clearest affirmation of unrestricted inerrancy ever to appear in a magisterial document. By citing *Dei Verbum* 11 in this same footnote, the doctrinal congregation also makes it clear that the "absence of error" (*sine errore*) of which Vatican II speaks is to be understood in the same way that Leo understood it: as a *total* absence of error.

So far we have made two main points. First, the Bible's unrestricted inerrancy, prior to Vatican II, had been proposed as a Catholic dogma inseparable from the still more basic revealed truth of the Bible's integral divine authorship. Secondly, we have argued that the clause in *Dei Verbum* 11 specifying the Bible's "salvific" purpose cannot legitimately be understood as implying the opposed thesis of restricted inerrancy; indeed, we have pointed out that such an interpretation of the conciliar text has been repeatedly ruled out, explicitly and implicitly, by the Church's teaching authority.

---

41   Pope John Paul II, Address to the Pontifical Biblical Commission (April 23, 1993), 6 (*SD*, 170–180, at 173; *EB* 1239–1258, at 1245).

42   *AAS* 90 (1998): 549, no. 11 (Lat.: "Absentia erroris in scriptis sacris inspiratis.")

43   *AAS* 90 (1998): 546, no. 5.

44   *AAS* 90 (1998): 549, n. 30, with references to *DS* 3293 and *Dei Verbum* 11.

MacKenzie, Brown and the Practical Implications of Restricted Inerrancy

It might be objected that my above criticism of MacKenzie is not entirely fair, in that it does not bring out the fact that, in arguing for restricted inerrancy, he appeals to the same conciliar *relatio* that I claim militates against that position. This point needs to be considered more thoroughly. Here is MacKenzie's complete footnote, with emphasis added to the words where he refers to the *relator's* announcement that the mention of salvific purpose in *Dei Verbum* 11 "indicates Scripture's *formal specification*" and "does *not imply any material limitation* of the truth of Scripture":

> The Bible was not written in order to teach the natural sciences, nor to give information on merely political history. It treats of these (and all other subjects) only insofar as they are involved in matters concerning salvation. It is only in this respect that the veracity of God and the inerrancy of the inspired writers are engaged. *This is not a quantitative distinction, as though some sections treated of salvation (and were inerrant), while others gave merely natural knowledge (and were fallible). It is formal, and applies to the whole text.* The latter is authoritative and inerrant in what it affirms about the revelation of God and the history of salvation. According to the intentions of its authors, divine and human, it makes no other affirmations.[45]

Now, by speaking of "sections" of Scripture and of their "whole text," MacKenzie shows that he has in mind here relatively lengthy passages of the Bible—paragraphs, discourses, and chapters taken as a whole, or perhaps whole books if they are short ones—as distinct from *discrete propositions*. But this fails to do justice to what the *relator* said, and indeed, makes his critically important explanation rule out nothing but a man of straw. For there are probably no advocates of restricted inerrancy who *claim* that whole "sections" of the Bible give "merely natural knowledge (and [are] fallible)". MacKenzie himself evidently thinks there are no such "sections"; but he also makes it clear (see the sentence beginning "It is only in this respect...") that he thinks there are errors in Scripture. All of these alleged errors, according to MacKenzie and others who restrict inerrancy, are of course *propositions*. For only of a proposition can either truth or falsity be predicated. Indeed, the whole point at issue between the respective defenders of restricted and unrestricted inerrancy is whether some biblical propositions, correctly understood, express mistaken judgments on the part of the inspired writers. Now, since it is in the very nature of propositions that they can be separated and quantified, the existence of false propositions expressed as judgments of the inspired authors would necessarily constitute "a *material limitation* of the truth of Scripture." Therefore, in denying

---

45   Abbott, *Documents of Vatican II*, 119, n. 31.

that the 'salvific' reference in *Dei Verbum* 11 implies any such limitation, the *relator* is denying that this conciliar text teaches restricted inerrancy.

The practical implications of a restricted view of inerrancy are immense. For instance, to start with the idea that only what is profitable for salvation is being affirmed in a given biblical text, so that one tries to deduce what, if anything, the author might be affirming in that text by first assessing whether or not its content and subject-matter appear to be "salvifically" relevant, reverses the correct and rational order of exegesis. Catholic interpreters who read *Dei Verbum* 11 correctly will begin, rather, with the faith-based awareness that whatever is affirmed in a given biblical text is there "for the sake of our salvation". Accordingly, they will *first* seek to understand what the biblical author affirms in a given text *and then* inquire as to how (not whether) that affirmation has some relevance to God's plan of salvation—at least in conjunction with others in that passage if not necessarily in isolation.

Meaning, after all, plainly precedes value *epistemically*, in the order of knowing. It is common sense that we first need to know and understand *what* someone is affirming before we can begin to evaluate the truth, importance, or usefulness of that affirmation. Once normal, common-sense linguistic rules for identifying a writer's affirmations are set aside in the way we have been criticizing, the way is opened to widely varying and subjective interpretations of the Bible. Indeed, far from *learning* from God's Word what is relevant for our salvation, exegetes who operate with assumptions of restricted inerrancy will necessarily bring to the text—and impose upon it—their own preconceived assumptions as to what sorts of information and ideas could or could not in principle be relevant for salvation. Exegete A will find little or no salvific value in a passage of Scripture which for Exegete B contains deep spiritual import.

This radical new hermeneutic bids fair to penetrate our Catholic doctrinal patrimony at a very deep level. The Church's creeds and doctrines all have a biblical basis. And the very confidence and firmness with which the popes and councils appealed to that basis was in turn founded on their unshakeable belief in the Bible's *unrestricted* inerrancy. So if that foundational belief is now conceded to be mistaken, how much strength and reliability will be left in the magisterial superstructure that has been so painstakingly erected on top of it? Indeed, would it not be logical for theologians who hold to restricted inerrancy to begin assessing the "salvific value" of each doctrine of the Church, just as they now evaluate each passage of Scripture? Restricting biblical inerrancy appears to undermine what the Church teaches about the infallibility of her magisterium.

For a concrete example of how these subjective *a priori* judgments of salvific relevance or irrelevance can make even articles of the Christian creed dissolve into doubt, we need look no further than the treatment of Jesus' virginal conception in the writings of Raymond Brown, probably the most renowned American biblical scholar since Vatican II and an outspoken partisan of restricted inerrancy.

The Church has, from its first formulations of the faith, taught that Jesus was conceived solely by the power of the Holy Spirit in the womb of the virgin Mary.[46] This doctrine is based on the assertions of the gospels of Matthew and Luke. Christian commentators for almost two millennia have recognized that Matthew is giving us a straightforward affirmation or assertion when, after telling us of the angel's reassurance to Joseph that the child Mary is carrying "is of the Holy Spirit," he states directly that Joseph "did not know her till she brought forth her first-born son."[47]

Brown, however, never grants "affirmed" status to this clear gospel statement. In his *The Birth of the Messiah*,[48] he admits that Matthew "*thought* that Jesus had been virginally conceived."[49] He also admits that both Matthew and Luke "*regarded* the virginal conception as historical"[50] and, indeed, that they "*presuppose* a biological virginity."[51] He even admits it to be "lucidly clear" that Matthew "*believed* in Mary's bodily virginity before the birth of Jesus."[52] But Brown avoids stating that Matthew actually *affirms* or *asserts* this fact. The reason for this reluctance is not hard to discern. Such an admission, in the light of *Dei Verbum* 11's teaching that the Holy Spirit affirms all that the sacred writers affirm, would discredit Brown's strenuously argued exegetical thesis—namely, that "the *scientifically controllable* biblical evidence leaves the question of the historicity of the virginal conception unresolved."[53]

Brown casts further doubt on the reliability of Matthew's statement by applying the very *a priori* litmus test that we have been criticizing: is the subject-matter "salvific" or not? Brown says "a faithful Catholic" considering whether or not to believe Matthew's testimony that Mary was a virgin when Jesus was conceived, "would have to ask" this question: "Should one rank the biological manner of Jesus' conception as a truth God wanted put into the sacred writings for the sake of our salvation?"[54]

---

46   See *Catechism of the Catholic Church*, 2d. ed. (Vatican City: Libreria Editrice Vaticana, 1997), nos. 496–498.

47   Matt. 1:20, 25.

48   Raymond E. Brown, *The Birth of the Messiah: A Commentary on the Infancy Narratives in the Gospels of Matthew and Luke* (New York: Doubleday, 1977).

49   Brown, *Birth of the Messiah*, 528; emphasis added.

50   Brown, *Birth of the Messiah*, 517; emphasis added.

51   Brown, *Birth of the Messiah*, 529; emphasis added.

52   Raymond E. Brown, *The Virginal Conception and Bodily Resurrection of Jesus* (New York: Paulist, 1973), 31, n. 37; emphasis added.

53   Brown, *Birth of the Messiah*, 527; emphasis in original.

54   Brown, *Birth of the Messiah*, 528, n. 28. See my "The Truth and Salvific Purpose of Sacred Scripture According to *Dei Verbum*, Article 11," *Living Tradition* 59 (July 1995): 8–9, nn. 27, 28.

Brown offers no answer to the question he poses. Nor does he suggest what sort of criteria would be needed to answer the question objectively. He did in fact profess his own personal belief in Jesus' conception without a human father. But he based his profession, not on the evidence of the Scriptures, but on the basis of Tradition and the Church's magisterium.[55] The trouble is that what the Tradition and the magisterium teach is based exclusively on the prior witness of Scripture. The Church's Fathers, Doctors, popes and bishops have all taught that Catholics must believe in the virginal conception simply because Matthew and Luke tell us it happened. But Brown holds that those Church authorities were mistaken in making that inference, because he denies the dogma upon which they relied—namely, unrestricted biblical inerrancy. Thus, by proceeding from an assumption of the limited inerrancy of Scripture, Brown's exegetical work reached conclusions that undermine the biblical foundations of this pivotal Church doctrine, not to mention the logical underpinnings of his own professed faith in the virginal conception.

Further Objections to Unrestricted Inerrancy

Rather than trying to limit Scripture's inerrancy on the basis of a prior judgment regarding the presence or absence of "salvific" content in various texts, some advocates of restricted inerrancy argue that the Council implicitly distinguished between the sacred writers' "stronger" statements, which are inerrant, and their "weaker" statements, which are not.

It is true that both the text of *Dei Verbum* 11 and the *relator's* explanation of it emphasize that it is what the sacred writers *affirm (asserere)* that is protected from error. Therefore, some argue that the Council is implicitly conceding that an inspired writer can sometimes fall into error—but without *affirming* his error. Again, with this way of reading *Dei Verbum* 11, the issue becomes what is being "affirmed" by the sacred text, and how to distinguish that from what the authors do not intend to affirm.

In order to distinguish "affirmed" from "non-affirmed" biblical statements, those who argue for this version of restricted inerrancy appeal not to an *a priori* judgment as to what seems relevant to salvation in the passage concerned, but rather, to the greater and lesser *degrees of commitment* seemingly shown by the sacred authors to the various things they say are true. When seeking to discern whether or not a given biblical statement is protected from error, the exegete who uses this criterion will ask, "How *strongly, deliberately* or *decisively* is this statement expressed?"

This approach, too, conflicts with the text of the conciliar document and the explanations given to it by the conciliar *relator*. As we have already noted, *any*

---

55 "I think this is infallibly taught ... I think this [Jesus' conception without a human father] is so." Raymond E. Brown, *Biblical Exegesis and Church Doctrine* (London: Geoffrey Chapman, 1985), 27, n. 11 and 36, n. 25.

erroneous statement coming from an inspired writer—whether "affirmed" or "non-affirmed"—would necessarily be a "material limitation" of the Bible's truth. And the *relator* made a point of telling the Council fathers that the text before them was not to be understood as allowing for any such limitation. In addition, any attempt to make this distinction between "stronger" and "weaker" statements in the Scriptures, like the attempt to decide *a priori* what does and does not have salvific value, is in practice likely to open a Pandora's box of widely varying and subjective applications.

Most importantly, those who invoke Vatican II to justify their claim that the inspired writers sometimes make mistakes, but without "affirming" them, invariably fail to notice that the last two of *Dei Verbum* 11's four Latin sentences—those that explicitly mention the Bible's freedom from error and salvific purpose—are not the only ones relevant to inerrancy. As we emphasized at the start of this article, inerrancy is not a "self-standing" dogma, but a consequence of the more fundamental revealed truth of integral divine authorship—with "authorship" being understood very fully and directly. It is precisely this sense of divine authorship that Vatican II explicitly confirms in the *second* sentence of *Dei Verbum* 11. The Council fathers state here that while the hagiographers were "true authors" who "used their own faculties and powers,"[56] they nevertheless wrote "all those things *and only those things* that [God] wanted."[57] Immediately following this, the third (and much better known) sentence begins with the words, "Since, therefore (*Cum ergo*) everything asserted by the sacred writers must be held to be asserted by the Holy Spirit."

The word "therefore" is nearly always neglected by commentators, but it clearly means that the kind of inerrancy taught in this third sentence is the kind that follows logically from Leo XIII's rigorous definition of divine authorship which has just been repeated word-for-word in the second sentence. And that of course can only be *unrestricted* inerrancy. For God could not have "wanted" the human authors to utter anything false, whether by "affirming" it or stating it less decisively. Indeed, this is confirmed by the first footnote to *Dei Verbum* 11, which directs us to the principal magisterial sources asserting the Bible's divine authorship and explaining what it means. Among those sources is a Pontifical Biblical Commission decision that explicitly rules out the idea that God is the author of all the hagiographers' "affirmations," but not of all their "statements." The commission's decree, confirmed by Pope Benedict XV, affirms that according to "the Catholic dogma of the inspiration and inerrancy of the Sacred Scriptures ... all that the sacred writer affirms, states, or implies must be held as affirmed, stated or implied by the Holy Spirit."[58]

---

56   Lat.: "Veri auctores . . . facultatibus ac viribus suis utentes."

57   Lat.: "Ea omnia eaque sola, quae Ipse vellet"; emphasis added.

58   Pontifical Biblical Commission, *Response On the Parousia or the Second Coming of Our Lord*

Why, then, did the Council's text and *relatio* on inerrancy emphasize what Scripture "affirms" and "teaches," if, as we have argued, the reason for this emphasis was not to make a distinction between 'stronger' statements (protected from error) and 'weaker' ones that might be erroneous?

First, in considering the reasons why the *relator* and the other conciliar fathers used and emphasized *asserere*, we need to note that in Latin it is hard to find two words that clearly differentiate between stronger ways of saying that something is the case ("affirmations") and weaker ways ("*mere* statements"). The verb *enuntiare* is sometimes used for "state"; but Latin-English dictionaries include stronger senses such as "declare," "affirm," and "assert" among its meanings, as well as weaker ones such as "say" and "express." So the fact that "assert" and "affirm" are strong verbs in English does not justify the conclusion that *asserere* has been used in *Dei Verbum* 11 in order to distinguish "stronger" biblical statements from "weaker" ones.

In fact, the drafting history of this sentence reveals a different reason. It should first be noted that, according to the *relator*, both *asserere* and *docere* ("teach") were to be understood as referring to the same parts or aspects of the Bible's overall content: "The word *teach*, which refers to those things which are truly affirmed, is to be retained."[59] In other words, *Dei Verbum* 11 means that whatever is taught in Scripture is affirmed, and vice versa. During the deliberations over the document, Cardinal Raúl Silva Henríquez had proposed using the word "teach" to indicate what it is that the biblical authors do "without error." He explained his proposal this way:

> *Reason:* the doctrine of biblical inerrancy is better expressed by speaking of the formal criterion of *teaching*, since it is according to that criterion that no error can be found. For in another sense, that is, the material sense, it is possible for expressions to be used by the sacred writer which are erroneous in themselves, but which, however, he does not wish to teach.[60]

The *relator* told the Council fathers that the doctrinal commission had accepted this proposal "substantially."[61] Thus we can take what Silva Henríquez

---

in the Letters of St. Paul the Apostle (June 18, 1915) (*EB* 415; *DS* 3629; *SD*, 207–208; Lat.: "Dogmate item catholico de inspiratione et inerrantia sacrarum Scripturam, quo omne id, quod hagiographus asserit, enuntiat, insinuat, retineri debet assertum, enuntiatum, insinuatum a Spiritu Sancto.")

59 *Acta Vaticani II*, vol. 4, pt. 5, 709 (Lat.: "Servetur vox docere, quæ agit de illis quæ proprie asseruntur.")

60 *Acta Vaticani II*, vol. 3, pt. 3, 799 (Lat.: "*Ratio*: doctrina de inerrantia Scripturarum melius exprimitur si de formali ratione *docendi*, secundum quam nullus error inveniri potest, loquitur, quia alio sensu, i.e. materiali, possunt locutiones de se erroneæ ab hagiographo adhiberi, quas tamen docere non vult."); emphasis in original.

61 *Acta Vaticani II*, vol. 3, pt. 3, 92 (Lat.: "quoad substantiam").

means as a guide to what the Council means. And we can see that he does not set up any dichotomy between a biblical author's "teachings" and his mere "statements," with inerrancy being guaranteed only for the former. Rather, his dichotomy is between what is taught and what is merely "used" (*adhiberi*) by the sacred writers, with the latter category possibly including expressions (*locutiones*) that are "materially" erroneous.

It would seem that "using" an erroneous expression without teaching or affirming it to be true could occur in one of two basic ways. One way would be citing someone else's words or ideas without expressing any judgment that they are true. The other would be the employment of a literary genre in which a series of verbs that are "materially" in the past tense are not intended to constitute a strictly historical narrative, or one in which certain words or expressions are not intended in their "material"—that is, their proper or literal—sense. For instance, "materially" the book of Ecclesiastes begins with an identification of the author as "the Preacher, son of David, king in Jerusalem" (that is, Solomon),[62] and the Book of Judith starts out depicting Nebuchadnezzar as King of Assyria, living at Nineveh, when he was in fact King of Babylon—and at a time when Nineveh had already been destroyed (in 612 B. C.) by his Father Nabopolassar. However, taking into account the ancient Near Eastern literary conventions, modern scholars are agreed that the authors would not have been formally teaching what their words "materially" expressed: they were "using" these names as symbols or archetypes. Any number of other similar examples could of course be given.

In short, we should see the Council's choice of the verbs *asserere* and *docere* in *Dei Verbum* 11 as ruling out the kind of superficial literalism that takes insufficient account of the Bible's diverse literary genres. It does *not* imply that we should draw a distinction between the hagiographers' stronger ("affirmed") and weaker (supposedly "non-affirmed") statements, and consider only the former to be immune from error. For even if this distinction could in practice be made with consistency and objectivity, any such hermeneutic of *Dei Verbum* 11's third Latin sentence will be in discontinuity not only with the whole of Catholic Tradition, but even with the preceding sentence of this same dogmatic constitution. For, as we have seen, the "ancient and constant faith of the Church," reaffirmed in that previous sentence, assures us that all the sacred writers' statements, along with all their "non-statements" (questions, aspirations, prayers, and the like) have God—who cannot err—as their author.

Thus does the whole of *Dei Verbum* 11, not just its last two sentences, uphold the Catholic dogma of unrestricted biblical inerrancy. There is no sound basis for reading the Council's teaching in discontinuity with this perennial and fundamental point of our faith.[63]

---

62 Eccl. 1:1.

63 There are other objections that might be raised against my twofold claim that the doctrine of

unrestricted biblical inerrancy is both true and upheld by Vatican Council II. I have answered them to the best of my ability in my earlier article, "Does Vatican Council II Allow for Errors in Sacred Scripture?" available in a slightly amplified form at www.rtforum.org/lt/lt145.html. To the objection that I do not explain how the many specific and well-known biblical problems can be solved without conceding error on the part of the sacred writer, see section 2.2 of that earlier article, (Also see the helpful article by Paul Zerafa ["The Limits of Biblical Inerrancy," *Angelicum* 39 (1962): 92–119], republished in this volume of *Letter & Spirit*.) At section 2.1 of my earlier article, I address the objection that, contrary to my interpretation of *Dei Verbum* 11, there are in fact many things in the Bible that have no relevance to salvation. Finally, the following objection can be raised: If, as I claim, the Council does *not* mean to teach that inerrancy is restricted to a "salvation-relevant" subset of all biblical propositions, then why did it insist—against initial objections from conservative council fathers—on inserting a reference to the Bible's salvific purpose in the sentence that explicitly affirms inerrancy? Why even mention salvific purpose in this context if inerrancy does not depend on it? Section 2.4 of my earlier article offers an answer to this question.

Letter & Spirit 6 (2010): 247-263

COMMUNAL OR SOCIAL INSPIRATION
A Catholic Critique

~: Robert L. Fastiggi :~
Sacred Heart Major Seminary

In analyzing the mystery of the divine inspiration of the Bible, it is important to distinguish the fact of this inspiration from the manner in which it was done. With respect to the fact of divine inspiration, the Church's teaching is well summarized by three statements from the *Catechism of the Catholic Church*:

> God is the author of Sacred Scripture. ...
>
> God inspired the human authors of the sacred books. ...
>
> The inspired books teach the truth.[1]

The fact of divine inspiration is a dogma of the Catholic faith. The Council of Trent (1546) spoke of God as the author of both the Old and New Testament because these writings have come down to us "by the dictation of the Holy Spirit" (*a Spiritu Sancto dictatus*).[2] The First Vatican Council (1870), taught that the books of the Old and New Testaments, "having been written under the inspiration of the Holy Spirit, have God as their author."[3] The Second Vatican Council, in its document on divine revelation, *Dei Verbum* (1965), repeats this teaching and adds: "all that the inspired authors or sacred writers assert must be held as asserted by the Holy Spirit."[4]

While the *fact* of divine inspiration is Catholic dogma, the manner by which the Holy Spirit inspired the human authors of the sacred books remains open to theological discussion. This is due, in part, to the mysterious nature of God's

---

1   *Catechism of the Catholic Church*, 2nd ed. (Vatican City: Libreria Editrice Vaticana, 1997), nos. 105–107.

2   Council of Trent, *Decretum Primum: Recipiuntur Libri Sacri et Traditiones Apostolorum* [First Decree: Acceptance of the Sacred Books and Apostolic Traditions], (April 8, 1546), in Heinrich Denzinger and A. Schönmetzer, eds., *Enchiridion Symbolorum Definitonum et Declarationum de Rebus Fidei et Morum* [Handbook of Creeds, Definitions and Declarations concerning Matters of Faith and Morals], 32nd ed. (Freiberg: Herder, 1963), 1501. Hereafter abbreviated *DS*. Translations from Denzinger are my own.

3   First Vatican Council, *Dei Filius* [The Son of God], Dogmatic Constitution on the Catholic Faith, (April 24, 1870), Chap. 2 (*DS* 3006; Latin: "quod Spiritu Sancto inspirante conscripti Deum habent auctorem").

4   Second Vatican Council, *Dei Verbum* [The Word of God], Dogmatic Constitution on Divine Revelation, (November 18, 1965), 11 (Lat.: "omne id, quod auctores inspirati seu hagiographi asserunt, retineri debeat assertum a Spiritu Sancto").

inspiration. How exactly the Holy Spirit moved and guided the human authors is not something that can be observed empirically. We have only the results of this divine inspiration—the sacred writings of the Old and New Testaments.

One traditional Catholic explanation of divine inspiration views the human authors as instruments of the Holy Spirit. St. Thomas Aquinas develops this explanation by looking upon God as the principal cause of the composition of the Bible, and the human authors as "instrumental causes."[5] Thomas also highlights the notion of instrumental causality in his discussion of prophecy, describing the prophet's mind as "an instrument moved by the Holy Spirit."[6] Pope Leo XIII, a key modern proponent of Thomism, draws upon the language of "instrument" in his encyclical letter, *Providentissimus Deus* (1893):

> Because the Holy Spirit employed men as his instruments in writing [*tamquam instrumenta ad scribendum*], we cannot therefore say that perhaps it was these inspired instruments who fell into error and not the primary author. For, by supernatural power, he so stimulated and moved them to write [*supernaturali ipse virtute ita eos ad scribendum*], and assisted them while they were writing that they conceived correctly with their minds and wished to write down faithfully all those things and only those things he ordered, and [these] they expressed in an apt manner with infallible truth: otherwise he himself would not be the author of all of sacred Scripture.[7]

Here we find a clear expression of the Catholic doctrine of divine inspiration. This teaching is repeated by Vatican II, though with greater emphasis on "the faculties and powers" of the human authors and their status as "true authors" (*veri auctores*) of the sacred texts.[8] In emphasizing the mysterious interplay of the divine and the human in the composition of the Bible, Vatican II invokes an analogy with the eternal Word's "assumption of human infirmity."[9] Just as the incarnation of Christ reveals God's loving-kindness and condescension, so does the composition

---

5   Thomas Aquinas, *Summa Contra Gentiles*, Bk. 3, Chap. 70, in *On the Truth of the Catholic Faith (Summa Contra Gentiles)*, 5 vols. (New York: Doubleday, 1955–1957).

6   Thomas Aquinas, *Summa Theologiae* [Summa of Theology], pt. 2a-2ae, q. 173, art. 4, in *Summa Theologica*, 3 vols. (New York: Benzinger Brothers, 1947).

7   Pope Leo XIII, *Providentissimus Deus* [The God of All Providence], Encyclical Letter on the Study of Scripture (November 18, 1893), 20 (*DS* 3293). It should also be mentioned that Leo XIII's understanding of inspiration manifests the influence of Johannes B. Franzelin (1816–1886), a *peritus* at Vatican I. See Raymond F. Collins, "Inspiration," in *The New Jerome Biblical Commentary*, eds. Raymond E. Brown, Joseph A. Fitzmyer, and Roland E. Murphy, (Englewood Cliffs, NJ: Prentice Hall, 1990), 1030.

8   *Dei Verbum*, 11.

9   *Dei Verbum*, 13.

of Scripture. God, making use of inspired human authors, adapts his Word to human language.

The theory of communal or social inspiration of Scripture developed in light of various aspects of higher biblical criticism, especially form criticism and redaction criticism. According to Raymond Collins, social theories of inspiration judge that "to a large extent, biblical books cannot simply be considered the literary production of an isolated individual, as modern books are." Instead, these theories presume that "the individual writers were members of faith communities which had more than a passing influence on the formation of the biblical literature itself."[10]

The principal Catholic proponents of "social inspiration" were three Jesuit scholars: Karl Rahner, John McKenzie, and Dennis McCarthy, who developed their theories in the late 1950s and early 1960s—prior to Vatican II's promulgation of *Dei Verbum* in 1965.[11]

McCarthy was focused chiefly on the Old Testament. His key insight is that "the ancient author was in all instances the spokesman of society, and society was the author of his book."[12] Inspiration for him is ultimately reduced to God's guidance of a "divinely chosen society," and "it is within this divinely guided community, through a complex process in which the community itself is deeply involved, that the inspired books come to be."[13]

McCarthy refers to both Rahner and McKenzie as the sources for his understanding of the social nature of inspiration and authorship.[14] Therefore, it seems fitting that we focus our attention on these two authors. After presenting the basic points of their analysis, we will critically examine their positions in light of the Catholic understanding of inspiration, especially that of *Dei Verbum*. I will argue that the social theory of inspiration fails to distinguish properly between the Holy Spirit's inspiration of the Bible and the Holy Spirit's guidance and protection of the Church's magisterium, or teaching authority.

10　Collins, "Inspiration," 1032.

11　See Collins, "Inspiration," 1032. See Karl Rahner, *Inspiration in the Bible*, trans. Charles H. Henkey (New York: Herder and Herder, 1961); compare Rahner, "Über die Schriftinspiration" [Concerning Scriptural Inspiration], *Zeitschrift für Katholische Theologie* 78 (1956): 137–168; John L. McKenzie, "The Social Character of Inspiration," *Catholic Biblical Quarterly* 24 (1962): 115–124; D. J. McCarthy, "Personality, Society and Inspiration," *Theological Studies* 13 (1963): 185–192. In Protestant circles, communal inspiration has been mostly associated with canonical criticism and names such as J. S. Semler and Brevard Childs. See Stephen B. Chapman, "Reclaiming Inspiration for the Bible," in *Canon and Biblical Interpretation*, eds. Craig G. Bartholomew, et al. (Gloucestershire: University of Gloucestershire and the British Foreign Bible Society, 2006), 168–174.

12　McCarthy, "Personality, Society and Inspiration," 554.

13　McCarthy, "Personality, Society and Inspiration," 574–575.

14　McCarthy, "Personality, Society and Inspiration," 553–554, n. 2.

The Influence of Rahner's "Inspiration in the Bible"

A prodigious author and *peritus* (expert) at Vatican II, Karl Rahner is widely recognized as one of the most influential Catholic theologians of the 20th century. His speculations on the nature of inspiration were articulated in his book, *Inspiration in the Bible* (1961),[15] one in a series of studies on "disputed questions," that Rahner conceived and promoted in conjunction with Heinrich Schlier.[16]

Rahner accepts as binding the traditional Catholic doctrine that "the Scriptures have God as their author...because he inspired the Scriptures."[17] He finds, however, "a certain formal abstractness" in the "material and factual description" of the process of inspiration.[18] He proceeds to analyze four problems surrounding this process that he believes must be faced.

The first problem involves the fact that we must acknowledge two authors: God and the human writers. As Rahner sees it, the human authors of Scripture "are not secretaries merely taking down divine dictations."[19] Instead, "they are real originators and authors."[20] Thus, the traditional concept of "instrumentality" must not be compared to that of a secretary. Rather, "human authorship...remains completely and absolutely unimpaired," for Rahner.[21] It is "permeated, embraced, but not diminished by the divine authorship."[22]

The second problem Rahner sees flows from the first: how does God inspire or illumine the consciousness of the author of Scripture? How does God affect the human author's intellect and will? Rahner believes that divine inspiration can be reconciled with a view of the divine working on the human author "by means of impulses, which are within the realm of the author's experience."[23] He cautions against reducing this process to something merely psychological. Nevertheless, he believes that divine inspiration not only tolerates human authorship, but it also requires it as something "formally different" from divine authorship.[24]

The third problem emerges from the question of how the Church can know which books are inspired. Rahner believes this question requires that the Church

---

15 Rahner, *Inspiration in the Bible*, 4. It should be noted that the English edition of this book bears an *imprimatur* from the Vicar General of the Archdiocese of Westminster, England, presumably designating that nothing offensive to Roman Catholic teaching on faith and morals has been found in it.

16 Leo J. O'Donovan, "Rahner, Karl," in *New Catholic Encyclopedia*, 2nd ed., 14 vols. (Detroit: Thomson Gale, 2003), 11:894.

17 Rahner, *Inspiration in the Bible*, 9.

18 Rahner, *Inspiration in the Bible*, 9.

19 Rahner, *Inspiration in the Bible*, 9.

20 Rahner, *Inspiration in the Bible*, 9.

21 Rahner, *Inspiration in the Bible*, 14.

22 Rahner, *Inspiration in the Bible*, 14.

23 Rahner, *Inspiration in the Bible*, 23.

24 Rahner, *Inspiration in the Bible*, 24.

have "a material content for the concept of inspiration," in order to determine which writings are inspired and, therefore, admitted into the *canon* of sacred Scripture. Recognizing canonicity "in fact means knowing inspiredness,"[25] even though there might not be any formal concept of inspiredness.

The fourth problem highlighted by Rahner is "the relationship between inspired and canonical writing on the one hand, and the teaching authority and tradition on the other."[26] Rahner sees a tension between the authority of the Bible and the authority of the Church needed to testify to the canonicity and inspiration of the individual texts that make up the Bible. For him, it seems that either the Church "weakens her own binding, 'infallible' teaching authority, which she needs in support of the Scriptures, or she weakens the Bible in favor of the teaching authority at the moment when she testifies to this authority."[27] Rahner sums up the problem this way:

> What is the point of an infallible teaching authority if there is an infallible Bible? What is the point of an infallible Bible if there is an infallible authority? If there is an infallible teaching authority, then it is certainly in a position, quite independently from a Bible, infallibly to select from the stream of opinions and of human tradition (at the beginning of which we have the oral tradition of the Christian events), what has been revealed by God, and to proclaim it to the world. What would be the point of an infallible Bible in the hands of an authority, which, in the Catholic Church did not always, even in her infallible decisions, rely upon the Scriptures, if it could also testify to divine revelation unerringly without the Bible?[28]

In response to these questions, Rahner admits that we could simply affirm that God has decided to provide two infallible authorities, the Bible and the Church. But he says this solution seems to involve "a rather dangerous theological positivism."[29] For him, a better solution to this problem—and to the others he has presented—is to recognize "that the Scripture is, from the beginning, the book of the Church who can testify to its inspiration because it is her book."[30] His thesis, therefore, is that the Scriptures are "are essentially books of the Church to be recognized only through her as Scripture given to her, to be interpreted through her and thus to

---

25 Rahner, *Inspiration in the Bible*, 30.

26 Rahner, *Inspiration in the Bible*, 30.

27 Rahner, *Inspiration in the Bible*, 31.

28 Rahner, *Inspiration in the Bible*, 31–32.

29 Rahner, *Inspiration in the Bible*, 34.

30 Rahner, *Inspiration in the Bible*, 37–38.

be actualized in their own nature through the Church."[31] This holds true for both the Old and the New Testament Scriptures, because "the Old Testament belongs *a priori* to the formation of the Church and not only of the synagogue, as part of her pre-history and as such remains actual forever; it can claim the same vitality as the New Testament."[32]

Ultimately, for Rahner, the Church affirms a particular writing as inspired because "the relevant writing emerges as a genuine self-expression of the primitive Church."[33] This means that we need not necessarily limit revelation or inspiration to the period up to the death of the last apostle. For one thing, Rahner believes that the idea of Church's "first generation is somewhat vague."[34] Furthermore, "the Scriptures are the canonical exposition of this teaching of the early Church."[35] Rahner's understanding thus removes the alleged tension between the two infallible authorities, the Bible and the Church. These two sources of authority "have reference to each other from the beginning like two instances of the same process."[36] For the later Church, this means that infallibility is expressed by "the inerrant interpretation of the Scripture because it includes by definition the link with the early Church."[37]

How does this thesis affect the traditional conception of the inspiration of the human authors? For Rahner, "the circle of personalities of the inspired authors" includes both apostles and others "inasmuch as their work at that time was representative of the Church, a means of her self-possession."[38] The authors of the Scriptures write as members of the Church. As such, what they write in the Scriptures is subject to the interpretation of the Church they represent.

Is God still the author of the Sacred Scriptures according to this thesis? Rahner would answer in the affirmative because "God wills and produces the Scriptures by a formal predefinition of a redemptive-historical and eschatological kind as a constitutive element of the foundation of the primitive Church."[39] God is the author of these Scriptures because "to effect such a book is to be its author in an actual sense," though, of course, authorship here is used only as "an analogous concept."[40] Rahner, therefore, locates inspiration in a type of "divine impulse, joined to God's will to establish the Church." This impulse "must always reach

---

31   Rahner, *Inspiration in the Bible*, 48.

32   Rahner, *Inspiration in the Bible*, 54.

33   Rahner, *Inspiration in the Bible*, 65.

34   Rahner, *Inspiration in the Bible*, 69.

35   Rahner, *Inspiration in the Bible*, 71.

36   Rahner, *Inspiration in the Bible*, 72.

37   Rahner, *Inspiration in the Bible*, 72.

38   Rahner, *Inspiration in the Bible*, 78.

39   Rahner, *Inspiration in the Bible*, 55.

40   Rahner, *Inspiration in the Bible*, 56.

down into the intellectual and volitive, spiritual sphere of man."[41] Ultimately for Rahner, the divine inspiration of Scripture is part and parcel of God's guidance and protection of the Church, which possesses the Bible as a "constitutive element"[42] of her "genuine self-expression."[43]

McKenzie and the Social Character of Inspiration

John McKenzie was one of the first American Catholic biblical scholars to embrace and promote the methods of higher biblical criticism. Yet his religious superiors were initially rather cautious about his methods. Jesuit censors held up publication of his first book, *The Power and the Wisdom: An Interpretation of the Old Testament* (1956) for three years before permission was granted for publication.[44] Eventually, his publications gained notice. He served as president of the Catholic Biblical Association and in 1966 became the first Catholic president of the Society of Biblical Literature.[45] His work continued to lead to conflicts with his superiors and, in 1970, he left the Jesuits while remaining a Catholic priest. [46]

McKenzie's view of inspiration shows the influence of Rahner, who had originally presented his position in a 1956 lecture at the University of Würzburg that was later published.[47] McKenzie cites this published lecture in his 1962 article, and approves of Rahner's thesis that "the charisma of inspiration in the New Testament is best understood as a charisma possessed by the Church herself and not by individual writers."[48] Rahner ultimately argues that, "the inspiration of the Scriptures…is but simply the causality of God in regard to the Church, inasmuch as it refers to that constitutive element of the apostolic Church, which is the Bible."[49]

McKenzie develops his description of the social character of inspiration around four major points. First, he notes that most of the books of the Bible have multiple authors or multiple layers of authorship. A theory of inspiration that works well with the idea of a single individual author does not work as easily "when it is applied to the compilation of the Pentateuch from scattered sources or to the 'school' of St. Matthew."[50]

McKenzie's second point is that the biblical texts are mostly "compilations" rather than "books" in the conventional sense, and "even compilation is an inexact

---

41   Rahner, *Inspiration in the Bible*, 57.

42   Rahner, *Inspiration in the Bible*, 51.

43   Rahner, *Inspiration in the Bible*, 65.

44   Francis T. Gignac, "McKenzie, John Lawrence," in *New Catholic Encyclopedia*, 9:402.

45   Gignac, "McKenzie," 9:402.

46   Gignac, "McKenzie," 9:402.

47   Rahner, "Über die Schriftinspiration."

48   McKenzie, "Social Character of Inspiration," 119.

49   Rahner, *Inspiration of the Bible*, 50–51.

50   McKenzie, "Social Character of Inspiration," 115–116.

term for the complex process of growth and development of which these books are the product."[51] Moreover, many books of the Bible are actually edited "re-readings" of earlier traditions. This reality of these multiple layers of history makes the search for inspired authors very difficult. As McKenzie writes: "unless we can answer such simple questions as who did what under the inspiring influence, there is much we do not know about inspiration."[52]

A third factor brought to bear by McKenzie is that of oral tradition. Regarding the Old Testament, he notes that most biblical scholars "postulate the survival of the traditions of the patriarchs, the exodus, the settlement, and pre-monarchic Israel by word of mouth"; he adds that "most of these traditions acquired not one but several variant oral forms."[53] A similar process he believes occurred with respect to the formation of the Gospels, though over a shorter interval of time. For McKenzie, the reality of multiple strands of oral tradition again makes tracing inspiration very difficult. Moreover, if ancient authors allowed a certain freedom in the revision and expansion of prior written traditions, they allowed even more flexibility with regard to oral traditions.

McKenzie's final point is actually the subtext of the preceding three: the reality of scriptural redaction and the question of where the gift of inspiration begins and ends. McKenzie writes:

> Who then, is the inspired author, and what does the inspired author produce? We find it difficult to believe that the final redactors of the Pentateuch, for instance, were the inspired authors who compiled quite uninspired material, and no one thinks that the final and terminal editor is the only inspired author, whoever he may have been. Therefore, we feel the need of distributing the charisma, so to speak, among the various men who contributed to the book—meaning the book we have. To me, at least, this has always seemed somewhat mechanical and contrived.[54]

Having made these four points, McKenzie believes he has provided sufficient evidence of the need to reformulate our understanding of biblical inspiration. What then, does he suggest as an alternate theory? Here, he is quite open in proposing the idea of the social character of inspiration, an idea he attributes not only to Rahner but also to Pierre Benoit, the French biblical scholar.[55] McKenzie believes that the social character of inspiration is "the most constructive theory of inspira-

---

51   McKenzie, "Social Character of Inspiration," 116.

52   McKenzie, "Social Character of Inspiration," 116.

53   McKenzie, "Social Character of Inspiration," 117.

54   McKenzie, "Social Character of Inspiration," 117-118.

55   See Pierre Benoit, O.P. *Prophecy and Revelation*, trans. Avery Dulles, and Thomas Sheridan (New York: Desclee, 1961). A more complete list of Benoit's publications can be found in James

tion in the last fifty to sixty years."[56] For McKenzie, inspiration is "a charisma possessed by the Church herself and not by individual writers."[57] Similar to the apostolic office, "inspiration is given to the Church only in her infancy, and yields to other charismata and functions in the more fully organized and established Church."[58] Finally, "those who write the inspired books of the New Testament write them as officers and representatives of the Church, which is the real author of the New Testament."[59]

McKenzie admits that this theory does not seem as applicable to the Old Testament as to the New. Yet he believes it can apply because the notion of "corporate personality" is operative in ancient Israel as well as in the Church. For both Israel and the Church, the sacred literature is not so much the work of individuals as it is the corporate voice of the people. Ultimately, inspiration is an expression of the Word of God, which McKenzie identifies as "a direct mystical insight and awareness of the divine reality."[60] Those who recite or record this experience do so as spokesmen for the community. McKenzie writes:

> The spokesman of God speaks for his society; when he speaks, he speaks not in virtue of his own personal experience and knowledge of God, but in virtue of the faith and traditions in which his experience occurs and without which his experience would not have meaning.[61]

This new formulation of inspiration raises important questions, as McKenzie himself acknowledges. For example, he is aware that this theory seems to obscure the differences between biblical inspiration and divine revelation. However, he believes that the traditional distinction between inspiration and revelation "is based on an inadequate conception of both."[62] He suggests that the experience of God and the expression given to that experience are intimately connected. The expression, though, is given form within a community of faith.

McKenzie also recognizes that his theory results in positing varying degrees of inspiration; that is, some books of the Bible might seem "more inspired" by others. He does not find this to be a major difficulty, for he believes it is already acknowledged that some biblical texts express revelation and inspiration with greater clarity and vigor than others.

T. Burtchaell, *Catholic Theories of Inspiration Since 1810: A Review and Critique* (Cambridge: Cambridge University, 1969), 308.

56 McKenzie, "Social Character of Inspiration," 118–119.

57 McKenzie, "Social Character of Inspiration," 119.

58 McKenzie, "Social Character of Inspiration," 119.

59 McKenzie, "Social Character of Inspiration," 119.

60 McKenzie, "Social Character of Inspiration," 121.

61 McKenzie, "Social Character of Inspiration," 121.

62 McKenzie, "Social Character of Inspiration," 122.

Finally, McKenzie speculates about where the Word of God is now and why the charisma of inspiration has passed away. His answer is that this charisma has *not* passed away because "the Spirit which seized the prophets has come to dwell in the Church."[63] For McKenzie:

> The Church does not write the Word of God because she is the Word of God; the charisma of her infancy has grown into her adult maturity. She does not write the Word of God because she is the living Word, which needs no written record.[64]

"Social Inspiration": A Catholic Critique

In evaluating any new theory, it is important to ask whether it has accurately and fairly assessed the inadequacies of an existing theory; to put this another way: have problems been raised that cannot be addressed by the existing theory? The new theory of inspiration must also be evaluated as to whether it introduces new problems and challenges to traditional Catholic teachings on biblical inspiration. There are, I believe, a number of problems created by the theory of the social character of biblical inspiration. Some are more evident in McKenzie, but others are also found in Rahner. I will have to divide these problems under four major headings.

The social concept of inspiration undermines inspiration as a charism of the Holy Spirit received by the biblical authors.

In the Nicene Creed (325), Christians affirm as a matter of faith that the Holy Spirit has "spoken through the prophets."[65] Likewise, the Letter to the Hebrews testifies that "God spoke…to our ancestors through the prophets."[66] The inspiration of the Scriptures, as well as of the biblical authors, is the work of the Holy Spirit. All Scripture is "God-breathed" or "inspired by God."[67] Writing in the theological encyclopedia, *Sacramentum Mundi*, edited by Rahner himself, Luis Alonso-Schökel offers this vivid description of how the Church understands inspiration:

> The very term "inspiration" refers us to the "Spirit." The inspiration of Scripture, then, must be something living, active, piercing. The "breath" of God that was breathed at creation, that gives man life, that raises up heroes of salvation, also inspires the prophet, the "man of the Spirit"; and since this Spirit is a

---

63   McKenzie, "Social Character of Inspiration," 123.

64   McKenzie, "Social Character of Inspiration," 123.

65   *DS* 150.

66   Heb. 1:1. All Scripture translations are from the New American Bible (NAB).

67   2 Tim. 3:17 (Greek: *Theópneustos*).

living, life-giving one, the inspired word too is something living and active (Heb. 4:12). Charisma is the name usually given to the action of the Spirit in the economy of salvation. Inspiration must be seen in the variegated setting of the charisms, as part of the total experience of Israel and the Church.[68]

Inspiration, therefore, is a charism, a special gift or anointing, given to the biblical authors. Rahner and McKenzie do not deny this "charism" of inspiration, but their social concept ultimately reduces it to some type of basic guidance of the faith community by God. Scripture itself, however, witnesses to the power of inspiration as something received by chosen individuals and not merely a type of charism given generically to the community. Jeremiah laments the derision and reproach his preaching of the Word of the Lord has brought him, and so he convinces himself, "I will speak in his name no more." But then he says the Word "becomes like fire burning in my heart, imprisoned in my bones; I grow weary holding it in, I cannot endure it."[69] Along these lines, 2 Peter 1:21 tells us that "no prophecy ever came through human will; but rather human beings moved by the Holy Spirit spoke under the influence of God."

McKenzie believes the idea of a "charism" of inspiration given to certain individuals is difficult to sustain because of the need to distribute it, so to speak, among those who participated in the complex history of the biblical text as it was handed down from oral tradition to its final redactors.[70] This leads him to embrace Rahner's thesis that the charisma of inspiration is one "possessed by the Church herself and not by individual writers."[71] This position fails to do justice to inspiration as a true charism or gift of the Holy Spirit. Albert Vanhoye notes that Rahner's treatment of inspiration fails to mention the biblical authors "at all," and this omission "favors the position of those who attribute the production of texts to the community rather than to persons."[72] In contrast to this idea of "communal inspiration," Vanhoye observes:

> Exegetical studies lead one to believe, however, that in the production of a given text, the charism can be stretched out over several persons, if they have all contributed to this production. It would be strange to limit inspiration to the final redactor,

---

68 Luis Alonso-Schökel, "Inspiration," in *Sacramentum Mundi, An Encyclopedia of Theology*, ed. Karl Rahner, et al., 6 vols. (New York: Herder and Herder, 1968–1970), 3:145–146.

69 Jer. 20:9.

70 McKenzie, "Social Character of Inspiration," 117–118.

71 McKenzie, "Social Character of Inspiration," 119.

72 Albert Cardinal Vanhoye, "The Reception in the Church of the Dogmatic Constitution, *Dei Verbum*," in *Opening Up the Scriptures: Joseph Ratzinger and the Foundations of Biblical Inspiration* edited by José Granados, et al. (Grand Rapids, MI: Erdmans, 2008), 117.

especially if his role were not so important, and to refuse it to the previous authors, whose contributions were much more substantial. One can speak of a "current" of inspiration, in a way, the action of which is stretched out over different stages in the formation of a text.[73]

Vanhoye's point is significant. The fact that a given biblical text might be the product of redaction does not, in itself, challenge the traditional notion that the charism of inspiration is given to individuals. As we have seen, McKenzie's four arguments are variations on a single theme—that modern biblical criticism's identification of multiple authors and traditions in biblical texts means we must reformulate our concept of divine inspiration.

McKenzie has not proven his point in this regard. Apart from the issue of whether his claims of multiple authorship for particular biblical books are always accurate, he offers no substantial argument against the idea that inspiration can be distributed to all who contributed to the production of the text; he simply states that this has always seemed to him "somewhat mechanical and contrived."[74]

The Church has long recognized modern scholarship's finding of multiple layers of oral tradition, writing, and redaction. For example, *Dei Verbum*, affirms the three stages in the formation of the Gospels, but it does not see this as any reason to reformulate the traditional concept of inspiration.[75] Earlier, Pope Pius XII acknowledged that the ancient sacred writers (*hagiographi antiqui*) might have drawn from popular narratives of non-biblical sources, but they did so "under the influx of divine inspiration (*divinae inspirationis afflatus*), which preserved them from all error in the choice and evaluation of these documents."[76] Thus, Pius recognized the divine inspiration of the redactors who put the Pentateuch into its final form; but this does not lead him to obscure inspiration as a charism given to individual biblical authors.

McKenzie notwithstanding, the fact of redaction in the biblical texts does not require that we abandon the traditional concept of inspiration as a charism given to certain individuals. Communal inspiration, ultimately, obscures inspiration as a charism given to the biblical authors themselves, so that, "moved by the Holy Spirit," they may speak "under the influence of God."[77]

---

73   Vanhoye, "Reception," 117.

74   McKenzie, "Social Character of Inspiration," 118.

75   *Dei Verbum*, 19; compare *Dei Verbum*, 11.

76   Pope Pius XII, *Humani Generis* [The Human Race], Encyclical Letter on Certain False Opinions Threatening to Undermine the Foundations of Catholic Doctrine (August 12, 1950), 38 (*DS* 3898).

77   2 Pet. 1:21.

The social concept of inspiration undermines the normative character of the written Word of God for the Church.

The social concept of inspiration makes it very difficult to accept what Vatican II teaches about the Church's magisterium being the servant of the Word of God.[78] If, as McKenzie claims, the Church "is the Word of God,"[79] then the Church would be servant to herself rather than servant to the Word of God. Moreover, while *Dei Verbum* specifically teaches that the Church is not superior to the Word of God, McKenzie's theory instead suggests an equivalence of the Church with the Word.

McKenzie's expression of social inspiration likewise lacks any appreciation of the importance of the written Word of God in the Church's sacred liturgy and in its theology. How can the Scriptures be the "soul" of sacred theology if inspiration is simply a function of the Church's early experience and expression of the Word of God?

The Fathers of the Church clearly distinguish between the written Word of God and the apostolic Tradition that preserves and interprets God's Word. St. Irenaeus, for example, teaches that, according to the will of God, the gospel that was preached by the apostles was "handed down to us in writings, to be the foundation and the pillar of our faith."[80] Speaking of the heretics, Irenaeus notes that what they teach "will not agree with either Scripture or Tradition."[81] Thus, he articulates the distinction that the Church recognizes to this day, between the inspired Scriptures and "the Tradition of the apostles."[82]

There is, of course, an intimate connection between Scripture and Tradition. Vatican II teaches that they both flow from "the same well-spring, come together in some fashion to form one thing and move towards the same goal."[83] Nevertheless, the Council recognizes the distinction between Scripture, which is "the speech of God as it is put into writing under the breath of the Holy Spirit,"[84] and Tradition, which "transmits in its entirety the Word of God which has been entrusted to the apostles by Christ the Lord and the Holy Spirit."[85] Nowhere does the Council teach that the transmission of the Word of God by Tradition is the same as divine inspiration. Yet both Rahner and McKenzie would seem to reduce divine inspiration to the Holy Spirit's guidance of the early Church.

---

78 *Dei Verbum*, 10.

79 McKenzie, "Social Character of Inspiration," 123.

80 St. Irenaeus, *Against the Heresies*, Bk. 3, Chap. 1, 1, in *Ante-Nicene Fathers*, 10 vols., eds. Alexander Roberts and James Donaldson (Peabody, MA: Hendrickson, 2004 [reprint]), 1:414. Hereafter abbreviated *ANF*.

81 Irenaeus, *Against the Heresies*, Bk. 3, Chap. 2 (*ANF* 1:415).

82 Irenaeus, *Against the Heresies*, Bk. 3, Chap. 2 (*ANF* 1:415).

83 *Dei Verbum*, 9; see also *Catechism*, no. 80.

84 *Dei Verbum*, 9 (Lat.: "locutio Dei quatenus divino afflante Spiritu scripto consignatur").

85 *Dei Verbum*, 9.

The social concept of inspiration undermines the concept of divine revelation as well as the "deposit of faith," the Word of God, written and handed down in Tradition.

As we have seen, McKenzie himself acknowledged that his theory called into question traditional distinctions made between revelation and inspiration. This was not a problem in his opinion, because these distinction were not altogether significant. It is, however, a major problem because the social theory of inspiration undermines important distinctions that the Church has always made concerning revelation, inspiration, the inerrancy of Scripture, and the infallibility of the Church.[86]

These distinctions are important again, in the Church's "service" to the Word of God. They enable the Church to clearly differentiate between the Word of God contained in Scripture and Tradition and the efforts of the Church's teaching magisterium to preserve and explain this Word.[87]

The social concept of inspiration confuses the biblical authors's inspiration by the Holy Spirit with the magisterium's protection and guidance by the Holy Spirit.

The role of the magisterium as the servant of the Word of God is, as already noted, obscured by the social theory of inspiration. Further, McKenzie's theory cannot be reconciled with what Vatican I teaches about the two-fold order of knowledge: the natural and the supernatural.[88] It is precisely because divine revelation discloses truths that we could not otherwise know, that the human authors require divine inspiration in the composition of the sacred Scripture.

Of course, McKenzie does not deny divine inspiration, but by reducing it to a charism of the Church rather than one given to certain individuals, the Church is no longer understood as the guardian, protector and teacher of divinely revealed truths. Rather, the Church becomes the source of these divinely revealed truths through this diffused communal inspiration.

Rahner likewise seems to reduce inspiration to the action of the Holy Spirit in guiding the early Church. Because of this, it is not clear how, in his position, an inspired author is really different than an apostolic Father preaching and teaching the faith. Either the biblical authors are reduced to the same status as the apostolic Fathers or the apostolic Fathers are elevated to the status of inspired authors. The

---

86 See, for example, Michaele Nicolau and Joachim Salavaerri, *Sacrae Theologiae Summa* [Summa of Sacred Theology], vol. 1 (Madrid: Biblioteca de Autores Cristianos, 1950), where a clear distinction is made between revelation as the speech or Word of God (*locutio Dei*) and inspiration as the influence of the Holy Spirit on the authors of sacred Scripture (at 96). In the same manual, further distinctions are made between the action of the Holy Spirit inspiring the authors of the sacred Scriptures and the assistance of infallibility (*assistentia infallibilitatis*) given to the magisterium under certain circumstances, an assistance that is not the same as divine inspiration (at 638).

87 It must be remembered that both Rahner and McKenzie were writing a few years before *Dei Verbum* (1965).

88 DS 3015.

Church, however, has never understood her magisterium or the writings of her saints to be divinely inspired in the way the authors of the Bible were divinely inspired. Infallibility is not the same as revelation, and the magisterium's guidance and protection by the Holy Spirit is not the equivalent of "divine inspiration."

Jared Wicks has noted that *Dei Verbum* does not offer "an explanation of just how inspiration has its impact on the biblical writers."[89] Instead, he says, it "respects the mystery of interaction between the Spirit's charism and the activities of these human authors of the text."[90]

The crucial point, however, is that the Holy Spirit operates differently in *inspiring* the authors of Scripture than he does in *protecting* and *guiding* the magisterium of the Church. Even when the magisterium interprets the Word of God handed down in Tradition, it is not doing so under divine inspiration. The Word of God handed down in Tradition does not come from inspired human authors but from Christ the Lord and the Holy Spirit.[91]

Theologians have explained these different influences of the Holy Spirit in different ways. One way is to understand inspiration as "principally the action of God moving man in an interior way [*actio principaliter Dei intrinsice hominem movens*], by means of whose power, man, as the instrument of God, expresses the truth that God wills, either orally (prophetical inspiration) or in writing (biblical inspiration)."[92] The "assistance of infallibility or the preservation from error is, in itself, the action of God assisting man in an exterior way [*est actio Dei per se ab extrinseco hominem adiuvans*] so that man, as the principal cause, may, without error, set forth the Word of God, whether revealed or inspired."[93]

The Word of God, written or handed down in Tradition, is divine revelation and the deposit of faith. When the Church teaches that a doctrine is "revealed by God" she is affirming that such a teaching is *contained* in the deposit of faith. Some doctrines or judgments of the Church, however, *pertain* to the deposit of faith. In the case of these secondary objects of infallibility, the assent given by the faithful is not specifically an assent to the authority of God's Word (*de fide credenda*) but an assent to a definitive decision or teaching of the Church. The assent to such a definitive judgment (which is not proposed as revealed by God) is an irrevocable assent "based on faith in the Holy Spirit's *assistance* to the magisterium and on the Catholic doctrine of the infallibility of the magisterium," doctrines that are "held as of the faith" (*de fide tenenda*).[94]

---

89   Jared Wicks, *Doing Theology* (New York: Paulist, 2009), 53.

90   Wicks, *Doing Theology*, 53.

91   *Dei Verbum*, 9; *Catechism*, no. 81.

92   Nicolau and Salavaerri, *Sacrae Theologiae Summa*, 638.

93   Nicolau and Salavaerri, *Sacrae Theologiae Summa*, 638.

94   Congregation for the Doctrine of the Faith, "Commentary on the Concluding Formula of the

All of this underscores the distinction that the Church makes between the inspiration of the Bible and the biblical authors by the Holy Spirit and the protection and assistance given by the Holy Spirit to the Church's magisterium. By their reduction of inspiration to the guidance of the Church under the "impulse" of the Holy Spirit, both Rahner and McKenzie seem to obscure this distinction

The social concept of inspiration ultimately allows for continuous alteration of the deposit of faith.

This last and most serious consequence is a logical extension of McKenzie's claim that the Church "is the Word of God."[95] If this is the case, the Church is not ruled or instructed by the inspired Word of God. Instead, the Word of God becomes a reality controlled by the Church which, according to McKenzie, has "the spirit of the prophets" dwelling within her.[96] Thus, the notion that God has "said everything" in speaking to us by his Son,[97] gives way to the possibility of a never-ending stream of "new revelations" given through the prophetic spirit of the Church. The social theory of inspiration, then, results in the relativizing of the inspired Word itself.[98]

Vatican II and the "Condescension" of Scripture

From what has been shown above, the social concept of inspiration is based on a false assertion that the traditional concept of divine inspiration is deficient in accounting for the findings of modern textual criticism. In many ways, Vatican II's *Dei Verbum* can be understood as a response to the various theories of social inspiration being proposed in the late 1950s and early 1960s. It is precisely because God, in his loving condescension, chose and inspired human authors to be instruments of his written Word that we have the precious gift of the sacred Scripture, which, together with sacred Tradition, forms the single deposit of the Word of God.

The Holy Spirit inspired the authors of the sacred Scripture and made use of them to reveal God's Word. There is a true communal aspect to the reception, proclamation, and interpretation of the divine Word under the guidance of the Holy Spirit. But this communal dimension is not the same as divine inspiration. According to God's most wise design:

> Sacred Tradition, sacred Scripture, and the magisterium of the
> Church are so connected and associated that one of them can-

---

Professio Fidei," (June 29, 1998), 8; text in Avery Cardinal Dulles, *The Magisterium: Teacher and Guardian of the Faith* (Ave Maria, FL: Sapientia, 2007), 163–173.

95 McKenzie, "Social Character of Inspiration," 123.

96 McKenzie, "Social Character of Inspiration," 123.

97 See *Catechism*, nos. 65–66.

98 This final consequence of "the social theory of inspiration" is more apparent in McKenzie than in Rahner, but we must recall that McKenzie understands himself as drawing upon the basic insights of Rahner and Benoit.

not stand without the others. Working together, each in its own way, under the action of the one Holy Spirit, they all contribute effectively to the salvation of souls.[99]

It was God's will that certain men be inspired by the Holy Spirit to disclose truths that we would never know "unless they are revealed by God."[100] The communal notion of inspiration obscures the mysterious and awesome truth of divine inspiration, a truth that keeps us humble before God, who, out of his great love for us, has chosen "to reveal himself and to make known the mystery of his will."[101]

---

99 *Dei Verbum*, 10; *Catechism*, no. 95.

100 *Dei Filius* (DS 3015).

101 *Dei Verbum*, 2; *Catechism*, no. 51.

Letter & Spirit 6 (2010): 265-280

The Modernist Crisis and the Shifting of Catholic Views on Biblical Inspiration

ᵔ: Jeffrey L. Morrow :ᵔ
Seton Hall University

On September 8, 1907, Pope St. Pius X condemned "modernism" as the "synthesis of all heresies" in *Pascendi Dominici Gregis*, an encyclical on the doctrines of the modernists.[1] Scholars typically date the modernist crisis to St. Pius X's promulgation of this encyclical. The crisis identified in *Pascendi*, however, reaches back into the nineteenth century and even earlier. Scholars of modernism typically emphasize several general trends as the root issues in the crisis: the focus on subjectivity in theological experience and the turn to the history of doctrinal development as opposed to engaging in theology as if doctrine was merely propositional. I argue, however, that at the root of the modernist crisis lies the biblical question. The full-flowering of the biblical question within Catholicism—that is, the issue of modern biblical criticism—arose with modernism. Modernism, at its heart, was about the full-scale appropriation of the modern historical-critical method into Catholic biblical interpretation. But it was much more than this. Modernism gave birth to the biblical question in the Catholic world.

This question over the role of modern biblical criticism, which has by and large come to be identified with the historical-critical method, is of fundamental importance for contemporary Catholic theology and exegesis. The near hegemonic status of historical criticism in the academy, with the attendant atrophy of theological exegesis has occasioned a crisis in Catholic biblical scholarship. This crisis involves the near absolute separation of Catholic biblical scholarship from Catholic systematic theology, wherein both ignore the other as though they were unrelated. At most, Catholic systematic theologians will occasionally rely on a truncated appropriation of the "assured" conclusions of historical criticism. In their pretentious claims of objectivity and neutrality, meanwhile, Bible scholars often remain blind to the particular philosophical, theological, and political commitments to which their methods remain wedded, thus prompting Joseph Cardinal Ratzinger to call for a "criticism of criticism."[2]

It is beyond dispute that Catholics must pay careful attention to history when it comes to biblical interpretation. Thus, some form of historical criticism

---

1 Pope St. Pius X, *Pascendi Dominici Gregis* [Feeding the Lord's Flock], Encyclical Letter on the Doctrines of the Modernists (September 8, 1907), 39, in *The Papal Encyclicals*, vol. 3: 1903–1939, ed. Claudia Carlen (Raleigh, North Carolina: McGrath, 1981), 71–98, at 89.

2 See Joseph Cardinal Ratzinger, "Biblical Interpretation in Conflict," in *God's Word: Scripture—Tradition—Office* (San Francisco: Ignatius, 2008 [2005]), 91–126.

is certainly necessary. If we take the incarnation seriously, and understand the Catholic doctrine of Scripture's "dual" authorship, which includes the human authors as true instrumental authors, we cannot avoid historical interpretation. The problem is when the canons of modern history take precedent in one's biblical hermeneutic. Magisterial teaching, the doctrine of the Church, and faith must always remain primary. Unfortunately, much of contemporary Catholic biblical scholarship makes it difficult for the study of Scripture to be the "soul of theology," as called for by the Second Vatican Council.[3] A resolution to this problem must be sought tirelessly.

This article will unfold in three parts. First, I will explain how the modernist crisis was the birth of the biblical question in the Catholic world. I will then proceed to show how problems with modernist appropriations of historical criticism continue to plague Catholic biblical studies and theology. Finally, I will suggest the importance of the Catholic doctrine of biblical inspiration for helping to unite faith and reason and tradition and history, in Catholic biblical interpretation. My overarching argument is that the Catholic doctrine of the dual authorship of Scripture requires a hermeneutic of faith wherein Catholic faith does not diminish or impair reason, but empowers it.

The Modernist Crisis and the Birth of the Biblical Question

Concerns over the use of biblical criticism in Catholic exegesis predate the modernist crisis by centuries. Indeed, the roots of historical criticism can be traced back at least as far as medieval nominalist philosophy, if not earlier in the polemical works of various Roman philosophers and Gnostic thinkers. But it is only in the nineteenth century that we see historical criticism come of age; in the Catholic world, we find its most complete appropriation in the works of modernists like Alfred Loisy. Hence, it is my contention that the modernist crisis was fundamentally about the uncritical appropriation of modern historical criticism into Catholic biblical scholarship, and moreover, that the modernist crisis gave birth to the biblical question in the Catholic world. By the very launching of the biblical question, the modernist crisis and its immediate historical preface initiated Catholic magisterial teaching on biblical inspiration. In order to understand how the modernist crisis gave birth to the biblical question, we need to take a brief look at the development of the historical critical method itself and its entrance into the Catholic world, as well as the politics which gave rise to the historical critical method and the modernist crisis.[4]

---

3   Second Vatican Council, *Dei Verbum* [The Word of God], Dogmatic Constitution on Divine Revelation, (November 18, 1965), 24. Latin texts of all citations from the documents of the Church ecumenical councils are taken from Norman P. Tanner, ed., *Decrees of the Ecumenical Councils*, 2 volumes (Washington, D.C.: Georgetown University, 1990).

4   I have summarized much of this history in Jeffrey L. Morrow, "The Politics of Biblical Interpretation: A 'Criticism of Criticism,'" *New Blackfriars* 91 (September 2010): 528–545.

A Criticism Forged in Theo-Political Polemics

Within both Jewish and Christian communities, certain hermeneutical assumptions and logical interpretive conclusions developed as the Scriptures were being canonized and rules for interpretation were being set forth. James Kugel maintains there were at least four basic assumptions implied in the exegesis of early Jewish and Christian interpreters. He explains:

> [1] They assumed that the Bible was a fundamentally cryptic text: that is, when it said A, often it might really mean B. ... [2] Interpreters also assumed that the Bible was a book of lessons directed to readers in their own day. It might seem to talk about the past, but it is not fundamentally history. It is instruction, telling us what to do. ... Ancient interpreters assumed this not only about narratives like the Abraham story but about every part of the Bible. ... [3] Interpreters also assumed that the Bible contained no contradictions or mistakes. It is perfectly harmonious, despite its being an anthology. ... In short, the Bible, they felt, is an utterly consistent, seamless, perfect book. ... [4] Lastly, they believed that the entire Bible is essentially a divinely given text, a book in which God speaks directly or through His prophets.[5]

Such views of Scripture came under attack even before the Christian period, and particularly on the issue of the divine origin of the Pentateuch. Early heretics attempted to curtail any Jewish claims to the divine authority of the Torah by attacking the history of its origins. The pre-Christian proto-gnostic group known as the Nasarenes attempted to do this by denying that Moses was the author of the Torah, which had been widely assumed throughout much of Jewish and Christian history.[6] In the Christian period, the third-century Roman neo-Platonist philosopher, Porphyry, also questioned the Mosaic authorship of the Pentateuch, as well as other traditional attributions of authorship and origin, in his polemical works against Christianity.[7] He and other polemicists attacked the history of Jewish and Christian claims concerning Scripture in order to denigrate assertion that these texts were divinely inspired.

In the medieval Muslim world, polemicists like Ibn Hazm and philosophers like Ibn Rushd (Averroes) followed suit. Ibn Hazm became one of the most im-

---

5 James L. Kugel, *How to Read the Bible: A Guide to Scripture, Then and Now* (New York: Free Press, 2007), 14–16. See also Thomas O'Loughlin, "The Controversy over Methuselah's Death: Proto-Chronology and the Origins of the Western Concept of Inerrancy," *Recherches de Théologie Ancienne et Médiévale* 62 (1995): 182–225.

6 Edwin M. Yamauchi, *Gnostic Ethics and Mandaean Origins* (Cambridge: Harvard University, 1970), 60.

7 Aryeh Kofsky, *Eusebius of Caesarea Against Paganism* (Leiden: Brill, 2000), 30.

portant medieval thinkers to use philological analyses and historical assertion to deconstruct traditional Jewish and Christian views of Scripture, particularly historical claims. Ibn Hazm wanted to eliminate all forms of spiritual interpretation, and his work spread far and wide.[8] Averroes, strongly influenced by Ibn Hazm, was even more important in the history of modern biblical criticism because he placed philosophy and reason as judge over faith and theology.[9]

Averroism spread throughout the Latin West at a rapid rate and became especially popular in university systems. We see this view enter biblical interpretation especially with the figure of Marsilius of Padua, who imbibed Averroist philosophy under the influence of Latin Averroists at the University of Padua. William of Ockham made similar exegetical moves, particularly in his attempts to curtail allegorical interpretation; for Marsilius and Ockham, there could be no spiritual interpretation. Nominalist biblical interpretation then spread throughout Europe from the University of Paris to the University of Heidelberg and elsewhere.[10] Much of the biblical work in which Marsilius and Ockham engaged, however, was tied to the politics of Ludwig of Bavaria, under whose protection they lived. Notably, Ludwig was in conflict with Pope John XXII.[11]

---

8   Abdelilah Ljamai, *Ibn Hazm et la Polémique Islamo-Chrétienne dans L'Histoire de L'Islam* [Ibn Hazm and Islamic-Christian Polemic in the History of Islam] (Leiden: Brill, 2003), 145–196; Theodore Pulcini, *Exegesis as Polemical Discourse: Ibn Hazm on Jewish and Christian Scriptures* (Atlanta: Scholars Press, 1998), 57–96; Hava Lazarus-Yafeh, "Some Neglected Aspects of Medieval Polemics against Christianity," *Harvard Theological Review* 89:1 (1996): 61–84; and Muhammad Abu Laila, "Ibn Hazm's Influence on Christian Thinking in Research," *Islamic Quarterly* 31 (1987): 103–115.

9   Roger Arnaldez, *Grammaire et Théologie chez Ibn Hazm de Cordoue: Essai sur la Structure et les Conditions de la Pensée Musulmane* [Grammar and Theology According to Ibn Hazm of Cordoba: An Essay about the Structure and Conditions of Muslim Thought] (Paris: Librairie Philosophique J. Vrin, 1956), 319; and Miguel Asín Palacios, *Abenházam de Córdoba y su Historia Crítica de las Ideas Religiosas II* [Ibn Hazm of Cordoba and his Critical History of Religious Ideas Volume II] (Madrid: Tipografía de la "Revista de Archivos, Bibliotecas y Museos," 1928), 74; see also 74, n. 105.

10   See A.J. Minnis, "Material Swords and Literal Lights: The Status of Allegory in William of Ockham's *Breviloquium* on Papal Power," in *With Reverence for the Word: Medieval Scriptural Exegesis in Judaism, Christianity, and Islam*, eds. Jane Dammen McAuliffe, Barry D. Walfish, and Joseph W. Goering (Oxford: Oxford University, 2003), 292-308; Frank Rosenthal, "Heinrich von Oyta and Biblical Criticism in the Fourteenth Century," *Speculum* 25:2 (1950): 178–179, 182, and 183, n. 5; and Erminio Troilo, "L'Averroismo di Marsilio da Padova" ["The Averroism of Marsilius of Padua"], in *Marsilio da Padova. Studi Raccolti nel VI Centenario della Morte* [Marsilius of Padua: Collected Studies on the Sixth Centenary of his Death], eds. Aldo Checchini and Norberto Bobbio (Rome: 1942), 47–77.

11   Jürgen Miethke, "Der Kampf Ludwigs des Bayern mit Papst und Avignonesischer Kurie in Seiner Bedeutung für die Deutsche Geschichte" ["The Struggle of Ludwig of Bavaria with the Pope and Avignon Curia and its Significance for German History"], in *Kaiser Ludwig der Bayer. Konflikte, Weichenstellungen und Wahrnehmung seiner Herrschaft* [Kaiser Ludwig the Bavarian: Conflicts, Choices, and Exercise of its Rule], eds. Hermann Nehlsen and Hans-Georg Hermann (Paderborn: Schöningh, 2002), 39–74; and Hermann Nehlsen, "Die Rolle Ludwigs des Bayern und seiner Berater Marsilius von Padua und Wilhelm von Ockham im Tiroler Ehekonflikt"

These very early examples of biblical exegetes exemplify polemics that are both theological and political. They are theological because they address biblical interpretation which has long-reaching implications for all aspects of theology. In some instances, matters of theological importance seem to be of primary concern. Political commitments, however, are present at every stage of the journey. The earliest polemics cannot be separated from the politics of the Roman Empire. When we reach medieval Muslim literature, and particularly the figure of Ibn Hazm, we encounter the politics of the Muslim caliphate structure and the concern over non-Muslims within that governmental structure. With Marsilius and Ockham, we see Christian concern with temporal authority, which they contended resided in state rulers. Ockham's insistence on evangelical poverty may have stemmed from sincere theological motivations but, practically speaking, his view would attempt to take property and wealth out of the hands of the Church and place them squarely with state rulers who were often in conflict with the pope.

Throne vs. Altar and the Rise of Modern Biblical Criticism

The conflict between state rulers and the Church would only increase as the centuries went by. In many ways the Renaissance period saw the development of new scholarly tools in philology and textual criticism that would place Scripture study on a firm footing. And yet, it was also during this time period that traditional authority was replaced by the authority of specialists. Renaissance scholarship continued a trend, already present in Ockham, of elevating the scholar over the Church's magisterium. We see this in the foundational work of Lorenzo Valla and especially Niccolò Machiavelli.[12]

The Protestant Reformation played an important role in continuing the trajectory set by nominalism and Renaissance philology. With their emphasis on the literal sense and their denigration of traditional Catholic spiritual exegesis, Protestant Reformers furthered the move towards modern biblical criticism, severing ties with the Catholic magisterium as the locus of biblical interpretive authority.[13] And yet, the Reformation could never be completely severed from the

---

["The Role of Ludwig of Bavaria and His Advisors Marsilius of Padua and William of Ockham in the Tyrolean Marital Conflict"], in *Kaiser Ludwig der Bayer*, 285–328.

12   Graham Maddox, "The Secular Reformation and the Influence of Machiavelli," *Journal of Religion* 82:4 (2002): 539–562; John H. Geerken, "Machiavelli's Moses and Renaissance Politics," *Journal of the History of Ideas* 60:4 (1999): 579–595; Steven Marx, "Moses and Machiavellism," *Journal of the American Academy of Religion* 65:3 (1997): 551–571; Riccardo Fubini, "Humanism and Truth: Valla Writes Against the Donation of Constantine," *Journal of the History of Ideas* 57 (1996): 79–86; James L. Kugel, "The Bible in the University," in *The Hebrew Bible and Its Interpreters*, eds. William Henry Propp, Baruch Halpern, and David Noel Freedman (Winona Lake, Indiana: Eisenbrauns, 1990), 143–165; and M.H. Goshen-Gottstein, "Christianity, Judaism and Modern Bible Study," in International Organization for the Study of the Old Testament, *Congress Volume: Edinburgh 1974*, Supplements to Vetus Testamentum 28 (Leiden: Brill, 1975), 69–88.

13   Travis L. Frampton, *Spinoza and the Rise of Historical Criticism of the Bible* (New York: T & T Clark, 2006), 23–42.

changing political order. Western Europe was undergoing its bloody transformation from complex feudal space to the modern centralized states that would ultimately subordinate the Church to the state.[14] European state rulers attempted to justify their opposition to the papacy. Regions which remained Catholic through the Reformation often had prior concordat agreements limiting the pope's arm within their realm, whereas the Protestant Reformation was most successful where no such agreements had been secured, and where rulers hence needed Protestant theology to justify their politics.[15] The case of England is paradigmatic; support for the Reformation was driven by state politics, and all opposition was crushed.[16]

It was in the seventeenth century, however, where the most important shift occurred in the course of modern biblical criticism, namely, the decisive turn to *modern* history devoid of explicit theological concerns.[17] The works of Isaac La Peyrère, Thomas Hobbes, Baruch Spinoza, and Richard Simon are pivotal;[18] these four built a foundation that would launch modern biblical interpretation far into the future. In supporting his employer, the Prince of Condé, and the prince's political aspirations of ousting King Louis XIV and becoming the first Protestant king of France, La Peyrère built upon the Renaissance tools of biblical criticism to deconstruct Scripture. He did this by utilizing the newest historical findings and hence sowing the seeds of doubt about biblical and ecclesiastical authority, so as to reinterpret Scripture to suit his own and the prince's political machinations.[19]

---

14   Jeffrey L. Morrow, "The Bible in Captivity: Hobbes, Spinoza and the Politics of Defining Religion," *Pro Ecclesia* 19:3 (2010): 285–299.

15   William T. Cavanaugh, *The Myth of Religious Violence: Secular Ideology and the Roots of Modern Conflict* (Oxford: Oxford University, 2009), 166–167.

16   Eamon Duffy, *The Stripping of the Altars: Traditional Religion in England c. 1400–c. 1580*, 2nd ed. (New Haven: Yale University, 2005 [1992]), 377–523; and Anthony W. Marx, *Faith in Nation: Exclusionary Origins of Nationalism* (Oxford: Oxford University, 2003), 128–139, 153–161, 175–184.

17   Moshe H. Goshen-Gottstein, "Foundations of Biblical Philology in the Seventeenth Century Christian and Jewish Dimensions," in *Jewish Thought in the Seventeenth Century*, eds. Isadore Twersky and Bernard Septimus (Cambridge: Harvard University, 1987), 77–94.

18   Moshe H. Goshen-Gottstein, "The Textual Criticism of the Old Testament: Rise, Decline, Rebirth," *Journal of Biblical Literature* 102:3 (1983): 365–399, at 376.

19   Fausto Parente, "Isaac de la Peyrère Interprète de Paul: Pourquoi le *Rappel des Juifs* a-t-il été Presque Entièrement Détruit au Moment de sa Publication?" ["Isaac de La Peyrère Interpreter of Paul: Why is *Rappel des Juifs* Almost Completely Destroyed at the Time of its Publication?"], *Revue des études juives* 167:1–2 (2008): 169–186; Élisabeth Quennehen, "'L'Auteur des *Préadamites*', Isaac Lapeyrère: Essai Biographique" ["'The Author of *Pre-Adamites*,' Isaac La Peyrère: A Biographical Essay"], in *Dissidents, Excentriques et Marginaux de l'Âge Classique: Autour de Cyrano de Bergerac: Bouquet offert à Madeleine Alcover* [Dissenters, Eccentric and Marginal, of the Classical Age: Around Cyrano de Bergerac: A Bouquet Offered to Madeleine Alcover], eds. Patricia Harry, Alain Mothu, and Philippe Sellier (Paris: Honoré Champion Éditeur, 2006), 349–373; and Richard H. Popkin, "Millenarianism and Nationalism—A Case Study: Isaac La Peyrère," in *Millenarianism and Messianism in Early Modern European Culture*, Vol. 4: Continental Millenarians: Protestants, Catholics, Heretics, eds. John Christian Laursen and Richard H. Popkin (Dordrecht: Kluwer Academic, 2001), 74–84.

Thomas Hobbes attempted in his biblical criticism to support the status quo in post-Reformation England where the state sovereign had absolute control over the spiritual and temporal realms within the land, including biblical interpretation, which was to be state-sponsored scholarship. Like La Peyrère, Hobbes used the newly forming modern discipline of history in order to support his claims, likewise deconstructing the sacred text, and naturalizing the supernatural in his biblical interpretations.[20]

Spinoza took both Hobbes's and La Peyrère's work further in laying the foundations for a more precise, ostensibly scientific, method of biblical interpretation than had thus far been developed.[21] Simon followed his predecessors's work even as he attempted to distance himself from them. Unlike his three exegetical forbears, Simon attempted to defend Catholic tradition, but he did so by tearing apart the Bible, piece by piece, to emphasize that without Catholic tradition all that remains is a bundle of contradictions. His prioritization of secular scholarship over Catholic orthodoxy, however, is demonstrated in his refusal to refrain from publication even after his book was placed on the Church's Index Librorum Prohibitorum ("List of Prohibited Books"). His work became instrumental in early modern English and German biblical criticism which furthered Spinoza's agenda into the eighteenth century.[22]

In the eighteenth century, several scholarly trends advanced the trajectory that had been set for modern biblical criticism in the seventeenth century works of La Peyrère, Hobbes, Spinoza, and Simon. La Peyrère and Hobbes had attempted

---

20 Jeffrey L. Morrow, "*Leviathan* and the Swallowing of Scripture: The Politics Behind Thomas Hobbes's Early Modern Biblical Criticism," *Christianity & Literature* (forthcoming); Frank M. Coleman, "Thomas Hobbes and the Hebraic Bible," *History of Political Thought* 25:4 (2004): 642–669; Michel Malherbe, "Hobbes et la Bible" ["Hobbes and the Bible"], in *Le Grand Siècle et la Bible* [The Great Century and the Bible], ed. Jean-Robert Armogathe (Paris: Beauchesne, 1989), 691–699; and Arrigo Pacchi, "Hobbes and Biblical Philology in the Service of the State," *Topoi* 7 (1988): 231–239.

21 Jeffrey L. Morrow, "The Early Modern Context to Spinoza's Bible Criticism," *Scottish Journal of Theology* (forthcoming); David Laird Dungan, "Baruch Spinoza and the Political Agenda of Modern Historical-Critical Interpretation," in *A History of the Synoptic Problem: The Canon, the Text, the Composition, and the Interpretation of the Gospels*, David Laird Dungan, Anchor Yale Bible Reference Library (New Haven: Yale University, 1999), 198–260; and R. David Freedman, "The Father of Modern Biblical Scholarship," *Journal of the Ancient Near Eastern Society* 19 (1989): 31–38.

22 Justin A.I. Champion, "Père Richard Simon and English Biblical Criticism, 1680–1700," in *Everything Connects: In Conference with Richard H. Popkin: Essays in His Honor*, eds. James E. Force and David S. Katz (Leiden: Brill, 1999), 39–61; John D. Woodbridge, "Richard Simon le 'Père de la Critique Biblique'" ["Richard Simon the 'Father of Biblical Criticism'"], in *Grand Siècle*, 193–206; Henning Graf Reventlow, "Richard Simon und seine Bedeutung für die Kritische Erforschung der Bibel" ["Richard Simon and his Importance for the Critical Study of the Bible"], in *Historische Kritik in der Theologie: Beitrage zu ihrer Geschichte* [Historical Criticism in Theology: Contributions to its History], ed. Georg Schwaiger (Göttingen: Vandenhoeck & Ruprecht, 1980), 11–36; and Paul Hazard, *La Crise de la Conscience Européenne (1680–1715)* [The Crisis of the European Consciousness (1680-1715)], vol. 3 (Paris: Boivin, 1935), 125–136.

to deconstruct the biblical texts, but they lacked the necessary philological skills and tools to make their project a success. Spinoza laid down a methodological framework that would be followed into the twenty-first century, and yet he never engaged sufficiently with the text critical tools forged in the Renaissance, which many of his contemporaries in the seventeenth century were using. In Simon we can see the Scripture begin to dissolve as a result of his more thorough incorporation of careful textual and philological analysis, in addition to his linguistic abilities which far surpassed those of La Peyrère and Hobbes. Although Simon used his methodological framework as an apologetic defense of Catholic tradition, in the eighteenth century, such methods began to erode Scripture further, setting firmly in place Spinoza's core hermeneutical method, which was nothing other than the entrance of Cartesian skepticism into the realm of biblical criticism.

Although Spinoza's and Simon's works were both brought into the world of German scholarship in the eighteenth century, the most significant shift in biblical studies that occurred then was in the work of Johann David Michaelis. Michaelis was not intending to deconstruct the Bible; in fact, his work represents a very sophisticated attempt to defend traditional views concerning Scripture. In the realm of Pentateuchal source criticism, for example, he provided a scholarly response to Jean Astruc, who, building upon Simon's work, divided Genesis into various sources. Astruc wanted to defend traditional attributions of authorship against La Peyrère, Hobbes, Spinoza, and Simon, but Michaelis believed that Astruc conceded too much ground. Where Michaelis's significance lies, however, was in his nearly complete transition of the study of the Bible from the realm of theology to the realm of history and culture. Michaelis was a faithful biblical exegete, but, basing himself on the reigning German classical scholarship of the day, he attempted to create a neutral and objective philological approach to biblical interpretation.[23]

The important context here is Prussian nationalism and the rise of Enlightenment universities in the German-speaking world, such as the University of Göttingen and the University of Berlin. These university systems existed to make productive civil servants for the Germanic state.[24] The burgeoning fields

---

23 For Michaelis, see Michael C. Legaspi, *The Death of Scripture and the Rise of Biblical Studies* (Oxford: Oxford University, 2010); on Astruc, see Legaspi, *Death of Scripture*, 136–140; Pierre Gibert, "De L'Intuition à L'Évidence: La Multiplicité Documentaire dans la Genèse chez H. B. Witter et Jean Astruc" ["From Intuition to Evidence: The Documentary Multiplicity in Genesis according to H.B. Witter and Jean Astruc"], in *Sacred Conjectures: The Context and Legacy of Robert Lowth and Jean Astruc*, ed. John Jarick (London: T & T Clark, 2007), 174–189; Aulikki Nahkola, "The *Memoires* of Moses and the Genesis of Method in Biblical Criticism: Astruc's Contribution," in *Sacred Conjectures*, 204–220; Jonathan Sheehan, *The Enlightenment Bible: Translation, Scholarship, Culture* (Princeton: Princeton University, 2005), 103–104, 114–115, 126, 180, 184, 186–187, 190, 197, and 210–215; and Anna-Ruth Löwenbrück, "Johann David Michaelis et les Débuts de la Critique Biblique" ["Johann David Michaelis and the Beginnings of Biblical Criticism"], in *Le Siècle des Lumières et la Bible* [The Enlightenment and the Bible], eds. Yvon Belaval and Dominique Bourel (Paris: Beauchesne, 1986), 113–128.

24 Legaspi, *Death of Scripture*, 27–51.

of classical studies and Pentateuchal source criticism influenced and shaped each other, as German scholars were attempting to cut their moorings from their Catholic past, with deep roots in Judaism and the Old Testament, and to seek a home elsewhere in ancient Rome and Greece. In so doing, they reconfigured their view of Christianity, not as flowing out of the Semitic ancient Near Eastern world, but as at its core Indo-European, which these scholars began to call Aryan.[25] Ancient Rome, Greece, and these scholars' own mythic pagan German past, became the new virtuous model on which to build a prosperous future.

Such scholarship culminated in the studies of Julius Wellhausen in the period just before and after Bismarck's anti-Catholic *Kulturkampf* ("culture war"). Many of the moves made within biblical studies, which soon became viewed as unquestioned starting points, as the assured results of "objective" scholarship, received their classical formulation in this period, in the wake of the First Vatican Council's definition of papal infallibility in 1870, and thus they represent the response of increasingly anti-clerical states to the Catholic Church. Judaism was denigrated as a symbol of Catholicism wherein Old Testament priesthood and modern Jewish traditions were viewed as representative of Catholic priests and Catholic traditions.[26]

The Politics of Modernism

As the twentieth century was beginning to approach its close, Edwin Yamauchi remarked that, "Catholic scholars are now accepting interpretations that were earlier proposed by antisupernatural critics of Christianity."[27] How this occurred is the story I wish to tell now. As we have seen, Catholics have been involved in the development of modern biblical criticism, at least as early as the medieval period with Marsilius and Ockham. Such scholarship, however, always remained on the fringe within the Catholic world, whereas it rapidly became dominant in the

---

25 Legaspi, *Death of Scripture*, 53–77; Tomoko Masuzawa, *The Invention of World Religions: Or, How European Universalism Was Preserved in the Language of Pluralism* (Chicago: University of Chicago, 2005), xii–xiii, 24–26, 145–206; Brian Vick, "Greek Origins and Organic Metaphors: Ideals of Cultural Autonomy in Neo-Humanist Germany from Winckelmann to Curtius," *Journal of the History of Ideas* 63:3 (2002): 483–500; and Suzanne Marchand, *Down from Olympus: Archaeology and Philhellenism in Germany, 1750–1970* (Princeton: Princeton University, 1996).

26 Michael B. Gross, *The War Against Catholicism: Liberalism and the Anti-Catholic Imagination in Nineteenth-Century Germany* (Ann Arbor: University of Michigan, 2004); William R. Farmer, "State *Interesse* [Interest] and Markan Primacy: 1870–1914," in *Biblical Studies and the Shifting of Paradigms, 1850–1914*, eds. Henning Graf Reventlow and William Farmer (Sheffield: Sheffield Academic Press, 1995), 15-49; and Arnaldo Momigliano, "Religious History Without Frontiers: J. Wellhausen, U. Wilamowitz, and E. Schwartz," *History and Theory* 21:4 (1982): 49–64.

27 Edwin M. Yamauchi, "The Episode of the Magi," in *Chronos, Kairos, Christos: Nativity and Chronological Studies Presented to Jack Finegan*, eds. Jerry Vardaman and Edwin M. Yamauchi (Winona Lake, Indiana: Eisenbrauns, 1989), 15–39, at 22.

Protestant world.[28] It was the modernists during the modernist crisis that brought such modern biblical hermeneutics into the heart of Catholic scholarship.

The scholarly assumptions of modernists like Loisy go back at least as far as Spinoza, and they pretended to be neutral and objective, that is, absent of prior commitments. This is not only false, but simply impossible. Such scholarship does not represent the absence of commitment, but rather the relocation of commitment.[29] This scholarship, devoid of traditional theological commitments, in fact represented state-sponsored biblical criticism.[30] Thus when anti-clerical violent revolutionaries appealed to the works of modernists like George Tyrrell, this made sense in the broader theo-political context.[31] The theoretical anti-Catholicism implied in such works was now made explicit in violent political action, as had already occurred centuries earlier with the Reformation and its violent liquidation of the monasteries.

The political context within the century leading up to the modernist crisis helps make the picture clearer. The early theological debate between throne and altar became a battle between the Church and ever more secular states in the modern period. States used their monopoly on coercive violence to remove Church lands from the public sphere, exile religious orders, and more. Portugal, Spain, Naples, Sicily, and France banned the Jesuits and deported them to the Papal States. In 1773 these states forced Pope Clement XIV to suppress the Jesuits, who were viewed as transnational since they circumvented the diocesan authority structures and were thus not under the direct control of state-appointed bishops.[32]

Within twenty years, Napoleon invaded the Papal States and compelled Pope Pius VI to agree to the Peace of Tolentino. On February 20, 1799, Napoleon's French soldiers captured Pius VI, who was deathly ill, and whisked him away to France where, six months later, he died as a prisoner. In 1801 Napoleon signed the Napoleonic Concordat with the Pope's successor Pius VII. Based on this Concordat, Pius VII reconstituted the hierarchy according to Napoleon's desires,

---

28   See Kugel's comment that, "It is no accident that, to this day, the great centers of modern biblical scholarship are to be found in largely Protestant countries—Germany and the Netherlands, Scandinavia and Great Britain, Canada and the United States." Kugel, *How to Read the Bible*, 28–29.

29   Jon D. Levenson, *The Hebrew Bible, the Old Testament, and Historical Criticism: Jews and Christians in Biblical Studies* (Louisville: Westminster/John Knox, 1993), 125.

30   Farmer, "State *Interesse*," 24.

31   William L. Portier, *Divided Friends: Portraits of the Roman Catholic Modernist Crisis in the United States* (New York: Paulist, forthcoming); and Paul Misner, "Social Modernism in Italy," in *Political and Social Modernism*, eds. Ronald Burke, Gary Lease, and George Gilmore (Mobile: Spring Hill College, 1988), 18–35.

32   Eamon Duffy, *Saints & Sinners: A History of the Popes*, 3rd. ed. (New Haven: Yale University, 2006 [1997]), 193–194, 203–204; and William L. Portier, "Church Unity and National Traditions: The Challenge to the Modern Papacy, 1682–1870," in *The Papacy and the Church in the United States*, ed. Bernard Cooke (New York: Paulist, 1989), 25–54.

and then crowned Napoleon emperor in France. After French troops occupied Rome, Napoleon asked Pius VII to give up his leadership of the Papal States. Pius VII refused, so Napoleon had his soldiers kidnap the Pope; he was only liberated when the Austrians forced Napoleon to abdicate his throne. Within his first three months back in Rome, Pius VII restored the Jesuits.

For the remainder of the nineteenth century, this political background leading up to the modernist crisis was a concern for both the magisterium as well as those espousing theological and philosophical views that would ultimately be condemned as modernist. In response to these threats, Pope Gregory XVI asked Austria to invade and occupy the Papal States. With the succession of Pius IX to the papal throne, the Piedmontese revolutionaries asked the Pope to join their forces in ousting the Austrians, which the Pope refused. In response, they assassinated the prime minister of the Papal States while he was in parliament. France entered the fray after the Austrians fled in fear of the Piedmontese. Vatican I ended early when the French left to fight the Prussians, leaving a vacuum in the Papal States that was filled by the Piedmontese who wrested the region from the Catholic Church.[33] This anti-clerical and anti-Catholic hostile political climate of the nineteenth century was in a very real sense the start of what would become known as the modernist crisis.

Some of the anti-modernist measures taken to stomp out modernism were overly harsh, in particular the clandestine operations of the semi-official group of theological censors known as the Sodalitium Pianum, or the Fellowship of Pius X. Pope Benedict XV, himself once suspected of being a modernist along with Pope John XXIII, ultimately suppressed this organization.[34] Marvin O'Connell's description of the Sodalitium Pianum's head, Umberto Benigni, as "sinister" and as "spy-master of a ragtag crew of informers and fanatics" is on target.[35] Their anonymous denunciations of Catholic professors, regardless of whether or not they were in fact modernists, created a climate of hostility and even terror throughout Europe and the United States. Pope Benedict XVI's reflections on this time period show that he is deeply saddened by the ways in which his own professors were hurt during this conflict. When he was still Prefect for the

---

33   Gary Lease, "Vatican Foreign Policy and the Origins of Modernism," in *Catholicism Contending with Modernity: Roman Catholic Modernism and Anti-Modernism in Historical Context*, ed. Darrell Jodock (Cambridge: Cambridge University, 2000), 31–55.

34   Portier, *Divided Friends*; Marvin R. O'Connell, *Critics on Trial: An Introduction to the Catholic Modernist Crisis* (Washington, DC: Catholic University of America, 1994), 321, 341, 348 n. 68, 361–365; and Émile Poulat, *Intégrisme et Catholicisme Intégral: Un Réseau Secret International Antimoderniste: La 'Sapinière' (1909–1921)* [Integralism and Integral Catholicism: A Secret International Anti-modernist Network: The "Piney Wood" (1909-1921)] (Paris: Casterman, 1969).

35   O'Connell, *Critics on Trial*, 361. O'Connell writes further that, "No one was safe. ... The files of the sodality eventually bulged with the names of such alleged malefactors, whose guilt was maintained simply by the fact that they had been denounced," at 363.

Vatican's Congregation for the Doctrine of the Faith, he wrote: "The danger of a narrow-minded and petty surveillance is no figment of the imagination, as the history of the modernist controversy demonstrates."[36] Despite the unfair and at times unchristian response to supposed modernism, however, the Church was undeniably threatened by modernism.

The case of Loisy is particularly instructive since he was the paradigmatic modernist. Loisy is the infamous Bible scholar who, in his *L'Évangile et l'Église* ("The Gospel and the Church") quipped that, "Jesus announced the Kingdom and what arrived was the Church."[37] Loisy's scholarship was not politically disinterested; in fact, political intrigue looms large behind much of his work. While writing his *L'Évangile et l'Église*, Loisy was lobbying to become a bishop. The anti-Catholic Prince of Monaco was attempting to get Loisy elected as bishop of Monaco. Of course the plan failed, but Loisy worked hard at rallying support for the position.[38]

Catholic Magisterial Teaching as a Response to Modernism

Long before Loisy was on the Vatican's radar, Pope Pius IX had called the First Vatican Council. The Council intended not only to resolve theological issues, but also to resolve the political problems that were inextricable from such theological issues. The clearest example is the document *Pastor Aeternus*, with its declarations on the authority of the papacy.[39] The theological issue involved whether ultimate authority rested with a council of bishops or with the pope. The closely related political issue can be seen by the fact that the majority of the world's bishops were appointed by heads of state, and thus the call for a council of bishops to trump the pope was a thinly veiled attempt to subjugate the Church to the concerns of modern European states.

When it comes to magisterial teaching on Scripture, modernists like Loisy were often in view, even though they went unnamed. Throughout most of the Church's history, Scripture's divine inspiration was assumed and clearly taught, but there were no systematic treatises on Scriptural inspiration. However, "the growing climate of intellectual skepticism," in the nineteenth century, first caused "the doctrine of inspiration" to be "subjected to serious examination."[40] The first

---

36   Joseph Cardinal Ratzinger, *The Nature and Mission of Theology: Essays to Orient Theology in Today's Debates*, trans. Adrian Walker (San Francisco: Ignatius Press, 1995 [1993]), 66.

37   Alfred Loisy, *L'Évangile et l'Église* [The Gospel and the Church] (Paris: A. Picard and Sons, 1902), 111.

38   Harvey Hill, "The Politics of Loisy's Modernist Theology," in *Catholicism Contending with Modernity*, 184–186; and Marvin R. O'Connell, "The Bishopric of Monaco, 1902: A Revision," *Catholic Historical Review* 71 (1985): 26–51.

39   First Vatican Council, *Pastor Aeternus* [The Eternal Pastor], Dogmatic Constitution on the Church of Christ (July 18, 1870), in *Decrees of the Ecumenical Councils*, vol. 1.

40   "Inspiration," in *Catholic Bible Dictionary*, ed. Scott Hahn (New York: Doubleday, 2009), 381–391, 383.

papal encyclical on Scripture was Pope Leo XIII's 1893 *Providentissimus Deus*, which, among other things, sought to counter specific trends in biblical criticism like Loisy's.[41] In the storm of the modernist crisis, Pius X issued his 1907 apostolic letter, *Lamentabili Sane*, clarifying Catholic teaching on divine inspiration against modernist attempts to limit inspiration.[42] In several magisterial documents, the Church continued to develop, hone, and clarify its dogmatic teaching on the dual authorship of Scripture, and on the unique divine inspiration that extends to every part of the sacred page: the Pontifical Biblical Commission's 1915 response to questions on the second coming of Christ in the letters of St. Paul; Pope Benedict XV's 1920 encyclical *Spiritus Paraclitus* ("The Holy Spirit the Comforter"); and Pope Pius XII's 1943 encyclical *Divino Afflante Spiritu* ("Inspired by the Divine Spirit"). These clarifications culminated in the Second Vatican Council's Dogmatic Constitution on Divine Revelation, *Dei Verbum* ("The Word of God"). Ironically, the birth of the biblical question in the modernist controversy is what necessitated the Church's clarification and detailed examination of the closely related questions of biblical interpretation and biblical inspiration.[43]

The Current Crisis in Biblical Interpretation

The hermeneutical problems identified in the modernist crisis are still with us. The abuses remain, as is evident in classrooms across the Catholic world. Unfortunately, the history has been misinterpreted and these misinterpretations have become the standard revised histories through which important teachings, such as contained in *Dei Verbum*, have been interpreted. Some trends within Catholic biblical scholarship have downplayed traditional patristic and medieval forms of exegesis, particularly typology, where Old Testament texts are read in light of their full flowering in the New Testament. The overwhelming majority of contemporary Catholic biblical interpretation in the academy virtually ignores magisterial teaching on Scripture's divine inspiration.[44] Since the focus of Catholic biblical scholarship leans heavily in the historical-critical direction, Scripture's hu-

---

41   Claus Arnold, "'Lamentabili Sane Exitu' (1907): Das Römische Lehramt und die Exegese Alfred Loisys" ["'Lamentabili Sane Exitu' (1907): Roman Teaching and the Exegesis of Alfred Loisy"], *Zeitschrift für Neuere Theologiegeschichte* 11:1 (2004): 24–51; and Harvey Hill, "Leo XIII, Loisy, and the 'Broad School': An Early Round of the Modernist Crisis," *Catholic Historical Review* 89:1 (2003): 40.

42   Pope St. Pius X, *Lamentabili Sane* [With Truly Lamentable Results], Syllabus Condemning the Errors of the Modernists (July 3, 1907), in *On the Doctrines of the Modernists, Pascendi Dominici Gregis: Encyclical Letter; and Syllabus Condemning the Errors of the Modernists, Lamentabili Sane* (Boston: St. Paul Editions, 1980).

43   For complete texts, see *The Scripture Documents: An Anthology of Official Catholic Teachings*, ed. Dean P. Béchard (Collegeville, MN: Liturgical Press, 2002).

44   On the Church's teaching on biblical inspiration, see Brant Pitre, "Catholic Doctrine on Scripture: Inspiration, Inerrancy, and Interpretation," in *The Sacred Text: Excavating the Texts, Exploring the Interpretations, and Engaging the Theologies of the Christian Scriptures*, eds. Michael Bird and Michael Pahl (Piscataway, NJ: Gorgias, 2010), 177–197.

man authorship tends to be the focus of such studies. But, like its modernist past, much of contemporary Catholic biblical scholarship implicitly calls into question magisterial teaching on the dual authorship of Scripture.

What has transpired is that the Catholic biblical scholarly guild has made its own the modern mythology of methodological neutrality to which the modernists subscribed.[45] As with the modern academic discipline of history, modern Catholic biblical scholarship in general tends to operate under the false assumption that the methods used are comparable to the laboratory methodology of the hard sciences like chemistry and physics.[46] Geometric reason and the discipline of mathematics, with its language of "proof," remains the paradigmatic example of rationality to many Bible scholars, Catholic or otherwise. Postmodern thought, now widespread in all humanities disciplines, simply takes farther the very modern project it seeks to transcend.[47]

In the retelling of the history of Catholic biblical scholarship, the modernists are cast as the heroes, and Church authorities such as Pope St. Pius X are the villains. Most of the actual historians of the modernist controversy are very careful historians who have done extremely valuable and important work in helping to shed light on a number of contextual matters that are essential in gaining an understanding of the events that transpired. Yet, even among such historians we find prejudicial exaggerations, for example, the description of Loisy as "among Roman Catholic biblical scholars the only one of outstanding distinction."[48]

Pope Benedict XVI has become one of the most significant voices in this discussion. In his programmatic 1989 essay on "Biblical Interpretation in Conflict," he pointed out the dangers of the failure to recognize and critique the philosophical positions giving life to various biblical hermeneutics. Modern biblical criticism styles itself on the hard sciences with a façade of neutrality and objectivity, but, as Benedict points out, even the hard sciences are bereft of a purely neutral objectivity. And yet, we cannot simply return to pre-modern biblical interpretation as if the historical-critical method was never created. Nor can we turn a blind eye to our

---

45   See Harvey Hill, "Henri Bergson and Alfred Loisy: On Mysticism and the Religious Life," in *Modernists and Mystics*, ed. C. J. T. Talar (Washington, DC: Catholic University of America, 2009), 104–136, at 120, where he writes that, "Loisy had insisted historical scholarship be free of theological or philosophical presuppositions and instead rely on those facts that historians could ascertain based on the available evidence. Philosophy and theology followed from history, in his view, not the reverse."

46   Constantin Fasolt, "History and Religion in the Modern Age," *History and Theory* 45 (2006): 10–26; Constantin Fasolt, "Red Herrings: Relativism, Objectivism, and Other False Dilemmas," *Storia della Storiografia* 48 (2005): 17–26; Constantin Fasolt, *The Limits of History* (Chicago: University of Chicago, 2004); and Peter Novick, *That Noble Dream: The "Objectivity Question" and the American Historical Profession* (Cambridge: Cambridge University, 1988).

47   David L. Schindler, *Heart of the World, Center of the Church: Communio Ecclesiology, Liberalism, and Liberation* (Grand Rapids, MI: Eerdmans, 1996).

48   Lawrence Barmann, "The Pope and the English Modernists," *U.S. Catholic Historian* 25:1 (2007): 31–54, at 40.

rich heritage in the patristic and medieval interpretive traditions. Rather, what we need to do is use the best of both traditional biblical exegetical traditions and of modern historical interpretation.[49] The guide to any such *ressourcement* ("return to the sources") has to be the Church's Tradition and magisterium so that the Bible is studied and read from the heart of the Church. This requires not only a hermeneutic of faith, as opposed to the Cartesian hermeneutic of skepticism that lies at the heart of modern biblical criticism, but also a hermeneutic of continuity. Pope Benedict XVI has shown us what this looks like in his seminal work, *Jesus of Nazareth.*[50]

The Mystery of Dual Authorship[51]

One of the fears modern Catholic Bible scholars apparently have is the eclipse of historical biblical interpretation. The magisterium has again and again stressed the importance of the literal sense of Scripture, of reading the Bible within its proper historical context. There should be no talk of the death of the historical-critical method if by such method is meant a scholarly historical study of Scripture. At their best, however, these methods are pre-theological and have very firm limits in what they can actually teach us. Too often contemporary exegetes make claims which far outreach the capabilities of the methods they employ.

What needs to return to Catholic biblical scholarship is something that was prominent in the work of Catholic exegetes prior to the modernist crisis, namely, the firm conviction that reason must be purified by faith. In the words of *Dei Filius* from the First Vatican Council, "faith is above reason." There are several explanations for this. One is that, in the words of the Council, "faith delivers reason from errors and protects it and furnishes it with knowledge of many kinds." But ultimately, as *Dei Filius* makes clear, "reason is never rendered capable of penetrating these mysteries in the way in which it penetrates those truths which form its proper object. For the divine mysteries, by their very nature, so far surpass the created understanding."[52]

Historical criticism is certainly indispensible, but it is not more indispensible than the Catholic doctrine of the divine inspiration of sacred Scripture. If anything, the mystery of the dual authorship of Scripture is more important than historical criticism, or any modern form of exegesis. Negatively this is because of historical criticism's limits, but positively it is also because of the implications

---

49 Paul T. Stallsworth, "The Story of an Encounter," in Richard John Neuhaus, ed., *Biblical Interpretation in Crisis: The Ratzinger Conference on Bible and Church* (Grand Rapids: Eerdmans, 1989), 107–108; and Ratzinger, "Biblical Interpretation in Conflict," 91–126.

50 Pope Benedict XVI, *Jesus of Nazareth: From the Baptism in the Jordan to the Transfiguration* (New York: Doubleday, 2007).

51 "Inspiration," in *Catholic Bible Dictionary*, 384.

52 First Vatican Council, *Dei Filius* [The Son of God], Dogmatic Constitution on the Catholic Faith (April 24, 1870), Chap. 4, in *Decrees of the Ecumenical Councils*, vol. 1.

of divine inspiration. Historical criticism by definition cannot demonstrate the mysteries of faith, and those sacred mysteries are of the utmost importance for Catholic biblical interpretation. Furthermore, the Church's teaching concerning the divine inspiration of sacred Scripture calls for an interpretation that does not exclusively rely on historical criticism. The Church's teaching that God is the primary author of Scripture imposes a hermeneutic of faith and of continuity on the biblical exegete.[53]

In this brief article we have taken a look at the roots of the modernist crisis in the Catholic Church at the end of the nineteenth century and at the dawn of the twentieth century. I argued that at its heart, the modernist controversy was not only fundamentally about the biblical question, but also gave birth to the biblical question in the Catholic world. Moreover, the issues involved in early twentieth century modernism have not left us; they remain in the contemporary debate over the future of Catholic biblical scholarship. It has been my goal to emphasize how the Church's teaching on the divine inspiration of Scripture demands a hermeneutic of faith and of continuity. Only by such a hermeneutic, which relies upon the best current methods of interpretation, and the best of the past, engaged in from the heart of the Church, can move us forward positively in reading and living the Scriptures as Catholics. All Catholic biblical exegesis should be oriented toward mystagogical exegesis; exegesis that draws us into participation in the divine liturgy where we become divinized. That is the ultimate goal of reading and studying Scripture.[54]

---

53 For a programmatic discussion of what such a biblical interpretation can look like see Scott W. Hahn, *Covenant and Communion: The Biblical Theology of Pope Benedict XVI* (Grand Rapids, MI: Brazos, 2009); Scott W. Hahn, "Worship in the Word: Toward a Liturgical Hermeneutic," *Letter & Spirit* 1 (2005): 101–136; and Scott Hahn, *Letter and Spirit: From Written Text to Living Word in the Liturgy* (New York: Doubleday, 2005).

54 I owe a debt of gratitude to a number of scholars for assistance at various stages of this project: William Portier for providing me with his work prior to publication, and for helping me see clearly the role of politics behind modern biblical criticism; Fr. Pablo Gadenz for providing me with resources and for numerous fruitful conversations on this topic; Timothy Furry for pointing me to the work of Constantin Fasolt; Michael Legaspi, Biff Rocha, and Michael Barber for fruitful conversations and correspondence on this topic; Brant Pitre for providing me with his own work prior to publication; Maria Morrow for her insightful comments and critiquing drafts of this manuscript; and finally Scott Hahn and Benjamin Wiker not only for important conversations on this topic but especially for providing me with drafts of their work tentatively entitled *The Bible Politicized* from which I learned a great deal, especially pertaining to Averroes, Marsilius, Ockham, Machiavelli, and Locke.

Letter & Spirit 6 (2010): 281-314

THE INSPIRATION OF SCRIPTURE
A *Status Quaestionis*

❧ Matthew Levering ☙

University of Dayton

This essay examines a representative sampling of recent literature on the doctrine of inspiration. My essay is divided into four sections. The first section summarizes briefly James Burtchaell's 1969 monograph *Catholic Theories of Biblical Inspiration Since 1810*. Burtchaell's book does two things: it displays the enormous intellectual effort that Catholic scholars put into trying to understand biblical inspiration, and it argues that inspiration has been vastly overblown. The book is thus helpful not only for surveying Catholic positions on this topic from 1810–1965, but also for appreciating why so little has been done since 1969 by Catholic scholars. The second section explores contemporary evangelical Protestant positions on inspiration, because debate about the doctrine (and the related doctrine of inerrancy) has continued and even intensified in recent decades among evangelical Protestants. I set the stage in this second section by summarizing the position of the nineteenth-century Princeton theologian B. B. Warfield, which remains influential, and then I turn to some important interventions from the early 1980s and from the 2000s.

The third section identifies the Second Vatican Council's Dogmatic Constitution on Divine Revelation, *Dei Verbum*, as a promising point of departure for contemporary Catholic reflection on inspiration. I argue that *Dei Verbum* exhibits the fruitfulness of the 1810–1965 period, by means of the identification of central principles that the doctrine of inspiration should affirm (even if *Dei Verbum* is unable to resolve the contested details). I also examine the *Catechism of the Catholic Church* (1994), which follows *Dei Verbum* while emphasizing spiritual exegesis, and the Pontifical Biblical Commission's "The Interpretation of the Bible in the Church" (1993), which sidelines the doctrine of inspiration. Lastly, the fourth section describes the approaches of two contemporary scholars who are attempting to reinvigorate the nearly dormant Catholic discussion of inspiration: Denis Farkasfalvy and Scott Hahn. These authors agree upon the importance of inspiration for Scripture's quasi-sacramental function, but they disagree about inspiration's relationship to inerrancy, among other matters.

A Once Vibrant Theological Discussion

Although dated by its late-1960s anti-authoritarian posture, Burtchaell's *Catholic Theories of Biblical Inspiration Since 1810* includes a wealth of scholarly reportage. Among the extraordinary range of scholars whose views on biblical inspiration Burtchaell surveys, we might note here the Jesuits Giovanne Perrone, Joseph

Kleutgen, Johann Baptist Franzelin, Louis Billot, Augustin Bea, Roderick MacKenzie, John McKenzie, Karl Rahner, Norbert Lohfink, Luis Alonso-Schökel, and René Latourelle; the Dominicans Thomas Pègues, Marie-Joseph Lagrange, Vincent McNabb, Paul Synave, Pierre Benoit, and Yves Congar; and other well-known figures such as Johann Sebastian von Drey, Johann Adam Möhler, Johann Evangelist von Kuhn, John Henry Newman, Heinrich Denzinger, John Acton, Friedrich von Hügel, Alfred Loisy, and George Tyrrell. Burtchaell's conclusion registers disappointment: "I am first of all led to feel that this has been an unhappy controversy. There was far too much ink spilled upon it; too many men struggled for too many years to such meagre advantage. ... Scant parturition has come forth from so many mountains in labor."[1] Burtchaell blames the usual suspects: deference to ecclesial authority, acceptance of biblical inerrancy, and failure to appreciate that God and humans are not competitive causes.[2]

In setting forth his constructive position on inspiration, Burtchaell emphasizes ambiguity, development of doctrine, and the claim that "no ancient statement or document ever quite puts forth the truth adequately for contemporary needs."[3] Doctrines of infallibility or inerrancy should be understood dynamically rather than statically, so as to allow the Church room to maneuver. Burtchaell describes the Bible as "the chief record of the faith's gestation," and the documents that comprise it are those that were found to serve the liturgical use of the community and to help the community define itself over against competing communities.[4] Eventually, as he explains it, the biblical canon arose as the collection of "those past writings which represent the mainstream of development from Abraham to Christ, and through Christ to wherever a particular Church stood."[5] The various texts of the Bible record the religious situation of believers at various eras and the paths open to believers in these eras. Ultimately these canonized texts trace the "route from paganism to Christ," and in this dynamic way they "inerrantly" display "the ability, not to avoid all mistakes, but to cope with them, remedy them, survive them, and eventually even profit from them."[6] Burtchaell concludes with the following definition of biblical inspiration:

> Inspiration is a charism that in no way interferes with a man's methods or mind as he writes or edits, but causes that he produce a composition which, in combination with others, can

---

1   James Tunstead Burtchaell, *Catholic Theories of Biblical Inspiration Since 1810: A Review and Critique* (Cambridge: Cambridge University, 1969), 281.

2   Burtchaell, *Catholic Theories*, 281.

3   Burtchaell, *Catholic Theories*, 296.

4   Burtchaell, *Catholic Theories*, 301.

5   Burtchaell, *Catholic Theories*, 303.

6   Burtchaell, *Catholic Theories*, 303.

serve the Church with an undeviating, or inerrant, reflection of how the faith grew from nothing to Christ.[7]

This definition raises numerous questions: Why would a "charism" of inspiration be needed for humans over the ages to write such texts? How could such texts err if all they do is to document the development of religious belief over time, culminating in belief in Jesus? If the charism of inspiration merely ensures that a set of texts emerges that faithfully records the development of religious opinion among some groups of educated Jews, then "inspiration" is extrinsic indeed, and the "inspiration" of the Bible consists simply in that its path ends with the earliest believers in Jesus. The Bible would have God as its "author" only in the sense that God ensured that the biblical record, despite its twists and turns, ended with testimony to faith in Jesus. Only the texts about Jesus would be directly related to Christian faith today. The other parts would be relevant for teaching us how to rise gradually from false worship. The Old Testament thereby loses much of its place as Christian Scripture. Indeed, Burtchaell's proposal exemplifies the "scant parturition" about which he complains.[8]

On the grounds that the antecedents of post-Vatican II "liberal theology" are found in the creative but suppressed theological work of the nineteenth century, however, Burtchaell argues that "one glaring fault of the contemporary discussion is precisely its deracination from the past."[9] The desire to fill this lacuna explains his detailed historical survey. I will summarize briefly the leading theories of inspiration that Burtchaell documents.

He begins with the "Tübingen School" of the early nineteenth century. Drey and Möhler conceived of inspiration as a charism that ensured that the authors of Scripture, and the Church as a whole, would find the right words by which to communicate the ideas that God sought to teach. Each human mind reshapes what it learns, so as to communicate this learning to others. Divine inspiration elevates the human mind for the task of communicating divine truth. Their student Franz Anton Staudenmaier takes this further by arguing that only the doctrinal

---

7   Burtchaell, *Catholic Theories*, 304.

8   As Robert Jenson, correcting his previous avoidance of the doctrine of inspiration, observes: "Christian exegesis of the Bible, and specifically of the Old Testament, does not itself work without something like the old doctrine of inspiration. … It was—I have now come to see—a function of the old doctrine of inspiration to trump the created author and first readers with a prior agent, the Spirit, and prior readers, the whole diachronic people of God, preserved as one people through time by that same Spirit." "A Second Thought about Inspiration," *Pro Ecclesia* 13 (2004): 393–398, at 393, 396. Lacking the agency of the Holy Spirit uniting the people of God over the centuries, reading the Old Testament christologically seems eisegetical—in which case, as Jenson says, "we should, in my judgment, acknowledge what our modern uneasiness suggests, and openly do what we have long done covertly: use the Old Testament not really as Scripture but as religious 'background' for the New Testament"; at 396. This is in fact what Burtchaell does.

9   Burtchaell, *Catholic Theories*, 304.

teachings of Scripture are inspired. Similarly, another student of theirs, Johann Evangelist von Kuhn, argues that while the content and essence of Scripture are divine, the matter and form are human. The position of these thinkers differs from earlier Catholic doctrines of inspiration, such as the view that inspiration consists in divine assistance and preservation from error, the view that a book can become inspired Scripture upon receiving the Church's later approval, and the view that the Holy Spirit supplied each word of the Scriptures to the human writers.

Burtchaell gives significant attention to Blessed John Henry Newman, the best known representative of the "partial inspiration" theory, according to which only Scripture's doctrinal and moral teachings are inspired.[10] This view is rejected in Pope Leo XIII's encyclical *Providentissimus Deus* (1893).[11] The mid-nineteenth century was dominated by a view of biblical inspiration that found its ablest exponent in the Jesuit Johann Baptist Franzelin and that Burtchaell calls "content inspiration." According to this view, God inspires the human authors so that they teach the saving truths (*res et sententiae*) that he wishes to communicate: "God has

---

10   For a fuller account of Newman's theology of Scripture, see Jeffrey W. Barbeau, "Newman and the Interpretation of Inspired Scripture," *Theological Studies* 63 (2002): 53–67; Jaak Seynaeve, *Cardinal Newman's Doctrine on Holy Scripture According to His Published Works and Previously Unedited Manuscripts* (Louvain: Publications Universitaires, 1953).

11   Leo XIII teaches that "it is absolutely wrong and forbidden either to narrow inspiration to certain parts only of Holy Scripture or to admit that the sacred writer has erred. As to the system of those who, in order to rid themselves of these difficulties, do not hesitate to concede that divine inspiration regards the things of faith and morals, and nothing beyond, because (as they wrongly think) in a question of the truth or falsehood of a passage we should consider not so much what God has said as the reason and purpose which he had in mind in saying it—this system cannot be tolerated. For all the books which the Church receives as sacred and canonical are written wholly and entirely, with all their parts, at the dictation of the Holy Spirit; and so far is it from being possible that any error can coexist with inspiration, that inspiration not only is essentially incompatible with error, but excludes and rejects it as absolutely and necessarily as it is impossible that God himself, the supreme Truth, can utter that which is not true. This is the ancient and unchanging faith of the Church, solemnly defined in the Councils of Florence and of Trent, and finally confirmed and more expressly formulated by the Council of the Vatican. These are the words of the last: 'The books of the Old and New Testament, whole and entire, with all their parts, as enumerated in the decree of the same Council (Trent) and in the ancient Latin Vulgate, are to be received as sacred and canonical. And the Church holds them as sacred and canonical not because, having been composed by human industry, they were afterwards approved by her authority; nor only because they contain revelation without errors, but because, having been written under the inspiration of the Holy Spirit, they have God for their author.' Hence, because the Holy Spirit employed men as his instruments, we cannot, therefore, say that it was these inspired instruments who, perchance, have fallen into error, and not the primary author. For, by supernatural power, he so moved and impelled them to write— he so assisted them when writing—that the things which he ordered, and those only, they, first, rightly understood, then willed faithfully to write down, and finally expressed in apt words and with infallible truth. Otherwise, it could not be said that he was the author of the entire Scripture." Pope Leo XIII, *Providentissimus Deus* [The God of All Providence], Encyclical Letter on the Study of Scripture (November 18, 1893), 20, in *The Scripture Documents: An Anthology of Official Catholic Teachings*, ed. Dean P. Béchard (Collegeville, MN: Liturgical Press, 2002), 37–62.

supplied the formal components of the sacred books on his sole responsibility."[12] God assists rather than inspires the human authors as regards the "material" components of Scripture, that is, the words and expressions (*signa, verba*) that do not directly impinge upon the saving truths. This position gives significance to the cultural milieu and human creativity of the biblical authors, while affirming God's authorship (by inspiring and assisting) of the entire Scriptures.

After the publication of Leo XIII's encyclical on Christian philosophy, *Aeterni Patris* (1879),[13] another view of biblical inspiration emerged, one that is most closely associated with Marie-Joseph Lagrange's early work on the topic and that Burtchaell describes as "plenary inspiration." Indebted to Aquinas's theory of instrumental causality, Lagrange argues that since the human author and God are non-competitive causes, both are fully authors of Scripture. There is no need, therefore, to distinguish God's sole responsibility for Scripture's truths from the human author's contributions. All Scripture is inspired, because God inspires the human author without compromising the human author's freedom and historicity. God wills to teach what the human author wills to teach. In willing to teach something as true, the human author makes a judgment of truth; thanks to God's inspiration, this judgment is infallible. Frequently, however, the human author presents material without making a judgment of truth. In such cases, inspiration ensures that the material is suitable for the particular purpose that the human author intends. In the years before Vatican II, Lagrange's position is extended by Pierre Benoit, especially with respect to distinguishing between the biblical author's speculative and practical judgment (the intention to teach something as true requires only the former).

In later work for which he incurred ecclesial sanction, Lagrange suggests that the Old Testament is largely a record of primitive and transitional beliefs rather than true teaching inspired by God. Among the leading figures of the modernist crisis, von Hügel understands Scripture as witnessing to the progressive development of understanding that continues in the Church. Even Jesus' teaching, von Hügel thinks, is marred by its cultural limitations. For his part, Loisy, prior to his excommunication in 1908, repudiates the view that God is the author of Scripture except for in the sense that God is the author of all things. Loisy supposes that to grant that God is the author of Scripture is to establish Scripture as the norm of human reason and thereby to place an ancient and largely mythological roadblock in the way of human intellectual progress.

---

12   Burtchaell, *Catholic Theories*, 99.

13   Pope Leo XIII, *Aeterni Patris* [The Eternal Father], Encyclical Letter on the Restoration of Christian Philosophy (August 4, 1879), in *Restoration of Christian Philosophy* (New York: Pauline, 1997).

Burtchaell describes a variety of positions set forth in the late 1950s and the 1960s. In his *Inspiration in the Bible*,[14] Karl Rahner focuses the doctrine of inspiration not on the human authors but on the Church. The first generation of the Church has the task of producing the norm of faith for all future generations. Only this first generation possesses the power to accept or reject writings as testifying to Christ. The Scriptures of Israel are not definitively inspired until they are accepted by the apostolic Church as witnessing to the Church's authentic "prehistory and prefaith."[15] In his founding of the Church, and not before, God is the author of the books of Holy Scripture. Inspiration thus has to do with the final form of the Church's faith rather than with the Holy Spirit's presence to individual authors in the process by which they teach saving truth.

Yves Congar responds to Rahner by emphasizing that the apostolic Church receives rather than constitutes the Scriptures. The apostles receive mission and authority from Christ, and their writings participate in their personal charism. The Church's faith is inconceivable absent the work of the Holy Spirit in and through the apostles and prophets, and so it would be a mistake to associate inspiration solely with the apostolic Church's certification of the whole Bible as the definitive record of her faith.

With regard to the relationship of inspiration and inerrancy, the views of two contemporaries of Rahner and Congar deserve mention. Norbert Lohfink argues that inerrancy belongs not to authors or books but to the whole Bible, which, when read as a whole (the Old Testament in light of the New), expresses the truth that God wills to convey to humankind. Luis Alonso Schökel holds that earlier theories of inspiration focused too strictly upon propositional truth. Just as we come to know a person by becoming familiar with the variety of his or her modes of self-expression, so too the inerrant truth of the Bible becomes known to us not through propositional fragments but through the dialogic reality of the literary whole. This emphasis on personal disclosure, on encounter with God, and on the inability of propositions to exhaust the mystery of revelation appears, Burtchaell observes, in a number of other authors publishing on this topic in the 1960s.[16]

The Evangelical Protestant Debate

In his writings on biblical inspiration, B. B. Warfield emphasizes that for the authors of the New Testament as well as in the view of Jesus himself, the Holy Spirit is the primary author of Scripture whose relationship to the human authors is one of "concursive" action. The inspiration of the human authors and the inspiration

---

14   Karl Rahner, *Inspiration in the Bible*, trans. Charles Henkey and Martin Pamer, 2nd ed. (New York: Herder and Herder, 1964).

15   Burtchaell, *Catholic Theories*, 253.

16   See also Maurice Blondel, "History and Dogma," in Blondel, *The Letter on Apologetics & History and Dogma*, ed. and trans. Alexander Dru and Illtyd Trethowan (Grand Rapids, MI: Eerdmans, 1994), 221–287, esp. 280–281.

of their writings are two sides of the same coin, because the words of Scripture are "the utterances of the Holy Ghost," who is the "responsible author" of every word.[17] Thus Scripture is "the Word of God in such a sense that whatever it says God says."[18] It follows that Scripture is inerrant and trustworthy in all particulars. Warfield criticizes efforts to distinguish between inspired and uninspired words of Scripture, and he also rejects the position, arising from Schleiermacher, that only those words are from God which resonate with the interior spiritual consciousness of the believer. In Warfield's view, it is clear that "the writers of the New Testament books looked upon what they called 'Scripture' as divinely safeguarded in even its verbal expression, and as divinely trustworthy in all its parts, in all its elements, and in all its affirmations of whatever kind."[19] Warfield holds, in short, that the first task is to understand "the doctrine of inspiration taught by the Bible as applicable to itself" and then test this doctrine by inquiring into the accuracy of the books of Scripture, where the doctrine will be found vindicated.[20]

I move from Warfield's writings to two books published by notable evangelical scholars in 1982, during a period that saw a flurry of evangelical scholarship on this topic. In his *Biblical Inspiration*, I. Howard Marshall begins, like Warfield, by arguing that the New Testament authors and Jesus consider the Scriptures to be the authoritative Word of God. He then describes seven ways of understanding the meaning of biblical "inspiration": the prophetic or dictation theory of inspiration; the view that Scripture is merely human eloquence; the view that the Bible is inspired only where it is spiritually inspiring; the view that the Bible is simply the

---

17 Benjamin Breckinridge Warfield, *The Inspiration and Authority of the Bible*, ed. Samuel G. Craig (Phillipsburg, NJ: Presbyterian and Reformed Publishing, 1948), 295. See the somewhat different edition of this book published as *Revelation and Inspiration* (Oxford: Oxford University, 1927).

18 Warfield, *Inspiration and Authority*, 106. Warfield remarks in passing, "The allegorical interpretation which rioted in the early days of the Church was the daughter of reverence for the biblical Word; a spurious daughter you may think, but none the less undeniably a direct offspring of the awe with which the sacred text was regarded as the utterances of God, and, as such, pregnant with inexhaustible significance"; at 109.

19 Warfield, *Inspiration and Authority*, 115.

20 Warfield, *Inspiration and Authority*, 223; compare at 222 where Warfield notes regarding inerrancy that "if in the midst of this marvel of general accuracy there remain here and there a few difficulties as yet not fully explained in harmony with it," one can reasonably assume that these difficulties will eventually be resolved. For a similar approach see Roger Nicole, "Induction and Deduction with Reference to Inspiration," in *Standing Forth: Collected Writings of Roger Nicole* (Fearn: Christian Focus, 2002), 151–158. See also Nicole's defense of Warfield (and of the Chicago Statement on Biblical Inerrancy). "The Inspiration and Authority of Scripture: J. D. G. Dunn versus B. B. Warfield," in *Standing Forth*, 159–222. Originally published in 1983, this essay responds to Dunn's "The Authority of Scripture According to Scripture," *Churchman* 96 (1982): 104–122, 201–225. Nicole's essay also includes a significant critique of the exegetical and theological positions that characterize Dunn's *Unity and Diversity in the New Testament: An Inquiry into the Character of Earliest Christianity* (London: SCM, 1975) and *Christology in the Making: A New Testament Inquiry into the Origins of the Doctrine of Incarnation* (Philadelphia: Westminster, 1980).

written record of divine revelation; the theory that this record of divine revelation becomes revelation for us when the Holy Spirit enables it to speak to us today (Karl Barth); the theory that the Holy Spirit inspires the gradual composition of the Bible rather than inspiring the biblical text itself (Paul J. Achtemeier);[21] the view that God inspires the human authors in the same way that a good teacher inspires his students to be able to spread his teachings in a broadly truthful but fallible manner (William J. Abraham); and the view that the Holy Spirit works concursively with the human authors in the literary process of the composition of the Scriptures (Warfield, J. I. Packer).

Marshall accepts this last position as the best one. He observes that "alongside and within this general concursive action of the Spirit in inspiring normal human forms of composition in the biblical books, we can trace special actions of the Spirit in bringing special revelations to prophets and apostles."[22] Beyond affirming this concursus, however, we cannot explain further the mysterious union of the two levels of agency. Marshall then explores whether inspiration requires

---

21 Marshall is commenting on the original 1980 edition of Achtemeier's book; a second edition appeared in 1999 as Paul J. Achtemeier, *Inspiration and Authority: Nature and Function of Christian Scripture* (Peabody, MA: Hendrickson, 1999). Indebted especially to G. C. Berkouwer's *Holy Scripture: Studies in Dogmatics* (Grand Rapids, MI: Eerdmans, 1975), Bruce Vawter's *Biblical Inspiration* (Philadelphia: Westminster, 1972), and Rahner's *Inspiration in the Bible*, Achtemeier rejects what he calls the "prophetic model" of inspiration, according to which "God inspired the author of a given book in the Bible to write down what God wanted written," with the result that Scripture is a unity because of the divine authorship (Achtemeier, *Inspiration and Authority*, 19; see also 25, 62–63, 85–89). In Achtemeier's view, the prophetic model has been discredited "by scholarly discoveries made over the past few decades about the way Scripture was produced" (at 63), specifically by the reality that "Church and Scripture grew up alongside each other—the traditions shaping the life of the Church, and the Church interpreting and reshaping the traditions in the light of its own proclamation of those traditions" (at 78), so that the Bible "reflects the life of the community of Israel and the primitive Church as those communities sought to come to terms with the central reality that God was present with them in ways that regularly outran their ability to understand or cope" (at 79; compare at 100–101). On the basis of the fact that some biblical books include words by numerous authors and redactors, Achtemeier holds that the model of inspired individual authors no longer works. After examining the various New Testament passages that are typically drawn upon to formulate the doctrine of biblical inspiration, Achtemeier locates "inspiration" largely in the community of faith and in the providential process by which the books were written and given final shape (at 102), while appreciating the role of those individuals who contributed "to the formulation and reformulation of tradition in specific situations" (at 116). As he puts it, "It is therefore in the interrelationship of the three components of Scripture—tradition, situation, and respondent—that the inspiration of Scripture is to be located. Inspiration thus describes more the process out of which our Scriptures grew than simply the final result in canonical form. This of course is not to disparage in any way that canonical form" (at 118–119). He goes on to define biblical inspiration "as the continuing presence of the Spirit with the community of faith as it preserved and renewed its traditions in response to the new situations into which God led it" (at 126). Taking issue with Marshall's formulation of Achtemeier's view, Achtemeier observes that "it is not the 'inspiredness of the resulting book' that is at issue ... but the inspiredness of what that book contains!" (at 125, n. 5).

22 I. Howard Marshall, *Biblical Inspiration* (London: Hodder and Stoughton, 1982), 43.

that Scripture be "inerrant" or only "infallible," that is, fully trustworthy for the saving purposes for which God inspired it. After providing a nuanced account of the ways in which biblical passages can be true (with attention to language and genre), he examines a set of exegetical problems that "inerrancy" faces. Can the trustworthiness of the Bible for accomplishing its saving purposes be affirmed without also affirming that the Bible has no historical errors? Although here he parts ways with Warfield and Packer, Marshall argues that "infallibility" occupies a salutary middle position between inerrancy and liberal skepticism, because Scripture's infallibility allows for some historical error but not for much.[23]

Marshall's position is in part a response to "The Chicago Statement on Biblical Inerrancy" set forth by the International Council of Biblical Inerrancy in 1978. The Chicago Statement teaches that Scripture is "without error or fault in all its teaching, no less in what it states about God's acts in creation, about the events of world history, and about its own literary origins under God, than in its witness to God's saving grace in individual lives."[24] This position is advocated by John Woodbridge in his *Biblical Authority*, published in the same year as Marshall's book. Woodbridge focuses upon refuting the historical claims made by the evangelical scholars Jack Rogers and Donald McKim in their *The Authority and Interpretation of the Bible*.[25] Somewhat like Marshall, Rogers and McKim suggest that the Bible possesses infallibility in matters pertaining to salvation but makes historical and scientific errors. On their view, the Bible is inerrant only in the sense that the biblical authors never intended to deceive.

In his book's introduction, Woodbridge comments, "Within the last two decades or so, evangelical Christians have become especially uneasy due to their

---

23 See also Stephen T. Davis, *The Debate about the Bible: Inerrancy versus Infallibility* (Philadelphia: Westminster, 1977), in which Davis, a philosopher of religion, defends biblical "infallibility." More recently, Davis describes his understanding of the Bible's truthfulness in the following manner: "We mean that our attitude toward the Bible is such that we believe what it says, we trust it, we lay ourselves open to it. We allow our rational structures and beliefs to be influenced by it. Such an attitude will include but not by any means be limited to accepting the truth (in the paradigmatic sense) of the assertions that we find in it. (What they are, obviously, will have to be interpreted.) It also means taking questions in the Bible ('Should we sin the more that grace may abound?') as legitimate and probing questions addressed to us. It also means taking biblical exhortations ('Give thanks to the Lord, for he is good') as exhortations addressed to us that we must heed. It also means taking poetic sections from the Bible ('We are his people, and the sheep of his pasture') as powerfully affective expressions of the way reality is." See Davis, "What Do We Mean When We Say, 'The Bible Is True'?" in *But Is It All True? The Bible and the Question of Truth*, ed. Alan G. Padgett and Patrick R. Keifert [Grand Rapids, MI: Eerdmans, 2006], 86–103, at 89–90. See also Kevin Vanhoozer, "Lost in Interpretation? Truth, Scripture, and Hermeneutics," *Journal of the Evangelical Theological Society* 48 (2005): 89–114.

24 Quoted in Marshall, *Biblical Inspiration*, 10. Marshall directs the reader to the text of the Chicago Statement as published in J. I. Packer, *God Has Spoken* (Downers Grove, IL: InterVarsity, 1979), 139–155.

25 Jack Rogers and Donald McKim, *The Authority and Interpretation of the Bible: An Historical Approach* (New York: Harper and Row, 1979).

growing awareness that scholars from their own ranks are proposing that the Bible is infallible for faith and practice but that it is susceptible to 'technical mistakes.'"[26] For Woodbridge, the trouble with the supposition that the Bible contains histori-cal and scientific errors is that it challenges God's authorship: God is truth, and so revelation that truly comes from God cannot be marred by errors. Rogers and McKim advance their argument by trying to show that historically—from the patristic and medieval periods through the Reformation, up until the rise of (ratio-nalistic) seventeenth-century Protestant scholasticism—Christians held biblical inspiration and "infallibility" but not biblical inerrancy. Rogers and McKim blame the nineteenth-century Princeton theologians, including Warfield, for contem-porary evangelicalism's emphasis on biblical inerrancy. In response, Woodbridge surveys the patristic, Reformation, Baroque, and nineteenth-century authors treated by Rogers and McKim, and Woodbridge finds that in fact they hold to the inerrancy and infallibility of all the words of Scripture.[27]

Evangelical Debate Today

This debate over inspiration and inerrancy continues today in evangelical scholar-ship. I will briefly survey four recent books plus one significant article: Peter Enns's *Inspiration and Incarnation: Evangelicals and the Problem of the Old Testament* (2005), N. T. Wright's *Scripture and the Authority of God* (2005), Craig Allert's *A High View of Scripture?: The Authority of the Bible and the Formation of the New Testament Canon* (2007), Stephen Chapman's "Reclaiming Inspiration for the Bible" (2006), and Ben Witherington III's *The Living Word of God: Rethinking the Theology of the Bible* (2007).

After describing modern biblical scholarship regarding the Old Testament, Peter Enns argues that the "conservative" evangelical response to this scholarship shares an assumption with modern disbelievers in the Bible's authority: namely, the assumption that "the Bible, being the Word of God, ought to be historically accurate in all its details (since God would not lie or make errors) and unique in its own setting (since God's Word is revealed, which implies a specific type of uniqueness)."[28] He argues that the lesson of the incarnation points in the opposite direction. Just as the incarnate Word is fully human, so also the biblical Word of God is fully human. God inspires the whole Bible in a way that allows for a diver-sity of portrayals of God. The Old Testament at times insists that there is only

---

26   John D. Woodbridge, *Biblical Authority: A Critique of the Rogers/McKim Proposal* (Grand Rapids, MI: Zondervan, 1982), 14; 20.

27   See also a related essay also originally published in 1982, Roger Nicole's "John Calvin and Inerrancy," in Nicole, *Standing Forth*, 103–132. Compare earlier historical studies such as Robert Preus, *The Inspiration of Scripture: A Study of the Theology of the Seventeenth Century Lutheran Dogmaticians* (Edinburgh: Oliver and Boyd, 1955).

28   Peter Enns, *Inspiration and Incarnation: Evangelicals and the Problem of the Old Testament* (Grand Rapids, MI: Baker Academic, 2005), 47; see also 17, 21.

one God, for example, while at other times it suggests that Israel's God is greater than the other gods. In a polytheistic world, the ancient Israelites's understanding of God developed in a human fashion, eventually arriving at the full affirmation of the truth that there is only one God, the Creator. Similarly, God allows the Bible to portray him at times as all-powerful and completely in charge, and at other times as grieving and changing his mind.

Enns affirms that "the Bible is God's Word, that it ultimately comes from him, that it is what the Spirit of God wanted it to be."[29] God inspires the Bible in a way that wills the human messiness of Scripture. Accommodating himself to our historical mode of existence, God reveals himself in a fully historical manner.[30] On this view, the Old Testament functions less as a source of timeless doctrine than as a witness to God's gradual self-revelation, culminating in Christ Jesus.[31] The unity of the Bible is found in Christ, since "it is to him that the Bible as a whole bears witness."[32] Indeed, the messiness or fully historical character of the books of the Old Testament bears witness to God's decision to become incarnate historically in Israel. The truth of the Old Testament, as a whole, appears not in its historical facts or its doctrines, but in the apostles's re-reading of the whole story in light of what God has done in Christ. The authors of the New Testament do not read the Scriptures with the goal of understanding the intended meaning of the original authors, but instead read them in light of extra-biblical traditions current in the Second-Temple period and with the purpose of showing that Christ and the Church bring the Old Testament story to completion. It is this completion, far more than a historical-critical recovery of the Old Testament's original facts and meanings, that reveals the inspired truth of the Old Testament.[33]

---

29 Enns, *Inspiration and Incarnation*, 108.

30 For related discussion of "accommodation," including its role in the Church Fathers, see Kenton L. Sparks, *God's Word in Human Words: An Evangelical Appropriation of Critical Biblical Scholarship* (Grand Rapids, MI: Baker Academic, 2008), 229–259. See also Nicholas Wolterstorff, *Divine Discourse: Philosophical Reflections on the Claim That God Speaks* (Cambridge: Cambridge University, 1995), 206–212; Achtemeier, *Inspiration and Authority*, 57–58.

31 See Enns, *Inspiration and Incarnation*, 67.

32 Enns, *Inspiration and Incarnation*, 110.

33 For a similar view see Achtemeier, *Inspiration and Authority*, 98. See also John Goldingay, *Models for Scripture* (Grand Rapids, MI: Eerdmans, 1994). Kenton Sparks extends and develops Enns's position, with which he agrees, in *God's Word in Human Words*. G. K. Beale offers an extended critique of Enns's position in Beale, *The Erosion of Inerrancy in Evangelicalism* (Wheaton, IL: Crossway, 2008), especially 25–122. See also, from a perspective in accord with Beale's, D. A. Carson's engagement with John Webster's *Holy Scripture*, Enns's *Inspiration and Incarnation*, and N. T. Wright's *The Last Word: Beyond the Bible Wars to a New Understanding of the Authority of Scripture* (New York: HarperCollins, 2005); Carson, "Three More Books on the Bible: A Critical Review," *Trinity Journal* 27 (2006): 1–62. Peter Leithart argues that Enns's position falls into a husk and kernel hermeneutics that fails to accord sufficient value to the letter of the text. Leithart proposes that the difficulties identified by Enns should instead prompt us to rediscover Jesus' and Paul's typological interpretation of Old Testament Scripture, on the grounds that texts are not timeless. For Leithart, the way forward is to recognize, with Jesus and

N. T. Wright explores the role of Scripture in God's accomplishment of his saving work. Wright warns against viewing Scripture as simply "conveying information" or as "divine self-communication" or a "record of revelation."[34] This view of Scripture imagines an absent God who seeks to give humanity a set of propositions about himself. Rather, Scripture depicts the living God who makes himself powerfully present in and with Israel, in order to heal and renew the entire creation through Christ Jesus and his Holy Spirit. The Bible belongs to this God's work of transforming us into a holy people who have a mission to the world. Although Wright's book is about what it means to speak about the Bible's authority in the context of the salvific authority of God, he notes that "some kind of divine inspiration of scripture was taken for granted in most of the ancient Israelite Scriptures themselves, as well as in the beliefs of the early Christians."[35] By his Spirit, God worked through the various authors and editors so as to bring about the books that God intended for his people. Wright explores the Old Testament understanding of the power of God's "Word" and of Israel's status as the hearers of God's Word. The "inner tensions and puzzles of the Old Testament" express the deeper tension of Israel as simultaneously bearing God's Word to the world and standing with the world under the judgment of God's Word. The Old Testament is not primarily a record of facts about the past, but instead is Israel's story of being called by God, a story set forth in various ways over the generations in service to Israel's mission.

In this sense, Scripture's "work" is accomplished definitively by Jesus Christ; he fulfills Israel's story and reorders it around himself, so as to bring it to the whole world. The relationship between the Old Testament and the New Testament is best understood not in terms of two sets of facts or propositions but in terms "of the entire storyline at last coming to fruition, and of an entire world of hints and shadows now coming to plain statement and full light."[36] The meaning of the Old Testament is revealed in Jesus. Jesus recognizes Scripture as authoritative because it is the story (the divine work) that he himself fulfills. His interlocutors recognize Scripture's authority in a more limited way, and so they fail to understand him when he speaks of Scripture's authority yet (for example) declares all foods clean. The New Testament authors understand that in writing about Jesus' fulfillment of Israel's story, they are writing "Scripture" in the sense of God's Word through which he transforms the world. They understand themselves to be living "under the *whole* Scripture" because Jesus' story is inseparable from that of Israel, as its

---

Paul (and the Fathers), that texts and events "say new things as they come into relationship with subsequent texts and events"; Leithart, *Deep Exegesis: The Mystery of Reading Scripture* (Waco, TX: Baylor University, 2009), 44; compare 67, 110–11, 138, 207–208.

34 Wright, *Last Word*, 30; compare 39.

35 Wright, *Last Word*, 37.

36 Wright, *Last Word*, 43. As Achtemeier says by way of relativizing the controversy over inspiration, "One gets the impression from Scripture that its chief task is to point away from itself to something or someone who is far more important." *Inspiration and Authority*, 92.

fulfillment.[37] Wright urges therefore that every part of Scripture (verse, chapter, book) be read in its biblical, historical, and canonical context. This awareness of context enables us to read the whole Scripture with appreciation for both its humanity and its divinity, the latter being its "inspiration." Wright suggests that so long as one keeps in mind that the comparison of Scripture's two dimensions with Jesus' two natures is an analogy, not a strict identity, the analogy proves helpful for understanding biblical inspiration and "the Spirit's power at work within the Bible-reading Church."[38]

Craig Allert takes up biblical inspiration in the context of his study of how the formation of the New Testament canon should shape our understanding of what Scripture is. Citing the trepidation with which Marshall entered into the debate over inspiration and inerrancy, Allert remarks that a "high view of Scripture" is often assumed to require the inerrancy of each and every word of Scripture (a "verbal plenary doctrine").[39] He connects this view with the position that the books in the biblical canon received their status when the apostles certified them as inspired. Regarding the formation of the canon, Allert argues that in fact the early Church did not conceive inspiration "to be the unique possession of only the documents that later came to be part of the New Testament canon. The Spirit was seen as living and active in the entire community of the faithful and therefore inspiring it."[40] The inspiration of the Church by the Holy Spirit cannot be separated from the inspiration of the canonical books of Scripture. In the final chapter of his book,

---

37   Wright, *Last Word*, 57.

38   Wright, *Last Word*, 130. Wright's approach is indebted to (among others) William J. Abraham, *Canon and Criterion in Christian Theology: From the Fathers to Feminism* (Oxford: Oxford University, 1998) and Telford Work, *Living and Active: Scripture in the Economy of Salvation* (Grand Rapids, MI: Eerdmans, 2002). See also David S. Yeago, "The Spirit, the Church, and the Scriptures: Biblical Inspiration and Interpretation Revisited," in *Knowing the Triune God: The Work of the Spirit in the Practices of the Church*, eds. James J. Buckley and David S. Yeago (Grand Rapids, MI: Eerdmans, 2001), 49–93, at 51 (compare 61–64, 70–71): "Over against *both* the hermeneutics of critical modernity *and* its inveterate foe, the Protestant doctrine of plenary verbal inspiration, this essay will suggest that classical scriptural interpretation proceeded from a rich and complex sense of Scripture's place and role within the economy of salvation; Scripture functions as a quasi-sacramental instrument of the Holy Spirit, through which the Spirit makes known the mystery of Christ in order to form the Church as a sign of his messianic dominion." Abraham's "canonical theism" likewise emphasizes the danger of viewing the canon of Scripture epistemologically rather than soteriologically. For Abraham's approach see also William J. Abraham, *The Divine Inspiration of Holy Scripture* (Oxford: Oxford University, 1981); Douglas M. Koskela, "The Authority of Scripture in Its Ecclesial Context," in *Canonical Theism: A Proposal for Theology and the Church*, eds. William J. Abraham, Jason E. Vickers, and Natalie B. Van Kirk (Grand Rapids, MI: Eerdmans, 2008), 210–223; and the concerns raised by Mark W. Elliott, *The Reality of Biblical Theology* (Bern: Peter Lang, 2007), 249–255.

39   Craig D. Allert, *A High View of Scripture? The Authority of the Bible and the Formation of the New Testament Canon* (Grand Rapids, MI: Baker Academic, 2007), 11.

40   Allert, *High View of Scripture*, 148. See also Achtemeier, *Inspiration and Authority*, 102–104.

therefore, he focuses on the implications of his view of canon formation for the doctrines of inspiration and inerrancy.

Aiming to critique positions such as Warfield's and Woodbridge's (especially their argument that God's truthfulness is at stake in the doctrine of inerrancy), Allert begins by examining what the Bible teaches about inspiration. Here he focuses in particular on 2 Timothy 3:15–17, 2 Peter 1:19–21, and John 10:35. With respect to 2 Timothy 3:15–17, he notes that Paul appeals first to the trustworthiness of those from whom Timothy has, from childhood, learned the gospel. Only after appealing to the trustworthiness of Timothy's teachers does Paul make his point about the inspiration and profitability of Scripture. This leads Allert to highlight the importance of ecclesial context or tradition for appreciating Scripture's inspiration. He also argues that what Paul means by "sacred writings" and "Scripture" is not yet the biblical canon, or even the canon of the Old Testament. Inquiring into the meaning of "*theopneustos*," he observes that it appears only once in Scripture and so one cannot conclude that it means that "God literally breathed out Scripture."[41] He points out that "the later Christian use of the term was not limited to the Scriptures and could include references to a commentary, a tomb inscription, and a conciliar decision."[42] Why suppose that Paul intends to suggest that Scripture alone is inspired? Regarding those (such as Warfield) who compare Paul's view to Philo's, Allert cautions against the dictation theory of biblical inspiration.

Allert is not of course denying that God inspired Scripture. He is simply arguing that Scripture does not itself mandate a particular theory of biblical inspiration. Whereas Warfield reads 2 Peter 1:19–21 as implying that God is the source of the whole of Scripture, Allert interprets the passage to be emphasizing the confirmation, in the prophetic books, of what the apostles saw. The passage does not offer an account of inspiration, but instead makes a claim about prophecy and about the eyewitness of the apostles. Likewise, for Allert John 10:34–35 is not a teaching about inspiration, but rather teaches about the authority of Scripture. One can affirm the authority of Scripture without holding to a particular account of the inspiration of Scripture.

After discussing these biblical texts, Allert addresses the Chicago Statement on Biblical Inerrancy, which holds to the view (as we found in Woodbridge) that Scripture makes no errors at all, including scientific or historical matters such as how many times the cock crowed before Peter's denial of Christ. Yet as Allert points out, Article 13 of the Chicago Statement clarifies that the biblical truth "is not negated by a lack of modern technical precision, irregularities of grammar or spelling, observational descriptions of nature, the reporting of falsehoods, the use of hyperbole and round numbers, the topical arrangement of material, variant

---

41   Allert, *High View of Scripture*, 154.

42   Allert, *High View of Scripture*, 155.

selections of material in parallel accounts, or the use of free citations."[43] According to the Chicago Statement, then, the diverse genres of the biblical texts must be taken into account in determining biblical truth, as must be the literary conventions that were standard at the time of composition. The effort to determine biblical truth can become complex, as shown by the response to Robert Gundry's proposal that Matthew deliberately embellishes historical information in order to make a theological point. Is this error, or is it, on the contrary, inerrant teaching of theological points about Jesus through the genre of midrash? If the latter, does Gundry's position—for which he was expelled from the Evangelical Theological Society in 1983—in fact uphold inerrancy as defined by the Article 13 of the Chicago Statement (as Gundry argued)?

Allert concludes that what the Bible teaches about inspiration neither mandates a particular theory of inspiration, nor mandates inerrancy as it is commonly understood. Instead, appreciation for the formation of the canon requires a different emphasis: namely, the affirmation of the Holy Spirit's inspiration not only of the biblical authors (and books) but also of the Catholic bishops who collected these books into a biblical canon. Writing as an evangelical, Allert challenges his fellow evangelicals to recognize that inspiration cannot do without the Church; the Bible cannot stand alone.

A somewhat different position is taken by Stephen Chapman, whose work advances Brevard Childs's project of canonical interpretation against the criticisms of such notable evangelical scholars as Carl Henry. Chapman argues that inspiration should be primarily associated not with the human authors (or editors) but with God's providential guidance of the canonical process, and therefore with the canonical text of Scripture.[44] Chapman recognizes the risk that a canonical focus will weaken the ability of the Bible to stand over against the traditions of the Church. He suggests that the Bible's uniquely authoritative status can be and should be maintained by applying inspiration to the canonical text, rather than to the authors and editors. Although he grants that Childs's approach values ecclesiology and tradition, he shows that Childs does this without undermining the preeminence of biblical authority.

Chapman includes a lengthy discussion of Carl Henry's theology of biblical inspiration and inerrancy. Focusing on the inspired authors and their inerrant original autographs,[45] Henry argues for the decisive role of the prophets and apostles. Comparing Henry's position to Childs's, Chapman observes, "The difference is that for Childs the prophetic-apostolic witness is more than simply what individual prophets and apostles originally said and wrote. Their witness

---

43   Allert, *High View of Scripture*, 161.

44   See Achtemeier, *Inspiration and Authority*, 104–108.

45   On the original autographs and related topics, see the discussion in Roger Nicole, "The Nature of Inerrancy," in Nicole, *Standing Forth*, 27–49.

continues to develop and deepen over time, a process reflected in the history of the biblical literature itself, until that witness is acknowledged by the community of faith to be complete."[46] The historical complexity of the formation of the biblical literature, until its recognition as canonical text, is for Chapman a good thing because it avoids liberal Protestantism's focus on individual experience (in this case of the human authors) and emphasizes instead the authority of the canonical text. History is always interpreted history; divine revelation in history includes this interpretation, and does so normatively in its canonical form. As Chapman points out, 2 Timothy 3:16 has to do with the inspiration of the biblical text, not the inspiration of its authors. Drawing on the scholarship of Peter Enns, Telford Work, and David Yeago, Chapman also argues that the incarnational analogy has value but only when seen in light of the work of the Holy Spirit—a work that takes place in the process of canonical formation through flawed human beings. Chapman concludes: "A canonical account of inspiration keeps the theological interpretation of Scripture focused where it should be—on the text."[47]

In his book on the Bible's inspiration, authority, and truthfulness, Ben Witherington finds that although the Bible contains "imperfections" such as grammatical errors, nonetheless when Scripture teaches on a topic (rather than simply touching upon a topic) it is inerrant. As he puts it, "on the occasions when an author was inspired by God's Spirit to say something specific, they were guided to speak truly without the admixture of error."[48] On this view, biblical inspiration requires inerrancy when the biblical authors are deliberately making judgments of truth. In this regard Witherington finds Enns's position to be inadequate. Although Enns argues for the coherence of the whole Bible when read in light of Christ, Enns also grants the presence in the Bible of a number of contradictory claims about God and humans. By contrast, Witherington wishes to affirm the coherence, consistency, and unity of the truth claims that the biblical authors (and texts) make about God and humans. An example is whether the authors of some of the psalms intend to teach a henotheistic, rather than monotheistic, doctrine of God. Enns thinks they do, whereas Witherington suggests that when the henotheistic language of

---

46 Stephen B. Chapman, "Reclaiming Inspiration for the Bible," in *Canon and Biblical Interpretation*, eds. Craig G. Bartholomew, Scott Hahn, Robin Parry, Christopher Seitz, and Al Wolters (Grand Rapids, MI: Zondervan, 2006), 167–206, at 179–180. See also Michael Fishbane, *Biblical Interpretation in Ancient Israel* (Oxford: Oxford University, 1988).

47 Chapman, "Reclaiming Inspiration," 200. See also John H. Sailhamer, *Introduction to Old Testament Theology: A Canonical Approach* (Grand Rapids, MI: Zondervan, 1995); Christopher R. Seitz, *Prophecy and Hermeneutics: Toward a New Introduction to the Prophets* (Grand Rapids, MI: Baker Academic, 2007); Seitz, *The Goodly Fellowship of the Prophets: The Achievement of Association in Canon Formation* (Grand Rapids, MI: Baker Academic, 2009).

48 Ben Witherington III, *The Living Word of God: Rethinking the Theology of the Bible* (Waco, TX: Baylor University, 2007), 197. See also Roger Nicole on "The Biblical Concept of Truth," in Nicole, *Standing Forth*, 133–149. As Nicole points out, "The primary New Testament emphasis is clearly on truth as conformity to reality and opposition to lies or errors" (at 142).

certain psalms is properly contextualized, such language can be shown to serve a monotheistic intention.

Even so, Witherington does not suppose that biblical inspiration and inerrancy require a modern standard of historical accuracy. He allows that 1–2 Chronicles, for example, intentionally rephrases and rearranges the earlier 1-2 Samuel. In his view, 1-2 Chronicles can take this liberty in order to make theological and homiletical points because 1-2 Chronicles presupposes that its audience knows 1-2 Samuel, which provides the historical foundation. Witherington similarly does not hold Genesis or other biblical texts to modern standards of historical precision, but he does hold these texts to "ancient standards of historical inquiry and truth telling."[49] On these ancient standards, the author of Genesis, for example, intends to convey a historical truth about the existence of Noah and the flood. Since the Bible is inspired, this basic claim regarding Noah's historical existence is true.

Here the distinction between what Scripture teaches and what it touches also comes into play. Witherington grants that no biblical author intends to teach natural science, so the biblical texts include erroneous cultural assumptions about things such as the rising of the sun or the age of the earth (as implied by the genealogies). But the author of Genesis does intend to affirm the historical existence of Adam and his Fall, and this affirmation is true. In accord with the standards of ancient historiography, the author of Genesis makes historical claims that "are more general and less precise than we perhaps would want to make today, but nonetheless, historical claims are being made."[50] Even in the terms of Enns's incarnational analogy, which Witherington critiques, Christ's humanity did not include our fallenness, and neither must the Bible include error as regards the historical judgments that the biblical authors wish to make.

Regarding inspiration, Witherington interprets 2 Timothy 3:16 to mean that "the whole Bible is suffused with divine inspiration, while also the whole thing is composed of human words. Some of it is more directly the Word of God (for example, the oracles), some of it more indirectly, but it is always the Word of God in human words."[51] Since God is speaking through the human authors, their words can mean more than they knew, although this deeper meaning must be consistent with the literal sense of the authors' words.[52] Reflecting its composition within an oral culture, the Old Testament already has a high view of God's presence in the texts of Scripture. In Mark 12:36 Jesus says that the Holy Spirit inspired David's words in Psalm 110.[53] Witherington emphasizes that both the person David and

---

49   Witherington, *Living Word*, 39.

50   Witherington, *Living Word*, 38.

51   Witherington, *Living Word*, 36.

52   Witherington, *Living Word*, 157–158.

53   Mark 12:36.

the written text are inspired by God. Paul understands his proclamation of the gospel as "the Word of God" rather than as "the word of men."[54] This Word of God, Paul continues, "is at work in you believers."[55] In the same vein Witherington explores such texts as 1 Corinthians 14:36–37, Acts 1:16, Acts 4:31, Acts 6:7, Acts 12:24, Hebrews 4:12–13, 1 Peter 1:23, and 2 Peter 1:21. He gives particular attention to the theology of inspiration articulated in 2 Timothy 3:16–17, and he concludes that "Paul does not envision any Scripture that is not God-breathed."[56]

Rather than explaining how inspiration works, Paul focuses on the reality that God is speaking in the words of Scripture and that these words are the word of God, "profitable for teaching, for reproof, for correction, and for training in righteousness."[57] In order to be profitable for teaching, God's inspired Word must be true. In Witherington's view, we can be confident that Paul here has in view essentially the canonical Old Testament books. Witherington adds that the New Testament authors envision a progressive revelation that culminates, in a full and definitive manner, in Christ Jesus.

For Witherington, then, the written words of the Bible all are inspired by God. As to the manner of inspiration, Witherington agrees with Marshall that God does not merely dictate his words through the human authors. He corrects Marshall's position with respect to the biblical authors' use of quotations from Persian kings or Greek poets: in this regard, "perhaps God providentially guided the biblical author to choose material which, while not originally part of inspired Scripture, nevertheless was true, and so could be included in a sacred text like Ezra's."[58] Inspiration by "dictation" only accounts for certain prophetic experiences, such as God's placing words in the mouth of Jeremiah in the context of God's personal relationship with Jeremiah. In his careful examination of the character of biblical prophecy, Witherington distinguishes between prophetic experience, oral expression, and written corpus. His main point is that inspiration must refer to all three: "The written word is God breathed as well as the oral word, according to the author of 2 Timothy 3:16."[59] Furthermore, the Bible does not merely contain inspired Scripture (let alone become inspired Scripture); every word of Scripture,

---

54   1 Thess. 2:13.

55   1 Thess. 2:13.

56   Witherington, *Living Word*, 9. See also Allen Rhea Hunt, *The Inspired Body: Paul, the Corinthians, and Divine Inspiration* (Macon, GA: Mercer University, 1996). Hunt focuses on 1 Cor. 2:6–16, where Paul describes his discourse as inspired by the Spirit. He argues that for Paul the whole community is inspired. His approach builds upon Karl Olav Sandnes's *Paul—One of the Prophets?: A Contribution to the Apostle's Self-Understanding* (Tübingen: Mohr, 1991). David Yeago underscores the importance of 1 Cor. 2:6–16 for the doctrine of inspiration; see "Spirit, the Church, and the Scriptures," 60.

57   2 Tim. 3:16.

58   Witherington, *Living Word*, 18.

59   Witherington, *Living Word*, 22.

as inspired by God, is God's Word. The Bible does not merely record or witness to revelation; God's Word in Scripture is revelation.

What about the more difficult texts of the Old Testament, such as Psalm 137's blessing of those who kill Babylonian babies? Such texts reflect truthfully the fallen human heart of the psalmist. As Witherington cautions, "moderns seem to assume that when you call something 'the word of God,' then one assumes in every passage it reflects God's character and will, rather than simply being a true revelation about some subject that God wanted us to know about, including our fallible selves."[60] Inspiration includes God's will that the human author tell the truth about the human condition. Exploring 2 Peter 1:19–21, Witherington explains that God uses the human authors to convey the truth he intends, but without overwhelming their human capacities and characteristics.

Wright's position is insufficient in Witherington's view. As we have seen, Wright focuses on God's authority exercised through Scripture, that is, on how Scripture functions in the saving economy of the triune God as an instrument of salvation rather than simply as a compendium of timeless truths. Wright also views Scripture through the lens of "story," a story that develops over time and whose meaning becomes clear only when it is completed in Christ. While agreeing with Wright's understanding of Scripture's function, Witherington argues that Wright needs to grapple more clearly with the question of Scripture's truth (which Witherington himself takes up through careful attention to genre). Unless Scripture is a "truthful instrument," it could not function for salvation in the way that Wright thinks it does.[61] The truth of God's inspired Word is salvific now and forever: "God's Word is indeed so God-breathed that it has no expiration date!"[62]

Vatican II and Biblical Inspiration

The solutions that these Protestant scholars propose have parallels in the nineteenth and twentieth-century Catholic discussions prior to 1965, as we have seen from Burtchaell's work. Burtchaell, however, makes a significant oversight by not discussing the doctrine of inspiration in the Second Vatican Council's constitution on divine revelation, *Dei Verbum* (1965).[63] He does briefly quote from the debate on the floor of the Council regarding the relationship of inspiration and inerrancy.[64] In passing, he also asserts that Vatican II, like the First Vatican Council, focuses on the doctrine of revelation while touching "but lightly on the biblical question"

---

60 Witherington, *Living Word*, 24.

61 Witherington, *Living Word*, 33.

62 Witherington, *Living Word*, 33.

63 Second Vatican Council, *Dei Verbum* [The Word of God], Dogmatic Constitution on Divine Revelation, (November 18, 1965), in *The Scripture Documents: An Anthology of Official Catholic Teachings*, ed. Dean P. Béchard (Collegeville, MN: Liturgical Press, 2002).

64 See Burtchaell, *Catholic Theories*, 268.

and refusing "to unpuzzle the inspiration problem."[65] What might *Dei Verbum* contribute to the theology of inspiration?

Dei Verbum teaches that the Word of God makes himself powerfully manifest in the New Testament writings, and especially in the Gospels. The Gospels arise from the preaching of the apostles and share in the apostles' charism. As *Dei Verbum* states, "The apostles preached, as Christ had charged them to do, and then, under the inspiration of the Holy Spirit, they and others of the apostolic age handed on to us in writing the same message they had preached, the foundation of our faith: the four-fold Gospel, according to Matthew, Mark, Luke and John."[66] The inspiration of the Holy Spirit ensures the Gospels' "historicity" (*historicitatem*), their faithful teaching of "what Jesus, the Son of God, while he lived among men, really did and taught for their eternal salvation."[67] The entirety of the New Testament was "composed under the inspiration of the Holy Spirit."[68] *Dei Verbum* regards the authors of Scripture, as well as the biblical text, as inspired by God. In support of this position *Dei Verbum* quotes 2 Timothy 3:16–17's teaching about the inspiration and function of Scripture.

According to *Dei Verbum*, revelation proceeds progressively, culminating in Christ Jesus. But even so, the Old Testament writings are "divinely inspired" and retain "a lasting value."[69] In the Old Testament, the sacred authors recount and explain God's work of salvation. This work of salvation "appears as the true Word of God in the books of the Old Testament." [70] The Old Testament writings reveal the truth about God and humanity, as well as about how God deals with humans in mercy and justice. Even in its inclusion of "imperfect and provisional" realities, the Old Testament provides "authentic divine teaching" (*veram paedagogiam divinam*). Not only has God ensured that the Old Testament writings provide "a lively sense of God" and "sublime teaching on God and … sound wisdom on human life,"[71] but also he has ensured that the mysteries of the New Testament are "hidden in the Old."[72]

---

65   See Burtchaell, *Catholic Theories*, 283. He quotes *Dei Verbum* once, in a footnote citation of the following sentence (without further discussion): "Since, therefore, all that the inspired authors, or sacred writers, affirm [asserunt] should be regarded as affirmed [assertum] by the Holy Spirit, we must acknowledge that the books of Scripture, firmly, faithfully and without error, teach that truth which God, for the sake of our salvation, wished to see confided to the sacred Scriptures." Burtchaell, *Catholic Theories*, 268, n. 1; compare *Dei Verbum* 11.

66   *Dei Verbum*, 18.

67   *Dei Verbum*, 19.

68   *Dei Verbum*, 20; compare at 11.

69   *Dei Verbum*, 14.

70   *Dei Verbum*, 14.

71   *Dei Verbum*, 15.

72   *Dei Verbum*, 16.

Dei Verbum affirms the compatibility of divine authorship and human authorship of the same texts. God does not overwhelm or negate the human author's capacities or culture. Rather, since God operates as a transcendent rather than a competitive cause, God authors Scripture in a way that allows for and requires the full operation of the human authors. God chooses the human authors, acts "in them and by them," and ensures that they write "whatever he wanted written, and no more," so that Scripture is entirely God's Word.[73] Like the action of grace, God's inspiration of the human authors involves their intelligent and free "full use of their powers and faculties" in writing the texts of Scripture; they are "true authors" rather than mere transmitters.[74] As *Dei Verbum* puts it (citing St. Augustine), "God speaks through men in a human fashion."[75] God expresses his meaning through human words and literary genres/conventions, which we must understand in light of the cultural context of the human authors. Quoting John Chrysostom, *Dei Verbum* praises the "marvelous *condescension*" of God in accommodating his divine truth to the limits of our human language, without thereby compromising his "truth and holiness." [76] Scripture expresses the words of God in human words that are "in every way like human language," fully human—just as the Word incarnate took on full humanity.[77]

In seeking to identify the realities that God intends to teach through the inspired words of Scripture, therefore, we need to investigate what the human authors intended to affirm. *Dei Verbum* holds that where the human author, in recounting, explaining, or foretelling the economy of salvation,[78] intends to affirm something, this affirmation is also affirmed by the Holy Spirit, so that "the books of Scripture, firmly, faithfully and without error, teach that truth which God, for the sake of our salvation, wished to see confided to the sacred Scriptures."[79] Yet the divine authorship of all Scripture requires that we cannot apprehend the meaning of Scripture solely by seeking the human authors' meaning. Rather, in order to appreciate the unified (divine) meaning of the whole Scripture, we must take "into account the Tradition of the entire Church and the analogy of faith."[80] Because of the divine authorship of Scripture, the ultimate interpreter of Scripture is the

---

73   *Dei Verbum*, 11; compare at 24.

74   *Dei Verbum*, 11.

75   *Dei Verbum*, 12.

76   *Dei Verbum*, 13.

77   *Dei Verbum*, 13.

78   *Dei Verbum*, 14.

79   *Dei Verbum*, 11. Lest the English translation imply a limitation of the scope of inerrancy, I quote the Latin: "Cum ergo omne id, quod auctores inspirati seu hagiographi asserunt, retineri debeat assertum a Spiritu sancto, inde scripturae libri veritatem, quam Deus nostrae salutis causa litteris sacris consignari voluit, firmiter, fideliter et sine errore docere profitendi sunt."

80   *Dei Verbum*, 12.

Church that carries forward, in the Holy Spirit, the apostolic mission of teaching the People of God.[81]

How do we know that the canonical books are the inspired ones? *Dei Verbum* states that with the Church of the apostles, the Church today "accepts as sacred and canonical the books of the Old and the New Testaments, whole and entire, with all their parts, on the grounds that, written under the inspiration of the Holy Spirit, they have God as their author, and have been handed on as such to the Church herself."[82] It is not the apostolic Church, let alone the Church today, that makes the books of Scripture "inspired"; rather the Church receives them because in faith the Church recognizes that the Holy Spirit has inspired them, as is attested by various New Testament passages.

Recall that for Burtchaell most of the Bible is simply "the chief record of the faith's gestation."[83] According to *Dei Verbum*'s doctrine of inspiration, by contrast, God inspires the books (and authors) of the Old Testament not simply as a record of revelation but so that the New Testament "should be hidden in the Old." All of the Old Testament books are "caught up into the Gospel message"[84] and are "authentic divine teaching,"[85] and "the true Word of God."[86] For Burtchaell, "inspiration is a charism that in no way interferes with a man's methods or mind as he writes or edits, but causes that he produce a composition which, in combination with others, can serve the Church with an undeviating, or inerrant, reflection of how the faith grew from nothing to Christ."[87] *Dei Verbum* agrees that the inspired human authors "made full use of their powers and faculties,"[88] but makes clear that the result is something more than what Burtchaell calls "a distinct selection of faith-leavings from a distinct epoch of faith-history."[89] Rather, "since they are inspired by God and committed to writing once and for all time, they present God's own Word in an unalterable form, and they make the voice of the Holy Spirit sound again and again in the words of the prophets and apostles."[90] They do so by teaching the truth about God and humanity, and about God's saving work.

---

81   See Ignace de la Potterie, "Interpretation of Holy Scripture in the Spirit in Which It Was Written," in *Vatican II: Assessment and Perspectives*, vol. 1, ed. René Latourelle (New York: Paulist, 1988), 220–266.

82   *Dei Verbum*, 11, citing John 20:31; 2 Tim. 3:16; 2 Pet. 1:19–21; 3:15–16.

83   Burtchaell, *Catholic Theories*, 301.

84   *Dei Verbum*, 16.

85   *Dei Verbum*, 15.

86   *Dei Verbum*, 14.

87   Burtchaell, *Catholic Theories*, 304.

88   *Dei Verbum*, 11.

89   Burtchaell, *Catholic Theories*, 303.

90   *Dei Verbum*, 21.

Dei Verbum holds that the Church, "relying on the faith of the apostolic age," receives the canonical books "on the grounds that [*propterea quod*], written under the inspiration of the Holy Spirit they have God as their author, and have been handed on as such to the Church herself."[91] The inspiration of Scripture precedes the decisions—inspired though they were—of the apostolic Church. *Dei Verbum* emphasizes that God inspired not simply the Church or the community, but individual authors: "To compose the sacred books, God chose certain men" who, under the inspiration of the Holy Spirit, "consigned to writing whatever he wanted written, and no more."[92] God's inspiration pertains both to the sacred writers and to the texts themselves. God is "the inspirer and author of the books of both Testaments." The inspiration of the Holy Spirit enables the apostles faithfully to proclaim the Gospel, and this same inspiration enabled the apostles and others to hand on "to us in writing the same message they had preached," the fourfold written Gospel.[93]

The distinction that Franzelin makes between formal and material components of Scripture, with God as the sole source of the formal components, is not found in *Dei Verbum*. Rather, the statements of *Dei Verbum* reflect Lagrange's view that God can employ the human authors as "instruments" without compromising their fully human authorship, because God's transcendent causality is not competitive with human causality. As we have seen, *Dei Verbum* affirms that the human authors make "full use of their powers and capacities" and are "true authors" whose words have their intended meaning within "a determined situation and given the circumstances of [their] time and culture."[94] *Dei Verbum* highlights the affirmations of the human authors, and states that these affirmations are also affirmed by the Holy Spirit. *Dei Verbum* instructs exegetes to seek to understand what the human authors are actually intending to affirm, in light of the genres in which they are writing and also in light of the divinely inspired unity of Scripture, which requires that we also attend to "the Tradition of the entire Church and the analogy of faith."[95]

---

91   *Dei Verbum*, 11, citing John 20:31; 2 Tim. 3:16; 2 Pet. 1:19–21; 3:15–16.

92   *Dei Verbum*, 11; compare at 20.

93   *Dei Verbum*, 18; compare at 7–8.

94   *Dei Verbum*, 11–12.

95   *Dei Verbum*, 12. For contemporary historical-critical understanding of the composition of the Old Testament texts, see Karel van der Toorn, *Scribal Culture and the Making of the Hebrew Bible* (Cambridge, MA: Harvard University, 2007). Van der Toorn comments that "the modern notion of authorship" is not "adequate to describe the realities of literary creation in antiquity. Books have authors, but the writers of texts of the ancient Near East are, as a rule, anonymous. ... The authors of antiquity were artisans rather than artists. Our preoccupation with originality would have been foreign to them, nor did they care about intellectual property. What they admired was skill, technical mastery. The texts they produced were often coproductions—if not by a collective of scribes, then by means of a series of scribal redactions. In most cases, then, the quest for an individual author is pointless. The making of the Hebrew Bible is owed to the scribal class

In short, although it leaves many problems unresolved, *Dei Verbum* defends a number of crucial principles regarding the doctrine of biblical inspiration, among them the following. First, inspiration has to do with both the human authors and the texts of Scripture: the charism of the human authors cannot be left out. Second, inspiration does not negate the limitations and cultural embeddedness of the human authors, but rather works in and through their graced intelligence and freedom. Third, the books of Scripture teach the truth about God and humanity in the economy of salvation. Fourth, the whole Scripture is inspired, although the Gospels have preeminence. Fifth, the inspiration of Scripture belongs within the context of divine revelation, so that Scripture is "constantly actualized in the Church"[96] as the Holy Spirit leads humans to salvation.[97]

Not surprisingly, the *Catechism of the Catholic Church* (1994) draws its teaching on the inspiration and truth of Scripture almost entirely from *Dei Verbum*. The Catechism affirms that "God inspired the human authors of the sacred books" and that these books "teach the truth."[98] Scripture has its purpose within the economy

---

rather than a limited number of individuals. We should not be looking for authors but seeking to penetrate the mind-set of the scribal elite" (at 5). He goes on to add that interest in individual authors is itself distinctively modern: "Until the dawn of modernity, neither theologians nor lay people had any great interest in the individual authors who wrote down the Bible texts. The Bible was the Word of God; whichever humans had been involved in its making were looked upon as mere channels for a heavenly voice. ... This lasted until the Enlightenment, when the dogma of the literal inspiration of the Bible was eroded. Only when the Bible was no longer literally the Word of God did its human authors gain in importance" (at 29). Notably, van der Toorn reduces the composition of Scripture to *techne*, leaving out entirely the role of practical wisdom (*praxis*, virtue), let alone prayerful contemplation or *theoria*. Far from envisioning the human authors as "mere channels for a heavenly voice," pre-modern theologians viewed them as holy people whom God had called into relationship with him, a relationship that provides the context for inspiration (of authors and texts in the compositional process). It is this insight— ultimately into the irreducibility of Scripture to extrinsic technological production—that *Dei Verbum* preserves through its refusal to break the link between what the human authors affirm and what the Holy Spirit affirms.

96   *Dei Verbum*, 8.

97   For examination of *Dei Verbum* with particular attention to the integration of the themes of *Dei Verbum*, 11–12, see Francis Martin, *Sacred Scripture: The Disclosure of the Word* (Naples, FL: Sapientia, 2006), 227–247. For background to the text of *Dei Verbum* see Joseph Ratzinger, "Origin and Background," in *Commentary on the Documents of Vatican II*, vol. 3, ed. Herbert Vorgrimler (New York: Herder and Herder, 1969). See also Jared Wicks's series of studies on Pieter Smulders and *Dei Verbum*, especially "Pieter Smulders and *Dei Verbum*: 3. Developing the Understanding of Revelation to Israel, 1962–1963," *Gregorianum* 83 (2002): 225–267; "Pieter Smulders and *Dei Verbum*: 4. Assessing the Mixed Commission's 1962 Work on Scripture/ Tradition and Biblical Inspiration," *Gregorianum* 85 (2004): 242–277; "Pieter Smulders and *Dei Verbum*: 5. A Critical Reception of the Schema *De revelatione* of the Mixed Commission (1963)," *Gregorianum* 86 (2005): 92–134. Robert J. Hill summarizes *Dei Verbum*'s position on inspiration in Hill, "Reading Symbols, and Writing Words: A Model for Biblical Inspiration," *New Blackfriars* 89 (2008): 22–38, at 26.

98   *Catechism of the Catholic Church*, 2nd ed. (Vatican City: Libreria Editrice Vaticana, 1997), nos. 106, 107.

of salvation, in which Christ and the Holy Spirit heal and elevate us and lead us to the Father. Without faith, therefore, the Scriptures "remain a dead letter."[99] Interpreting Scripture requires reading it in the same Spirit by whom Scripture was inspired.[100] Both the Old Testament and the New Testament are inspired, and "the New Testament lies hidden in the Old and the Old Testament is unveiled in the New."[101] These points are all found in *Dei Verbum*, although the Catechism places a greater emphasis on spiritual exegesis.

Attention to the doctrine of inspiration is absent from the Pontifical Biblical Commission's "The Interpretation of the Bible in the Church" (1993), as is appreciation for spiritual exegesis. The topic of God's inspiration of Scripture comes up most significantly in the document's discussion of "fundamentalism." The Biblical Commission affirms that Scripture is inspired and inerrant, but it argues that fundamentalism falls into a dictation theory of inspiration. In general, however, the document adheres to its promise not "to adopt a position on all the questions which arise with respect to the Bible—such as, for example, the theology of inspiration."[102] The document instead focuses on historical-critical, literary, sociological, and liberationist methods of biblical interpretation, as well as hermeneutical questions and other issues.

In his April 23, 1993 address on the Pontifical Biblical Commission's "The Interpretation of the Bible in the Church," Pope John Paul II urges that the biblical texts be understood "in their historical, cultural context." He criticizes the view that "since God is the absolute Being, each of his words has an absolute value, independent of all the conditions of human language."[103] On the contrary, in expressing himself in human language, God accepts its limitations, including historical and cultural ones. God can do this while maintaining the truth of his biblical word because "the God of the Bible is not an absolute Being who, crushing everything he touches, would suppress all differences and nuances."[104] But Pope John Paul quotes verbatim, with approval, Pope Pius XII's statement in his encyclical *Divino Afflante Spiritu* (1943): "Just as the substantial Word of God became like men in every respect except sin, so too the words of God, expressed in human languages, became like human language in every respect except error."[105] Pope John Paul warns, too, against focusing solely on the human dimensions of the biblical texts:

---

99 *Catechism*, no. 108.

100 *Catechism*, no. 111.

101 *Catechism*, no. 129.

102 Pontifical Biblical Commission, "The Interpretation of the Bible in the Church," (Boston: St. Paul, 1993), 34.

103 Pope John Paul II, Address to the Pontifical Biblical Commission (April 23, 1993), 8, in *Scripture Documents*, 170–180.

104 John Paul II, Address (April 23, 1993), 8.

105 John Paul II, Address (April 23, 1993), 6.

the exegete needs faith in order to perceive God's Word and thus to perceive the true nature and meaning of the Scriptures.

In his monograph on the Pontifical Biblical Commission's document, the Catholic exegete and theologian Peter Williamson touches briefly on inspiration at various points. Citing Pope John Paul's address, Williamson observes that "although all Scripture and all of its parts are inspired, not every verse or paragraph is of equal theological value," because (for example) some sentences express theological truths explicitly whereas others do not.[106] In addition, the human authors' writings are not exempt from the influence of the historical circumstances in which they were written. For the Biblical Commission, as Williamson says, divine inspiration/authorship does not override the limited capacities and resources of the human authors, including for instance faulty memory and mistaken historical and scientific opinions. As Williamson puts it, "neither the human authors nor the divine Author intended absolute precision in historical details or in scientific matters."[107]

Williamson addresses Pope John Paul's citation of the passage from *Divino Afflante Spiritu* which takes a high view of inerrancy. Noting that the problem with the incarnational analogy is its lack of specificity with respect to how Scripture reflects divine perfections and human limitations, Williamson concludes that the Biblical Commission's document should have included "more serious reflection on the nature of Scripture [e.g. inspiration] and its implications for interpretation."[108] Williamson also discusses the position of a member of the Pontifical Biblical Commission, Lothar Ruppert, who along with some others argued during the composition of the document that because of the complexity of the process of redaction, "the charism of inspiration and the literal sense should be considered to belong to the biblical text itself, rather than to the intention of an inspired author."[109] Williamson suggests that the Church will continue to affirm the inspiration of the biblical authors but, following the lead of historical-critical exegesis,

---

106 Peter S. Williamson, *Catholic Principles for Interpreting Scripture: A Study of the Pontifical Biblical Commission's The Interpretation of the Bible in the Church* (Rome: Editrice Pontificio Istituto Biblico, 2001), 36.

107 Williamson, *Catholic Principles*, 37.

108 Williamson, *Catholic Principles*, 40; compare at 331. For criticism of the document along these lines, see especially Avery Dulles, S.J., "The Interpretation of the Bible in the Church: A Theological Appraisal," in *Kirche sein: Nachkonziliare Theologie im Dienst der Kirchenreform* [His Church: Conciliar Theology in the Service of Church Reform] (Freiburg: Herder, 1994), 29–37.

109 Williamson, *Catholic Principles*, 166, n. 9. See Lothar Ruppert, "Kommentierende Einführung in das Dokument," [Introductory Commentary on the Document], in *Die Interpretation der Bibel in der Kirche: das Dokument der Päpstlichen Bibelkommission vom 23.4.1993 mit einer kommentierenden Einführing von Lothar Ruppert und einer Würdigung durch Hans-Josef Klauck* [[The Interpretation of the Bible in the Church: The Document of the Pontifical Biblical Commission of April 23, 1993, with a Commentary by Lothar Ruppert and an Assessment by Hans-Josef Klauck] (Stuttgart: Verlag Katholisches Bibelwerk, 1995), 9–61.

may in the future accentuate the inspiration of the text rather than the inspiration of the authors and editors.[110]

Whither the Catholic Doctrine of Biblical Inspiration?

Since Vatican II, the great majority of Catholic exegetes and theologians have ignored the doctrine of inspiration. Two notable exceptions are Abbot Denis Farkasfalvy and Scott Hahn.[111]

Farkasfalvy bemoans the precipitous decline of interest in the doctrine of inspiration after Vatican II. In accord with Burtchaell's findings, Farkasfalvy observes that "right before the Council, the question of biblical inspiration was perceived by both dogmatic and biblical theologians as a question of great importance and full of challenge."[112] Before the Council, he notes, the dominant interpreters of biblical inspiration were the Jesuits Augustin Bea and Sebastian Tromp and the Dominicans Paul Synave and Pierre Benoit. The contributions to this topic offered by the *nouvelle théologie's* recovery of the Fathers came too late to be absorbed by the Council, as did the work of Luis Alonso-Schökel. The result, Farkasfalvy thinks, was that *Dei Verbum* failed to attain the standard of constructive thinking with respect to inspiration that other documents, such as those on the Church, the liturgy, and ecumenism, achieved in their domains.[113]

In response to this situation, Farkasfalvy calls for scholarly monographs on the theologies of inspiration offered by the Fathers, parallel to his own dissertation on biblical inspiration according to Bernard of Clairvaux. He points for instance to the contribution that could be made by a study of Origen's introduction to his *Commentary on John*, where Origen reflects at length on the meaning of *"euangelion."*[114] Farkasfalvy explains that the Fathers' understanding of biblical inspiration has two aspects: first, the charism of the inspired author whose mind is illumined to understand the realities about which he writes (and whose interpreter

---

110 On this point see also Hill, "Reading Symbols," 35.

111 For another Catholic approach, see Robert Hill, "Reading Symbols." Hill summarizes his position as follows: "With biblical inspiration, therefore, the writer is inspired by a higher level (Holy Spirit) to respond to symbols of divine disclosure" (at 38). Hill is indebted to Avery Dulles, for his theology of revelation, and to Paul Ricoeur for his theology of symbol. Hill also mentions his indebtedness to T. A. Hoffman, "Inspiration, Normativeness, Canonicity, and the Unique Sacred Character of the Bible," *Catholic Biblical Quarterly* 44 (1982): 447–469. Hoffman explores what the Bible means when it depicts human beings as animated by the Spirit of Christ.

112 Denis Farkasfalvy, "How to Renew the Theology of Biblical Inspiration?," *Nova et Vetera* 4 (2006): 231–254, at 231. For context see Anthony Dupont and Karim Schelkens, "Scopuli Vitandi: The Historical-Critical Exegesis Controversy between the Lateran and the Biblicum (1960–1961)," *Bijdragen, International Journal in Philosophy and Theology* 69 (2008): 18–51.

113 For this view see also Denis Farkasfalvy, "Inspiration and Interpretation," in *Vatican II: Renewal within Tradition*, eds. Matthew L. Lamb and Matthew Levering (Oxford: Oxford University, 2008), 78–100.

114 See Farkasfalvy, "How to Renew the Theology of Biblical Inspiration," 248.

must therefore be enlightened by faith); second, "the structure of the inspired text in which the literal sense veils and reveals a deeper sense of doctrinal, moral, and eschatological dimensions."[115]

The first aspect expresses the principle of mediation in God's revelation to his people: he reveals himself through the inspired words and deeds of chosen persons, leaders of the people of God. Indebted to Rahner, however, Farkasfalvy suggests that the doctrine of inspiration may be equally applicable "to collectivities of concrete historical human beings, who, in the same process by which the Church came about, played their role of leadership and mediation under the guidance of the Holy Spirit, bringing the memory of prophetic and apostolic preaching into written forms in the way God wanted these to be recorded in his Church's sacred books."[116] From this perspective, the Scriptures are both a record of God's history with his people and a prime exemplar (in their composition and development) of that historical encounter.[117] Within that history, moreover, the Scriptures function to advance God's history with his people by mediating "(analogously) inspired encounters with God within the Church, by both communities and individual believers."[118] Emphasizing the social character of human existence and of the life of grace, Farkasfalvy seeks to extend our conception of inspired prophets and apostles: "God's self-disclosure constitutes 'prophets and apostles'—charismatically gifted human beings whose ministry transmits the knowledge of God in the world. ... The 'prophets' mean those who anticipate his word and presence; the 'apostles' mean in a wider sense all those who extend his mediating role until the end of times."[119]

In shifting inspiration away from the individual authors and toward the ecclesial community (without thereby negating the role of the individual authors),[120]

---

115 Farkasfalvy, "How to Renew the Theology of Biblical Inspiration," 248. Regarding the human authors of Scripture, Farkasfalvy adds that "there are ample indications that, in their own way, the Church Fathers saw that the scriptural documents were depositories of traditions held in firm possession by a collectivity and also were the product of a plurality of authors" (at 242). He also thinks that "the conceptual differentiation between 'inspired authors' (subjective inspiration) and 'inspired texts' would have immensely helped the work of the conciliar subcommittee" (at 242–243).

116 Farkasfalvy, "How to Renew the Theology of Biblical Inspiration," 249.

117 Farkasfalvy explains, "Jesus and his apostles spoke and acted 'in fulfillment of the Scriptures,' the prophetic Word accumulated, distilled, and redacted into sacred literature through the special history that prepared the coming of the Incarnate Word. By their ministry, Jesus and his apostles enlightened the believers about the inspired character of the written records of Israel's salvation history. In this sense the Christian canonicity of the Old Testament, although ultimately also 'prophetic' (that is, based on the tradition of Israel), is 'apostolic' (that is, its guarantee and credibility are received from their apostolic attestation)." "How to Renew the Theology of Biblical Inspiration," 251–52.

118 Farkasfalvy, "How to Renew the Theology of Biblical Inspiration," 249.

119 Farkasfalvy, "How to Renew the Theology of Biblical Inspiration," 251.

120 Commenting on the development of historical-critical biblical scholarship since the 1960s,

Farkasfalvy has in view the way that the Church doctrinally and liturgically mediates God's gracious gifting. The inspiration of the Scriptures enables the Scriptures to mediate God's outpouring of himself. This outpouring should not primarily be conceived in the propositional terms of "inerrancy," but rather should be primarily conceived as the quasi-sacramental "presence of a spiritual fullness in the biblical text, a capability to reveal not only truths but ultimately the One who said 'I am the Truth.'"[121] Inspiration ensures that in Scripture we encounter not simply historical facts guaranteed by the Holy Spirit, but the inexhaustibly rich tri-personal God who cannot be known simply by knowing historical facts. This vision of inspiration is Trinitarian: the Father authors the biblical drama, the Son is its central protagonist, and the Holy Spirit guides the biblical authors and readers to a personal encounter in faith with the realities of the drama, which the letter of the text can only partially reveal.[122]

Farkasfalvy defends the inspiration of all the words of Scripture, but he emphasizes that divine "authorship" must be understood analogously:[123] God

---

Farkasfalvy states, "While the Council's theologians wrestled with their respective schemes of linking human and divine authorship, biblical scholars began to leave behind the concept of a biblical author (the 'hagiographus' of the Council's text) as an individual and adopted various models of 'collective authorship' or theories of multiple authorship, as has been required by the emergence of source theories, the modern assumptions about strains of traditions, 'emerging thoughts,' and developing documents." "How to Renew the Theology of Biblical Inspiration," 241. Indeed, *Dei Verbum* itself exemplifies such "collective authorship" and redaction history. For many biblical texts, Farkasfalvy envisions "a chain of authors and redactors working in dialogue with a community of believers and directed by providential guidance to an ultimate and final redaction, working also under inspiration, so that the process would indeed produce a fully inspired text." "How to Renew the Theology of Biblical Inspiration," 242. See also Hill, "Reading Symbols, and Writing Words," 27.

121 Farkasfalvy, "How to Renew the Theology of Biblical Inspiration," 249.

122 From a Lutheran perspective, David P. Scaer similarly emphasizes the role of Christ and the Father in the inspiration of Scripture; see "Biblical Inspiration in Trinitarian Perspective," *Pro Ecclesia* 14 (2005): 143–160. In the same vein see Jenson, "Second Thought about Inspiration," 396–398, which focuses attention on the *Logos*.

123 Farkasfalvy criticizes *Dei Verbum* for failing to include "the focal issue of Rahner's book on inspiration, the distinction between 'author' and 'originator,'" with the result that "the question of God's transcendental authorship—and thus the fact that human and divine roles in inspiration can both be called 'authorship' only in an analogous sense—receives no attention. Instead, the document concentrates on the question of how to conceive a linkage between the two authors, one human, the other divine. God exercises his 'authorship' as he 'puts together (*confecit*)' the inspired books through selecting human beings through whom and in whom he acts (*Ipso in illis et per illos agente*). In other words, from the concept 'Deus auctor scripturarum' the document jumps to a concept of *double authorship*, divine and human, which it then promptly applies to all scriptural texts." "How to Renew the Theology of Biblical Inspiration," 237. In a footnote, Farkasfalvy points to the significance of Alonso-Schökel, along with Alonso-Schökel's student and translator Francis Martin, for re-thinking the concept "Deus auctor scripturarum." Farkasfalvy goes on to extend his criticism: "The conciliar text fails to deal with the transcendence of the divine author. One does not see how to avoid a false conclusion that in the process of divine inspiration, the human being's consciousness sets limits to the divine meaning. Whatever the author does not intend consciously cannot be truly in any form or shape

providentially ensures that the biblical books, as a whole and in their parts, are his Word, and in this sense God makes no errors. But God does allow the human authors, as must be expected from truly human writing, to make grammatical errors, to lack eloquence, and so forth—deficiencies that God certainly does not possess but that God condescends to employ. Farkasfalvy thus argues that *Dei Verbum's* teaching on inerrancy needs to be revised in order to make it less propositional and more sacramental. Inerrancy would be better understood, he suggests, along the following lines: "By its inspired character each part of the Bible offers a path to Christ who is that Truth that God offered mankind for the sake of salvation."[124] He adds that inspiration and inerrancy ensure not super-human propositional accuracy but rather our access, through each and every part of Scripture, to the divine realities that constitute our salvation: "This fullness of meaning or 'spiritual sense' that the Church Fathers affirmed to be accessible through each and every part of Scripture is not a collection of propositions in one-to-one correspondence with the individual grammatical units of the biblical text, but the ultimate sense of the whole, in which the unity, sacredness, relevance, and sanctifying force of the Bible lies."[125] We have this access to God's inspired and inerrant Word when we read it in faith, in the same Spirit in which it was written.

Another recent article on inspiration by Farkasfalvy deserves mention. In "Biblical Foundations for a Theology of Inspiration," he first explores the relationship between the first Christians' understanding of Israel's Scriptures and their faith in Christ. The first Christians claimed the Scriptures of Israel (not yet a canon) as their own because Christ has fulfilled the covenants and prophecies recorded in Israel's Scriptures. According to the New Testament writings, Israel's Scriptures are God's authoritative Word. The Gospels carefully attach themselves to the apostolic preaching. Other New Testament writings connect themselves to the apostles Peter, Paul, or John while in fact having been written after the deaths of these apostles: this practice parallels the attribution of large parts of the Old Testament to Moses, David, and Solomon, and it signals that the pseudepigraphic

---

a part of the authentic meaning of the text. Moreover one remains baffled by such a narrow 'must' imposed on the reader to reconstruct the human author's intention in its original setting. Such a reconstruction is often not even possible or is of no central concern for the divinely intended meaning of a text. For the divine author's intention does not appear only in the context of a biblical book's historical setting, but also in its canonical context. In fact, there is much content in the biblical text of which the human author, according to his historically limited perspective, remains partially or fully unaware. ... Moreover, an inspiration theory that exalts the importance of the author's state of mind at the expense of the meaning of the text, fleshed out in its literary and grammatical properties, does not reflect the Church's exegetical practice and tradition." "How to Renew the Theology of Biblical Inspiration," 239–240.

124 Farkasfalvy, "How to Renew the Theology of Biblical Inspiration," 252; compare at 244–246, where he discusses the debate over inerrancy during the drafting of *Dei Verbum*.

125 Farkasfalvy, "How to Renew the Theology of Biblical Inspiration," 253.

writing has a legitimate claim to participate in the charism of the prophets and apostles.

In Farkasfalvy's view, both 2 Timothy and 2 Peter are pseudepigraphic. Perhaps as a result, these two books provide the most help for the doctrine of inspiration. 2 Timothy 3:16 identifies every scriptural text as divinely inspired and useful for teaching. 2 Peter 1:21 identifies God as the source or inspirer of all biblical prophecy. Indeed, Farkasfalvy suggests that the author of 2 Peter views the entire Old Testament as prophecy, since the entire Old Testament points to Christ. Whereas 2 Timothy identifies inspiration with the text, 2 Peter 1:21 locates inspiration in the inspired author, the prophet "moved by the Holy Spirit." Only interpreters who have this same Spirit can interpret the biblical text.[126]

In his book *Letter and Spirit* (2005), Scott Hahn emphasizes that God's breath both creates the universe and inspires the Scriptures, so that Paul can call the Scriptures "God-breathed."[127] Quoting a lengthy passage from Augustin Bea, whose work is surveyed by Burtchaell, Hahn notes that Jesus and his disciples clearly accepted the unique authority of Scripture. This authority becomes particularly apparent in liturgical proclamation: the Scriptures "are the documents of the covenant, which is solemnly renewed in the ritual worship of God's people."[128] In the Scriptures, we discover the terms of God's covenant with us; God makes his saving power present to us through his trustworthy Word. As Hahn says, with reference to the passage from *Divino Afflante Spiritu* quoted by Pope John Paul II in his above-mentioned address, "Scripture's authority is thus an extension of Christ's own authority, and its characteristics are analogous to those of Christ himself."[129] Just as Christ is divine and human, so analogously Scripture has the Holy Spirit as its primary author and human beings as its "instrumental" authors.

Hahn points out that *Dei Verbum*, indebted to *Divino Afflante Spiritu* as well as to Pope Leo XIII's *Providentissimus Deus* and to the tradition of the Fathers, connects inspiration with inerrancy: "*Dei Verbum* makes clear that inspiration is not merely for the sake of an unerring text, but 'for the sake of our salvation.' Still, an unerring text 'follows' logically from the doctrine of inspiration. Divine authorship is an act of God and, as such, it precludes error."[130] Hahn observes that this

---

126 See Denis Farkasfalvy, "Biblical Foundations for a Theology of Inspiration," *Nova et Vetera* 4 (2006): 719–745. See also the Catholic philosopher Michael Gorman's response to this article in the same issue of *Nova et Vetera*: "Inspired Authors and Their Speech Acts: A Philosophical Commentary on the Essay by Denis Farkasfalvy," 747–759, especially Gorman's point that "taking the human intentions of the scriptural authors seriously is important for taking them seriously as authors" (at 753).

127 2 Tim. 3:16. See Scott Hahn, *Letter and Spirit: From Written Text to Living Word in the Liturgy* (New York: Doubleday, 2005), 78–79.

128 Hahn, *Letter and Spirit*, 80.

129 Hahn, *Letter and Spirit*, 81.

130 Hahn, *Letter and Spirit*, 83.

understanding of Scripture's authority is a liturgical one: the saving realities an-nounced authoritatively and truthfully in Scripture are actualized in the Church's Eucharistic liturgy.[131] The inspiration and truthfulness of the Old Testament make it possible for the Church to "remember" in the liturgy God's saving work in Israel. Were the Old Testament's (inspired) truthful memory to be denied, the Church's liturgical remembering would be cut off at its roots.[132] For Hahn, it is a profoundly liturgical and participatory sensibility, rather than the usual suspects of rationalism or rigidity, that requires Christian biblical interpretation "to preserve and even exalt the historical and literary integrity of the Old Testament," without which "Christian liturgy—which depends upon deeply historical concepts such as *anamnesis* and covenant—makes no sense at all."[133]

Hahn's point is that if the covenantal history of the Old Testament is in er-ror, what sense would it make to "remember" liturgically the covenant's fulfillment by the trustworthy God of the covenant?

Conclusion

I agree with Farkasfalvy that the spiritual sense sheds light on Scripture's inspira-tion and inerrancy, and that biblical inspiration means that Scripture plays its role fully within the mediation of God's gracious gifting in and through the people of God. Farkasfalvy also rightly argues that divine authorship must be understood analogously, a point that affects arguments about inerrancy. Despite the complexi-ties that attend the human authorship of the biblical texts (noted by Farkasfalvy, Chapman, and others before and after *Dei Verbum*), however, the theology of Scripture cannot do without *Dei Verbum*'s insistence upon the Holy Spirit's inspi-ration of particular human beings. Although our understanding of the charism of the prophets and apostles can be expanded in the directions Farkasfalvy indicates, the fully personal character of God's relationship with his people means that his Spirit guides not merely canonical texts (or in the canonizing Church) but also the persons who, sharing the charism of prophets and apostles, compose the texts.[134]

---

131 See Hahn, *Letter and Spirit*, 99–100, 144, 171–72, and indeed the whole book.

132 See Hahn, *Letter and Spirit*, 165–167.

133 Hahn, *Letter and Spirit*, 165. See also Hahn's "Canon, Cult and Covenant: The Promise of Liturgical Hermeneutics," in *Canon and Biblical Interpretation*, 207–235. For his "liturgical hermeneutics," Hahn notes a particular debt to the following: Jean Daniélou, S.J., *The Bible and the Liturgy* (Notre Dame, IN: University of Notre Dame, 1956); Oscar Cullman, *Early Christian Worship* (London: SCM, 1953); Yves Congar, *Tradition and Traditions: An Historical and a Theological Essay* (London: Burns and Oates, 1966).

134 Consider Augustine's insistence, faced with the differences between the Septuagint and the Hebrew version of the Old Testament, that the Holy Spirit inspired both the authors *and* the translators: "anything in the Septuagint that is not in the Hebrew texts is something which the same Spirit preferred to say through the translators, instead of through the prophets, thus showing that the former and the latter alike were prophets." *City of God*, Bk. 18, chap. 43, (New York: Penguin, 1984), p. 822. Augustine comments, "For the very same Spirit that was in the prophets when they uttered their messages was at work also in the seventy scholars when they

Hahn's liturgical and covenantal understanding of Scripture brings out the way in which divine inspiration of particular human beings, which Thomas Aquinas describes as "the raising of the mind" by God, avoids an individualistic or strictly propositional focus.[135]

Through its inclusion of the doctrine of inspiration within the doctrine of revelation, *Dei Verbum* supports a theocentric, liturgical, and participatory understanding of Scripture.[136] From this perspective, Allert's emphasis that inspiration cannot only involve the Scriptures but must also involve the Church is clearly correct. Wright's understanding of Scripture as part of God's saving work in Israel as fulfilled by Christ and his Spirit-filled Church is also profoundly helpful, despite his skeptical view of the Church's ability to interpret Scripture. Both Allert's and Wright's positions are enriched by Hahn's understanding of how the Scriptures are properly read liturgically, and thus how their meaning and truth is inseparable from our ecclesial participation in the realities that they proclaim. Chapman's insistence upon divine providence in the unfolding of the canonical process recognizes that the messiness of human history participates in the divine wisdom which guides all things to fulfillment. Farkasfalvy's appreciation of the spiritual sense recognizes that every passage of Scripture opens up into the eschatological realities that God intends from eternity, realities which are inexhaustible in their truth and meaning. Enns's discussion of the value of the way in which the New Testament authors interpret and employ Old Testament Scriptures points in this same participatory direction, although he should also note that sustaining this kind of reading requires sacramental communion.

---

translated them. And the Spirit could have said something else as well, with divine authority, as if the prophet had said both things, because it was the same Spirit that said both. The Spirit could also have said the same thing in a different way, so that even though the words were not the same, the same meaning would still shine through to those who properly understood them. He could also have omitted something, or added something, so that it might be shown in this way too that the task of translation was achieved not by the servile labour of a human bondservant of words, but by the power of God which filled and directed the mind of the translator" (at 821).

135 Thomas Aquinas, *Summa Theologiae* [Summary of Theology], pt. 2a-2, q. 171, art. 1, reply obj. 4, in *Summa Theologiae*, 3 vols. (New York: Benzinger Brothers, 1947).

136 This broader context is likewise emphasized, within the Protestant discussion, by (among others) William J. Abraham, *Crossing the Threshold of Divine Revelation* (Grand Rapids, MI: Eerdmans, 2006); Abraham, *Canon and Criterion*; Work, *Living and Active*; Yeago, "The Spirit, the Church, and the Scriptures"; and Koskela, "The Authority of Scripture." Koskela recognizes that it is "crucial for Christian communities of faith to designate particular persons within the church to regulate and order their interpretive judgments" (at 217). Although he holds that "it would be unwarranted simply to transpose biblical authority unambiguously to the authority of particular persons within the church," Koskela cites Dulles to show that "what is ultimately authoritative is a dynamic process of the church's reception of revelation as demonstrated in particular beliefs and practices" (at 218). See Avery Dulles, "Scripture: Recent Protestant and Catholic Views," in *The Authoritative Word: Essays on the Nature of Scripture*, ed. Donald K. McKim (Grand Rapids, MI: Eerdmans, 1983), 260. See also my *Participatory Biblical Exegesis: A Theology of Biblical Interpretation* (Notre Dame: University of Notre Dame, 2008).

When the doctrine of inspiration spills over into the doctrine of inerrancy, how should theologians respond? Inerrancy cannot be separated from inspiration, for the simple reason that what is involved in both doctrines is the truth of Scripture (and thus Scripture's power truly to transform). Can we hold with Marshall and Witherington to a view of inerrancy that allows for some, but not many, historical and scientific errors? Should we argue, with many of the Catholic thinkers whom Burtchaell chronicles and with *Dei Verbum*, that inerrancy pertains to what the human authors intend to affirm? Does this mean that when the human authors are not making judgments of truth, the inerrancy of their writings is not affected by historical or scientific errors? Should we suppose, with Enns and Farkasfalvy, that inspiration accords with a broad range of historical and scientific error in Scripture? Given the Fathers' high view of biblical inerrancy, have Woodbridge and especially Hahn succeeded in identifying a high view of inerrancy with the power and plausibility of worshipping the God of Israel?

On the basis of an understanding of history's participation in God's eternal presence and plan, a participation that is both revealed in Scripture and characteristic of Scripture, we can affirm *Dei Verbum*'s teaching (referencing 2 Timothy 3:16–17) about the truthfulness of Scripture: "we must acknowledge that the books of Scripture, firmly, faithfully and without error, teach that truth which God, for the sake of our salvation, wished to see confided to the sacred Scriptures."[137] What this means for particular biblical texts differs, insofar as God and the human authors teach truth in biblical texts in diverse ways.[138] The diversity of these ways rules out the quest for Cartesian certitude and instead invites us to understand biblical inspiration as rooted in "the power of God"[139] in those chosen to bear witness to "the wisdom of God, which God decreed before the ages for our glorification."[140] *Dei Verbum* calls us to this liturgical path: "Hearing the Word of God with reverence, and proclaiming it with faith, the sacred synod assents to the words of St. John, who says: 'We proclaim to you the eternal life which was with the Father and was made manifest to us—that which we have seen and heard we proclaim also to you, so that you may have fellowship with us; and our fellowship is with the Father and with his Son Jesus Christ.'"[141]

---

137 *Dei Verbum*, 11.

138 See Thomas Aquinas, *De potentia dei*, Bk. 1, q. 4, art. 1, in *On the Power of God*, (Eugene, OR: Wipf and Stock, 2004), 8–9; see also Vanhoozer, "Lost in Interpretation," 97, 104, 107–108.

139 1 Cor. 2:5.

140 1 Cor. 2:7.

141 *Dei Verbum*, 1, citing 1 John 1:2–3.

Letter & Spirit 6 (2010): 315-332

Tradition & Traditions

~:~

Divinely Inspired for Teaching Truth and Refuting Error
A Catena of Catholic Sources

~: Pope St. Clement of Rome (80) :~

Brethren, be contentious and zealous for the things which lead to salvation! You have studied the Holy Scriptures, which are true and are of the Holy Spirit. You well know that nothing unjust or fraudulent is written in them.

Letter to the Corinthians, 45, 1–3
(*PG* 1:300–302; *ANF* 1:17)[1]

~: St. Justin Martyr (155) :~

If you spoke these words, Trypho ... because you imagined that you could throw doubt on the passage, in order that I might say that the Scriptures contradicted each other, you have erred. I will not have the effrontery at any time either to suppose or to

---

1   The following abbreviations are used: *AAS* = *Acta Apostolicae Sedis* [Official Acts of the Holy See]; available online: http://www.vatican.va/archive/aas/index_sp.htm. *ACW* = *Ancient Christian Writers: The Works of the Fathers in Translation* (Mahwah, NJ: Paulist, 1946–); *ANF* = *Ante-Nicene Fathers*, 10 vols., eds. Alexander Roberts and James Donaldson (Peabody, MA: Hendrickson, 2004 [reprint]); *CCL* = *Corpus Christianorum: Series Latina* (Turnhout: Brepols, 1953–); *CSEL* = *Corpus Scriptorum Ecclesiasticorum Latinorum* (Vienna, Prage, and Leipzig: Tempsky, 1865–); *DS* = Henirich Denzinger, ed., *Enchiridion symbolorum definitonum et declarationum de rebus fidei et morum* [Handbook of Creeds, Definitions and Declarations concerning Matters of Faith and Morals] (Freiberg: Herder, 1911); Eng.: *The Sources of Catholic Dogma* (Fitzwilliam, NH: Loreto, 2002). *EB* = *Enchiridion Biblicum: Documenti della Chiesa sulla Sacra Scrittura* [Documents of the Church Concerning Sacred Scripture], eds. Alfio Filippi and Erminio Lora, 2nd. ed. (Bologna: Dehoniane, 1993); *GCS* = *Die Griechischen Christlichen Schriftseller der Ersten Drei Jahrhunderte* [The Greek Christian Scriptures of the First Three Centuries] (Leipzig: Hinrichs, 1897–); *NPNF1* = *A Select Library of Nicene and Post-Nicene Fathers of the Christian Church*, 1st series, 14 vols., ed. Philip Schaff (Peabody, MA: Hendrickson, 1994 [reprint]); *NPNF2* = *A Select Library of Nicene and Post-Nicene Fathers of the Christian Church*, 2nd series, 14 vols., ed. Philip Schaff (Peabody, MA: Hendrickson, 1994 [reprint]); *PG* = *Patrologiae Cursus Completus: Series Graeca*, ed. J. P. Migne, 161 vols. (Paris: Garnier and J. P. Migne, 1857–1866); *PL* = *Patrologiae Cursus Completus: Series Latina*, ed. J. P. Migne, 221 vols (Paris: Garnier and J. P. Migne, 1844–1864); *SD* = *The Scripture Documents: An Anthology of Official Catholic Teachings*, ed. Dean P. Béchard, S.J. (Collegeville, MN: Liturgical Press, 2002).

say such a thing. If a Scripture which appears to be of such a kind be brought forward, and there be a pretext for regarding it as contradictory, since I am totally convinced that no Scripture is contradictory to another, I shall admit instead that I do not understand what is spoken of, and shall strive to persuade those who assume that the Scriptures are contradictory to be rather of the same opinion as myself.

Dialogue with Trypho, Chap. 65
(PG 6:625–628; ANF 1:230)

~: St. Justin Martyr (260) :~

Neither by nature nor by human reasoning is it possible for men to know things so great and so divine; but such knowledge can be had only as a gift, which in this case descended from above upon the holy men, who had no need of the art of words, nor of saying anything in a quarrelsome or contentious manner, but only of presenting themselves in a pure manner to the operation of the divine Spirit, so that the divine Plectrum himself, descending from heaven and using righteous men as an instrument like a harp or lyre, might reveal to us the knowledge of things divine and heavenly.

Exhortation to the Greeks, Chap. 8
(PG 6:255–258; ANF 1:276)

~: St. Irenaeus of Lyon (190) :~

If however we are not able to find explanations for all those passages of Scripture which are investigated, we ought not on that account seek for another God besides him who exists. This would indeed be the greatest impiety. Things of that kind we must leave to God, the one who made us, knowing full well that the Scriptures are certainly perfect, since they were spoken by the Word of God and by his Spirit.

Against the Heresies, Bk. 2, Chap. 28, 2
(PG 7:804–805; ANF 1:399)

❧ St. Hippolytus of Rome (204) ☙

Neither does Scripture falsify anything, nor does the Holy Spirit deceive his servants, the prophets, through whom he is pleased to announce to men the will of God.

Commentary on Daniel, 4, 6
(PG 10:641–700; GCS, vol. 1, pt. 1, 1–340)

❧ St. Hippolytus of Rome (230) ☙

But that those who use the arts of unbelievers for their heretical opinions and adulterate the simple faith of the divine Scriptures by the craft of the godless, are far from the faith, what need is there to say? They have not feared to lay hands upon the sacred Scriptures, saying that they have corrected them. … Nor is it likely that they themselves are ignorant of how very bold their offense is. For either they do not believe that the sacred Scriptures were spoken by the Holy Spirit, in which case they are unbelievers; or, if they regard themselves as being wiser than the Holy Spirit, what else are they but demoniacs?

Against the Heresy of Artemon,
In Eusebius, *History of the Church*, Bk. 5, Chap. 28, 15
(GCS, vol. 9, pt. 1; *NPNF2* 1:248)

❧ Origen (230) ☙

I do not condemn [the Gospel writers] if, to serve the mystical aims they had in view, they have in some way rearranged actual historical events in an order other than that in which they occurred, so as to tell of what happened in one place as if it had happened in another, or of what happened at a certain time as if it had happened at another time, and to introduce into what was said in a certain way some variations of their own. For they proposed to speak the truth where it was possible both spiritually and materially and, where this was not possible, it was their intention to prefer the spiritual to the material. The spiritual truth was often preserved in what some might say the material falsehood.

Commentary on John, Bk. 10, 4
(PG 14:314–315; *ANF* 9:383)

❧ Origen (244) ☙

With complete and utter precision the Holy Spirit supplied the very [words of Scripture] through his subordinate authors, so that you might ever bear in mind the weighty circumstance of their writing, according to which the wisdom of God pervades every divinely inspired writing, reaching out to each single letter. Perhaps it was on account of this that the Savior said: "Not one iota nor even a serif thereof shall be lost from the Law until all is accomplished" (Matt. 5:18).

Commentary on the Psalms, Ps. 1, 4
(PG 12:1081–1082)

❧ St. Cyril of Jerusalem (350) ☙

For concerning the divine and holy mysteries of the faith, not the least part may be handed on without the holy Scriptures. Do not be led astray by mere plausibility and artifices of speech. ... The salvation in which we believe is proved not from clever reasoning but from the holy Scriptures.

Catechetical Lectures, Lect. 4, 17
(PG 33:331–1128)

❧ St. Gregory of Nazianzen (362) ☙

We who extend the accuracy of the Spirit to the merest stroke and serif [of Scripture], will never admit the impious assertion that even the smallest matters were dealt with in a careless and hasty manner by those who have recorded them.

In Defense of his Flight to Pontus After his Ordination, Orat. 2, 105 (PG 35:503–506; NPNF2 7:225)

❧ St. Epiphanius of Salamis (377) ☙

And it is impossible, especially for a human nature, to see God. It is not allowed the visible to see the invisible. But the invisible God, in his love of mankind and strengthening the powerless with power, will bring about by his own power a way that it may see both the invisible and the infinite, not as the infinite is, but accordingly as our nature has been enabled to do so, and to the extent of the power in which the powerless have been empowered. And nothing of discrepancy will be found in sacred Scripture, nor will there be found any statement in opposition to any other statement.

Panacea Against All Heresies, Her. 70, 7
(PG 42:349–352)

~: St. Augustine of Hippo (400) :~

If we are perplexed by an apparent contradiction in Scripture, it is not allowable to say, "The author of this book is mistaken." Rather, either the manuscript is faulty or the translation is wrong, or you have not understood it. … But in consequence of the distinctive peculiarity of the sacred writings, we are bound to receive as true whatever the canon shows to have been said by even one prophet or apostle or evangelist. Otherwise not a single page will be left for the guidance of human fallibility, if contempt for the wholesome authority of the canonical books either puts an end to that authority altogether or involves it in hopeless confusion.

Against Faustus the Manichean, Bk. 11, 5
(PL 42:249; NPNF1 4:180)

~: St. Augustine of Hippo (400) :~

These things are true; they are faithfully and truthfully written of Christ, so that whosoever believes his Gospel may be thereby instructed in the truth and misled by no lie.

Against Faustus the Manichean, Bk. 26, 8
(PL 42:484; NPNF1 4:324)

~: St. Augustine of Hippo (400) :~

It is reasonable enough to suppose that each of the evangelists believed it to have been his duty to proceed with his narrative in the same order in which God had willed to suggest to his recollection the matters he was engaged in recording. At least this might hold good in the case of those incidents with regard to which the question of order, whether it were this or that, detracted nothing from the authority and truth of the Gospel.

> *The Harmony of the Gospels*, Bk. 2, Chap. 21
> (PL 34:1102; NPNF1 6:127)

❧ St. Augustine of Hippo (405) ☙

I have learned to hold those books alone of the Scriptures that are now called canonical in such reverence and honor that I do most firmly believe that none of their authors has erred in anything that he has written therein. If I find anything in those writings which seems to be contrary to the truth, I presume that either the codex is inaccurate, or the translator has not followed what was said, or I have not properly understood it. ... I think that you, dear brother, must feel the same way. And I say, moreover, that I do not think you would want your books to be read as if they were the books of prophets and apostles, about whose writings, free of all error, it is not lawful to doubt.

> *Letter* 82, Chap. 1, 3 [to St. Jerome]
> (PL 33:277; NPNF1 1:350)

❧ St. Augustine of Hippo (415) ☙

There is a danger that a man uninstructed in divine revelation, discovering something in Scripture or hearing from it something that seems to be at variance with the knowledge he has acquired, may resolutely withhold his assent in other matters where Scripture presents useful admonitions, narratives or declarations. Hence, I must say briefly that in the matter of the shape of heaven the sacred writers knew the truth, but that the Spirit of God, who spoke through them, did not wish to teach men these facts that would be of no avail for their salvation.

> *On the Literal Meaning of Genesis*, Bk. 2, Chap. 9, 20
> (PL 34:270–271; ACW 41:59)

❧ St. Jerome (386–415) ☙

The Lord's words are true; for him to say it means that it is.

> *Commentary on Micah* 4:1
> (PG 25:1188B)

The apostles are one thing, while profane writers are another; the former always tell the truth but the latter, as being mere men, sometimes err.

Letter 82, 7 [to Theophilus]
(PL 22:740; CSEL 55:114; NPNF2 6:173)

Scripture cannot lie.

Commentary on Jeremiah 6:27
(PL 24:729; CSEL 59:407)

∻ St. Thomas Aquinas (1256–1259) ∾

It is unlawful to hold that any false assertion is contained either in the Gospel or in any canonical Scripture, or that the writers thereof have told untruths, because faith would be deprived of its certitude which is based on the authority of Holy Writ.

Summa Theologiae, pt. 2a–2ae, q. 110, art. 3, reply obj. 1[2]

∻ St. Thomas Aquinas (1256–1259) ∾

We believe the prophets only in so far as they are inspired by the spirit of prophecy. But we have to give belief to those things written in the books of the prophets even though they treat of conclusions of scientific knowledge, as in Psalms (Ps. 136:5): "Who established the earth above the waters," and whatever else there is of this sort. Therefore, the spirit of prophecy inspires the prophets even about conclusions of the sciences. ...

In all things which exist for the sake of an end the matter is determined according to the exigency of the end. ... But the gift of prophecy is given for the use of the Church, as is clear in the first Epistle to the Corinthians (1 Cor. 12:7): "And the manifestation of the Spirit is given to every man unto profit." The letter adds many examples among which prophecy is numbered. Therefore, all those things the knowledge of which can be useful for salvation are the matter of prophecy, whether they are past, or future, or even eternal, or necessary, or contingent. But those things which cannot pertain to salvation are outside the matter of prophecy. Hence, Augustine says: "Although our

---

2   Thomas Aquinas, *Summa Theologica*, 3 vols. (New York: Benzinger Brothers, 1947), 2:1666.

authors knew what shape heaven is, [the Spirit] wants to speak through them only that which is useful for salvation." ...

Moreover, I say necessary for salvation, whether they are necessary for instruction in the faith or for the formation of morals. But many things which are proved in the sciences can be useful for this, as, for instance, that our understanding is incorruptible, and also those things which when considered in creatures lead to admiration of the divine wisdom and power. Hence, we find that mention of these is made in Holy Scripture.

Disputed Questions On Truth, q. 12, art. 2, contra., resp.[3]

~: Pope John XXII (1323) :~

Since among not a few scholarly men it often happens that there is called into doubt, whether to affirm pertinaciously, that our Redeemer and Lord Jesus Christ and his apostles did not have anything individually, nor even in common, is to be censured as heretical, diverse and opposite things being opined concerning it, We, desiring to put an end to this contest, after [having taken] the counsel of our brothers [the cardinals] by this perpetual edict do declare that a pertinacious assertion of this kind, when sacred scriptures, which assert in very many places that they had not a few things, expressly contradict it, and when it supposes openly that the same sacred Scripture, through which certainly the articles of orthodox faith are proven in regards to the aforesaid things, contains the ferment of falsehood, and consequently, as much as regards these things, emptying all faith in them, it renders the Catholic faith doubtful and uncertain, taking away its demonstration, is respectively to be censured erroneous and heretical.

Quum Inter Nonnullos,
Dogmatic Definition on the Poverty of Christ and the Apostles
(November 13, 1323) (*EB* 44)

~: Pope Clement VI (1351) :~

[To determine whether you are obedient to the true faith of the Church] We ask: ... In the fourteenth place, if you have believed

---

3   Thomas Aquinas, *The Disputed Questions on Truth*, 3 vols. (Chicago: Regnery, 1952–1954), 2:110–112.

and now believe that the New and Old Testaments in all their books, which the authority of the Roman Church has given to us, contain undoubted truth in all things, without the possiblity of error.

Errors of the Armenians (September 29, 1351) *(EB 46)*

❧ Council of Florence (1442) ☙

It [the Council] professes that one and the same God is the author of the old and the new Testaments—that is, the law and the prophets, and the Gospel—since the saints of both testaments spoke under the inspiration of the same Spirit. It accepts and venerates their books.

Session 11, Bull of Union with the Copts
(February 4, 1442) *(EB 47)*

❧ Council of Trent (1546) ☙

The sacred and holy, ecumenical and general Council of Trent … has always this purpose in mind: that errors being removed, the purity itself of the Gospel be preserved in the Church. This Gospel was promised of old through the prophets in the sacred Scriptures; our Lord Jesus Christ, the Son of God, first promulgated it from his own lips; he in turn ordered that it be preached through the apostles to all creatures as the source of all saving truth and rule of conduct.

The Council clearly perceives that this truth and rule are contained in the written books and unwritten traditions which have come down to us, having been received by the apostles from the mouth of Christ himself or from the apostles by the dictation of the Holy Spirit, and have been transmitted as it were from hand to hand.

Following then the example of the orthodox Fathers, [the Council] receives and venerates with the same sense of loyalty and reverence all the books of the Old and New Testaments—for the one God is the author of both—together with all the traditions concerning faith and practice, as coming from the mouth of Christ or being inspired by the Holy Spirit and preserved in continuous succession in the Catholic Church.

First Decree: Acceptance of the Canonical Scriptures and Apostolic Traditions (April 8, 1546) (*EB* 57; *SD*, 3–4)

❧ First Vatican Council (1870) ☙

Now this supernatural revelation, according to the belief of the universal Church, as declared by the sacred Council of Trent, "is contained in written books and unwritten traditions, which were received by the apostles from the lips of Christ himself, or came to the apostles by the dictation of the Holy Spirit, and were passed on as it were from hand to hand until they reached us."

The complete books of the Old and the New Testament with all their parts, as they are listed in the decree of the said Council and as they are found in the old Latin Vulgate edition, are to be received as sacred and canonical. These books the Church holds to be sacred and canonical not because she subsequently approved them by her authority after they had been composed by unaided human skill, nor simply because they contain revelation without error, but because, being written under the inspiration of the Holy Spirit, they have God as their author, and were as such committed to the Church.

Dei Filius [The Son of God],
Dogmatic Constitution on the Catholic Faith, Chap. 2, 5–7
(*EB* 77; *SD*, 16–17)

❧ Pope Leo XIII (1893) ☙

But it is absolutely wrong and forbidden, either to narrow inspiration to certain parts only of holy Scripture, or to admit that the sacred writer has erred. For the system of those who, in order to rid themselves of these difficulties, do not hesitate to concede that divine inspiration regards the things of faith and morals, and nothing beyond, because (as they wrongly think) in a question of the truth or falsehood of a passage we should consider not so much what God has said as the reason and purpose which he had in mind in saying it—this system cannot be tolerated.

For all the books which the Church receives as sacred and canonical are written wholly and entirely, with all their parts, at the dictation of the Holy Spirit; and so far is it from being possible that any error can co-exist with inspiration, that inspiration not only is essentially incompatible with error, but excludes and rejects it as absolutely and necessarily as it is impossible that God himself, the supreme Truth, can utter that which is not true.

This is the ancient and unchanging faith of the Church, solemnly defined in the Councils of Florence and of Trent, and finally confirmed and more expressly formulated by the Council of the Vatican. ...

Hence, because the Holy Spirit employed men as his instruments, we cannot therefore say that it was these inspired instruments who, perchance, have fallen into error, and not the primary author. For, by supernatural power, he so moved and impelled them to write—he was so present to them—that the things which he ordered, and those only, they, first, rightly understood, then willed faithfully to write down, and finally expressed in apt words and with infallible truth. Otherwise, it could not be said that he was the author of the entire Scripture. Such has always been the persuasion of the Fathers. "Therefore," says St. Augustine, "since they wrote the things which he showed and uttered to them, it cannot be pretended that he is not the writer; for his members executed what their head dictated."[4] And St. Gregory the Great thus pronounces: "Most superfluous it is to inquire who wrote these things—we loyally believe the Holy Spirit to be the author of the book. He wrote it who dictated it for writing; he wrote it who inspired its execution."[5]

It follows that those who maintain that an error is possible in any genuine passage of the sacred writings, either pervert the Catholic notion of inspiration, or make God the author of such error. And so emphatically were all the Fathers and Doctors [of the Church] agreed that the divine writings, as left by the hagiographers, are free from all error, that they labored earnestly, with no less skill than reverence, to reconcile with each other those numerous passages which seem at variance—the very passages

---

4   Augustine, *The Harmony of the Gospels*, Bk. 1, Chap. 35 (CSEL 43:60; NPNF1 6:100–101).

5   Gregory the Great, *Morals on the Book of Job*, Pref. 1, 2 (CCL 143:8).

which in great measure have been taken up by the "higher criticism"—for they were unanimous in laying it down, that those writings, in their entirety and in all their parts were equally from the afflatus of Almighty God, and that God, speaking by the sacred writers, could not set down anything but what was true.

> *Providentissimus Deus* [The God of All Providence],
> Encyclical Letter on the Study of Scripture
> (November 18, 1893), 21–22 (*SD*, 55–56)

~: Pope Benedict XV (1920) :~

No one can pretend that certain recent writers really adhere to these limitations [on the "the absolute immunity of Scripture from error"]. For while conceding that inspiration extends to every phrase—and, indeed, to every single word of Scripture—yet, by endeavoring to distinguish between what they style the primary or religious and the secondary or profane element in the Bible, they claim that the effect of inspiration—namely, absolute truth and immunity from error—are to be restricted to that primary or religious element. Their notion is that only what concerns religion is intended and taught by God in Scripture, and that all the rest—things concerning "profane knowledge," the garments in which divine truth is presented—God merely permits, and even leaves to the individual author's greater or less knowledge.

Small wonder, then, that in their view a considerable number of things occur in the Bible touching physical science, history and the like, which cannot be reconciled with modern progress in science!

Some even maintain that these views do not conflict with what our predecessor [Pope Leo XIII] laid down since, so they claim, he said that the sacred writers spoke in accordance with the external, and thus deceptive, appearance of things in nature. But the Pontiff's own words show that this is a rash and false deduction. For sound philosophy teaches that the senses can never be deceived as regards their own proper and immediate object. Therefore, from the merely external appearance of things—of which, of course, we have always to take account as Leo XIII, following in the footsteps of St. Augustine and St. Thomas, most wisely remarks—we can never conclude that there is any error in Sacred Scripture. ...

Those, too, who hold that the historical portions of Scripture do not rest on the absolute truth of the facts but merely upon what they are pleased to term their relative truth, namely, what people then commonly thought, are—no less than are the aforementioned critics—out of harmony with the Church's teaching, which is endorsed by the testimony of St. Jerome and other Fathers.

Yet they are not afraid to deduce such views from the words of Leo XIII on the ground that he allowed that the principles he had laid down touching the things of nature could be applied to historical things as well. Hence they maintain that precisely as the sacred writers spoke of physical things according to appearance, so, too, while ignorant of the facts, they narrated them in accordance with general opinion or even on baseless evidence; neither do they tell us the sources whence they derived their knowledge, nor do they make other peoples' narrative their own. Such views are clearly false, and constitute a calumny on our predecessor. After all, what analogy is there between physics and history? For whereas physics is concerned with "sensible appearances" and must consequently square with phenomena, history on the contrary, must square with the facts, since history is the written account of events as they actually occurred. If we were to accept such views, how could we maintain the truth insisted on throughout Leo XIII's encyclical—namely, that the sacred narrative is absolutely free from error?

> *Spiritus Paraclitus* [The Holy Spirit, the Comforter],
> Encyclical Letter Commemorating the Fifteenth Centenary
> of the Death of St. Jerome
> (September 15, 1920), 19–22 (*SD*, 88–89)

∻ Pope Pius XII (1943) ∻

The first and greatest care of Leo XIII was to set forth the teaching on the truth of the sacred Books and to defend it from attack.[6] Hence with grave words did he proclaim that there

---

6   Pope Leo XIII, *Providentissimus Deus* [The God of All Providence], Encyclical Letter on the Study of Scripture (November 18, 1893), 21–22 (*SD*, 55–56).

is no error whatsoever if the sacred writer, speaking of things of the physical order "went by what sensibly appeared" as the Angelic Doctor says,[7] speaking either "in figurative language, or in terms which were commonly used at the time, and which in many instances are in daily use at this day, even among the most eminent men of science." For "the sacred writers, or to speak more accurately—the words are St. Augustine's[8]—'the Holy Spirit, who spoke by them, did not intend to teach men these things (that is to say, the essential nature of the things of the universe), things in no way profitable to salvation.'"

This principle "will apply to cognate sciences, and especially to history," that is, by refuting, "in a somewhat similar way the fallacies of the adversaries and defending the historical truth of sacred Scripture from their attacks." Nor is the sacred writer to be taxed with error, if "copyists have made mistakes in the text of the Bible" or "if the real meaning of a passage remains ambiguous."

Finally it is absolutely wrong and forbidden "either to narrow inspiration to certain passages of holy Scripture, or to admit that the sacred writer has erred," since divine inspiration "not only is essentially incompatible with error but excludes and rejects it as absolutely and necessarily as it is impossible that God himself, the supreme Truth, can utter that which is not true. This is the ancient and constant faith of the Church."

This teaching, which our predecessor Leo XIII set forth with such solemnity, we also proclaim with our authority and we urge all to adhere to it religiously.

> *Divino Afflante Spiritu* [Inspired by the Divine Spirit],
> Encyclical Letter Promoting Biblical Studies
> (September 30, 1943), 3–4 (*SD*, 116–117)

~: Pope Pius XII (1950) :~

For some go so far as to pervert the sense of the [First] Vatican Council's definition that God is the author of holy Scripture, and they put forward again the opinion, already often condemned, which asserts that immunity from error extends only

---

7 Aquinas, *Summa Theologiae*, pt. 1a, q. 70, reply obj. 3.

8 Augustine, *On The Literal Meaning of Genesis*, Bk. 2, Chap. 9, 20 (*PL* 34:270–271; *ACW* 41:59).

to those parts of the Bible that treat of God or of moral and religious matters. They even wrongly speak of a human sense of the Scriptures, beneath which a divine sense, which they say is the only infallible meaning, lies hidden. In interpreting Scripture, they will take no account of the analogy of faith and the Tradition of the Church. Thus they judge the doctrine of the Fathers and of the teaching Church by the norm of holy Scripture, interpreted by the purely human reason of exegetes, instead of explaining holy Scripture according to the mind of the Church which Christ our Lord has appointed guardian and interpreter of the whole deposit of divinely revealed truth.

Humani Generis [The Human Race],
Encyclical Letter on Certain False Opinions Threatening to
Undermine the Foundations of Catholic Doctrine
(August 12, 1950), 22 (*SD*, 141)

~: Second Vatican Council (1965) :~

Those divinely revealed realities which are contained and presented in Sacred Scripture have been committed to writing under the inspiration of the Holy Spirit. For holy mother Church, relying on the belief of the apostles,[9] holds that the books of both the Old and New Testaments in their entirety, with all their parts, are sacred and canonical because written under the inspiration of the Holy Spirit, they have God as their author and have been handed on as such to the Church herself.[10]

In composing the sacred books, God chose men and while employed by him[11] they made use of their powers and abilities, so that with him acting in them and through them,[12] they, as true

---

9   See John 20:31; 2 Tim. 3:16; 2 Pet. 1:19–20; 3:15–16.

10 First Vatican Council, *Dei Filius* [The Son of God], Dogmatic Constitution on the Catholic Faith, Chap. 2, (*EB* 77); Pontifical Biblical Commission, *On the Parousia or the Second Coming of Our Lord in the Letters of St. Paul the Apostle* (June 18, 1915) (*EB* 420; *SD*, 207–208); Sacred Congregation of the Holy Office, Letter *Iam pluribus* (December 22, 1923) (*EB* 499).

11 Pope Pius XII, *Divino Afflante Spiritu* [Inspired by the Divine Spirit], Encyclical Letter Promoting Biblical Studies (September 30, 1943) (*EB* 556).

12 For references in the Latin Vulgate edition to God acting "in" (*in*) or "through" (*per*) human agents, see 2 Kings [Samuel] 23:3; Matt. 1:22; Heb. 1:1; 4:7; see also First Vatican Council, Schema on Catholic Doctrine, note 9, in Gerhard Schneemann and Theodore Granderath, eds., *Acta et decreta Sacrorum Conciliorum recentiorum Collectio Lacensis* [Collection of the Acts and Decrees of Recent Sacred Councils], 7 vols. (Freiburg: Herder, 1870–1892), 7:522.

authors, consigned to writing everything and only those things which he wanted.[13]

Therefore, since everything asserted by the inspired authors or sacred writers must be held to be asserted by the Holy Spirit, it follows that the books of Scripture must be acknowledged as teaching firmly, faithfully, and without error that truth which God wanted put into sacred writings[14] for the sake of salvation. Therefore "all Scripture is divinely inspired and has its use for teaching the truth and refuting error, for reformation of manners and discipline in right living, so that the man who belongs to God may be efficient and equipped for good work of every kind."[15]

Dei Verbum [The Word of God],
Dogmatic Constitution on Divine Revelation
(November 18, 1965), 11 (*SD*, 24)

❧ Vatican Congregation for the Doctrine of the Faith (1998) ☙

The first paragraph [of the Profession of Faith[16]] states: "With firm faith, I also believe everything contained in the Word of God, whether written or handed down in Tradition, which the Church, either by a solemn judgment or by the ordinary and universal magisterium, sets forth to be believed as divinely revealed." The object taught in this paragraph is constituted by all those doctrines of divine and catholic faith which the Church proposes as divinely and formally revealed and, as such, as irreformable.[17]

These doctrines *are contained in the Word of God, written or handed down, and defined with a solemn judgment as divinely revealed truths either by the Roman Pontiff when he speaks "ex cathedra," or*

---

13   Pope Leo XIII, *Providentissimus Deus* [The God of All Providence], Encyclical Letter on the Study of Scripture (November 18, 1893); *EB* 125.

14   Compare Augustine, *On the Literal Meaning of Genesis*, Bk. 2, Chap. 9, 20 (*PL* 34:270–271; *ACW* 41:59); Augustine, *Letter* 82, 3 (*PL* 33:277; *CSEL* 34:2; *NPNF1* 1:350); St. Thomas Aquinas, *On Truth*, q. 12 art. 2, contra.; Council of Trent, Decree Concerning the Canonical Scriptures; Leo XIII, *Providentissimus Deus* (*EB* 121, 124, 126–127); Pius XII, *Divino Afflante Spiritu* (*EB* 539).

15   2 Tim. 3:16–17 (Greek text).

16   Congregation for the Doctrine of the Faith, *Profession of Faith and Oath of Fidelity* (January 9, 1989), *AAS* 81 (1989) 105.

17   *DS* 3074.

by the College of Bishops gathered in council, or infallibly proposed for belief by the ordinary and universal magisterium. ...

To the truths of the first paragraph belong the articles of faith of the Creed, the various christological dogmas[18] and Marian dogmas;[19] the doctrine of the institution of the sacraments by Christ and their efficacy with regard to grace;[20] the doctrine of the real and substantial presence of Christ in the Eucharist[21] and the sacrificial nature of the eucharistic celebration;[22] the foundation of the Church by the will of Christ;[23] the doctrine on the primacy and infallibility of the Roman Pontiff;[24] the doctrine on the existence of original sin; the doctrine on the immortality of the spiritual soul and on the immediate recompense after death;[25] the absence of error in the inspired sacred texts [absentia erroris in scriptis sacris inspiratis];[26] the doctrine on the grave immorality of direct and voluntary killing of an innocent human being.[27]

Doctrinal Commentary on the Concluding Formula of the
Professio Fidei, 5, 11[28]
(*AAS* 90 [1998] 546, 549)

---

18 *DS* 301–302.

19 *DS* 2803, 3903.

20 *DS* 1601, 1606.

21 *DS* 1636.

22 *DS* 1740, 1743.

23 *DS* 3050.

24 *DS* 3059–3075.

25 *DS* 1000–1002.

26 *DS* 3293; Second Vatican Council, *Dei Verbum,* 11.

27 Pope John Paul II, *Evangelium Vitae,* Encyclical Letter on the Value and Inviolability of Human Life (March 25, 1995), 57 (*AAS* 87 [1995] 46).

28 Also published in *L'Osservatore Romano,* English edition, (July 15, 1998): 3, 4. Compare Pope John Paul II, *Ad Tuendam Fidem* [To Protect the Faith], Apostolic Letter Moto Proprio by which certain norms are inserted into the Code of Canon Law and into the Code of Canon Law of the Eastern Churches (May8, 1998) (*AAS* 90 [1998] 457–461).

Letter & Spirit 6 (2010): 333–343

The Gospels as History

∼: Thomas McGovern :∼

University of Navarre

It is not infrequent in contemporary biblical exegesis that one finds assertions that certain aspects of the life of Christ as recorded in the gospels are unhistorical. With striking confidence it is declared that particular events and teachings are the outgrowth of the evangelists' imaginations, or a retrospective projection of events and sayings, which amplify the personality of Christ in the light of the resurrection.

Thus it is alleged, for example, that the infancy narratives in Luke and Matthew are creations of the sacred writers in the light of some parallel Old Testament events, and that this is a literary device to give status to the birth of Jesus. Consequently, according to some exegetes, there is no historical basis for the message of the angels to the shepherds, or the visit of the magi to Bethlehem. The historical authenticity of central doctrines of the faith such as the virginal conception of Christ, Jesus' self-knowledge as the pre-existing Son of God, the fact that he instituted the priesthood and the episcopacy are frequently impugned—doctrines the certainty of which the Church has always seen affirmed in the gospel accounts.

What we are confronted with is essentially a denial of the fundamental historical character of the gospels. It is an attitude of mind which is nourished by several different influences. At one level there is an implicit denial of the supernatural character of the incarnation. At another, the influence of the Bultmann school of exegesis ("form criticism") is still very much with us. This postulates a complete discontinuity between the Jesus of history and the Christ of faith, with the consequent need to "demythologize" the gospel accounts to get to the basic kerygma. To explain the genesis of the gospels, form criticism affirmed that the environment in which the gospels crystallized was the primitive Christian community. This community, form critics say, was "anonymous" and "creative," and was influenced by contiguous pagan cultures in such a manner that it provided the type of popular setting in which legends are born. The gospel stories are thus a product of "faith" and not of history, because faith and scientific history are incompatible. This exegetical approach, as can be clearly seen, undermines both the historicity of the gospels and the doctrine of divine inspiration of Scripture as the Church has always understood this charism.

How important is it for our faith that we be certain the gospels are truly historical?

Catholic faith is based on God's revelation of himself to man. This revelation centers on the incarnation, life and teaching of Jesus Christ, Son of God, the Word made flesh. We are reminded by *Dei Verbum*, the Second Vatican Council's constitution on divine revelation that "God graciously arranged that the things he had once revealed for the salvation of all peoples should remain in their entirety, throughout the ages, and be transmitted to all generations."[1] It was part of this design that, at the prompting of the Spirit, a written record would be compiled of the life and teachings of Christ. Among these inspired writings, the gospels have a special place because, according to the same conciliar text, "they are our principal source for the life and teachings of the Incarnate Word, our Saviour."[2]

Consequently, if the historicity of the gospels were controverted in any way, the very basis of our faith would be undermined. It is not surprising then that the magisterium of the Church has diligently defended the historical reality of these writings.[3] Historicity is a fundamental characteristic of the Judeo-Christian revelation. The Bible presents a history of salvation in which people, events and institutions are portrayed in a space-time framework. Christ is the central figure of this history; his life on earth, his actions and his words are, at the same time, the subject both of history and of faith.

The gospel message that Jesus of Nazareth is the Messiah, the Son of God, is a testimony of faith which has a historical reference and implies a historical event. At the same time, the historical fact of Jesus of Nazareth is something which is not fully comprehensible at the rational level alone; it is only by reference to faith that we begin to understand the implications of the essentially supernatural reality of the Word Incarnate.

For the Catholic exegete and believer, the distinction between the "Jesus of history" and the "Christ of faith" has no validity. They are one and the same Lord Jesus Christ, the knowledge of whose life and teaching is faithfully transmitted to us by the Church. My faith assures me that the personality of Jesus which the gospels portray, his life and teachings which have been taught to me by the Church, are true, and that they have not been falsified or deformed in any way by the process of transmission. On the other hand, critical research can help us to deepen our knowledge of Christ's life and mission, by giving us more historical background to the gospel tradition which culminated in the literary record of the evangelists. However, access to Jesus through the gospels as an exegetical task cannot be reduced to mere literary and historical criticism; it must seek faith and be supported by it.

---

1   Second Vatican Council, *Dei Verbum* [The Word of God], Dogmatic Constitution on Divine Revelation, (November 18, 1965), 7, in *The Scripture Documents: An Anthology of Official Catholic Teachings*, ed. Dean P. Béchard (Collegeville, MN: Liturgical Press, 2002), 19–33.

2   *Dei Verbum* 18. For an excellent survey of the teaching of the Catholic magisterium in this area, see Edith Black, "Historicity of the Bible," *Homiletic and Pastoral Review* (December 1980): 12–23; (January 1981): 24–32.

3   See *Enchiridion Biblicum: Documenti della Chiesa sulla Sacra Scrittura* [Documents of the Church on Sacred Scripture] 2nd ed., eds. Alfio Filippi and Erminio Lora (Bologna: Dehoniane, 1993), 558–560. Hereafter abbreviated *EB*.

From a Catholic point of view, since God is the principal author of Scripture, the dogma of biblical inspiration guarantees the historicity of the doings and sayings of Jesus Christ, while recognizing at the same time that the differences between the four gospels give rise to certain difficulties. Pope Pius XII, in his encyclical *Divino Afflante Spiritu*, helped overcome some of these difficulties through his recognition of the validity of applying the theory of literary genres to the Bible.[4] Research along these lines led to the conviction that these four canonical books constituted a unique genre in the field of literature, and even within the Bible itself. Without ceasing to have a general historical character, they could not, however, be fitted easily into the category of either classical or modern history.

Nevertheless, as Vatican II points out, there are different ways of writing history, all of which have their own validity.[5] The fact that the gospels do not give us a life of Christ according to the canons of modern historiography in no way detracts from the truth of what they tell us.

Historical validity is intrinsically related to the supernatural message. The primary objective of the evangelists was to transmit the good news of salvation for the benefit of future generations, as drawn from the life and teaching of Jesus Christ. The literary form they intended was not biographical, but the form of preaching—announcing the message of salvation in such a manner, on the basis of historical events, as to evoke a response of faith in those who would hear it or read it.[6] It was a supernatural message, but its capacity to convince was intrinsically related to its historical validity.

Stages in the Redaction of the Gospels

Research in the present century has shown that the redaction of the gospels was in fact the result of a much more complex process than was envisaged previously. This was confirmed by the instruction of the Pontifical Biblical Commission on the historicity of the gospels.[7] This instruction throws immense light on the much controverted question of the gospels as history, and consequently its principal characteristics deserve to be recalled.

---

4   Pope Pius XII, *Divino Afflante Spiritu* [Inspired by the Divine Spirit], Encyclical Letter Promoting Biblical Studies (September 30, 1943) (*EB* 558–560).

5   *Dei Verbum*, 12. The Theological Commission of Vatican II, which drafted this document, clarifies that the history we find in the Gospels is authentic history (*historicitas proprie dicta*). See *Acta Synodalia Sacrosancti Concilii Oecumenici Vaticani II* [Synodal Acts of the Ecumenical Council Vatican II], 32 vols. (Rome: Typis Polyglottis Vaticanis, 1970–), vol. 3, pt. 3, 101.

6   *Dei Verbum*, 19.

7   Pontifical Biblical Commission, *Sancta Mater Ecclesia* [Holy Mother Church], Instruction on the Historical Truth of the Gospels (April 21, 1964), in *Scripture Documents*, 223–235. The translation used in this article is from the Appendix to Augustin Bea, *The Study of the Synoptic Gospels: New Approaches and Outlooks*, ed. Joseph A. Fitzmyer (London: Chapman, 1965), 79–89.

Looking at the gospels as purely human documents, the scriptural evidence is very clear that the primitive Christian community was not in any way anonymous, but one that is well known to us, which is guided by the apostles. We see how Peter acts and preaches as head of the apostolic college and of the newly born Church.[8]

The apostles and the gospel writers had a real interest in the historical dimension of Christ's life and teaching. This attitude is reflected clearly at the very beginning of Luke's gospel.[9] The apostles were very conscious that the reliability of what they preached derived from the fact that they had received this teaching from the lips of Christ himself, and that they were eye-witnesses of the events they recounted. "You shall be my witnesses," Christ had said to them.[10] After his ascension, as a guarantee of their authenticity, they frequently referred to themselves as precisely that, direct "witnesses" of the doings and teachings of the Lord.[11]

The Biblical Commission instruction outlines the context in which the historical character of the gospels should be defended and explained. This context is apostolic tradition, and, specifically, the three stages by which the life of Jesus has come down to us.

The first of these stages is the historical life and teaching of Christ himself, together with his own interpretation of the salvific significance of what he did and taught. During this time Christ chose disciples who followed him from the beginning of his public life, and lived in close intimacy with him; who heard his teaching and saw his miracles, and who understood the salvific purpose of all of this.

The second stage is the preaching of the apostles, who were guided into all truth by the Holy Spirit.[12] Also, through his special assistance, they were able to recall all Christ had taught them,[13] and, in the light of the resurrection, were able to see the full significance of the deeds and teaching of Christ. The instruction tells us that they faithfully explained his life and words, and passed on to their listeners all that Our Lord had taught them.

In the third stage of this apostolic tradition, the evangelists, under the inspiration of the Holy Spirit, drawing on this historical and doctrinal tradition, wrote down "that truth which God, for the sake of our salvation, wished to see confided to the sacred Scriptures."[14] From the many things handed down, the Biblical Commission instruction tells us, the sacred writers selected some of the events and teachings; they made a synthesis of others; still others were explicated

---

8   See Acts 2:14–20; 3:12–26; 4:8–12.

9   See Luke 1:1–3.

10   Acts 1:8; compare Luke 24:48.

11   Acts 1:22; 2:32; 3:15; 5:32.

12   See John 16:13.

13   See John 14:26.

14   *Dei Verbum*, 11.

bearing in mind the situations of the different communities. Hence the variety and individuality of the four gospel traditions.[15]

These same three stages of apostolic tradition are reiterated in *Dei Verbum*, where it deals with the historicity of the gospels. It also repeats the three elements which characterize the work of the gospel writers—selection, synthesis and explication.[16]

The Starting Point for Exegesis

For Catholic exegesis, then, the historical truth of the gospels is "a principle to be taken as a starting point for all work of interpretation of the sacred books; it is not, therefore, a conclusion or end product of critical research."[17]

If it is to be truly theological, exegesis must throw light on the gospels considered as divinely inspired writings, that is, it must have something to say from the point of view of the hermeneutical criteria of the faith, otherwise it is a merely human science which never penetrates the theological depth of the inspired word. In his book, *The Study of the Synoptic Gospels*, Augustin Cardinal Bea adumbrates a number of principles which lead to a deeper understanding of the historicity of the Gospels viewed as inspired books.[18] How is the historical character of the gospels affected by the fact that they are inspired writings, that is, that God is their principal literary author? The fact of inspiration leads directly to the conclusion that "the gospels not only enjoy a genuine historical credibility in what they affirm and in the way in which they affirm it, but also that perfect form of it which is called inerrancy."[19]

However, at first sight there are many parallel passages in the different synoptic accounts where there appear to be contradictions, for example the healing of the centurion's servant, or the description of the Sermon on the Mount, both of which are recorded with significant differences in Matthew and Luke. It might also be reasonably asked, if in such a centrally important event as the institution of the Eucharist there is quite a variation in the words of the formula of institution, how can we be sure that the evangelists are reliable authors?

Many of these problems can be solved, as Pius XII recommended, by a deeper penetration of the doctrine of divine inspiration from the point of view of instrumental causality.[20] According to this approach the human author, although under the influence of the Holy Spirit, leaves the imprint of his own character

---

15   In Bea, *Synoptic Gospels*, 82–85.

16   *Dei Verbum*, 19.

17   Paul Cardinal Taguchi, "The Study of Sacred Scripture," *L'Osservatore Romano* (May 15, 1975): 6.

18   Bea, *Synoptic Gospels*, 45–51.

19   Bea, *Synoptic Gospels*, 45.

20   Pius XII, *Divino Afflante Spiritu* (*EB* 556).

and distinctive genius on the document he writes, no less than any other human author. And yet, by divine design, he writes exactly what God wills and only what he wills.[21] The doctrine of instrumental causality, articulated so clearly by Pius XII, is affirmed again by *Dei Verbum*,[22] avoiding, however, the type of technical terminology which would be inappropriate in a document which was intended to be primarily pastoral in orientation: "To compose the books, God chose certain men who, all the while he employed them in this task, made full use of their powers and faculties so that, though he acted in them and by them, it was as true authors that they consigned to writing whatever he wanted written, and no more."[23]

As we have seen, in spite of the desire of the sacred authors to be faithful to the truth, differences are to be expected in the way the gospel message is presented. This is so in the first place because, as already explained, the gospels are a form of literary "preaching" rather than biography.

As Bea has pointed out, many of the differences in the gospel accounts can be explained by basic human psychology. It is a well known phenomenon that the capacity of human observation to grasp particular events is quite limited and varies conciderably from person to person. Precisely because of the principle of divine condescension, we can expect similar variation in reportage of the same events in the life of Christ. These differences, however, can be such that they complete one another.[24]

The differences between parallel passages are due not only to limitations of observation and memory, but arise also because of differences in the narrative skills of the various writers. Indeed one of the points highlighted by *Dei Verbum* was the fact that the Scripture writers were authentic authors (*veri auctores*) with all that that implies for the reflection of human personality of the hagiographer in his written work. Matthew writes with a keen eye to the implications of what he says for a predominantly Hebrew audience. Luke has a unique capacity to capture the compassion of Christ in a number of incidents related more soberly in other accounts. The same evangelist shows a particular refinement in relating incidents involving women (for example his telling of the events related to the Samaritan woman, the widow of Naim, the woman taken in adultery).

Another factor which has to be taken into account is that we are considering writers of the Near East of two thousand years ago. This was a specific culture with a particular outlook and mentality, very different from our own. It would therefore

---

21   Pope Leo XIII, *Providentissimus Deus* [The God of All Providence], Encyclical Letter on the Study of Scripture (November 18, 1893) (*EB* 125).

22   *Dei Verbum*, 11.

23   *Dei Verbum*, 11.

24   Bea, *Synoptic Gospels*, 51–54.

be perverse to judge these writers according to the standards of contemporary historical science developed in Western culture.[25]

It should therefore not surprise us to find these differences in the gospel narratives. Indeed God used them to provide us with a richer perception of the truths of salvation because of the complementary nature of these writings. The treasures of divine revelation are inexhaustible,[26] and thus human language or literature is incapable of conveying all the riches of the inspired word.

What should be the attitude of a believer when confronted with such difficulties in the gospel text? The Catholic who accepts the divinely guided teaching of the Church on the inspiration of Scripture will respond with that certitude which faith alone can give. St. Augustine forewarns us that God allows these difficulties to be scattered through the biblical text so that, on the one hand, we would study it with greater diligence, and on the other, being more conscious of our intellectual limitations, we would approach it with greater humility.[27] In addition, there is no reason for any fear or inferiority complex in relation to the findings of the sciences—historical, philological, archaeological, and the like. It is the same God who is the author of Scripture and of nature, and, as Pope Leo XIII pointed out in his great biblical encyclical *Providentissimus Deus*, "truth can never contradict truth."[28]

The assent of faith to the truths transmitted in the gospels precludes any question of doubt about their certainty. Tradition, we are reminded by Vatican II, "transmits in its entirety the Word of God which has been entrusted to the apostles by Christ the Lord and the Holy Spirit," and "thus it comes about that the Church does not draw her certainty about all revealed truths from the holy Scriptures alone."[29] Consequently the Catholic exegete will, for example, approach the study of the virginal conception of Christ in the Matthean and Lucan infancy narratives with the prior advantage of knowing that this truth is part of the deposit of faith. His exegesis will thus inevitably shed more light than that of the biblical scholar who begins from a perspective of doubt or skepticism about this mystery.

While the Pontifical Biblical Commission instruction considerably increased our understanding of the way in which the gospels are to be understood as historical, the most authoritative statement of the magisterium on this topic is, of course, *Dei Verbum*. This conciliar document confirms the historicity of the gospels in its fullest sense, in continuity with the previous teaching of the magisterium.

---

25 Pius XII, *Divino Afflante Spiritu* (*EB* 558–559). See also Pontifical Biblical Commission, *Sancta Mater Ecclesia*, in Bea, *Synoptic Gospels*, 85–87.

26 See Pope Pius XII, *Humani Generis* [The Human Race], Encyclical Letter on Certain False Opinions Threatening to Undermine the Foundations of Catholic Doctrine (August 12, 1950) (*EB* 611).

27 Pius XII, *Divino Afflante Spiritu* (*EB* 563).

28 Leo XIII, *Providentissimus Deus* (*EB* 131).

29 *Dei Verbum*, 9.

The Church's "Absolute Certainty" Concerning the Gospels

The theme of the historicity of the gospels is introduced in *Dei Verbum* with a certain solemnity of tone: "Holy Mother Church has firmly and with absolute certainty maintained, and continues to maintain [*tenuit ac tenet*], that the four Gospels, whose historicity she unhesitatingly affirms, faithfully hand on what Jesus, the Son of God, while he lived among us, really did and taught for their salvation until the day when he was taken up."[30]

It is of particular interest to recall the editorial itinerary of this important paragraph. During the process of redacting this conciliar document, which went through five different drafts spread over the life-time of the Council (1962–1965), some council fathers proposed that the clause "maintained and continues to maintain" (*tenuit ac tenet*), be substituted by "believed and continues to believe" (*credidit et credit*), since this was a truth which had always been accepted in the Church through an act of faith. Nevertheless the council's Theological Commission, which was entrusted with the task of redrafting the schema of the constitution, replied that *tenuit ac tenet* had been written because in this way the idea was more clearly affirmed that the historicity of the gospels was a truth which could be accessed both by faith and reason, and not just by faith alone.[31] This argument was accepted and approved by the Fathers and confirmed by Pope Paul VI in the definitive text of *Dei Verbum*.

The historicity of the gospels is thus presented to us in *Dei Verbum* as a datum which has been, and continues to be, an object of the faith of the Church. It is therefore a truth which claims the full assent of faith of the believing Christian, even though there are objective difficulties in understanding it, both from the point of view of the internal structure of the Scriptures (relating texts among themselves), as well as from the scientific confirmation of the events narrated. As a datum of faith, it is an essential premise of theological research, especially in the exegetical area, since theology as a science is developed from first principles which are the principles of the faith.

At the same time, the apologetic intent of giving rational support to faith in the historicity of the gospels, as underlined by the conciliar text, is a valid one. Exegesis has been encouraged by *Dei Verbum* to present testimony which endorses gospel historicity, objective historical proofs which oblige a rational adherence to it. Rational justification does not make faith in the historicity of the gospels vain, but demonstrates the appropriateness of accepting it. Faith, for its part, is necessary to adhere to this truth, overcoming the existing obscurities and human resistance to admit a reality which escapes us because of its transcendence.[32]

---

30   *Dei Verbum*, 19.

31   *Acta Synodalia Sacrosancti*, vol. 4, pt. 5, 722–723.

32   See M. A. Tabet, "Cristologia y Historicidad en *Dei Verbum*" [Christology and Historicity

The constitution affirms that "the Gospels are the principal witness we have to the life and teaching of our Saviour, the Word made Flesh."[33] The question of the historical truth of the gospels is thus not just a matter which affects the Christian apologetic and fundamental theology; it is the solid bedrock on which christology, ecclesiology, exegesis of the New Testament, and other doctrinal and pastoral areas are firmly grounded.

By following closely the history of the redaction of paragraph 19 of *Dei Verbum* one is left in no doubt about the desire of the Council fathers to emphasize clearly the historical nature of the gospels. As we have already seen, the first sentence of this paragraph contains the phrase "whose historicity she unhesitatingly affirms." This was introduced in the final draft of the schema of *Dei Verbum*, as a result of the direct intervention of Paul VI.

A number of Council fathers had raised the question of the inadequacy of the phrase at the end of paragraph 19 of the fourth schema, the penultimate draft, to express the historicity of the gospels: the gospels were written in such a way, it says, so that "they always tell us true and sincere things about Jesus" (*ita semper ut vera et sincera de Iesu nobis communicant*).[34] The Holy Father, unhappy with the direction which the debates in the Council were taking, had a letter drawn up by the Secretary of State,[35] and sent to the president of the Theological Commission, in which he invited commission members to reconsider, among other points, the question of the historical truth of the gospels. He requested that this doctrine would be explicitly articulated, and suggested that the phrase *vera et sincera* of the penultimate schema be replaced by the phrase *vera seu historica fidei digna* (true; worthy of historical belief). "It would seem," the letter continues, "that the first does not guarantee the real historicity of the gospels; and on this point, as is obvious, the Holy Father could not approve a formula which would leave the slightest doubt about the historicity of these most holy books."[36]

The Theological Commission studied this suggestion, and proposed the phrase "whose historicity she unhesitatingly affirms," which was approved by the Council fathers. In this context it is of particular interest to recall what *Dei Verbum* affirms about the consequences of the divine inspiration of Scripture, a point which has no small significance for the historicity of the gospels. In *Dei Verbum* we read: "Since, therefore, all that the inspired authors, or sacred writers, affirm should be regarded as affirmed by the Holy Spirit, we must acknowledge that the books of

---

in *Dei Verbum*], in *Cristo, Hijo de Dios y Redentor del Hombre* [Christ, the Son of God and Redeemer of Man] (Pamplona: University of Navarre, 1982): 302–306.

33   *Dei Verbum*, 19.

34   *Acta Synodalia Sacrosancti*, vol. 4, pt. 5, 723.

35   Dated October 18, 1965.

36   See G. Caprile, "Tre Emendamenti allo Schema sulla Rivelazione" [Three Amendments to the Schema on Revelation] in *Civilta Cattolica*, 117:1 (1966): 216–231, at 228.

Scripture, firmly, faithfully, and without error, teach that truth which God, for the sake of our salvation, wished to see confided to the sacred Scriptures."[37]

It is no accident that this text on the truth of Scripture, together with the text on historicity, constituted two of the most debated points in the whole of the Council discussion on the text of *Dei Verbum*. The inerrancy of Scripture was in fact one of the other points which Paul VI draws attention to in the letter of October 18, 1965. His concern was again to ensure that the final text of *Dei Verbum* would not leave itself open to ambiguity of interpretation about the nature of the truths contained in the inspired books. Many of the Council fathers had expressed concern that the text of the penultimate draft could be interpreted as saying that scriptural inerrancy extended only to those affirmations which related directly to the religious and moral teaching of the Bible. As a result of the intervention of the Holy Father, the text was revised to make it clear that the salvific truth which the Bible contains referred to all the affirmations of Scripture.[38]

Some biblical commentators have tried to make a case to show that *Dei Verbum* teaches a restricted doctrine of scriptural inerrancy by comparison with previous documents of the Magisterium. However, a careful study of the redaction of the conciliar text, together with a detailed analysis of the documents referred to at this point, provide no basis for attenuating the scope of the traditional concept of biblical inerrancy.[39] Gospel historicity and inerrancy are correlative and coextensive concepts. They either stand or fall together. From what we have seen, there can be no doubt that, in *Dei Verbum*, they mutually reinforce one another, while making due allowances for the use of different literary genres by the inspired writers.

Twenty years after the Council, Pope John Paul II, in *Dominum et Vivificantem*, his encyclical on the Holy Spirit, reaffirms the historicity of the gospels and situates it in a wider theological perspective.[40] He reminds us that the Holy Spirit is always present in the Church as "teacher of the same good news that Christ proclaimed." The Pope gives us an authoritative interpretation of John 14:26 ("He will *teach you* all things and *bring to your remembrance* all that I have said to you"),[41] which has profound implications for the historical authenticity of the gospel texts. He says:

---

37   *Dei Verbum*, 11.

38   *Acta Synodalia Sacrosancti*, vol. 4, pt. 5, 708.

39   See G. Aranda, "Santo Tomás en la Constitución Dei Verbum" [St. Thomas in the Constitution *Dei Verbum*], *Scripta Theologica* 11(1977): 403–407.

40   Pope John Paul II, *Dominum et Vivificantem* [Lord and Giver of Life], Encyclical Letter on the Holy Spirit in the Life of the Church and the World (May 18, 1986), in *The Encyclicals of John Paul II*, ed. J. Michael Miller, C.S.B. (Huntington, IN: Our Sunday Visitor, 2001), 244–302.

41   John Paul II, *Dominum et Vivificantem*, 4; emphasis in original.

> The words "he will teach" and "bring to your remembrance" mean not only that he, in his own particular way, will continue to inspire the spreading of the Gospel of salvation but also that he will help people to understand the correct meaning of the content of Christ's message; they mean that he will ensure continuity and identity of understanding in the midst of changing conditions and circumstances. The Holy Spirit, then, will ensure that in the Church there will always continue the same truth which the apostles heard from the Master.[42]

There is thus no question of any difference between the meaning given to the apostolic preaching by the gospel writers and the way in which the Church understands it today. This is because it is the Holy Spirit, the soul of the Church who leads us into all truth, who is the permanent guarantor of the historicity of the gospels down through the centuries.

---

42 John Paul II, *Dominum et Vivificantem,* 4.

Letter & Spirit 6 (2010): 345-348

Verbum Dei Incarnatum and Verbum Dei Scriptum in the Fathers

~: Joseph Hugh Crehan, S. J. :~

Frequent appeal has recently been made to the analogy by which the written Word of God, the *Verbum Dei Scriptum*, produced in the Scriptures by God's power and man's operative union, is compared to the mystery of the incarnation, the *Verbum Dei Incarnatum* where godhead and manhood are united in the person of Jesus Christ.

It has been quoted with approval by theologians of such different views as Loisy, Hurter, Bainvel, and G. B. Bentley,[1] and it is admitted into a recent encyclical of Pope Pius XII.[2] It was rejected by no less a theologian than Cardinal Billot as being inapplicable.[3] Even in Hurter, where the analogy is set forth most fully, the only early authority invoked is that of Hrabanus Maurus, the eighth-century Archbishop of Mainz who wrote in the afterglow of the patristic age, saying:

> As in these last times the Word of God, clothed with flesh taken from the Virgin Mary has come forth into this world, though there is one element in him that is visible and another that is hidden, even so when the Word of God is set before men by prophet or legislator, it is set forth in befitting garments, the letter being visible like the flesh of Christ, while the spiritual meaning is hidden within like his divinity.[4]

---

1   Alfred Loisy, *Études Bibliques* [Biblical Studies] (Paris: Alphonse Picard, 1901), 34; Hugo Hurter, *Theologia Generalis Complectens Disputationes Quator* [General Theology], vol. 1 (Innsbruck: Wagner Academic, 1900), 174; Jean Vincent Bainvel, *De Scriptura Sacra* [The Sacred Scripture] (Paris: Gabriel Beauchesne, 1910), 121; Geoffrey Bryant Bentley, *The Resurrection of the Bible* (Paris: Dacre, 1940), 40–47.

2   Pope Pius XII, *Divino Afflante Spiritu* [Inspired by the Divine Spirit], Encyclical Letter Promoting Biblical Studies (September 30, 1943), 41, in *The Scripture Documents: An Anthology of Official Catholic Teachings*, ed. Dean P. Béchard, S.J. (Collegeville, MN: Liturgical Press, 2002), 19–31.

3   Louis Billot, *De Inspiratione Sacrae Scripturae: Theologica Disquisitio* [The Inspiration of Sacred Scripture: A Theological Disquisition] (Rome: Society for the Propagation of the Faith, 1903), 129.

4   Latin: "Sicut in novissimis diebus Verbum Dei ex Maria virgine carne vestitum processit in hunc mundum, et aliud quidem erat quod videbatur in eo, aliud quod tegebatur, ... ita et cum per prophetas vel per legislatorem Verbum Dei profertur ad homines, non absque competentibus profertur indumentis ... ut litera quidem aspiciatur tanquam caro, latens vero intrinsecus spiritualis sensus tanquam divinitas sentiatur," in *Patrologiae Cursus Completus: Series Latina*, ed. J. P. Migne, 221 vols. (Paris: Garnier and J. P. Migne, 1844–1864), 108:248. Hereafter abbreviated *PL*.

It does not seem therefore to be out of place to examine here a few of the patristic evidences on which this analogy can be based.

Even if no patristic text gave an express statement of the analogy, it would be correct to say that the foundations for it are in the Fathers. On the one hand, Eusebius and St. John Damascene speak of Christ using his humanity as an instrument, just as a musician might show forth his wisdom by means of a harp[5]; on the other hand the Fathers generally, from the days of Athenagoras and Theophilus of Antioch, call the inspired writers of the Bible the instruments of God breathed upon by the Spirit of God as a piper might play upon his pipe.[6]

It is true that Christ's humanity is not merely the instrument of his godhead, but then again, neither are the inspired writers mere instruments in the production of the Scriptures, for they are both living and intelligent instruments. The analogy holds good up to the point where one examines the nature of the union between divine and human elements, and here the union of Holy Spirit and inspired writer in the production of the *Verbum scriptum* has yet to yield precedence to the hypostatic union between divine and human natures in Christ.

The first evidence of the analogy in the Fathers I find is in St. Ignatius of Antioch's epistle to the Philadelphians where he speaks of himself "fleeing to the Gospel as to the flesh of Jesus."[7] The word "Gospel" is changing its sense in the time of Ignatius from the good news preached, to denote something written. Here the context implies that a written gospel (or gospels) is intended, for Ignatius goes on to say that his other refuges are the apostles and the prophets; thus, he uses the common second-century designation of the Old Testament and New in these terms of "prophets" and "apostles." His thought is further clarified in his epistle to the Trallians, where faith is said to be the flesh of Christ and charity his blood.[8] "Faith" as it was understood in these early times means the elementary creed that was adhered to rather than the act of adherence itself, a creed which the gospels amplified, explained, and defended.

If Ignatius does not say *how* the Gospel is to be likened to the flesh of Christ, Origen and later writers show no such reticence. In his homilies on Leviticus,

---

5   Eusebius, *Proof of the Gospel*, Bk. 4, Chap. 13, in *Patrologiae Cursus Completus: Series Graeca*, ed. J. P. Migne, 161 vols. (Paris: Garnier and J. P. Migne, 1857–1866), 22:285. Hereafter abbreviated *PG*. See also John Damascene, *The Orthodox Faith* Bk. 3, Chap. 15 (*PG* 94:1060); also in *The Fathers of the Church: A New Translation* (Washington, DC: Catholic University of America, 1947–) 37:277–278. Hereafter abbreviated *FC*. Athanasius also has the idea that the humanity is the instrument of the Godhead: *Treatise on the Incarnation of the Word of God*, 8, 41 (*PG* 25:109, 169).

6   Athenagoras, *A Plea for the Christians*, 9, in *Ante-Nicene Fathers*, 10 vols., eds. Alexander Roberts and James Donaldson (Peabody, MA: Hendrickson, 2004 [reprint]), 2:133. Hereafter *ANF*. Theophilus, *To Autolycus*, Bk. 2, Chap. 9 (*PG* 4:1064; *ANF* 2:97).

7   Ignatius, *To the Philadelphians*, 5, 1 (*ANF* 1:82; Greek: "prosphugōn tō euangeliō hōs sarki Iēsou").

8   Ignatius, *To the Trallians*, 8 (*ANF* 2:69; Gk: "en pistei ho estin sarx tou Kuriou.")

Origen writes: "With the flesh and blood of his word as with pure materials does he give food and drink to the whole human race. Next after his flesh are Peter and Paul and all the apostles to be regarded as pure food, and in the third place, their disciples."[9]

Origen has no doubts about the nature of the Eucharist; he shows his mind about this later in the same set of homilies.[10] The food that Christ gives us is the Word of the Scriptures; the words that he spoke to us are spirit and life, as St. John records;[11] Origen loved this text: "We are said to drink the blood of Christ not only at the sacred liturgy but when we take to ourselves those words of his in which are spirit and life, according to his own saying in John."[12] The principal food Christ offers us is his body and blood, and there is analogy, but not strict identity, between the food that is himself and the food that is his written word.

"Blessed Is He who Discerns the Marrow in this Corn"

The analogy is now fairly launched. It reappears in Eusebius, again in conjunction with the text from John 6.[13] One may in passing remark how much the exegesis of this chapter of John would have gained, and how much Reformation controversy we should have been spared, if this analogy had been familiar at an earlier age when a strict dichotomy was being urged—either the Bible or the Eucharist but not both. Had the interest of theologians then been turned on the problem of authorship, divine and human, of the Scriptures, as in this psychology-ridden age it is now turned, perhaps the analogy would have emerged from its cover much sooner.

One of the most interesting uses of the analogy is made by the author known as pseudo-Jerome, identified with St. Columbanus by the older editors of the *Breviarium in Psalmos* (A Brief Treatise on Psalms). He says, commenting on the words of the Psalm 147: "He shall fill thee with the fat of corn [Latin: *adipe frumenti saturavit te*]," that this food is the Word of God. "Blessed is he who discerns the marrow in this corn. We read the holy Scriptures. I consider the Body of Jesus

---

9   Origen, *Homilies on Leviticus*, Hom. 7, 5 (FC 83:146; Lat.: "Carnibus enim et sangiune verbi sui tanquam cibo ac potu potat ac reficit omne humanum genus. Secundo in loco post illius carnem mundus cibus est Petrus et Paulus omnesque apostoli; tertio loco discipuli eorum."); also in *Die Griechischen Christlichen Schriftseller der Ersten Drei Jahrhunderte* [The Greek Christian Scriptures of the First Three Centuries] (Leipzig: Hinrichs, 1897–), 6:387. Hereafter abbreviated GCS. See also, Clement of Alexandria, *The Instructor*, Bk. 1, Chap. 6, 38 (GCS 1:113; ANF 2:219–222).

10   Origen, *Homilies on Leviticus*, Hom. 9, 10 (GCS 6:438).

11   John 6:63.

12   Origen, *Homilies on Numbers*, Hom. 16, 9 (GCS 7:152; Lat.: "Bibere autem dicimur sanguinem Christi non solum sacramentorum ritu sed et cum sermones eius recipimus in quibus vita consistit, sicut et ipse dicit: Verba quae ego locutus sum, spiritus et vita est.")

13   Eusebius, *Church History*, Bk. 1, Chap. 3, 12. (GCS 4:168). Also in *A Select Library of Nicene and Post-Nicene Fathers of the Christian Church*, 2nd series, 14 vols., ed. Philip Schaff (Peabody, MA: Hendrickson, 1994 [reprint]), 1:86. Hereafter abbreviated NPNF2.

is the Gospel, the holy Scriptures, his doctrine."[14] This writer has gone back to the original statement of the analogy in Ignatius. The marrow of the corn was indeed the written Word of God, especially when it told of Christ.

But does not the whole Scripture tell of him? "Search the Scriptures; the same are they that give testimony of me," as Origen was never tired of quoting from John.[15] This idea, that the whole Scripture looks forward to, or is concerned with Christ, was best brought into relation with our analogy by a medieval writer, Rupert of Deutz. Taking a text from Isaiah: "Before she was in labor, she brought forth," he finds in it this meaning (which he must have gathered from the Fathers, though I cannot discover his source):

> That Word which the Virgin Mary bore incarnate, that same
> Word did the souls of patriarch and prophet conceive by faith
> and bring forth in speech and writing at an earlier time.[16]

Origen had said as much in another connection: "This honey is good which is found in the Scriptures; and just as among bees there is one that is called king, even so the prince of bees is my Lord Jesus Christ, to whom the Holy Spirit sends me that I should eat honey, for that is good."[17]

---

14   *PL* 26:1334; see also Ps. 147:14.

15   John 5:39.

16   Rupert of Deutz, *On Isaiah*, Bk. 2, Chap. 31 (*PL* 167:1362; Lat.: "Quod Virgo Maria Verbum parturivit incarnatum, ipsum fide conceptum dicto ac scripto pepererunt prius animae patriarcharum et prophetarum.)"; compare Isa. 66:7. It has been suggested to me that St. Gregory the Great was Rupert's source. Gregory does indeed throw out a lapidary phrase ("Learn the heart of God in the words of God [*disce cor Dei in verbis Dei*]") *when* writing to Theodore the imperial physician; see *Epistles*, Bk. 4. Ep. 31 (*PL* 77:706; NPNF2 12:156). But to my mind Athanasius is more likely in view of his striking statement that when the Logos comes to be in the prophets, then they give forth prophecies in the Holy Spirit. See *Epistle 1 to Serapion*, 31 (*PG* 26:601).

17   Origen, *Homilies in Isaiah*, Hom. 2, 2 (*PG* 13:227; GCS 8:252; Lat.: "Bonus est hoc mel quod in scripturis invenitur; ... et quomodo inter apes rex quidam est, qui nominatur esse rex, sic princeps apum Dominus meus est Iesus Christus, ad quem mittit me Spiritus sanctus ut comedam mel, bonum est enim.").

Letter & Spirit 6 (2010): 349-357

"As I Break Bread for You"
St. Augustine's Method in Preaching

~: Thomas F. Stransky, C. S. P. :~

It is impossible to appreciate St. Augustine's technique of planning and delivering a sermon without alluding to the saint's use of his primary sourcebook—the Bible. The Bible, from which Augustine once recoiled because of its supposedly barbaric style and unintelligible meanings, became his most precious book. As he came to see it, the Bible was filled with words of "marvelous sublimity joined to the most wholesome simplicity,"[1] written for our salvation, entrusted to the Church for its support and guidance, and given to authorized preachers to provide old things and new for the spiritual needs of the flock.[2]

Augustine judges the intellectual effectiveness of a sermon on its correct utilization of sacred Scripture. "A man speaks more or less wisely in proportion

---

1 Joseph Christopher's translation of the paranomastic "*altitudinis salbueririmam*" (*De Catechizandis Rudibus, Liber Unus*, trans. Joseph Patrick Christopher [Washington, DC: Catholic Unveristy of America, 1926], See Augustine, *On the Catechizing of the Uninstructed*, Chap. 8, 12, in *Patrologiae Cursus Completus: Series Latina*, ed. J. P. Migne, 221 vols. (Paris: Garnier and J. P. Migne, 1844–1864), 40:319. Hereafter abbreviated *PL*. Also in *A Select Library of Nicene and Post-Nicene Fathers of the Christian Church*, 1st series, 14 vols., ed. Philip Schaff (Peabody, MA: Hendrickson, 1994 [reprint]), 3:290. Hereafter abbreviated *NPNF1*. Augustine put away his early distaste for the Bible. See his *Confessions* Bk. 3, Chap. 5, 9 (*PL* 32:686; *NPNF1* 1:62); Bk. 6, Chap. 5, 8 (*PL* 32:709; *NPNF1* 1:93); Bk. 7, Chap. 20, 26 (*PL* 32:747; *NPNF1* 1:114); Bk. 7, Chap. 21, 27 (*PL* 32:747; *NPNF1* 1:133); Bk. 9, Chap. 5,13 (*PL* 32:769; *NPF*, 1:93, 114, 133). He became convinced that the Bible is "a sound and substantial study; it does not allure the mind with embellished language, nor strike a flat or wavering note by means of any deceit of the tongue." *Epistle* 132:1 (*PL* 33:508; *NPNF1* 1:470). Scripture conquered Augustine as it conquered many others, "not by violence and warfare, but by the resistless force of truth," and he who attacks that truth injures none but himself. *Against Faustus the Manichee*, Bk. 22, 60 (*PL* 42:438; *NPNF1* 4:295); 22, 83 (455); Augustine, *Epistle* 138, 4 (*PL* 33:526; *NPNF1* 1:482).

2 The Scriptures are lamps lit in the night of this world for our guidance to the next world where they will be needed no longer. See Augustine, *Sermon* 23, 3 (*PL* 38:156); *Tractates on the Gospel of John*, Tract. 35, 9 (*PL* 35:1662; *NPNF1* 7:207). Maurice Pontet remarks that Augustine "always extolled the Bible as a book written to save men. He sees in it not so much a beautiful text as a powerful remedy, and he assures us that before charming us, it will heal us." *L'Exégèse de S. Augustin, Prédicateur* [The Exegesis of St. Augustine, Preacher] (Paris: Aubier, 1946), 112. The Church, like a mother, feeds her children from her two breasts—the two Testaments. See Augustine, *Homilies on the First Epistle of John*, Hom. 3, 1(*PL* 35:1998; *NPNF1* 7:476); Augustine, *On the Morals of the Catholic Church*, Chap. 30, 62–63 (*PL* 32:1335–1336; *NPNF1* 4:58); *The True Religion*, Chap. 7, 12 (*PL* 34:128). The Church is the custodian and interpreter of the Scripture. See *Confessions*, Bk. 7, Chap. 7, 11 (*PL* 32:739; *NPNF1* 1:106); Bk. 13, Chap. 29, 44 (*PL* 32:864; *NPNF1* 1:205). For Augustine, "I would not believe the Gospel unless the authority of the Church moved (*commoverit*) me thereto." *Against the Epistle of Manichaeus*, Chap. 5, 6 (*PL* 42:176; *NPNF1* 4:131).

as he makes more or less progress in holy Scripture."[3] He was so convinced of this that shortly after his ordination, when Valerius insisted on making him preach, he writes to the bishop:

> I ought to study carefully the remedies God has provided in his Scriptures. By prayer and reading I must gain the proper strength for my soul, that it may be prepared for this perilous task. For I was ordained just at the vacation time when I was planning how I could best learn the sacred Scriptures. I was planning on some leisure to do this. Indeed, to tell the truth, I knew not at that time how ill-prepared I was for this present task which now fills me with anxiety and threatens to crush me.[4]

Augustine then begs the bishop to grant him a little time to study the Bible for the profit of those committed to his care. After his episcopal consecration, he bargained with his flock to give him some time so he could study the Bible. The compact was soon violated, as he acknowledged: "I am not permitted to have the leisure for the work I wish to do."[5]

Even after long, toilsome years of study, he still felt that he had learned so little from the Bible that he wanted a co-adjutor bishop in his diocese to lighten his burden. In 426 he begs the flock, "Let me now, if God grants me a little longer time to live, devote that little space, not to sloth or idleness, but to his holy Scriptures wherein, as far as he allows and strengthens me, I may exercise myself."[6] From beginning to end, Augustine saw the need of feeding upon the Bible, this "daily bread of my soul," in order to feed his hungering flock.[7]

As Bishop of Hippo, Augustine outlined his approach to preaching in the opening words of a sermon commenting on the multiplication of the loaves:

> In explaining the Holy Scriptures to you, I, as it were, break bread for you [*Scripturas sacras vobis, quasi panes frangimus vobis*]. As hungering, receive it. ... And you who are rich in your banquet, be not meager in good works and deeds. What I deal out is not my own. What you eat, I eat. What you live upon, I

---

3   Augustine, *Christian Doctrine*, Bk. 4, Chap. 5, 7 (PL 34:92; NPNF1 2:576). He adds, "I do not mean in the extensive reading and memorizing of them, but in a thorough understanding and the careful searching into their meanings."

4   Augustine, *Epistle* 21, 3–4 (PL 33:88–89; NPNF1 1:238).

5   Augustine, *Epistle* 213, 5 (PL 33:968; NPNF1 1:570).

6   Augustine, *Epistle* 213, 6 (PL 969; NPNF1 1:570).

7   He often refers to the daily bread of the Our Father prayer as the bread of the Scriptures. See also *Sermon* 56, 6, 10 (PL 38:381); 57, 7 (PL 38:389).

live upon. We have in heaven a common storehouse; from there comes the Word of God.[8]

Italicized scriptural references sprinkle throughout almost every page of Jacque-Paul Migne's edition of Augustine's sermons.[9] The language of the Bible is habitual with him. Its peculiar turns and favorite expressions are constantly on his lips.[10] Here is how he considers his duty:

> In expounding the Word of God and more especially, the holy Gospel, we must, brethren, as much as we can, dwell fully on every part of the sacred text, *not leaving one single passage unnoticed.* In addition, we ourselves must be nourished according to our capacity. I must minister to you whence I am nourished.[11]

Sowing Trouble in Order to Instruct

His type of biblical preaching centered on glossing the Bible. This was an adoption of the classical Roman teacher of literature and language, the *grammaticus* who explained Virgil and Homer by breaking the text into fragments, and analyzing each word under the microscope of encyclopedic learning. Augustine's process was identical; only the text had been changed.[12]

Scrupulous to explain every passage, he encountered many difficulties. Of course, he would rather read the Gospel to the people than discuss in his own words the questions he finds in it,[13] but he understands that these questionings have been willed by God: "The Teacher has given trouble in order to instruct, has sown a difficulty in order to excite earnest attention."[14] "For there are in holy

---

8   Augustine, *Sermon* 95, 1 (*PL* 38:581).

9   See *PL* 38–39.

10   Besides his ingenious adaptations and unconscious allusions, there are 13,276 formal citations from the Old Testament and 29,540 from the New Testament, according to Maurist editions, the eleven-volume edition of Augustine's complete works published by the Benedictine community at St. Maur, 1679-1700, and reprinted in the Migne edition, *PL* 32–47. See also Henri Iréné Marrou, *Saint Augustin et l'Augustinisme* (Paris: Editions du Seuil, 1956), 57; Eng.: *St. Augustine and His Influence through the Ages*, trans. Patrick Hepburne-Scott (New York: Harper, 1956). Célestin Douais affirms that from Augustine's works, two-thirds of the Bible can be constructed. "Augustin," *Dictionnaire de la Bible, Supplément*, eds. Louis Pirot, André Robert, Jacques Briend, and Édouard Cothenet (Paris: Létouzey et Ané, 1926), 1:1240.

11   Augustine, *Gospel of John*, Tract. 2, 1 (*PL* 35:1388; *NPNF1* 7:13).

12   See Fredrik Van de Meer, *Saint Augustin, Pasteur d'âmes*, 2 vols. (Paris: Editions Alsatia, 1955), 2:246; Eng.: *Augustine the Bishop*, trans. Brian Battershaw and G. R. Lamb (New York: Sheed and Ward, 1962).

13   Augustine, *Sermon*, 356, 1 (*PL* 39:1574).

14   Augustine, *Sermon*, 126, 8, 10 (*PL* 38:703).

Scripture deep mysteries which are hidden lest they should be held cheap; sought, that they may employ us; opened, that they may feed us."[15] As he wrote Volusian:

> The very language in which the holy Scripture is expressed is accessible to all, but penetrable by few. In its easily understood parts, it speaks to the heart of the learned and unlearned like a familiar friend who uses no subterfuge. Even those truths which it veils in mystery, it does not set forth with such lofty eloquence that the slow and unskilled mind dares not approach—like a poor man fearing to draw near to a rich one; rather, in simple speech holy Scripture invites all. It not only feeds them with evident truths but even exercises them with the hidden ones, for truth exists in both what is clear and what is hidden. But lest the obvious truths should cause disgust, the hidden ones arouse longings; longings bring on certain renewals; renewals bring sweet inner knowledge. By these means depraved minds are set straight, small ones are nourished, great ones are filled with delight.[16]

The preacher searches for Scriptural difficulties and solutions and presents them to his audience, thereby gaining attention and provoking thought. Augustine, I think, is certain of the effectiveness of this technique. Almost every sermon contains a scriptural problem; some sermons, in fact, center around one problem and its solution. Psychologically, the technique is sound. Curiosity springs from a love of the known rather than the unknown. We are conscious of the knowledge we already possess but we cannot know the limitations of that knowledge unless we know that other things exist, that our knowledge can unfold and flower. An explicit problem awakens this consciousness of ignorance or deficiency and this in turn becomes an impetus to sound reflective thinking and hard reasoning, whereas thinking without the perception of an actual problem is often barren.[17]

The role of the preacher as teacher is to prod the mind: "The reason why you question another is no other than to teach the one you question," writes Augustine in his early work, *The Teacher*.[18] The teacher suggests that the student's present knowledge has a privation. He then guides the mind to march from the known to the unknown in order to conquer new ground. Every word in the Bible is true.

---

15   Augustine, *Expositions of the Psalms*, 140, 1 (PL 37:1815; NPNF1 8:641).

16   Augustine, *Epistle* 137, 18 (PL 33:524; NPNF1 1:480).

17   Augustine, *On the Trinity*, Bk. 10, Chaps. 1–2 (PL 42:971–975).

18   Augustine, *The Teacher*, Chap. 1, 1 (PL 32:1194), also in *The Fathers of the Church: A New Translation* (Washington, DC: Catholic University of America, 1947–), 59:7. Hereafter abbreviated FC.

Contradictions that appear in the text cannot be true contradictions.[19] Present a contradiction and curiosity is aroused, for the mind wishes to rest in a resolution of the problem.

Sermon 71 is a good example. In Matthew's gospel, Christ emphatically declared: "Whoever speaks against the Holy Spirit will not be forgiven, either in this age or in the age to come."[20] For Augustine this was the most difficult problem in Scripture, and also the most important. He shows the difficulty: "What will become of those whom the Church desires to gain? When they have come into the Church from whatsoever error, is the hope in the remission of sins a false hope?" He then elaborates on the problem. Non-believers who blaspheme believers' sanctification blaspheme the Holy Spirit. Some of the Jewish leaders believed that Christ cast out devils through the prince of devils, not through the Holy Spirit. Heretics deny that the Holy Spirit is in the Catholic Church; some even deny his existence. Apostates, having received the Holy Spirit through baptism, leave the Church, apparently ungrateful of the gift. Are all these people forever without hope of forgiveness? Moreover, every doctrine contrary to truth is against the Holy Spirit, "and yet the Church does not cease to reform and gather out of every error those who shall receive the remission of sins and the Holy Spirit himself."

Thus having set up the problem, Augustine preaches that God wills "to exercise us by the difficulty of the question and not to deceive us by a false decision." He has taken an apparently uninteresting text, presented a practical difficulty, thereby creating interest. He then proposes the solution.

Proposing Problems in Scripture and their Solutions

Augustine develops sermon after sermon in this way. Space permits but a few examples of the Scriptural problems he poses and proceeds to propose solutions for:

> "For the flesh lusts against the spirit, and the spirit against the flesh; for these are opposed to each other, so that you do not what you would." Does this mean that we can use as an excuse for our sins, "I am forced, I am overcome by evil"?[21]

---

19 Inerrancy is intimately connected with inspiration; see Augustine, *On the Literal Meaning of Genesis*, Bk. 4, Chap. 34, 53 (*PL* 34:319), also in *Ancient Christian Writers: The Works of the Fathers in Translation* (Mahwah, NJ: Paulist, 1946–), 41:143. Hereafter abbreviated *ACW*. See also *The City of God*, Bk. 21, Chap. 7, 1 (*PL* 41:719; *NPNF* 2:458). It is the duty of the interpreter to see that in his explanations he does not leave the impression that Scripture is contradicting itself, a thing which is impossible. Augustine, *Our Lord's Sermon on the Mount according to Matthew*, Bk. 1, Chap. 22, 76 (*PL* 34:1267; *NPNF* 6:31).

20 Matt. 12:32.

21 Augustine, *Sermon* 128, 5, 7 (*PL* 38:716); see also Gal. 5:17.

God saw the world, that it was good. But is not the Creator overlooking all the evil in the world?[22]

How can the dead bury the dead?[23]

More often Augustine combines two scriptural passages that appear to be contradictory or at least create confusion:

"God tempts no man" (James 1:13). But: "The Lord our God tempts you" (Deut. 13:3); furthermore, Christ "tempts him [Philip]" (John 6:5).[24]

Christ apparently contradicts himself in the same sentence: "In praying, do not multiply words ... for your Father knows what you need before you ask him" (Matt. 6:7–8). But: If the Father knows, why ask at all? And what of this declaration of Christ: "Ask, and it shall be given you" (Matt. 7:7).[25]

"Thou art beautiful above the sons of men" (Ps. 45:2). But: "There is no beauty in him, nor comeliness." (Isa. 53:2).[26]

"I am not sent, but unto the lost sheep of Israel" (Matt. 15:24). But: "Other sheep I have which are not of this fold" (John 10:16).[27]

"Let your light shine before men, in order that they may see your good works" (Matt. 5:16). But: "Take heed not to do your good before men, in order to be seen by men" (Matt. 6:1).[28]

A man wants to bury his father: "Honor thy father and thy mother." But: "Let the dead bury their dead" (Luke 9:60).[29]

The constant use of this pedagogical method gives both preacher and audience a "cautious attitude of mind"[30]—a realization that not every line of Scripture can be

---

22 Augustine, *Sermon* 96, 4 (*PL* 38:586–588); see also Gen. 1:31.

23 Augustine, *Sermon* 100, 1, 2 (*PL* 38:603); see also Luke 9:60.

24 Augustine, *Sermon* 71, 10, 15 (*PL* 38:452-453).

25 Augustine, *Sermon* 80, 2 (*PL* 38:494).

26 Augustine, *Sermon* 95, 4 (*PL* 38:582).

27 Augustine, *Sermon* 77 (*PL* 38:483–490).

28 Augustine, *Sermon* 54 (*PL* 38:372–377).

29 Augustine, *Sermon* 100, 1, 2 (*PL* 38:603).

30 Augustine, *Teacher*, Chap. 10, 31 (*PL* 32:1213; *FC* 59:45).

understood at first glance.[31] Buried beneath the lines are treasures which cannot but enrich the soul. The cautious and zealous investigator digs deep, finds, and shares—aware all the while that it is "hazardous to consider as known what is not known." In preaching the Bible this caution is far superior to rash assertions.[32] Augustine preaches:

> Remember this: not to be disturbed by the Scriptures which you do not yet understand, nor be puffed up by what you do. What you do not understand, wait for with submission; and what you do understand, hold fast with charity.[33]

In addition to this submission of the soul (*animi subjectio*),[34]Augustine asks for prayers to enlighten both himself and his flock. For example, in putting forth the problem, the apparent contradiction between Jesus' admonition, "Tell him his fault, between you and him alone," and the advice of St. Paul: "Rebuke them in the presence of all"—Augustine says:

> Are we listening to this controversy as judges? That be far from us! Yes, rather as those whose place it is to be under the Judge. Let us knock that we may obtain, that it may be opened to us. Let us fly beneath the wings of the Lord God.[35]

The searching in common, under the action of the Holy Spirit, for an understanding of the text, follows from the delicate balance of Augustine's sermons, carefully planned, yet delivered extemporaneously. As one student of Augustine's method has noted: "There is not the slightest reason to believe that Augustine ever wrote or dictated a sermon and then read it or delivered it from memory."[36] This *ex tem-*

---

31 "For such is the depth of the Christian Scriptures, that even if I were attempting to study them and nothing else from early boyhood to decrepit old age, with the utmost leisure, the most unwearied zeal, and talents greater than I have, I would be still daily making progress in discovering their treasures; not that there is so great difficulty in coming through them to know the things necessary to salvation, but when any one has accepted these truths with the faith that is indispensable as the foundation of a life of piety and uprightness, so many things which are veiled under the manifold shadows of mystery remain to be inquired into by those who are advancing in the study, and so great is the depth of wisdom not only in the words in which these things have been expressed, but also in the things themselves, that even the most advanced in years, the most penetrating of mind, the most ardent zealous one in learning, might find himself described by what Scripture says, 'When a man hath finished, then he shall begin.'" *Epistle* 137, 3 (*PL* 33:516–517; *NPNF1* 1:474); see also Sir. 18:7.

32 Augustine, *Epistle* 95, 4 (*PL* 33:353; *NPNF1* 1:402).

33 Augustine, *Sermon* 51, 14, 35 (*PL* 38:354).

34 Augustine, *Sermon* 145, 1 (*PL* 38:791).

35 Augustine, *Sermon* 82, 5, 8 (*PL* 38:510); see also Matt. 18:15; 1 Tim. 5:20.

36 Roy J. Deferrari, "St. Augustine's Method of Composing and Delivering Sermons," *The American Journal of Philology* 43 (1922):119. According to Deferrari, stenographers (*notarii*) took

pore preaching necessitates vast remote preparation: an awareness of the Church's teaching, the careful reading and memorizing of the Bible, acute observations of daily life in order to draw ready examples, development of sensitivity to the immediate needs and capacities of the people, rapid adaptability, and a quick mind coupled with a sure flow of words. True, when we read Augustine, we are listening to a master who had triumphantly carried off the prize for rhetoric against brilliant Roman competitors. Nevertheless, a master can teach underlings.

Augustine wants the preacher to have a working knowledge of biblical languages, plus natural history, music, history, logic, and philosophy.[37] He should not only read extensively and memorize accurately the Bible, but thoroughly understand it and carefully search into its meaning.[38] He should develop Augustine's habit of pinning down ideas in writing—the ideas that arise while meditating "during brief moments on the Law of God."[39] If he does possess a well-stored mind, he will look to the works of others as well, especially to Scripture commentaries and printed sermons.

But above all Augustine would have the preacher develop a devout attitude towards his use of Scripture. It is the Lord who will give him the proper understanding of the text, and it is the Lord who will enlighten the hearts of his hearers. Even in his sermons, Augustine remained ever the Doctor of Grace:

> All that I have said has been said only to make the difficulty
> of the question increase. You yourselves see how valid it is and
> almost insoluble. May the Lord help me to solve it. May he who
> deigned to put it before us deign also to explain it. Pray with me

---

down in shorthand the sermons as they were being delivered. Van de Meer suggests the *notarii* may have been recruited from the clerics of Augustine's community. *Saint Augustin,* 2:208. Certainly this position helps explain the vigorous, controversial tone, and many irregularities found in the discourses. Apparently the bishop sometimes delivered even impromptu talks, as when he prepared a short psalm (138) to expound, but saw that the flustered lector had sung a different one at the last moment: "So I prefer to follow God's will in the lector's mistake rather than my own in my original purpose" (*PL* 37:1784).

37 Augustine, *Christian Doctrine,* Bk. 2, Chap. 11, 16 (*PL* 34:42–43; *NPNF1* 2:540); Bk. 2, Chap. 16, 24 (*PL* 47; *NPNF1* 2:543); Bk. 2, Chap. 29, 45 (*PL* 34:56–57; *NPNF1* 2:549–550); Bk. 2, Chap. 28, 42 (*PL* 34:55–56; *NPNF1* 2:549); Bk. 2, Chap. 31, 48 (*PL* 34:58; *NPNF1* 2:550); Bk. 2, Chap. 40, 60 (*PL* 34:63; *NPNF1* 2:554). Augustine does not think it pedantic to trace a word back to its original Greek for the simple people. For example in his commentaries on St. John, see Tract. 3, 8 (*PL* 35:1399; *NPNF1* 7:21); 82:1 (*PL* 35:843; *NPNF1* 7:346); 83:2 (*PL* 35:1845; *NPNF1* 7:348); 100:1 (*PL* 35:1891; *NPNF1* 7:385); 104:3 (*PL* 35:1903; *NPNF1* 7:395).

38 Augustine, *Christian Doctrine,* Bk. 4, Chap. 5, 7 (*PL* 34:92; *NPNF1* 2:576).

39 Hugh Pope, *Saint Augustine of Hippo* (London: Sands, 1937), 167. Because of frequent repetition of phrases and thoughts, Joseph Christopher thinks Augustine probably kept a commonplace book wherein he noted down turns of expressions and metaphors that particularly appealed to him. See *De Catechizandis Rudibus,* 217.

for some issue. Give me your ears; give him your heart. What he wishes to suggest to me, I will communicate to you.[40]

---

40   Augustine, *Sermon* 244, 2 (*PL* 38:1149).

Letter & Spirit 6 (2010): 359-376

THE LIMITS OF BIBLICAL INERRANCY

~: Peter Paul Zerafa, O. P. :~

Unlike other dogmas of the Church, the dogma of biblical inerrancy was not defined in special historical circumstances and in opposition to heretical views; it was the professed doctrine of the Church from the very beginning. The early Church Fathers certainly experienced difficulties in tackling some obscure biblical texts but this did not shake their faith; all dutifully adhered to the unshakable belief in biblical truth while admiring the liberty that the Holy Spirit permitted to the sacred authors.[1]

The example of St. Augustine is enlightening. He would acknowledge his own incapacity for catching the fleeting manifestations of divine thought when he could not find a reasonable solution to the scriptural problems that tormented him.[2] But the clearest interpretation of the Church's mind is the testimony of St. Thomas Aquinas. He declared that it would be heretical to say that anything false is contained in some canonical Scripture.[3]

Thus, the Church has not found it necessary to make inerrancy the object of a separate dogmatic definition. The Roman pontiffs have, from time to time, called the attention of exegetes to this undisputed doctrine;[4] in addition, the Pontifical Biblical Commission[5] and the Holy Office[6] have promptly intervened when some opinion threatened to obscure it.

By its very nature, the notion of biblical inerrancy is universal. That is to say, it would be impossible to posit a mistake anywhere in the inspired text; the inerrancy of the text is co-extensive with the divine inspiration of the text. The Church

---

1   The principal difficulties are discussed in G. Courtade, *"Inspiration et Inerrance,"* in *Dictionnaire de la Bible, Supplément,* eds. Louis Pirot, André Robert, Jacques Briend and Édouard Cothenet (Paris: Létouzey et Ané, 1926), 4:526.

2   St. Augustine, *Epistle* 82, 1, 3, in *Patrologiae Cursus Completus. Series Latina,* ed. J. P. Migne (Paris: Garnier and J. P. Migne, 1844–1864), 26:417A. Hereafter abbreviated *PL.*

3   St. Thomas Aquinas, *Commentary on the Book of Job,* Chap. 13, 1. Compare Aquinas, *Summa Theologiae* [Summary of Theology], pt. 1a, q. 68, art. 1; *Quaestiones Disputatae De Potentia Dei* [Disputed Questions on the Power of God] (Westminster, MD: Newman, 1952), q. 4, art. 1, contra. 4; *Quaestiones Quodlibetales* [Miscellaneous Questions], q. 12, art. 26, reply obj. 1.

4   *Enchiridion Biblicum: Documenti della Chiesa sulla Sacra Scrittura* [Documents of the Church Concerning Sacred Scripture], 4th ed. (Bologna: Dehoniane, 1961), 44; 46; 124–127; 205; 450; 538–540. Hereafter abbreviated *EB.*

5   *EB* 420.

6   *EB* 499.

reproves all efforts to "limit" the scope of inerrancy[7] or to restrict it to certain texts or expressions in the Scriptures.[8]

As the word implies, innerancy is a negative concept that involves the exclusion of errors;[9] to this negative concept, there corresponds a positive one that involves the assertion of the truth of Scripture. But these two concepts, as applied to a given writing, are not necessarily co-extensive, for they are governed by different conditions. It is sufficient for the former that nothing is said against truth, but it is required for the latter that truth itself be positively expressed. And since not everything that is free from error contains truth, it could happen that a particular text fulfils the requirements of negative inerrancy without implying the positive one.

The magisterial documents of the Church, always intent on safeguarding the truth of the inspired Word, acknowledge negative inerrancy, but do not deal direcly with "positive inerrancy," which must be established in each case by the principles of sound exegesis. The difference between the absence of error and the position of truth is a commonsense principle that has been given a forceful wording by Pierre Benoit. Benoit emphatically asserts that positive inerrancy is not co-extensive with inspiration, insofar as not all of the inspired text is the bearer of a particular truth.[10] It is the "limits" of positive inerrancy, or rather the extension of biblical truth, that interests us in this article.

The Study of Literary Forms

In attempting to attain the truth of the Bible and defend it against attack, the exegete relies on the Church's official interpretation and the unanimous teaching of the Fathers.[11] Where this secure lead cannot be found, the surest means of encompassing the divine truth is to employ the method of "literary forms," according to the principles of sound interpretation set out by the Church. As G. Courtade has stated, since the Bible does not err, it is enough to understand it well in order to reach its truth and uncover its inerrancy.[12]

In fact, difficulties with the Church's belief in biblical inerrancy have generally proceeded from a new appraisal of the biblical literature spurred on by the progress of modern science. In other words, with the advance of scientific under-

---

7   *EB* 124; 455.

8   *EB* 454.

9   Hildebrand Hopfl and Louis Leloir. *Introductio Generalis in Sacram Scripturam* [A General Introduction to Sacred Scripture], 6th ed. (Rome: Neapoli 1958), n. 130.

10   Pierre Benoit, *"L'Inspiration,"* in *Initiation Biblique: Introduction a L'Etude des Saintes Ecritures*, 3rd. ed., eds. André Robert and Abbé Tricot (Paris: Desclee & Cie, 1954), 6–45, at 35; Eng.: *Guide to the Bible: An Introduction to the Study of Holy Scripture* (Rome: Society of St. John the Evangelist, 1951).

11   *EB* 565.

12   Courtade, *"Inspiration et Inerrance,"* 4:533.

standing, we are becoming ever more conscious that familiar biblical ideas express more the heritage of the ancient culture than the findings of scientific truth as we now know it. However, at the same time, the historical and literary methods for studying the ancient "forms" or genres of the biblical texts permits us to separate the divine message from the baggage of outdated ideas that often accompany it. In this way, inerrancy is reduced to its proper boundaries where it can ward off any possible attack.

The study of literary forms is neither peculiar to the Bible nor is it a modern invention. The biblical texts have been clothed in an apparatus that lies far away from us, both in time and in mentality. The Semitic mentality, more or less shared by the various ethnic groups of the ancient Near East, was already at variance in biblical times with the mentality of the Western civilization of which we are heirs. The gap between the Semitic and the Western mentality has not decreased in the ensuing millennia; in fact, it has grown wider. We continue to use the same biblical terms, but we have different notions; we continue to employ the same idioms, but for different categories; we discuss the same reality but with different evaluation.

The Bible will remain forever what it has been from the very beginning— perennial divine truth incorporated in a fixed literary apparel that obeys predetermined literary laws. We will never be able to separate the biblical message from the literary form in which it is conveyed to us. We will never be able to drop this literary apparatus and transpose the biblical imagery into our own context. The concordists of the last century made a last try to read contemporary science into the Bible, but their efforts evoked the disapproval of biblical scholars[13] and a call to order by Church authorities.[14] We cannot conform the Bible to our mentality; it is we, as scholars and believers, who must conform ourselves to the mentality of the Bible if we are to catch its message.

This fundamental principle of interpretation was already traced by Augustine, who had to steer a difficult way between two different but equally erroneous currents. On the one hand, he confronted those who wanted by all means to bridge the gap between the sacred text and their scientific ideas by imposing these ideas on the Bible. Augustine rejected this as an exercise in "pulling the Scriptures to one's own opinions, while we should rather conform ourselves to the sense of the Scriptures."[15] On the other hand, Augustine had to rebuke those who questioned the truth and inerrancy of the Scriptures because they could not find confirmation for their scientific knowledge in the holy books. To these, Augustine counseled humility and recognition that the the Bible is susceptible to multiple interpreta-

---

13   Ferdinand Prat, *La Bible et l'histoire* [The Bible and History], 5th ed. (Paris: Desclee. 1908), 23–25.

14   *EB* 330.

15   Augustine, *On the Literal Meaning of Genesis*, Bk 1, Chap. 18, 37 (*PL* 34:260), also in *Ancient Christian Writers: The Works of the Fathers in Translation* (Mahwah, NJ: Paulist, 1946), 41:41. Hereafter abbreviated *ACW*.

tions: "They should keep low, who stigmatize as ignorant and rough the words of Scripture, chosen as they are to nourish all pious spirits."[16]

It is no wonder, then, that the Church in our day calls on the exegetes to look upon the study of literary forms as a grave duty. Pope Leo XIII had already insisted that biblical teachers and theologians know the original languages of the Bible and be well versed in the art of biblical criticism. These tools are important for defending against those who would impugn the biblical truth. For the same reason, exegetes and theologians should study the physical sciences and be familiar with the historical sciences.[17] Although Leo did not mention expressly the study of the literary forms, his words laid down fundamental principles for this study. It was Pope Pius XII who gave definitive authorization for the study of the literary forms, declaring this study not only acceptable to the Church but also imperative to biblical scholars.[18]

When first introduced, form study was presented as a remedy for apparently insoluble difficulties with select texts of the Bible. Especially as it was developed by the Jesuit exegete, Franz von Hummelauer,[19] the emphasis on the human authors's use of literary genres seemed to admit some sort of diminished truth in the inspired writings. This led to long discussion as to which literary forms are admissible, with some authors distinguishing between worthy and unworthy forms.[20] When the discussion threatened to get out of hand, Pope Benedict XV tightened the reins and called for moderation.[21]

Pius looks at the problem from a different point of view and beats another track. These literary genres or manners of expression, as he calls them, [22] are simply a means of communicating one's ideas; all of them can be admitted provided that the holiness and truth of the Bible are not jeopardized.[23] In the same way, modern scholars no longer try to fix beforehand what forms could have been employed by God.[24] They rather search for the forms actually employed by the sacred writer.

The interpreter must, as it were, go back wholly in spirit to those remote centuries of the East and accurately determine what modes of writing, so to speak, the

---

16   Augustine, *Meaning of Genesis*, Bk. 1, Chap. 20, 40 (*PL* 34:262; *ACW* 41:44).

17   *EB* 118–123.

18   *EB* 560.

19   Franz von Hummelauer, *Exegetisches zur Inspirationsfrage*: Mit besonderer Rücksicht auf das Alte Testament [Exegetical Questions of Inspiration: With Respect Especially to the Old Testament] (St. Louis: Herder, 1904).

20   Louis Billot, *De Inspiratione Sacrae Scripturae: Theologica Disquisitio* [The Inspiration of Sacred Scripture: A Theological Inquiry], 4th ed. (Rome: Society of the Propagation of the Faith, 1929), 141–166.

21   *EB* 461.

22   *EB* 558–560.

23   *EB* 559.

24   Courtade, *"Inspiration et Inerrance,"* 4:538.

authors of that ancient period would be likely to use, and in fact did use. For the ancient peoples of the East, in order to express their ideas, did not always employ those forms or kinds of speech which we use today; but rather those used by the men of their times and countries.[25]

By way of example the pontiff mentions "certain fixed ways of expounding and narrating, certain definite idioms, especially of a kind peculiar to the Semitic tongues, so-called approximations, and certain hyperbolic modes of expression, nay, at times, even paradoxical." [26] He singles these out without excluding other possible genres, as appears clearly from the general comparison established between the written and the substantial Word of God.

Form Study and Objections to Biblical Inerrancy

Widely used by modern commentators, the study of literary forms has borne abundant fruit and has dissipated many of the objections once levelled against the inerrancy of the Bible. The most famous of these objections stems from the Scriptures's use of outdated terms based on unreliable visual observation of such objects as the movement of the heavenly bodies, the peculiar qualities of animals, and the like. In these matters, the biblical terminology reflects the first impressions which may not always correspond to the intimate nature of things.

Leo[27] quoted Aquinas's remark that Moses described the movement of the heavenly bodies as it appears to the external senses,[28] and the pontiff added that our modern scientific age has retained the same expressions. One could also mention in this connection that we continue to speak of people being affected by a "bad spirit," which is the source of all ailments in ancient literature.[29] Today we are perhaps better able to diagnose the pathological state of King Saul, and can perhaps give a better classification of the ailments of so many people grouped together as demoniacs in the New Testament.[30]

The point is that the Scripture's use of this and similar terminology does not invalidate our belief in its inerrancy. The same is true for its use of numbers and numerology. Mathematical accuracy has never been a Semitic strong point or priority. Figures are generally rounded and may be used as conventional expressions of determined durations and quantities. A generation can be described as a passage of forty years, regardless of its actual length. Grandeur is also communicated by numbers. We read that after only a few generations, and notwithstanding the

---

25   *EB* 558.

26   *EB* 559.

27   *EB* 121.

28   Aquinas, *Summa*, pt. 1a, q. 70, art. 1, reply obj. 3.

29   Compare Olegario Garcia de la Fuente, *Los Dioses y el Pecado en Bailonia* [The Gods and Sin in Babylon] (El Escorial: Madrid Centro Biblico Hispano-Americano, 1963), 135–140.

30   Courtade, *"Inspiration et Inerrance,"* 4:535.

oppressive measures of Pharaoh, the insignificant group that entered Egypt under Joseph had soared up to more than six hundred thousand men-at-arms,[31] which would postulate a population of more than two million. This great figure stands to prove the exceptional protection of God who led the people safely through all their troubles.

More than large figures or quantities, it is totality itself that bears out clearly the idea of exceptional greatness. This is why we so often find such expressions as "not one escaped,"[32] and "every nation under heaven."[33] A special emphasis on a given thing could be expressed by a denial of its opposite. The importance of the inner love of God is illustrated by the rejection of external cult,[34] and the strong attachment to Christ implies the hate of all that is outside him.[35] Here the attention should be focused on what is affirmed; the denial is of secondary importance.

Another literary form is the use of stereotyped pictures and old traditions; these play a great part in the biblical descriptions of events. Jeremiah gives a vivid depiction of the fall of Babylon. The details are borrowed from typical siege stories—demolition of the ramparts,[36] burning of the gates,[37] followed by a general devastation.[38] We know, however, from other sources, that Babylon did not suffer any harm under the Persian conqueror, King Cyrus. In other instances, literary figures are taken from old mythological traditions, such as the prophet's mention of Rahab,[39] or from apocryphal story, as that used in the epistle of Jude.[40]

Also, we know from the study of ancient forms that lengthy actions and elaborate speeches are often used to signal and enhance the importance of a message being conveyed. The prophet Ezekiel must have gone through laborious acting the better to express the coming siege of Jerusalem; the author of Job expresses his doctrine in the form of a protracted discussion by which he gradually demolishes the theological views against which he is reacting. In these cases it is not the highly finished presentation that should attract our attention, but rather the divine message hidden therein.

The principle of literary forms has also proven useful for answering objections to inerrancy in historical narratives. Pius is very positive on this matter:

---

31   Num. 1:46.

32   1 Macc. 7:47.

33   Acts 2:5.

34   Hos. 6:6.

35   Luke 14:26.

36   Jer. 50:15; 51:44, 58.

37   Jer. 51:58.

38   Jer. 50:3, 13; 51:3, 37.

39   Isa. 51:9.

40   Jude 9.

Not infrequently—to mention only one instance—when some persons reproachfully charge the sacred writers with some historical error or inaccuracy in the recording of facts, on closer examination it turns out to be nothing else than those customary modes of expression and narration peculiar to the ancients, which used to be employed in the mutual dealings of social life and which in fact were sanctioned by common usage.[41]

The same pontiff later applied this principle in his encyclical letter, *Humani Generis*, where he confirmed that the first eleven chapters of Genesis contain real history, but not as that history is presented in Greek, Roman, or modern historiography.[42] The poetical descriptions throughout the Bible are also to be interpreted according to their literary form, especially when they deal with the interventions of God in favor of his people.

An honest appraisal of the biblical message arrived at through the study of the literary forms eliminates those difficulties that flow from a faulty interpretation of the text itself. But Pius has not presented it as the primary rule for defending the truth of the Bible; it is just one principle of interpretation, one means of understanding the literal sense of the text. He has written:

What is the literal sense of a passage is not always as obvious in the speeches and writings of the ancient authors of the East, as it is in the works of the writers of our own time. ... The interpreter must ... accurately determine what modes of writing, so to speak, the authors of the ancient period would be likely to use, and in fact did use.[43]

In this way "many difficulties" can be solved, because "not infrequently" apparent inaccuracies are only the result of special literary forms peculiar to the ancients.

By bracketing together interpretation and inerrancy, Pius makes it clear that the limits of inerrancy can be only established by determining, with the help of the literary study, the literal sense of the text. Once we know what the sacred writer has in mind, we are able to mark the limits of inerrancy, for "all that is contained in the sacred Scripture is true."[44]

What is the "Formal Object" of Scripture?

Some modern scholars advocate a different means for establishing the limits of Scripture's inerrancy. They search for what they call the "formal object" of the

---

41   *EB* 560.

42   *EB* 618.

43   *EB* 558.

44   Aquinas, *Quodlibetales*, q. 12, art. 26, reply. obj. 1.

Bible.[45] This has some immediate appeal and much can be said in favor of this method. Setting out the object of any judgement is the basic requirement for comprehension, and it is quite clear that the limits of truth have to be measured according to the limits of the object in question. It is also clear that along with the object of an affirmation one could find many secondary developments that serve to illustrate this object without forming a part of the affirmation itself; these secondary developments fall under the judgement only insofar as they are connected with the object. In themselves, they remain outside the sphere of the judgement.

The actual limits of the object of the Bible can be established by the study of the literary forms.

Augustine articulated this principle in his polemic against Felix the Manichean. Teaching about the constitution and origin of the world falls outside the scope of divine revelation, he argued. "It is enough for men to know about these things what they learned at school, for their own use." He added: "It is not written in the Gospel that the Lord said: 'I shall send you the Paraclete who will teach you about the courses of the sun and the moon.' He wanted to form Christians, not mathematicians."[46]

Some modern scholars would widen this principle and apply it as an independent general rule in conjunction with the study of literary forms.[47] They insist on the fact that God has given us our natural faculties by which we can attain the knowledge of natural objects. The divine inspiration is not intended to replace our investigation of the natural world through our natural faculties; inspiration intends to elevate the intellect to a higher level in order to grasp a supernatural truth. The Bible is written in view of this higher truth, which in turn, they argue, forms the object of inspiration and inerrancy; everything else in the sacred text falls under inerrancy only insofar as it is connected with this object.

Thomas Aquinas on Prophecy and Sacred Writing

This general limitation of inerrancy to a predetermined biblical object, while superficially attractive, cannot be squared with the Church's traditional understanding and leads to numerous theological difficulties. Thomas Aquinas followed Augustine's lead in excluding the fashioning of the heavenly bodies from the object of the Bible.[48] But he did not present this restriction as a general principle. He offers only one limitation: God reveals to the prophets what is necessary for the in-

---

45 Compare Paul Synave and Pierre Benoit, *Prophecy and Inspiration: A Commentary on the Summa Theologica II-II, Questions 171–178* (New York: Desclee, 1961), 134–137.

46 Augustine, *Against Felix the Manichee*, Bk. 1, Chap. 10 (*PL* 42:525).

47 André Baruco and Henri Cazelles, "*L'inerrance des Livres Inspiré*" [The Inerrancy of the Inspired Books], in *Introduction à la Bible*, 2 vols., eds. André Robert and André Feuillet (Tournai: Desclee, 1959), 1:58–68, at 61–65.

48 Aquinas, *Questiones Disputatae de Veritate* [Disputed Questions on Truth], q. 12, art. 2, reply, in *Truth*, 3 vols. (Chicago: H. Regnery, 1952–1954).

struction of the faithful.[49] But the extension of this doctrine cannot be established beforehand.

Thomas places prophecy midway between the beatific vision and faith. In the beatific vision, the human intellect is elevated by a supernatural light through which it can see the divine essence and other objects in it. No human intellect, adorned with this light can totally penetrate the divine essence; each one comprehends God in proportion to the participation in this divine light granted to him, according to God's degree of charity.[50] And the extent of the other objects visible in the divine essence varies with one's comprehension of the divine essence.[51] Thus, while the divine light is not of itself limited to determined objects, it is actually restricted by one's degree of participation in that light, which in turn depends on the divine charity.

The limits of the object of faith are established by different criteria, for the act of faith is governed by different rules. The believer does not see the truth in which he believes: he assents to a truth visible to others.[52] All that Thomas would concede is that the believer perceives by some external signs that a given truth is to be believed, and that faith itself confirms this credibility;[53] but this perception does not bear on the truth itself.[54] The object of faith is God; many other things fall under faith because of their connection with God and insofar as they help man in his trend towards the fruition of God.[55] This general statement is elsewhere limited by two negative qualifications. Speaking about heresy, Thomas distinguishes those matters that directly or indirectly pertain to faith from the "questions of geometry and suchlike topics which cannot belong to the faith by any means."[56] Then, since faith is an assent to an invisible truth, it cannot bear on any object that is either seen or known.[57] To be noted however is that for Thomas all that is contained in the Scripture falls under the object of faith,[58] at least indirectly.[59]

These two restrictions do not apply to the object of prophecy. Unlike the believer, the prophet does not assent to invisible truth: he sees it.[60] Under this aspect

---

49   Aquinas, *Summa*, pt. 2a–2ae, q. 171, art. 4 reply obj. 1; Aquinas, *De Veritate*, q. 12, art. 2.

50   Aquinas, *Summa*, pt. 1a, q. 12, art. 6.

51   Aquinas, *Summa*, pt. 1a, q. 12, art. 8.

52   Aquinas, *Summa*, pt. 2a–2ae, q. 2, art. 1.

53   Aquinas, *Summa*, pt. 2a–2ae, q. 1, art. 4, reply obj. 3; compare pt. 2a–2ae, q. 1, art. 5, reply obj. 1.

54   Aquinas, *Summa*, pt. 2a–2ae, art. 4, reply obj. 2.

55   Aquinas, *Summa*, pt. 2a–2ae, q. 1, art. 1.

56   Aquinas, *Summa*, pt. 2a–2ae, q. 11, art. 2.

57   Aquinas, *Summa*, pt. 2a–2ae, q. 1, arts. 4, 5.

58   Aquinas, *Summa*, pt. 2a–2ae, art. 5.

59   Aquinas, *Summa*, pt. 1a, q. 32, art. 4.

60   Aquinas, *Summa*, pt. 2a–2ae, q. 173, art. 4; compare *Summa*, pt. 2a–2ae, q. 171, art. 5.

prophecy comes very near to the beatific vision, from which it is distinguished by the fact that it is not a permanent habit but a transitory passion:

> The divine essence cannot be seen by a created intellect save through the light of glory, of which it is written (Ps. 36:9): *In Thy light we shall see light.* But this light can be shared in two ways. First by way of an abiding form, and thus it beatifies the saints in heaven. Secondly by way of a transitory passion ... of the light of prophecy.[61]

It follows that the act of prophecy can stand together with the habit of faith but not with the act of faith.[62] Since therefore in prophecy the intellect is perfected for its own sake, and not in view of its subjection to the will,[63] there is no ground for limiting its object to those matters which are unattainable by human activity.

Thomas does seem to restrain the object of prophecy to invisible things, as he does when he deals with the object of faith. Starting from the fact that prophecy is a knowledge of what is remote from us, he mentions the following possible objects of prophecy: First, the future contingencies that are in themselves unknowable and are the chief matter of prophecy and belong to it most properly.[64] Second come the divine mysteries that are unattainable by our intellect because of its weakness. Finally come those things that are within reach of some men, and remote from others. In this way, what is known to one can be communicated to another through a prophetic revelation. These things are not of themselves the object of prophecy, but only with reference to those who ignore them.[65]

In this case however Aquinas is speaking of prophecy in a restricted sense. Prophecy has a wide range of degrees, and not all that is said of a special degree can be applied to the whole range. Sometimes Aquinas considers prophecy only as a prediction of future events;[66] at other times he widens his perspective to include all those things that cannot be known except by revelation,[67] thus excluding what is already known by human investigation; but generally he includes within the object of prophecy all that can fall under divine cognition,[68] even if it is attainable

---

61 Aquinas, *Summa*, pt. 2a–2ae, q. 175, art. 3, reply obj. 2; compare *Summa*, pt. 2a–2ae, q. 171, art. 2; pt. 2a–2ae, q. 173, art. 1.

62 Aquinas, *Summa*, pt. 2a–2ae, q. 175, a. 3, reply obj. 3.

63 Aquinas, *De Veritate*, q. 12, art. 1, reply.

64 Aquinas, *Summa*, pt. 2a–2ae, q. 171, art. 3.

65 Aquinas, *De Veritate*, q. 12, art. 2.

66 Aquinas, *Summa Contra Gentiles*, Chap. 154, art. 10, in *On the Truth of the Catholic Faith (Summa Contra Gentiles)*, 5 vols. (New York: Doubleday, 1955–1957); *Summa*, pt. 2a–2ae, q. 171, art. 3, reply obj. 1.

67 Aquinas, *Summa*, 2a–2ae, q. 171, art. 3, reply obj. 2.

68 Aquinas, *Summa*, 2a–2ae, q. 171, pref.

by human reason.[69] The restriction that he construes by analogy with the object of faith does not apply to prophecy as such, but to a special kind of prophecy.

The limitation of the object of prophecy to what is useful for our salvation is very misleading. Thomas admits that those matters which cannot have any relation to our salvation are alien to the object of prophecy,[70] but when he explains what is required for something to be useful to the faithful he drops every shadow of discrimination. Among the natural truths which he accepts, he mentions first of all such facts as the incorruptibility of the intellect, which is postulated by other revealed truths, and is admitted in the Bible because of its connection with them. Then he passes on to other matters which are not postulated by higher truths, but are handed down through prophecy because they induce us to admire God's wisdom and might.[71] Now, there is no natural truth that could not lead to this admiration of God, and therefore no truth can of itself be excluded from prophecy.

It is also to be noted that when prophecy bears on a topic that can be attained by human reason, the truth that is in the mind of the prophet does not differ from that which is possessed by the ordinary man. For the divine power can produce without the collaboration of the natural qualities and faculties the same effects that are normally produced by these qualities and faculties.[72] It follows that it is not necessary to be always searching for higher meanings hidden under the cover of natural events. Very often the natural facts are admitted in the Bible as conveyors of a supernatural message, but this is not always the case. Sometimes a modest natural truth is transmitted to the prophet, and falls under inerrancy for its own sake, because it occupies a peculiar place in God's plan of salvation.

One cannot, therefore, determine in advance the boundaries of the object of prophecy and inerrancy.

Distinguishing Inspiration in Prophets and Hagiographers

The distinction between prophet and hagiographer, or sacred writer, has also been harnessed to the cause of setting the limits of inerrancy; this is the object of an important treatise by Pierre Benoit.[73] He presents this distinction as the fundamental principle for judging the inerrancy of the Bible, in that it separates

---

69 Aquinas, *De Veritate*, q. 12, art. 12; *Summa*, 2a–2ae, q. 174, art. 2, reply obj. 3.

70 Aquinas, *De Veritate*, q. 12, art. 2.

71 Aquinas, *De Veritate*, q. 12, art. 2; compare q. 12, art. 2, reply obj. 3.

72 Aquinas, *De Veritate*, q. 12, art. 2, reply obj. 4.

73 Synave and Benoit, *Prophecy and Inspiration*, 103; see also the shorter discussion by Benoit, "L'Inspiration," 34–35. Some useful remarks upon this theory may be found in Michel Labourdette, "Les Charismes: La Prophétie les Problèmes Scripturaires" [The Charisms: The Problem of Prophecy in Scripture], *Revue Thomiste* 50 (1950): 404–421. Joseph Coppens, "L'Inspiration et L'Inerrance Bibliques" [The Inspiration and Inerrancy of the Bible], *Ephemerides Theologicae Lovanienses* 33 (1957): 36–57; J. Terrance Forestell, "The Limitation of Inerrancy," *Catholic Bible Quarterly* 20:1 (January 1958), 9–18.

the practical judgement from the speculative one, which is the sole guarantee of truth and inerrancy. Discarding his earlier categories,[74] he now distinguishes three possible formalities in the divine charism: *revelation, cognitive inspiration*, and *scriptural inspiration*.

According to Benoit's schema, these may be found either singly or united together in different combinations.[75] *Revelation* is the characteristic of the prophet and does not necessarily include a speculative judgement and inerrancy. *Scriptural inspiration* is an impulse to compose a book or a discourse. Of itself this charism does not include an inerrant judgement; it belongs most properly to the sacred writer. *Cognitive inspiration* is a light that illuminates the speculative judgement; it carries with it truth and inerrancy, and is the normal case with the genuine prophet. Cognitive inspiration may also be found in the sacred writer if he is moved to form a speculative judgement, just as scriptural inspiration could also be found in a prophet if he is called to compose a book. It follows that the genuine prophet has a speculative judgement with inerrancy, while the sacred writer as such requires only practical judgement without inerrancy, but can at times be graced, for the sake of his book, with the inerrant speculative judgement proper to the prophet.

Benoit bases his distinction in part on the different roles incumbent on the prophet and the sacred writer; he also cites some expressions found in Aquinas that seem to affirm this duality of function. The author observes that in addition to the different functions that St. Paul ascribed to the Scriptures,[76] the biblical writings also function to threaten and console, encourage and call to penance, delight and entertain. Sometimes they intend to simply transmit to posterity a recollection of past events without intending to inculcate them or to teach them.

Benoit concludes that these different tasks can be grouped in two categories. First, there are those that deal with the transmission of the truth. These require a speculative judgement and fall to the lot of the prophet, who does nearly nothing of his own initiative. Second, there are those intended to produce some determined effect; these are left to the sacred writer, to whom is assigned the laborious task of literary composition.

In this regard we might distinguish two distinct vocations, as it were: the first one impels one *to repeat an oracle* which has come down from heaven; the other impels one to *compose a book*. We shall designate them by the two standard terms, *"prophet"* and *"sacred writer."*[77]

---

74   In the original French edition of his commentary on the section on prophecy in Thomas ("*La Prophétie*" [Prophecy], in *Somme Théologique*, ed. Paul Synave and Pierre Benoit [Paris: Desclee, 1947], 319), he had adopted the following terms: *révélation prophetique* [prophetic revelation], *inspiration prophétique* [prophetic inspiration], *inspiration scripturaire* [scriptural inspiration]; compare the English translation, Synave and Benoit, *Prophecy and Inspiration*.

75   Synave and Benoit, *Prophecy and Inspiration*, 110.

76   2 Tim. 3:16.

77   Synave and Benoit, *Prophecy and Inspiration*, 106.

This distinction, however, should not be reduced to a mere question of speaking or writing. Benoit continues:

> The essential differentiating factor in these two typical cases …
> is the nature of the message which God confides to his repre-
> sentative. In the case of the prophet, God reveals to him super-
> natural truths which he could never have attained by himself
> and which he therefore has only to repeat. The sacred writer, on
> the other hand, retains the task of acquiring and ordering by
> himself—with God's help, to be sure—natural truths, or even
> supernatural ones, which he has been able to learn by human
> methods of inquiry.[78]

For Benoit, the most fundamental difference between sacred writer and prophet comes from the final cause. In prophecy, the inspiration first affects the intellect, for the prophet is sent to teach—his judgement is principally speculative. The sacred writer acts initially on the impulse of the will, for he has to attain more extensive and more varied ends: his judgement is principally practical.[79]

As a result of Benoit's imposing apparatus, one has to admit that the speculative judgement is not a universal characteristic of the Bible. We must not search for inspired truth in all that is said by the sacred writer, since some apparent judgements are incorporated in the Bible for practical reasons, and not as representing divine thought. This conclusion is sound, and it is exactly the duty of the exegetes to ascertain, by studying the literary forms, where the sacred writer expresses speculative judgements and to disclose their import.

However, one has to question the usefulness and advisability of presenting the prophet and the sacred writer as the principal beneficiaries of the speculative and the practical judgements, respectively. Benoit admits that normally both judgements appear together in the Scripture[80] and that the scriptural inspiration, and consequently the practical judgement, are found alone when "a sacred writer [is] quoting on the authority of another or writing about incidentals, without vouching for the truth of the matter."[81] One fails to see why this rare phenomenon of scriptural inspiration should be given as a fundamental distinction for biblical interpretation.

The distinction between prophet and sacred writer, based on a difference in their respective judgement, is indeed hard to justify. Benoit considers the practical judgement as the principal requirement for the composition of a book. And it is true that not every writing is composed with the intention of communicating a

---

78   Synave and Benoit, *Prophecy and Inspiration*, 109.

79   Synave and Benoit, *Prophecy and Inspiration*, 110.

80   Benoit, *"L'Inspiration,"* 22.

81   Synave and Benoit, *Prophecy and Inspiration*, 111.

speculative truth. A book may be written with the exclusive intention of entertaining the reader, and in this case the writing of the book does not entail more speculative activity than the sketching of a portrait or the composition of a symphony.

But this is not the case of the Bible. The scriptural message leads man to God by instructing him in the faith and by guiding him in his actions.[82] The latter function of the Scripture presents no difficulty: God guides us by his precepts, entreaties, and the like. Here nobody has ever searched for speculative truth—the object of this message is practical truth. The difficulty lies in the first object of God's Word, which is often attained through narratives and descriptions that do not always tally with reality. Can we get around this difficulty by supposing that in such cases the principal judgement applied by the writer is a practical one? Hardly ever. The biblical message is delivered in a human and pleasing way, and therefore the writer makes use of all his literary talent. But all his faculties are mobilized in view of the message he is delivering; this message remains the principal factor of the book, and brings with it the speculative judgement as his principal intellectual activity.

The study of the literary forms is very precious here. It shows us that to bring home his message, the writer may use poetical descriptions, old traditions, fictitious and parabolic narratives, and more. Even more, the sacred writer can relate false assertions and impious actions. We have to sift the divine truth that is carried by this great diversity of literary form; we do this by dropping out the literary apparel, whether good or bad, that is incorporated in the Bible not for its own sake but as a vehicle to convey this divine truth. But one cannot affirm that the judgement underlying the composition of such passages is principally a practical one. It is principally a speculative judgement, but it naturally postulates the practical judgement, without which the sacred writer cannot transmit his truth to others.

Nor is there any reason for Benoit to restrain the literary activity of the genuine prophet to a simple repetition of an oracle.[83] If Christ delivered his message in highly elaborate parables, why could not a prophet repeat his oracle in carefully developed literary forms? Supposing that the prophetical speeches preserved in the Bible are a reliable sample of prophetical oratory, one has to admit that the divine Spirit allowed great liberty in literary composition to the prophets. These speeches in fact show that the prophets made use of all their talent in handing down the divine revelation. Moreover, even under this supernatural impulse, the prophets normally retained their liberty of action:[84] they could accept or reject this charism,

---

82   Compare Aquinas, *Summa*, 2a–2ae, q. 174, art. 6.

83   All that Benoit would admit here is that, "At the very most he has to make a choice about the method of presentation, the form of his discourse." But this activity does not extend itself to the composition of a discourse, which already surpasses the proper role of the prophet. *Prophecy and Inspiration,* 107, 110, n. 2.

84   Compare Aquinas, *De Veritate*, q. 12, art. 4: "But the use of any prophecy is within the power of the prophet. It is in keeping with this that the first Epistle to the Corinthians (14:32) says:

which shows that even in the case of the prophets the practical judgement plays an important part. One can admit, however, that the liberty left to the human instrument is susceptible of various degrees. Only that the difference between the prophet and the hagiographer should not be taken as a criterion for measuring the degree of the divine light and of the human initiative.

Thomas and the Grace of Inspiration

The authority of Thomas Aquinas cannot be called upon to confirm the distinction that Benoit would make between prophet and sacred writer. In some places[85] Thomas mentions them separately, and this has led some authors to think that he assigns a different role to each. Domenico Zanecchia, for instance, thinks that for Thomas the sacred writer's role is to judge supernaturally and to consign to the Church natural truths obtained by human means. By contrast, the prophet's function consists not only of judging and transmitting, but also of receiving from God those truths which cannot be reached by the human intellect. In other words, the distinction is based on the provenance—and on the nature—of the truths in question. Whenever there is a revelation of a supernatural truth, there is also prophecy; otherwise there is only a scriptural inspiration.[86]

The general lines of this distinction between revelation and biblical inspiration is universally accepted; everybody in fact admits that the sacred writer does not necessarily receive a revelation from God. But some authors proceed much further. Benoit thinks that Thomas did not examine the scriptural inspiration, because the condition of the biblical studies in his time did not demand it, and therefore we must be very cautious in applying to scriptural inerrancy what he says about prophecy. He notes Thomas's distinction between the prophets, who speak as representatives of God (*ex persona Dei*), and the sacred writers, who write in their own name (*ex persona propria*). For Benoit this suggests the difference in the messenger's initiative, which can be explained in terms of greater or smaller importance of the practical judgement.[87]

Thomas, however, never dreamt of these distinctions, nor is it exact to say that he did not discuss the scriptural inspiration. Although he was not beset by the many problems that have to be tackled by present day exegetes and theologians, he did discuss biblical inspiration, and not prophecy in general. The charism that

---

'And the spirits of the prophets are subject to the prophets.' Therefore, one can prevent himself from using prophecy. And the proper disposition is a necessary requirement for the proper use of prophecy, since the use of prophecy proceeds from the created power of the prophet."

85 Aquinas, *De Veritate*, q. 12, art. 12, obj. 10; *Summa*, 2a–2ae, q. 174, art. 2, reply obj. 3.

86 Dominico Zanecchia, *Divina Inspiratio Sacrarum Scripturarum ad Mentem S. Thomae Aquinatis* [The Divine Inspiration of Sacred Scripture in the Thought of St. Thomas Aquinas] (Rome: F. Pustet, 1898), 96.

87 Synave and Benoit, *Prophecy and Inspiration*, 113; compare Aquinas, *Summa*, 2a-2ae, q. 174, art. 2, reply obj. 3.

falls under his scrutiny is the canonical prophecy, which is a *gratia gratis data*,[88] that is, an external grace granted principally for the utility of the Church.[89] All the examples of canonical prophecy given by St. Thomas are taken from the Bible, because he considers the Scripture as the embodiment of this divine charism. One can therefore safely transfer to the Scripture what he affirms about prophecy, without any risk of misrepresenting his thought. In fact, in his opuscula on the Bible,[90] he applies to the Scripture the principles discussed in connection with prophecy.

The difference between prophets and hagiographers mentioned by St. Thomas[91] does not correspond to our modern distinction. In the texts in question, Aquinas falls back on the *Prologus Galeatus* ("Helmeted Preface") of St. Jerome which, following the familiar Jewish division, distinguishes three orders in the Bible—the torah, the prophets, and the hagiographers—and in the end he mentions the apocrypha among which he includes the so-called deuterocanonicals. This distinction does not oppose the Scripture to the prophets, but separates different parts of the Scripture itself. Thomas retains this Jewish distinction for practical purposes, but he does not feel himself bound by it. He departs from it in the question of the deuterocanonicals, which he brackets together with the last collection, and he prefers to admit Daniel into the second order instead of leaving him among the hagiographa.[92] Moreover, when he speaks about the modalities proper to each order, he uses such terms as "more frequently" (*plures frequentius*)[93] and "all, or almost all" (*omnes, aut fere omnes*),[94] by which he shows that there is no clear cut distinction between the three orders.

In the first of his biblical opuscula, St. Thomas explains what he means by *ex persona Dei*, and *ex persona propria*. This terminology in no way reflects the degree of the human initiative in prophecy, but simply alludes to the way in which the divine message is transmitted by the prophets. The first part of this message contains a coercive mandate, and therefore it is delivered under the form of a precept. The second part induces man to observe this mandate through the heralds and the messengers: these are the prophets who speak *ex persona Dei*. The third part contains a persuasive message, and is announced by the hagiographer in the form of a paternal instruction *ex persona propria*. The deuterocanonicals are grouped together with the hagiographers, because they also speak in a persuasive

---

88 Aquinas, *Summa*, 2a–2ae, q. 171, pref.

89 Aquinas, *Summa*, 2a–2ae, q. 172, art. 4, reply obj. 1.

90 Aquinas, *De Commendatione et Partitione Sacrae Scripturae* [The Commendation and Division of Sacred Scripture], in *Selected Writings* (Penguin, 1998).

91 Aquinas, *De Veritate*, q. 12, art. 12, obj. 10; *Summa*, 2a–2ae, q. 174, art. 2, reply obj. 3.

92 Aquinas, *Commendatione et Partitione*.

93 Aquinas, *Summa*, 2a–2ae, q. 174, art. 2, reply obj. 3.

94 Aquinas, *De Veritate*, q. 12, art. 12, obj. 10.

manner.[95] On the other hand, Daniel was a prophet: he received a divine revelation and predicted the future, but he did not speak *ex persona Dei* because he was not sent by God as a messenger. Joshua too was a prophet, but he can be placed among the hagiographers because he was not sent to prophesy to the people.

The distinction between prophet and hagiographer based on the provenance of their message does not render full justice to the texts of Aquinas. He never in fact said that what constitutes the hagiographer is the supernatural judgement, and that the eventual supernatural reception is proper to the prophet and accidental to the hagiographer. In the text quoted by Zanecchia,[96] Thomas does not distinguish between judging and receiving, but between an imaginative and a non-imaginative revelation;[97] Thomas further asserts that while the prophets received imaginative visions, the hagiographers were granted intellectual ones.[98] The revelation of divine truths does not therefore surpass the role of the hagiographers.

All of this stands to prove that for Thomas Aquinas there cannot be any real distinction between prophet and sacred writer. There is only one prophetic charism that is shared in different ways by different beneficiaries. Commenting on the distinction between the imaginative and the intellectual visions in Aquinas, Cajetan explains that one is more properly called a prophecy than the other, but both are properly called a prophecy.[99] And Thomas categorically affirms that there is only one kind of prophecy because all the prophets participated of the same divine light.[100] Whenever we find this divine light with the ensuing judgement there is also prophecy, for knowledge is accomplished in judgement;[101] where this judgement is absent, there is no place for prophecy. The hagiographers possessed the full charism of prophecy: they did not always receive intellectual revelations, but they always had a supernatural judgement.[102]

---

95   "Because there is the same manner of speaking in them and in the hagiographical works, they are for now counted among them" (*Quia tanem idem modus loquendi in eis [the deuterocanonicals] et in agiographis observatur, ideo simul cum eis computentur ad praesens.*] Aquinas, *Commendatione et Partitione.*

96   Zanecchia, *Divina Inspiration*, n. 96.

97   "But, of those whom he [St. Jerome]calls the prophets, all, or almost all, received revelation under the imagery of imagination. But many of those whom he calls writers of sacred books received revelation without imagery." (*Sed illi quos nominat prophetas, omnes, aut fere omnes, revelationem acceperunt sub figuris imaginativis; plures autem eorum quos inter agiographas nominat, sine figuris revelationem acceperunt.*) Aquinas, *De Verbis*, q. 12, art. 12, obj. 10.

98   "They, however, are called sacred writers who had only intellectual visions supernaturally, whether in judgment alone or in judgment and reception together." (*Agiographae autem dicuntur qui supernaturaliter solum visiones intellectuales habuerunt sive quantum ad judicium tantum, sive quantum ad judicium et acceptionem simul.*) Aquinas, *De Veritate*, q. 12, art. 12, reply obj. 10.

99   Cajetan, *Commentary in Summa Theologiae* (London: R & T Washbourne, 1914), pt. 2a–2ae, q. 174, art. 2.

100 Aquinas, *Summa*, 2a–2ae, q. 171, art. 3, reply obj. 3.

101 Aquinas, *Summa*, 2a–2ae, q. 173, art. 2.

102 Aquinas, *De Veritate*, q. 12, art. 12; q. 12, reply obj. 10; *Summa*, 2a–2ae, q. 173, art. 2; q. 174, art.

The different manifestations of prophecy are to be explained within the framework of the same charism, and are reduced by Thomas to different degrees of the same quality.[103] These distinctions remain totally outside the sphere of the supernatural judgement. As far as this is concerned, there is not the slightest difference between the different degrees of prophecy, nor should one present them as a possible means of determining the limits of inerrancy by separating the speculative from the practical judgement.

Literary Forms and the Delimiting of Inerrancy

The limits of inerrancy cannot be established by any general speculation about the object of inspiration, for every kind of truth may be manifested by God to his prophets. Nor does the distinction between prophet and hagiographer or between speculative and practical judgements help much here. The prophetical charism is absolutely uniform as far as the judgement is concerned. For those texts which have not yet been clarified by the interpretation of the Church, the only means of delimiting the object of biblical inerrancy remains the study of the literary forms. This study brings us in close contact with the sacred writer and qualifies us to understand his message.[104]

2, reply obj. 3.

103 Aquinas, *De Veritate*, q. 12, art. 13, reply obj. 2. The highest grade of prophecy is the rapture (*Summa* 2a–2ae, q. 171, pref.), which he treats separately because of its special object (*Commentary in Isaiah* 1; *Summa*, 2a–2ae, q. 175, art. 3), and its special way of attaining it (*Summa*, 2a–2ae, q. 175, art. 4). Of the other aspects of prophecy, the noblest is that in which a supernatural truth is contemplated in an intellectual vision, followed by the manifestation of a supernatural truth in an imaginative vision (*Summa*, 2a–2ae, q. 174, art. 2). Last of all comes the prophecy that deals with natural truths. But prophecy connotes some sort of obscurity and remoteness from the intelligible truth (*Summa*, 2a–2ae, q. 174, art. 2, reply obj. 2), and therefore the most proper kind of prophecy is that in which the truth is attained through an imaginative vision. The second member in order of nobility comes first in order of propriety.

104 This approach however will not solve all the difficulties. There is something in the Scripture that cannot be directly attained by the literary forms, and that is the *plenary sense* of the text. Since the prophet is a defective instrument (Aquinas, *Summa*, 2a–2ae, q. 173, art. 4), he does not always catch the full import of his message; nor do we, who try to approach as much as possible to the level of the prophet. The plenary sense becomes manifest through successive revelation or through the interpretation of the Church. It falls under the study of the literary forms only in so far as the later revelation and interpretation are also made manifest by some literary mode of expression.

Vatican II and the Truth of Sacred Scripture

~: Augustin Cardinal Bea, S. J. :~

Biblical inspiration is intimately connected with the question of the firmness and faithfulness with which it hands down to man the great treasure of revelation.

Dei Verbum, the Second Vatican Council's Constitution on Divine Revelation, says of the divine books: "Inspired by God and committed once and for all to writing, they impart the Word of God himself without change"[1]). The intimate connection between this faithfulness and certainty of Holy Scripture—called by theologians "inerrancy"—and its divine inspiration is also noted in the Constitution. Indeed, the inerrancy of Scripture is presented as the logical conclusion of the doctrine on inspiration: "Therefore, since everything asserted by the inspired authors or sacred writers must be held to be asserted by the Holy Spirit, it follows that the books of Scripture must be acknowledged as teaching firmly, faithfully, and without error that truth which God wanted put into the sacred writings for the sake of our salvation" (no. 11).

Let us consider briefly the composition of this passage. It clearly consists of two parts: the premise and the conclusion to be deduced from it. The premise is this: "Everything asserted by the inspired authors or sacred writers must be held to be asserted by the Holy Spirit." This statement is in its turn presented as a conclusion derived from what has gone before, for it is introduced with "therefore." The previous argument is that if God has so moved the inspired authors that, although writing as true authors, they nevertheless wrote "all and only those things which he wished to be written,"[2] then there can be no doubt that all that these authors assert is to be considered as asserted by the Holy Spirit which has inspired them.

The second part of our text, the conclusion deduced from the premise, is this: "The books of Scripture ... teach firmly, faithfully, and without error that truth which God wanted put into the sacred writings for the sake of our salvation." This conclusion presupposes a self-evident truth—that God surely obtains what he desires, and that he cannot make a mistake or cause a mistake to be made. This obvious presupposition is explicitly formulated further on in this same chapter of the Constitution where it is affirmed that when God condescends to speak to men in a human manner through an inspired book, his truth and holiness must always remain inviolable.[3]

Concerning the proof of the doctrine of the inerrancy of Scripture, the document itself quotes as its foundation passages from St. Augustine, St. Thomas

---

1   Second Vatican Council, *Dei Verbum* [The Word of God], Dogmatic Constitution on Divine Revelation, (November 18, 1965).

2   *Dei Verbum*, 11.

3   *Dei Verbum*, 13.

Aquinas, and the Council of Trent and some recent documents of the supreme magisterium of the Church.

The doctrine of inerrancy was put forward and expounded chiefly by Leo XIII in his encyclical, *Providentissimus Deus*, which is largely dedicated to establishing and defining this doctrinal point. The encyclical first expounds the doctrine of inspiration in order to affirm that of inerrancy, asserting: "Therefore it is so impossible for divine inspiration to contain any error that, by its very nature, it not only excludes even the slightest error but must of necessity exclude it, just as God, the Supreme Truth, must also necessarily be absolutely incapable of promoting error."[4]

The encyclical therefore concludes: "Consequently, any who were to admit that there might be error in the authentic pages of the sacred books must certainly either betray the Catholic concept of divine inspiration or make God himself the author of error."[5] The encyclical bases this teaching on the doctrine of the popes, from among whom it quotes largely St. Gregory and St. Augustine. The same theme of inerrancy is fully dealt with also in the encyclical *Spiritus Paraclitus*, which illustrates with particular care St. Jerome's doctrine about this. The teaching of Leo XIII on this question is recalled by Pius XII's encyclical *Divino Afflante Spiritu*.

The Inerrancy of Scripture in Scripture

The source and foundation of this conviction held by the first Fathers of the Church and the magisterium concerning the inerrancy of Scripture is Scripture itself—or more precisely the way in which Christ and the apostles used and quoted it.

According to the New Testament, there exists a collection of writings which are called "Scripture"[6] or "the Scriptures,"[7] or the "Holy Scriptures."[8] This collection is considered by both Christ and the apostles to be of divine origin and to it is attributed divine authority. With the words "it is written," Christ repeatedly appealed to the Scriptures as to an irrefutable authority.[9] So did the apostles.[10]

The divine origin of these Old Testament books is also implied by their being called simply "oracles of God"[11] or described as "prophetic" and their words as "prophecies"[12]—prophetic being the term used to describe a man who brings to other men the message, the Word of God.

---

4   Pope Leo XIII, *Providentissimus Deus* [The God of All Providence], Encyclical Letter on the Study of Scripture (November 18, 1893), 20.

5   Leo XIII, *Providentissimus Deus*, 21.

6   See John 2:22; 10:35; Gal. 3:8; 1 Pet. 2:6; 2 Pet. 1:20.

7   Matt. 21:42; 22:29; John 5:39; Acts 17:2, 11; 18:24; Rom. 15:4.

8   Rom. 1:2.

9   Matt. 4:4–10; 22:31, 43; John 10:34–35.

10   Acts 15:15–18; Rom. 1:17.

11   Rom. 3:2

12   See Matt. 13:14; 15:7; Rom. 16:26; 1 Pet. 1:10; 2 Pet. 1:19–20.

Moreover, in a series of texts, Christ and the apostles, referring to the Old Testament, affirm that God himself is present in these writings because he himself speaks in them, or because the human authors speak "in the Holy Spirit" or are "inspired by the Holy Spirit."[13] Hebrews introduces a quotation from Psalm 95 with the words: "the Holy Spirit says."[14] Moreover, in Matthew, quotations from the Old Testament are introduced with the words: "All this took place to fulfil what the Lord had spoken by the prophet."[15] Because God was considered the Author of Scripture, it was considered necessary and inevitable that the Scripture should "be fulfilled."[16] This argument from Scripture is summed up in the encyclical *Spiritus Paraclitus*:

> Who is there who does not know and remember that when speaking to the people, either on the mountain by the lake of Genazareth, in the synagogue of Nazareth or in the city of Capernaum, Jesus our Lord drew the principal points and proofs of his doctrine from the sacred books? Was it not from these that he took invincible weapons for his discussions with the Pharisees and the Sadducees? Whether he was teaching or discussing he always derived his assertions and examples from every part of holy Scripture; he refers, for example, to Jonah, to the inhabitants of Nineveh, to the Queen of Sheba and Solomon, to Elijah and Elisha, to David, Noah, Lot, the inhabitants of Sodom, and Lot's own wife.[17]

"For the Sake of Our Salvation"

Let us now proceed to determine the meaning of the Constitution's doctrine on inerrancy. We have already said that it does not use here the theological term itself, but instead, for greater precision, says that the Scriptures "teach firmly, faithfully and without error." The basic idea of the absolute truth of the Scriptures is always the same, although it may be differently expressed. The Constitution expresses most forcefully the notion that Scripture absolutely guarantees the faithful transmission of God's revelation.

On the other hand, it is more difficult to define another point of our text—that is, the object of the infallible teaching of Scripture, "the truth which God wanted put into the sacred writings for the sake of our salvation."

---

13   Acts 1:16–18; 2:30–31; Matt. 22:31–32, 43; 2 Pet. 1:19–21; 2 Tim. 3:16–17.

14   Heb. 3:7; 4:4–5; 9:8; 10:15.

15   Matt. 1:22; see also 2:15.

16   Matt. 5:18–19; Luke 24:44; Acts 1:16.

17   Pope Benedict XV, *Spiritus Paraclitus* [The Holy Spirit, the Comforter], Encyclical Letter Commemorating the Fifteenth Centenary of the Death of St. Jerome (September 15, 1920), 29.

At first sight, the meaning of these words seems clear and obvious. In fact, the whole Constitution illustrates the truth—the revelation of God is intended to bring about man's supernatural salvation. It is therefore to be expected that the truth taught by Scripture should be with reference to this salvation. Nevertheless, there is a certain difficulty here which needs to be explained.

In order to understand this point let us re-consider the preparatory work for this Constitution. An earlier *schema* or draft (the third in succession), said that the sacred books teach "truth without error." The following *schema*, the fourth, inspired by words of St. Augustine, added the adjective "saving,"[18] so that the text asserted that the Scriptures taught "firmly, faithfully, wholly and without error the saving truth." In the voting which followed, one hundred and eighty-four council fathers asked for the adjective "saving" to be removed, because they feared it might lead to misunderstandings, as if the inerrancy of Scripture referred only to matters of faith and morality, whereas there might be error in the treatment of other matters. The Holy Father, to a certain extent sharing this anxiety, decided to ask the drafting commission to consider whether it would not be better to omit the adjective, as it might lead to some misunderstanding. After a long and wearisome debate, with much discussion and several ballots, the present text was accepted, the adjective "saving" being omitted: "the truth which God wanted put into the sacred writings for the sake of our salvation."

This incident concerns us only in so far as it helps us to understand more precisely the meaning of the present definitive text of the Constitution. The actual question is as follows: It is evident that the purpose which God wished to be expressed in Scripture was the revelation of God to man, in the fullest sense, a revelation by means of "deeds and words," which aims at man's eternal salvation. Now we must consider whether the "truth" (that is, the truth "which God wanted put into the sacred writings for the sake of our salvation") implies some limit set to the inerrancy of Scripture—meaning that it taught "without error," not everything that it asserts, but only all that concern our salvation (or those things also which closely and directly affect our salvation).

Let us explain at once what we mean. In order to describe those manifestations of God occurring in "deeds and words," which form the "history of salvation" (see no. 2), Scripture must necessarily set them in an authentic historical framework. Our question, therefore, about the possible existence of a limit set to inerrancy refers, not to the events in which God truly reveals himself, but to those events which form their historical setting and which Scripture frequently describes in great detail. Does the inerrancy asserted in this document cover also

---

18   We mention that this is a question of principle which does not admit of any compromise such as would, for example, be inherent in a declaration that only those events which are "closely connected" with the history of salvation are described without error, and not those where the connection is somewhat fragile. This distinction is, at least in practice, impossible to maintain.

the account of these historical events? In other words, is the historical background also described "without error"?

In the 'Background' of Salvation History

For my own part I think that this question must be answered affirmatively, that is, that these "background" events also are described without error. In fact, we declare in general that there is no limit set to this inerrancy, and that it applies to all that the inspired writer, and therefore all that the Holy Spirit by his means, affirms.

Our reasons are these. First of all, the Constitution itself says that in holy Scripture the truth and holiness of God must always remain inviolable.[19] This thought, which re-occurs in various forms in the documents of the magisterium of the Church,[20] is here clearly understood in a sense which excludes the possibility of the Scriptures containing any statement contrary to the reality of the facts.

In particular, these documents of the magisterium require us to recognize that Scripture gives a true account of events, naturally not in the sense that it always offers a complete and scientifically studied account, but in the sense that what is asserted in Scripture—even if it does not offer a complete picture—never contradicts the reality of the fact.

If therefore the Council had wished to introduce here a new conception, different from that presented in these documents of the supreme teaching authority, which reflects the beliefs of the early Fathers, it would have had to state this clearly and explicitly.

Let us now ask whether there may be any indications to suggest such a restricted interpretation of inerrancy. The answer is decidedly negative. There is not the slightest sign of any such indication. On the contrary everything points against a restrictive interpretation.

First of all: even at that stage of the discussion when the Conciliar Theological Commission put forward the term "the saving truth," it explained that by this expression it did not mean to restrict the inerrancy of the Bible to matters of faith and morals. In order to show that this had not been its intention, it explained that the text spoke of "truth" in the singular, not of "truths," as if it had wished to discriminate between those which are necessary for salvation and others which are not. Moreover, in spite of this prudent explanation, the word "saving" was finally eliminated from the text and replaced with another expression—in order to prevent any possibility of implying that the inerrancy was restricted.

Does the text of *Dei Verbum* we have before us now imply a restrictive interpretation of inerrancy? Here also the answer is firmly negative. The first proof

---

19   *Dei Verbum*, 2.

20   See also *Enchiridion Biblicum: Documenti della Chiesa sulla Sacra Scrittura* [Documents of the Church Concerning Sacred Scripture], eds. Alfio Filippi and Erminio Lora, 2nd. ed. (Bologna: Dehoniane, 1993), 124, 279, 450, 539, 559.

of this is seen in the fact that all those (and in the first place the Pope himself) who had been anxious to prevent the possible misunderstandings that might have arisen from the expression "the saving truth" have instead accepted the present form. This means that they consider that this does not present the same danger of misunderstanding. In fact, the phrasing we now have does not admit of any such interpretation because the idea of salvation is no longer directly linked with the noun "truth," but with the verbal expression "wanted put into the sacred writings." In other words, the phrase in which the text speaks of salvation explains God's purpose in causing the Scriptures to be written, and not the nature of the truth enshrined therein.

Let us then conclude: all that the inspired writers assert is asserted through them by the Holy Spirit. Consequently, in all their assertions the sacred books teach "firmly, faithfully and without error, what God wanted put into them for the sake of our salvation." The paragraph we are commenting upon (no. 11) ends with St. Paul's words: "All Scripture is inspired by God and useful for teaching, for reproving, for correcting and, for training in righteousness; that the man of God may be perfect, equipped for every good work."[21]

---

21 2 Tim. 3:16–17, Greek text.

Letter & Spirit 6 (2010): 383-400

Sacred Scripture and the
Errors of the "New" Exegesis

~: Paul Cardinal Taguchi :~

In the epilogue of his gospel, St. John points out:

> Many other signs also Jesus worked in the sight of his disciples,
> which are not written in this book. But these are written that
> you may believe that Jesus is the Christ, the Son of God, and
> that believing you may have life in his name.[1]

He is reminding us that the aim of his gospel—and, we might say—the aim of all
the gospels and the whole of sacred Scripture, is that we should have faith in Christ,
the Son of God, true God and true man, and, further, that we should put that faith
into practice. This is how it has always been interpreted in the life of the Church.
Reading the sacred books is solid nourishment for the Christian in his task of
molding his conduct to the words of God himself found written in their pages. St.
Augustine liked to call the books of sacred Scripture "letters which reach us from
our distant homeland while we are away from it on our travels."[2]

The Church has always encouraged those who read and study the holy Bible
to approach it with the proper dispositions of faith and piety, reminding us time
and again that it is the written word of God, given in safekeeping to the Church to
be watched over, defended, and authentically explained. Yet over the years, there
has been no shortage of opinions expressing an apparent ignorance of the divine
character of Scripture and of the duty of reverence and faith incumbent on those
who read, study, or interpret it.

There has been a growing tendency among some Catholics specializing in
scriptural studies to question the divine origin, authority, and contents of the
Bible. The divine element is sometimes denied or ignored, as if the Bible were just a
human work subject to the conditioning, limitations, and evolution of any revered
document of antiquity. Its veracity and its literal and historical meaning are at
times either refuted or given a twisted meaning. The exegesis of the Fathers of
the Church is discredited; and there are even some who argue against the Church
having the right to interpret the sacred books at all.

Catholic doctrine is being undermined by various writers who we could call
the "modern exegetes." Whereas the correct Catholic interpretation draws on the

---

1   John 20:30–31.

2   St. Augustine, *On the Psalms*, 90, in *St. Augustine on the Psalms* (Westminster, MD: Newman,
1960).

immense wealth of Tradition, the declarations of the Magisterium and the analogy of the faith, compiled over two thousand years of prayerful scholarship, the new exegesis is based on research that turns its back on all that has gone before and plunges instead into a whole series of dangerous speculations based on a total commitment to philosophies diametrically opposed to faith and the supernatural. It is thus deeply influenced by naturalism and the rationalist criticism of liberal Protestantism, in which subsidiary data are stressed to the detriment of the content.

In the face of all this, it seems more opportune than ever to restate some of the main points of the doctrine of the Church on sacred Scripture.

The Basic Doctrines: Scripture, Tradition, and Magisterium

According to the Second Vatican Council (1963–1965):

> In his goodness and wisdom, God chose to reveal himself and to make known to us the hidden purpose of his will, by which through Christ, the Word made flesh, man has access to the Father in the Holy Spirit and comes to share in the divine nature. Through this revelation, therefore, the invisible God out of the abundance of his love speaks to men as friends, and lives among them, so that he may invite and take them into fellowship with himself.[3]

God has revealed himself to us, and this revelation makes up a body of truths, a divine *depositum* ("deposit") entrusted to the safekeeping of the Church.[4] This *depositum* is contained in sacred Scripture and in Tradition.[5] When the hierarchical Church received this *depositum* it was also given the promise of divine help for its safekeeping and interpretation. According to Catholic faith, therefore, there is an intimate union between Scripture, Tradition, and the Magisterium of the Church;

---

3   Second Vatican Council, *Dei Verbum* [The Word of God], Dogmatic Constitution on Divine Revelation, (November 18, 1965), 2, in *The Scripture Documents: An Anthology of Official Catholic Teachings*, ed. Dean P. Béchard. (Collegeville, MN: Liturgical Press, 2002), 19–31. Hereafter abbreviated *SD*.

4   "The doctrine of the faith which God has revealed has not been proposed as philosophical findings which should be perfected by human intelligence, but it has been given to the Spouse of Christ as a divine deposit to be faithfully guarded and infallibly declared." First Vatican Council, *Dei Filius* [Son of God], Dogmatic Constitution on the Catholic Faith (April 24, 1870), Chap. 4, 13, in *Decrees of the Ecumenical Councils*, 2 vols., ed. Norman P. Tanner (Washington: Georgetown University, 1990).

5   "This supernatural revelation, according to the faith of the universal Church declared by the holy Council of Trent, is contained in the written books and in the unwritten traditions which were received by the apostles from the lips of Christ himself and were passed from hand to hand down to us from those same apostles, under the inspiration of the Holy Spirit." *Dei Filius*, Chap. 2, 5.

it would be clearly against God's designs to seek his revelation in any one of these three without also consulting the other two.[6]

For any interpretation of sacred Scripture to conform with Catholic faith, it must, of necessity, be done in the light of and with the guidance of Tradition, keeping as its touchstone all that the Magisterium has said so far. This is nothing more than the old and reliable principle: *The Church is the only authentic interpreter of the sacred books.*[7] Revealed truth is kept, transmitted, illustrated, and set forth by the Church chiefly through the organ of its sacred Magisterium. This role of the Magisterium has been repeatedly asserted in pontifical documents.[8] The preservation of this unity between Scripture, Tradition, and the Magisterium is essential if exegesis is to give fruitful results leading to a better understanding of the Word of God. The excellence of Scripture and the sacred character granted it by the Church is based on one fact alone: *that God is its principal author.* When we speak of "inspiration" we refer to that divine and supernatural action whereby God raised the human writer above his natural capacity in order to make him an instrumental cooperator in the composition of the sacred books.

The truth is affirmed in Scripture itself. St. Paul wrote: "All Scripture is inspired by God and useful for teaching, for reproving, for correcting, for instructing in justice: that the man of God may be perfect, equipped for every good work."[9] As if foreseeing that some would attempt to deny the divine origin of these books, St. Peter adds: "No prophecy of Scripture is made by private interpretation. For

---

6   "It is clear, therefore, that sacred Tradition, sacred Scripture, and the teaching authority of the Church, in accord with God's most wise design, are so linked and joined together that one cannot stand without the others, and that all together and each in its own way under the action of the Holy Spirit contribute effectively to the salvation of souls." *Dei Verbum*, 10.

7   "If the heavenly doctrine of Jesus Christ, contained for the most part in the books inspired by God, had been given over to the thoughts of men, it could not, on its own, unite their spirits; rather would it become the object of their own differing interpretations. And this would happen not only because of the depth of its mysteries but also because of the diversity of the minds of men, and because of the turmoil that would result from the clash and struggle of opposing passions. For, from differing interpretations, there would inevitably spring differing sentiments, and these would provoke controversies, disagreements, and quarrels. … In order, therefore, to unite spirits and to foster and preserve harmony of feeling, it was necessary for there to be another principle, in addition to the existence of sacred Scripture. The divine wisdom required it; for God could not have wished for the unity of faith without also providing the suitable means to preserve that unity." Pope Leo XIII, *Satis Cognitum* [It is Sufficiently Well-Known], Encyclical Letter on the Unity of the Church (June 29, 1896), 7 (Kansas City, MO: Angelus, 2005).

8   "The task of authentically interpreting the Word of God, whether written or handed on, has been entrusted exclusively to the teaching office of the Church, whose authority is exercised in the name of Jesus Christ. … This teaching office is not above the Word of God, but serves it, teaching only what has been handed on, listening to it devoutly, guarding it scrupulously, and explaining it faithfully by divine commission and with the help of the Holy Spirit; it draws from this one deposit of faith everything which it presents for belief as divinely revealed." *Dei Verbum*, 10.

9   2 Tim. 2:6.

not by will of man was prophecy brought at any time; but holy men of God spoke as they were moved by the Holy Spirit."[10]

The Church's belief in the divine origin of Scripture has figured again and again in documents of the Magisterium and was solemnly proclaimed by the First Vatican Council (1868–1870). Vatican II reaffirmed it once more: "Those divinely revealed realities which are contained and presented in sacred Scripture have been committed to writing under the inspiration of the Holy Spirit."[11]

The role of the human writer is clarified when he is considered as one who, "in composing his sacred book, is a living and intelligent tool or instrument of the Holy Spirit."[12] However it is equally true that this divine inspiration does not deprive the human instrument of his liberty, while he remains perfectly attuned to the will of God, faithfully reproducing what God wishes to say. As Pope Benedict XV said:

> The books of sacred Scripture were composed under the inspiration, suggestions, promptings, or even at the dictation of the Holy Spirit; and, furthermore, they were written and edited by the Holy Spirit himself; and yet, this does not call into question the fact that each of the human authors has cooperated with God's inspiration according to his own individual character and personal traits.[13]

The Magisterium of the Church has further stated that the divine inspiration applies to *all the books in all their parts*.[14] In Vatican II's constitution on Scripture, *Dei Verbum* ("The Word of God") we read: "Everything asserted by the inspired authors or sacred writers must be held to be asserted by the Holy Spirit"[15]

---

10   2 Pet. 1:20–21.

11   *Dei Verbum*, 11.

12   Pope Pius XII, *Divino Afflante Spiritu* [Inspired by the Divine Spirit], Encyclical Letter Promoting Biblical Studies (September 30, 1943), 33 (*SD*, 115–139).

13   Pope Benedict XV, *Spiritus Paraclitus* [The Holy Spirit, the Comforter], Encyclical Letter Commemorating the Fifteenth Centenary of the Death of St. Jerome (September 15, 1920), 8 (*SD*, 81–111).

14   "Anyone who does not accept these books as sacred and canonical in all their parts, as they are wont to be interpreted in the Catholic Church and as they are contained in the Latin Vulgate edition ... will be excommunicated." Council of Trent, *De Libris Sacris et de Traditionibus Recipiendis* [On the Sacred Books and the Reception Tradition], Decree on the Reception of the Sacred Books and Apostolic Traditions (April 6, 1546), in Henirich Denzinger, ed., *Enchiridion symbolorum definitonum et declarationum de rebus fidei et morum* [Handbook of Creeds, Definitions and Declarations concerning Matters of Faith and Morals] (Freiberg: Herder, 1911), 1504; English text in *The Sources of Catholic Dogma* (Fitzwilliam, NH: Loreto, 2002). Hereafter abbreviated: *DS*.

15   *Dei Verbum*, 11.

Since all the books of both the Old and the New Testament have but one author—the Holy Spirit—there is in them a unity of content. All the pages of both Testaments move toward Christ as to their center.[16] The constant teaching of the Fathers of the Church, as well as the doctrine so often given by the Magisterium, have fully clarified that the *realities* of the New Testament are contained in prophecy and prefiguration in the Old. The New Testament reveals explicitly and contains *really* what in the Old was only foretold.[17] In short, the New Testament completes and perfects the Old. This unity of sacred Scripture also implies a total harmony of content, so that the various texts illustrate one another. This is what is usually known as the *analogy of scriptural faith.*[18]

Scripture's Freedom From Error

Inerrancy means that the sacred books are totally free from error in all their statements. This is very closely linked to the belief in inspiration; for, if Scripture has God for its author, and God is the supreme truth, then, obviously, there can be no error in the sacred books, for otherwise it would be tantamount to imputing the authorship of error to God himself. The Magisterium has often referred to this truth of faith.[19]

So the Magisterium has never ceased to come out strongly against any theory which tries to resolve the *apparent* inexactitudes of the sacred books by chafing against the limitation placed, *not* by inspiration, but by inerrancy, as if errors were possible in an inspired passage. Everything written in Scripture comes from God and, as such, is true. In other words, the formal reason for biblical inerrancy lies

---

16 Benedict XV, *Spiritus Paraclitus*, 63.

17 "God, the inspirer and author of both Testaments, wisely arranged that the New Testament be hidden in the Old and the Old be made manifest in the New." St Augustine, *Questions on the Heptateuch*, Bk. 2, q. 73, in *Patrologiae Cursus Completus: Series Latina*, ed. J. P. Migne, 221 vols (Paris: Garnier and J. P. Migne, 1844–1864), 34:623. Hereafter abbreviated *PL*; compare *Dei Verbum*, 16.

18 Vatican II teaches that "since holy Scripture must be read and interpreted according to the same Spirit by whom it was written, no less serious attention must be given to the content and unity of the whole of Scripture, if the meaning of the sacred texts is to be correctly brought to light. The living tradition of the whole Church must be taken into account along with the harmony which exists between elements of the faith." *Dei Verbum*, 12.

19 "For all the books which the Church receives as sacred and canonical are written wholly and entirely, with all their parts, under the inspiration of the Holy Spirit; and so far is it from being possible that any error can coexist with inspiration, that inspiration not only is essentially incompatible with error, but excludes and rejects it as absolutely and necessarily as it is impossible that God himself, the supreme truth, can utter that which is not true." Pope Leo XIII, *Providentissimus Deus* [The God of All Providence], Encyclical Letter on the Study of Scripture (November 18, 1893), 20 (*SD* 37–61). Pius XII, after indicating these words to be the constant belief of the Church, adds: "This teaching which our predecessor Leo XIII set forth with such solemnity. We also proclaim with Our authority, and We urge all to adhere to it religiously. No less urgently do we inculcate obedience in the present day to the counsels and exhortations which he in his day so wisely enjoined." *Divino Afflante Spiritu*, 4.

in the very nature of inspiration. As Pope Leo XIII taught: "It follows that those who maintain that an error is possible in any genuine passage of the sacred writings, either pervert the Catholic notion of inspiration, or make God the author of such error."[20]

There is no margin for distinctions within the sacred Scriptures which would allow inerrancy to some texts and deny it to others, be it on account of their content, their ultimate aim, or for any other reason. Scripture is the Word of God and is true *because it is inspired*; that is, not only because (and insofar as) it is revealed; nor only insofar as it is matter of faith and morals.[21] To again quote *Dei Verbum*:

> Therefore, since everything asserted by the inspired authors or sacred writers must be held to be asserted by the Holy Spirit, it follows that the books of Scripture must be acknowledged as teaching firmly, faithfully, and without error that truth which God wanted put into the sacred writings for the sake of our salvation.[22]

One particular area of inerrancy that has a special relevance these days is that of freedom from error in historical matters. This is not to say that everything written in the sacred books is an actual historical event. There are scores of allegories, parables, and the like; these have no need of an historical basis since they belong to a different type of instruction. But with these exceptions (which must be established on the grounds of substantial evidence and a careful avoidance of sweeping generalizations), *the historical truth of sacred Scripture is a principle to be taken as a starting point for all work of interpretation of the sacred books; it is not, therefore, a conclusion or end-product of critical research.* Judging by the results of modern hypotheses, it is quite clear that this point has often been ignored. Nowadays in fact, it seems as if the *onus probandi* ("burden of proof") is being placed on the defenders of the historical truth or literal meaning.

The Church's thinking is made clear in the answer given by the Pontifical Biblical Commission to this question: "Is it possible to admit as a principle of sound

---

20 Leo XIII, *Providentissimus Deus*, 21.

21 In this context, Pius XII wrote: "A number of things are proposed or suggested by some even against the divine authorship of Sacred Scripture. For some go so far as to pervert the sense of the [First] Vatican Council's definition that God is the author of holy Scripture, and they put forward again the opinion, already often condemned, which asserts that inerrancy extends only to those parts of the bible that deal with God himself, religion, or morals. They even wrongly speak of a human sense of Scripture, beneath which a divine sense, which they say is the only infallible meaning, lies hidden." Pius XII, *Humani Generis* [The Human Race], Encyclical Letter on Certain False Opinions Threatening to Undermine the Foundations of Catholic Doctrine (August 12, 1950), 22 (*SD*, 141).

22 *Dei Verbum*, 11.

exegesis that books of sacred Scripture which are regarded as historical, at times do not relate, either wholly or in part history properly so-called and objectively true, but present only the appearance of history with the purpose of expressing some meaning differing from the strictly literal or historical sense of the words?" The commission's responded:

> Answer: In the negative. Except in the case neither easily nor rashly to be admitted, in which, the mind of the Church not being contrary and without prejudice to its judgment, it is proved by solid arguments that ... under the guise and form of history, a parable, an allegory, etc. is set forth.[23]

With reference to the historical truth of the gospels, we have a particularly strong and unanimous tradition, expressed and approved in numerous documents of the Magisterium. In these it is unequivocally affirmed that the inspired books quite rightly demand our unwavering belief in their historicity.[24] The latest statement in this regard comes in *Dei Verbum*:

> Holy Mother Church has firmly and with absolute constancy held, and continues to hold, that the four gospels ... whose historical character the Church unhesitantly asserts, faithfully hand on what Jesus Christ, while living among men, really did and taught for their eternal salvation until the day he was taken up into heaven.[25]

Doctrinal Deviations of the "New" Exegesis

Of the doctrinal deviations now being adopted by some Catholic exegetes, perhaps the most harmful is the application of the Protestant principle of *sola Scriptura* ("Scripture alone"). Those who uphold this principle assert that the only source of revelation is the Bible itself; they completely ignore Tradition and the Magisterium of the Church. This assertion is incompatible with the unity of Scripture. It is as if they were trying to wrench the Holy Spirit who wrote the books from the same Holy Spirit who interprets them through the organs of Tradition.

The falsity of this position shows itself in two main tendencies. First, one comes across frequent references to a so-called "scientific investigation" of Scripture that is said to be opposed to a "Catholic interpretation"; it is almost as if

---

23 Pontifical Commission for Biblical Studies, *Responsum de Narrationibus Specietenus Tantum Historicis in Sacrae Scripturae Libris qui pro Historicis Habentur* [Response Concerning Historical Narratives] (June 23, 1905) (*SD*, 188).

24 Compare the responses from the Pontifical Commission for Biblical Studies dated June 19, 1911, June 26, 1912, and May 29, 1907 (*SD* 190, 197–202).

25 *Dei Verbum*, 19.

the Magisterium and Tradition were superfluous to a correct understanding of the Bible. Consequently, total reliance is placed on the critical and historical methods of study, while Catholic interpretations are regarded as mere impositions.

This approach, in practice if not in theory, denies the Magisterium's right to guard, interpret, and explain Scripture.[26] The important word here is *interpret*; for it is the Magisterium's supreme task to interpret the truths of faith in its care. The exegete should do his work with the Magisterium as his support—directed by the Magisterium, defended by it, joyfully submitting to it, sure in the knowledge that the Magisterium has always maintained the continuity of the Church's teaching.

The second tendency one sees is that the opinion of contemporary exegetes, and particularly Protestant exegetes, is rated higher than those of the Fathers of the Church and of Tradition. Some Catholic workers in the field of biblical studies seem to take as their yardstick the commonly held opinions of their contemporary Protestant counterparts, in preference to what has at all times and in all places been the unanimous belief of the Church. It follows that the exegesis of the Fathers, when not openly ridiculed, is considered worthless and outdated. In doing so, Catholic exegetes appear to be influenced by a certain inferiority complex which makes them oblivious to Pope Leo XIII's words:

> The holy Fathers... are of *supreme authority whenever they all interpret in one and the same* manner any text of the bible as pertaining to the doctrine of faith and morals; ... The opinion of the Fathers is also of very great weight when they deal with these matters in their own personal capacity as private doctors; not only because they excel in their knowledge of revealed doctrine and in their acquaintance with many things which are useful in understanding the apostolic books, *but because they are men of eminent sanctity and of ardent zeal for the truth, on whom God has bestowed a more ample measure of his light.*[27]

These words are systematically ignored by those who prefer to accept the authority of the modern exegetes as supreme.[28] To overvalue the work of the modern exegetes, betrays a lack of faith as well as a faulty methodology. It amounts to

---

26 Compare *Dei Filius*, chap. 4.

27 Leo XIII, *Providentissimus Deus*, 14.

28 This situation also seems to have been foreseen by Leo XIII, when he wrote: "It is most unbecoming to pass by, in ignorance or contempt, the excellent work which Catholics have left in abundance, and to have recourse to the works of non-Catholics, and to seek in them, to the detriment of sound doctrine and often to the peril of faith, the explanation of passages on which Catholics long ago have successfully employed their talent and their labor. For ... the sense of holy Scripture can nowhere be found incorrupt outside the Church, and cannot be expected to be found in writers who being without the true faith, only gnaw the bark of the Sacred Scripture and never attain its pith." *Providentissimus Deus*, 15.

rejecting material of superior quality in favor of an inferior product. It would be naïve indeed to accept some of these "new" views simply because they are often talked about and frequently appear in print. The propaganda campaign behind them may be stronger than the *scientific proofs* that would seem to support them.

Another false approach is that of considering the exegesis of the Fathers merely as a *pious exegesis*. It is good to remember that, as Pope Pius XII has written, the Fathers are valued for their intellect as well as their faith: "By reason of the office assigned to them by God in the Church, *they are distinguished by a certain subtle insight into heavenly things and by a marvelous keenness of intellect*, which enables them to penetrate to the very innermost meaning of the divine Word and bring to light all that can help to elucidate the teaching of Christ and promote holiness of life."[29]

In general, one might say that the notion of inspiration, in the hands of the modern exegetes, has lost its supernatural and dogmatic-value and has acquired in its place a somewhat vague content derived from rationalistic reflection. Modern exegetes will not, of course, deny outright the divine origin of the inspired books, but it is obvious from their writings that they rely on exclusively human methodology—philology, historical research, and sociology as if this were the correct way to show their true content.

In other words, the production of these sacred books is looked upon as the result of a purely human effort. This effectively precludes mention of God's inspiration as something positive, as a *supernatural charisma* elevating the powers of the writer and making him an instrument of God to write all that God wanted him to write, and only that. Any biblical passage, any institution or action due to the supernatural intervention of God in history is explained away in a human fashion (even when such explanation happens to go against the obvious meaning of the words or against the whole context of a passage); appeal is made to "ancestral taboos," or a "centralizing mentality," or the sacred writer is said to be "personifying" God or ascribing to God words that really come from other sources.

Modern exegetes would have us believe that the writer's inspiration comes, not from God, but from his community; they contend that the sacred books are the result of evolutionary elements at work among the people of Israel. Again, instead of affirming the profound unity of the Old and New Testaments, modern exegetes believe Christ's preaching should be interpreted in harmony with the historical setting he lived in—namely, the world of the Old Testament, with its emphases on collective responsibility, social determinisms, punishment or reward dealt out to the nation as a whole, and so on. They try to present Christian doctrine as an antidote to an exaggerated acceptance of collectivity and things temporal—not as the fullness of revelation or as the redemptive intervention of God.

---

29 Pius XII, *Divino Afflante Spiritu*, 28.

Another problem is the excessive value given to the social background of neighboring ancient nations as the key to understanding the literal meaning of the sacred books. The "analogy of faith" existing in Scripture is replaced by a "cultural and ethnical analogy." In this view, the Bible is the purely human work of many authors of an unimportant nation, who were influenced by the cultural, political, and economical policies of more affluent neighboring states; what they wrote and the way they wrote it did not basically differ from the literature of those neighboring peoples, so the literal meaning of the Bible can be found through comparative philology and the interpretation of Israel's history discovered through comparative sociology.

A Mistaken View of Inerrancy

One natural consequence of this mistaken view of inspiration is that modern exegetes accept the possibility of falsehood in the Bible while insisting that this does not detract from inerrancy. This leads them to seek a critical examination of the Bible so as to draw a line between what *can be deemed truthful* and what can be considered owing to the imagination of the sacred writer or the influence of his social background.

The moderns also draw a line between so-called fundamental and secondary elements in the Bible and consider inerrancy as applying only to the former in such a way that it is not affected by "inaccuracies" in the secondary elements. However, the Magisterium has quite clearly disapproved of "those who distinguish between the primary or religious element of Scripture and the secondary or profane element and quite openly admit that inspiration affects all the sentences, even every word of the Bible, yet who restrict its effects, and above all its immunity from error and its absolute truth, to the primary or religious elements only."[30]

Faith tells us that everything in sacred Scripture which appears as historical narrative should be understood in its literal meaning, unless there are sufficient and proven reasons for thinking otherwise, in which case it should be submitted to the judgment of the Church. In contrast, current exegetes think that the reader should put no trust in this literal and historical reading but should rather go in search of whatever historical nucleus the probings of philological and historical investigations might happen to bring to light.

It is a doctrine of the Church that, since the faith is one, there must be a perfect adequacy or similarity of content between the way an ordinary Catholic with no theological training understands the Bible, and that in which a scholar of exegesis understands it.[31] The plea of the modern exegetes is that the advances

---

30   Benedict XV, *Spiritus Paraclitus*, 19.

31   Compare Pope Pius X, *Lamentabili Sane* [With Truly Lamentable Results], Syllabus Condemning the Errors of the Modernist (July 3, 1907), 32, in *Encyclical Letter of His Holiness Pope Pius X on the Doctrines of the Modernists* (London: Catholic Truth Society).

made in exegesis have left the ordinary Christian behind, and now only the experts are qualified to understand Scripture. And so, as in the case of liberal Protestantism and modernism, the Bible ends up appearing as a *double history*. First, there is the historical version that a straightforward reading of the books would give. However this, they say, is riddled with dramatic personifications, epic historifications, and borrowed myths; the true history is said to be reached only by delving beneath the surface with their own particular critical tools.

When faced with errors like the ones we have been outlining here, we must remember that sacred theology cannot come to conclusions at variance with the doctrine of the Church. *Faith is not a conclusion to be reached; it is the premise to use as a starting point.* Theological research does not discover faith, but rather it studies it more deeply, and not in any new sense, but in the way it has always been understood by all the faithful. Theologians in general, and exegetes in particular, should make it very clear to the faithful that their conclusions in no way change or increase the content of our faith, but simply attempt to clarify further what has always been believed.

Exegesis as "Pseudo-Science"

The whole question of literary genres as dealt with in the new exegesis is closely bound up with the question of the historical truth of the sacred books.

The doctrine outlined by Pius XII—that any literary genre may be postulated as long as it is not opposed to the truth and sanctity of God[32]—is no longer accepted by the new exegetes. They have replaced it with the arbitrary assertion that any literary genre is possible, whether it goes against the sanctity and truth of God or not, so long as it conforms to the mentality of the ancient Middle East. The Fathers and Doctors of the Church were, of course, very much aware of the different genres of the Bible, and had much to say on the subject in terms of historical books, psalms, canticles, parables, and the like.

What some writers are now affirming is not only without precedent, it is also in direct opposition to what the Church has always understood and believed. In the name of the so-called mentality of the ancient Middle East, the new exegetes multiply the number of literary genres (*midrash, etiological narrative, historical epic, lament,* etc.), and proceed to question the historical truth of the books of Joshua, Judges, Judith, Esther, and Daniel, as well as the childhood of Christ as narrated in the gospels; they even go so far as to cast doubt on the whole framework of prophecies and miracles throughout sacred Scripture. They would say, for example, that in the gospel account of the annunciation, Mary's question and the archangel's answer would not imply that such an exchange actually took place; instead they are to be understood as a literary device of the author in order to describe the virginal

---

32   Compare Pius XII, *Divino Afflante Spiritu*, 38.

conception of the Messiah. There are countless examples of such pseudo-scientific nonsense.[33]

Other abuses in this pseudo-scientific vein concern the history of forms (German: *Formgeschichte*) and the history of composition (*Redaktiongeschichte*). The first dwells mainly on the creative role of the community, and the second on the creative genius of the writer. In practice, these methods take their origin and growth from rationalistic conceptions of philosophy and theology, which are opposed to the supernatural character of sacred Scripture. So it is only natural that they should be out of focus with respect to the object upon which they are supposed to be used, namely, a book written by God via human instruments, which is not simply a record of the history of a people but rather a narrative of the intervention of God in that history.

Let loose upon the gospels, these theories have remarkable effects. The first theory leads to the suggestion that the authors of the gospels were no more than editors who more or less arbitrarily pieced together the *creations* of the primitive and impersonal community. Consequently, the only things we can know about Jesus Christ are what the primitive community thought about him. The second theory presents the idea that the evangelists were actually theologians who added their own opinions, interpretations, and philosophies of life to the gospels to give them a theological unity.

The net result of both of these approaches is that inspiration, authenticity, and historical accuracy all go by the board. In the name of "internal criticism," the sacred books have been torn apart. Their integrity is sometimes accepted, sometimes rejected; and the order of the passages is radically changed because of mere hypotheses affecting the dating. Thus, for example, chapters 40–66 of Isaiah are no longer considered to be written by the prophet; the author of 2 Peter is no longer supposed to be St. Peter; similarly, St. Paul is robbed of the authorship of his letter to the Hebrews; and in St. John's gospel the passage about the woman taken in adultery is thought to be out of harmony with the rest of his message.

Leo XIII spoke out strongly against this high-handed procedure as unacceptable not only for the study of the sacred books but even for that of any purely human work: "It is clear that in historical questions such as the origin and the handing down of writings, the *witness of history is of primary importance* and that historical investigation should be made with the utmost care and that, in this matter, *internal evidence is seldom of great value except as confirmation.*"[34]

In other words, when it is a question of authenticity and integrity, the weight of argumentation ought to lie on external evidence: Christian tradition, the liturgy,

---

33 It was with a note of sorrow that Benedict XV wrote: "Holy Scripture is assailed by detractors of every class. We speak particularly of those who abuse certain principles—which, if rightly used, would be legitimate—to the point where the foundations of the truth of the Bible are whittled away, and the Catholic doctrine taught by all the Fathers is destroyed." *Spiritus Paraclitus*, 26.

34 Leo XIII, *Providentissimus Deus*, 17.

Jewish tradition, manuscripts; and not, for instance, on the computer analysis of the occurrence rate of the Greek participle *kai* ("and") in one of the sacred books. This is a basic ruling of scholarship even for a non-believer who sees the Bible as nothing more than a human document.

"Demythologization" and the Myths of Modernism

One cannot forget how the encyclical *Pascendi Dominici Gregis* ("Feeding the Lord's Flock"), condemned the attempt to adapt faith to the demands of "modern thought." It showed that its consequent vision, based on the "principle of immanence," was necessarily agnostic and opposed to the supernatural. In fact, the campaigners for this false position would consider the supernatural as only a particular way in which the evolution of religious feeling manifests itself.

Nearly all the modernist errors condemned by Pope St. Pius X boiled down to an open profession—by a handful of Catholics—of the theories of schools which sprang from the seedbed of nineteenth century liberal Protestantism. For several decades it appeared that this tide had been stemmed. But in the last ten or twelve years, perhaps partly due to the feeling of revision which attended many of the debates of Vatican II, the hermeneutical principles of liberal Protestantism and Catholic modernism have again raised their heads. This time they appear mainly in the work of some Catholic exegetes who write essay-type articles for magazines and reviews of wide circulation.

The job of exegesis is now seen to be *demythologization*. This means that everything in the sacred books that implies the supernatural is dubbed as a *myth*, a relic of the *primitive reality*, which is said to be repulsive to the modern mind. In principle, they reject the existence of miracles, prophecies, and any divine intervention in the history of the chosen people. "Demythologization" may be a new name, but the idea behind it is as old as Christianity itself. Even Peter had occasion to condemn it when he wrote: "For we were not following fictitious tales when we made known to you the power and coming of our Lord Jesus Christ, but we had been eyewitnesses of his glory."[35]

Modern existentialist philosophy has been raised to the category of a fundamental hermeneutical principle for the interpretation of Scripture. By observing how some moderns now explain our Lord's resurrection, we can clearly see how the criteria of modern philosophy (existentialism and rationalism in particular) are being used to banish supernatural elements from the bible. This is alluded to in a letter from the German bishops:

> The words in the gospel which affirm that *Jesus has risen from the dead* are, they [modern exegetes] tell us, the result of the pious reflection of the primitive community in their attempts to explain

---

35 2 Pet. 1:16.

their paschal experience, a 'happening' that cannot be expressed in precise historical terms. It expresses their conviction that the cause of Jesus had not ended with the cross, but that it continued. This somewhat vague experience had first been understood as the missionary task entrusted to the apostles. Later, it was termed as a *vision* of the Risen One; and finally it stabilized into the formula *'Jesus has risen from the dead.'*[36]

It is clear that this hermeneutical assumption amounts to a denial of the faith of the Church, which definitely affirms and professes that the resurrection of Jesus was a *real fact*. The resurrection cannot be understood as the result of an inner experience, conditioned by time and expressible in other terms.

Finally, we are witnessing a new-styed *gnosis*. In the type of interpretations we have just been discussing, all coming from ideas opposed to faith, one thing stands out clearly, and that is that the truths of faith revealed by God, which ought to be the starting point and objective for everything, have been entirely lost. When supernatural reality is demoted to a mere by-product of evolutionary factors and inner experiences of the community, then these truths are replaced by human "thoughts" or "decisions." Thus, instead of objective truth, modern exegetes put forward explanations which they know are not fully satisfactory and which, consequently, can be justifiably replaced by new ones as human knowledge progresses.

How to Read, Study, and Explain the Scriptures

Now when Jesus came into the district of Caesarea Philippi, he asked his disciples, "Who do men say that the Son of man is?" And they said, "Some say John the Baptist, others say Elijah, and others Jeremiah or one of the prophets."

He said to them, "But who do you say that I am?" Simon Peter replied, "You are the Christ, the Son of the living God." And Jesus answered him, "Blessed are you, Simon Bar-Jona! For flesh and blood has not revealed this to you, but my Father who is in heaven."[37]

In his own time, afterwards, and up to our own days, we men have taken various attitudes towards Jesus. Sometimes it is one of human esteem, or admiration; or we regard his as a man with a prophetic religious mission. But there is only one attitude which Jesus Christ praised, and that is Simon Peter's. Only the man who

---

36   Letter from the German Bishops, September 22, 1967.

37   Matt. 16:13–17.

confesses that Jesus is the Messiah, the Son of God, true God, has grasped the truth; only he has fully understood.

But to do so requires two things. The first is beyond the reach of purely human effort; for it is the free gift of faith, a grace of God. The second is the human cooperation with that grace of God, man's noble and sincere acceptance of it. From this we can draw the following consequences for the dispositions of those who read and study the sacred books:

Any Christian, whether he is an ordinary member of the faithful or a theologian, must necessarily begin by having *obedience to the faith*[38] of the one Church of Jesus Christ in order to penetrate the written Word of God. This means *the faith of the Church in the canonicity, the inspiration, the inerrancy, the historicity, and the authenticity of the holy Bible*. Faith, in other words, in God's being the principal author of the sacred books, and in their containing truth unmixed with error.

This faith, however, cannot be attained outside the Church, nor is it compatible with error. Through it, we accept what God revealed to us and which is proposed by the Magisterium as such, "not by the intrinsic truth of things, viewed in the natural light of reason, but by the authority of God who reveals them and who can neither deceive nor be deceived."[39]

Since faith is a free and supernatural gift of God, man can neither make himself worthy of it, nor can he acquire it with his human strength alone. As he grows in the knowledge of the written Word of God, man should so dispose himself in prayer that he will be able to receive the light which comes to us freely from the Holy Spirit.[40] In this spirit, anyone who reads, studies, or meditates upon sacred Scripture should seek the meaning of the holy Word in earnest prayer and in his contact with God. Understanding of the secrets of the divine words is not to be found in philology, sociology, psychology, or any other branch of human knowledge, but, quite simply, in holiness of life.

Through his relationship with God in prayer, a man becomes humble and learns to walk in the dazzling light of faith without being blinded. Only the love of God can bring him this familiarity with things divine, for they cannot come through neat rationalist formulas. This, too, is of the very nature of sacred Scripture. As Pius XII stated:

> For the sacred books were not given by God to men to satisfy their curiosity or to provide them with material for study and research, but, as the Apostles observe, in order that these divine oracles might *instruct us to salvation, by the faith which is Christ*

---

38 Compare Rom. 16:26.

39 *Dei Filius*, Chap. 3.

40 See Dan. 9:1–23.

Jesus, and that the man of God may be perfect, equipped for every good work.[41]

The Christian must show humility and love in the work of exegesis; he must be prudent in not even considering injudicious opinions which are at variance with what the Magisterium of the Church and Tradition have always taught. He must be firmly convinced that he can never actually demonstrate truths of a supernatural order, and that it is not a question of getting to the bottom of what God has revealed but of joyfully accepting it exactly in the way it is interpreted by the teaching authority of the Church.

These virtues must also be shown in the way he firmly rejects any new opinions which are not in line with the doctrine of faith and morals. Also, the exegete should give an example of humility and Christian charity when, in his work, done in full realization of his duty to God and to souls, he refrains from publishing theories which may seem brilliant but are also imprudent and would only lead to confusion. In short, when a Christian exegete makes the bringing of souls to God the first aim of his work, then he can be sure that he is doing that work as God would wish it to be done.

The exegete makes of faith a science; that is, he seeks a better understanding of what we believe. It would be ridiculous for him to argue with faith, since faith is the first principle of his science. If he does not begin his work in obedience to faith, then he can never by rational dialectic come to the true pillars of his science, which are the dogmas of faith.

It is not the job of the theologian or exegete to change the faith, to pick away at the truths in the *depositum* by denying them and offering other "truths" in their place. It is their job to make more explicit the truths that have always been believed, but perhaps in a more general sense. With the light of their knowledge they should pinpoint what was before believed and admired for its beauty; they should try to clarify things that were believed but not fully understood; they should strive to make more precise the language used to express truths which have always been wholeheartedly believed. This last point, especially, merits careful consideration, for theologians in general and exegetes in particular should avoid false novelties which would render their work ineffective. To forfeit the terminology which the patient work of centuries has succeeded in making precise, and to replace it by a new one on the pretext that it is more "evangelical" would be sheer folly.

From all that has been said, it should be clear that it is essential for the exegete to have a wide, deep, and mature knowledge of theology. If his work were that of a philologist, he should be noted for his flair for oriental and Semitic languages. If he were a historian, he should be renowned for his knowledge of the dynasties of the Pharaohs of Egypt, of the kings of Assyria, and the like. But since his work

---

41   Pius XII, *Divino Afflante Spiritu*, quoting 2 Tim. 3:15–17.

is to research into the written Word of God, which is inseparable and indeed complementary to the Word of God transmitted orally and by the Magisterium of the Church, then "the professor of holy Scripture ... must be well acquainted with the whole circle of theology and deeply read in the commentaries of the holy Fathers, the Doctors, and other interpreters of note," as Leo XIII has written.[42]

When there is no authentic interpretation of the Magisterium on a certain passage, it is up to the exegete to go into the writings of the Fathers and Doctors of the Church, and to set forth his conclusions in continuity with the doctrine commonly held by those holy men. He should not suggest something in opposition to what they would have unanimously affirmed in matters of faith and customs, and he should always work within the analogy of faith.

Logically, the exegete should make correct use of all the human means within his reach. But if, for example, he limited himself to only a philological analysis of some words used in sacred Scripture, or to the social background of a particular hagiographer, then he would end up knowing practically nothing of the sacred books. These texts are the living word of God, not even fully understood by the inspired writers themselves. Their theological content is both deep and precise, and only accessible to those to whom God chooses to reveal it. They are for this reason inseparable from the Tradition of the Church and from the living, constant, and universal Magisterium. Critical, historical, and philological procedures alone stand no chance of attaining their true meaning. They are the Word of God, which can only be understood in the light of the infallible help of his Spirit and his Church.

If the above are the criteria which guide the exegete in his research work, how much more firmly should he adhere to them in the publication of his findings and in teaching. Hence, the really essential part of an exegete's work is showing the theological content of each passage or book, and how the doctrine of the Church is contained in sacred Scripture.

The words of Pius XII addressed to Scripture teachers can be fittingly quoted here by way of conclusion:

> With special zeal should they apply themselves not only by ex-
> pounding exclusively these matters which belong to the historical,
> archeological, philological, and other auxiliary sciences. ... Their
> exegetical explanation should aim especially at the theological
> doctrine, avoiding useless discussions and omitting all that is
> calculated rather to satisfy idle curiosity than promote true
> learning and solid piety. They should expound what is called
> the literal meaning and most especially the theological meaning
> so carefully, explain it so clearly, and implant it so deeply, that
> in their students there might take place in a certain way what

---

42   Leo XIII, *Providentissimus Deus*, 14.

happened to the disciples on the way to Emmaus when, having heard the words of the Master, they exclaimed: "Was not our heart burning within us while he was speaking on the road and explaining to us the Scriptures!"[43]

---

43   Pius XII, *Divino Afflante Spiritu*, 54.

Letter & Spirit 6 (2010): 401-432

HOLY SCRIPTURE AND THE SCIENCE OF FAITH

~: Romano Guardini :~

Translated by Scott G. Hefelfinger

Translator's note: Romano Guardini's "Heilige Schrift und Glaubenswissenschaft" was originally published in the little-known German review, Die Schildgenossen 8 (1928): 24–57. The essay, translated into Italian and in an abridged form in French, played an influential role in Catholic discussions of biblical interpretation and theology in the years prior to the Second Vatican Council. Cardinal Joseph Ratzinger, now Pope Benedict XVI, cited the importance of this essay in his classic 1988 Erasmus Lecture, "Biblical Interpretation in Crisis."[1] This marks the first time Guardini's text has been translated into English. In the text that follows, all footnotes are from the original publication, with slight amendments made for style.

The New Testament consists of numerous texts brought together in a canon—a word meaning "order," or official collection. These are the four Gospels, the Acts of the Apostles, the letters of the Apostles Paul, Peter, Jude, James, and John, and the Letter to the Hebrews, and the Book of Revelation. In what way can these texts be sources of knowledge for a science, theology? They present themselves as historical documents—as reports of events, messages of teachings, ordinances, commands; the aftermath of religious occurrences. The most obvious thing would be to treat them simply as historical sources, just as we would do to other sources as well. If we were to do that, would we do them justice?[2]

We stand here before a fundamental question concerning the teaching regarding knowledge in general and religious knowledge of the Christian sort in

---

1   For background on Guardini's "Heilige Schrift und Glaubenswissenschaft," see "Biblical Interpretation in Crisis: On the Question of the Foundations and Approaches of Exegesis Today," in *The Essential Pope Benedict XVI: His Central Writings and Speeches*, eds. John F. Thorton and Susan B. Varenne (New York: HarperCollins, 2007), 243–258, at 254; 438–439, n. 25. See also the long appreciation by Ignace de la Potterie, "Biblical Exegesis: A Science of Faith," in *Opening Up the Scriptures: Joseph Ratzinger and the Foundations of Biblical Interpretation*, eds. José Granados, Carlos Granados, Luis Sanchez-Navarro (Grand Rapids, MI: Eerdmans, 2008), 30–64.

2   The present essay appears in the first instance to concern only the theologian. Nevertheless, the editorial staff believes it ought to be included here. There is today a double danger: on the one hand, that theology ends up falling outside the context of concrete, religious living and its accompanying experiences; on the other, that concrete, religious living declares itself to be disinterested in theology and deteriorates into mere praxis—of feeling, or method, or any sort of experiment. This essay is concerned, under particular aspects, to present the essence of the properly theological, beginning from the first realities. In this way, it will perhaps be able to make the meaning of the properly theological perceptible also to the non-specialist. Because it takes as its point of departure not the specialist but the common way of thinking and speaking about the things of faith today, although this thinking and speaking is very blurred, we hope the essay will be excused for going into more details or making more repetitions than might appear necessary to some readers. — The Editors of *Die Schildgenossen*.

particular. The question touching upon the theory of knowledge contains first of all a general problem: what does that act which we designate as "knowing" mean? What does it mean, not according to its psychological process but according to its content, its signification? This particular act claims to apprehend "objects"; is this correct? What are these objects? How are they related to the apprehending subject? What limits are placed upon this apprehension? The general question of the theory of knowledge deals then with the specific relation that obtains between the bearer of knowledge and the object of knowledge in the act of knowing in general.

But then the question reaches further: Is this relation universally the same? Or does it signify a difference, when in one instance it has to do with comprehending a chemical process, whereas in another instance it tries to understand the motives that led Charlemagne in his political policies against the Saxons? Thinking is not law-giving formation of the object through spontaneous categories, as Kant and the school of Idealism would assert, if we simplify the problem. Thinking apprehends, rather, reality existing in itself and in a determined way, and it must do so as this reality demands to be apprehended.

But this apprehension does not mean a simple mirroring of reality. Cognition is not a dead mirror that reflects an object. It is not an apparatus of logical forms that are brought to a unity in the subject, nor does it receive every object that comes "before the lens." Cognition is a living motion of the real man to the object; it is an encounter between man and object. But in this movement and encounter, there emerges a meaning valid beyond the concrete event: "truth."[3] If that becomes clear to us, then we can no longer suppose that it happens as a matter of course, the way a mechanical apparatus functions. Rather, a concrete interplay of powers is carried out, a living happening and encountering, and we must ask: when does it come to pass?

The emergence of the content of validity, the truth, depends on that concrete act of knowing of the living man coming to pass. What are the—not abstract, but living—preconditions of its coming to pass? In the concrete act of knowing, I am not concerned with "subject in general," but with the living subject; not with "object in general," but with the "concrete object." What does this mean for the act of knowing?

Being is in itself not homogenous, but qualitatively diverse. It is diverse according to great realms of being, and within these realms it is once again diverse according to types, subtypes, all the way down to the fullness of individual determinations. Let us remain with the realms of being, and let us further distinguish these realms with very rough delineations: the realm of the mechanical-dead; that

---

3   Thus, the idealistic understanding is here fundamentally denied. This understanding separates cognition into the concrete process and the ideal frame of reference; the former really and the latter effectively. In truth, there is only living cognition in which, being concretely one, the ideal frame of reference stands in the real act, and the essence of which lies precisely in this concreteness.

of the biological and psychic-living; of the spiritual-personal; of the pneumato-logical-supernatural. Finally, not in the same category, God.[4] These realms are qualitatively diverse, not deriving from one another even if they stand at the same time in a certain relation to each other.[5] The qualitative diversity now also relates to their knowability, to how it becomes a reality for the knower.

There is no singular, sweeping, superficial cognition for the whole world, no knowing that could be directed in a uniform way upon a chemical reaction, a mechanical apparatus, the growth process of a plant, the development of an animal, a human stirring of emotion, the formation of a concept, an ethical decision, a philosophical problem of essence, the religious phenomenon of prayer. A largely dominant way of thinking thinks so. But such a knowledge simply does not exist! The supposition is false as such and to tolerate it at all reveals a spiritual feebleness!

In the face of such a will to know, precisely the essential element within the various realms of objects closes itself off. If this essential dimension is to be apprehended, then knowing must be living. The ontological particularity of things must correspond to a noetic particularity of the act of knowing; the specific sort of object must be apprehended within the appropriate specific categories.

What is Knowledge and How is it Acquired?

Let us sharpen the question: Cognition is a special way that the concrete subject apprehends through a living movement the real thing—in its being, in its essence, in its meaning; for itself and in its relation to other things; in its concrete unique-ness, as well as according to its general characteristics.

This cognition is a living, concrete act. Certainly, it has a general "meaning" that goes beyond this uniqueness. The generality of the meaning of knowledge becomes, however, an empty specter if it does not remain related to the living act. It is not in the generality of meaning alone that the essence of knowledge lies, but rather in the fact that this generality radiates in an individual act, as the knowledge belonging to this man. Furthermore, the object of this act is the concrete thing, which contains a validity that exceeds its singularity; an intelligible concept, a norm, a law, a meaning.

Once again, however, this general validity must not be taken detached and in itself, otherwise it becomes an empty specter. It must remain related to the concrete thing. The meaning of knowledge is not found in an intelligible concept, value, or law; it is found in the general to the extent that it is something general from something concrete. Is all of this mechanically apprehended? Does it force

---

4   On this point, see Guardini, "Gedanken über das Verhältnis von Christentum und Kultur" ["Thoughts Concerning the Relation Between Christianity and Culture"], *Die Schildgenossen* 6 (1926): 281–315.

5   See Guardini, "Gedanken," for more concerning this and also the relation of analogy, order, expression, etc.

itself of its very nature upon the one knowing, as things placed before a camera's lens impress themselves onto the camera's film?

Let us follow then the act of knowing in its endeavor to reach the various contents of objectivity. Here is reality as such. The real existence of a thing appears to be a simple, readily graspable matter. That this thing is right here seems to impose itself on us. But let us think perhaps of the phenomenon of attentiveness. Some things we grasp keenly and clearly. Others we have undoubtedly seen one time, then later, at some other opportunity, they come to mind; but in the very act of seeing, we failed to notice them at all; conscious attentiveness was not directed towards them. Between both extremes of grasping reality—from absolutely nothing to complete clarity—there are an infinite number of intermediate forms.

Such a gradation of perceiving reality can come into play even with very clear consciousness. For certain natures, the world has something peculiarly unreal, dreamlike. Perhaps each person experiences such times in the age of development, or at certain hours of the day, or given certain interior conditions. There also appear to be periods in history where this becomes generally stronger; consider, for example, the Romantic period. On the other hand, for other natures, things have a great intensity of actual existence; so much so that they nearly invade the mind and can engender an angst before things and the world. What is here distinctive is that the Platonic type of philosophical thinking adopts a gradation of reality, degrees of the real. Just as this model adopts this gradation based on original experience, the antithetical inductive-analytical model rejects it. Clearly then, the apprehension of reality is in no way an automatic thing.

Even less so is the apprehension of quality, the grasping of the intelligible notion in the multiplicity of its determinations and the unity of its structure. It ought to be seen: this thing is such and such; it is different from other things. Wholeness and particularities should be discovered, associated, penetrated. The final result will be the completely grasped, distinguished, understood concept. This does not, however, happen easily. How could it otherwise have come to pass that materialism—and not only the primitive sort but also the scholarly variety—understood "life" as a function of chemical and physical powers? That it was capable of stating that the brain secretes thoughts as the bodily excretory organ the waste product of metabolism? That was a crude example; but innumerable others, and of a more refined sort, can convey the point.

Before such misperceptions, we first of all raise the technical objection: this and that fact stand against it, the assertion is provably false, and the like. If we regard the matter precisely, we will note that with this objection something else resonates. We not only sense that the assertion is erroneous but say also: something is not right here, something is blind. And indeed, it is a blindness that we make into a reproach against the thinker. He is not allowed to have this blindness! To mix up the qualitative realm in this way is not only untrue, it is impermissible; and the impermissibility can go so far that we basically render a judgment of a certain insignificance. Thus, the task of formation, indeed the ethical task, touches upon knowing—just as, by the way, the problems of attentiveness in the widest sense, the difficulties of order or purifying of the relation to reality, are not only noetic issues but also pedagogical and ethical ones.

If we observe ourselves, then we shall see how easily we mix up the qualitative realms! How intractably inclined we are to grasp living things with the categories of physical thinking, psychic things with those of the biological, spiritual things with those of the psychological; how often we jumble up ethical, political, economic determinations. If standing before reality it is necessary to have a sensitivity towards the encounter with it, so also, standing before quality it is necessary to have an attentiveness towards this specific property. These things, however, encompass a whole series of theoretical and practical questions that we will take up below.

Apprehending the object becomes even less self-evident as soon as values and norms are concerned. There are dispositions whose certain values become a reality for the knower basically not at all, or only very imperfectly. We probably have all regretfully noticed how inaccessible for us, in contrast to others, the beauty of an artwork was, or even the beauty of an entire branch of the fine arts. Or we were receptive for such things at certain times and not at others; or the receptivity to these things changed according to the mood of the moment. But all of this determines our cognitive judgment.

The meaning of our daily work or our relations with other people was sometimes living and clear; at other times, fluctuating, or everything could be twisted towards the obnoxious. But this had once again an influence on our value judgment. There are times of indifference, when everything loses its meaning for our perception. If we know ourselves well, we then take care in such moments not to render a judgment or make a decision. Moral obligations—of fidelity, gratitude, responsibility—are clear when a living and open disposition allows them to clearly become apparent. But they can also recede and become nebulous. Indeed, they can appear to our sensibilities as loathsome, so that the whole vigilance of conscience is required in order to fulfill such obligations with consistency of judgment and faithfulness of character.

Along these lines there would be much to say. It is possible, looking to someone's disposition, to point out a plain model of his way of viewing the world and his values; an unconscious technique of interpreting, of attenuating and emphasizing, of transforming meanings, even of falsifying norms and values due to the influence of mood, passion, situation and environment, mannerism and habit, the results of which, supported by reasons and theories, then present themselves in the apparently objective form of a judgment.

Even what appears to be the most exact moment of apprehending an object—finding a thing's measure in the widest sense of the word, its size, weight, intensity, need, urgency—is subjected to subjective presuppositions. The psychology of estimation and deception reveals how little a false estimation can be traced back only to the poor workings of eye or ear; rather, it is to be traced back to the fact that psychological impulses mislead us. The whole system of the senses functions wrongly—because it is meant to function wrongly, because subconscious interests have an effect on the process of apprehending an object and thus falsify matters of fact.

The Knowing Subject and the Objects of Knowledge

The adequate apprehension of a thing in its essence is therefore anything but self-evident. It sets up rather certain prerequisites, which are often fulfilled either not at all or only imperfectly. And this is the case not only because man's powers are not up to the demands of the object, but also because an inner will is at work, a will that, with a delicate game of selecting, weakening, sharpening, and transforming influences, does not let the objects become a reality for the knower as they are, but as they are wished to be, thus making them to be an atmosphere in which the individual feels confirmed in his self-desire and borne along by it.

The world of objects divides into a multitude of qualitatively distinguished realms. Coming to know them sets up however certain presuppositions in the knowing disposition. There is not only the general problem of epistemology, but also the difficulty of a knowledge differentiated according to its proper object as well as its preconditions. The latter extend from the realm of the psychological to the most deeply held moral convictions; from questions of attentiveness to difficulties regarding the formation of knowledge. In this regard, I will try to point out a few aspects.

Here we find above all the qualitative adequation of the knowing power to the object. Cognition is not a stiff apparatus but a living and pliable power of that spiritual and corporeal unity that we call "man." "I perceive" means that in that special, fundamental, receptive disposition, one that cannot be traced further back, I direct "myself" towards the object. The entirety of this act calls into play many powers of apprehension: powers of eyes, hands, ears; of imagination, distinction, comparison; of insight and understanding; of combining and judgment.

In the movement of cognition, the living act of knowing transcends itself—intentionally—towards the object standing in itself; it conforms to its specifying characteristic, inspects it, takes it up, takes hold of it, enables it to give witness to its own identity. If this self-conforming of the knowing subject is not present, the object fails to become a reality for the subject. It is discarded. To the extent that I approach the object without being "receptive," actively receptive, I discard it from the horizon of my perception.

This self-assimilation of the knowing power to the object becomes possible through the fact that all the contents of the world are given along with the living existence of man. Here, the old theory of microcosmic nature is pertinent. Man is in fact the living abbreviation of Being. Every knowing means a simultaneous self-actuation. In the knowledge of an object, something in man corresponding to this object rises up and enters into the living act. Throughout the whole history of epistemology, the awareness of this issue is traceable, though often misconstrued in an actualistic or monistic manner.

This self-conforming of the knower to the object may not be pushed as far as the assertion: "I know only what I myself am." I need not concretely be an animal in order to understand an animal. The content of the act of knowing as such is not real, but represented. In order that something can become the content of awareness, can become "known," it is not demanded that it be concretely a component of the knower's very reality.

To this extent "to have knowledge about" is precisely not "to be." But the act of knowing, since its content comes to be something of our consciousness, is not the merely logical act of an abstract logical subject, but rather the real act of a living subject. This subject stands in the act with everything it is. In this way, a mobilization of an existing power proportioned to the object is required if this object is really to be known.

In stating this, however, certain questions result: On what does this ability to come to actuality and conformity depend? How does correct cognition depend on the condition of the whole subject? In what way does it depend on the subject's integrity, acuteness, spiritualization, or even his personal perfection? To what extent are certain sorts of objects and certain levels in every realm of the object bound up with certain presuppositions of moral, spiritual, personal "formation"?

And still the question leads deeper: that qualitative conformity cannot take place in indifference. The matter at hand is not the functioning of a machine but a living act. "Act" however signifies that it is "performed" by the living subject. Knowledge does not mean a mechanical reflection of the object by a rigid surface; it means, rather, the living reception of the object in the interiority of the person. An object becomes truly known when, in the act of knowing, it actualizes this interiority, and this in a specific way: through the fact that this object is taken into this interiority, and that in the knower a realm of this inner life corresponding to the object is called up or introduced. A life filled with interiority realizes itself only in objects; and here we mean in knowing them.

Objects, for their part, arrive at being known—they stand before us in the inner sphere of living consciousness—only by this consciousness actualizing itself as a living process. And, importantly, this does not happen in a general way, directed towards some "object in general"; instead it regards this particular object. Diverse objects demand the realization not only of a different measure, but also of a qualitatively different sort of content belonging to man's living interiority. The objects establish a certain hierarchy characterized by the fact that the individual things require to an ever-increasing degree coming close, being received. But this means simultaneously that there comes about each time the introduction of a new, qualitative interior realm. And only when the knower in this way welcomes the objects and takes them into himself—thereby committing himself to the very knowledge of these objects—only then will they really be known. Otherwise such objects are not known, but merely "registered."

Every object—even the dead, mechanical sort—necessitates a certain degree of earnest consideration. I consider something in earnest when I allow it to impact me. Otherwise I see it without its qualitative force. The moment I truly approach a thing to know it, I simultaneously commit myself to it somehow; I thereby also admit that, for me, "this object matters." This is not only a matter of objective "correctness"—a purely objective, unconcerned disposition towards the object remains barren.

Only that disposition bears fruit which enacts the earnestness of committing oneself to the object. Every being is intrinsically valuable, every existing thing is ranked among things worthwhile. But values are not dead existents: they have power over the one feeling, and this power is the power of values. When the subject perceiving values admits them into his lived experience, then it portends a threat to his world of values closed in upon itself. But this happens only to the extent that he is receptive, committed, and earnest in knowing. This "crisis" can produce an expansion, provoke an explosion, promote a bending and buckling within the subject. The subject reacts, struggles. Here the battle of the living thing for self-assertion acquires metaphysical significance.

This involvement of the subject with the object through the subject's self-commitment grows ever more demanding in proportion to the ascending hierarchical order of objects. Standing before a human being considered as object, it attains to a very high level. I can understand something about man by way of feeling along with the mechanical aspects, as I can with a dead object. For other things, a vital resonance will suffice. But everything having to do with character, personality, personal life, heart, and interiority—these I only know to the extent that I am really involved with it. I have to become active in a particular sense of the word; I have to live *with* the life happening before my eyes; I have to let it penetrate me. And this means a new self-commitment. I am put under the active power of the other's personality, under the dynamism of his character and the force of his destiny. But this is necessary, otherwise I do not understand him.

The notion that the person is in no way an object but is always only realized in action, is false. A person is not only the shining point of the act, but also an abiding countenance, a lasting form. However, a person is all this as something interior, and I can only know him when I "take" him as something interior, which is something I can do by participating in his life and experience. Precisely in this way do I take this person into my own interior life and expose my interiority to the power of a foreign form.

"Lived Faithfulness" and "Knowing" God

Indeed, the cognition of ultimate, personal values makes still further demands. Let us take an example: faithfulness, as the essential relation of one person to another, as a value and a task. The salvation of a person depends upon his being faithful. Now, how can I acquire knowledge of "faithfulness"? Through manifold observations, I can discover the generally recurring psychological fact of a relation characterized by faithfulness; I can purify it conceptually, and then through observation and analysis, through an intuition of the essence as well as the work of logic, I can extract the general phenomenon of "faithfulness."

The result, however, would still not do justice to the object. Faithfulness is not a way of acting that applies to "person in general"; rather, it is a way of acting that applies to a specific person in relation to another specific person. If we talk about a "power of soul," for example, then it is of no concern who has it—a "power of soul" is something that follows upon the general species, in relation to which the individual developing this power is only accidental. In contrast to this, the essential aspect of faithfulness is not given in the general phenomenon. It is not a property of the general species, which is realized in the individual as a bearer of the species; instead, it is a property, or more precisely a characteristic of the person as such. A person, however, only exists as "this person." In regard to person, there is a general notion only in a very provisional sense, because in a very essential way it only exists as this unique person.

What we call "personal" constitutes an objective order of its own sort.[6] For this reason, the problem of "faithfulness" is truly the problem of "the faithfulness of this human being with respect to this other human being." In this way, I can then do what we have already discussed: grasp the faithfulness of a specific person by means of a sympathetic involvement; experience with the other how someone holding to faithfulness roots himself in his personal worth, or how a different person, who does not live out faithfulness, falls into misery. Would this then mean that our task would be solved? Not yet.

When I say "faithfulness" meaning the process serving as the foundation of salvation, is it—in this context and according to the deepest sense of our task—a matter of indifference whose "salvation" is meant, when it has to do with only a particular one? I think not. As soon as I say "salvation" without any further qualification, then at the heart of the matter, it is my salvation that is meant. As soon as I say "person," then at the heart of the matter, it is my person that is meant. Here we reach the point where the theoretical task of knowing the object is anchored in the practical task of becoming sanctified. And at this point, we must say that being "objective" is no longer of value; it is, rather, an uprooting.

This does not mean that the general problem of personal salvation is of no concern for me; or that the question could not be put forward and answered. It also does not mean a sort of pragmatism that would assert that truth consists in how something concerns me. Nor does it mean that the problem of another person's

---

6   Here, see Guardini, "Über Sozialwissenschaften und Ordnung unter Personen" ["On Social Science and Order Among Persons"], *Die Schildgenossen* 6 (1926).

salvation is inaccessible for me. All of this is a concern for me, is accessible, and is of great value. But the essential form of the question concerning salvation is the question regarding the salvation of myself. Only from this point begins the way to the salvation of the other.[7] In this way, the question, "What is faithfulness?" becomes in its ultimate form the question, "What is my faithfulness?" But this means again, the faithfulness that I live out. Not as a person in general, but as myself, who I am. And not as faithfulness towards a person in general, but towards this person. And, finally, not faithfulness in general, but in this moment, and then in the next, and then again in the next.

What this means, then, is that I cannot construct this faithfulness *a priori* [prior to any experience]. I cannot deduce it from observations and general psychic data, nor can I win it from an awareness of how I otherwise am. Rather, I have to live faithfulness. In its formal constitution, which is in fact personal, faithfulness is simply not present until I live it. What faithfulness means in this strictest sense of the phenomenon is something that becomes a reality for me only when I practice it.

This is the existential way of thinking, as Kierkegaard demanded it with such tremendous intensity in response to an objectivistic, noncommittal way of thinking. Kierkegaard showed—admittedly in "catastrophic" exaggeration that exploded every possibility—that there are things, including of course things spiritual such as the ethical and religious realm, which cannot be swallowed, so to speak, in a purely objective way without any inner involvement. Instead, such things only become realities at the moment they are personally realized, lived out. There are ultimate things that are only given to me in such a way that I can only *know* them when I *do* them. Kierkegaard overextends this thought—even in these questions there is also objective reality. But he is certainly right in one point: the essential aspect of the problem of salvation is only noticed in its personal realization.

To this extent, the measure of my knowing depends upon the measure of my doing. The more intensively I act, the more I act from a pure disposition, the more I do this from a greater passion—that much clearer and complete will be the result of my knowledge. "Do what I tell you, and you will notice that it is from the truth." What is said here is certainly not to be expressed in general terms; it is precisely the un-general, the personal and particular. But it flows into general notions and gives to them their credibility and binding force.

To these objects belong all the beings, realities, relations, values, and claims that have to do with the salvation of the person. This means first of all the relation of the person to himself, those things such as: interiority, purity, character. It also means the relation to another person: faithfulness, love, marriage, friendship, fellowship, mastership and discipleship. Then there is the relation to worth and to responsibility; the whole world of moral values, relations, attitudes; the world of

---

7   Herein lies an important approach to the words of Christ: "You should love your neighbor as yourself."

religious values and realities. They are all valid in themselves; they are not created by us; they are not constituted only through our experience or through categorical determination. About such things as well can a wealth of general statements be made.

All efforts towards an objective teaching of values, an objective ethics, a philosophy of religion, theology—these are all correct and meaningful. It is only the very last realm of the problem, the personal connection to salvation, that becomes a reality for the subject in an existential way of thinking, not an objective one. This happens in living execution, in a living disposition, in doing. *In doing*—or at least in the real readiness to act, a readiness that already anticipates something of this doing.

Everything stated here holds in the highest way with respect to God. By many and various means, I can come to know many things of great significance about God: through a serious wanting to see, accompanied by clear thinking; through observing the world and its characteristics; through the recollection and openness brought about by participating in religious acts. But this is not the final word. God is not like a tree, about which one can say all sorts of things and just leave it at that. God addresses himself to me in a demanding way. My salvation depends entirely upon him. If there is a God, then his being and essence signify a living and absolute claim on me. On me, and not on the other.

God is, in the first moment, a matter of salvation. As the Greek Fathers hold, he is not given to me as *Theos pros heauton*, "God for himself." As such, he is his own sanctuary. He is given to me only as *Theos pros hemas*, "God for us." I have no claim on him, and he does not need me; but in his existence, he makes a claim on me, and I need him. Thus, only when I take God as the salvation of my person does he enter into the reality that is possible, full, and decisive for me. Not when I say "God"; but only when I say "my God." And then he becomes a reality for me—to the extent that I deal with him seriously; to the degree that I, in ever deeper interiority, take him seriously; to the measure that I realize the "my" in the expression "my God." But this means: to the extent that I "accomplish his will."

The New Testament as a "Pneumatic" Text

What does all of this mean for our question?

With the New Testament, we stand before texts. Thus it is first of all a literary object. Such an object wants to be grasped from a disposition different from, for example, a natural process or a sociological event. The one considering has to open himself to the peculiarities of the spiritual event of its creation. Then he will see its character and from this character he will shape concepts and words. He will recognize the mechanisms of a psychological or sociological type that are moreover contained in the object; only they receive from the unique particular their actual meaning: they are mechanisms within a human, creative, spiritual, personal event.

Literary works, for their part, must always be considered according to their specific, literary character. The histories of Thucydides are historical sources: they relate events. Justice is done to them when they are taken as such, when the tidings of former happenings are drawn from them. Or, the Homeric epics can also be taken as historical sources and considered with the whole historical apparatus. In this way, one will make meaningful historical discoveries. The essence, however, the poetry, remains mute if one does not draw closer to it with the disposition demanded by it, with the aesthetic disposition. Without this, all historical research remains a fragment. Within the realm of literary objects, therefore, the diverse genres require diverse dispositions of knowledge, and this precisely according to the measure of true science.

At the same time, the fundamental laws of methodical research remain universally the same. But these laws are not mechanical and the sovereign stipulation of scientific method holds that an object is grasped not with a "general method" but rather with the "method corresponding to the object." This has nothing to do with something mysterious or fanciful; it has rather to do with the problem of attentiveness, with the question of apprehending quality, with the limits of the field of perception, and with the processes of selection, revision, accentuation of what is understood rightly or wrongly. It is, to say it once more, a matter of our thinking being a process, in which a very different measure of power can be applied in each case; a process which is confronted with the various qualities of the object not in a mechanically uniform way but in living reaction, and in which different qualitative realms of living being can become actualized.

In the New Testament it is a matter first of all of historical sources, that is, of earlier developments; it is a matter of reports, letters, records. Thus, they must be taken and excavated as such. The result would be the history of those segments of time and those events related by these texts.

Would that be enough for them? What if we would treat them as perhaps the annals of Tacitus, the epistles of Seneca, the visions of Virgil? In so doing, we would have gained very much. We would have heard of the environment in which the texts emerged, of their historical presuppositions, of parallel appearances, and so forth. But still we would not have touched upon the essential element. What is that?

The New Testament is a holy text, the aftermath of a religious event, the expression of revelation. That it is precisely this is presupposed. All the facts from which we gain the conviction that God speaks here and which justify it if we bind ourselves to it in faith, are here presupposed. "The New Testament," according to its literary character is a collection of chronicles concerning personalities, teachings, and happenings; it is a collection of letters and prophetic texts; it is not a manifestation of a purely natural sort. Rather, it traces back to an event of revelation. It is carried by the power of that event, filled by its contents, and supported by its worth and validity.

God spoke here into history. This he did not only in some general sense according to which everything that comes to pass essentially reaches into eternity somehow; rather, asserting that God spoke in history means that a special, free, and personal self-revelation of God took place. This is the context out of which these texts arose. They emerged out of the *pneuma*, the Holy Spirit, through whom revelation occurs and becomes understandable; the Spirit who interiorizes Christ within man, who works such that man takes hold of, makes his very own, recognizes, and lives out Christ and what has been opened up in Christ.

Scripture is the work of Christ's *pneuma*; it is inspired. It is a pneumatic text, a holy text. Thus, this text forms over and above its purely literary determination a particular realm for a special sort of object. It therefore also demands a specific disposition corresponding to the text: a disposition capable of grasping its qualitative specificity; of characterizing as its own the categories that do justice to the text's essence; of saying in what way the "givens" of other points of departure (historical, psychological) are applicable to it.

It is possible to treat the gospels as any other source that claims to put forth history—the histories of Thucydides, for example—and according to this method the gain would be invaluable. The only question is whether the text, according to its proper character, belongs in the same class of objects as Thucydides. It is a dogma, and a false one, to suppose *a priori* that each text speaking of what has transpired must be treated as Thucydides.

In reality, the gospels are reports of events which are certainly historical, but which happen in a wholly different manner than the Peloponnesian War. Their coming to pass stems from God; they are salvific events, pneumatic happenings. They are accounts that work "with ink and paper"; they employ the usual words and grammatical structures of the time; they contain the then-current views; they are built into a concrete social and historical milieu; all of this is just as other narratives. Nevertheless, it is a particular sort of reporting grounded in the pneumatic, in men who themselves stand in the experience of revelation and speak from it. These accounts, therefore, are completely and objectively something other than the histories of Thucydides. The events are of a special sort; the points of view, purposes, and standards are different; the existential layers of man and things present in this narrative are other; and above all, the fundamental reality presented here is a supernatural reality: God and his holy action constitutive of our salvation. It is a matter of sacred history—and that may not, despite every analogy, be taken simply as profane history.

The Pauline letters can be treated as ancient treatises concerning moral objects, like those of Seneca, Epictetus, or Marcus Aurelius, and in this way much will be gained. But in essence these letters have to do with something else. They have to do with the breaking through of a supernatural way of life for the individual and the community. This is not about ethics, but about leading a Christian, holy life. And if the disposition of the one studying is living, then he must notice that he will come no further with a purely humanistic method of formulating his questions.

What then is the particular disposition corresponding to the holy text that must be had if the text is to become clear in its specific meaning? Evidently, a religious disposition. But this remains insufficient if one understands this as only a general religious openness. Such a disposition is also a prerequisite for the speech of Buddha and the sayings of Lao Tzu. Christianity is—presupposing what was earlier taken as presupposed—not only "a religion"; it is, rather, the positive revelation of the living God, the Father, in his incarnate Son. It is unique and binding. With this we step out of the domain of general religiousness. This demand is immense and even—from the perspective of the contemporary conception of history—absurd. It is "an offense and a folly."[8] Christianity itself knows this, but maintains the demand. Thus, this particular object corresponds to a particular, positive, religious disposition: Christian faith.

The Cognitive Disposition for Knowing the Believing Word

Faith is the cognitive disposition proportioned to revelation. The New Testament is the word of God in a particular, positive sense. This word only becomes perceptible in its actual meaning when it is taken as what it is—that is, as a believing word. Only when I approach it in a believing way do I open myself for its specific content, for the supernatural and holy that is in it, for the holy event, the holy way and form of life, the reality of God expressing itself in the holy and supernatural.

What is faith? Above all: an event creating a point of departure and a new horizon. It cannot be traced back to other acts. It establishes a beginning. Sense perception cannot be traced back to something else; it too establishes a beginning—the one perceiving stands face-to-face with the thing perceived. Aesthetic experience establishes a beginning: the one aesthetically experiencing stands face-to-face with the work of art; it is a relation that in its very essence and meaning cannot be derived from psychological presuppositions, but instead arises in a primordial way from the aesthetic act itself. So also in this case: faith is not an antecedent or derivative of thinking; it is not the result of intuiting, of the power of symbol, of an interpretation of the world, or anything of this sort. Faith is rather an act of a unique character with which a new relation to a new level emerges: the believing man stands face-to-face with revelation.

This relation has its own particular, irreducible content. The standing face-to-face of the sensing perceiver and the perceived has its own content: the perception of the thing. The aesthetic experience has its particular content as well: the experience of an expression of an essence. So also does the standing face-to-face

---

8   It is, by the way, a whole problem unto itself what significance the moment of the "absurd" has in its position towards Christianity and in the motive of the act that takes a stand in faith.

of the believer and revelation have its proper content: the perception of the divine Word.

What happens in faith? Let us take the more simply constructed case in which a person, who earlier did not believe, comes later to the faith. What happens in this step? This person has a collection of facts confronting him—historical witnesses, historical events, personages, thoughts handed down across generations, and other such things. He has gained insights, acquired experiences, perceived values, seen goals. He immerses himself in all of that; he tests and weighs to the point where in all of this he grasps—more or less quickly, with more or less certainty—a reality implied by these appearances, values, forms, events; a reality that finds expression in these things; a reality that expresses itself "in the world" and yet as becomes clear is not "from the world"; the God who lives and speaks to us.

The one searching recognizes this reality, scoops it up, secures it, emphasizes it. He acknowledges that it exists, confesses it as normative for his life; he professes himself to it and, through a personal act of loyal joining, binds himself to this personal reality through a personal act of pledged faithfulness. He knows that a realm of his personality is called, one that lies deeper than anything else that otherwise could be called. This realm, the religious core, relates to that reality. He receives in some sense a participation in the otherness of that reality. He steps towards God and stands together with him, facing him, on a level altogether different from the material, the psychological, the natural-personal. On this level, a new life now arises—a new set of acts, contexts, and orders, all with new contents.

The event appears to be most fittingly compared with a bond of a definitive, personal sort. A man gets to know another person, establishes contact with the other until he is confronted by the actual spiritual person, the self which emerges from the various physical and spiritual realities and yet lies beyond all of them. He grasps this out of all the residual aspects, recognizes it, establishes a bond to it. He experiences that something stands out in this I-you relation: a deeper reality, a deeper level of something coming to pass. Based on this relation, a new life, a new way of life becomes possible: friendship, work-partnerships, marriage, each with their own particular content.

In faith, what was demanded above for a new grasping of the object comes to pass. The self constitutes itself in a new and indeed definitive way. The reality here at hand is that which quite simply constitutes salvation—it is the absolute salvation, eternal life through the love of God. The act that grasps it is, according to its meaning, an absolute participation. I can only believe in my God, in my Savior, in my Father.[9] An objectivity that does not participate is not possible here. Faith is essentially the appropriation of salvation, fundamentally the "gifting of the soul." Faith exists to the extent that I, in my innermost self, am involved; to the

---

9   Which of course in no way means subjectivism. The "my" indicates the participation in contrast
    to mere contact with an object.

degree that this reality is accepted and taken into my own life: "I live; no longer I, but Christ lives in me." That means, however, being shaken up: "The new wine in the old wine skins"; the "taking off of the old man"; the "passing away of the former man"; the cross.

The content of faith and the act of faith are grace; they are gifted to us. And precisely in this grace is man's innermost actualized, that innermost of innermosts and soul of souls. It is clearly something different than the self-actualization discussed earlier. Revelation does not belong to the "world" in such a way that some aspect of man's essence would correspond to it in a microcosmic way. It is also not the case of a purely natural knowledge of God: there the actualized in man would be his being in the image of God. Revelation is not only transcendent, but also supernatural. At the same time, something lives within man that anticipates it. That is what St. Augustine means when he says, the soul is "Christian by nature;" what Bl. John Duns Scotus, St. Francis de Sales, and Matthias Scheeben mean when they say that God would have become man even had there been no sin, in order to lead creation to the communion of grace. This something—which human thought, in trying to determine it more precisely, easily winds up distorting the mystery of grace—this something that awakes actualizes itself in faith, as the human bearer of the grace of faith.

That reality apprehended in faith, that relation in which the believer stands to this reality, is higher than the psychological realm, loftier than the natural-personal realm. It cannot be derived from them. It also cannot be judged by them. It lives in the awareness of being sovereign with respect to these realms. Faith in its relation to life knows itself to be so much higher than everything natural that it judges only from itself and not from logical and psychological presuppositions: the essence of faith itself can, once again, only be believed; its tasks, its crises, and all such things can only be assessed from faith itself. And still more: after faith is constituted, it defends itself against the threats coming from the soul's store of experiences, from theoretical objections and ethical crises; this it does no longer on the level of those experiences, objections, and crises, but purely from itself, in the form of resistance.

In the final analysis, faith does not discuss at all—it asserts itself in fidelity to itself. Here we find the justification for the Church's conviction, so disconcerting at first, that doubt is a sin and that therefore a real and serious occasion of doubt is not at all allowed. Is this not a circle? If I assert that the reality of God, the reality of Christ cannot be deduced from natural phenomena, is this not a circle? Not "deduced," I say, though certainly "shown, manifested, evidenced." It is otherworldly, supernatural, grasped through an act given by God himself and in the end only judged by this same act itself. It has been repeatedly asserted that this constitutes a circle. But in so doing two fundamentally different things are confused: "circle" and "beginning." It is not a circle, but it *is* a beginning of life.

From exterior and interior experience, I am able to discover a plethora of indications and evidences for realities lying beyond the natural realm and I can pursue them in the form of intellectual considerations, experiences of value, or grasping certain expressions; but all of this is not yet faith. Faith does not originate from all of this, as something like a psychological process originating from another or a logical conclusion from its premises. All of that certainly justifies faith in the face of intellectual and ethical conscience; but faith itself arises spontaneously from a more profound center of action, which is itself only actualized in the act of faith.[10] When faith comes to be, then an eruption of new life emerges out of its own beginning. In the foreground, this is certainly carried out in psychological acts of thinking, deciding, etc. But still, there is the consciousness that behind all of this stands something more. This "more"—this center, the proper subject of faith—is "the new man," the one born anew, the child of God, who is only created through grace.

The act of faith as well as the relation arising with it can express themselves in a logical and psychological way. But still they know themselves to be something that in the final analysis is independent of all of that. The stronger faith becomes, the more purely and decisively it rejects legitimizing itself through natural presuppositions; the stronger it grows, the more there emerges what, understood falsely, looks like a circle: faith's being a beginning. And still more! Standing against the indications and proofs of the faith are inhibitions, objections, value conflicts, insoluble riddles of the most diverse sort.

Were faith as such qualitatively founded upon natural presuppositions it would then need to remain in doubt until such difficulties would be clarified. But this is not the case. The logical, psychological, historical scope of the problem is only the field upon which faith appears. These aspects have a certain meaning for faith, since faith should be able to justify itself—at least to some extent—on an intellectual basis, an ethical basis, and other bases of value. (Consider the demand in 1 Pt 3:15, to "always be ready to give an explanation...") But still faith does not found itself upon these bases and therefore, when it has become a living faith, it is also able to overcome the most difficult theoretical and practical burdens. As Ven. John Henry Newman says: "Faith means being able to bear doubt."

Perhaps the example drawn above can clarify what is meant here. The act of binding oneself in faith, out of which a relation of genuine love arises, is prepared by psychological processes. A plethora of reasons and motivations can be offered for this act. But the act itself is not derived from them. A love that can be traced back to psychological presuppositions is indeed only a psychic process that may

---

10 This is said in a human way. In itself, the act of faith is in no way a purely human act. In a fundamental way, the act of faith is executed through the power of grace, through the "infused divine virtue"—which is itself, of course, a *credendum* [something to be believed]. Here we are speaking of the human "incarnation" of this grace; we are touching upon the observable material of a human act, in which grace is operative.

find itself extinguished once again by the same psychic causes that gave rise to it. A properly personal love cannot be derived, rather it arises in the very midst of various preparatory dimensions from a deeper core. It establishes a beginning. It lives from itself, it is able to overcome all psychic fluctuations, and—always presupposing that it is truly love—it alone is able to judge itself.

But the final word is still to come. If the object of faith is God, understood through his Word, his appearance, his becoming man in time, then God and his appearance can never be coextensive—the divine content and the perceptible word can never be entirely correlative. For God is certainly the archetype of all finitude and thus related; but nevertheless as the Absolute he is finally incommensurable with it. In this way, his relation to the world is allegorical, enigmatic, and insoluble from the world's perspective. Given this situation, carrying out the act of faith involves an irresolvable problem: how can what is beyond this world and wholly "other" be grasped beginning from natural realities? How can what is incommensurable and divine be understood beginning from the finite? It is the moment that despite every analogy is always perceived in Christian consciousness as a "dare." To put it in an extreme way we could say, as a paradox or as the moment of the "absurd." To put it in an antagonistic way, as an "annoyance and foolishness."

In this way, faith is a beginning, the being born of a new life. It is a similar situation between faith and waking up. The condition of consciousness in the morning, when I can perceive, make up my mind, and act—this condition is not derivable from the physical and psychological process of sleeping and its lightening. Rather, it emerges as something new that lives from itself. It is newly present. It is somehow a repetition of being born. So also, analogously, is faith.

And in regard to those thoughts or experiences that menace faith, faith acts as a living thing among the living: it does not discuss how it would come about that at the same level one argument would win out over another. Instead, it asserts itself through its living power. Where there is true faith it cannot be refuted, only challenged. It cannot be proven false; it can only sicken and perish.

Subordinate Dispositions for the Critical Study of Scripture

Faith is the specific cognitive disposition that corresponds to the Word of God. In holding to this formulation, the other cognitive dispositions are not abolished— the psychological, the historical-critical, that of the humanities, the philosophical. The philological-historical disposition need not be abrogated as soon as I take the *Iliad* as what it essentially is, as poetry; such a disposition, however, will be subordinated to another way of understanding, namely, the aesthetic. In a corresponding way this is also the case in our question: all of those dispositions and results retain their full weight when it comes to holy Scripture. They are simply subordinated to that which is here specifically responsible, namely, the one believing.

Reality constitutes a highly differentiated order and within this order each realm must first be seen from its specific particular significance. When that happens, when what is proper to it is certain not to be confused and when the essential notions and categories are gained from it, then the question is justified: to what extent are the other realms of being found in the object under consideration and what can be applied from those realms to this one? But then they will not be applied "univocally" but rather "analogously." The essence of a living thing can only be determined from the perspective of one who lives, with categories taken from himself. When that takes place, then we can ask how the chemical and mechanical processes of inanimate things are rediscovered in the realm of the living. They will find themselves within this inquiry, but analogously; that is, they will retain their particular meaning in the perspective of the specific categories of the living. This applies in a corresponding way to the realm of the personal with respect to the vital and psychic.

The correspondence applies also to the case at hand. The proper essence of the holy text remains cut off, in the strictest sense of the word, as long as the adequate disposition is not present—that is, faith. The one considering the holy text in a merely historical way does not see the proper object at all. He sees only the external appearances, psychological contexts, philological and cultural meanings of the word. One can conceive the word of revelation, "grace," from the perspective of the history of religion, in a religio-psychological way, a philosophical way, or whatever. In this way, one would arrive at psychological or religio-philosophical concepts while at the same time completely missing the fact that the word "grace" in its proper sense does not have meaning at all in the categories of psychology or philosophy of religion. Rather, it is a name for something unique—that something that broke out into the open in Jesus and in his vicinity; that something that Paul and John indicated when they used the word and its synonyms. But that only opens up when one believes—or at least has an inner readiness and openness to the faith.

Our language used in the science of religion is teeming with secularized holy words, with words not accepted in faith but somehow taken in a general way. And today, the task is plainly given to the faithful individual to do away with these words and their meanings, and instead to listen to them anew in their original meaning based on the matter at hand, revelation. Holy Scripture itself knows of this difficulty. Over and over again in Scripture, words appear, such as the unveiling of the eyes and the opening up of the heart, beginning from the psalms and prophets. Christ speaks of "hearing and not understanding"; he speaks of "unlocking the text." Paul talks of "the spiritual that can only be spiritually understood" and of the pneumatic man "who himself judges the others, but he cannot be judged."

Indeed, the "pneumatic gospel" of St. John is full of the fact that what comes "from above" cannot be understood by that which comes "from below"; or again, Christ and his word cannot be grasped by the merely natural man. The great shock in the life of the apostle, which still causes shivers to run through his gospel and letters, was certainly that the Light came into the world, ready to illuminate the darkness, and yet the darkness did not understand it. This line of thought is carried forward by the Fathers and theologians. Augustine knows that only he who has love understands the world of love. St. Anselm of Canterbury teaches: whoever does not experience what is revealed in a spiritual way, cannot grasp it rationally; but whoever does not believe cannot experience things in a spiritual way.[11] Bonaventure goes as far as saying, one must be holy in order to be a theologian. The mystics teach that there is a stepladder of spiritual objects which, if they are to be understood, presuppose a hierarchy of spiritual degrees realized in a living way.

All of these things are realities that have long since been forgotten, breaking down at the same time as the great order of being and living established in the Middle Ages. (I do not speak pessimistically. There will be a new one, but so far none has arisen since that of the Middle Ages. And the task of once again bringing into a new order the individual taken out of the old order is a task that remains absolutely unaccomplished!) Everything is leveled into a general schema of intellectualistic cognition, in which an abstract, homogenous cognitive apparatus, the subject, stands before an object, which is just as homogenous in its abstract objectivity, whether we are dealing with a stone or a plant or a person. And this disposition has been dogmatized in the name of being scientific according to that science which stems from comprehending mechanical things.

Theology, a Science of Reality

We confront the New Testament as the Word of God, as a pneumatic text that speaks from the spiritually-filled disposition of the hagiographer to address the "spiritual," the supernatural. We understand it through faith. Faith is not the last link of a syllogism, a link that must have a rational character just as the syllogism does; it is not the final stage of a psychological process, a stage that would then be just as psychological as any other. Rather, faith is a new beginning. The act of faith may as always be supported by the rational and the psychological; but when the proper act is carried out, then it constitutes something new. In and through this act, a new aspect of reality and a new qualitative realm enters into the solid world of reality.

The contents of holy Scripture can, as the Word of God, only be grasped in faith. Indeed, even this characteristic and dignity itself, the fact that it is the Word of God, can as such only be comprehended by faith. Before this point, all the explanations of reason and feelings serve only as preparations, *praeambula* [preambles], pre-steps. They belong to a qualitatively different order of reality, the natural order. Only the act of faith corresponds adequately and qualitatively to the Word of God as such. The act does not emerge from those natural preparations; they prepare the way for it. It arises from the free center of the living, redeemed spirit; it is generated

---

11   See Guardini, *Auf dem Wege* [On the Way] (Mainz: Matthias-Grünewald, 1923), 37.

by the grace that creates a higher life. It is a divine, infused "virtue." Despite this, or in fact in virtue of this, it is the act of man that is most his very own—here is the paradox of God's action, that it makes the creature acted upon freer to perform its own proper act in proportion to the intensity of God's acting upon it.

Precisely how this act arises is not something that can be resolved or even observed, just as little as I can observe or explain how I wake up or how I am born. It is a process through which I appear as one living in a new reality of life, in a new degree of life. One cannot know it but can only experience it.

Then, when it is present, one can try to penetrate into the act itself or into the realities that appear in virtue of the act and thereby come to a steadily deeper knowledge: the knowledge of faith, Christian *gnosis* [knowledge]. Of course, it will always remain but a penetration and never attain to comprehension, because what is revealed is not merely partially, but is essentially mystery. Faith will always remain the presupposition, never to be superseded by knowledge, for faith establishes the level at which this mystery is given.

As soon as that penetration happens in a methodical way, with a critical consciousness of judgment and systematic order of procedure, it becomes the science of faith, theology. Belonging to the objects and sources of this science are the text and its contents as the Word of God. Theology has the task of determining on the basis of faith the essence and content of God's Word, and to shape words and concepts based thereupon. Theology accepts as help everything placed into its hands by the historical, psychological, and philological methods of examination. But theology does not transfer it all directly or univocally but rather analogously; it orders everything under the specific categories of the sacred and supernatural.

But theology remains always carried by faith. Presupposing that even the most distinguished theologian should truly lose his faith, he will also lose his object. He would not even understand his own earlier writings. He would be vexed by his own elucidations. Just as the teachings of Jesus cannot be separated from his mouth and just as there is no "essence of Christianity" apart from the person of Christ—in the same way there is no theology detached from faith. (This is not meant in a subjectivistic way in the least, but rather it is much more meant in an eminently objective way.) It then also follows that the intensity and breadth of theological understanding—scholarly competence assumed—grows and diminishes with the liveliness of faith.

Theological understanding depends upon the life of faith, upon prayer, upon Christian deeds, upon holiness. In the New Testament itself this is self-evident. Also in the earliest period of Christianity. And in the Middle Ages, for Anselm, St. Bonaventure, St. Thomas Aquinas—not even to mention the mystical schools. Thus it has basically remained until this historical hour. But coming to predominate over this basic relationship was in fact another one. The autonomism of modern, methodological science—with its fiction of a detached, objectivistic understanding operating from and for itself—transferred itself more or less into theology also.

With this shift, however, not only do Christian life and theological thought diverge so that practically speaking they run alongside each other to the great harm of both; but theological science in itself is also endangered, since it threatens to take away the given act and with that the specific object of the science.

When Thomas Aquinas states that he carried out his *Summa theologiae* on his knees, it is not a pious remark but rather a methodological principle valid for every genuine theology. It indicates not only that a theologian must be pious and ask for God's assistance; all of this would only have personal consequences. Even more so, it means that the living act of faith and its concrete activity, in prayer and Christian deeds, are together the methodological foundation of theological thought—just as the perception of a work of art is the basis for every possible aesthetic science. It is not at all accidental that the truly great theologians were saints—men of prayer. This was not incidental but rather essential. And it is here that the properly creative theological forces originate primarily—only secondarily in the historical, psychological, and the like. Here, the theologian stands before Christian realities; here, he seeks the living face of God; here, he perceives the real demands placed upon time by the Father governing his kingdom—and at this point I certainly need not mention that I have in mind not only the individual life of religiosity but also and even more, that the reality of the Church be lived, and this in a religious way, with man's inner being, with living self-commitment, all the while believing, loving, and carrying it in heart and conscience. …

Theology is a science of reality. This reality is the living, triune God, as he works in the Church and in souls. The man of faith and faith-filled deeds approaches this reality through meditation and liturgy, through actively supporting the Church, through actions and overcoming challenges. … In all of this he grasps that reality which constitutes the matter of theology, what theology works through conceptually—here, of course, dogma and the magisterium of the Church play the role of giving to the object of faith its guaranteed form and to the act of faith its law. This also belongs to the foundations of theological method and should be explicitly noted in order that what is stated is not misunderstood in the sense of an experimenting subjectivity (more on this point later). Here it comes down to one thing for us: that theology is a science of realities, given in faith and in the fullness of the life of faith—not a piece of literary history or conceptual analysis.

Theology thus determined can encounter difficulties from the findings of purely natural science. Holy Scripture belongs to the spheres of both faith and experience. Thus, observations arriving from different points of departure collide within Scripture, and the results of faith's consideration and those of an inductive-historical judgment can stand opposed to each other. We take this possibility into account from the very outset. It is, in fact, given with the divine-human structure of holy Scripture, as well as with the supernatural-natural structure of the believer.

As soon as such a difficulty enters the scene we will resist it. We will not seek to solve it rashly, prematurely. We will neither weaken the perspective of faith nor accommodate the historical judgment. We will test both. Regarding the first, we will test whether or not it is also one of faith's components, truly and correctly seen. It is indeed possible to make a mistake in this regard, and clearly there have been occasions where a later time rectified what an earlier time put forward. Regarding the second, we will test whether or not it is really a matter of a scientific insight. And similarly here, a later time—often only a decade later, or sometimes even shorter—has seen something change which has been put down with emphasis as scientifically certain. Particularly scientific research—carried out by real men, not their ideology—is indeed prejudiced, and apart from that there also exists the strange thing of scientific fashion.

By testing in this way, apparent contradictions will be resolved. Should, however, a situation present itself in which a proposition of faith and a scientific result truly stand in opposition to each other, then we will have the courage to let it go at *non liquet* [it is not clear]. We will be convinced that the tension does not arise from a real contradiction, since truth cannot contradict truth, but from the fact that we do not yet have a sufficiently broad standpoint to behold as a unity what at a lower level appears to be a contradiction but at a higher level is truly consistent and not merely through some appearance.

The Word of God, Grasped in History and in Faith

We took as our point of departure the proposition that holy Scripture is the Word of God and demands a corresponding cognitive disposition. It leads us even further. Scripture confronts us first of all as a text of historical genesis. It is a collection of reports written in a particular time, letters that arose from assignable circumstances of time and place, prophetic utterances made by particular persons. All of this is attached to a specific historical environment and the fundamental principle is valid that one must understand an historical expression from within its own presuppositions. If one wants to understand the Word of God in accord with this principle then he must ask: when was it written? From which human author? What did the words used by the text mean in the time they were written? Which circumstances does it bear upon? What spiritual conditions does it presuppose?

In this way, the Word of God could only be understood through proper historical inquiry—of course always under the directive categories of the holy text and from the governing fundamental disposition of faith. Our way to it went into the past. We reached the text and its sense only by going backwards along the path upon which the text came to us, through the various forms of historical mediation. That this is indeed the case is clear. It results from what was said about the historical way of treating the holy text. But this cannot exhaust the relation to Scripture as a holy text. For the questions—which is the assured form of the text; at which time it arose; how the individual elements are related to each other; what is the historical meaning of its vocabulary; what the fundamental historical circumstances are and with that the particular meaning of persons, relationships, and conditions it speaks of—for all of this and similar things, the historical mode of questioning is responsible.

The Word of God is an historical word. So it must also be historically grasped as such. But with no need for further consideration it is clear that this cannot be the only way to the Word of God as such; indeed seen at the most essential level, it cannot even be the most important. Let us call to mind the number of problems that arise here, as well as the amount of work and knowledge, and moreover the rarely met presuppositions that are required—all of this must be addressed if the questions are to be answered in an adequate way. Thus we see immediately that concerning these points, only a very few people are capable. And all the fewer the more seriously the question of historical critique is taken up. It is good when there are such men, who fulfill this task in the great working group of humanity. But this cannot be the only or even just the normal way of the believer to the text as Word of God.

I will try to state more precisely this thought so that it is not misunderstood. What is certainly not meant is that in addition to the historical conception of Scripture as the truly serious way productive of science, we ought to admit another more tentative, more arbitrary, practically oriented way. So much effort would not have been necessary to say that. Instead: the moment we take as our point of departure the first presupposition—that holy Scripture is the Word of God, a holy text presenting a clearly determined genus of spiritual entities—then it demands accordingly a proportionate way of cognition, so that it can become a reality for us and be grasped according to its properly essential content, and not only its edifying, practical effect; only when it becomes a reality for us can a science be established upon it.

If all of this is so, then the way to Scripture cannot be only the historical way; indeed, this cannot even be the primary way. Otherwise, it would be reserved to very few and moreover on the basis of natural talent and social grace; it would be a privilege of the learned. If this were the case, then this would run counter to the essence of a revealed text. Revelation is directed to humanity. Thus, the way to understanding it must be one open for humanity.

Thus, the matter at hand is not one of granting permission for the practical, religious consideration of Scripture; rather, it is a matter of the fundamental precondition for the understanding of faith and the science of faith at all. Faith's understanding is itself still not "science," as little as aesthetic experience is science. It is a form of a vital grasping of the object. There is, however, a science built upon the aesthetic grasping of objects, in that it treats of these acts and their results in a conceptually critical way. Similarly, there is a science of the understanding of faith; a methodically ordered, critically circumspect treatment of the act of faith and its contents: this is theology. If aesthetics as a science is to become possible, then aesthetic experience must be a prerequisite. If theology is to become possible, then faith's cognition must be presupposed, as it takes place among other things, in the cognitive grasping of Scripture as the product of revelation.

Scripture as the Word of God is therefore something completely different than a document relating a governing deed of Charlemagne. This deed presents a purely historical happening, determined by that day and in that environment. If I want to understand it, then I must try to come as close as possible to that time and those circumstances; this is to say, I have to tread the historical way.[12] Holy Scripture, however, arises from revelation, from that paragon of personalities, events, deeds, through which God spoke and worked in time. This incident certainly bears first upon particular people; but according to its proper sense, it is not restricted to that time and person it immediately concerns, but is directed towards all men and all times. An event from the life of Charlemagne relates to me primarily through the mediation of reports telling of it, as well as through the chain of historical consequences running from it to me. Thus, if I want to reach it, I must go back along that path of mediation—unless its general understandability allows for an immediate relation. Revelation, on the contrary, aims essentially and fundamentally at every time, including my own. Thus it relates immediately to me and my time.

As a message of salvation for humanity, as the Word of God historically spoken but nevertheless transcending history to address all men, myself included—it is precisely as such that revelation, also in its written expression, is grasped in faith. This, then, is exactly what the science of faith is about, the Word of God grasped in faith.

Let us reach deeper still. Revelation is an event originating from eternity but bearing upon time. Here the eternal God, who is simply and perfectly one, his whole being and action an "eternal now," speaks his Word into time. This Word lies in the revelation event, in the person and life of Christ, in what he did and what was done to him, what he spoke and instituted. As the Word of the eternal God, it does not remain trapped within the years between Jesus' proclamation and departure; rather, it coexists in all times. God is eternal, timeless; but he carries time, fulfills it. He coexists in every time. He who stands in *aeternitas* [eternity] fulfills the *aevum* [time], is *aeviternal*. Every time can come to him without needing to go back to some "way back then," for example the primordial beginning when he created the world. No, every time can go to him as this time, as today. It is the same with his Word. It was spoken in a particular time, but it was uttered as the Word of God. Thus it coexists in every time. And if my time or I myself in this very moment want to come to God's Word, then I need not return to some "way back

---

12 Even here the situation is not only historical, since that document is written by man and has to do with the things of men. Given that, it has therefore a certain super-historical and general aspect. This becomes greater the more significant the man who wrote it is, the more humanly comprehensive the object concerned is, the more strongly fundamental human circumstances are expressed in it.

then," the time at which it was historically written, I need not possess a disposition of historical understanding; rather I can as a man of today and from within my contemporary situation go to his Word as if to a word spoken into my today.

It has always been a part of Christian consciousness that the individual man in his own time relates differently to the living Word of God, to Christ, his life and words, to the event of salvation and revelation, than he does to any other historical event. The understanding has always been that he stands in an immediate relation to Christ and his Word. Of course Christ did exist at that time, as a real, historical figure. He is not an idea, a myth, a projection of a religious or metaphysical experience into the historical past. He is history, he *happened* back then. But he simultaneously coexists in every time, since he is the living Son of God, the essential Word of God, coming from eternity and existing as eternal life.

Historicism and the "Today" of the Word

Today Christ is born. Today he lives and acts and speaks. Today he dies and goes home to the Father. Today the Holy Spirit arrives. This happens either today also, or never. If the faith were a matter of a savior who happened to be only historical, only "back then," then it would have nothing to accomplish. All of this however does not mean a merely religious experience, a literary or dialectical affair; it means reality. A form of reality of a particular sort, of course—namely a form that in the language of the Church is called mystical. It is the form in reality of the Christ encountered by faith, the Christ who once was, but simultaneously is, "always with us." It is a pneumatic reality. If we want to feel this reality in all of its force then we must consequently read the letters of St. Paul, paying attention especially to those passages in which the discussion of Christ's being "in us" surfaces or man's being, living, and acting "in Christ"[13] comes to the fore.

Now, holy Scripture is a part of the revelation event. That the apostles wrote these texts is—according to time, occasion, power, validity, and content—a part of a revelation that happens in history, while emerging from eternity, taking aim at and therefore coexisting with every time period. Thus, the objective constitution of holy Scripture corresponds to the subjective aspect of faith. Faith sets out from its particular *now* and heads in the direction of eternity. This it does through the form of revelation, a form in which eternity directs itself towards every *now*.

In this way, the Word of God orients itself towards every time and asks for faith. This includes our time and it includes me. And each person has the right, indeed the corresponding task, to examine the faith directly from his own time, from the historical understanding of his own condition and environment. The Word of God in Scripture is "pan-historical" and the whole of history is charged with extracting its meaning. Within this general mission, each time period has its par-

---

13   See on this point Guardini, "Das liturgische Mysterium" [The Liturgical Mystery], *Die Schildgenossen* (1925).

ticular task. Naturally the Word of God is materially determined by the concrete situation in which it was written. Nevertheless, it has something indeterminate in itself, an indeterminate meaning that awaits the impression of its particular character by each time period. This is not in the least meant in a relativistic way, or in a way that would weaken the objective clarity of revelation. Rather, the Word of God is a message and every message perfects itself only from the heart of the one hearing it.

The Word of God is a living, generative power—generative truth that achieves a new fullness in each time period. It is not only a mere statement or a logical message from this or that person; it is rather a living Word striving to enter into life and to generate life. And if it is believed, then this does not mean some sort of mechanical consent, but rather that it is accepted into life and there it bears fruit. Christian consciousness has never thought in any way other than this way—the dominant empirical turn of the academic world to the contrary—and it has confidently acted in accord with this way of thinking.

This is once again important for the correct conception of the essence of theology. Our biblical scholarship falls by and large into historicism. Understanding holy Scripture in a scholarly way is largely equivalent with understanding it historically. Prescinding entirely from the danger of historical relativization, the consequence of this is ominous—the properly theological threatens to slip away; so too the sacred, the pneumatic. And the threat extends further still to the reading, unlocking, and drawing from the Word of God, which is absolute and eternal. The divine authority of the holy text is also under the threat of losing what is to be understood in adoration. And, in a rarer but profoundly more reasonable correspondence to this: there is the danger of losing the present-ness, the *today* in which theologians stand as listeners.

Historicism loses in its *yesterday* the *eternal* and also the *now*. Thus, it becomes irrelevant, academic. The Word of God however is not only in pastoral "usage," but also essentially practical. It is essentially God's call from out of eternity and into time—not time in general, but the time of today. Thus, it is also not properly theologically understood if it is not understood from its temporal immediacy. That which essentially belongs to the Word falls out of sight: the "hearer of the Word," for he is the hearer of today. In precisely this way, theology becomes a matter of indifference.

Thus, the theological matter at hand is a deep, comprehensive penetration of the holy text, one that welcomes working carefully through historical findings but still arises fundamentally from the consciousness that this text calls out to our daily *now*. It is a message from God's eternity to our present.

Then the living and religious question, our question concerning the Word of God, raises itself wholly on its own accord: "Lord, what should we do?" And the question will call out the answer. Then the countenance of God will disclose its features, including those features he intended precisely for our own time, and out of the matter and events of our time—a time certainly also included in the plan of Providence—he who is eternal will "prepare that praise" of knowledge and of deed which can only be prepared from time.

The Living Divine Word as an Object of Science

When someone advancing in his best abilities and in accord with his present understanding tries to penetrate Scripture; when he uses that which an historical understanding offers to him; at that point still, there is more that must happen. All of this expresses only the empirical side of the process. The essential process of examining the Word of God and coming to understand Scripture is a spiritual one. Scripture itself often speaks of this. Over and over we find thoughts such as these: that Scripture must be opened up if one is to understand what he reads; that man is sluggish when it comes to understanding everything the prophets said and for this reason the prophets' meaning must be opened up for him; that our eyes must be opened, our view unveiled, our soul moved, our innermost enflamed.

Scripture is the living, divine Word, the power of truth hovering and ready to beget. Its meaning and intention is realized by an interior event that involves becoming clear, understood, illuminated, enflamed, and fructified. This is so because whenever God approaches the soul—to elaborate upon the thoughts of a friend—he does not bring about finished results and perfect circumstances; instead, it happens in the manner of a seed, which operates only slowly and is only scarcely perceived at the beginning. It is a matter of God's action and has to do with an opening of self, an assimilation, a decision, and a cooperation arising from the deepest part of the soul. It is an event of grace.

It follows from this that one cannot willfully force this particular perception of the text, this specific understanding of Scripture. The only thing one can do is to stand ready, to prepare oneself. In the life of faith, what can be wished for and practiced is to "watch and pray," to direct a living discipline and attentiveness towards God. Beyond this, all those things are good and necessary which aid the penetration of the work of reason and of the heart.

From a scholarly perspective, the question naturally follows: can something that depends upon such conditions be an object of science? Is not science in its essence the sort of investigation of realities which renders at all times a rational account of what it does and accepts, and which can present at any time its process by way of repetition?

This would hold true the moment we understand "science" as the limited activity of dealing with concepts. If, however, we understand it as the rational handling of the great insights, then it does not hold. The great insight of natural science, history, and philosophy is never only a matter of logical exertion. Rather, it is a process encompassing a person's entirety, an interior realization; things become lucid, the soul is moved, the senses highly attuned, and a flourishing fruitfulness results. It is a process which is always perceived as a gift by those who participate in it. Preparations can be undertaken for it, but it can never be forced. Once the first view is gained, however, then begins the conceptual work that understands the process and its finding. This work can be presented again at any time. But it too always appeals in some way to the fact that this living insight is constantly thought through and comprehended anew, lest it come up empty.

If we have perceived the whole process in its pure form with the great thinkers, then we easily see that something comparable happens with us also. Our truly living insights are not rationally coerced, but instead just "happen." The whole of our living knowledge depends ultimately on those insights that come to us as gifts. And incidentally, it also depends on that form of vital knowing that does not allow itself to be determined by specific acts of knowing, but rather plays out in a gradual clarification, deepening, increasing, and unfolding drawn from the whole of life's experience.

Thus, our viewpoint here. The proper process of apprehending Scripture is a religious one. It cannot be forced. The work of reasoning leans on this process and tries to render an account of it and its contents. Of course the result of this is the consequence discussed earlier: the measure of the scientific apprehension of Scripture as the Word of God depends on the power and depth of the individual's religious understanding. Yes, that is in fact how the situation stands. For the one understanding Scripture scientifically, for the theologian, his scientific measure—taking "scientific" in the strictest sense—is determined first of all by the power of the believing perception of revelation, and only secondarily by the power of conceptual apprehension, explanation, and processing. This is an evident truth for all truly religious thinking. Accordingly, a hierarchy is established in which it is fitting that he who is more humble has reverence before he who is greater. Religious cognition and its science are not mechanical matters in which, to state it fundamentally, everything is accessible for everyone. Rather, they are carried out in a hierarchy of persons, and only reverence and discipleship lead beyond the proper measure, the reverence and discipleship that think along with the insight of the higher one and thus participate in it.

The Church, the Individual, and the Address of the Word

But having said this, we are then led to a last question: to what extent is the individual responsible? Is not the Word of God handed over to the subjective experience of the individual if we found the scientific treatment of Scripture upon the religious relation? That would admittedly happen if the foregoing were exhaustive.

The Word of Scripture, as revelation in general, is not a private word. It is not directed to the individual as such. Accordingly, perceiving this Word of God is not a private concern, not a concern of the individual as such. Certainly, knowledge of Scripture is a concern of the person. The Word of God is directed "to me, and not to another." It is a matter of my salvation, of my relation to God, which no one can take away from me. I am involved in all of this with the uniqueness, irrepresentability, irreplaceability of my person. But it is not my concern as a sheer individual, as someone isolated from every context. The Word is rather directed to man, who is "private" and "public" at the same time. There is no such thing as an isolated individual. Such an individual is only a limit case, a construct for fighting and defending against a certain stereotyping of man. What exists in truth is the person, standing in itself but simultaneously in relation to the whole. This is the one to whom the Word of God is directed.

The man whom Christ addresses is the individual in his irreplaceable uniqueness, but ordered to the whole. But in saying "to the whole," what is meant is the whole as it subsists in personal individuals. In itself, revelation would also be thinkable as private. In fact, this has also taken place: think, for example, of the revelations of the mystics. These revelations however take a wholly different direction of meaning; they are characterized as private. In contrast, revelation proper, the one we designate as "Christian" is directed towards the living, variously connected order of the whole and the individual. Thus, it can only be properly understood from within this order and its tension; it can only be correctly grasped from the Christian individual who is integrated into the Christian whole, that is, the Church.

It is a Catholic conviction that holy Scripture is entrusted to the Church and that the individual can examine and understand Scripture only from within the living connection with the Church. One who thinks individualistically has an "anti-Churchly disposition," which makes him perceive such a claim of the Church as placing pressure upon religious freedom, as a socialization of the personal religious sphere. But this claim of the Church does not spring from a disdain for the person and religious interiority. Rather, it springs from the fact that the person standing entirely on his own does not exist; it arises from the realization that the conception of such a person is not an ontic concept [one rooted in reality] but a dialectical concept [one fashioned wholly by the mind] and through this unreal concept the person is not valued higher in reality, but brought into an impossible situation. The event of revelation is directed towards the real person. In this way, it addresses itself from the outset to the individual standing in the Church and to the Church standing in individuals.

In regard to this point, the Church, as the Christian whole, as the objective instantiation, has, according to its essence, primacy over the individual. It is not a primacy of value but of representation, authority, function, guidance, and leadership. "Whoever does not listen to the Church let him be to you as a Gentile and a public sinner." "Whoever hears you, hears me."

No one believes only on their own private account; rather, the believer believes as a member of the Kingdom of God. As little as I can pray, "Thy kingdom come to me" when it ought to be "to us," just as little can I think of revelation as being entrusted to my personal interpretation. The religious "we" stands at the heart of being Christian. And this "we" is meant not only in the sense of a freely flowing, subjectively bound community, nor again only in the sense of a community resting in the similarity or identity of a way of life; no, it is meant in the sense of the formed whole of the Church, a whole that stands in its own right. "Church" belongs just as profoundly in the center of what it is to be a Christian as does "person."

In this way, the Church also stands essentially within faith's act of knowledge. An exclusively individual knowledge of the faith does not exist. This sort of knowledge is a limit case. What actually exists is the individual's knowledge of the faith but stemming from the Church's consciousness of the faith as it bears upon its surroundings, in the synchronic relations of the present Church community as well as the diachronic relations of Church history as it runs through the ages. Indeed the individual's knowledge of the faith springs from the Church in its last consequence: as representative and authoritative wholeness, as magisterium and Tradition.

The act of faith arises from the insight, decision, and responsibility of the individual; it does so simultaneously, however, from obedience and self-enlargement of the individual disposition into the disposition of the Church. And both are not related as if hanging next to each other nor as if one is only the corrective of the other. Rather, they are as a living unity, in which one moment cannot in any way be separated from another. The individual decision is from the very outset determined by the Church. From the very outset, the essence of the act of faith is personally determined to the Church and obedience. Once again, however, not in the sense of a synthesis. There is nothing here that can be synthesized. Instead, it is a primordial, unified act, indeed the Christian-Catholic religious act that realizes itself essentially in the tension of these two poles.[14]

In the particular person, the fact of the Church can of course affect his individual Christian life in an inhibiting way. It can do the same for a critical examination, for the historical or psychological analysis and commentary. In view of the whole, however, the influence of the Church is a positive one, and this in three ways:

First: it makes it possible for the individual to elevate himself above psychological determinations arising from aptitude, heredity, environment, course of education, and the like. This determination runs very deep and is often recognizable in one's thoughts and views, which appear along with the demand for strict objectivity. Often, theoretical judgment and practical assessment are determined through and through by precisely such aspects of psychological aptitude. The sup-

---

14 Today, thoughts regarding personal decision are very strongly emphasized. This is understandable given the relativistic flowing together of qualities, forms, and values. It is understandable given the chaos of the turning point and it stands historically under the influence of spirits that likewise wanted a clarification of thought and deed to come out of a chaos of thought and deed. This will to decide is not allowed to create a spell that wants to decree away the foundational fact of life's tension lying in the concrete. It may combat the relativistic disposition, but it may not forget that it is necessarily confronted by the will to see the concrete being and therein the inexistence of the contrary moments. This is just as much ethically assigned as is "decision."

posed truth of judgment is often a function of existence, indeed often enough of subconscious desires. The Word of God, however, demands freedom. It seeks to be examined from the perspective of an at least relative surmounting of individual determination of essence.

Herein lies the liberating action of the Church. Presenting a tremendous integration of typical, human possibilities and standing within a history measured in millennia, the Church possesses a certain objective general form, which might not come to the fore so clearly in the individual case but in the general direction is unmistakable for whoever opens himself to it. Participating in this relative surmounting of individual determination is the believer. His act of faith undergoes a purification and enlargement that goes beyond the individual.

Second: the Church's influence safeguards the individual from letting the interpretation of Scripture degenerate into the currently reigning trends of a cultural and academic sort. It makes it possible for the individual to hear the Word of God coming from eternity with a certain timeless disposition.

Third: it is certain that the greatest danger of an individual understanding of Scripture consists in its being seen in only a natural way, where the supernatural and Christian element slips away into what is purely historical, psychological, philosophical. If we hold before our eyes the disposition of the Church regarding the individual, with all of its narrowness, hardships, intolerance, then considering the matter rather superficially we will admittedly see very often that the Church has set herself against scientific progress. But considered more profoundly, the situation is rather that the Christian and supernatural substance of the faith is safeguarded against the danger of being made into something merely natural, and thus the proper and qualified science of God's Word attains to the object with which it stands and falls.

In this way, the Church is ultimately the atmosphere and order in which the eye of the individual fully sees its object, beholds revelation.

Having said this, those questions arising from the whole relation of Church and individual are not forgotten. The task remains to surmount them ever anew. Moreover, given that these questions arise from the fact that both the Church and the individual are human, they must be treated accordingly.

COVENANT AND COMMUNION
THE BIBLICAL THEOLOGY
OF POPE BENEDICT XVI

BY SCOTT W. HAHN

"A superb introduction to the way in which the theology of Pope Benedict XVI has been shaped by the Bible. Hahn's crisp and clear analysis puts the reader at the very center of this remarkable pope's thought."

Gary Anderson,
University of Notre Dame

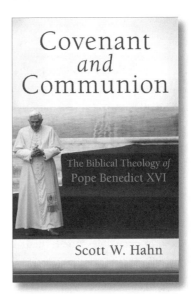

Cardinal Joseph Ratzinger's election as Pope Benedict XVI brought a world-class biblical theologian to the papacy. There is an intensely biblical quality to his pastoral teaching and he has demonstrated a keen concern for the authentic interpretation of sacred Scripture.

Here Scott Hahn, a foremost interpreter of Catholic thought and life, offers a probing look at Benedict's biblical theology and provides a clear and concise introduction to his life and work. Hahn argues that the heart of Benedict's theology is salvation history and the Bible and shows how Benedict accepts historical criticism but recognizes its limits. The author also explains how Benedict reads the overall narrative of Scripture and how he puts it to work in theology, liturgy, and Christian discipleship.

160 pages | Publisher: Baker Brazos Press (October 1, 2009) | $21.99

KINSHIP BY COVENANT
A CANONICAL APPROACH TO THE
FULFILLMENT OF GOD'S SAVING PROMISES

SCOTT W. HAHN

"Both well-written and exhaustive, this impressive work will fascinate readers with New Testament truths about God's unyielding covenant with his chosen, fallible people." — David Noel Freedman

While the canonical scriptures were produced over many centuries and represent a diverse library of texts, they are unified by stories of divine covenants and their implications for God's people. In this deeply researched and thoughtful book, Scott Hahn shows how covenant, as an overarching theme, makes possible a coherent reading of the diverse traditions found within the canonical scriptures.

Biblical covenants, though varied in form and content, all serve the purpose of extending sacred bonds of kinship, Hahn explains. Specifically, divine covenants form and shape a father-son bond between God and the chosen people. Biblical narratives turn on that fact, and biblical theology depends upon it. With meticulous attention to detail, the author demonstrates how divine sonship represents a covenant relationship with God that has been consistent throughout salvation history. A canonical reading of this divine plan reveals an illuminating pattern of promise and fulfillment in both the Old and New Testaments. God's saving mercies are based upon his sworn commitments, which he keeps even when his people break the covenant.

ANCHOR YALE BIBLE REFERENCE LIBRARY

H608 PAGES • PUBLISHER: YALE UNIVERSITY PRESS (JUNE 16, 2009) •$50

THE ST. PAUL CENTER
FOR BIBLICAL THEOLOGY
Reading the Bible from the Heart of the Church

Promoting Biblical Literacy for Ordinary Catholics . . .

- Free Online Bible Studies
- Online Library of Scripture, Prayer, and Apologetics Resources
- Conferences and Workshops
- Popular Books and Textbooks
- Pilgrimages: to Rome, the Holy Land, and other sacred sites
- Journey Through Scripture: a dynamic parish-based Bible study program

...and Biblical 'Fluency' for Clergy, Seminarians, and Teachers

- Homily Helps: lectionary resources for pastors and RCIA leaders
- Reference Works: including a Catholic Bible Dictionary
- Letter & Spirit: a Journal of Catholic Biblical Theology
- Scholarly Books and Dissertations
- Seminars and Conferences
- Studies in Biblical Theology and Spirituality: reissues of classic works

ST. PAUL CENTER
FOR BIBLICAL THEOLOGY

2228 Sunset Boulevard, Suite 2A
Steubenville, Ohio 43952-2204
(740)264-9535
www.SalvationHistory.com